ABROAD

WORK, STUDY, TRAVEL ABROAD

THE WHOLE WORLD HANDBOOK

TWELFTH EDITION
1994–1995

EDITED BY LÁZARO HERNÁNDEZ
AND MAX TERRY

ASSISTANT EDITORS
Amy Carden, Richard Christiano, Jon Howard,
Priscilla Tovey

Council on International
Educational Exchange

ST. MARTIN'S PRESS
NEW YORK

IMPORTANT NOTE

All information cited in this book, including prices, is subject to change. To the best of its ability, CIEE has verified the accuracy of the information at the time *Work, Study, Travel Abroad* went to press. However, at press time, international airfares for peak summer travel in 1994 had not yet been announced. Most of the fares listed throughout this edition are those which were valid for the summer of 1993. For information on all CIEE services, get a free copy of the latest edition of CIEE's *Student Travels* magazine or check with any Council Travel office.

ISBN 0-312-10578-9

LC# 84-646778

Twelfth edition: March 1994

10 9 8 7 6 5 4 3 2 1

CONTENTS

PREFACE

The 1994–1995 edition of *Work, Study, Travel Abroad: The Whole World Handbook* marks the twelfth edition of the book. The Council on International Educational Exchange has been updating and revising this book every other year since the first edition was prepared in 1972. Although this new edition generally follows the format developed for the eleventh edition, the number of countries covered has increased, especially in Africa, Asia, and the South Pacific. This edition includes brief descriptions of more than 1,200 study, work, and travel programs abroad, and new maps with more detailed information than in previous editions. In addition, you'll find expanded recommendations of books to read and movies to see before going to specific countries.

Two years of effort have gone into producing the twelfth edition of this book. Hundreds of people—including professors and advisers on college campuses, students recently returned from abroad, and CIEE personnel from Hong Kong to Bonn—have been involved in the project. We've researched the latest on international travel, updated program offerings, reviewed books and movies, created maps, put together fact sheets, and collected useful suggestions from people who've recently been overseas. We hope you'll be able to use some of the information we've gathered to make your trip more rewarding. We also hope that when you return from your trip abroad, you too will be part of the effort to revise and update the 1996–1997 edition.

WE WANT TO HEAR FROM YOU

Can you tell us anything you found out during your travels that will help make the next edition of *Work, Study, Travel Abroad: The Whole World Handbook* more informative? Do you want to write a country introduction, suggest some reading material, or share some travel tips in our next edition? Persons whose country introductions we use will receive a free copy of the next edition of this book. Send correspondence to the Editor, *Work, Study, Travel Abroad*, CIEE, 205 East 42nd Street, New York, NY 10017.

ACKNOWLEDGMENTS

So many people in so many countries have been involved in the two-year effort to rewrite and update this edition that any attempt to name all the individuals who contributed would be futile. First and foremost, gratitude must be expressed to the publications staff at the Council on International Educational Exchange, especialy Lázaro Hernández and Max Terry, who served as the book's editors. Overseeing a project of this magnitude and scope requires a combination of sharp organizational skills as well as excellent writing ability. Their dedication to produce a more comprehensive and up-to-date edition is manifest in the quality of the book. Thanks also to the other members of CIEE's publications staff, Amy Carden, Richard Christiano, Jon Howard, and Priscilla Tovey, who assisted in many phases of producing this edition.

Thanks to the many CIEE staff members around the world who updated program information and offered suggestions and advice. Gratitude also needs to be expressed to the people at Council Travel, including Greg Posey, who provided travel information and verified fares. The staff people at CIEE's Creative Services Department, Michele Garfield in particular, deserve our appreciation for creating the maps that appear throughout the book. Also vital to the compilation of this book have been the CIEE representatives at the colleges, universities, and other organizations that are members of CIEE. These people provided information about programs abroad, suggested books to read and films to see, and helped establish contact with students across the U.S. who recently returned from work, study, and travel experiences abroad. A collective thank-you to all of them. Additional thanks to the writers of the country introductions, whose names appear at the end of the introductions.

The literature and film sections owe their usefulness to the information provided by a variety of persons familiar with certain countries or regions. Special thanks are also in order for CIEE Deputy Executive Director Joe Hickey and Assistant Executive Director Margaret Shiba for their support and suggestions for this project.

Finally, we would like to thank all the readers who have sent in comments and information. Receiving reactions and contributions from users of the book is especially helpful and encouraging. We hope that readers will continue to provide the feedback necessary for a useful book serving the needs of young people going abroad for study, work, or travel experience.

Del Franz
Director, Information and Student Services
Council on International Educational Exchange

ABOUT CIEE

The Council on International Educational Exchange (CIEE) is a nonprofit organization with offices in the U.S., Europe, and Asia. In its 47 years of service to the educational community, CIEE has emerged as one of the foremost organizations promoting international education and student travel.

CIEE was founded in 1947 to help reestablish student exchange after the Second World War. In its early years, CIEE chartered ocean liners for trans-atlantic student sailings, arranged group air travel, and organized orientation programs to prepare students and teachers for educational experiences abroad. Over the years, CIEE's mandate has broadened dramatically as the interests of its ever-incresing number of members have spread beyond Europe to Africa, Asia, and Latin America. Today, CIEE assumes a number of important responsibilities that include developing and administering programs of international educational exchange throughout the world, coordinating work-abroad programs and international workcamps, and facilitating inexpensive international travel for students, teachers, and other budget travelers.

This section will give you an idea of what CIEE does and how it can help you. For more information on any of the following services, contact the appropriate department at CIEE in New York. Be as specific as possible about your request.

University Study Programs

Among CIEE's most widely recognized educational services are the academic programs that it administers in Argentina, Australia, Belgium, Brazil, Chile, China, Costa Rica, the Czech Republic, the Dominican Republic, France, Germany, Hungary, Indonesia, Japan, Korea, the Netherlands, Poland, Russia, Spain, Thailand, the United Kingdom, and Vietnam. These programs are administered by CIEE's University Programs Department on behalf of sponsoring colleges and universities that participate in policy and curriculum formation, assure academic credibility and quality control, and serve the particular academic field for which the program has been developed.

Work Abroad

CIEE operates a series of work-exchange programs that enable U.S. college and university students to work in other countries, primarily during summer vacation periods. Through these programs, students are able to obtain temporary employment in Britain, Canada, Costa Rica, France, Germany, Ireland, New Zealand, and the United States. Many governments are unwilling to issue work permits to foreign students. The process involves time consuming red tape and bureaucratic regulations which make it an extremely difficult, if not impossible, task for students to do on their own. Because of the reciprocal nature of CIEE's work-exchange programs, governments have enabled it to avoid these processes and issue the necessary work permission directly to the student. Along with the necessary employment authorization, work-abroad participants receive general information on the country, tips on employment, and helpful hints on housing and travel. In each country the program is offered in cooperation with a national student organization or CIEE office that provides an orientation on the country's culture and society, advises on seeking jobs and accommodations, and serves as a sponsor during the participant's stay.

International Voluntary Service

CIEE's International Voluntary Service Department operates an international workcamp program for young people interested in short-term voluntary service overseas. International workcamps bring together 10 to 20 volunteers from different countries to work on environmental and community service projects for a period of two to four weeks. Volunteers are placed with organizations conducting projects in Algeria, Belgium, Canada, the Czech Republic, Denmark, France, Germany, Ghana, Hungary, Japan, Morocco, the Netherlands, Poland, Russia, Slovenia, Spain, Tunisia, Turkey, Ukraine, and the United Kingdom. Some examples of the types of projects available are taking part in trailbuilding and in a nature conservation project; restoring a historical site; working with children or the elderly; and constructing low-income housing. Volunteers receive room and board and the opportunity to become involved in a local community. CIEE also operates workcamps at various locations around the U.S.

Secondary School Programs

CIEE administers School Partners Abroad, which matches U.S. secondary and middle schools with counterpart schools in Europe, Asia, and Latin America. The program involves participating schools in an array of year-round curriculum-related activities, the centerpiece of which is an annual reciprocal exchange of students and teachers. During the short-term exchange, visiting students and teachers participate fully in the life of the host school, attending regular classes, joining in extracurricular activities, and living with local families.

Also for U.S. high school students is Youth in China, a unique summer study program in Xi'an, China. The program combines travel with a period of residence and language study at a Chinese secondary school. American participants live with Chinese roommates and participate in a full academic program.

Adult/Professional Programs

Continuing education is another area of extensive CIEE activity. The Professional and Continuing Programs Department designs and administers a wide array of short-term seminars and in-service training programs for groups of international professionals, including secondary-school teachers and administrators, university faculty, business managers, and other "adult learners." As an additional service, CIEE is able to custom-design international education programs on behalf of CIEE-member or cooperating institutions.

The Professional and Continuing Education Programs Department also offers the International Faculty Development Seminar series for faculty and administrators at two- and four-year institutions of higher education. These overseas seminars and professional interchange opportunities are designed to assist institutions with internationalizing home campus curricula.

Student Services

Through its Information and Student Services Department, CIEE sponsors the International Student Identity Card in the United States. Over 170,000 cards are issued each year by CIEE's New York headquarters, its 41 Council Travel offices, and more than 450 issuing offices at colleges and universities. Cardholders receive travel-related discounts, basic accident/medical insurance coverage while traveling abroad, and access to a 24-hour toll-free emergency hotline. Also sponsored by CIEE are the GO 25 International Youth Travel Card for those under 25, and the International Teacher Identity Card for full-time faculty—both of which provide benefits similar to the International Student Identity Card.

The department also administers the International Student Identity Card Fund. Supported by the sale of the International Student Identity Card in the United States, the fund offers travel grants to U.S. high school and undergraduate college students participating in educational programs in the developing countries of Africa, Asia, and Latin America.

In its role as the ''information clearinghouse'' of CIEE, the department answers more than 100,000 inquiries on work, study, and travel abroad each year. To keep campus advisers and others in the field of international education informed, CIEE publishes *Update*, a free newsletter.

Publications

Probably the most widely circulated publication in the student travel field is *Student Travels* magazine, read by hundredes of thousands of students each year. Featuring articles on the hottest international destinations for students, each issue brings readers travel tips, a calendar of interesting events around the world, and short takes of the overseas adventures of student travelers plus detailed information on studying, working, or volunteering abroad. Published twice a year by CIEE, *Student Travels* is available free of charge at Council Travel offices and at colleges and universities all over the country. Your school's study-abroad office or international center might have copies on hand. If not, you can order a copy from CIEE, Information and Student Services, 205 East 42nd Street, New York, NY 10017; (212) 661-1414, ext. 1108.

In addition to *Work, Study, Travel Abroad: The Whole World Handbook*, CIEE publishes the following titles:

- *Going Places: The High-School Student's Guide to Study, Travel, and Adventure Abroad*, compiled by CIEE and published by St. Martin's Press, an award-winning compendium of short- and long-term overseas opportunities for youth 12 to 18 years of age; updated every other year.
- *Volunteer! The Comprehensive Guide to Voluntary Service in the U.S. and Abroad*, published jointly by CIEE and the Council of Religious Volunteer Agencies (CRVA), a guide to hundreds of short-, medium-, and long-term opportunities for voluntary service in every corner of the world; updated every other year.
- *Where to Stay USA*, a state-by-state listing of more than 1,200 places to spend the night from $4 to $35, with special city sections and general travel advice for anyone touring the United States; updated every other year by CIEE and published by Prentice-Hall.
- *Smart Vacations: The Traveler's Guide to Learning Adventures Abroad*, compiled by CIEE and published by St. Martin's Press, features more than 200 organizations offering learning vacations for adults. Information on study tours, outdoor adventures, language institutes, environmental projects, and much more is included. Updated every other year.

Educators, administrators, and researchers in the field of international education can request a free publications catalog describing the books, pamphlets, studies, reports, and occasional papers produced by CIEE.

Travel Services

Council Travel operates a network of 41 retail travel offices across the country that provide travel assistance to students, teachers, and other budget travelers planning individual or group trips to any part of the world. Here are some samples of what they offer:

- low-cost flights from the U.S. to destinations around the world on scheduled and charter carriers; flights from Europe to Africa, the Middle East, and Asia; intra-European flights; intra-Asian flights; and domestic flights (many of these fares are available only to students or young people and offered exclusively through Council Travel offices)
- rail passes, including Eurail and individual country passes
- the International Student Identity Card, the GO 25 International Youth Travel Card, and the International Teacher Identity Card
- car rental plans worldwide
- language courses in 18 European cities as well as Japan
- travel insurance, guidebooks, and travel gear
- complete land services catalog including car, hotel, and land packages

In addition to services for individuals, Council Travel provides educational institutions with a complete range of travel services designed to simplify travel planning for groups. Group Services departments in Austin, Boston, Chicago, New York, San Diego, San Francisco, and Seattle can arrange anything from transportation and accommodations to lectures, study programs, special events, sightseeing, and meals.

Charter Flights

Council Charter, a subsidiary of CIEE, offers budget flights between the U.S. and Europe on scheduled and charter carriers that are open to students and nonstudents alike. Cities served vary slightly each year; in 1993 flights were available to Amsterdam, Brussels, London, Madrid, Milan, Málaga, Paris, and Rome. Council Charter allows you to fly to one city and return from another, and offers a low-cost cancellation waiver that allows you to cancel your flight as late as three hours before your departure with no penalty.

CIEE Membership

At present, over 250 educational institutions and organizations in the United States and abroad are members of CIEE. As members, they may take advantage of CIEE's information and publication services; become involved in CIEE's advocacy, evaluation, and consultation activities; and participate in conferences and services organized by CIEE. Membership allows educational institutions and organizations to play a central role in the operation and development of exchanges at a national and international level. See Appendix I for a list of CIEE members.

Council on International Educational Exchange
205 East 42nd Street
New York, NY 10017

COUNCIL TRAVEL OFFICES

ARIZONA
Tempe
120 East University Drive, Suite E
Tempe, AZ 85281
(602) 966-3544

CALIFORNIA
Berkeley
2486 Channing Way
Berkeley, CA 94704
(510) 848-8604

Davis
University of California—Davis
Memorial Union Building,
Room 162
Davis, CA 95616
(916) 752-2285

La Jolla
UCSD Price Center
9500 Gilman Drive
La Jolla, CA 92093-0076
(619) 452-0630

Long Beach
1818 Palo Verde Avenue, Suite E
Long Beach, CA 90815
(310) 598-3338
(714) 527-7950

Los Angeles
1093 Broxton Avenue, Suite 220
Los Angeles, CA 90024
(310) 208-3551

Palo Alto
394 University Avenue, Suite 200
Palo Alto, CA 94301
(415) 325-3888

San Diego
953 Garnet Avenue
San Diego, CA 92109
(619) 270-6401

San Francisco
530 Bush Street, Suite 700
San Francisco, CA 94108
(415) 421-3473

919 Irving Street, Suite 102
San Francisco, CA 94122
(415) 566-6222

Santa Barbara
903 Embarcadero del Norte
Isla Vista, CA 93117
(805) 562-8080

COLORADO
Boulder
1138 13th Street
Boulder, CO 80302
(303) 447-8101

CONNECTICUT
New Haven
Yale Co-op East
77 Broadway
New Haven, CT 06520
(203) 562-5335

DISTRICT OF COLUMBIA
Washington, DC
3300 M Street NW, 2nd Floor
Washington, DC 20007
(202) 337-6464

FLORIDA
Miami
One Datran Center, Suite 320
9100 South Dadeland Boulevard
Miami, FL 33156
(305) 670-9261

GEORGIA
Atlanta
Emory Village
1561 North Decatur Road
Atlanta, GA 30307
(404) 377-9997

ILLINOIS
Chicago
1153 North Dearborn Street,
2nd Floor
Chicago, IL 60610
(312) 951-0585

Evanston
1634 Orrington Avenue
Evanston, IL 60201
(708) 475-5070

INDIANA
Bloomington
409 East 4th Street
Bloomington, IN 47408
(812) 330-1600

LOUISIANA
New Orleans
Joseph A. Danna Center
Loyola University
6363 St. Charles Avenue
New Orleans, LA 70118
(504) 866-1767

MASSACHUSETTS
Amherst
South Pleasant Street
(2nd floor, rear)
Amherst, MA 01002
(413) 256-1261

Boston
729 Boylston Street, Suite 201
Boston, MA 02116
(617) 266-1926

Carl S. Ell Student Center
Northeastern University
360 Huntington Avenue
Boston, MA 02115
(617) 424-6665

Cambridge
1384 Massachusetts Avenue,
Suite 201
Cambridge, MA 02138
(617) 497-1497

Stratton Student Center
MIT W20-024
84 Massachusetts Avenue
Cambridge, MA 02139
(617) 225-2555

MICHIGAN
Ann Arbor
1220 South University Drive,
#208
Ann Arbor, MI 48104
(313) 998-0200

MINNESOTA
Minneapolis
1501 University Avenue SE,
Room 300
Minneapolis, MN 55414
(612) 379-2323

NEW YORK
New York
205 East 42nd Street
New York, NY 10017
(212) 661-1450

New York Student Center
895 Amsterdam Avenue
New York, NY 10025
(212) 666-4177

148 West 4th Street
New York, NY 10012
(212) 254-2525

NORTH CAROLINA
Chapel Hill
137 East Franklin Street, Suite 106
Chapel Hill, NC 27514
(919) 942-2334

OHIO
Columbus
8 East 13th Avenue
Columbus, OH 43201
(614) 294-8696

OREGON
Portland
715 SW Morrison, Suite 600
Portland, OR 97205
(503) 228-1900

PENNSYLVANIA
Philadelphia
3606A Chestnut Street
Philadelphia, PA 19104
(215) 382-0343

Pittsburgh
118 Meyran Avenue
Pittsburgh, PA 15213
(412) 683-1881

RHODE ISLAND
Providence
171 Angell Street, Suite 212
Providence, RI 02906
(401) 331-5810

TEXAS
Austin
2000 Guadalupe Street
Austin, TX 78705
(512) 472-4931

Dallas
6923 Snider Plaza
Suite B
Dallas, TX 75205
(214) 363-9941

UTAH
Salt Lake City
1310 East 200 South
Salt Lake City, UT 84103
(801) 582-5840

WASHINGTON
Seattle
1314 Northeast 43rd Street, Suite 210
Seattle, WA 98105
(206) 632-2448

219 Broadway Avenue East
The Alley Building, Suite 17
Seattle, WA 98102
(206) 329-4567

COUNCIL TRAVEL OFFICES ABROAD

FRANCE
Aix-en-Provence
12, rue Victor Leydet
13100 Aix-en-Provence

Lyon
36, quai Gailleton
69002 Lyon

Montpellier
20, rue de l'Université
34000 Montpellier

Nice
37bis, rue d'Angleterre
06000 Nice

Paris
22, rue des Pyramides
75001 Paris

16, rue de Vaugirard
75006 Paris

GERMANY
Düsseldorf
Graf-Adolf Strasse 18
4000 Düsseldorf 1

Munich
Adalbert-Strasse 32
80799 Munich 40

JAPAN
Tokyo
Sanno Grand Building, Room 102
14-2 Nagato-cho, 2-chome
Chiyoda-ku, Tokyo 100

SINGAPORE
110D Killiney Road
Tai Wah Building
Singapore 0923

UNITED KINGDOM
London
28A Poland Street
London, W1V 3DB

CIEE ADMINISTRATIVE CENTERS

UNITED STATES
CIEE International and North
American Regional
Administrative Center
205 East 42nd Street
New York, NY 10017
(212) 661-1414

FRANCE
CIEE European Regional
Administrative Center
66, Champs-Elysées, Immeuble E
75008 Paris
(33) 1-40759510

CIEE
Centre Franco-Américain Odéon
1, Place de l'Odéon
75006 Paris
(33) 1-44417474

GERMANY
CIEE
Thomas-Mann-Strasse 33
53111 Bonn 1
(49) 228-659746

CIEE
Hagenauerstrasse 1
10435 Berlin
(49) 30-2317297

HONG KONG
CIEE
Prince's Building
Suite 1408
Central, Hong Kong
(852) 5269837

ITALY
CIEE
Via della Lungara 233
00165 Rome
(39) 6-6832109

JAPAN
CIEE Asia Regional
Administration Center
Sanno Grand Building, Room 205
14-2 Nagato-cho, 2-chome
Chiyoda-ku, Tokyo 100
(81) 3-35817581

CIEE Western Japan Regional
Liaison Office
Kyoto International Community
House
2-1 Toriicho, Awataguchi
Sakyo-ku, Kyoto-shi 606
(81) 75-7521130

SPAIN
CIEE
C/Carranza, 5, 1° Deha.
28004 Madrid
(34) 1-5941886

UNITED KINGDOM
CIEE
33 Seymour Place
London W1H 6AT
(44) 71-7063008

CHAPTER ONE

GOING ABROAD

"Travel is fatal to prejudice, bigotry and narrow-mindedness, all foes to real understanding. Likewise tolerance, or broad, wholesome, charitable views of men and things cannot be acquired by vegetating in our little corner of the earth all one's lifetime."
—Mark Twain

This book is not a traditional travel guide. In it you won't find the best night spots in Helsinki, where to stay in Moscow, or what to see in Kyoto. Most bookstores are packed with travel guides that provide this information for virtually any country or region you may want to visit.

This book is something different. It's for the international traveler who wants to be more than just a tourist; it's for those who want to go beyond just seeing the sights to try to really get to know and understand another country and culture. In this book you'll find information that will help you to experience another country as an insider—as a student, worker, volunteer, or intern. Want to know about study-abroad programs, study tours, or summer language programs? What about voluntary service, international workcamps, summer jobs, or internships in other countries? All of these are included, as well as information about low-cost flights, money-saving rail passes, student and youth discounts, and more.

Most readers of this book will be college students who want to consider all the options before deciding what kind of experience is right for them. But *Work, Study, Travel Abroad* is for anyone thinking about international travel, whether they are going abroad for the first time or simply want their next trip abroad to be the best possible.

Why Travel Abroad?

CIEE's worldwide staff represents a vast spectrum of beliefs, but we all agree on one thing—the need to encourage all types of international educational exchange. Americans must learn more about the rest of the world, not simply to help our nation compete in international markets or maintain its role as a world leader, but also in order to understand global issues and battle global problems. Whether you're concerned with human rights, the environment, poverty and hunger, or questions on war and peace in a "new world order," you'll need to understand the world beyond our national borders. Increasingly, issues that used to be considered only of local or national importance—like the unemployment rate, industrial development, even civil wars—are ones that now require understanding of the transnational systems of which our own economy, political system, and environment are only one part. Firsthand experience abroad is probably the best way to increase one's knowledge of the world we share with so many other nations and peoples.

Experiencing life firsthand in another country will not only broaden your understanding of the world around you, it also will give you a new perspective on the things most familiar to you. Most people who experience a foreign culture find that at least as important as the knowledge they gain about a different part of the world is the chance to see their own country and culture from a new, broader perspective.

Fortunately, we need not spend too much effort extolling the benefits of going abroad, since most people find that it's not only an enriching educational experience—it's also lots of fun. But don't expect everything to be wonderful all the time. If you really try to get the most out of your experience abroad, you'll find that coping with a new culture and possibly a new language isn't always easy. To keep problems to a minimum and to get the most out of your time abroad, you'll have to do some careful planning. And that's exactly why we've written this book.

Where to Go and What to Do

Everyone thinking of going abroad faces two basic questions: Where should I go and what should I do? Should you tour Europe or be more adventurous and explore Asia, Africa, or Latin America? Should you work, study, travel, or do a little of all three? This book will help you explore the possibilities. And once you've made up your mind, it will help you make the necessary preparations.

Before you decide where to go, be sure to consider all your options. While most Americans going abroad still travel to Europe, an increasing number are opting for study, work, voluntary service, or educational travel experiences in the countries of Africa, Asia, and Latin America. Why not seriously consider helping to build an irrigation system in Latin America or studying Chinese business and society in Beijing? What about traveling the Nile by felucca or seeing for yourself the effects of deforestation in the Brazilian rain forest? Because non-Western countries provide such vivid social, economic, and cultural contrasts with our own way of life, you'll find a radically different perspective from which to examine your beliefs, values, and assumptions. And, with over three-quarters of the world's population living in Africa, Asia, and Latin America, an understanding of these regions is valuable preparation for living and working in an increasingly interdependent world.

Wherever you decide to go or whatever you decide to do, we have a couple of suggestions before you plunge in. Be open and flexible, but be realistic about yourself and your trip. Consider all the options, talking to family, friends, foreign students, academic advisers, or anyone you know who's been abroad. In the end, however, the decision is yours. To help you decide what to do abroad, you'll find general information about working, studying, and traveling in Chapters Three, Four, and Five. But don't leave the country without looking at Chapter Two, which provides the practical information you need to know about passports and visas, student identity cards and discounts, as well as travel insurance and money matters. Each of the remaining chapters focuses on a specific world region—11 in all. These chapters will give you information on specific countries and the work, study, and travel opportunities available in each.

Ecotourism

Most countries benefit economically from tourism. In fact, tourism is the number-one source of income for some countries, particularly in the Caribbean. But foreign visitors can unwittingly cause harm. This is especially true in developing countries and traditional societies, where large numbers of tourists can damage the environment and disrupt the routine way of life. The concept of ecotourism implies a sensitivity to the local population. This can be as simple as showing respect for local customs or as complicated as analyzing what effect your money has on the local economy or what effect your hiking expedition has on the environment. There are now a number of organizations that conduct tours with a socially responsible focus, but even solo travelers can be socially and environmentally conscious. For more information on responsible tourism, contact the **North America Coordinating Center for Responsible Tourism**, PO Box 827, San Anselmo, CA 94979; (415) 258-6594; fax (415) 454-2493. Another organization, **Cultural Survival**, encourages responsible travel in its support for indigenous peoples around the world. You can contact Cultural Survival at 215 First Street, Cambridge, MA 02142; (617) 621-3818; fax (617) 621-3814.

For Further Reading

The Intrepid Traveler, by Adam Rogers, is an excellent primer on world travel. Drawing on years of experience as a solo traveler, Rogers gives tips on getting the most out of your travels while remaining sensitive to local cultures. *The Intrepid Traveler* is available for $14.95 (plus $2 postage) from Global View Press, 7095 Hollywood Boulevard, Suite 717, Los Angeles, CA 90028.

For a regular update on educational opportunities abroad, read *Transitions Abroad*, a bimonthly magazine geared to economy travel, overseas study programs, work opportunities, and educational travel. Each issue focuses on a specific subject area or country. *Transitions Abroad* emphasizes practical, usable information in timely and informative articles and firsthand reports. Each year's July issue includes the "Educational Travel Resource Guide," a compilation of the best and most current information sources—by country and subject—on work, study, travel, and living abroad. Submissions from readers (feature stories, short information pieces, and photographs) are encouraged. For writer's guidelines and a sample copy ($4.50), contact *Transitions Abroad*, 18 Hulst Road, PO Box 344, Amherst, MA 01004. One-year subscriptions (six issues) cost $19.95 and can be obtained by writing *Transitions Abroad*, Department TRA, PO Box 3000, Denville, NJ 07834.

A good source of books on the intercultural experience is **Intercultural Press**, PO Box 700, Yarmouth, ME 04096; (207) 846-5168; fax (207) 846-5181. Intercultural Press's catalog includes such titles as *Intercultural Communication: A Reader*, which includes articles and studies about verbal and nonverbal cross-cultural communication by Edward T. Hall and other experts in the field; *On Being Foreign: Culture Shock in Short Fiction*, an anthology of short selections from well-known writers including Herman Hesse, Jorge Luis Borges, Paul Theroux, and Albert Camus; and *Survival Kit for Overseas Living*.

CHAPTER TWO

THE ESSENTIALS

Leaving the U.S. isn't as easy as grabbing a backpack and buying a plane ticket. There are a lot of details that you'll have to deal with—like visas, passports, immunizations, and traveler's checks. Be sure to take care of all these details before you go; it will make a big difference. As soon as you decide to leave the U.S., you should start getting the formalities out of the way.

Passports

U.S. citizens need a passport to enter just about any foreign country and to return to the United States. Exceptions include short-term travel between the United States and Mexico and Canada. For travel to many Caribbean countries, a birth certificate or voter registration card is acceptable proof of U.S. citizenship. However, even when it's not specifically required, a valid U.S. passport is the best travel documentation available, even within the United States.

Passports for U.S. citizens 18 and older are valid for 10 years and cost $55 plus a $10 execution fee (see below for details). For anyone under 18, they are valid for five years and cost $30, plus the $10 execution fee. Between March and August the demand is heaviest and the process will take longer than at other times of the year. Apply several months before departure, and if you're going to need visas, allow yourself even more time. It takes at least three weeks to process first-time applications.

If you have never applied for a passport before, you must apply in person at (1) a U.S. post office authorized to accept passport applications; (2) a federal, state, or county courthouse; or (3) one of the passport agencies located in Boston, Chicago, Honolulu, Houston, Los Angeles, Miami, New Orleans, New York, Philadelphia, San Francisco, Seattle, Stamford, or Washington, DC. To apply, you'll need to bring proof of U.S. citizenship (a certified copy of a birth certificate, naturalization certificate, or consular report of birth abroad) and proof of identity (such as a valid driver's license, not a Social Security or credit card). You'll also need two recent, identical photographs two inches square. Photographs can be color or black and white, but they must be taken against a white background. The distance from your chin to the top of your head may not exceed one and three-eighths inches. Most photo shops will know exactly what you need. Finally, you must complete the form DSP-11, "Passport Application."

You may apply by mail and avoid the $10 execution fee if (1) you have had a passport within 12 years of the new application; (2) you submit your most recent passport with the application; and (3) your previous passport was not issued before your eighteenth birthday. Complete form DSP-82, "Application for Passport by Mail," which can be obtained from a post office, courthouse, or passport agency as above. Attach your previous passport and two new passport-size photographs and mail these items to the **National Passport Center**, Passport Lockbox, PO Box 371971, Pittsburgh, PA 15250-7971.

You should keep your passport with you at all times while traveling. American passports are coveted by those wishing to work or live in the U.S. but can't due to visa restrictions. On the international black market, U.S. passports can sell for more than $1,000. One good way to assure that *your* photo remains in your passport is to carry it in a pouch that is tied at the neck or worn around the waist like a belt. This pouch can hold traveler's checks, too, and should always be kept inside your clothing. All Council Travel offices (see pages xiii–xvi) sell passport holders and pouches.

Loss, theft, or destruction of a valid passport is a serious matter and should be reported immediately to local police and to the nearest U.S. embassy or consulate. If the loss occurs in the U.S., you must report the loss in person when you reapply for a new passport. If you lose your passport in another country, you will need to get a replacement at a U.S. embassy or consulate. This process will be much easier if you have with you two extra passport photos and a photocopy of your original showing the number and date and place of issuance. In case your passport is stolen or lost, you also should have with you—but in a separate place from your passport—both proof of citizenship (an expired passport or copy of your birth certificate) and proof of identity (a driver's license or other photo ID).

You should also be aware that a number of countries will not permit visitors to enter and will not place visas in passports that have a remaining validity of less than six months. If you return to the U.S. with an expired passport, you are subject to a passport waiver fee of $80.

Non-U.S. citizens without a valid passport from another country who have permanent residency in the U.S. can apply for a U.S. travel permit. This permit functions much like a passport and can be obtained from the Immigration and Naturalization Service in the state where the applicant resides. Note, however, that the requirements for obtaining visas are usually different from those that apply to U.S. citizens. The information on visa requirements provided throughout this book is applicable only to U.S. citizens. Non-U.S. citizens—whether traveling with a travel permit or a valid passport from another country—will have to consult the embassy or consulate of the country they want to visit to obtain the appropriate visa requirements.

For more information about passports, contact the **Office of Passport Services**, 1425 K Street NW, Department of State, Washington, DC 20520; (202) 647-0518.

Visas

Depending on the country you visit and the length and purpose of your stay, you may also need a visa. A visa is an endorsement or stamp placed in your passport by a foreign government permitting you to visit that country for a specified purpose and a limited time, such as a three-month tourist visa. To study in a particular country, you may need a special student visa. In most cases, you'll have to obtain visas before you leave the U.S. Apply directly to the embassies or consulates of the countries you plan to visit, or check with a travel agent. The Department of State *cannot* help you get a visa.

In this book, you'll find visa requirements as of summer 1993 described briefly in the individual country sections. Another source of information is the booklet, *Foreign Entry Requirements*, which lists the entry requirements for U.S. citizens traveling to most foreign countries and tells where and how to apply for visas. Single copies are available for 50¢ from the **Consumer Information Center**, 3A, R. Woods, PO Box 100, Pueblo, CO 81002. Although this publication is updated periodically, changes can occur without notice at any time. For the latest information, your best sources are the embassies or consulates of the countries you plan to visit.

Since the visa is usually stamped directly onto one of the blank pages in your passport, you'll need to fill in a form and give your passport to an official of each foreign embassy or consulate. You'll have to pay for most visas, and you may need one or more photos (have extras made when you're having passport pictures taken). The whole process can take several weeks, so if you have more than one to get, start well in advance of your trip. Also, bear in mind that some countries require evidence that you have enough money for your trip and/or ongoing or return transportation tickets.

Some countries have reciprocal arrangements with the United States in which they allow U.S. citizens to travel as tourists for a limited time (often, three months) without applying for visas ahead of time. In such cases, the temporary tourist visa is usually stamped in your passport upon arrival. Other countries, such as Mexico, allow U.S. citizens to enter and stay without a passport or visa but require visitors to obtain a tourist card. These cards are distributed on flights to the country, at airports, and at border stations.

Customs

When you come back to the U.S., you'll have to go through customs. The U.S. government prohibits Americans from bringing back certain articles and imposes import fees or duties on other items. Everything that you'll need to know about customs regulations for your return to the U.S. can be found in *Customs Tips For Travelers*, a pamphlet available for 50¢ from the Consumer Information Center (see "Visas," above). Another helpful pamphlet is *Know Before You Go*, available free from **U.S. Customs Services**, Box 7407, Washington, DC 20044; (202) 927-6724.

Health

Certificates of inoculation against such diseases as yellow fever and cholera are required before you go to some countries. For others, certain inoculations are recommended for your personal safety but not required for entry. Check your health care records to ensure that your measles, mumps, rubella, polio, diptheria, tetanus, and pertussis (whooping cough) immunizations are up to date. **The Centers for Disease Control** has an International Traveler's Hotline for determining whether any special vaccinations are needed to visit a country: (404) 332-4559.

The two greatest threats to travelers' health today are diseases against which you *cannot* be inoculated: diarrhea and malaria. The most common causes of traveler's diarrhea and other gastrointestinal ailments are parasites and other organisms to which your body isn't accustomed, but which may be common to the water supply and certain foods, especially fresh produce, in other countries. Malaria is spread through the bite of the female anopheles mosquito. Some travel agents and tourist bureaus don't tell you about the malaria risk in certain countries. Most types of malaria can be prevented, but you must begin taking antimalarial drugs *before* you arrive in the infected area and must continue taking them after you leave.

One organization that has been working energetically to alert travelers about the risks of malaria and other health problems worldwide is the **International Association of Medical Assistance to Travellers (IAMAT)**. IAMAT is a nonprofit organization with centers in 450 cities in 120 countries. Its members receive a pocket-size directory listing IAMAT centers abroad, a world immunization chart (which we particularly recommend), and various publications and maps that alert travelers to existing health problems throughout the world.

Contact IAMAT at 417 Center Street, Lewiston, NY 14092. Membership in this organization is free but donations are appreciated.

As always, when traveling you should be aware of the risk of contracting AIDS (Acquired Immunodeficiency Syndrome). Don't let exaggerated or distorted information alter your travel plans, but do be aware of the risks and prepare ahead. Be aware that some countries may require HIV (human immunodeficiency virus) antibody tests before they'll grant a visa for an extended period of time; tourists staying for 30 days or less are usually exempt. You might want to be tested before you depart; do so only at a center that offers pre- and post-test counseling. Allow two weeks for the testing process. While traveling, remember: the best way to deal with AIDS is through knowledge, foresight, and action, not ignorance and fear.

The Centers for Disease Control has issued the following advisory: "AIDS has been reported from more than 130 nations, but adequate surveillance systems are lacking in many countries. Because HIV and AIDS are globally distributed, the risk to international travelers is determined less by their geographic destination than by their individual behavior. HIV infection is preventable. There is no documented evidence of HIV transmission through casual contacts; air, food, or water routes; contact with inanimate objects; or through mosquitos or other arthropod vectors. HIV is transmitted through sexual intercourse, blood or blood components, and perinatally (at birth) from an infected mother. Travelers are at increased risk if they have sexual intercourse (homosexual or heterosexual) with an infected person; use or allow the use of contaminated, unsterilized syringes or needles for any injections, e.g., illicit drugs, tattooing, acupuncture, or medical/dental procedures; or use infected blood, blood components, or clotting factor concentrates."

There are several things that you can do to avoid contracting HIV. First and foremost, if you plan on being sexually active, bring condoms and/or dental dams with you. You may not have access to these items in certain parts of the world, and conditions, manufacturing, and storage of condoms in other countries may be questionable. More importantly, use them—even if you are aware of the HIV status of your partner and yourself. Remember, testing HIV negative does not necessarily mean that a person has not been in contact with the virus. If you require a blood transfusion, try to ensure that screened blood is used. If you are concerned about needing a blood transfusion while abroad, contact others in your academic program or traveling group; you can arrange with those that have your blood type to be blood donors if necessary. For more information, write CIEE or stop by any Council Travel office (see pages xiii–xvi) for a free copy of Council Travel's brochure, *AIDS and International Travel*. Another good resource for information is the **Centers for Disease Control's AIDS Hotline**: (800) 342-AIDS.

The following books are recommended reading for overall health issues affecting travelers. You won't need to consult all of them, but do try to look through at least one.

- *The Pocket Doctor*, by Stephen Bezruchka, M.D., is a pocket-size publication written especially for travelers. You can order it from The Mountaineers Books, 1011 SW Klickitat Way, Suite 107, Seattle, WA 98134, for $4.95.
- *Health Information for International Travel* is published by the Centers for Disease Control and available for $6 from the Superintendent of Documents, U.S. Government Printing Office, Washington, DC 20402; (202) 783-3238.
- *Staying Healthy in Asia, Africa, and Latin America*, by Dirk Schroeder, is

basic enough for the short-term traveler yet complete enough for someone living or traveling off the beaten path. Formerly published by Volunteers in Asia, it's now available for $10.95 from Moon Publications. For ordering information, see page 56.

- *The International Travel HealthGuide* ($16.95), by Stuart Rose, M.D., is updated annually. It's a little large to stuff in your backpack, but has country-by-country immunization, health, and safety listings. It also has chapters on AIDS, travel and pregnancy, and traveling with disabilities. Look for it in good bookstores or contact the publisher, Travel Medicine, Inc., 351 Pleasant Street, Suite 312, Northampton, MA 01060.

Some general advice: Make sure you're in good general health before setting out. Go to the dentist before you leave on your trip, have an extra pair of eyeglasses or contact lenses made up (or at least have your doctor write out your prescription), and if you take along any prescription drugs, pack them in clearly marked bottles, and have the prescription with you in case a customs officer asks for it.

Safety

Leaving the U.S. is not dangerous in and of itself; in fact, travelers will encounter few countries where the crime rate—especially the frequency of violent crime—equals that of the United States. But it is important to remember one thing: while traveling, you *will* be recognized as a foreigner. To some, this means you will be a novelty; to others, a rube. This means that you must be aware and thoughtful at all times because you can no longer rely on your instinctive knowledge of what may be considered unsafe, insulting, or provocative. This doesn't mean that you should not explore or stray away from the beaten path. It does mean that you should be aware of your passport and money at all times and consult a good guidebook that will give you a rough idea of manners and customs of the country you're visiting. Try to determine areas to avoid alone or at night and avoid arriving in strange cities late at night unless you have a confirmed place to stay and a secure means of getting there. You can't control everything that happens to you—at home or abroad—but you can sway the odds.

Women should be especially aware of situations in which they might be harassed, robbed, or molested. When traveling, there is not only the usual burden of sexism to deal with but also the fact that, as a recognizable Westerner, you will be treated according to stereotypes of Western women (thought in some parts of the world to be promiscuous, immodest, and wealthy). *Women Travel: Adventures, Advice, and Experience*, in the *Real Guides* series published by Prentice Hall Travel, is highly recommended. For each country, the book lists suggested styles of dress, valuable contacts, and advice for women travelers.

If you're planning a trip to a spot where political problems or high crime rates exist, you should obtain a **Consular Information Sheet** for that country from the U.S. Department of State. Replacing the Department of State's former travel advisory system, the new series of country-specific Consular Information Sheets can provide information on health and safety conditions in countries around the world, as well as unusual currency and entry regulations, locations of U.S. embassies and consulates, and other useful facts. In extreme circumstances, the Department of State will issue warnings advising travelers to avoid certain countries. Consular Information Sheets are available at any of the 13 regional passport agencies (see "Passports," above), field offices of the U.S. Department of Commerce, and U.S. embassies and consulates abroad. To receive sheets by mail, send a stamped, self-addressed envelope to the **Citizens Emergency Center (CEC)**, Bureau of Consular Affairs, Room 4811, 2201 C Street N.W., U.S. Department of State, Washington, DC 20520-4818. The information on the sheets can be heard anytime by calling (202) 647-5225 from a touch-tone phone. It can also be accessed via modem at (202) 647-9225. For information by fax, dial (202) 647-3000 from your fax machine.

The U.S. Department of State also distributes several pamphlets that can help you make your trip a safe one. A good source of basic information, including such subjects as how to judge a travel program, information on charter flights, and where to get help when you are in trouble abroad, is *Your Trip Abroad. A Safe Trip Abroad* reminds travelers of some common-sense precautions and also gives tips on protecting against the possibility of terrorism. Finally, *Tips for Americans Residing Abroad* introduces the reader to topics such as tax considerations and voting procedures while abroad. These can be ordered for $1 each from the U.S. Government Printing Office, Washington, DC 20402; (202) 783-3238.

Insurance

Check to see whether your medical and accident insurance policies are valid when you are traveling outside the United States. You should never underestimate the importance of being insured when traveling abroad. If you purchase an **International Student Identity Card** (see the following section of this chapter), you will automatically receive basic accident/sickness insurance for travel outside the U.S., valid from the time of purchase until the card's expiration date. Also included is a toll-free emergency hotline number for travelers needing legal, financial, or medical assistance.

You should also investigate the various plans for baggage and flight insurance. Baggage or personal effects insurance covers damage to or loss of your personal belongings while traveling. Flight insurance covers the cost of your fare if you are unable to take a flight you have already paid for. One insurance package, **Trip-Safe**, provides a variety of options that may be purchased in any combination for any period from one month to one year. You can find details in *Student Travels* magazine. Insurance can also be obtained at any Council Travel office (see pages xiii–xvi).

International Student Identity Card

More than a million students worldwide purchase the International Student Identity Card each year. If you are a junior high, senior high, college, university, or vocational student planning to travel outside the U.S., you should investigate the benefits this card provides.

Holders of the International Student Identity Card get student discounts on transportation and accommodations, and reduced admissions to museums, theaters, cultural events, and other attractions. The best-known discounts are student/youth fares on regular international flights connecting cities in the United States, Africa, Asia, Europe, Latin America, and the South Pacific. Cardholders can save up to 50 percent over commercial fares on the same routes. Information on worldwide student and youth fares is available from any Council Travel office (see pages xiii–xvi). A listing of participating student travel organizations in 62 countries and a U.S. discounts directory is contained in the *International Student Identity Card Handbook,* distributed free to all purchasers of the International Student Identity Card. Even in countries that do not have their own national student travel bureau, the International Student Identity Card is often recognized as proof of student status and can be helpful in securing whatever student discounts are around. New to the 1994 card are a discount on AT&T's USADirect Service and a rebate on American Express moneygrams. There are also growing numbers of cardholder discounts within the U.S., including budget motel chains and car rentals.

Besides the student discounts, the International Student Identity Card provides basic medical and accident insurance. Every student who obtains the card in the U.S. receives coverage while they're abroad for as long as their card is valid. Also available to cardholders is a toll-free hotline for travelers in need of assistance in a legal, medical, or financial emergency. CIEE's free *Student Travels* magazine (see page xi) has all the details.

The International Student Identity Card was initiated in 1968 by the **International Student Travel Confederation (ISTC)**, made up of student travel organizations in 74 countries around the world. If imitation is the sincerest form of flattery, the card has had more than its share. Forgeries and imitations of the International Student Identity Card are marketed from time to time, both in the U.S. and abroad. The best way to protect yourself from a worthless forgery or imitation is to buy from a reputable student travel organization.

To obtain the International Student Identity Card, submit a passport-size photo and proof of student status at a junior or senior high school, college, university, or vocational school in a program leading to a degree or diploma. To get the 1994 card, valid from September 1, 1993, to December 31, 1994, you must be a student in the fall of 1993 or the spring or summer of 1994. College students can prove student status with a letter from the registrar or dean stamped with a school seal; a clear photocopy of a transcript or grade report; or a bursar's receipt. High school students can prove student status with a photocopy of a report card or a letter from a principal or guidance counselor on school stationery. You must be at least 12 years of age, but there is no maximum age limit (although age restrictions may apply on some discounts).

In the United States the International Student Identity Card is sponsored by the Council on International Educational Exchange, the U.S. member of the ISTC. Available in 1994 for $16, it may be obtained at any Council Travel office, (see pages xiii–xvi) or one of 479 authorized issuing offices at colleges and universities across the country. You can also order by mail; call 1-800-GET-AN-ID for an application form. *Student Travels* magazine (see page xi) contains a form that can be used to apply for the card by mail.

For details on the **International Student Identity Card Fund,** which provides travel grants to students studying or doing voluntary service in the Third World, see page 40.

International Teacher Identity Card

In the last several years the International Student Travel Confederation, creator of the International Student Identity Card, has worked to open its low-cost educational travel network to elementary, secondary, vocational, and college faculty. The International Teacher Identity Card provides teachers with some of the same benefits that students holding the International Student Identity Card enjoy, including the insurance and traveler's assistance service. Teachers can also get some of the same special fares on international flights that students get by booking with travel services that honor the card, such as Council Travel. Cardholders can also take advantage of discounts on AT&T USADirect

Service, Eurocentre teacher refresher courses, and Berlitz language classes. In North America, cardholders are eligible for discounts at Alamo Rent a Car, Howard Johnson's, Days Inns, and Ramada locations. All purchasers receive the *International Teacher Identity Card Handbook,* which outlines the benefits of the card. The 1994 International Teacher Identity Card, which costs $17, is issued at all Council Travel offices (see pages xiii–xvi) and a number of campus issuing offices. It can also be obtained by mail from CIEE. The center insert of *Student Travels* magazine contains an application form.

GO 25 Card

Anyone over the age of 12 and below age 26 is eligible for the GO 25 International Youth Travel Card (formerly known as the International Youth Card), sponsored by the Federation of International Youth Travel Organizations (FIYTO). This card allows all young people to take advantage of many of the same discounts students get, including discounts on many international flights. Cardholders receive a free booklet, the *GO 25 Travel Handbook*, that lists youth discounts in 40 countries. GO 25 Cards issued through CIEE also carry the same insurance and traveler's assistance benefits as the student and teacher cards described above. The GO 25 Card costs $16 and is valid for one year from the date of issue. For more information on the GO 25 Card, contact CIEE or any Council Travel office (see pages xiii–xvi).

Mail

If you want to receive mail while you are abroad but do not have a mailing address, you can have mail sent to you in care of **Poste Restante** (General Delivery) at the central post office in the cities you'll be visiting. Simply go to the post office and pick up any mail that has arrived for you; usually, you'll have to pay a small charge for each item received.

If you have **American Express** traveler's checks or an American Express card, you can have your letters (but not packages) sent to an overseas American Express office. *Traveler's Companion,* a brochure published by American Express, includes a list of offices abroad as well as other helpful information. It can be picked up at any American Express office.

Money

The safest way to carry your money abroad is in traveler's checks, which can be replaced if lost or stolen. Most traveler's checks cost one percent of the total dollar amount you're buying (for example, a $5 charge for $500 in traveler's checks). Traveler's checks in U.S. dollars are widely accepted around the world. However, it is also possible to purchase traveler's checks in other major currencies such as British pounds, German marks, and Japanese yen. If the dollar is falling in value relative to other major currencies, your money will go farther if it is denominated in marks, pounds, or yen.

The most common traveler's checks are American Express, Citicorp, Thomas Cook, and Visa. In deciding what kind of traveler's checks you should buy, try to determine how widely the check is recognized and the number of offices the issuing agency has abroad (in case your checks are lost or stolen). You won't have to go to an overseas branch of the issuing agency if you just want to convert your checks to local currency. Most banks will cash them readily; in fact, in many countries you'll get a better exchange rate with traveler's checks than with cash. Try to avoid changing your money in hotels or restaurants where the rate of exchange is usually less favorable.

Daily **currency exchange rates** are quoted in the financial pages of most major newspapers; overseas, try the *International Herald-Tribune, The Financial Times*, or the *Asian Wall Street Journal*. Note that newspaper rates are for wholesale transactions usually exceeding $1 million. The reason exchange rates differ from one place to another is that most currency dealers include a variable service charge for small exchanges. Thus, the rate you actually receive will almost never be as good as the wholesale rate. Be sure to investigate all options for the best rate of exchange, especially if you're going to be changing large amounts of money. But be wary of currency exchange with money changers on the street; in most countries this type of transaction is illegal. In many countries, you can convert currency in exchange shops (known in French and Spanish as *bureaux de change* and *cambios*). These shops have longer hours than banks, but in Europe the rate of exchange will not be as good; elsewhere, the rate offered in the currency exchange shops is often better than what you'll find in a bank. You can also usually buy foreign currency in an air, ship, or train terminal when you arrive. It's a good idea to obtain some local currency before you first arrive in a country (assuming you haven't already changed money back home), but rates are often better once you're in town.

If you run short of money, traveler's checks or cash can be cabled to you from the U.S. in care of a bank or an agency, such as American Express, Western Union, or Thomas Cook. If your bank has a foreign branch, you can have money transferred to you there. It is best to do this in major cities and to make arrangements as far in advance of imminent destitution as possible. You can get more information on wiring money abroad from the agencies that issue your traveler's checks or from a Western Union office.

One of the best-kept secrets of international travel is that most U.S. bank cards are able to obtain cash from **automated teller machines (ATMs)** overseas. Accessing your home account from abroad is easier than ever before with the proliferation of ATM networks around the world. When withdrawing cash in local currency, the dollar equivalent is charged to your home bank. The best part is that you get charged the wholesale exchange rate, giving you more for your money than you can get with traveler's checks or cash. To make it easier, all overseas ATMs are required to include instructions in English. Note that most overseas ATMs only accept four-digit personal identification numbers (PINs); if your card's PIN exceeds four digits, you'll have to change it before departing. Consult your bank or the financial institution that oversees your ATM network to ask for a location directory and make sure that your card will function overseas. Cardholders connected to the CIRRUS system can obtain information on ATMs abroad by calling (800) 424-7787. Plus System cardholders can receive a free 520-page directory of worldwide ATM locations by writing Plus System Inc., 950 17th Street, Suite 2210, Denver, CO 80202.

A Word of Warning: Many countries restrict the entry of persons who can't demonstrate that they have a return plane ticket and/or a certain amount of money for each day they plan to spend in the country. Check with the consulate of the country you plan to visit to see what kind of proof of solvency you will be expected to show.

Drugs

In 1992, almost 3,000 U.S. citizens were arrested abroad. More than 1,000 of those arrested were held on charges of using or possessing drugs. Many others were arrested for violating local laws regarding the use of alcohol in public and the behavior associated with it.

Many Americans assume that, as U.S. citizens, they are immune from prosecution under foreign laws. The truth is that Americans suspected of drug violations can face severe penalties, even the death penalty, in some foreign countries. It is not uncommon to spend months or even years in pretrial detention without bail, only to be sentenced to a lengthy stay without parole.

Once you leave U.S. soil, U.S. laws and constitutional rights no longer apply. U.S. consular officers can visit jailed Americans to see that they are being fairly and humanely treated, but cannot get them out of jail or intervene in a foreign country's legal system on their behalf.

Be particularly wary of persons who ask you to carry a package or drive a car across a border. Also, be sure that if for medical reasons you are required to take drugs containing narcotics you have your prescription bottle and a doctor's certificate attesting to the facts along with you. Remember too that the U.S. Customs Department will inspect your baggage upon your return to the United States, and that it is tightening its enforcement procedures.

For more information, a free brochure, *Travel Warning on Drugs Abroad*, is available from the Bureau of Consular Affairs, Public Affairs Staff, Room 5807, Department of State, Washington, DC 20520-4818.

For Persons with Disabilities

In the last decade a growing number of persons with disabilities have been participating in the world of international travel and exchange. This is partly the result of laws passed by the federal government that reflect a national commitment to end discrimination on the basis of disabilities and to bring persons with disabilities into the mainstream of American life. But it is primarily the result of a growing number of people with disabilities insisting upon their right to face the challenges and enjoy the benefits of international travel and exchange.

One organization that is active in the advocacy of the disabled traveler is **Mobility International**. The organization, with its main office in London, was founded in 1973; the U.S. branch was opened in 1981. Working both with persons with disabilities and with the organizers of international educational exchange programs, Mobility International USA (MIUSA) has helped persons with disabilities participate more fully in the world community.

Besides publishing its quarterly newsletter, *Over the Rainbow*, MIUSA has put together several highly recommended publications. *A World of Options for the 90's: A Guide to International Educational Exchange, Community Service and Travel for Persons with Disabilities* ($14 for members, $16 for nonmembers) contains more than 300 pages of programs for volunteer, study, and host-family living, especially for persons with disabilities. It also contains useful information on travel, accommodations, and publications. Participants provide firsthand accounts of what can be learned from international exchange. *A New Manual for Integrating Persons with Disabilities into International Educational Exchange Programs* ($16 for members, $18 for nonmembers) is targeted to the staff of service and exchange organizations. It costs $16 for MIUSA members, $18 for nonmembers. *You Want to Go Where? A Guide to China* ($7.95 for members, $8.95 for nonmembers) is an invaluable resource written for travelers with disabilities and anyone interested in disability issues in China. MIUSA's latest publication is *Global Perspectives on Disability: A Curriculum* ($40).

MIUSA's video series includes *Mi Casa es Su Casa*, describing a Costa Rica exchange in Spanish or English; *Looking Back, Looking Forward*, featuring interviews with participants with disabilities; *Home Is in the Heart*, dealing with homestays; and *Emerging Leaders*. All MIUSA videos are available with or without captions for the hearing-impaired.

In addition, MIUSA sponsors month-long international exchanges for persons with or without disabilities; recent programs have been offered in Germany, the People's Republic of China, Costa Rica, U.K., countries of the former Soviet Union, Bulgaria, and Mexico. For more information contact Mobility International USA, PO Box 3551, Eugene, OR 97403; (503) 343-1284 (voice or TDD).

Travelers with disabilities might also want to read a new book in the *Real Guides* series, *Able to Travel* ($20), which collects more than 100 stories by disabled travelers describing their adventures around the world. For more information on *Real Guides*, see page 57.

For Gay and Lesbian Travelers

A worldwide movement for gay and lesbian rights has brought the issue of homosexuality to the forefront of public discourse in many countries. This step toward recognition of a historically oppressed minority, however, has in many instances met with harassment and violence. Attitudes toward homosexuality differ according to many variables within a particular country or culture and according to the individual people you will meet. Some travel guide series such as *Let's Go* and the *Real Guide*s include sections on issues of interest to gay and lesbian travelers. Many books and other publications provide information on the political and social climate that gay and lesbian travelers can expect from specific destinations. The publications listed below are available at bookstores throughout the U.S., and most can also be ordered from the address listed or from **Giovanni's Room**, 345 South 12th Street, Philadelphia, PA 19107; (215) 923-2960; or from **Renaissance House**, PO Box 292, Village Station, New York, NY 10014; (212) 674-0120.

Are You Two . . . Together?, by Pamela Brandt and Lindsey Van Gelder, is a guide to Western European capitals and gay resorts. It is published by Random House and is available in bookstores for $18. *Spartacus International Gay Guide* is the standard, most comprehensive international guide for gay men that lists hotels, bars, bookstores, hotlines, and more. It also describes the culture of the country as it pertains to homosexuals. It is available in the U.S. for $28.95 from 100 East Biddle Street, Baltimore, MD 21202; (301) 727-5677. *Gaia's Guide* is an annually revised international guide for women that lists lesbian, feminist, and gay information numbers, publications, cultural centers and resources, hotels, and more; available for $12 from 9-11 Kensington High Street, London W8, England.

Out & About, a travel newsletter published 10 times a year, provides general travel information for gay and lesbian travelers as well as specific city briefs with detailed information on popular destinations. It is available on a subscription basis for $49 a year in the U.S. from 542 Chapel Street, New Haven, CT 06511; (203) 789-8518 (back issues are $5). *The Guide* (available at newsstands for $2.95 or 12 monthly issues for $25 from Fidelity Publishing, PO Box 593, Boston, MA 02199; [617] 266-8557) is a monthly magazine that features articles on travel and entertainment, and includes maps of major cities in the U.S. and abroad.

The Women's Traveler, a travel guide for lesbians that lists hotels, restaurants, bookstores, and more, is available for $11 from PO Box 11270, San Francisco, CA 94101; (415) 777-0113. *Places of Interest* is a series of three books including maps. International guides *Places of Interest for Men* ($12.95) and *Places of Interest for Women* ($10) are available from Ferrari Publications, PO Box 37887, Phoenix, AZ 85069; (602) 863-2408. *Inn Places: U.S. and Worldwide Gay Accommodations* is available for $14.95 from the same address.

Packing

On their first trip abroad, everybody seems to take more than they need. A good way to avoid this is to pack everything you want to bring and then walk around the block with it. Then bear in mind that most hotels and youth hostels are going to be a healthy jaunt from the train station, or at least a crowded bus ride. Remember, clothes can be washed and laid out to dry overnight for use the next day. Keep in mind that you will probably want to purchase some clothing and souvenirs; save room in your bags for things you pick up. Fashion is not a necessity when you're traveling; being comfortable and able to enjoy your surroundings is.

A backpack is probably your best bet if you're going to be touring. Check out the new conversion packs, which act as a backpack but can easily separate into other smaller bags. Be sure to get a good one that won't fall apart on the plane trip over. Also, bring a canvas bag or day-pack for wallet, camera, maps, passport—stuff you'll want with you during the day and shouldn't leave with your backpack at the hotel or stored in a locker at the train station. Be sure to take a passport-holder that you can wear around your neck or a sturdy, inconspicuous money-belt. It may be a good idea to get a backpack or suitcase that you can lock. At night you'll also want to lock it to something immovable: the luggage rack of a train, for example.

Bring good, comfortable walking shoes and a pair of plastic thongs for scary showers. A pocketknife is sure to come in handy, as will a small flashlight, but most basic toiletry items can be purchased outside of the U.S. This is especially true if you are traveling to Europe or to large cities elsewhere. Plan ahead if you wear glasses or contact lenses, and bring any special medication you might need along with a signed note from your doctor explaining what it is (handy in emergencies or when dealing with suspicious border guards). Keep in mind that it is easier to pack light and buy any necessities you may have forgotten.

Be sure to take clothes that are sturdy, climate-friendly, and easy to care for. Plan to dress comfortably but be sensitive to local customs; for example, in many countries people wear shorts only when involved in sports or at the beach. Bring a pair of long pants or a long skirt or you won't be let into many places of worship; it's no fun to have to wait outside. Remember too that without an electrical converter and an adapter plug, your U.S. electrical appliances will be worthless in most other countries. For suggestions on what to pack, check guidebooks for the region you are going to or talk to someone who has recently been there.

Becoming Informed

No matter where you go, you'll be asked questions about U.S. foreign policy, especially matters that directly affect the countries you visit. The best thing to do is prepare yourself a little in advance by reading newspapers like the *New York Times*, the *Washington Post*, the *Wall Street Journal*, and the *Christian Science Monitor*, which, although not always objective or without bias, are known for their coverage of international affairs. Especially valuable are the publications of the **Foreign Policy Association**, a nonprofit, nonpartisan organization dedicated to informing the public of the complexities of foreign-policy issues. One of the best ways to quickly inform yourself about foreign-policy topics is to read *Great Decisions*, which describes the pros and cons of alternative courses of action on eight different foreign policy issues each year. The 1993 edition of *Great Decisions* costs $10 (plus $3 postage and handling) and is one of many publications on foreign policy topics available from the Foreign Policy Association, 729 Seventh Avenue, New York, NY 10019; (212) 764-4050; fax (212) 302-6123.

For a quick introduction to the culture of various countries, we recommend *Culturegrams*, published by Brigham Young University's **David M. Kennedy Center of International Studies**. These country-specific profiles briefly describe the customs, manners, and lifestyles you'll encounter in more than 100 countries. The four-page briefings also discuss typical greetings and attitudes, religion, and politics. Single *Culturegrams* cost $1; educational discounts are available. For ordering information, contact the Center's Publication Services, 280 HRCB, Brigham Young University, Provo, UT 84602; (800) 528-6279.

CHAPTER THREE

WORKING ABROAD

Have you ever considered picking grapes in southern France? A business or marketing internship in Japan? What about volunteering to work in a clinic in Kenya or teaching school in Bolivia? Each year, CIEE receives about 50,000 inquiries on the subject of working overseas. Getting a job abroad can help finance the trip, furnish valuable job experience, and provide a good way of really getting to know a country and its people.

Finding a job abroad is not easy, but it is most certainly possible. To deal with the wide range of options available, we've divided this chapter into four general sections: Short-Term Jobs, Voluntary Service, Teaching Abroad, and Long-Term Employment.

SHORT-TERM EMPLOYMENT

Summer Jobs

For most countries, you will be required to have a work permit before you can obtain work. Some countries will not grant a permit until you have a promise of a job from an employer, and some employers say they cannot hire you without a work permit. This can be frustrating, to say the least, and many students never get beyond this catch-22 situation.

Fortunately, there is an easy way to avoid these difficulties. For over 20 years, **CIEE** has been operating a unique work program that eliminates the red tape and enables students to get work permits in Canada, France, Germany, Britain, Ireland, New Zealand, Spain, and Costa Rica. In 1993, more than 5,000 American students took advantage of the program. As a participant in the CIEE Work Abroad program, you receive the necessary authorization to work in the country you have chosen to visit, along with a program handbook containing general information on the country, tips on employment, a list of possible employers to contact, and helpful hints on housing and travel. In each country, the program is offered in cooperation with an overseas national student organization whose staff is available to advise you on hunting for a job, as well as a place to live, and will provide you with an orientation upon arrival. For most countries in this program, work authorization is for summer jobs only. But in France, Ireland, and the United Kingdom, work authorization for short-term employment can be arranged any time of the year. For details on the program, write the Work Exchanges Department at CIEE, 205 East 42nd Street, New York, NY 10017.

Working a short-term unskilled job in another country probably will earn you enough to cover food, lodging, and day-to-day living expenses. You should not expect to earn enough to pay for your air transportation, but if you are lucky you may save enough to cover some of your travel costs after you leave your job. Whatever job you find probably will not be glamorous, although two students participating in the program found themselves serving the Queen during Prince Andrew's royal wedding reception. Remember that in the final analysis employers only want someone who will do the job well and are not interested in any romantic notions you may have about working in a foreign country.

CIEE's Work Abroad Program is open only to U.S. students. Canadians who wish to go on a working holiday abroad should contact **Travel CUTS/ Canadian Federation of Students—Services**, 243 College Street, Fifth Floor, Toronto, Ontario MST 2YI. This member organization of CIEE operates SWAP (Student Work Abroad Programme), which sends students to a number of overseas destinations.

Another possibility for summer employment abroad is working as a group leader with one of a number of U.S. organizations that offer international programs, such as **World Learning Inc.** (founded in 1932 as the U.S. Experiment in International Living). This organization, which sends small groups of high school and college students abroad, has summer leader and semester academic director positions available around the world. You must have experience in cross-cultural living and working with American teenagers or college students. Language proficiency is required for some countries.

One of the best sources for more information is the *Directory of Overseas Summer Jobs*, which lists more than 50,000 jobs worldwide from Australia to Yugoslavia. Listings include names and addresses of employers, length of employment, rates of pay, how and when to apply, duties, and qualifications sought. Published by Vacation Work (Oxford: United Kingdom), this book is revised annually. It is available from Peterson's Guides, PO Box 2123, Princeton, NJ 08543; (800) 338-3282, for $14.95 plus $4.75 shipping and handling.

Another useful publication is *Work Your Way Around the World*, which contains good advice for anyone planning a long working trip. Although at times the advice verges on the bizarre, overall it's very practical and comprehensive. The book, written by Susan Griffith, is published by Vacation Work (Oxford: United Kingdom), and available in the U.S. through Peterson's Guides for $17.95 plus $4.75 shipping and handling (see address above).

Finally, *Working Holidays*, which is updated annually, contains approximately 300 pages of information on paid and voluntary work opportunities worldwide. Published in the United Kingdom, it's available from the Institute for International Education, 809 United Nations Plaza, New York, NY 10017, for $19.95 plus $3.00 shipping and handling.

Internship and Trainee Programs

Although finding internships or trainee programs abroad may require some research, they have become quite popular. Interns not only get the opportunity to learn the skills required for a specific profession, but also the chance to develop the cross-cultural understanding and communication skills that have become vital in the global environment in which many professionals and business executives now function.

Internships may be paid or unpaid positions—more often the latter—in a company, an organization, or an educational institution. The motivating factor is the applicant's overall desire to train, update, or strengthen a particular skill or field of study. Some assignments may include tedious or clerical tasks in addition to the more meaningful project work. Remember, too, that an overseas internship will no doubt require some economic initiative on your part, since few positions are salaried and most likely you will have to spend some money getting there.

Begin planning your internship experience abroad as far in advance as possible. You'll find internship/traineeship opportunities described under the "Work" heading of the individual country sections later in this book. Also check under the "Study" heading for internship options that may be part of the study abroad programs offered by U.S. colleges and universities. You should also be aware of three organizations that arrange traineeships around the world for students possessing certain skills:

- **AIESEC—US.** The International Association of Students in Economics and Commerce (known by its French initials, AIESEC) is a worldwide association of students that offers opportunities for college/university students to gain practical management and leadership skills with a global perspective. Opportunities include organizing and participating in international conferences and working abroad through a reciprocal internship exchange program in a variety of business-related fields. Internships are offered in 74 member countries lasting 6 weeks to 18 months. Living expenses are covered by the hosting firm. The programs are restricted to full-time undergraduate or graduate students active in local AIESEC chapters at 70 U.S. colleges and universities. To find out if your institution has an AIESEC chapter, check with the career placement or study abroad office on your campus. For more information, contact AIESEC—US, 135 West 50th Street, 20th Floor, New York, NY 10020; (212) 757-3774.
- **IAESTE Trainee Program.** The International Association for the Exchange of Students for Technical Experience (IAESTE) provides on-the-job training for students in engineering, architecture, mathematics, computer sciences, and the natural and physical sciences in 60 countries around the world. Juniors, seniors, and graduate students enrolled in an accredited college or university are eligible to apply. Each trainee is paid a maintenance allowance to cover living expenses while training. Fluency in the language is required for some countries. The application deadline for summer placements is December 10; for long-term placements of from 3 to 12 months, a minimum of 4 months' processing time is required. For more information, contact IAESTE Trainee Program, c/o Association for International Practical Training, 10 Corporate Center, Suite 250, 10400 Little Patuxent Parkway, Columbia, MD 21044-3510; (410) 997-2200.
- **People to People International.** In collaboration with the University of Missouri–Kansas City, People to People sponsors two-month summer internship programs in England, Ireland, Germany, Australia, France, the Czech Republic, Mexico, and Russia. Prospective interns submit a completed application and placements are arranged based on the applicant's background and interests. Six semester hours of academic credit (undergraduate/graduate) may be earned from the University of Missouri; noncredit participation is also available. For further information contact Collegiate and Professional Studies Programs, People to People International, 501 East Armour Boulevard, Kansas City, MI 64109; (816) 531-4701.
- **YMCA Intern Abroad.** The YMCA Intern Abroad program, conducted by the YMCA of Metropolitan Washington, offers an opportunity to volunteer with YMCA staff members in project countries. Participants live in local YMCAs or with YMCA host families; most assignments are for the summer and range from teaching English or sports to working in camps or with development projects. Internships have been conducted in Australia, Austria, the Bahamas, Bangladesh, Brazil, Chile, Colombia, Costa Rica, Egypt, England, France, The Gambia, Gaza, India, Ireland, Kenya, Sri Lanka, Switzerland, Tanzania, Thailand, Trinidad, Uruguay, Venezuela, Zambia, and Zimbabwe. Contact National Capital YMCA, 1711 Rhode

Island Avenue NW, Fourth Floor, Washington, DC 20036, for further information.

Before taking off, be certain to plan your project carefully with a study abroad or academic adviser. Talk to someone who has completed an internship abroad—if possible, one in your field of study. And keep an open mind even if the feedback you get is not all positive—some individuals require a more structured program.

One of the most helpful resource books on internships is the *Directory of International Internships*, which is put together by various offices at Michigan State University. Listed are descriptions of international internships offered by educational institutions, government agencies, and private organizations. It is available for $20 and can be ordered from the Office of Overseas Study, 108 International Center, Michigan State University, East Lansing, MI 48824; (517) 353-8920.

Another helpful book, *Internships*, is revised annually and focuses mostly on internships available within the U.S. but also includes a chapter on positions overseas. You can check your library or career placement office for a copy; it can also be ordered from the publisher, Peterson's Guides, PO Box 2123, Princeton, NJ 08543; (800) 225-0261. The 1994 edition costs $29.95 plus $5.75 postage.

For a good reference that combines internship opportunities with voluntary service programs, consult *International Internships and Volunteer Programs*, by Will Cantrell and Francine Modderno. This publication includes descriptions of organizations that sponsor internship and voluntary service opportunities abroad, including businesses, development firms, educational institutions, government agencies, and more. While some programs require applicants to have specific skills or experience, others welcome those with a more general background. This book is available for $18.95 (postage included) from the publisher, Worldwise Books, PO Box 3030, Oakton, VA 22124; (703) 620-1972.

Au Pairs, Nannies, and Mothers' Helpers

If you enjoy working with children, you may want to consider becoming an au pair, nanny, or mother's helper overseas. As largely live-in jobs, these positions will provide you with firsthand exposure to family life in another culture.

Au pair positions are primarily geared toward young, single people who are interested in learning the language and culture of a foreign country. Working about 30 hours per week, six days per week, an au pair cares for children but usually has less responsibility than a nanny. Nannies usually have sole responsibility for the children around-the-clock, with one or two days off per week. Certification or substantial experience working with children is required. Mothers' helpers usually work with the mother; sometimes they will have complete charge of the children. Household tasks such as cooking or cleaning may also be required. The helper usually works eight hours per day and babysits a few nights a week.

World Learning sponsors an "Au Pair/Homestay Abroad" program that places young people between the ages of 18 and 26 with families in France, Germany, Great Britain, Norway, Spain, and the Netherlands. Basic foreign language proficiency is required for placements in France, Germany, and Spain. English-speaking families are available in Great Britain, Norway, and the Netherlands. Host families provide full room and board and a weekly stipend. The participant's length of stay is flexible, ranging from 3 to 12 months. Contact **Au Pair/Homestay Abroad** at 1015 15th Street NW, Suite 750, Washington, DC 20005; (202) 408-5380. You can also reach them at 303 S. Craig Street, 2nd Floor, Pittsburgh, PA 15213; (412) 681-8120.

For further information consult *The Au Pair and Nanny's Guide to Working Abroad*, by Susan Griffith and Sharon Legg. Updated in 1993, this book discusses the pros and cons of working as an au pair, nanny, or mother's helper and provides suggestions on preparing for and coping with the experience. Also included is a discussion of working regulations in different countries and a listing of agencies that provide placement services. This guide is available for £8.95 plus shipping from Vacation Work, 9 Park End Street, Oxford OX1 1HJ, England; (44) 865-241978; fax: (44) 865-790885. Checks should be payable in British pounds and made out to Vacation Work.

Farm Camps

Have you ever been enticed by the notion of working on a farm? Farm camps bring together an international group of students during the summer to help with labor-intensive farm work, usually picking grapes or strawberries. Workers get paid by the amount of fruit they pick but must pay for their own room and board. Wages are not lucrative, but depending on how long and how fast you work, it is possible to earn some extra money. For specific information, see the sections on France and the United Kingdom in Chapter Six.

VOLUNTARY SERVICE

Workcamps

Workcamps bring together groups of people from various parts of the world to work (usually manual labor) on projects as varied as building a school in Africa or restoring a castle in France. The focus is on projects that meet community needs such as health care, education, environmental conservation, construction of low-cost housing, or restoration of historical sites.

Hundreds of workcamps all over the world are open to Americans. Usually there are no special requirements for participants other than a willingness to work. Most participants are young and often time is set aside for cultural activities, group discussions, and field trips.

CIEE recruits several hundred volunteers for placement each year with workcamp organizations in Algeria, Belgium, Canada, the Czech Republic, Denmark, France, Germany, Ghana, Hungary, Lithuania, Japan, Morocco, the Netherlands, Poland, Russia, Slovenia, Spain, Tunisia, Turkey, Ukraine, and Wales (U.K.), as well as in its own workcamps in the U.S. The camps are located in a wide variety of settings, from small villages to big cities, from national parks and forests to archaeological digs, and from farmhouses to historic monuments and castles. They usually last two, three, or four weeks. No salary is paid, but room and board are provided. U.S. residents should write CIEE's International Voluntary Service Department for further information on current workcamps.

For Canadian citizens, the **Canadian Bureau for International Education (CBIE)** offers a program of international workcamps in most European countries that is similar to those described for CIEE. Canadians should contact CBIE, 85 Albert Street, Suite 1400, Ottawa, Ontario K1P 6A4.

The **World Council of Churches** sponsors short-term workcamp projects during the summer in several countries of Africa, Asia, and the Middle East. Locations vary from year to year. Some workcamps require a knowledge of French; for others, English is sufficient. Most involve the construction of schools or other community buildings or rural development work. Local people often work alongside the volunteers on the project. Volunteers must be 18 to 30 years old, pay their own travel expenses, and contribute to their living expenses (which vary according to the project). For further information on what workcamps are planned in a particular year, write to Ecumenical Youth Action, World Council of Churches, 150 route de Ferney, PO Box 2100, 1211 Geneva 2, Switzerland.

In addition, the **Fourth World Movement** sponsors work/information camps that are committed to the rights of the poor in Belgium, Canada, the Netherlands, and Switzerland. Participants work for 10 days during the summer on projects that may involve construction, gardening, sewing, typing, and library or research activities. Volunteers are housed in cabins or tents and are responsible for their own meals, the cost of preparing the camp, and health insurance. For more information contact the Fourth World Movement, 7600 Willow Hill Drive, Landover, MD 20785; (301) 336-9489.

Also be sure to check the work sections in the country-by-country descriptions later in this book. The workcamp programs of CIEE-member organizations and institutions are described under the countries in which they are located.

Other Short-Term Voluntary Service

Workcamps, which involve an international group of volunteers working together on a project for two or three weeks, are only one type of short-term voluntary service experience. Some other volunteer opportunities for persons who are interested in spending part of their summer or academic year as a volunteer are described below.

- **The American Friends Service Committee** offers short-term voluntary service opportunities in Mexico and Cuba. Projects involve working in construction, recreation, education, and more. Volunteers must be 18 to 26 years of age and able to speak Spanish. The Mexico program lasts for about seven weeks during July and August; there is a participation fee of $750 plus transportation costs. The Cuba program takes place for three weeks in July and the participation fee is $300 plus transportation costs. Contact the American Friends Service Committee, 1501 Cherry Street, Philadelphia, PA 19102; (215) 241-7295.
- **Amigos de las Americas** conducts summer programs that provide community health services in a variety of Latin American countries. Volunteers need no experience in health care but must have at least one year of high school Spanish or Portuguese. Service training is provided and the minimum age for participation is 16. Programs last from four to eight weeks and the cost ranges from $2,300 to $3,000, depending on where the volunteer is placed. For further information contact Amigos de las Americas, 5618 Star Lane, Houston, TX 77057; (800) 231-7796.
- **YMCA's International Camp Counselor Program (ICCP) Abroad** offers U.S. students with camp counseling or YMCA experience an opportunity to work in a youth camp overseas. Positions in previous years have been offered in Austria, Colombia, England, France, Germany, Ghana,

Greece, Hungary, Italy, Japan, Nepal, New Zealand, Nigeria, Peru, Spain, Sweden, and Switzerland. Camps provide room and board (and sometimes a small stipend) in return for four to eight weeks of service. Participants pay a $125 (approximate) placement fee along with international transportation costs. For more information and applications contact YMCA International Program Services, 356 West 34th Street, New York, NY 10001; (212) 563-3441.

- **AFS Intercultural Programs** sponsors Global Service Projects for adults interested in offering their professional and life experiences in a variety of settings in Russia, Thailand, Ghana, China, and Mexico. These intercultural exchanges provide participants with the opportunity to engage in such activities as teaching English; providing lectures on American culture in high schools and universities; working on community service projects; and participating in daily village life. Projects run from three to seven weeks during the summer and are open to interested participants who are at least 19 years old; for the program in Mexico, working knowledge of conversational Spanish is required. For more information contact AFS Intercultural Programs, 313 East 43rd Street, New York, NY 10017; (800) 237-4636.

Archaeological Digs and Field Research Projects

Field research projects and archaeological digs offer the opportunity to be an active rather than passive learner and to expand in some small way what is known about the world in which we live. Possibilities include helping to excavate a Bronze Age city in Israel, studying sea lions off the coast of Mexico, or scuba diving to explore a long-submerged French settlement in the Caribbean. While some organizations require volunteers to make a rather large ''contribution'' to the project they will be involved in, it is still possible to find inexpensive opportunities where you can trade your hard work in the sun for room and board.

Some archaeological excavations accept inexperienced volunteers while others insist on volunteers who have some training or experience. The best source of information on archaeological fieldwork is the **Archaeological Institute of America (AIA)**. Each January, AIA publishes *Archaeological Fieldwork Opportunities Bulletin*, which includes a listing of opportunities for volunteers at excavations, field schools, and educational programs in several countries, including the U.S. Good health is always required for participants in archaeological field work, as well as adaptability to unusual foods or other local conditions. The *Bulletin* costs $11.50 for AIA members and $13.50 for nonmembers (postage included) and can be ordered from Kendall-Hunt Publishers, Order Department, 4050 Westmark Drive, PO Box 1840, Dubuque, IA 52004; (800) 228-0810. The Institute is also the publisher of *Archaeology* magazine, which twice yearly presents the ''Travel Guide,'' a special feature listing excavations in progress, as well as archaeological sites that welcome visitors as observers or active members of the field crew. To order a subscription, contact *Archaeology* magazine, 135 William Street, 8th Floor, New York, NY 10038; (800) 829-5122.

The University of California sponsors a **University Research Expeditions Program (UREP)** to support research in the natural and social sciences and provide educational opportunities for students, teachers, and the general public. Expeditions take place all over the world, and activities range from excavating archaeological remains to surveying wildlife and collecting marine specimens. Expeditions last from two to three weeks and no experience is necessary.

Participants are expected to make tax-deductible contributions to cover program costs and pay for their own transportation. Programs range anywhere from a low of $950 to a high of about $2,000. Scholarships are available for high school and college students and grants are available for K through 12 teachers; academic credit can be arranged. For more information, contact UREP, University of California, Berkeley, CA 94720; (510) 642-6586.

The **Foundation for Field Research** is a nonprofit organization that supports scientific projects by recruiting volunteers willing to donate their labor and pay a fee to participate. Projects in the disciplines of archaeology, botany, geology, mammology, ornithology, paleontology, and primatology are conducted all over the world and vary in length from two days to one month; the contribution can range from $649 to $990. The Foundation also publishes *Explorer News*, a free newspaper describing the projects volunteers can join. Contact the Foundation for Field Research, PO Box 771, St. George's, Grenada; (809) 440-8854.

Another nonprofit organization, **Earthwatch**, recruits volunteers 16 and over, for field research expeditions in 50 countries and 25 states in the U.S. Projects include helping with archaeological excavations in France and England and gathering data on volcanos in Costa Rica. Expeditions are directed by university professors, and volunteers participate for two to three weeks. Membership in Earthwatch costs $25 per year, which includes six issues of *Earthwatch* magazine. Though no special skills are required to participate, volunteers must be members of Earthwatch and pay a tax-deductible fee to cover the cost of room and board, equipment, and ground transportation; this fee ranges from $500 to $3,000, depending on the project. For further information, contact Earthwatch, 680 Mount Auburn Street, Box 403N, Watertown, MA 02272; (800) 776-0188.

Long-Term Voluntary Service

Many people prefer a longer term of voluntary service abroad than is available through a workcamp or field research project. Fortunately, the options in the field of voluntary service are unlimited with programs all over the world involving individuals in all sorts of voluntary-service opportunities lasting anywhere from a few weeks to several years. All share the same underlying goal: to involve participants in cooperative projects that respond to human needs and enrich people's lives. Volunteers in such programs are motivated by a sense of commitment, as well as by the rewards of personal and professional growth that derive from this type of work. A sample of such organizations is listed below; a more complete listing is available in the CIEE book *Volunteer! The Comprehensive Guide to Voluntary Service in the U.S. and Abroad.* Be sure to check the country sections later on in this book for voluntary-service programs specific to a particular country.

- **Brethren Volunteer Service** is a Christian service program dedicated to advocating justice and peace, as well as serving basic human needs in the U.S. and 18 countries overseas. Volunteers, who must be at least 18 years old, provide a variety of community services, including education, health care, and assistance for the homeless and hungry. Participants are required to serve for two years abroad. Contact Brethren Volunteer Service, 1451 Dundee Avenue, Elgin, IL 60120, for further information.
- **The Episcopal Church's Volunteers for Mission** matches volunteers with projects in the U.S. and abroad. Assignments last from six months to two

years and include teaching, health care, social work, technology, agriculture, and other fields. For further information, contact Volunteers for Mission, Episcopal Church Center, 815 Second Avenue, New York, NY 10017.

- **International Christian Youth Exchange (ICYE)** offers persons ages 18 to 30 voluntary-service opportunities in the fields of health care, education, environment, construction, and more. The one-year program has homestay and academic credit options; participant scholarships are also available. Service opportunities are offered in Austria, Belgium, Brazil, Bolivia, Colombia, Costa Rica, Denmark, Finland, West Germany, Ghana, Honduras, Iceland, India, Italy, Japan, Kenya, South Korea, Mexico, New Zealand, Nigeria, Norway, Sierra Leone, Spain, Switzerland, and Taiwan. For more information, contact International Christian Youth Exchange, 134 West 26th Street, New York, NY 10001; (212) 206-7307.
- **The International Liaison of Lay Volunteers in Mission** is the official center for the U.S. Catholic Church's promotion, referral, and recruitment of lay mission volunteers. While it does not have its own voluntary-service programs, it does serve as a clearinghouse for others. *The Response,* its free, annual publication, provides information on over 144 organizations with openings for volunteers in the U.S. and abroad. Contact the International Liaison of Lay Volunteers in Mission, 4121 Harewood Road NE, Washington, DC 20017; (800) 543-5046 for further information.
- **International Voluntary Services (IVS)** is an independent, nonprofit organization that provides skilled and experienced volunteer technicians for projects serving the needs of low-income people in the Third World. The organization recruits internationally for technicians with relevant overseas experience to work with locally based groups in agriculture, health care, business cooperatives, community development, water resources, and AIDS education. IVS volunteers serve a minimum of two years and receive an "allowance package" to cover the costs of food, housing, and local travel. Benefits include life and health insurance, an education allowance for families with school-age children, and round-trip transportation to the country of assignment. Contact International Voluntary Services, Recruitment, 1424 16th Street NW, #603, Washington, DC 20036; (202) 387-5533.
- **The Mennonite Central Committee (MCC)** offers overseas programs that enable volunteers with skills in agriculture, rural development, public health education, water development, and appropriate technology to serve in about 50 countries in Asia, Africa, Latin and North America. Requirements include Christian faith; membership in a Christian church; and a belief in nonviolence. In most cases a college degree is essential. A three-year commitment is required for overseas placements; a two-year commitment is required for service in North America. MCC also offers the Youth Discovery Team Program, which combines service work with the study of language and culture and the exploration of faith. Three-month to one-year terms are available. For further information on any of MCC's programs, contact MCC, 21 South 12th Street, Akron, PA 17501; (717) 859-1151.
- **The Presbyterian Church's Mission Volunteers/International Program** offers overseas voluntary-service opportunities for periods usually ranging from one to two years. Requirements include a B.A./B.S. degree and active church membership (not necessarily Presbyterian). The *Mission Service Opportunities* bulletin, published through the MV office, lists information about positions available. To receive a copy of the bulletin or additional information contact the Mission Service Recruitment Office, Presbyterian

Church (USA), 100 Witherspoon Street, Room 3420, Louisville, KY 40202-1396; (502) 569-5295.

Service-Learning

You may also want to consider an interesting, relatively new opportunity that combines the concept of voluntary service with academic credit. In the words of Howard Berry, founder of an organization called the **Partnership for Service-Learning,** "Service-learning is a powerful union of two traditional goals, academic study and service to the world. Through service-learning programs for a semester, a summer, or a year, college students or recent graduates may continue formal learning and, at the same time, have the experience of working with others to address human needs."

The Partnership offers programs in England, Ecuador, Jamaica, the Philippines, France, India, Mexico, and South Dakota (with Native Americans). Projects in the fields of health care, education, and community development are available during the academic year, the January interim, and the summer. Students spend 15 to 25 hours per week in a service capacity while taking a full academic load at the university affiliated with the program. There is an administrative fee covering academic instruction, service placement and supervision, orientation, room, basic board, and field trips; airfare is extra. Financial aid and loans usually may be applied to program costs. For more information, contact the Partnership for Service-Learning, 815 Second Avenue, Suite 315, New York, NY 10017; (212) 986-0989. Most colleges and universities grant academic credit for participation in the programs of the Partnership for Service Learning; check with your own institution before applying.

Publications on Voluntary Service

CIEE compiles *Volunteer! The Comprehensive Guide to Voluntary Service in the U.S. and Abroad*, a guide to short-, medium-, and long-term service programs worldwide. Copublished with the **Council of Religious Volunteer Agencies (CRVA)**, the book lists over 170 organizations that place participants on voluntary-service assignments. Opportunities may last a week, a month, six months, or up to a year or two and range from positions for highly skilled professionals to assignments for people with nothing more than a sincere desire to help. *Volunteer!* costs $8.95 (plus $2.50 for first-class or $1 for book-rate postage) and can be ordered directly from CIEE, 205 East 42nd Street, New York, NY 10017.

Another publication on the subject, written primarily for a British audience, is *The International Directory of Voluntary Work*, by David Woodworth. Published by Vacation Work (Oxford, England) this book is available from Peterson's Guides, PO Box 2123, Princeton, NJ 08543; (800) 338-3282, for $15.95 plus $4.75 shipping and handling.

If you're interested in short-term voluntary service, you may want to consult *Volunteer Vacations*, by Bill McMillon. Revised in 1993, the fourth edition includes opportunities in the U.S. and overseas. Available for $11.95 plus $3.50 for shipping from Chicago Review Press, Inc., 814 North Franklin Street, Chicago, IL 60610; (312) 337-0747.

TEACHING ABROAD

Teaching is perhaps the most common way that Americans have found to support themselves during extended stays overseas. Teaching opportunities range from informally teaching English as a private tutor to working as an intern, aide, or regular teacher in a public school abroad; from volunteering to teach in a Third World country to working as a regular faculty member in an "American" school abroad. Other long-term employment possibilities are discussed later in this chapter.

Teaching English

Most American college graduates possess a skill that's in demand throughout the world: they know how to speak English. Today, for mostly economic reasons, English is being used as an international language more than ever before, and more and more people are being encouraged to learn it. New English-language schools are popping up all over Europe and Asia. Private companies conduct in-house language classes for their staff, and families look for tutors for their children. Most Americans, as native speakers, can easily find work teaching English overseas.

Your university's career development office may have information on overseas companies or language institutes in need of recent college graduates to fill teaching positions. You can also look through the want ads in foreign English-language newspapers. Arranging employment before you go gives you the security of a legal work permit. The other route, finding work after arrival, may leave you little option but to teach privately without legal authorization. In fact, however, teaching privately is often more profitable than teaching for an institute or business. On the other hand, it is less secure. Schools and companies maintain different standards for their teachers. Many do not require certification in Teaching of English as a Foreign Language (TOEFL), but most prefer some teaching experience. It's a good idea anyway to gain some experience before you leap into teaching, even if you're planning only to teach informal conversation. Consider volunteer work in your university community before you go abroad.

Other Teaching Positions Abroad

WorldTeach, a program based at the Harvard Institute for International Development, has placed over 700 volunteer teachers in Africa, Latin America, Central Europe, and Asia. In 1993–1994, volunteer opportunities were available in China, Costa Rica, Namibia, Poland, Thailand, Russia, and South Africa. Volunteers teach English, math, or science; in South Africa, they also coach soccer and teach physical education. No special language skills or teaching experience are necessary. A bachelor's degree from an accredited college or university and a one-year commitment are required for all programs except the Shanghai Summer Teaching Program, which is open to undergraduate and graduate students. For further information, contact WorldTeach, Harvard Institute for International Development, One Eliot Street, Cambridge, MA 02138-5705; (617) 495-5527.

If you are a recent college/university graduate interested in teaching abroad, you may want to contact the **International School's Internship Program (ISIP)**. Whether you have teaching experience or not, ISIP can arrange an internship for you. Opportunities are available for 10 months on the elementary, junior-, and senior-high school levels. Interns receive a cost-of-living stipend, health insurance, and round-trip transportation to the program site. For further information, contact the International School Internship Program, PO Box 103, West Bridgewater, MA 02379; (508) 580-1880.

Another teaching program that has employed many American teachers abroad is operated by the **Department of Defense**. This program maintains approximately 240 elementary, junior-, and senior-high schools, along with a community college, in 19 countries for children of U.S. military and civilian personnel overseas. It is responsible for staffing these schools with teachers, counselors, librarians, nurses, psychologists, and social workers. Some of the elementary schools are small, and teachers are required to teach more than one grade; some junior-high schools require that you teach two or more subjects. Assignments are for one or two years. The Department of Defense is emphatic that applicants must "agree to accept an assignment to any location throughout the world where a vacancy exists and where their services are needed." For the latest copy of *Overseas Employment Opportunities for Educators*, write to the Department of Defense, Office of Dependents' Schools, Recruitment and Assignment Section, 2461 Eisenhower Avenue, Alexandria, VA 22331-1100.

Teachers interested in positions abroad might find a job opening through the **International Schools Services (ISS)**, a private, not-for-profit organization that recruits and recommends personnel for American and international schools abroad. At present, ISS serves over 200 schools in Africa, Europe, Asia, Latin America, and the Middle East. Applicants must have a bachelor's degree and at least two years of current experience at either the elementary or secondary level. There is a $50 registration fee, and an additional fee if the candidate finds a position through ISS. For information on registration procedures, contact the ISS Educational Staffing Program, 15 Roszel Road, PO Box 5910, Princeton, NJ 08543. ISS also publishes a directory of American schools abroad, *The ISS Directory of Overseas Schools* ($34.95 plus shipping and handling), available from Peterson's Guides, PO Box 2123, Princeton, NJ 08543; (800) 338-3282.

Another organization that might be of assistance is the **European Council of International Schools (ECIS)**, which comprises 250 affiliated schools at the pre-university level, chiefly in Europe, but also in other locations. Every fall ECIS publishes an *International Schools Directory* giving detailed descriptions of its member schools and a listing of more than 500 other English-speaking, independent international schools throughout the world. The directory may be ordered from Peterson's Guides (address above); the cost is $29.95 plus $5.75 postage.

Publications on Teaching Abroad

A directory that's useful for those seeking teaching positions abroad is *Schools Abroad of Interest to Americans*. Now in its eighth edition, the book is written for parents who wish to send their children to school abroad. Over 800 elementary and secondary schools in 130 countries are described. The book is available from the publisher, Porter Sargent Publishers, 11 Beacon Street, Boston, MA 02108 ($35 plus $1.98 for postage and handling).

Divided into country-by-country sections, *Teaching English Abroad*, by Susan Griffith, provides an introduction to the range of opportunities available overseas, including training requirements; how to start the job search; and a listing of specific schools that have openings for teaching English as a Second Language. Published by Vacation Work (Oxford, England), this book is available from Peterson's Guides, PO Box 2123, Princeton, NJ 08543; (800) 338-3282, for $13.95 plus $4.75 shipping and handling.

The *ISS Directory of Overseas Schools 1992–93*, a comprehensive guide to American-style elementary and secondary schools abroad, is a useful reference for information on schools abroad. It is available for $34.95 plus $5.75 for shipping from Peterson's Guides, PO Box 2123, Princeton, NJ 08543; (800) 338-3282.

LONG-TERM EMPLOYMENT

Finding a long-term job outside the U.S. is not easy. It can be done, and has been done, but it takes a great deal of patience and perseverance. Most governments are extremely strict about the employment of foreigners in their country. In most countries, before a work permit is issued, the employer must convince his or her government that the job being given to a foreign citizen can be done only by that person and that there isn't a local worker who can do the job. What this means is that your chances of getting a job overseas are related directly to the skills you've acquired before you apply. If you're a doctor, nurse, or teacher, you may be needed. If you've had a liberal arts education with little specialization, you have problems.

There are plenty of horror stories about people who have paid substantial fees to employment agencies that lure people with promises of foreign positions and then do absolutely nothing for them. Very often these organizations go unpunished since they word their advertisements cleverly and are careful not to promise anything at all in writing. Your best bet, whether you decide to use an employment agency or not, is to become informed using some of the directories and other resource materials listed in this chapter.

Jobs with the U.S. Government

The U.S. government, the largest single employer of American citizens working abroad, assigns over 150,000 civilian personnel overseas. The U.S. Department of State, the U.S. Department of Commerce, the U.S. Department of Agriculture, the U.S. Information Agency, and the Agency for International Development all hire personnel for positions abroad. Overseas assignments are made primarily to about 260 diplomatic and consular posts abroad.

How to Find an Overseas Job with the U.S. Government, by Will Cantrell and Francine Modderno, describes 17 government agencies as well as the specialized agencies of the United Nations. Information on internship, entry-level, and mid-level employment opportunities is included, as well as tips on how to prepare for the Foreign Service exams. This book is available for $28.95 (postage included) from the publisher, Worldwise Books, PO Box 3030, Oakton, VA 22124; (703) 620-1972.

One option to consider is the **Foreign Service**. Foreign service officers manage overseas posts and perform political, economic, consular, administrative, and cultural functions. They are selected through a rigorous written and oral examination process. Interested applicants for entry-level foreign service positions in the Department of State, the United States Information Agency, and the Department of Commerce's Foreign Commercial Service should write to the Recruitment Division, Department of State, PO Box 12226, Rosslyn Station, Arlington, VA 22219.

The Department of State has a number of other employment opportunities within the Foreign Service, including Foreign Service Specialists, who perform vital technical, support, and administrative services overseas and in the United States. Candidates for these positions must possess a high school diploma or its equivalent, and meet any other stated qualifications for the particular position. A current vacancy listing and corresponding vacancy announcements that describe the application procedures can be obtained from the Recruitment Division, Department of State, PO Box 9317, Rosslyn Station, Arlington, VA 22219.

The **Peace Corps** is another government agency that offers positions abroad, and although remuneration is not great, a living allowance is provided. Both generalists and specialists are in demand, including health-care workers, civil engineers, industrial arts teachers, architects, accountants, agriculturalists, urban planners, and forestry experts. The Peace Corps requires that participants have either a four-year degree from a college or university, or five years of experience in the field of placement. Volunteers serve for two years with an additional 7 to 14 weeks of training, including intensive language, cultural, and technical studies. The living allowance corresponds to what the volunteer's counterpart in the host country would earn. In addition, a readjustment allowance of $200 per month is payable upon completion of service. Applications for Peace Corps positions are available from Peace Corps, Public Response Unit, 1990 K Street NW, Washington, DC 20526; (202) 606-3000.

Jobs with International Organizations

There are many nongovernmental organizations that are active worldwide and that hire U.S. citizens for posts abroad. Included are organizations like the American Red Cross and CARE. Their needs and requirements are as varied as the organizations themselves. The best way to investigate employment possibilities in this category is to find out what organizations of this type exist. The three-volume *Encyclopedia of Associations*, published by Gale Research Company and available at most libraries, contains one of the most complete and best annotated listings of organizations in the United States; check especially the "Public Affairs" and "Foreign Interest" listings.

Another source of information on long- or short-term employment opportunities with international development organizations is the *Job Opportunities Bulletin*, published by TransCentury, a consulting group based in Washington, DC, that recruits highly qualified people to work in the Third World on various development projects. A year's subscription to the *Bulletin* (six issues) is $25 in the U.S. and $40 overseas. For information, write to TransCentury, 1724 Kalorama Road NW, Washington, DC 20009.

Jobs in International Business

U.S. companies seldom hire people for overseas positions unless the person has already had considerable experience living and working in that country. If an overseas job is not filled by a person with this type of experience, it is almost always filled by someone who has been working for the company for a number of years in the U.S. Generally, a company will take very few risks on untried personnel in overseas positions. If you'd like to work for a bank or some other international business operation, you might have to resign yourself first to serving a few years on U.S. soil. Be sure, though, that your employer knows that you'd eventually like to go abroad.

If you want to apply for business positions abroad, a useful publication is the three-volume *Directory of American Firms Operating in Foreign Countries*. It describes some 3,000 U.S. corporations with more than 22,500 subsidiaries and affiliates in 122 countries. The *Directory* is published by World Trade Academy Press Inc., 50 East 42nd Street, Suite 509, New York, NY 10017, and is available in most college as well as many public libraries. Many foreign embassies also put out lists of the U.S. companies that have branches in their countries.

Publications on Long-Term Employment

You may want to begin by reading *Careers in International Affairs*, compiled by the Georgetown School of Foreign Service, which provides you with an overview of opportunities available in the field. Listed are organizations that are recognized for hiring graduates with an international background. Included are chapters on the U.S. government, banking, business, consulting, international organizations, media, and nonprofit and educational organizations, as well as research organizations. Also included are helpful tips written by insiders in the field. Published in 1991, this book is available for $15 from Careers in International Affairs, PO Box 344, Mt. Vernon, VA 22121; (202) 687-2612. The *International Employment Hotline* is a monthly newsletter that lists current jobs and advice for ‘‘career’’ international job seekers; information on short-term opportunities abroad is also provided. A year's subscription is $36; contact *International Employment Hotline*, PO Box 3030, Oakton, VA 22124.

A useful booklet that realistically discusses all of the major considerations involved in seeking employment overseas is *Employment Abroad: Facts and Fallacies*. It's available for $7.50 from U.S. Chamber of Commerce, International Division, 1615 H Street NW, Washington, DC 20062.

The *Guide to Careers in World Affairs*, published by the Foreign Policy Association (729 Seventh Avenue, New York, NY 10019), is a paperback that presents more than 250 listings of some of the best sources of international employment in business, government, and nonprofit organizations. Published in 1993, the *Guide* costs $14.95 and can be ordered from Cornell University Press Services, (800) 477-5836.

Another source of information on the subject is *International Jobs: Where They Are, How to Get Them* (1989), by Eric Kocher, published by Adison-Wesley, Route 128, Reading, MA 01867 for $12.95. Aimed at college students, this book begins by offering a strategy for job-hunting abroad and then lists international businesses and organizations that might have openings. The second part is all quite general; don't take the title too literally.

The Overseas List: Opportunities for Living and Working in Developing Countries (1985), by David M. Beckmann, Timothy J. Mitchell, and Linda L. Powers, is for those looking for a job in the Third World. Written especially for Christians who are interested in service work, this book includes information on teaching, journalism, commerce, and government employment. It describes opportunities for salaried work and volunteering in Asia, Africa, or Latin America. Although the book is dated, the organizations described are still worth contacting. Published by Augsburg Fortress (426 South Fifth Street, Box 1209, Minneapolis, MN 55440), this book is available for $14.95 plus postage; (800) 328-4648.

The *Directory of Work and Study in Developing Countries* (1990), by David Leppard, is divided into three parts: paid work, voluntary work, and study. Described are nonprofit organizations, employment agencies, government offices, educational institutions, and business firms that provide opportunities for work, study, or voluntary service in the Third World. It's available from the publisher, Vacation Work, 9 Park End Street, Oxford OX1 1HJ, United Kingdom, for £7.95, plus £1.50 for surface mail shipping to the U.S. Checks should be made out in British pounds and payable to Vacation Work.

The Canadian Guide to Working and Living Overseas for Entry-Level and Seasoned Professionals, written for Canadians, includes such helpful general information on conducting an international job search as developing long-term career strategies; acquiring international skills; the resumé-writing and interviewing process; as well as reviews of 230 publications (many are published in the U.S.) and profiles of 750 employers. The 1992 guide is available from the publisher, ISSI, PO Box 588, Station B, Ottawa, Ontario K1P 5P7,

Canada, for US $37 (includes delivery). For VISA orders, call (613) 238-6169. The next edition is slated for publication in 1995.

Finally, a helpful guide for job-seekers interested in working in the Pacific Rim is *How to Get a Job in the Pacific Rim*, by Robert Sanborn and Anderson Brandao. It includes information on how to conduct a job search in over 20 countries (including Japan, China, Taiwan, Hong Kong, Thailand, Malaysia, Indonesia, Philippines, Australia, New Zealand, and Fiji); a discussion of short-term and career opportunities; and listings of potential employers in such industries as retail and wholesale, service, and tourism. Also included are major American firms operating in each country. This book is available for $17.95 from Surrey Books, 230 East Ohio Street, Suite 120, Chicago, IL 60611; (800) 326-4430.

CHAPTER FOUR
STUDYING ABROAD

There was a time not all that long ago when study abroad was the exclusive privilege of the rich. Now, for many reasons, study abroad has become a possibility for all—and the opportunities are boundless. The number of American students studying abroad continues to grow; figures gathered from colleges and universities across the U.S. indicate that more than 70,000 U.S. undergraduate students study abroad each year. Why do they choose to pursue part of their education overseas? A survey commissioned by CIEE in the mid-1980s indicates that nearly one-fifth of the participants in study programs abroad sponsored by U.S. institutions said career goals influenced their decision; many felt an overseas experience would add a new dimension to their schooling, improve foreign-language skills, and help them to become more independent. Of Americans preparing for a second trip abroad, the survey found that as a result of their first international experience, "an overwhelming number became more interested in international events, saw an improvement in academic performance, and became more self-confident."

The experience of living and studying abroad is one that enhances understanding, helping people see beyond their own world views to empathize with and truly comprehend other cultures. In fact, the belief that international understanding would promote peace and stability brought about the formation of CIEE shortly after the end of the Second World War. Today, in addition to the goal of achieving international peace and understanding, more selfish concerns about the United States' international competitiveness in the global arena of business and finance prompt leaders in business, government, and education to emphasize the need for enhanced foreign-language training and improved international education.

Like everything else, studying abroad means different things to different people. To one student it may mean a three-week summer course in French culture on the Riviera; for another it may mean a year of research on a doctoral thesis in the stacks of a German library. First, you'll have to decide what kind of study experience you want. Your choice will depend on things like your field of interest, your capabilities (particularly language skills), the amount of time available to you, and the amount of money you can afford to spend. You should also ask yourself: Am I independent and outgoing? Serious and academic? How organized and academically focused am I? How hesitant am I about going on my own?

Be certain to talk with your academic adviser or with your school's study-abroad adviser early in your planning. Your adviser will help you decide what kind of study-abroad experience you want, evaluate program possibilities, and arrange for credit transfers and the continuation of any financial aid package you might be receiving. If you don't have a study-abroad or academic adviser, make an effort to speak with your school's admissions officer, registrar, or dean of students for advice and assistance. Other good sources of practical information are foreign students or students who have returned from study abroad.

Also, think ahead to the time of your return to your home, friends, and school. There's a phenomenon in foreign travel that has been termed "culture shock." First of all, the process of preparing for a trip and then leaving behind familiar customs and values, as well as family and friends, can be very difficult. Then, while overseas, you may find that you change your outlook about many important things. This may include changing goals—both personal and educational. And finally, depending on the length and type of experience you have had, you may find readjustment to your old life difficult. Most things have probably stayed the same while you were gone, but you most likely have changed quite a bit.

STUDY-ABROAD OPTIONS

Once you have set your personal and academic goals, you need to look at all the different types of systems available to you. Should you enroll directly in a university abroad or should you participate in the study-abroad program of a U.S. institution? Do you want to be integrated into classes with regular students at the university or in classes specially designed for foreigners? Below are the basic program models for study abroad and the advantages and disadvantages of each.

Study-Abroad Programs of U.S. Colleges and Universities

Due to the challenges of direct enrollment in a foreign university, most Americans studying abroad choose a program sponsored by a U.S. institution. American colleges and universities sponsor hundreds of these programs. In fact, you should first check to see whether your own school sponsors an overseas program or is a member of a consortium (an association of colleges and universities) that sponsors such a program. Going abroad with your own university will ease the problems of transferring academic credit and maintaining any scholarships or loans you might have.

It's possible, though, that your college may not sponsor the type of program that you are looking for. If this is the case, don't be discouraged. Of the hundreds of colleges and universities that sponsor overseas study programs, most accept students from other campuses. In fact, there are so many programs to choose from that selecting a course from the listings in *Work, Study, Travel Abroad* (or one of the other books described later in this chapter in "For Further Information") can be a formidable task. Of course, you'll eliminate many of them after taking into consideration such things as language requirements, cost, academic focus, and the possibility of academic credit transfer to your own school. In making your selection, be sure to consult the office on your own campus that advises students on foreign study or administers your school's foreign-study programs. People in this office may be personally familiar with some of the programs you are considering and might also be able to direct you to students on campus who were participants at an earlier time.

Programs sponsored by American institutions grant academic credit that is usually fairly easy to transfer to your home college or university, although this should not be taken for granted. In order to avoid wasting your time and money, make sure to get your courses approved for credit by your college or university before you commit yourself to a program.

The study-abroad programs of U.S. colleges and universities encompass a wide range of program types. In many programs you can enroll in the regular courses of a university abroad. Others place students in special courses for foreigners offered by a college or university abroad. Often courses are designed by the U.S. institution and are taught by a regular member of the school's faculty. Most of the study-abroad programs of U.S. colleges and universities involve a mix of options that can be adjusted to the individual's needs and language abilities.

Study-Abroad Programs of Other U.S. Organizations

In addition to colleges and universities, a number of other U.S. organizations also offer study-abroad programs. One option is to enroll in a study-abroad program offered by a consortium of colleges and universities. Examples of organizations that offer study-abroad programs on behalf of their member colleges and universities are the Great Lakes College Association, the Associated Colleges of the Midwest, and the Council on International Educational Exchange. In a program sponsored by a consortium of colleges and universities, one or more of the participating colleges grant academic credit. As with any study-abroad program, be sure to check on the transfer of credit at your school before you sign up. Programs sponsored by consortia of colleges and universities generally are no different from those sponsored by an individual college and university; the same advantages and disadvantages apply (see previous section). In the country and regional sections later in this book, you'll find listed all the study programs of CIEE-member institutions, both individual schools and consortia of colleges and universities.

If you are considering a study-abroad program offered by an organization other than a college or university (or consortium of colleges and universities), make sure you know whether the organization is a nonprofit educational institution or a profit-making company. If you are considering a program offered by a for-profit organization, it is especially important to look into credit transfer in advance; most U.S. colleges and universities transfer credits only from other nonprofit educational institutions. All study programs listed in this book are offered by nonprofit educational institutions.

American Colleges Abroad

Another possibility for U.S. students is to study at one of the "American" colleges and universities that have been established abroad. Two of the better-known institutions of this type are the American University in Cairo and Sophia University in Japan. Organized like U.S. institutions, these universities generally host an international student body and offer a varied curriculum. You can enroll for a term or a year and transfer credits to your home institution, or you can enroll in a regular degree program offered by the school. Since most of these American colleges abroad are accredited by the same institutions that accredit colleges and universities in the United States, you shouldn't have much trouble transferring credit. However, be sure to check on credit transfer before you leave.

Some of these U.S.-style institutions abroad have a student body largely made up of Americans. Others, however, are designed to give local students the option of obtaining an American-style education in their own country. More information on these schools is available in two publications of the Institute of International Education: *Vacation Study Abroad* and *Academic Year Abroad* (see "For Further Information" near the end of this chapter).

Special Courses for International Students at Foreign Universities

Many universities abroad offer specially designed classes for foreigners, which usually include language classes and courses in the history and culture of the country. Some of these courses are taught during the academic year but most are given during the summer when foreign universities usually suspend their regular classes. Your classmates will be students from around the world, but not local students. For these courses you won't be expected to be completely fluent in the language or deeply knowledgeable about the country. However, credit granted by the foreign university for these courses may not be readily accepted by a U.S. university. Students who want to transfer credit to a university in the United States should make arrangements before going abroad.

The two best sources to consult for this kind of program are *Vacation Study Abroad* and *Academic Year Abroad*, both published by the Institute of International Education (see "For Further Information," near the end of this chapter). Also be sure to talk with the study-abroad adviser at your school.

Enrollment in a Foreign University

Direct enrollment in a foreign university can be an exacting venture and is best suited to the independent and highly motivated individuals who already have experience living abroad and are fluent in the language of the country where they plan to study. Others will probably need the support system of a program sponsored by a U.S. institution (see the above sections).

Students considering enrolling directly in a university overseas should be well aware that university systems and teaching methods in other countries are very different from those in the United States. For one thing, students entering a university in Europe are, generally speaking, at about the same educational level as juniors in a U.S. college or university. This makes it very difficult for an U.S. freshman or sophomore to enroll in a university abroad except in a special program of some kind.

Because of the differences between higher education systems from country to country, credit is not easily transferred from a foreign university to a U.S. university. Students who want to transfer credit earned at an institution abroad to a university in the United States are strongly advised to make an arrangement with the U.S. institution before going abroad; many American students return to the States to find that their home institution will not give them full credit.

Besides the problems of adapting to another educational system and transferring credit, there is also the problem of language. Study-abroad advisers at U.S. institutions report that a number of students without proficiency in a foreign language ask about the possibilities of direct enrollment at universities where the language of instruction is not English. According to one adviser: "The fact of the matter is that most Americans do not have sufficient foreign language skills to qualify for enrollment as a regular student at foreign universities in non-English-speaking countries. Many Americans grossly underestimate the time it takes to acquire the proficiency in a foreign language necessary to follow a formal lecture, take notes, participate in class discussions, and then compete on tests on an equal footing with those students who are native speakers of the language."

SELECTING A PROGRAM

Once you have explored the different study-abroad options, you will need to make even more detailed decisions about the length of your program, the teaching methods used, living arrangements, and spending money.

The Specifics

There are a number of factors students should consider in deciding how long to study abroad: timely fulfillment of graduation requirements, pertinence of courses to a particular field of study, degree of strain placed upon personal financial resources, and personal maturity and independence. It is generally assumed that the traditional year abroad (usually at the junior-year level) is the most rewarding. A growing number of students are participating in more than one study-abroad program during their college career, often going for a summer or other short-term experience initially, and later for a semester or year abroad. Although almost anything is possible, most programs do not accept first-year college students.

A semester or an academic year of study abroad will probably give you enough time to become involved in the student life of the country. Many students on semester programs, however, comment that just as they were finally gaining a firm grasp of the language and culture and had started to form meaningful friendships, it was time to go home. At the same time, other students feel a year only gives them enough time to get miserably homesick. After all, being away from home and friends for a year, or even six months, and having to cope with the pressure of another culture and academic system doesn't appeal to everyone. On the other hand, periods of homesickness or alienation are often inevitable phases in the process of expanding one's cultural awareness. Most students abroad feel that these somewhat negative experiences pass with time and, in fact, make them stronger for having endured them.

If you can't, or don't, want to interrupt your regular course of studies and go abroad for a semester or year, a summer program might be best for you. An extraordinary variety of opportunities is available. You can study journalism in London, botany in Brazil, or archaeology in Israel, for example. Taking a summer course might also be a good way to find out whether you would like to study abroad for a longer period of time.

More and more colleges and universities have switched to calendars that have an "interim" period between terms. During the interim, usually in January between the fall and spring semesters, students can select one of a variety of programs, many of which involve an off-campus experience. An example of an interim program might be an architecture tour in which participants spend a week attending classes in London and the rest of the time in an organized "tour" studying important works of architecture in several countries of Europe. Classes are usually taught by professors from the sponsoring school. Students can join such programs arranged either by their own or another school.

In the country sections of this book, we've arranged the listings into two broad groups: (1) semester and academic-year programs and (2) summer programs. You'll find interim programs—although they are short-term in character—listed in the "Semester and Academic Year" section, since they take place at various times during the school year.

In addition to the length of the program, another major consideration will be the manner in which the courses are taught. Does the program provide American-style courses in English or does it enroll you in a foreign university whose classes are likely to be large lectures in the local language? Or will you be taking special courses set up by the foreign university for all of their international students which are sometimes, but not always, taught in English? Will you be taught by U.S. professors or by professors from the host country? How much individual attention will you receive? There is a wide array of possibilities, and some programs offer several different options. Decide what's best for you.

Also of major importance are living arrangements. Will they involve you in the social life of the students of the host country? Some programs arrange for all U.S. students to live together in a hotel or dormitory; others house participants in university dormitories with students from the host country. Still others provide housing in rented rooms, apartments, or in private homes. (Students living with foreign families generally acquire a better understanding of the host country and its language, although they also may face particular difficulties in adapting to an unfamiliar family setting.)

Of course, there are personal preferences to take into account as well. How do you feel about the size of the institution? Would you like to be part of a cohesive group of fellow U.S. students, or would you rather be responsible for your own activities? Would you prefer studying in a major city or in a more rural setting? And last (but certainly not least), what should you expect to spend in the way of daily living expenses? Does the sponsoring institution provide any of these expenses?

Each country section later in this book contains listings, by subject area, of study programs for undergraduate and graduate students. These programs are sponsored by member colleges, universities, and organizations of the Council on International Educational Exchange. Addresses for the institutions offering these programs appear in Appendix I.

Evaluating a Program

Once you've decided to join a study-abroad program, you'll soon discover how many there are to choose from. Chances are that at first they will all sound good to you—and probably most of them are. But there are some that will not suit your purposes and some that are just not worth the money. Unfortunately, there have been incidents in which students have enrolled in programs only to find, on the eve of their trip, that the organization has disbanded and there is no program. The U.S. Information Agency often receives complaints from people who have found themselves taking courses of limited academic value as well as complaints from students who have discovered, too late, that they had paid fees far exceeding the value of the services received. Often, if the right questions had been asked before the student committed his or her time and money, the disappointments would have been avoided.

Lily von Klemperer, one of the pioneers in the field of study abroad, wrote a useful guide entitled "How to Read Study-Abroad Literature." We have borrowed most of what follows in this section on evaluating a program from this now-classic article.

Spend Your Summer in Sunny Spain!

(1) Live in a Medieval Castle or with a Local Family
(2) Learn Spanish at a Renowned Academic Institution
(3) Outstanding Faculty
(4) International Student Body
(5) Academic Credit Available
(6) Limited Enrollment—All Ages Eligible
(7) All-inclusive Charge
(8) Write to the Director of Admissions, PO Box 000, Cambridge, MA

Above is the text of an imaginary advertisement. How does this program sound? Let's take this mock advertisement line by line and see what it really does and does not say.

First, the emphasis seems to be on spending the summer in sunny Spain. Not an unappealing idea, of course, but if your objective is to learn the language, how will that be accomplished? How serious does the program sound if it uses as its "hook" a travel brochure's view of Spain?

Line 1: A medieval castle sounds great, but how close is it to the place where you will study or to town? Are there places to eat nearby? It may be a castle, but how has it been converted? Will you sleep in a dorm with six other students? And what about the host family? Is it going to turn out, in fact, to be someone who simply wants to make some extra money by having an American boarder?

Line 2: Just what is this famous university? Why isn't it named? Foreign universities do not have regular classes during the summer, so what is probably referred to here is a special course for foreigners—not a regular university class. Whenever the ad or brochure uses the words "recognized" or "accredited" to describe a learning institution, find out exactly who does the recognizing or accrediting, and what are the criteria they use.

Line 3: This reference to outstanding faculty needs to be explained carefully in any brochure. Their names, titles, and affiliation should be given. This phrase is much too vague.

Line 4: Get specifics on this. The students who are categorized as "international" may actually be sons and daughters of U.S. parents working abroad. Find out how many countries really are represented.

Line 5: This vague reference to credit is of little use, since the transfer of credit is such an individual matter. Whether or not you can get credit where you want it is something that only you can determine. You should, however, ask the sponsor to give you a list of institutions that have granted credit for the program in the past. This will be excellent ammunition if you need to approach your own guidance counselor or academic dean to request credit.

Line 6: How selective is this organization? What are the standards for limited enrollment? Are there, indeed, standards? And if all ages are eligible, how will you like being together with people much younger or older than you? If some are working for credit and others aren't, will that affect the seriousness of the work?

Line 7: "Inclusive charge" is much too vague. This is where the small print comes in. Find out exactly what is included and get an estimate of the total expenses, whether or not they are included.

Line 8: The actual name of a responsible person would be better here. When the backup brochure arrives, it should list (besides the director of faculty) a board of advisers, trustees, and so on. Don't let the Cambridge address mislead you into assuming that the program is affiliated with Harvard. Remember that anyone can get a post office box anywhere.

We obviously aren't able to give you an absolute qualitative framework for evaluating a program. In the final analysis, you have to decide what's best for the goals you have identified for yourself. We do suggest that you judge whether the costs of any particular program seem fair and representative of the course offerings and objectives. If you have questions, ask a study-abroad adviser if he or she has heard about the program.

SCHOLARSHIPS, LOANS, AND FELLOWSHIPS

You may be surprised to learn that study abroad, even with transportation included, is not necessarily more expensive than study in the United States. In fact, studying in many Third World countries, where the U.S. dollar generally has more purchasing power than it does at home, may even be cheaper than studying at your own institution.

Your school may be willing to apply your regular scholarship or loans to the cost of study abroad. Check with your academic dean or financial-aid office. And if financial factors are important to you, remember that your tuition costs may be lower if you apply for programs available through public universities in the state of which you are a resident.

The U.S. Department of Education's **Office of Student Financial Assistance** administers six financial-aid programs for students who are enrolled at least half-time in a regular course of study at a school that participates in the programs: the Pell Grant, the Supplemental Educational Opportunity Grant, the College Work-Study Program, the Perkins Loans, the Stafford Loans, and the Supplemental Loans for Students Program. Call the **Federal Student Aid Information Center** at (800) 433-3243 for more information. A student attending a foreign school may receive aid from one of these programs if that school is affiliated with an eligible institution located in the United States. Students attending school abroad may receive guaranteed student loans if they are attending an eligible foreign institution. To find out if a particular U.S. school is eligible, contact that school's financial-aid office.

CIEE's **International Student Identity Card Fund** provides travel grants to high school and undergraduate college students participating in educational programs in the developing nations of Africa, Asia, and Latin America. Students involved in any type of educational program including study, work, voluntary service, internship, and independent research programs are eligible to apply. Awarded twice a year, the grants cover the minimum cost of transportation to and from the program site. To apply, students must be attending a CIEE-member institution or planning to participate in a program sponsored by CIEE or one of its members. Application deadlines are October 15 and March 15. For more information contact CIEE, Information and Student Services Department, 205 East 42nd Street, New York, NY 10017; (212) 661-1414.

In their effort to further international understanding, the **Rotary Foundation** of Rotary International offers three types of scholarships especially for students who want to study abroad. Offered to students who have completed two years of university work (or equivalent professional experience), they include the Academic-Year Scholarships, Multi-Year Scholarships, and Cultural Scholarships (for three- to six-month study periods). Contact your local Rotary Club to inquire about the availability of scholarship types in your area and to obtain application forms. Deadlines vary by club, but most will probably fall between March and July of the previous year. If you cannot find your local club, the headquarters is One Rotary Center, 1560 Sherman Avenue, Evanston, IL 60201; (708) 866-3000.

While there are only a limited number of scholarships set aside for undergraduates who wish to study abroad, a greater number of grants are available to graduate students. *Fulbright and Other Grants for Graduate Study Abroad*, a free brochure put out each year in May by the **Institute of International Education (IIE)**, describes fellowships and scholarships administered by that organization. This 85-page booklet includes grants offered by foreign governments, universities, corporate and private donors, as well as U.S. government grants for graduate study abroad funded under the Fulbright-Hays Act. Application deadlines for these awards are not until the following October; the period for which these grants apply begins in the next academic year. Call U.S.

Student Programs at the Institute of International Education in New York at (212) 984-5330.

In New York City, a good place to do research on all kinds of foundation grants is the information library at **The Foundation Center**, open and free to the public. The library, at 79 Fifth Avenue, is open 10 A.M. to 5 P.M. Monday through Friday (Wednesdays until 8 P.M.). Another excellent source of information on fellowships and scholarships is the **Information Center of the Institute of International Education** (see page 42).

A number of directories, usually available in college and university libraries, provide information on specific scholarships, grants, and fellowships available for study abroad. However, most of the scholarships and grants in the directories listed below are available only at the graduate level.

- *Foundation Grants to Individuals*, updated in 1993, contains information on more than 2,300 independent and corporate foundations which award grants to individuals. It is very user-friendly, with six indexes—including ones by subject area and geographic area—to help you target prospective grants. This book is available for $55 (plus $4.50 shipping and handling) from the Foundation Center, 79 Fifth Avenue, New York, NY 10003-3076; (212) 620-4230.
- *The Grants Register 1993–95* offers a detailed compendium of graduate-level awards offered for study, research, and training for nationals of all countries. Compiled by Lisa Williams and published by St. Martin's Press, it costs $89.95 and can be ordered by calling (800) 221-7945.
- *Financial Aid for Study and Training Abroad* and *Financial Aid for Research and Creative Activities Abroad*, edited by Gail Ann Schlachter and R. David Weber, has been updated and expanded in 1993. The grants in these books are thoroughly indexed by title, sponsoring agency, geographic location, subject of study, and even by application deadline, and include a bibliography of other financial aid directories. They are available for $30 and $40 respectively, plus $4 per book for postage and handling from Reference Service Press, 1100 Industrial Road, Suite 9, San Carlos, CA 94070; (415) 594-0743.
- *The International Scholarship Book*, edited by Daniel Cassidy and recently updated by Prentice Hall in 1990, provides a comprehensive list of scholarships, grants, and internships available in the public and private sector for study in dozens of countries. The author states that $6.6 billion in funds from corporations is unclaimed, "not because people were unqualified, but because no one knew where to look." The cost of the book is $22.95. Call (800) 223-2336 to order.
- *Study Abroad* is an international directory of fellowships, scholarships, and awards that can be applied to study and travel opportunities in over 100 countries. The 1993–94 edition, produced by UNESCO, is available from UNIPUB, 4611-F Assembley Drive, Lanham, MD 20706-4391; (800) 274-4888. It costs $24 (order #U7154).
- *Fellowships, Scholarships, and Related Opportunities in International Education* is published by the Center for International Education, 201 Aconda Court, University of Tennessee, Knoxville, TN 37996-0620; (615) 974-3177. The cost of the 1993 edition is $10, including postage; make checks payable to the University of Tennessee.
- *Free Money for Foreign Study* offers information on hundreds of sources that fund undergraduate and graduate study in 68 countries around the

world, indexed by country and by academic discipline. It costs $14.95 and can be ordered from Facts on File, 460 Park Avenue South, New York, NY 10016-7382; (800) 322-8755.
- The seventh edition (1989) of the *Fellowship Guide for Western Europe* is available from the Council for European Studies, Box 44 Schermerhorn Hall, Columbia University, New York, NY 10027; (212) 854-4172. The cost is $8 (make checks payable to Columbia University).

A special note for veterans: Many university-sponsored study-abroad programs are open to veterans, in-service students, or eligible dependents. The Department of Veterans Affairs (VA) awards educational assistance for the pursuit of an approved program leading to a degree at an institution of higher learning. Additional information may be obtained at VA regional offices located in each state, or from the Director, Education Services (22), Department of Veterans Affairs, 810 Vermont Avenue NW, Washington, DC 20420.

FOR FURTHER INFORMATION

There are several places to go for additional information on study abroad. Start on your campus at the study-abroad adviser or international programs office. Also of assistance might be the placement office, the dean's office, or the library. One of the best and most often overlooked source of study information on any given country is that country's embassy or consular offices in the U.S. Most of these offices will provide, at no charge, lists of the specific courses available to you and instructions on how to go about enrolling in them. Addresses of representatives of foreign governments and the titles of useful information packets are included in the individual country sections later in this book.

If you are in or near New York City, you may want to stop at the **Information Center of the Institute of International Education (IIE)**, 809 United Nations Plaza, open Tuesday through Friday (except major holidays) from 11 A.M. to 4 P.M. Volunteers will assist you with the extensive resources of the Center, which include books, brochures, and audiovisual materials.

Publications on Study Abroad

The most comprehensive guide to study programs outside the U.S. open to Americans is *Academic Year Abroad*. Updated annually, this book by IIE lists, country by country, nearly 1,900 semester and academic-year study programs abroad for undergraduates and graduates. Full of necessary information on each program, this directory also offers guidelines for choosing a program and, with five indexes, is very easy to use. The cost is $42.95 (plus $3 shipping and handling). Write or call IIE Books, 809 United Nations Plaza, New York, NY 10017; (212) 984-5412.

The companion volume to the book above is *Vacation Study Abroad*, also published annually by IIE. It includes information on over 1,400 programs abroad that are open to U.S. students. Most take place during the summer but short-term programs at other times of the year, including the January interim and spring break, are also included. The cost is $36.95 (plus $3 shipping and handling). Order from IIE Books at the above address or phone number. Most international centers and study-abroad offices at U.S. universities also have copies of these two books.

For students planning to study at a foreign university—either through direct enrollment or by participating in a program sponsored by a U.S. institution—several of the following reference works might be useful. Since these are quite expensive, you'll probably want to check a library for a copy rather than purchasing your own.

Study Abroad is a directory of universities in over 100 countries that accept foreign students. It explains how to enroll directly in these schools and also gives financial aid information. For ordering information, see "Scholarships, Loans, and Fellowships." *The World of Learning* (London: Europa Publications, $370), which is updated annually and lists over 26,000 academic institutions around the world, is widely regarded as the most accurate and comprehensive guide of its kind. Universities in the Commonwealth countries (typically English-speaking ones) are detailed in the *Commonwealth Universities Yearbook* (New York: Stockton Press, $199). Facts on File publishes the *Guide to the Universities of Europe* ($35), by Storm Boswick, a country-by-country directory including information on academic requirements and scholarships for foreigners. If you choose to order this guide, contact Facts on File, 460 Park Avenue South, New York, NY 10016-7382; (800) 322-8755.

Another useful source is *Higher Education in the European Community: A Directory of Courses and Institutions in 12 Countries*, produced by the European Community Information Service (2100 M Street NW, Washington, DC 20037). It can be ordered from UNIPUB for $24.95 (plus $2.50 shipping and handling) at 4611-F Assembly Drive, Lanham, MD 20706-4391; (800) 274-4888. The *World Education Encyclopedia* (1988, Facts on File, $195), by George Kurian, provides descriptions of the educational system of every country in the world, from Afghanistan to Zaire. A similar publication is the *World Education Series*, which is a series of profiles of foreign education systems from the American Association of Collegiate Registrars and Admissions Officers (AACRAO), in cooperation with NAFSA. Although designed for U.S. admissions officers evaluating foreign academic credentials, these publications are also of use to the prospective student. For ordering information or catalogs, contact AACRAO, One Dupont Circle, Suite 330, Box 7822, Washington, DC 20036-1171; (202) 293-9161.

Medical students can find various resources on studying abroad as well. *The World Directory of Medical Schools*, compiled by the World Health Organization (WHO) and updated in 1988, costs $31.50 (plus $3 for postage and handling) and is available prepaid from WHO Publications Centre, USA, 49 Sheridan Avenue, Albany, NY 12210; (518) 436-9686. **Note**: Some agencies promising to place U.S. students in foreign medical schools charge large fees for their service; the Association of American Medical Colleges warns that these agencies usually charge fees for information that is available without cost from other sources.

High School Programs

Although the focus of this book is on work, study, and travel opportunities for college students, there is also a rapidly expanding number of programs abroad for high-school and junior-high-school students. Too numerous to be listed here, these programs are described in *Going Places: The High-School Student's Guide to Study, Travel, and Adventure Abroad* (see page xi).

It has become fairly common for students to take off the year between high school and college to do something "different" for a while before settling down to the academic routine again. *Going Places* is the best reference for such opportunities. Also check the sections on international workcamps, voluntary service, service-learning, and field research projects in Chapter Three of this book.

Programs for Adults

The number of educational programs abroad designed specifically for adults is growing by leaps and bounds. CIEE receives brochures almost daily describing programs abroad sponsored by museums, alumni organizations, and the continuing-education divisions of foreign universities. While the focus of this book is on work, study, and travel opportunities for college students, many of the programs described here are also open to adults not currently attending any type of school. To find these, check through the eligibility requirements for the study and travel programs listed in the country sections later in this book. To find learning vacations, you might also look at the various sections on workcamps, field research projects, and voluntary service in Chapter Three.

Traditionally, one of the most popular ways of taking a learning vacation has been to enroll in a language center in a foreign country and to spend a few weeks immersed in the study of the language. These language centers exist everywhere. Some are quite well known, like the Instituto Allende in San Miguel de Allende, Mexico. **Eurocentres**, a nonprofit organization based in Switzerland, operates 28 language centers in nine countries around the world. Holiday courses last from two to six weeks, and intensive courses up to three months. Students can live with host families or in hotel/pension facilities. More information and application information on Eurocentres is available from Council Travel offices across the country (see listing on pages xiii–xv) or from Eurocentres' new United States location at 101 North Union Street, Suite 300, Alexandria, VA 22314; (703) 684-1494.

One of the best sources of information on unusual educational opportunities for adults is CIEE's own *Smart Vacations: The Traveler's Guide to Learning Adventures Abroad*. Featuring more than 200 one- to six-week learning vacations throughout the world, *Smart Vacations* contains information on study tours, outdoor adventures, voluntary service, field research/archaeological digs, language institutes, environmental and professional projects, fine arts, and much more. For ordering information, see page xi.

For more information on learning vacations, Athabasca University in Canada puts out *Educational Travel*, a 230-page directory of programs around the world. It includes study tours and research expeditions offered by Canadian universities and colleges, volunteer and socially responsible travel opportunities, language and eco tours, art appreciation, archaelogical digs, and the like. Last updated in 1993, it is available for US $16.26 for Canadian addresses and US $18 for U.S. addresses from Marketing and Communications, Athabasca University, Athabasca, Alberta T0G 2R0, Canada; (403) 675-5864.

People 60 years and older seeking a learning vacation can participate in the popular **Elderhostel** program, which "combines the best traditions of education and hosteling." Elderhostel is based on the belief that retirement doesn't have to mean withdrawal but, on the contrary, can be an opportunity to enjoy new experiences. Besides an extensive network of Elderhostels in the U.S., where participants spend a week on a college campus studying different topics and enjoying activities in the local setting, the organization sponsors programs in 47 countries including Australia, Bermuda, Canada, France, Germany,

Great Britain, Holland, India, Ireland, Israel, Italy, Mexico, Scandinavia, and Spain. International programs usually last two to four weeks, involving one-week stays at each of several colleges or universities. For example, in a typical Elderhostel in Australia, participants spend a week at Dunmore Lang College studying the city of Sydney, a week on Heron Island focusing on the Great Barrier Reef, and a week at the Gippsland Institute in rural Victoria studying the relationship between man and the environment. For details on Elderhostel offerings, contact Elderhostel, 75 Federal Street, Boston, MA 02110; (617) 426-8056.

CHAPTER FIVE

MAKING YOUR TRAVEL PLANS

By now you're ready to see the world, be it as a student, volunteer, or tourist. Whether you plan to trek the Himalayas or simply find your way to a school in London, you need to know a little about your travel options in order to make the best decision about how to get to where you're going. And once you're there, you'll probably have to make some plans for getting around. Good research and planning can help you make the most of the time you have and can make a big difference in keeping your costs low.

If you live near a **Council Travel** office, your research will be a bit easier. Council Travel offices are full-service travel agencies that specialize in providing services for students and other budget-minded travelers. There are 43 of them in the United States, as well as a number in Europe and Asia (see pages xiii–xvi). Many are located near university campuses. All are staffed by trained personnel who can answer your questions about student discount fares, rail passes, and other ways to save money while traveling. CIEE's other travel subsidiary, Council Charter, is discussed later in this chapter.

Whether or not you live near a Council Travel office, your research should begin with a copy of *Student Travels* magazine, published twice a year by CIEE. It's available free of charge at Council Travel offices and distributed to colleges and universities all over the country. Your school's study-abroad office or international center might have copies on hand. If not, you can order a copy from CIEE, Information and Student Services, 205 East 42nd Street, New York, NY 10017; (212) 661-1414, ext. 1108. Featuring articles on the hottest destinations for students around the world, each issue brings you travel tips, a calendar of exciting local events, first-person accounts of overseas adventures, and detailed information on studying, working, or volunteering abroad. Remember: Research is the only way to make your overseas experience an economical one.

GETTING THERE

Finding the Best Airfare

The extremely competitive nature of the airline industry, which seems to be growing fiercer every year, keeps airfares affordable. Prices for tickets to some international destinations are actually falling. Because of low airfares, more and more travelers are heading to non-European destinations such as Asia, the South Pacific, and South America. Before you begin researching fares, you'll need to make a few decisions about your trip. You should have a rough idea of your general itinerary, your travel budget, how many stopovers you plan to make (if any), what time of year you plan to travel, and the length of time you plan on staying.

Airfares are generally determined by the "high" and "low" travel seasons.

For example, transatlantic flights are most expensive between June 1 and August 31. If you want to go for the summer, you should consider a May departure or, if possible, a September return. Conversely, South American and South Pacific destinations are most expensive between December 1 and March 1. Planning at least one leg of your trip at an off-peak time may save you money. Know too that fares go up during the weeks before and after major holidays, such as Christmas. However, if you don't mind traveling on the date of the holiday itself, when most people stay at home, you might be able to find a rare bargain. But whatever dates you choose, plan early—at least seven or eight weeks ahead of departure if you want to get the lowest fares available.

Be aware, too, that although some advertised fares may be lower than others, there are usually certain restrictions attached that you'll learn about only by reading the fine print. In some situations you may even be better off buying a more expensive ticket, particularly if you wish to make stopovers or need the flexibility to change travel dates. More expensive fares may allow you a number of "free" stopovers, resulting in an airfare that's better suited to your particular itinerary. As you do your research, keep in mind that inexpensive fares abound; they just require a certain amount of investigation, flexibility, and a good deal of creative planning. Let this be your guiding principle when it comes to airfares: Usually, the more conditions attached to a certain fare, the cheaper it's going to be.

If you're a student, you'll find that your **International Student Identity Card** (see pages 9–10) is worth many times what you paid for it. This card entitles you to travel on a student-fare basis to almost any destination in the world at savings of up to 50 percent off regular economy-class fares. If you're not a student but are under 26, you are eligible for most of the discounts if you get a **Go 25 Card** (see page 11). Educators also are eligible for some discounts on airfares at Council Travel offices if they have a valid **International Teacher Identity Card** (see pages 10–11). For more information, see "Student and Youth Airfares," below.

With all that in mind, it's not possible at press time for us to tell you exactly what international fares will be when you want to travel. What we can do, though, is advise you on how to go about getting the latest consumer information on the best fares available. Council Travel publishes "Airfare Updates," fact sheets that provide the latest information on nearly every type of international airfare; you can request these from a Council Travel office or have them mailed to you automatically by completing the appropriate form in *Student Travels* magazine. Also check the Sunday travel sections of large metropolitan newspapers such as the *New York Times*, the *Chicago Tribune*, the *Los Angeles Times*, and the *Washington Post*. Usually, these are full of ads for competitive airfares and contain the latest travel information in columns or feature articles.

Student and Youth Airfares

For those who are eligible, student/youth fares can save as much as 50 percent off the regular economy fare on a scheduled flight. Besides the low cost, student/youth fares have the advantage of having few of the restrictions that apply to most budget airfares. Student/youth fares are valid on regularly scheduled flights of a number of major international airlines. In order to qualify for most student/youth airfares, you must have either the **International Student Identity Card** or the **Go 25 Card** (see pages 9–11).

Council Travel offices can issue these cards in person when booking your flight; students not living in the vicinity of one of these offices often book their flight with Council Travel by phone after obtaining an International Student Identity Card at their school. Since a number of these student and youth fares are the result of contracts between CIEE and the various airlines, many student/youth fares are available only from Council Travel and other specially authorized travel agents. Student/youth fares are generally not sold directly by the airline, and airline ticketing offices will not have information about them. If you are dealing with a travel agency, make sure that it has access to student/youth flights.

Since student/youth flights are generally the lowest fares to most parts of the world, these are the fares that you'll find quoted as examples in the "Getting There" sections throughout this book. Some international airlines also allow teachers with the **International Teacher Identity Card** (see pages 10–11) to take advantage of the same low fares for students and young people. However, although students of any age are eligible for the International Student Identity Card, a number of airlines have placed age restrictions on student fares.

Charter Flights

A charter flight is one in which a tour operator reserves a plane to fly a specific route on certain dates. Booking an entire planeload of seats usually gives charter companies a price advantage, often allowing them to beat even the price of promotional fares and discount tickets. There are a lot of pros and cons to consider in deciding whether to take a charter flight. For example, most charters depart only from major cities; however, some operators offer low-cost "add-on" fares for connecting flights to other cities. Also, many charter flights have seasonal availability. Generally, charter flights depart less frequently than regular scheduled carriers.

Perhaps the biggest drawback to some charter flights is the difficulty of getting a refund or exchanging your ticket if you have to cancel your flight. If you book with **Council Charter**, however, tickets are refundable (less a $75 cancellation fee) as long as you cancel before your scheduled departure from the United States. Council Charter return flights can be changed in Europe for a fee of $75 as well. If you shop around early enough, using a charter company could result in substantial savings.

When making any travel arrangements, be sure to ask for the policy in writing. Some companies, Council Charter included, put your payment into an escrow account until departure, which protects you should the airline go under. In layperson's terms, this means that the company opens an account into which it places all the money it receives for a specific flight. By law, this money cannot be touched until the flight takes off.

If you decide to book a charter flight, here are some tips on avoiding an unpleasant experience:

- Read the fine print of ads—"OW" fares, for example, often represent one-way fares based on round-trip purchase.
- Get the ticket as soon as possible, perhaps by overnight mail; you'll have time to correct any scheduling errors. Also, make sure there are no alterations (flight times or dates covered with revalidation stickers).
- Pay by credit card, if at all possible. This way, you can cancel payment if problems aren't corrected.
- Try to book with a company that places your money in an escrow account.

Council Charter, which offers discounted seats on regularly scheduled flights, has more than 40 years of experience in the budget travel field. Two features that make its service unique are the mix-and-match plan, which lets you fly into one city and return from another, and the trip cancellation waiver. The latter, an optional waiver, is available for a modest fee at the time of booking and guarantees a full refund of all money paid if the cancellation notice is received anytime up to your scheduled check-in time. Although the actual cities served vary slightly from year to year, Council Charter's destinations generally include Amsterdam, Brussels, London, Madrid, Málaga, Paris, Rome, and other European cities. Many of the destinations are offered on a year-round basis. Council Charter also offers special low-cost, add-on fares from a variety of U.S. cities including Chicago, Cleveland, Denver, Las Vegas, Los Angeles, Minneapolis, Portland, Salt Lake City, San Diego, San Francisco, Seattle, and Spokane. You'll find fares for Council Charter flights across the Atlantic listed in the "Getting There" section of the chapter on Europe. For more information contact a Council Travel office or call Council Charter's toll-free number: (800) 800-8222.

Other Budget Airfares

If you aren't eligible for a student or youth fare and you can't find a charter flight to your destination, there are several other options to explore. Except for consolidator tickets, the options discussed in this section can generally be obtained directly from the airline. If you use a travel agent, however, select one who is interested in selling budget travel. Many agents simply aren't interested in scrolling through their computer databases on your behalf in return for the small commission a budget fare earns them. Similarly, those agents who don't normally devote a good deal of time to reading and studying bargain fares won't be of much help to you.

Below you'll find listed a variety of budget fares available for scheduled flights in 1993. Remember that in the highly competitive airline industry, fares, restrictions, and special promotions change frequently and without notice.

- **Economy Fares:** The term "economy," when applied to an airline fare, is a contradiction in terms. As it is used today, "economy" usually indicates an unrestricted, full-fare ticket for economy-class seating. Usually, you'll be able to find a cheaper fare, but it you are making reservations at the last minute or if you intend to make a number of stopovers en route, an economy fare may be your best—or only—option.
- **Advance Purchase Excursion (APEX) Fares:** In some ways the airline industry's answer to charters, APEX fares are between 30 and 40 percent lower than regular economy class. Since low fares seem to go hand in hand with restrictions, however, be aware that there are minimum- and maximum-stay requirements, cancellation and change penalties, and stopover restrictions. You must also purchase your ticket anytime from 7 to 30 days in advance.
- **Promotional Fares:** Bargain fares pop up sporadically; usually, they are part of a "quick sale" strategy that airlines use to fill seats during slow periods or price wars. One drawback is that they usually require the traveler to act immediately rather than meticulously plan an itinerary ahead of time. However, if you have the luxury of flexibility, promotional and bargain fares can be a dream come true.
- **Round-the-World Tickets:** Most major carriers sell round-the-world tickets, which are good for a certain number of stops over a specified period, usually one year. Travel must continue in one direction, with no backtracking. However, you can always arrange side trips and purchase addi-

tional stops for a small fee. Round-the-world tickets can be an economical alternative, but only if you really intend to be a world traveler. The average price in 1993, departing from the U.S., was $2,700. Better deals can often be found abroad (see end of this section). There are usually no student discounts for these passes, but around-the-world itineraries for students and young people can also be custom-designed using a combination of various student and discount fares linked together. This option is often cheaper than purchasing a single round-the-world ticket. Again, be sure to consult with a travel agent familiar with student fares, such as Council Travel Services.

- **Consolidator Tickets:** When airlines can't fill seats, they sell them to a consolidator at a big discount. Consolidators, also known as "bucket shops," offer these tickets at about 20 to 50 percent below normal prices to travel agents or directly to the public through newspaper ads. Often these tickets are nonrefundable and cannot be changed. Consolidated tickets are available for most major carriers. However, many smaller or foreign airlines use consolidators when they have difficulty selling tickets. In case any problems arise, it's wise to pay by credit card; although this may add a bit to the price, it makes it easier to get your money back.

In addition, to flights embarking from the United States, there are many special low-cost excursion fares on commercial routes connecting cities outside the U.S. Many of these can only be sold in the country where the flight originates. Check with the airlines wherever you are to see if such fares exist on the route you intend to travel. Certain cities have emerged as excellent places to look for inexpensive air travel. Amsterdam, London, Bangkok, Hong Kong, and Singapore, for instance, are famous as starting points for inexpensive flights to other parts of the world. These are also excellent cities to search for round-the-world tickets.

Flying as an International Air Courier

International courier companies use regularly scheduled flights on major airlines to ship items like film, documents, blueprints, advertising material, and canceled checks. While there are professional couriers, many courier companies operate by selling regular tickets at a significant discount to single travelers in exchange for using their luggage space. Most courier companies don't sell tickets directly, but instead through clearinghouses specializing in courier travel. Most of these agencies charge a membership fee of about $50, which entitles you to use their service for one year. Most courier services won't schedule flights more than two months in advance. Generally, the best deals are found at the last minute. Most courier services also require round-trip purchase, and stays are usually limited to periods between a weekend and one month. Although couriers can usually bring only carry-on baggage, this is not always the case. As you can see, courier travel is geared to those with flexible schedules and a spirit of adventure.

Some round-trip courier fares from New York in 1993 included London for $280, Milan for $200, and Singapore for $359. For further information contact one of the many agencies that screen and select couriers. In New York, one such agency is **Now Voyager**; (212) 431-1616. In Los Angeles, there's **Way to Go**; (213) 466-1126. Although courier information dates itself rapidly, a good general resource is *The Insider's Guide to Air Courier Bargains*, by Kelly Monaghan. The index lists courier services from around the globe, including flight patterns, sample fares, even the names of friendly agents at each company. You might not find it in your local bookstore, but it can be ordered from The Intrepid Traveler, Box 438, New York, NY 10034 for $14.95, plus $2 postage and handling. For a monthly update of sample fares, a subscription to the newsletter *Travel Unlimited* might be a good investment. The newsletter, $25 for 12 issues, can be ordered from *Travel Unlimited*, PO Box 1058, Allston, MA 02134.

TRAVELING AROUND

Because there are so many options for traveling around once you've arrived at your destination, you'll have to make some choices. Do you want to travel by yourself or with a group of people? Do you want to see as much as possible or stay in one place and really get to know it? How do you want to travel—by foot, bus, train, car, boat, or bike?

One of the questions you should ask yourself is if you would feel safer, less isolated, and more at home with a group. Certainly, there is safety in numbers, and a tour means you'll always have somebody to talk to—traveling solo can be lonely sometimes. And if you take an organized tour, you won't have to worry about planning the logistics of your trip and arranging transportation, accommodations, and meals. But there are disadvantages to traveling in a group, too. A lot of the adventure is planned out of your trip, and since you have to go along with the group, your individual needs may not always be served. If you really want to meet the people of the country and learn another language, the worst thing you can do is travel with a bunch of Americans. Remember, too, that most organized tours are usually more expensive than traveling on your own; tours always have an administrative fee built into them.

Many people choose to travel with one or two friends. This can be one of the best ways to go, being a compromise between the tour group and solo adventure. Traveling with a friend gives each of you the support of a familiar face with the freedom to be somewhat independent. Keep in mind, however, that choosing a traveling partner is much like selecting a roommate. You'll be spending a lot of time with your companion, probably more than you're already used to even with a close friend. Make sure not only that your personalities are compatible but also that you both have similar expectations of your trip. It's terrible to spend half your time fighting over where to go next.

Getting Around

Every country has its own transportation system, dictated by geographical and economic conditions. While some countries in Europe and elsewhere have succeeded in linking their national systems in an efficient transnational network, travel among many countries is more of a challenge. Throughout this book, we'll discuss all the options you have for local modes of transportation in particular regions and countries. In general, however, you should consider the following possibilities.

- **By Train:** In many countries, travel by train is the least expensive, safest, and most convenient way to get around. You can eat, sleep, read, view the countryside, and meet interesting people. When you arrive at your destination, you usually find yourself in the city center without having to worry about traffic or parking. Even in nations without extensive rail networks, like most Latin American nations, trains are usually cheaper (though slower) than buses and can make for a comfortable and interesting trip. Most countries with extensive rail systems offer special rail passes for foreign visitors. These are generally good for a period of unlimited travel or for a set number of days of travel during a similar period. A good source of information on train travel around the world is the *Eurail Guide—How to Travel Europe and All the World by Train*, which covers 141 countries in detail. The 816-page 23rd edition is available for $14.95 in bookstores. To order by mail, send $17 to Eurail Guide Annual, 27540 Pacific Coast Highway, Malibu, CA 90265. For more information on travel by train in Europe, see Chapter Six.

- **By Bus:** Buses are the world's most common form of public transportation. In many countries, buses are the only means of public transportation. Buses go everywhere—and relatively cheaply—although the level of comfort varies greatly depending on the bus, the road, the mood of the driver, the weather, and the number of passengers. Many countries also issue bus passes.
- **By Car:** The independence and flexibility that a car offers the traveler can't be matched. But a car that is useful in getting to out-of-the-way places can become a major headache in a traffic-choked city where you don't know your way around. Traveling by car in most foreign countries means renting. When renting, however, always proceed with caution. The December 1992 Consumer Reports Travel Letter reports that in a test of 60 rental cars in Greece and Spain, 20 were found to be "dangerous" or "very dangerous." Only 6 of the 60 cars were judged to be in "fine" shape. Be sure to inspect the car before you rent it—especially vital components such as tires, brakes, lights, and wipers—and if there are any minor dents or scratches, make sure they're noted on your contract. Your best bet may be to rent through Council Travel (see pages xiii–xvi), which offers economical car-rental plans around the world.

  Most English-speaking countries allow American citizens 18 years of age and over to drive with a valid U.S. driver's license. Your U.S. license is all you need in a number of other countries where American tourists are common, including Belgium, France, Israel, Mexico, Spain, Portugal, and most of the Caribbean. Most other countries will require an **International Driving Permit**. This document provides an official translation of the information on your regular license, which you must also carry with you. The permit, established by a 1949 United Nations treaty, must be obtained in the country where your regular license is issued. In the United States, the International Driving Permit can be obtained at any local office of the **American Automobile Association (AAA)**. If you apply in person, a permit will be issued while you wait; however, it will take at least two weeks if you apply through the mail. You'll have to complete an application form and provide two passport-size photos and a fee of $10. The International Driving Permit is valid for one year unless your regular license expires earlier. Some South American countries do not honor International Driving Permits and instead require an **Inter-American Driving Permit**, which can also be obtained through AAA. If you do plan on driving abroad, you may want to become a member of AAA. AAA membership gives you access to a number of international travel services, such as discounts on car rental, and emergency assistance. For more information, visit your local AAA, or contact the American Automobile Association at 1000 AAA Drive, Heathrow, FL 32746-5063; (407) 444-7000.

- **By Boat:** Affordable transatlantic cruises are something from a bygone era. However, lake, river, and maritime connections provide vital links to many parts of the world. Hovercraft shuttle across the English Channel; hydrofoils connect the Mediterranean coasts of Europe and North Africa; steamers navigate the Amazon and Nile rivers; ferries link the East Asian countries of China, Korea, Taiwan, and Japan. Many national and regional rail passes are also valid for some forms of waterborne transportation. The **International Student Identity Card** (see pages 9–10) is also good for special rates on a number of boat trips around the world.
- **By Bicycle:** It's easy to take your bike along with you; most airlines will let you bring one on board for little or no extra charge. You also can rent or buy one overseas. Many national rail networks offer special bike rental deals in combination with rail passes that allow you alternate travel by bike and train. Youth hostels in most countries also cater to cyclists. Bicycle touring is a great way to see the country up close and at your own pace, stopping at will and choosing your route. Of course, long-distance touring is serious exercise and—depending on weather, terrain, and equipment failure—can be hazardous. If you plan a long trip, consider touring with a friend.

  You might also consider participating in a group tour. Most organized bicycle tours include around 20 participants and two to three leaders and are graded according to ability and experience. Check the listings of travel programs in the remaining chapters of this book for the bicycle tours abroad offered by Hostelling International/American Youth Hostels and Council Travel. An excellent organization that specializes in bike tours of Africa is the **International Bicycle Fund/Bicycle Africa**, 4887 Columbia Drive South, Seattle, WA 98108-1919; (206) 628-9314. Other organizations that offer bicycling programs abroad include **Backroads Touring**, 1516 Fifth Street, Suite Q452, Berkeley, CA 94710-1740; (800) 245-3874; **Breaking Away Bicycle Tours**, 1142 Manhattan Avenue, Suite 253, Manhattan Beach, CA 90266; (310) 545-5118; and **EUROPEDS**, 761 Lighthouse Avenue, Monterey, CA 93940; (800) 321-9552.

Budget Accommodations

If you know where to look, low-cost accommodations can be found in all parts of the world. In fact, staying in major cities abroad is often cheaper than staying in U.S. cities. Of course, the options vary in type as well as in quality. In some countries, you can stay in four-star hotels with all the amenities for the same cost as the average American roadside motel. In other countries, you might have to settle for a shared room with a shower down the hall for the same amount of money.

Private **boardinghouses** are generally one of your best bets. Most small pensions are family-run. Some are geared to tourists staying only a few days, while others cater to longer-term guests. Finding a good pension in an unfamiliar city can be an exhausting process, requiring lots of legwork. Most guidebooks include a list of pensions and low-cost hotels; but often you'll find their prices have doubled. It is a good idea to talk to as many other travelers as you can to gather information. Another valuable resource is the local tourist information center; the staff will usually point you to several places in your price range and some will even call ahead for you.

There's a worldwide network of accommodations operated by **YMCAs** and **YWCAs**. As in the U.S., international Ys usually offer a range of activities and events as well as recreational and exercise facilities. Some are single-sex, but many welcome both men and women. Their prices vary, however, from cheap to somewhat expensive. One of the most convenient services offered by YMCAs is their central computerized reservation system, which allows you to book accommodations in many countries around the world. For more information, or for a *Y's Way* travel brochure, write to The Y's Way, 224 East 47th Street, New York, NY 10017; (212) 308-2899; fax (212) 308-3161.

Hostelling International (the new name for the International Youth Hostel Federation) oversees more than 6,000 youth hostels around the world where you can spend the night for approximately $10. Accommodations are dormitory style, although many hostels offer a few more expensive private rooms for couples or families. You are provided with a mattress and blankets, although a sleeping sack (a sheet sewn up on three sides) is usually required. Different regulations exist for youth hostels in each country, and although they vary, there are certain similarities from country to country. Hostelers usually are expected to share in the cleanup, to abstain from drinking or using drugs in the hostel (and smoking in some areas), and to stay no more than a few days. Most hostels, especially in rural areas, have a curfew of 10 or 11 P.M., although many urban hostels have later curfews or no curfew. Some hostels embrace the lockout system, which saves them from having to employ help during the day but can translate into major hardships for hostelers. During the lockout period, usually from 10 A.M. to 5 P.M., no one is allowed back into the hostel. However, this policy is undergoing change and many hostels now have daytime access.

In order to stay in many hostels around the world you must have a membership card. In the U.S., these are issued by Hostelling International/American Youth Hostels (HI/AYH). Some hostels will admit you without a card, but cardholders usually get priority so it is recommended that you get one before you leave. The cost of membership varies according to age: $10 if you are under 18; $25 if you are over 18 but under 55; and $15 for persons 55 or over. HI/AYH also offers a family membership for $35, which includes all children under the age of 18 (16 in Europe). Cards are valid for 12 months from the date of purchase. You'll find a listing of hostels by country and information on hostel rules in the annual *Budget Accommodations Guide* available from HI/AYH in two volumes: Volume I covers Europe and the Mediterranean; Volume II covers Asia, Australia, Africa, and the Americas ($10.95 each plus $3 postage per book). For membership applications, book orders, and general information on hosteling, contact Hostelling International/American Youth Hostels, PO Box 37613, Washington, DC 20013-7613; (202) 783-6161.

In addition, many universities around the world offer inexpensive dormitory accommodations for use by travelers when school is out of session. In many cases, you can obtain information on this sort of service by contacting national tourist offices and student travel agencies. An excellent resource for university housing and other inexpensive lodgings around the world is *The U.S. and Worldwide Travel Accommodations Guide*. Updated annually, the guide is available for $12.95 (plus $1.05 book-rate postage) from Campus Travel Service, PO Box 5486, Fullerton, CA 92635; (800) 525-6633 or (714) 525-6625.

Organized Tours

If you think an organized tour is the way to go, prepare for it by having realistic expectations. There are different types of tours, from a standard tour of European capitals to a horseback tour of the Inner Mongolian grasslands. Check the travel programs offered by CIEE-member institutions and organizations listed in the chapters that follow. You will also find a wide selection of tours listed in newspapers and travel magazines.

Whatever your choice, be sure it's run by a reliable operator or an institution with proven experience. If possible, you should talk to a previous participant. Licensed tour operators should belong to a professional organization with clearly defined operating standards. If you want to avoid the risk of losing your entire vacation budget, try to check them out before putting your money down.

Among the tours worth checking into are those offered by student travel bureaus around the world. These student travel bureaus—many of which are nonprofit or run by the government—organize a number of interesting tours in their individual countries geared especially to students and youths. Holders of the International Student Identity Card receive a discount on most tours offered by student travel bureaus. You'll find the addresses for these student travel bureaus listed in the appropriate country sections later in this book. CIEE itself organizes student/youth tours to Russia, China, and Thailand through its travel subsidiary, Council Travel (see tour descriptions in the appropriate country sections).

If you're looking for a tour that requires some physical exertion, there are a number of organizations with outdoor adventure packages, including some of those mentioned above. A good guide to such programs is *Adventure Holidays*, which covers all sorts of adventure travel, from scuba diving in the Red Sea, to mountain climbing in Wales, to camel caravanning in the Sahara. Updated annually, it's available for $12.95 (plus $4.75 postage) from Peterson's Guides, PO Box 2123, Princeton, NJ 08543; (800) 225-0261.

Meeting the People

If you want to spend a short time with local people while you travel, there are organizations in many countries—including government tourist offices—that will arrange an afternoon or evening home visit for you. Such organizations are listed throughout this book. Another possibility is what's called a homestay, in which you stay with a host family for anywhere from a few days to several weeks. Many countries have their own homestay organizations, and a number of organizations in the U.S. also specialize in arranging homestay programs.

One such organization, founded by Jimmy and Rosalynn Carter, is **Friendship Force**, Suite 575, South Tower, 1 CNN Center, Atlanta, GA 30303; (404) 552-9490. Another is **AFS Intercultural Programs**, 313 East 43rd Street, New York, NY 10017; (800) AFS-INFO.

A good organization to contact for short-term homestays is **SERVAS**, which sponsors a worldwide program of person-to-person contacts for travelers in over 100 countries, with the ultimate aim of helping to build world peace, goodwill, and understanding. Here's how SERVAS works: After applying, you are interviewed by a local SERVAS representative; if accepted, you receive a personal briefing, written instructions, a list of SERVAS members in the area that you are going to visit, and an introductory letter. Using this introductory letter, you can arrange to stay with listed families. The average stay with SERVAS hosts is two nights, although it's possible to stay with several different members in the same area. SERVAS also recruits members to serve as hosts in the U.S. For more information write to U.S. SERVAS, Inc., 11 John Street, Room 407, New York, NY 10038. If you use its services, SERVAS asks for a travel membership fee of $55 and a refundable host list deposit of $25.

A good resource for finding homestay programs not mentioned in this book is the *Directory of Low-Cost Vacations with a Difference*, compiled by

J. Crawford, a former chairman of the board for SERVAS. Other listings include bed-and-breakfasts, vacation work programs, and home exchanges. It is available for $5.95 from Pilot Books, 103 Cooper Street, Babylon, NY 11702. A complete listing of meet-the-people programs in 35 countries can be found in the *International Meet-the-People Directory* ($6), compiled by the International Visitors Information Service, 733 15th Street NW, Suite 300, Washington, DC 20005.

More Resources for the Traveler

A good guidebook is indispensable on any trip; however, don't let your guidebook dictate your experience. Never free from error, guidebooks represent the perceptions of their authors, each as unique as your own. The best guidebooks provide more than just listings of hotels, cheap restaurants, and museums. They should give you a sense of both history and contemporary life, helping you to understand the people in whose midst you travel. The drawback of every guidebook, of course, is that it is consulted by thousands of travelers like yourself. If you follow a very popular guidebook, the places you choose to frequent may well be swarming with other readers. For this reason, it's best to use guidebooks to acquaint yourself with your destination and to consult with periodically, but try to strike out on your own as much as possible.

There are a number of guidebook series, each suited to people of differing interests and financial conditions. Two series actually written by college students, and therefore tailored to the student budget, are the *Let's Go* guides, written by Harvard Student Agencies and published by St. Martin's Press, and the *On the Loose* guides, written by students of the University of California at Berkeley. *Let's Go* guides have been spotted in the hands of student travelers trekking through Europe for more than 30 years. *On the Loose* guides are the new kids on the block, with only four titles in print at press time but intending to rival *Let's Go* on all fronts. Individual titles and prices are listed in the appropriate country chapters of this book. Both series are available in bookstores and at Council Travel offices (see pages xiii–xvi).

Both *Let's Go* and *On the Loose* guides are mostly confined to European and North American destinations; for other locations, check out the guidebooks published by Lonely Planet and Moon Publications. Both specialize in nontraditional (albeit increasingly frequented) destinations and provide historical and cultural background in addition to tips on where to stay, what to eat, and so on. In general, both are geared to the budget traveler. Lonely Planet's *Travel Survival Kits* cover specific countries in Africa, Asia, Latin America, and, most recently, Europe. Their *On a Shoestring* guides cover broader geographic regions such as West Africa or Eastern Europe. If you can't find these books in your local bookstore, you can order them directly from Lonely Planet Publications, Embarcadero West, 155 Filbert Street, Suite 251, Oakland, CA 94607-2538; (800) 275-8555. Include $2 for fourth-class postage and $4 for first-class (add 50¢ for each additional book). *Moon Handbooks* have not yet branched into Europe, but are known for the high quality of their guides to South Pacific and Southeast Asian destinations, among others. *Moon Handbooks* can be found in most bookstores or ordered (include $3.50 postage for first book and 50¢ for each additional title) from Moon Publications, 722 Wall Street, Chico, CA 95928; (916) 345-5473. Titles from both series can also be purchased at any Council Travel office (see pages xiii–xvi). In addition, both Moon Publications and Lonely Planet distribute free newsletters packed with travel information.

Two other highly recommended guidebook series not necessarily limited to budget travel are *Real Guide*s and *Cadogan Guides*. *Real Guide*s are comprehensive yet concise, providing a wealth of practical information with opinionated, critical advice. *Cadogan Guides* are outstanding for the depth and richness of the historical and cultural information they convey. *Real Guide*s are available in bookstores or from Simon & Schuster, Order Department, 200 Old Tappan Road, Old Tappan, NJ 07675; (800) 223-2336. *Cadogan Guides* can be ordered ($3 postage per book; orders of three or more books postage-free) from The Globe Pequot Press, PO Box 833, Old Saybrook, CT 06475-0833; (800) 243-0495. Globe Pequot publishes a number of other useful publications, such as *Europe by Eurail*.

A number of useful books on travel in Europe and Asia are published by John Muir Publications, including their series of *2 to 22 Days* itinerary planners. For ordering information, contact John Muir Publications, PO Box 613, Santa Fe, NM 87504; (800) 888-7504. Outdoors enthusiasts will find plenty of titles on biking, hiking, and climbing in the U.S. and abroad from The Mountaineers Books, 1011 SW Klickitat Way, Suite 107, Seattle, WA 98134; (800) 553-4453.

One more series deserves special mention: *Insight Guide*s. While they do provide basic travel information, these books are not traditional guidebooks. Rather, *Insight Guide*s provide fascinating introductions to a number of countries with brilliant photographs and incisive writing. With a number of writers and photographers contributing to each country-specific volume, *Insight Guide*s provide interesting perspectives on history, culture, art and literature, modern life, and natural surroundings by focusing on the people who give each locale its distinctive character. Perhaps best read before departure to stimulate your imagination, *Insight Guide*s can be ordered from Houghton Mifflin Company, Attn: Order Processing, Wayside Road, Burlington, MA 01803; (800) 225-3362.

A growing number of magazines cater to world travelers with low budgets and high expectations. One worth investigating—although you might not find it on your local newsstand—is *Great Expeditions*, which features firsthand information from travelers, free classified ads, and an information exchange. Feature articles in recent years have included "Biking Baja California," "Fly Cheap as an Onboard Courier," and "Streetsmarts for South America." Four issues cost $18; request a free sample copy from *Great Expeditions*, Box 18036, Raleigh, NC 27619; (800) 743-3639.

CHAPTER SIX

EUROPE

A few short years ago, after the dismantling of the Berlin Wall and the breakup of the Soviet Union, Europe seemed headed for a bright future. The much-heralded unification of the 12-nation European Community promised a kind of super-state in which Europeans could find a common bond. As of 1993 goods, services, and capital can move freely across borders, but the super-state seems farther away than ever. Instead, Europeans seem to have retreated back into provincialism as French farmers destroy shipments of foreign produce and right-wing German youths persecute Turkish immigrants.

Yet even as Europe undergoes trying moments, it offers more opportunities to students and travelers than ever before. Europe's historical sights and natural beauty have long held an irresistible attraction for young people in the U.S. To reap the maximum benefits from your experience abroad, we suggest that you concentrate on a particular region or even a single country. Rushing from city to city may be an exhilarating experience, but chances are you'll emerge from such a whirlwind tour with only a blur of images.

GETTING THERE

As we noted in Chapter Five, your options for travel to Europe are limited to international flights, unless you have a lot of money to spend on a cruise ship. If you skipped Chapter Five, be sure to read it now for more complete information about your options for air travel to Europe, including student airfares, charters, consolidators and flying as a courier. One thing we will repeat here is that most prices quoted throughout the book are for comparison purposes only, owing to the constantly changing nature of airfares. Fares quoted below were those available in 1993. For more up-to-date information, contact your nearest Council Travel office (see pages xiii–xvi) or pick up a copy of *Student Travels* (see page xi).

Student/Youth Fares

Students and young people are often able to find special discount fares on regular scheduled airlines. Although regulations vary depending on the carrier, generally you must be under the age of 26 or, if a student, under the age of 31. In most cases, you will need proof of your student or youth status, such as the International Student Identity Card (see pages 9–10) or GO 25 Card (see page 11). Examples of *round-trip* youth and student fares available through Council Travel in 1993 were as follows:

	Off-peak Season	Peak Season
New York–London	$390	$550
New York–Paris	$450	$670
Boston–Brussels	$518	$588
Boston–London	$398	$538
Chicago–Amsterdam	$570	$688

Dallas–Frankfurt	$598	$858
Seattle–London	$630	$718
New York–Warsaw	$690	$810
New York–St. Petersburg	$658	$750
Chicago–Warsaw	$670	$898

Consolidator and Charter Flights

Consolidator and charter fares continue to be some of the best bargains in air travel to Europe. Council Charter destinations include Amsterdam, Brussels, London, Madrid, Milan, Paris, and Rome, among others. Council Travel offices (see pages xiii–xvi) can help you make connections from many points in the U.S. to one of Council Charter's cities of departure. Sample round-trip fares for the 1993 peak travel season were as follows:

From New York:

Amsterdam	$538
Brussels	$638
London	$578
Madrid	$728
Málaga	$728
Milan	$795
Paris	$518
Rome	$795

From Boston:

Brussels	$638
Paris	$728
London	$578

From Los Angeles/San Francisco:

Paris	$918

TRAVELING AROUND EUROPE

If you're a student or if you are 25 or under, and you have an International Student Identity Card or a GO 25 Card, you can benefit from a number of travel discounts offered by student travel bureaus in each country. Refer to Chapter Two for basic information on how to obtain these cards.

By Train

Train travel in Europe is an unexpected pleasure for Americans, who have the chance to experience a way of getting around quite different from those available at home. In a land where train travel is still the popular choice for daily commuters and long-distance travelers alike, rail networks are widespread, fast, and efficient. Trains can also be quite comfortable, although you should be prepared for crowded cars on some of the most popular routes during peak travel seasons.

To suit travelers with different needs, European trains come in many varieties, from suburban commuter trains to long-distance expresses. Long-distance routes always feature first- and second-class cars, and most give you a choice

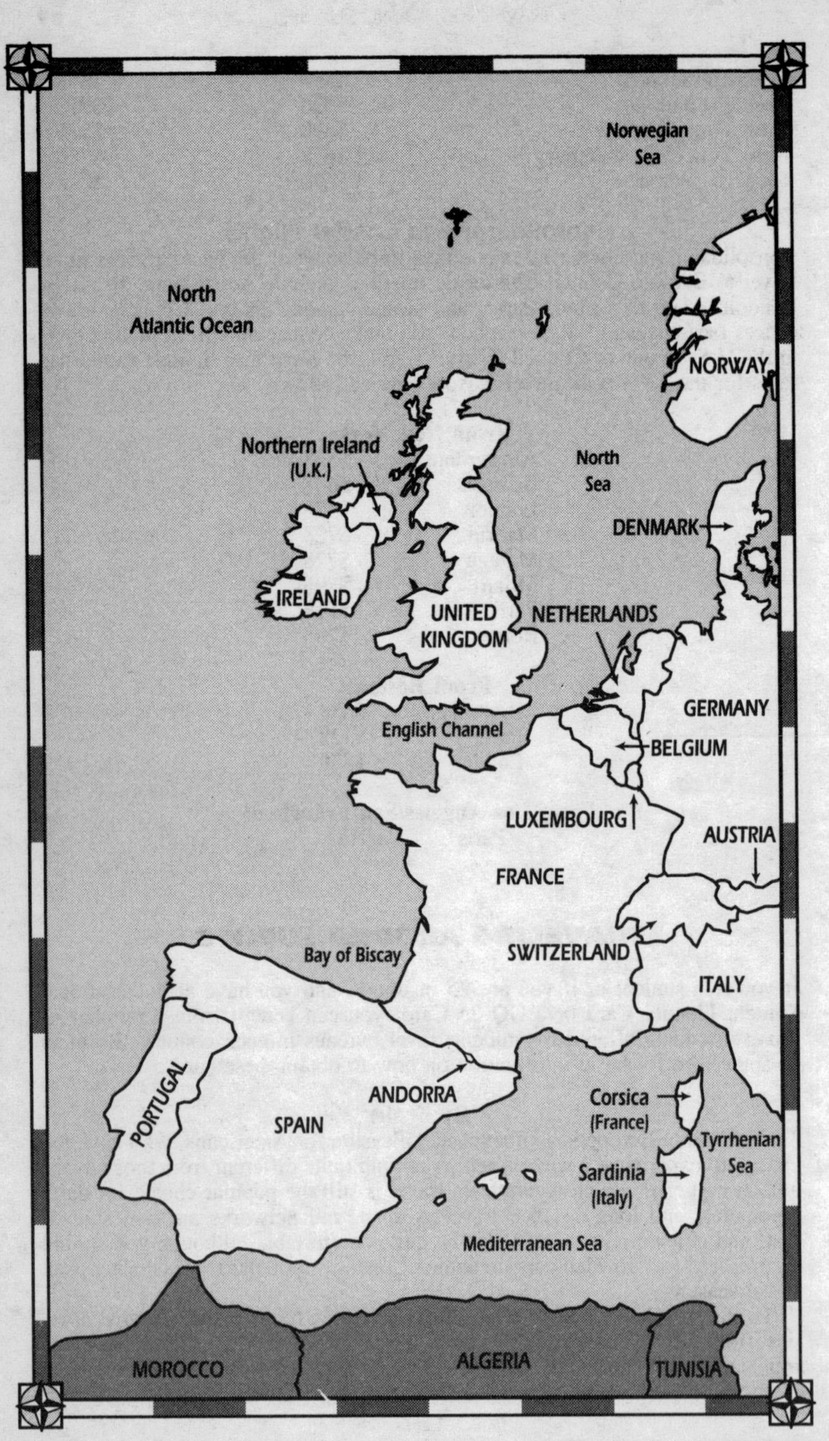
Norwegian Sea
North Atlantic Ocean
NORWAY
Northern Ireland (U.K.)
North Sea
DENMARK
IRELAND
UNITED KINGDOM
NETHERLANDS
GERMANY
English Channel
BELGIUM
LUXEMBOURG
AUSTRIA
FRANCE
SWITZERLAND
Bay of Biscay
ITALY
PORTUGAL
ANDORRA
SPAIN
Corsica (France)
Tyrrhenian Sea
Sardinia (Italy)
Mediterranean Sea
MOROCCO
ALGERIA
TUNISIA

NORWAY
SWEDEN
Gulf of Bothnia
FINLAND
RUSSIA
ESTONIA
LATVIA
Baltic Sea
LITHUANIA
RUSSIA
BELARUS
GERMANY
POLAND
UKRAINE
CZECH REPUBLIC
SLOVAKIA
MOLDOVA
AUSTRIA
HUNGARY
ROMANIA
CROATIA
SLOVENIA
BOSNIA HERCEGOVINA
YUGOSLAVIA
Black Sea
Adriatic Sea
BULGARIA
MACEDONIA
ITALY
ALBANIA
TURKEY
GREECE
Aegean
Ionian Sea
Sicily (Italy)
MALTA
Crete (Greece)
CYPRUS

between coach cars and compartment cars on day trains, and couchettes or private sleepers on overnight trains. Your costs will vary according to the option you choose.

The main factor affecting your cost, of course, is the total distance you travel. If you only plan one trip, you need only to purchase a single point-to-point ticket. But if your itinerary takes you on a number of different routes, you have the choice of purchasing individual tickets for each leg of your trip or a rail pass. The best way to decide if a rail pass is for you is to calculate the cost per mile of each leg of your trip. Find out the cost of a regular ticket and divide it by the miles traveled. You can do this easily by consulting Eurail's brochure *Europe on Track* (available from Rail Europe or most travel agents), which also lists prices for major point-to-point trips. Then figure out how many miles you have to travel to save money with a rail pass. The March 1993 *Consumer Reports Travel Letter* has a convenient table of European rail pass options, complete with the number of miles you need to travel to break even with each. For example, *Consumer Reports* estimates you need to travel 2,419 miles to break even on a one-month Eurail Youthpass ($508).

The greatest hidden cost contained in all rail passes is the **reservation fee**. Your rail pass entitles you to travel, but does not guarantee your seat. And even if you hold a rail pass, you cannot board certain trains (such as high-speed TGV and ICE trains) without making a reservation. To make a reservation, you must pay a surcharge ($10 per person, per train, if reserving from the U.S. through Rail Europe). A second-class couchette will cost you $24. Of course, you will have to pay these costs anyway, regardless of whether you have a rail pass or a point-to-point ticket; just be sure to keep these extra costs in mind.

Rail Europe offers a variety of Eurailpasses. All Eurailpasses are valid for travel in 17 European countries: Austria, Belgium, Denmark, Finland, France, Germany, Greece, Hungary, Ireland, Italy, Luxembourg, The Netherlands, Norway, Portugal, Spain, Sweden, and Switzerland. (Travelers to eastern Europe can find information on the European East Pass below.) Eurailpasses are also valid on many lake and river steamers, ferry boats, and buses. Since not all available discounts will be listed in your brochure, always ask to see if your pass is valid. All of the Eurailpasses mentioned below must be purchased in the U.S.; you can get them at most travel agencies, including Council Travel (see pages xiii–xvi), or directly from Rail Europe, 226-230 Westchester Avenue, White Plains, NY 10604; (800) 848-7245.

- **Eurail Youthpass.** If you are under 26, the Eurail Youthpass entitles you to unlimited *second-class* travel for one or two months. In 1993, a one-month pass cost $508; a two-month pass cost $698.
- **Youth Flexipass.** This pass, also restricted to *second-class*, allows travelers under 26 years to choose a number of travel days within a two-month period. Costs in 1993 were $220 for five days, $348 for 10 days, and $474 for 15 days. Considering that most people don't travel every day of their trip, the Youth Flexipass is often more economical than the Youthpass.
- **Eurailpass.** The regular Eurailpass, which has no age limit, entitles you to unlimited *first-class* travel. Since some trains get very crowded on certain routes during peak travel seasons, such as summer, first class may be the way to go if comfort is your main concern. In 1993, a pass valid for 15 days cost $460; for 21 days, $598; for one month, $728; for two months, $998; and for three months, $1,260.
- **Eurail Flexipass.** Like the Youth Flexipass, the *first-class* Flexipass allows

a number of travel days within a two-month period. Costs in 1993 were $298 for 5 days, $496 for 10, and $676 for 15 days.

- **Eurail Saverpass.** If you travel with a group, you and your companions can purchase the Eurail Saverpass ($390 in 1993), good for 15 days of unlimited *first-class* travel. Three people must travel together sharing the same itinerary to be eligible for this pass between April 1 and September 30; at other times, only two people are required to travel together.

Introduced in 1993, the Eurail Pass Protection Plan is included with each Eurailpass purchase. In case of loss or theft, this plan allows for reimbursement of the unused portion of your pass, minus a 20-percent deductible. For an additional $10 per pass, you can enroll in the Zero Deductible option, which allows for reimbursement of 100 percent of the unused portion of your pass. However, the above reimbursement plans take effect only upon return to the U.S. While in Europe, you must purchase a replacement pass.

While Eurailpasses cover a lot of territory, they are not accepted in the United Kingdom, Russia, or most of eastern Europe. Those planning to travel widely in the U.K., Russia, or any other European country should look into the national rail pass options described in the country sections of this chapter. Special regional passes are also described in the country sections. For travel in eastern Europe, Rail Europe offers the **European East Pass**, valid in Austria, the Czech Republic, Slovakia, Hungary, and Poland. In 1993, prices for the European East Pass were $169 for five days of travel in a 15-day period, and $275 for 10 days of travel in one month.

As noted above, buying individual tickets instead of a rail pass may be the cheaper option. Point-to-point tickets can be purchased in the U.S. through Rail Europe. Travelers under 26, however, can get a better rate at any number of European travel agencies selling **BIJ** tickets (*Billets Internationals de Jeunesse*). Two agencies that sell them are Eurotrain and Transalpino. Wasteels sells similar youth tickets. These agencies have offices all over Europe. Make sure you check with local student travel bureaus; they usually have good deals on these tickets.

If you are going to be living in Europe for a while before traveling, you may be eligible for the **Inter-Rail Pass**. This pass allows European youth a one-month rail plan similar to the Eurail Youthpass offered to North Americans. If you are under 26 and can prove that you have resided in a European country for at least two months, you too are eligible. Inter-Rail holders receive a 50-percent discount on train fares in the country of purchase and unlimited free travel in all other countries subscribing to the plan. The pass is available at many European train stations and at student travel bureaus throughout Europe.

There are a number of good guidebooks geared especially to train travel in Western Europe. *The Eurail Guide*, by Kathryn Turpin and Marvin Saltzman, highlights 715 one-day excursions from 132 European cities, recommends the most scenic routes, and includes information on schedules for intercity train travel (see page 52 for more information). Since *The Eurail Guide* describes train travel not just in Europe but throughout the world, it presents information in a rather sketchy manner. A more detailed guide to the myriad rail excursions throughout Europe is *Europe by Eurail* (1992 edition, $13.95), by George and LaVerne Ferguson. *Europe by Eurail* is available from The Globe Pequot Press (see page 57).

Camp Europe by Train (eighth edition, 1994), by Lenore Baken, is a complete rail and campground guide for backpackers. Its 520 pages include 117 maps and information on rail passes, train schedules, scenic rail routes, how to reach campgrounds using public transportation, packing, and more. The book is available for $16.95 plus $3 postage from Ariel Publications, 14417 SE 19th Place, Bellevue, WA 98007; (206) 641-0518.

The most complete guide to all European train and ferry schedules is the *Thomas Cook European Timetable* ($24.95); picking up a copy will save you the hassle of waiting in endless lines trying to get complicated information from harassed ticket officers behind glass partitions—a chore unless you're incredibly multilingual, extremely patient, and good at reading lips. You might also want to check out the companion publication, the *Thomas Cook Rail Map of Europe* ($9.95). You can find both publications in the travel section of most bookstores, or order from Forsythe Travel Library, PO Box 2975, Shawnee Mission, KS 66201; (800) 367-7984.

By Air

While traveling on a European train can be a delightful experience, the charm quickly dwindles as the number of uninterrupted days and nights of train travel increases. Trans-European train trips are best broken down into shorter segments with stops along the way. If you have only a few far-flung destinations on your itinerary you should investigate air travel options. Not only will this save you valuable time, but intra-European student/youth airfares also are usually comparable to the price of a long-distance train ticket.

There are a number of student flights as well as special student/youth fares on scheduled flights connecting the major European cities. In many cases, savings can be more than 50 percent off the regular economy fares. As with transatlantic student discounts, regulations vary depending on the airline, but generally you must be a student under the age of 31 or a young person under the age of 26 and have either an International Student Identity Card or a Go 25 Card (see pages 9–11). Student/youth fares on most of these flights can be booked at Council Travel offices in the U.S. Here are some sample *round-trip* fares within Europe from 1993:

Paris–London	$138
Paris–Copenhagen	$270
Rome–Madrid	$330
Nice–Barcelona	$170
Copenhagen–Rome	$408
London–Moscow	$455
London–Budapest	$378
Frankfurt–Warsaw	$298
Frankfurt–Moscow	$610

Another option is to purchase a book of the new **Euro Flyer Passes**, valid on Air France, Air Inter, Czechoslovak Airlines, and Sabena. Passes come in the form of coupons costing $120, each the equivalent of a one-way ticket. Each book contains three to nine coupons. Compare with the price of a regular ticket and see if you'll save. Euro Flyer Passes must be purchased in conjunction with a flight from the U.S. to Europe. For more information, contact Council Travel (see pages xiii–xvi).

By Bus

Bus travel is not as popular as train travel in Europe primarily because the various national railway systems are so good. As a result, buses are usually used for tour groups rather than for regular international transportation. They are fairly cheap, however, and there is one bus plan that will save you money if you have a Eurailpass or Youthpass. It's administered by **Europabus**, the motorcoach division of the European railroads, and has 70,000 miles of scheduled lines throughout Europe. Holders of the Eurailpass and Eurail Youthpass are entitled to substantial reductions on most European lines. For information and reservations, contact a student travel bureau or the ticket offices of the European railroads.

By Ship

Boats continue to serve as vital transportation links between many European countries. You'll find boats of all types connecting Britain and Ireland to the mainland. In northern waters, a number of ferry routes link the Scandinavian countries to Britain, Germany, Poland, the Baltic republics, and Russia. Ferries and passenger boats are most numerous in the Mediterranean region. Ships connect the mainland to numerous islands including Sicily, Sardinia, Corsica, and Crete. They also provide an economical way to get from Europe to North Africa, Israel, and Turkey. Especially popular with tourists are the boats to the resort isles of the Mediterranean such as Mallorca, Ibiza, Capri, Mykonos, and Corfu. If you're interested in exploring the southern Mediterranean coast and nearby islands, check out *Undiscovered Islands of the Mediterranean*, by Linda Lancione Moyer and Burl Wiles; the second edition (1992) is available for $13.95 (plus $3.75 postage and handling) from John Muir Publications, PO Box 613, Santa Fe, NM 87504; (800) 888-7504.

Several national student travel bureaus offer special student rates on English Channel, Baltic, and Mediterranean sailings. For example, an International Student Identity Card will give you a discount on ferries between Finland and Sweden, Norway and Denmark, Italy and Greece, and Britain and various countries on the Continent. Information and bookings can be made at any of the student travel bureaus in Europe. Your Eurailpass also entitles you to discounts on many boats and ferries.

By Car

If you have a fairly loose itinerary, try ride-sharing. In most countries it's quite easy to find drivers looking for riders, both for company and the sharing of expenses. Sharing a ride costs you less than taking the train and it's also a great way to meet people. Your driver will probably be familiar with your destination and might even extend an offer of hospitality or an evening out. Of course, ride-sharing carries some of the same hazards as hitchhiking, but it is generally a more businesslike arrangement.

University student-center bulletin boards are especially good sources for finding ride-shares. Students frequently seek riders for weekend trips. And driving with an American is as much as a diversion for them as it is for you.

Another alternative is to register with a ride-share agency, which for a small fee puts you in touch with drivers. Drivers who register with agencies have certain contractual obligations, such as gasoline-cost limits, that protect the rider. If you have your own car and want to list with such an agency, the service should cost you nothing. The largest network of ride-share agencies in Europe is **Eurostop International**, known as Allostop in France and Verband der Deutschen Mitfahrzentralen in Germany.

The pros and cons of driving abroad are discussed in Chapter Five. If the idea appeals to you, there are numerous options for purchasing, leasing, and renting cars in Europe. If you plan to travel with friends and cover a lot of territory in Europe, renting a car may actually be cheaper than travel by rail or bus. However, you may end up paying quite a bit for one-day rentals made on the spot. You'll get the best deal if you reserve your car before you depart from the U.S. Remember, too, that gasoline prices are much higher in Europe than in the United States—usually around $6 a gallon. European roads are generally in good condition and the network of superhighways is extensive, especially in Germany, where superhighways originated. One agency that specializes in European rentals is **Auto Europe**, PO Box 1097, Camden, ME 04843; (800) 223-5555. Council Travel offices can arrange leases or rentals with a selection of companies (like Auto Europe and Renault) that offer cars with unlimited mileage at budget rates as low as $20 a day. If you plan to drive through Europe for two or three months, it will actually cost you less to lease a car or to purchase one from a company that will guarantee to repurchase it at the end of your trip.

You may need an **International Driving Permit** (see page 52). Even if the permit is not required, it's helpful to have it along when traveling in a non-English-speaking country where your regular license might not be understood. Also, when making car-rental arrangements, be sure to check whether insurance coverage is included in the cost. Most companies take care of this for you; they'll also provide you with the **International Insurance Certificate** or "green card," required for all European countries. If you buy or lease a car, you can obtain insurance coverage and the green card through the dealer.

By Bicycle

Traveling by bicycle allows you to slow down, enjoy the pleasures of the countryside close-up, and get away from the tourist trail. Most major highways in Europe have separate bicycle lanes.

Most international airlines permit bicycles in the luggage compartment. You do, however, have to take the pedals off, turn the handlebars sideways, and pack it into a special bag. Costs vary with the destination and the carrier, so make sure to ask. If you want to avoid the hassle, you can always buy or rent top-quality bicycles in Europe. In fact, many train stations have bike rental facilities, and most rail lines will let you carry your bike as baggage.

In most countries, bicycling is very popular indeed, especially in regions where the terrain is relatively flat, as in Denmark, Holland, and France's Loire Valley. If you're thinking of biking through Europe, the following books might be helpful. *Europe by Bike: 18 Tours Geared for Discovery* (second edition), written by Karen and Terry Whitehill, gives detailed information on touring routes ranging from 100 to 800 miles in length. It's available for $14.95 from The Mountaineers Books, 1011 Klickitat Way, Suite 107, Seattle, WA 98134; (800) 553-4453. *Biking Through Europe*, by Dennis and Tina Jaffe, describes 17 cycle tours of varying difficulty, suggests accommodations and restaurants along the way, and gives advice on selecting your bicycle and gear. It's available for $13.95 (plus $2.50 postage and handling) from Williamson Publishing, Box 185, Church Hill Road, Charlotte, VT 05445; (800) 234-8791. Also, don't forget to check with government tourist offices; each will have information on biking in its respective country, and in most cases can put you in touch with national bicycle clubs or similar organizations.

Hiking

For those who want to escape the cities, railways, and highways to enjoy the peaceful beauty of the countryside, mountain trails and cross-country paths can be found throughout Europe. In the Swiss Alps, for example, you'll find not only well-maintained and scenic mountain trails, but also a network of comfortable trailside chalets that accept phone reservations in advance. For an introduction to the wide range of trails that await you, read *100 Hikes in the Alps*, which describes alpine routes in Austria, France, Germany, Italy, Liechtenstein, and Switzerland. It can be ordered for $14.95 from The Mountaineers Books (for ordering information, see "By Bicycle," above). The Mountaineers also publishes a number of more specific regional hiking guides. If you have a particular country in mind, call the government tourist office and ask for information on hiking clubs and parks services.

Hitchhiking

Hitchhiking, or "autostop," as it is frequently called on the Continent, is a popular way for European students to get around. It's risky, but some argue that it's a cheap and interesting way of getting around. For anyone who is going to hitchhike in Europe, here are a few pointers:

- Look legitimate; dress in a way that will make car drivers feel they can trust you.
- Find out the local conditions for hitchhiking—your best source is the people who are doing it.
- Carry a sign that states clearly the direction in which you are headed and your destination.
- Women: Don't hitchhike alone. The best team is a man and a woman.
- Travel light—you should be able to jump in and out of a car quickly and not burden the driver with having to find room for your luggage.

For more detailed information on hitching, read *Europe: A Manual for Hitchhikers*, a unique book that gives country-by-country information on hitching techniques, route planning, and local attitudes towards hitchers. The book is available for £3.95 from the publisher, Vacation Work, 9 Park End Street, Oxford, OX1 1HJ, England; (44) 865-241978; fax (44) 865-790885. Checks should be made out in British pounds and payable to Vacation Work.

Organized Tours

On the other hand, if you prefer the security and companionship offered by an organized tour, there's a wealth of options for you in Europe. In fact, a number of national student travel organizations offer organized, escorted tours by bus, bike, or on foot throughout Europe. You can find more information on these in the individual country sections that follow.

Hostelling International/American Youth Hostels (see page 54) organizes biking and hiking tours through several European countries. Cycling tours range from 8 to 15 days and include France's Loire Valley, the Scottish Highlands, and the Danube River. Backpacking and hiking tours take place in Switzerland, Mont Blanc, England, and Israel. For information on a host of other tour packages, contact **Council Travel** (see pages xiii–xvi).

Student Travel Bureaus

In nearly every European country, you'll find a student travel organization that is affiliated with the **International Student Travel Confederation (ISTC)**. In the individual country sections that follow, we've included the addresses of the headquarters of these organizations. In addition, most have a network of branches around the country, usually in university cities. As ISTC members, these offices issue the International Student Identity Card and can arrange discounted tickets for student travel. Many also provide information on travel and accommodations, arrange tours, conduct language courses, and more. If you're going to be spending some time traveling in a country, be sure to make use of the information, discounts, and services offered by that country's student travel bureau.

Finding a Place to Stay

For decades, young Americans traveling in Europe have been greeted by a wide variety of inexpensive lodgings. Today, these bargains are harder to find. While the budget traveler can still go a long way on the dollar in Portugal, Greece, and the countries of eastern Europe, prices in northern Europe are generally quite high. And, of course, the price for food and accommodations increases during the high tourist season.

Still, if you use your head (and your feet), you can find affordable pensions, budget hotels, and hostels anywhere you go. You'll find many listed in booklets put out by tourist offices and in the guidebooks mentioned later in this chapter. But beware—once many of these places get into a guidebook like *Let's Go*, they raise their rates or become so popular that it's difficult to get a room. However, there is a network of **student hostels** and **youth hostels** (see page 54) whose prices remain consistently affordable. In most European cities of any size you will find a general tourist office—usually in or near the railroad station, airport, or another central location—that lists accommodations and will often call and book your stay for you, saving you the legwork.

If, however, you decide to stay in one city for an extended period of time (say, one year) you'll find that the price of renting a room becomes considerably less expensive. Often, if you arrive a few weeks before the school year begins, you'll be able to share an apartment with local students. Check out the local university bulletin boards for apartment-share notices. International and English-language book stores are also likely to have bulletin boards with similar information.

The accommodations situation in eastern Europe deserves special mention. Because the hotel industry in former Soviet-bloc countries is relatively undeveloped, a fortunate alternative to the usual paid lodgings has cropped up in recent years: rented rooms in **private homes** and apartments. Eager to meet Westerners and to earn a little extra income as well, many families in the Czech Republic, Slovakia, Hungary, and Poland enthusiastically open their doors to foreign travelers. Rooms are homey and comfortable, helpings of local food are generous, and your host will be happy to make conversation. To find a room in a private home, visit a tourist information center or ask a fellow traveler. These accommodations are much less expensive than hotels.

Camping

There are campgrounds located all over Europe—on the outskirts of large cities, along major highways, and in resort areas at beaches, lakes, and mountains. Many are accessible by foot or by public transport, although having a car is usually more convenient. Most are well equipped with hot and cold running water, stoves, electrical outlets, laundry facilities, and a small store. Each person using the campsite will have to pay a small fee per night plus a nominal charge for a car or motorcycle.

If you are going to camp in Europe, you might want to get an **International Camping Carnet**, issued by the National Campers and Hikers Association,

4804 Transit Road, Building 2, Depew, NY 14043-4704; (716) 668-6242. While not all campgrounds require this card, many privately owned campgrounds do. At other campgrounds it can get you a small discount off the regular price, but unless you're planning to camp for an extended period of time, don't expect to save much money. The card costs $10, but you must also become a member of the National Campers and Hikers Association; a one-year membership costs $10. The National Campers and Hikers Association can also put you in touch with hikers' groups and supply you with information on camping.

You don't necessarily need a campground to camp. Most Scandinavian countries permit you to camp for one night anywhere in the countryside except on fenced land. And in the other countries of western Europe, camping for a night in the open countryside is generally acceptable as long as you are discreet and ask permission before setting up camp on a farmer's land. Not only will you save money, you'll also avoid the crowds found at most European campgrounds during July and August. One good source of information on getting around between campgrounds, and many other helpful camping hints, is *Camp Europe By Train*, by Lenore Bakken (see "By Train," above).

Suggestions for Further Reading

Let's Go: Europe, updated each year by Harvard Student Agencies ($18.99), is probably the most popular guidebook for Europe-bound students. It includes basic information on getting around, seeing the sights, and finding inexpensive places to sleep and eat. Published by St. Martin's Press, it's available in bookstores and Council Travel offices (see pages xiii–xvi). A number of more specific regional guides are listed later in the appropriate country sections.

Let's Go is full of practical travel information and covers the entire continent, but if you want a lot of detail about a particular region of Europe, try these new (1993) guidebooks by the well-seasoned staff at Lonely Planet Publications: *Western Europe on a Shoestring* ($24.95), *Mediterranean Europe on a Shoestring* ($24.95), and *Scandinavian and Baltic Europe on a Shoestring* ($17.95). Lonely Planet's *Eastern Europe on a Shoestring* ($21.95) is also good, but because it was published in 1992 it isn't as up-to-date as the others. Lonely Planet publications are available at most bookstores as well as all Council Travel offices.

Veteran traveler Rick Steves has written a number of helpful primers on European travel. *Europe 101* ($15.95) serves as a humorous introduction to European art and culture. *Mona Winks* ($14.95) is a guide to Europe's museums and how to get the most out of each. *Europe Through the Back Door* ($16.95) shows the traveler how to enjoy Europe on a budget. Steves has also written *2 to 22 Days in Europe* ($12.95), an itinerary planner. All of Steves's books are available from John Muir Publications.

WORKING IN EUROPE

If working in Europe appeals to you, there are organizations listed within each country section that can help you do just that. In addition, pick up a copy of *How to Get a Job in Europe*, by Robert Sanborn. Included are the nuts and bolts of conducting a job search, tips on summer jobs and opportunities for career seekers, as well as a country-by-country look at potential employers in such fields as tourism, banking and finance, and the retail and wholesale industries. This book is available for $17.95 from Surrey Books, 230 East Ohio Street, Suite 120, Chicago, IL 60611; (800) 326-4430.

STUDYING IN EUROPE

The options for study in Europe are virtually unlimited. In the individual country sections that follow, you'll find descriptions of the academic programs in Europe offered by CIEE-member institutions. In this section, we've listed only those study programs that take place in more than one country of the region. Unless otherwise noted, consult Appendix I for the addresses of the sponsoring institutions.

Semester and Academic Year

Art and Architecture

Associated Colleges of the Midwest. *London and Florence: Arts in Context.* Spring semester. Eight weeks in each city. Sophomores to seniors with 2.75 GPA. Apply by October 15.

Beaver College. *Year in Art History at the University of East Anglia.* Norwich, England, and Venice, Italy. Academic year with winter term in Venice. Juniors and seniors with 3.0 GPA overall and 3.2 in art history. Apply by April 20.

Butler University. *Academic Year at University of East Anglia with Term in Venice.* Norwich, England; and Venice, Italy. Academic year. Fully integrated program for majors in the history of art with a spring term of study in Venice. Juniors and seniors with 3.0 GPA. Apply by April 15. Contact: Institute for Study Abroad, Butler University, 4600 Sunset Avenue, Indianapolis, IN 46208-3485; (800) 858-0229.

General Studies

Antioch College/Great Lakes College Association. *European Academic Term.* Germany, Poland, and England. Fall term. Interdisciplinary program analyzing social, economic, and political changes of contemporary Europe. Lectures and independent research projects. Juniors and seniors. Apply by March 15. Contact Antioch College. Contact: (800) 874-7986.

Council on International Educational Exchange. *Europe and the European Community at the University of Amsterdam and the Free University of Brussels.* Amsterdam, the Netherlands; and Brussels, Belgium. Semester and academic year. Offered in conjunction with European Studies Consortium. Broad European studies focus for fall semester in Amsterdam, and European Community focus for spring semester in Brussels. Sophomores to seniors with 2.75 GPA. Apply by April 1 for fall and academic year; October 15 for spring. Contact University Programs Department.

Eastern Michigan University. *European Cultural History Tour.* 45 cities in Western and Eastern Europe, Russia, and the Mediterranean. Fall semester. History, art, literature, and political science taught in an interdisciplinary context. Sophomores to seniors with 2.5 GPA. Apply by May 15. Contact: (800) 777-3541.

Moorhead State University. *European Humanities Tour.* Spring quarter. Eight-week program beginning in Oxford with tour through Paris, Florence, Rome, Venice, and Berlin. Sophomores to seniors. Apply by November 15. Contact: International Programs, Moorhead State University, Moorhead, MN 56563; (218) 236-2956.

University of Alabama. *Alabama in Eastern Europe.* Berlin, Cracow, Warsaw, Prague, and Budapest. June. Political, social, and cultural consequences of the political revolution of 1989–90. Undergraduates, graduate students, and adults. Apply by March 15.

University of Nebraska—Lincoln. *Nebraska Semester Abroad.* Olomouc, Czech Republic; and Leuven, Belgium. Spring semester. Humanities and social sciences. Sophomores to seniors at member institutions of the Association of Big Eight Universities. Rolling admissions.

University of Wisconsin at River Falls. *Semester Abroad.* Fall semester. Independent study. Juniors and seniors; students must attend orientation seminar during preceding spring semester. Apply by end of fall semester for following year.

World Learning/School for International Training. *College Semester Abroad.* Weimar and Dresden, Germany; and Prague, Czech Republic. Fall and spring semesters. Intensive language, interdisciplinary seminar, field-study methods seminar, and independent-study project. Homestays. Sophomores to seniors with 2.5 GPA. Apply by May 7 for fall; October 7 for spring. Contact: College Semester Abroad Admissions, (800) 336-1616.

Women's Studies

Antioch University. *Comparative Women's Studies in Europe.* The Netherlands, Germany, Poland, and England. Fall term. Lectures and individual research projects. Juniors and seniors. Apply by March 15. Contact: (800) 874-7986.

Summer and Short-Term

Agriculture

Iowa State University. *ISU/Ag Travel Course.* Italy, England, Portugal, Spain, and Morocco. Three weeks in May and June. Agriculture, agronomy, farm management, and international agriculture. Undergraduates and graduate students. Apply by January 15. Contact: Ken Larson, 1126 Agronomy Hall, ISU, Ames, IA 50011; (515) 294-3281.

Michigan State University. *Food and Agricultural Systems in Europe.* The Netherlands, France, Germany, and Switzerland. Mid-May to mid-June. Policy and marketing issues affecting American and European agricultural systems. Excursions. Juniors to graduate students. Apply by April 15. Contact: Office of Overseas Study, 108 International Center, Michigan State University, East Lansing, MI 48824-1035; (517) 353-8920.

Art and Architecture

Miami University. *European Design Workshop.* London, Paris, Luxembourg, Florence, and Venice. Summer. Interior design and architecture. Sophomores to seniors. Apply by January 20.

Michigan State University. *Interior Design in Europe*. London and Paris. Summer. Interior design and architecture from 16th century to present; contemporary design optional in Italy. Juniors to graduate students. Apply by April 15. Contact: Office of Overseas Study, 108 International Center, Michigan State University, East Lansing, MI 48824-1035; (517) 353-8920.

Syracuse University. *The Medieval Pilgrimage Routes from Southern France to Santiago de Compostela: Romanesque Art in the Making*. Summer. Sophomores to graduate students and professionals. Apply by March 1. Contact: (800) 235-3472.

University of Minnesota. *Interior Design in Europe*. London, Paris, Luxembourg/Trier, and Florence. Summer. Interior design, architecture, and decorative arts. Sophomores to graduate students and adults. Apply by March 14. Contact: The Global Campus, 106C Nicholson Hall, 216 Pillsbury Drive SE, University of Minnesota, Minneapolis, MN 55455-0138; (612) 625-3379.

University of Nebraska—Lincoln. *Visual Arts in London and Paris*. London and Paris. Winter break. Introduction to European art in museums and galleries with focus on drawing, painting, and sculpture. First-year college students to graduate students. Apply by October 12.

Business

Michigan State University. *International Management in Europe: Sweden, Denmark, France, Switzerland, and Germany*. Summer. Juniors to graduate students. Apply by April 15. Contact: Office of Overseas Study, 108 International Center, Michigan State University, East Lansing, MI 48824-1035; (517) 353-8920.

Communications

Michigan State University. *Telecommunications in Europe*. Paris, Geneva, Brittany, and Brussels. Summer. Juniors to graduate students. Apply by April 15. Contact: Office of Overseas Study, 108 International Center, Michigan State University, East Lansing, MI 48824-1035; (517) 353-8920.

Engineering

Council on International Educational Exchange. Technology in the European Community at the Aachen University of Technology and the University of Limburg. Four weeks in Aachen, Germany, and two weeks in Maastricht, the Netherlands. Excursions. Sophomores to graduate students in good academic standing and with a major in engineering or in the sciences. Apply by March 1. Contact University Programs Department.

Fashion

Syracuse University. *Fashion in Paris and London*. Five weeks in June and July. International fashion industry, principal fashion designers of England and France, and history of fashion in England and France with site visits and fashion shows. Undergraduates and graduate students. Apply by March 1. Contact: (800) 235-3472.

General Studies

Eastern Michigan University. *European Cultural History Tour*. Includes 35 cities in Western and Eastern Europe and the Mediterranean. Summer. History, art, literature, and political science taught in interdisciplinary context. First-year college students to seniors. Apply by April 1. Contact: (800) 777-3541.

Michigan State University. *Social Science in Scandinavia.* Helsinki, St. Petersburg, and Stockholm. Summer. First-year college students to graduate students. Apply by April 15. Contact: Office of Overseas Study, 108 International Center, Michigan State University, East Lansing, MI 48824-1035; (517) 353-8920.

State University of New York College at Oneonta. *Cultures and Cities of Europe.* London, Paris, and Berlin. Two and a half weeks in January. Study of selected European cities in their historical and geographical settlement and growth, economic development, culture, arts and architecture, and ethnicity. High-school students to graduate students and continuing education students. Rolling admissions. Contact: International Education Office, Netzer Building 332C, SUNY College at Oneonta, Oneonta, NY 13820-4015; (607) 436-3369.

Syracuse University. *Shaping a New Future in East-Central Europe.* Frankfurt and Berlin, Germany; Prague, Czech Republic; Budapest, Hungary; and Vienna, Austria. Five weeks in June and July. Traveling seminar on problems of transition from communism to democracy, supplemented by meetings with government officials, political activists, journalists, and union leaders. Undergraduates and graduate students. Apply by March 1. Contact: (800) 235-3472.

Health and Medicine

State University of New York College at Brockport. *Comparative Health Systems Overseas Study Programs.* Scotland and the Netherlands. Summer. Graduate students in health administration with 2.5 GPA. Apply by May 1. Contact: Office of International Education, SUNY College at Brockport, Brockport, NY 14420; (716) 395-2119.

International Relations

University of Alabama at Birmingham. *UAB in Europe.* Brussels, Belgium; Berlin, Germany; and Prague, Czech Republic. Late June to late July. Social, political, economic, monetary, and environmental issues of European Economic Community, reunified Germany, and post-communist Eastern Europe. High-school graduates to graduate students. Contact: Dr. James Trent, Department of History, University of Alabama at Birmingham, Birmingham, AL 35284-1150; (205) 934-5634.

AUSTRIA

"There are no kangaroos in Austria," declares a popular T-shirt, indicative of the confusion foreigners sometimes have regarding this historic country in the heart of Europe. Its neighbors include the Czech Republic, Germany, Hungary, Italy, Liechtenstein, Slovakia, Switzerland, and Slovenia. Due to its geographic position and its traditional political neutrality, this small, landlocked nation often serves as a crossroads between East and West and is the site of one of three United Nations complexes.

From Innsbruck in the west, the Alps stretch east to Austria's capital and most populous city, Vienna. Small towns dot the Alps, their architecture closely Bavarian and the country pristine. Remote inhabitants of the alpine region still wear lederhosen, 19th-century leather garb, and still dance to ancient refrains, including waltzes. Salzburg, a small city in the heart of the Alps, overflows each summer with tourists eager to see the picturesque medieval city where

Mozart was born and *The Sound of Music* was filmed. In the east lies Vienna, spreading from the Alpine foothills to the Danube and across the plain towards Hungary.

In general, the standard of living is very high. Most families can afford cars and electronics imported from Germany and Japan. Austria produces most of its food and manufactures many products exported to its Central and Eastern European neighbors. Due to economic agreements that Austria has with the Common Market, it has access to a free-trade area that includes most West European countries.

It was an Austrian monarch's assassination—Archduke Franz Ferdinand—in Sarajevo in 1914 by a Serbian nationalist that precipitated World War I. The monarch was a Hapsburg from a dynasty that for hundreds of years ruled a large central European empire including all or part of what is now Germany, Italy, Hungary, former Yugoslavia, Romania, the Czech Republic, Slovakia, Poland—and Austria.

The country still contains a diverse mix of peoples. Descendants of Bavarians and Swiss reside in the west; descendants of Turks, Slavs, and Hungarian Magyars in the east. The various groups are fiercely protective of their ethnicity. Austrians of all backgrounds resent being thought of as German; their country ruled much of Europe more than 500 years before Germany arose as a nation-state. German is Austria's language, but it is distinct in many ways from its northwestern neighbor's tongue, particularly in a lilting dialect often unfathomable to northern German speakers.

—Peter Stadtfeld, Ypsilanti, Michigan

Official name: Republic of Austria. **Size:** 32,374 square miles (about the size of Maine). **Population:** 7,665,000. **Population density:** 236 inhabitants per square mile. **Capital and largest city:** Vienna (pop. 1,500,000). **Language:** German. **Religion:** Roman Catholic. **Per capita income:** US$17,360. **Currency:** Schilling. **Literacy rate:** 99%. **Average daily temperature:** Vienna: June, 65°F; December, 34°F. **Average number of days with precipitation:** Vienna: June, 19; December, 13.

TRAVEL

U.S. citizens need a passport to travel to Austria; however, a visa is not required for a stay of up to three months. Persons planning a stay longer than three months should check with the Consular Office of the **Austrian Embassy**, 3524 International Court NW, Washington, DC 20008-3035; (202) 895-6767.

Getting Around

A good deal for anyone who wants to travel by rail is the **Rabbit Card**, valid for 4 days of second-class travel within a 10-day period. For travelers under 26, the pass costs AS700 (US$60). Regular Rabbit Passes cost AS1070 (US$90). The Rabbit Pass may be obtained at all Austrian rail stations.

The **European East Pass** can be used for travel in the Czech and Slovak Republics, Austria, Hungary, and Poland. Available in first class only, it costs $169 for 5 days of travel in 15 or $275 for 10 days in one month. It's available in the U.S. through Rail Europe (see page 62) or Council Travel (see pages xiii–xvi).

Most Austrian railway stations rent **bikes** from April through October. Rental fees are AS90 per day, with a 50-percent reduction if you submit a railway ticket showing you arrived at the station that day. Bicycles may be returned to any station with a rental outlet. Pick up a list of participating train stations from any Austrian Federal Railways office. There is a fee of AS40 to transport bikes on trains.

For those who want to see the Alps as the Austrians do, a walking trip from one mountain hut to the next is an energetic option. Huts are open from early July until mid-September. Some are extremely basic while others are equipped with hot showers. To help plan your itinerary, *Walking Austria's Alps Hut to Hut* describes 82 tours from 4 to 11 days in length through craggy peaks and flower-filled meadows for both novices and experienced hikers. The book is available for $10.95 from The Mountaineers Books (see page 57).

Eating and Sleeping

Austria has more than 100 youth hostels sponsored by two youth hostel organizations. For further infomation on youth hostels and special travel discounts for Hostelling International members, contact Hostelling International/American Youth Hostels (see page 54) or the travel sections of the following organizations:

- **Österreichischer Jugendherbergsverband**, 1010 Vienna, Schottenring 28; (43) 222-5335353; fax (43) 222-5350861
- **Supertramp**, Österreichisches Jugendherbergswerk, 101 Vienna, Helferstorferstrasse 4; (43) 222-5335137; fax (43) 222-533183381

A number of Austrian universities also offer affordable dormitory housing to travelers. For more information, contact one of Austria's student travel organizations (see "Especially for Students and Young People," below) or consult Campus Travel Service's *U.S. and Worldwide Travel Accommodations Guide* (see page 54).

Especially for Students and Young People

Students going to Austria should be aware of two student travel organizations, both issuers of the International Student Identity Card:

- **ÖKISTA** provides an accommodation service in hotels, pensions, or private homes (minimum stay: three weeks); sightseeing tours; and student discount tickets for flights and trains. The organization also arranges German-language courses in different cities. ÖKISTA branches are located in Graz, Innsbruck, Linz, and Salzburg. For further information, contact ÖKISTA, Türkenstrasse 4, A-1090 Vienna; (43) 222-3475260.
- **Buro für Studentenreisen (BfSt)** offers a student accommodation service, student discount tickets for flights and trains, and language courses. You can contact them at Schreyvogelgasse 3, A-1010 Vienna; (43) 1-5333589; fax (43) 1-5333499.

For Further Information

The best source of general tourist information is the **Austrian National Tourist Office**, 500 Fifth Avenue, New York, NY 10110; (212) 944-6880.

Let's Go: Austria ($16.95) is tailored to the student budget. An excellent book to read in preparation for your trip is *Insight Guide: Austria* ($19.95). For more information on *Let's Go* and *Insight* guides, see pages 56–57.

WORK

Getting a Job

According to the Austrian Consulate General, government regulations regarding employment in Austria have been tightened. Foreigners wishing to work in the country must be in possession of a valid work permit, which is issued by the local State Employment Office (Arbeitsamt) upon application by the prospective employer. Visas are only issued to holders of valid work permits. Further information is included in *Employment of Foreigners in Austria*, which is available from the **Austrian Press and Information Service**, Austrian Embassy, 3524 International Court NW, Washington, DC 20008-3035.

For information on teaching in Austria, contact **The Austrian Cultural Institute**, 11 East 52nd Street, New York, NY 10022; (212) 759-5165; fax (212) 319-9636. Ask for their fact sheet, "Teaching in Austria," which lists organizations that administer teacher exchange programs and hire teachers for overseas assignments. The Institute also has a list of addresses of boards of education for the various Austrian provinces and suggests that teaching positions often exist in the smaller cities of these provinces. A good command of the German language is necessary for teaching in an Austrian public school.

Internships/Traineeships

Programs offered by members of the Council on International Educational Exchange are described below. Consult Appendix I for the addresses of the organizations sponsoring these programs. In addition to those listed here, Moorhead State University sponsors a program open only to its own students.

Association for International Practical Training. *IAESTE Trainee Program.* On-the-job training for undergraduate and graduate students in technical fields such as engineering, computer science, agriculture, architecture, mathematics, the natural and physical sciences. See page 19 for more information.

Hospitality/Tourism Exchanges Program. On-the-job training for young people beginning a career in the hotel and food service industries. Participants must have graduated, or be currently enrolled in a university or vocational school and possess at least six months of training or experience in the chosen field. Training usually runs 6 to 18 months.

Voluntary Service

One possibility for persons interested in voluntary service work in Austria is the "Year Abroad Program" sponsored by the International Christian Youth Exchange. Open to persons 18 to 24 years of age, it offers long-term voluntary service opportunities in the fields of health care, education, the environment, construction, and more. See page 25 for more information.

STUDY

The Austrian Cultural Institute (see "Work," above) distributes several free publications on study opportunities at Austrian universities, including *Information for Foreign Students Intending to Study at an Austrian Institute of Higher Learning, Summer Courses in Austria*, and *American Educational Programs in Austria*, a listing of U.S. colleges and universities that sponsor their own programs in Austria open to students from other schools. They can also provide you with information about grants and scholarships for studying in Austria.

Described below are the academic programs of CIEE-member institutions. Unless otherwise noted, consult Appendix I for the addresses where you can write for more information.

Semester and Academic Year

Business

Northern Illinois University. *International Business in Salzburg*. Spring semester. Economics, business, finance, and marketing plus internship. Homestays. Sophomores to seniors with 2.7 GPA. Apply by November 1. Contact: Foreign Study Office, Semester/Academic Year Programs, Northern Illinois University, Williston Hall 100, DeKalb, IL 60115-2854; (815) 753-0420/0304.

University of North Carolina at Chapel Hill. Vienna. Semester and academic year. Study at the Wirtschaftsuniversität Wien. International management and economics. Sophomores to graduate students. Apply by February 14 for fall and academic year; October 1 for spring.

Communications

Northern Illinois University. *Communications Studies and International Relations*. Salzburg. Semester and academic year. Comparative analysis of mass media systems in North America and Europe and introduction to central European practice and theory of public relations; emphasis on case study and field work. Sophomores to seniors with 2.75 GPA. Apply by June 1 for fall and academic year; November 1 for spring. Contact: Foreign Study Office, Semester/Academic Year Programs, Northern Illinois University, Williston Hall 100, DeKalb, IL 60115-2854; (815) 753-0420/0304.

European Studies

Beaver College. *Vienna Semester Programs in Comparative European Studies: Central European Studies*. Fall semester. Offered in cooperation with Austro-American Institute of Education. Excursions to Czech Republic, Slovakia, Poland, and Germany. Juniors and seniors with 3.0 GPA. Apply by April 20.

Vienna Semester Programs in Comparative European Studies: European Integration Studies. Spring semester. Offered in cooperation with Austro-American Institute of Education. Excursions to Belgium, France, Italy, Germany, and the Netherlands. Juniors and seniors with 3.0 GPA. Apply by October 15.

Vienna Semester Programs in Comparative European Studies: Southeast European Studies. Spring semester. Offered in cooperation with Austro-American Institute of Education. Excursions to Bulgaria, Hungary, Romania, and selected republics of Yugoslavia. Juniors and seniors with 3.0 GPA. Apply by October 15.

Northern Illinois University. *European Studies in Salzburg.* Semester and academic year. Business internships available during spring semester. Homestays. Sophomores to seniors with 2.7 GPA. Apply by June 1 for fall and academic year; November 1 for spring. Contact: Foreign Study Office, Semester/Academic Year Programs, Northern Illinois University, Williston Hall 100, DeKalb, IL 60115-2854; (815) 753-0420/0304.

General Studies

Alma College. *Midwest Consortium for Study Abroad—Vienna.* See listing under American Heritage Association.

American Heritage Association. *Midwest Consortium for Study Abroad—Vienna.* Fall and spring semesters. Excursions and homestays. Sophomores to seniors. Apply by June 15 for fall; November 1 for spring. Contact: (800) 654-2051.

Ball State University. *Midwest Consortium for Study Abroad—Vienna.* See listing under American Heritage Association.

Brigham Young University. *BYU Study Abroad.* Vienna. Fall semester. Study at Austrian-American Educational Institute. Excursions and homestays. Apply by February 1.

Central Michigan University. *Midwest Consortium for Study Abroad—Vienna.* See listing under American Heritage Association.

International Student Exchange Program (ISEP). Academic year. Direct reciprocal exchange between U.S. institutions and Karl Franzens University in Graz. Full curriculum options. Rolling admissions. Open only to students at ISEP-member institutions. Contact ISEP for list of members.

Iowa State University. *ISU/Iowa Regents' Program in Austria.* St. Radegund and Vienna. June to August. German language, literature, and culture. Students with two years of college German. Apply by March 15. Contact: Mark Rectanus, Foreign Languages and Literatures, 300 Pearson Hall, ISU, Ames, IA 50011; (515) 294-4046.

Northern Michigan University. *Midwest Consortium for Study Abroad—Vienna.* See listing under American Heritage Association.

St. Lawrence University. *Vienna Fall Semester Program.* Sophomores to seniors with 2.8 GPA. Apply by February 20.

Southern Illinois University at Carbondale. *Study in Austria.* Bregenz. Semester and academic year. German language, social sciences, and humanities. Excursions and homestays or dormitory housing. Juniors and seniors with 2.75 GPA. Apply by April 1 for fall and academic year; November 1 for spring.

State University of New York at Binghamton. Graz. Semester and academic year. Austrian culture and full university curriculum options at Karl Franzens University. Juniors and seniors with four semesters of college German. Apply by April 1. Contact: Department of German, Russian, and East Asian Languages, SUNY at Binghamton, PO Box 6000, Binghamton, NY 13902-6000; (607) 777-2000.

University of Maine. *New England Study Abroad Program.* Salzburg. Spring semester and academic year. Sophomores to graduate students with four semesters of German. Apply by April 15 for academic year; November 15 for spring.

University of Notre Dame. *International Study Program in Innsbruck.* Innsbruck. Academic year. German language, Austrian history and culture study. Sophomores and juniors with 2.5 GPA and one year of college German with 3.0 GPA in German. Apply by December 1.

Webster University. *Study Abroad in Vienna.* Quarter, semester, and academic year. High-school graduates to graduate students. Apply four months before projected start of study. Contact: (800) 753-6765.
Wilmington College. *Midwest Consortium for Study Abroad—Vienna.* See listing under American Heritage Association.

German Language and Austrian Culture

Adventist Colleges Abroad. St. Peter am Hart. Semester and academic year. Undergraduates with 3.0 GPA in German and 2.5 overall. Open only to students at Adventist Colleges Abroad consortium institutions. Apply by March 25 for fall and academic year; November 15 for spring.
Longwood College. *Junior Year Abroad at University of Salzburg.* Semester and academic year. Juniors with four semesters of college German and 2.5 GPA. Apply by July 1 for fall and academic year; December 1 for spring. Contact: Dr. John F. Reynolds, International Studies Program, Longwood College, Farmville, VA 23901; (804) 395-2172.
Macalester College. *Associated Colleges of the Twin Cities German Program.* Spring semester. Intensive German language study in Germany during January and February; culture and literature study in Vienna from March to May. Sophomores to seniors with two years of college German. Apply by October 15.
Ohio University. *Intensive German Abroad.* Salzburg. Spring quarter (late March to early June). Advanced German language, culture, and literature. Students and nonstudents with two quarters of college German. Apply by December. Contact: Dr. Barry Thomas, Modern Languages Department, 220 Ellis Hall, Athens, OH 45701; (614) 593-2765.
University of Minnesota. *German and Austrian Studies in Graz.* Winter and spring quarters. Language, culture, history, and literature. Spring quarter internships available. Direct enrollment at Karl-Franzens Universität for advanced students. Homestay and excursions. First-year college students to graduate students and adults with 2.5 GPA and four quarters (three semesters) of German. Apply by October 15 for winter; January 15 for spring.

International Relations

American University. *Vienna Semester.* Fall and spring semester. Politics and foreign policy of Austria, Germany, and Switzerland. Internships with international organizations and Austrian agencies. Second-semester sophomores to seniors with 2.75 GPA. Apply by March 15 for fall; October 15 for spring. Contact: World Capitals Programs, American University, Dunblane House—Tenley Campus, Washington, DC 20016-8083; (202) 895-4900/4937.
Beaver College. *Study in Austria: Peace Studies at the EPU.* Stadtschlaining. Semester and academic year. Intensive 12-week program in peace and conflict studies, in cooperation with the European University Center for Peace Studies. Juniors and seniors with 3.0 GPA. Apply by February 15 for fall and academic year; October 15 for spring.

Performing Arts

DePauw University. *DePauw Music Program in Vienna.* Vienna. Fall semester. Theory and applied music. Homestays and excursions. Sophomores to seniors with one semester of college German. Rolling admissions.

Summer and Short-Term

Business

University of Kentucky. *College of Business and Economics Summer Program in Vienna.* Vienna. Summer. Juniors to graduate students with lower level courses in business, art history, or history. Apply by April 15.

University of North Carolina at Chapel Hill. *Summer in Vienna.* Study at the Wirtschaftsuniversität Wien. International management and economics. Sophomores to graduate students. Apply by March 15.

General Studies

Brigham Young University. *BYU Study Abroad.* Vienna. Six-week program from June to August. Homestays and excursions. Apply by February 1.

Hope College. *Vienna Summer School.* June and July sessions. Austrian history, music, art, economics, German language and literature, and independent studies. First-year college students to seniors. Excursions and homestays. Apply by March 1.

North Carolina State University. Vienna. Summer. Art, architecture, music, theater, turn-of-the-century Vienna, and German language. Sophomores to seniors with prior knowledge of German preferred. Apply by March 1.

Southern Methodist University. *SMU in Austria.* Salzburg. Summer. German language and liberal arts studies with focus on Austria and Central Europe. Homestays and excursions. Sophomores to seniors. Apply by March 1. Contact: Office of International Programs, SMU, 100 McFarlin Auditorium, Dallas, TX 75275-0391; (214) 768-2338.

University of New Orleans. *The European Centre.* Innsbruck. Three weeks in summer. Excursions. Students and nonstudents. Apply by April 1. *UNO–Innsbruck International Summer School.* Innsbruck. Six weeks in summer. Field trips. First-year college students to graduate students and adults. Apply by April 7.

Webster University. *Study Abroad in Vienna.* Summer. High-school graduates to graduate students. Apply four months ahead. Contact: (800) 753-6765.

German Language and Austrian Culture

Adventist Colleges Abroad. St. Peter am Hart. Summer. Six-week intensive courses at advanced, intermediate, and beginning levels. Excursions. High-school students, high-school graduates not enrolled in college, and college students with 2.5 GPA. Open only to students at Adventist Colleges Abroad consortium institutions. Apply by March 25.

Beaver College. *Study in Austria: Intensive German Language.* Vienna. August and January pre-semester sessions of four weeks. Offered in cooperation with Austro-American Institute of Education. Sophomores to seniors with beginning to intermediate German. Apply by April 20 for August; November 15 for January.

Eastern Michigan University. *Intensive German Language Program.* Graz. Summer. Intermediate and advanced levels. First-year college students to graduate students. Apply by March 1. Contact: (800) 777-3541.

Indiana University. *Summer Language Study in Graz.* Intermediate German language program. First-year college students to seniors with three semesters of college German. Apply by February 1.

University of Arkansas at Little Rock. *Summer in Austria.* Graz. Early July to mid-August. Offered in cooperation with Karl Franzen University, Graz,

Austria. German language at intermediate and advanced levels, and Central European studies. Homestays or dormitory housing with Austrian students. Undergraduates with intermediate German. Apply by March 1. Contact: Office for International Programs, UALR, 2801 South University Avenue, Little Rock, AR 72204; (501) 569-3374.
University of Kentucky. *Kentucky Institute for International Studies in Bregenz, Austria.* Bregenz. Summer. Language study. Excursions. First-year college students to graduate students and adults. Apply by March 1.
Kentucky Institute for International Studies in Salzburg, Austria. Salzburg. Summer. Language study. Excursions. First-year college students to graduate students and adults. Apply by March 1.

EXPLORING AUSTRIAN CULTURE

Readings

After the disappearance of the Austro-Hungarian Empire, Austrian literature developed a tendency toward dark introspection. This cult of despair is manifested perfectly in the writings of Georg Trakl. *Helian*, his most widely respected work, is strongly influenced by his fascination with death.

Peter Handke, perhaps the most famous Austrian writer today, has been one of greatest defenders of literary form over moral content. *The Goalie's Anxiety at the Penalty Kick* (1971) portrays a former soccer player and pathological killer who subjects every detail of his life to semiotic analysis; it was made into a German film the same year it was published. His latest collection of musings is titled *The Weight of the World: A Journal*. Ingeborg Bachmann, a writer who favors the stream-of-consciousness style, has written many short stories, some of which are collected in *The Thirtieth Year*, in addition to writing a novel entitled *Three Paths to a Lake* (1989).

The bitter humor and cynicism directed towards his country won novelist and playwright Thomas Bernhard perhaps as many enemies as admirers. In *Heldenplatz* (1988), a drama written just before his death, Bernhard risked a head-on collision with his countrymen, once again bringing up their Nazi past and connecting this with the moral state of the country today. Bernhard's less controversial works include *The Chalk Factory*, a novel about a misanthropic man who kills his wife in order to write a scholarly paper, and *The Ignoramus and the Madman*, a drama about alienated individuals who have lost the ability to be spontaneous. Bernhard's *Concrete* presents the hilarious philosophical ravings of a pessimistic intellectual dominated by his worldly sister, while *Wittgenstein's Nephew* portrays the author's friendship with the nephew of Austria's most famous philosopher.

BELGIUM

Although Belgium has existed as an independent state since 1830, there is no Belgian language and there are no real Belgians. Two cultures—the Flemish and the Walloons—coexist within the state's borders. About 55 percent of the people speak Flemish (Dutch), while the remainder are French-speaking Walloons. Today, as the importance of the historic forces that have unified

Belgium (such as a common religion and king) have weakened, linguistic battles and other disputes between these two groups have become more pronounced. While an international soccer championship can sometimes unify the two groups to do justice to the national motto, "*L'union fait la force* (Union makes strength)," Belgium is evolving into two separate semi-autonomous regions within a federal system.

The Flemish region (known as Flanders) encompasses the flat lowlands of the northern part of the country. In the late Middle Ages, the area produced some of the wealthiest trading cities in the world. Visitors to the cities of Antwerp, Ghent, and Bruges will find the inhabitants intensely proud of their rich heritage of art and architecture from the "Golden Century."

Farther south, in the French-speaking area known as Walloonia, the countryside becomes progressively more hilly and more scenic. Here travelers enjoy hiking and biking, exploring quaint villages and castles, and visiting caves and spas (in fact, the Belgian town of Spa gave its name to the whole concept).

In the center of the country lies the booming "Eurocity" of Brussels. Although the capital of Belgium, Brussels is now more important as headquarters for NATO and the European Community, as well as European headquarters for a growing number of multinational corporations. New high-rise buildings surround the city but the Grand Place, the town's medieval center, retains its charm. South of Brussels is Waterloo, site of Napoleon's crushing defeat in 1815.

In this small bilingual and bicultural country tucked between France, Germany, Luxembourg, and the Netherlands, people are used to dealing with cultural and linguistic differences. Most people speak more than one language and many, especially the young, speak some English.

Paradoxically, although Belgium is split by ethnic rivalry, it has consistently been a leading supporter of greater European unity. Such a stand is not surprising. The country's modern industrial economy is dependent on international trade and the nation's very existence depends on friendly relations between its much more powerful neighbors. Greater European unity might lead to the denouement of the country's ethnic rivalry and end the international conflicts between Belgium's neighbors which have, twice in this century, made the small nation a world battlefield.

—Vera van Brande, New York, New York

Official name: Kingdom of Belgium. **Size:** 11,780 square miles (slightly larger than Maryland). **Population:** 9,979,000. **Population density:** 325 inhabitants per square mile. **Capital and largest city:** Brussels (pop. 954,000). **Language:** Dutch, French. **Religion:** Roman Catholic. **Per capita income:** US$10,890. **Currency:** Belgian franc. **Literacy rate:** 98%. **Average daily high/low:** Brussels: January, 42/31°F; July, 73°/54°F. **Average number of days with precipitation:** Brussels: January, 12; July, 11.

TRAVEL

A passport is required for Americans visiting Belgium. A visa is not required for business or tourist stays of up to 90 days. For longer stays, a temporary residence permit is required. For residence authorization, check with the **Belgian Embassy**, 3330 Garfield Street NW, Washington, DC 20008; (202) 333-6900.

Getting Around

Most travelers to Belgium will also want to visit neighboring countries. Eurailpasses, of course, are a good option for multi-country rail travel (see page 00). Those planning to spend most of their time in Belgium, the Netherlands, and Luxembourg would do well to inquire into the **Benelux Tourrail Pass**, which allows 5 days of travel throughout the three countries during a 17-day period. Youths under 26 pay $92 for second class. The Benelux Tourrail Pass can be purchased from Rail Europe (see page 62) or Council Travel (see pages xiii–xvi).

For travel exclusively within Belgium, the **Belgian Tourrail "B" Pass** allows unlimited travel on any 5 days within a 17-day period. Youths under 26 receive special discounts; BF1,300 ($36) second-class. The **16-Day Pass** is good for 16 days of consecutive travel year-round and costs BF3,050 ($86) second-class. The **Half-Rate Card** costs BF500 ($14) for one month and gives the bearer a 50-percent reduction on first- or second-class rail tickets bought in Belgium for travel within the country. These passes can only be bought in Belgium.

Another way to explore Belgium is by bike, as most major roads are accompanied by bike paths. Bicycles can be rented year-round at most train stations, can be taken on Belgian trains at no extra charge, and can be returned at any station.

Eating and Sleeping

Belgium has over 30 youth hostels operated by two independent youth hostel organizations:

- In the Dutch-speaking, northern half of Belgium (Vlaanderen), contact **Vlaamse Jeugdherbergcentrale**, Van Stralenstraat 40, 2060 Antwerp; (32) 3-2327218; fax (32) 3-2318126.
- In the French- and German-speaking south (Walloonia), contact: **Les Auberges de Jeunesse**, Rue Van Oost 52, B-1030, Brussels; (32) 2-2153100; fax (32) 2-2428356.

Both organizations operate hostels in the capital city of Brussels. For more information, you can also contact Hostelling International/American Youth Hostels (see page 54).

In addition, several Belgian universities offer affordable dormitory lodgings to travelers. For more information, contact one of Belgium's student travel organizations (see "Especially for Students and Young People," below) or consult Campus Travel Service's *U.S. and Worldwide Travel Accommodations Guide* (see page 54).

Especially for Students and Young People

Belgium has two student travel bureaus, both issuers of the International Student Identity Card. One is **ACOTRA**, rue de la Madeleine 51, B-1000 Brussels; (32) 2-5128607; fax (32) 2-5123974. ACOTRA also operates a Welcome Service at Brussels Airport. The other is **Connections**, Kolenmarktstraat 13 rue Marché au Charbon, 1000 Brussels; (32) 2-5125060; fax (32) 2-5126801. Connections also has offices in Antwerp, Ghent, Leuven, Liège, and Louvain-la-Neuve. Both organizations are good sources of information on discounts available to students in Belgium.

For Further Information

You can get maps and information on camping, budget hotels, excursions, and more from the **Belgian Tourist Office**, 745 Fifth Avenue, New York, NY 10151; (212) 758-8130. Also available from the tourist office is *Windrose*, a listing of accommodations with host families in Belgium. In Belgium, pick up a copy of the English-language weekly *Bulletin*, which lists cultural events as well as job opportunities.

The best guide to Belgium and neighboring countries is *The Real Guide: Holland, Belgium, and Luxembourg* ($16). Also good is *Frommer's Belgium, Holland, and Luxembourg* ($18). Both are published by Prentice Hall Travel.

WORK

It is necessary to obtain a work permit for employment in Belgium. The permit is issued by the appropriate Belgian authorities upon application by the prospective employer in Belgium. If you are planning to stay for more than 90 days, it is necessary to obtain a temporary residency permit as well. For further information, contact the Belgian Embassy (see "Travel," above).

Internships/Traineeships

A program offered by a member of the Council on International Educational Exchange is described below. Consult Appendix I for the address where you can write for more information. In addition, Moorhead State University sponsors an internship program open only to its own students.

Association for International Practical Training. *IAESTE Trainee Program.* On-the-job training for undergraduate and graduate students in technical fields such as engineering, computer science, agriculture, architecture, mathematics, and the natural and physical sciences. See page 19 for more information.

Voluntary Service

CIEE places volunteers in Belgian workcamps organized by Compagnons Batisseurs in Marche-en-Famenne. At these workcamps, groups of volunteers from around the world work on a variety of construction projects. Applicants must be at least 18 years of age. Applications of U.S. residents are processed by CIEE. For more information, contact CIEE's International Voluntary Service Department.

For persons interested in longer term voluntary service work, the Year Abroad Program sponsored by the International Christian Youth Exchange offers persons ages 18 to 24 opportunities in the fields of health care, education, the environment, construction, and more. See page 25 for more information.

STUDY

For those who want to study in Belgium, the Embassy of Belgium (see "Travel," above) can supply you with a list of Belgian universities plus brochures on direct enrollment programs there. They can also supply you with applications for fellowships for study in Flemish universities offered by the Ministry of the Flemish Community. There are two fellowships for undergraduates and three for graduate students. The deadline is March 1.

For predoctorate graduate students wishing to pursue independent study and research in Belgium, the **Belgian American Educational Foundation** offers an $11,000 fellowship for a 10-month period. Candidates must speak and read either German, French, or Dutch. The application deadline is December 31. For details, write to the Belgian American Educational Foundation, 195 Church Street, New Haven, CT 06510; (203) 777-5765.

Described below are the academic programs sponsored by CIEE-member institutions. Unless otherwise noted, consult Appendix I for the addresses of the colleges and universities listed in this section.

Semester and Academic Year

Business

Bentley College. *Bentley's Business Program in Belgium*. Brussels. Semester and academic year. Offered in association with Vesalius College of Vrije Universiteit Brussels. European Community, European culture, and other subjects. Excursions and visits to NATO and EC headquarters. Sophomores to seniors with 2.7 GPA. Apply by April 15 for fall and academic year; November 1 for spring.

University of Alabama. *Study Abroad in Belgium*. Hautes Etudes Commerciales in Liege. Academic year. Sophomores to seniors with 3.0 GPA. Apply by March 1. Contact: (205) 348-5256.

General Studies

International Student Exchange Program (ISEP). Academic year. Direct reciprocal exchange between U.S. institutions and Katholieke Universiteit te Leuven. Full curriculum options. Rolling admissions. Open only to students at ISEP-member institutions. Contact ISEP for list of members.

University of Pennsylvania. *European Culture and Society*. Leuven. Semester and academic year. Study at the Katholieke Universiteit. Juniors and seniors with 3.0 GPA. Apply by February 15 for fall and academic year; October 15 for spring.

International Relations

American University. *Brussels Semester*. Fall and spring semesters. International relations between U.S. and Western Europe; function and role of the European Community. Internships with multinational organizations. Second-semester sophomores to seniors with 2.75 GPA. Apply by March 15 for fall; October 15 for spring. Contact: World Capitals Programs, American University, Dunblane House—Tenley Campus, Washington, DC 20016-8083; (202) 895-4900/4937.

Summer and Short-Term

General Studies

Lehigh University. *Lehigh in Brussels*. Leuven (near Brussels). June. Five-week program in European history and/or marketing. Internships possible.

First-year college students to seniors with 2.8 GPA. Apply by March 15. Contact: Office of Summer Studies, 205 Johnson Hall, 36 University Drive, Lehigh University, Bethlehem, PA 18105; (215) 758-3966.

International Relations

Michigan State University. *International Relations in Brussels.* Summer. Political science and international relations. Sophomores to seniors. Apply by April 15. Contact: Office of Overseas Study, 108 International Center, Michigan State University, East Lansing, MI 48824-1035; (517) 353-8920.

EXPLORING BELGIAN CULTURE

Readings

Because Belgium did not exist as an independent country until the early 19th century—and because it is even further divided into Flemish- and French-speaking regions—a distinctly Belgian cultural tradition has been slow to develop. Perhaps the most internationally known modern Belgian writer is Georges Simenon, the famed author of psychological mysteries. His ability to penetrate the pathological mind is especially apparent in *The Man Who Watched the Trains Go By* and *The Little Saint* (1965). His novel *Monsieur Hire* was made into a French thriller movie in 1989. It focuses on a disliked middle-aged voyeur suspected of murder and his sexual obsession with a young girl. Simenon's most famous sleuth—Inspector Jules Maigret of the Paris police—is the subject of 76 of his novels. Many of them were made into films, the best probably being *Maigret Sets a Trap* (1957), directed by Michel Audiard. Simenon himself is quite a fascinating character, as the 1993 biography by Patrick Marnham proves. *The Man Who Wasn't Maigret* is an engrossing account of this author who once claimed he had made love to 10,000 women.

Belgium's foremost Flemish novelist is Hugo Claus. Many of Claus's works show his concern with the effects of World War II. *The Sorrow of Belgium* (1983), for example, is about a young boy growing up in Flanders during the Nazi occupation. Another of his novels, *The Sacrament* (1963), which takes place in a typical Flemish village in the 1950s, was made into a film directed by Claus himself. A satirical look at a community under the thumb of the Catholic church, it centers on the latent frustrations and grudges that explode during a gluttonous, drunken feast.

Belgian playwright Fernand Crommelynck's *The Magnificent Cuckold* (1920) is a naughty sex comedy about marital infidelity and jealousy. The 1966 film was an Italian production directed by Antonio Pietrangeli. Crommelynck's other plays, set in Flemish towns and written in a poetic style, include *Carine* (1929) and *Hot and Cold* (1936).

BULGARIA

Bulgaria is one of the least visited of the countries formerly known as the "Soviet Bloc." The Bulgaria of today, however, can no longer be considered an intimidating place to visit. The adventurous traveler who makes the trip will encounter people with a fresh interest in visitors and a fascinating country that has been largely spared the crush of Western tourism.

A common alphabet and real gratitude for being freed from Ottoman Turks in the late 1800s are but two of the ties that contribute to the closeness Bulgarians feel toward Russia. Perhaps because of this, the changes that have swept through Eastern Europe have had different effects on Bulgaria than on Hungary or Poland, for example. But Bulgarians, like the other peoples of Eastern Europe, are searching for new directions, and the country's economy and society are engaged in a difficult, fascinating period of transition.

The capital city of Sofia, with its historic ruins, university centers, and nearby modern alpine skiing facilities on Mount Vitosha, frequently hosts international sports competitions and conferences. The ancient city wall and ruins just off the main city square, the lively market area with its live chickens and varied aromas, and the structures and monuments of several cultures are all linked by an inexpensive public transportation system.

Visitors to the area near Varna on the Black Sea coast will find a very different Bulgaria—one designed to attract the tourist and to offer vacation packages. Russians and Ukrainians mingle with Western tourists, often from the United Kingdom, who fly in to enjoy an inexpensive seacoast holiday; here the visitor is more apt to find English or German understood.

Travel away from Sofia and Varna reveals another perspective on the country. Monasteries in the remote mountains have survived hundreds of years and remain in remarkable condition, relics of the various cultures that Bulgaria has seen throughout the centuries. There is a strong sense of history in Bulgaria, and the preparation time spent in reading a little about the country's past and learning a few phrases of the language will be richly rewarded with warmth, smiles, and helpfulness.

Memories of countless roses will linger with those who travel to the countryside. Exporting rose nectar for perfumes is a Bulgarian tradition and a key source of hard currency. Extensive vineyards produce excellent local wines that are developing an international following. An extensive but crowded rail network provides the independent traveler with inexpensive access to a countryside that sharply contrasts the urban centers. Lines for train tickets can be annoying, but your patience will be rewarded with insights on Bulgarian culture and daily life.

Bulgarian students and businesspeople alike are intensely interested in the world of ideas, and you can easily find yourself debating the merits of von Mises or Piaget over a tiny cup of the strong, dark, local coffee. It's always useful to understand some of the local body language: the thumb is used to indicate one (such as in ordering coffee) and the "yes/no" head nods are reversed from the United States custom. As always, there is no substitute for a healthy sense of humor and a willingness to accept things as they are.

—Bill Peirce, Forestdale, Massachusetts

Official name: Republic of Bulgaria. **Area:** 44,365 square miles (about the size of Ohio). **Population:** 8,910,000. **Population density:** 200 inhabitants per square mile. **Capital and largest city:** Sofia (1,200,000). **Language:** Bulgarian, Turkish. **Religion:** 85% Bulgarian Orthodox. **Per capita income:** US$5,300. **Currency:** Leva. **Literacy rate:** 98%. **Average temperature:** Sofia: June, 66°F; December, 33°F. **Average number of days with precipitation:** Sofia: June, 12; December, 12.

TRAVEL

Holders of a U.S. passport do not need a visa to travel in Bulgaria for a stay of up to 30 days. Visas for stays over 30 days cost $27. For more information, contact the **Bulgarian Embassy** at 1621 22nd Street NW, Washington, DC 20008; (202) 387-7969; fax (202) 234-7973.

Getting Around

Bulgaria's **rail** network is extensive and inexpensive. Bulgaria's trains do, however, have a reputation for being quite crowded and slow, and lines to purchase tickets can be quite long. Purchase tickets well in advance, if possible. To do this, find the central ticketing offices in each city; in the stations themselves, tickets go on sale two hours before departure. Alternatively, you can avoid lines by buying tickets on the train for twice the regular price.

Trains do not run along the Black Sea coast, but **buses** do. In general, private bus lines go wherever trains do, costing less and getting there faster. However, most buses don't adhere to strict schedules. A good way to beat the crowds is to hop on a **Balkan Air** shuttle flight. Airfares have risen dramatically in the last couple of years, but domestic flights are still affordable. **Hydrofoil** service between coastal towns is also fast and comfortable.

Eating and Sleeping

Bulgaria has more than 60 **youth hostels**. For more information, contact Hostelling International/American Youth Hostels (see page 54) or the **Bulgarian Youth Hostel Federation**, Boul Vassil Levski 75, Sofia 1000; (359) 2-883821; fax (359) 2-802414. A network of **student hotels** is operated by Orbita (see "Especially for Students and Young People," below).

Especially for Students and Young People

Bulgaria's student travel office and issuer of the International Student Identity Card is **Orbita**, 45A Stambolijski Boulevard, Sofia; (359) 2-879552; fax (359) 2-800102. There are Orbita branches throughout the country. Besides serving as an information source, Orbita runs a chain of student hotels, for which Westerners must make advance reservations. Orbita also sponsors several tours and offers sports and cultural activities. Holders of the International Student Identity Card receive discounts on train fare to other eastern European countries. Ask Orbita about other student discounts.

For Further Information

At press time, there were no good guidebooks focusing solely on Bulgaria. However, you can find reliable information on traveling in Bulgaria in *Eastern Europe on a Shoestring*, available for $21.95 from Lonely Planet Publications. An excellent book to read in preparation for your trip is *Insight Guide: Eastern Europe* ($19.95). For more information on Lonely Planet and *Insight Guides*, see pages 56–57.

WORK

It's virtually impossible for Americans to obtain regular employment in Bulgaria. However, internship and voluntary service opportunities are described below.

Internships/Traineeships

A program sponsored by a member of the Council on International Educational Exchange is listed below.

Association for International Practical Training. *IAESTE Trainee Program.* On-the-job training for undergraduate and graduate students in technical fields such as engineering, computer science, agriculture, architecture, mathematics, and the natural and physical sciences. See page 19 for more information.

EXPLORING BULGARIAN CULTURE

Readings

Bulgaria did not develop a literature of its own until the 19th century, when intellectuals reacted against Turkish rule by expressing their feelings of rage and nationalism. One such writer was Khristo Botev, whose revolutionary and patriotic works are still popular. *Under the Yoke* (1893), a novel by popular writer Ivan Vazov about the struggle against the Turks, won international recognition.

After the communist takeover in 1944, several authors attempted to escape the Socialist-imposed realism by glorifying the past. The finest example of this kind of writing is Dimitur Talev's famous trilogy—*The Iron Candlestick* (1952), *Elijah's Day* (1954), and *The Bells of Prespa* (1954)—a family saga centering on the fight for independence. A more recent book, *The October Circle* (1976), by Robert Littell, is about a group of Bulgarian performers who resist the 1968 Soviet invasion of Czechoslovakia.

In *Balkan Ghosts: A Journey Through History* (1993), veteran journalist Robert Kaplan's explorations of the countryside and his meetings with people from priests to peasants gives the reader an enlightened look into the psyche and culture of this troubled region. Anton Gill's experiences and conversations in *Berlin to Bucharest: Travels in Eastern Europe* (1990) also offers a fascinating introduction to the history, politics, and culture of this region.

CYPRUS

The Mediterranean island nation of Cyprus was the site of early Phoenician and Greek colonies. Because of its strategic position in the eastern Mediterranean, it has fallen prey to numerous other conquerors over the centuries. The British seized the island from the Turks in the First World War and held it until 1960, when it was granted independence.

Turkish-Greek animosity on the island is rampant. In fact, the majority of the population regard themselves as either Greeks or Turks, rather than Cypriot nationals. To make matters worse, violence between Greek and Turkish Cypriots has been provoked by the interference of Greece and Turkey in the island's affairs. In 1974, Turkish troops invaded Cyprus in defense of the Turkish minority, and Turkey still controls about a third of the island. Greek Cypriots—most of whom support self-determination for the island (that is, union with Greece)—have fled to the southern and western parts of the country. Turkish Cypriots, however, have set up a government in the area they control and proclaimed their independence. While the international community still recognizes Cyprus as a single independent state, in fact the island is split into two belligerent states, divided by linguistic, religious, and ethnic differences.

In addition to Cyprus's strategic position, its natural attributes have long made it a coveted possession and a popular vacation spot. Streams flow down from its high mountain ranges to water the foothills and the fertile plain. The rich natural landscape is adorned with ancient Roman and Greek ruins, Orthodox monasteries and castles built by the crusaders, landmarks that attest to the rich history of this land. However, tourists are prohibited from crossing the militarized border ("Green Line") between the Greek and Turkish sections of the island. Most tourists visit the Greek section, which is linked by plane to Western Europe and the Middle East and by ferry to Greece, Israel, and Lebanon. Good beaches, a warm sunny climate, and inexpensive food and accommodations have made the Greek section popular with tourists in spite of the continuing conflict between Greeks and Turks.

—Michael LaPierre, New York, New York

Official name: Republic of Cyprus. **Area:** 3,572 square miles (one and a half times the size of Delaware). **Population:** 708,000. **Population density:** 194 inhabitants per square mile. **Capital and largest city:** Nicosia (pop. 166,000). **Language:** Greek, Turkish (both official); English. **Religion:** Greek Orthodox, Islam. **Per capita income:** US $7,585. **Currency:** Cypriot pound. **Literacy rate:** 95%. **Average daily high/low:** Nicosia: January, 58/42°F; July, 97/69°F. **Average number of days with precipitation:** Nicosia: January, 10; July, less than 1.

TRAVEL

U.S. citizens will need a passport to travel to Cyprus; however, a visa is not required. For specific requirements, check with the **Embassy of the Republic of Cyprus**, 2211 R Street NW, Washington, DC 20008; (202) 462-5772.

Getting Around

The southern part of Cyprus has more to offer the tourist than does the Turkish-controlled north. Remember, travelers cannot pass from either part of the island to the other. Cyprus's main airport is in Larnaca. Most European boats disembark at Limassol, a western port; Cyprus provides regular sea connections with the Mediterranean coastal countries of Europe, the Middle East, and North Africa.

The routes between major towns and cities are served by **buses** and **shared taxis**. Taxis and buses follow regular routes, departing when they are full and picking up and dropping off passengers along the way. **Hitchhiking** is relatively easy, and on secondary routes it may be the only alternative if you don't have your own transportation. **Car** rentals can be arranged; remember that driving is on the left side of the road.

You can also rent motorcycles and bicycles throughout Cyprus. For information on bicycling, contact the **Cyprus Cycling Federation**, 5 Vizinos Street, Nicosia; (357) 2-459056.

Eating and Sleeping

You should have no problem finding inexpensive hotels in Cyprus. In addition, you can find **youth hostel** accommodations in Larnaca, Nicosia, Paphos,

Stavros, and Troodos. For more information, contact Hostelling International/American Youth Hostels (see page 54) or the **Cyprus Youth Hostel Association**, 34Th. Theodotou Street, PO Box 1328, Nicosia; (357) 2-442027; fax (357) 2-442896. The southern coast of Cyprus offers several inexpensive **campgrounds** with sanitary facilities, grocery stores, and restaurants.

For Further Information

Let's Go: Greece and Turkey contains a chapter on Cyprus with helpful information for the budget traveler. It's available for $16.95 in most bookstores and at Council Travel offices (see pages xiii–xvi). A great introduction to the country is *Insight Guide: Cyprus* ($19.95). General tourist information and wonderful maps are available from the **Cyprus Tourism Organization**, 13 East 40th Street, New York, NY 10016; (212) 683-5280. The Cyprus Tourism Organization can also provide information on modern Greek-language classes and other educational opportunities.

WORK

In order to work in Cyprus you need to obtain a work permit; positions are granted only to foreigners who possess a needed skill that can't be filled by a Cypriot national. It is difficult to get a permit while in the country unless you have a prearranged position with a company in the private sector. For more information contact the **Consulate of Cyprus**, 13 East 40th Street, New York, NY 10016.

Internships/Traineeships

The following program is sponsored by a member of the Council on International Educational Exchange.

Association for International Practical Training. *IAESTE Trainee Program.* On-the-job training for undergraduate and graduate students in technical fields such as engineering, computer science, agriculture, architecture, mathematics, and the natural and physical sciences. See page 19 for more information.

STUDY

For a list of Cyprus's private institutions of higher education that are recognized by the Cyprus Ministry of Education, contact the **Press and Information Office** of the Embassy of Cyprus (see "Travel," above).

Described below are the educational programs offered by CIEE-member institutions. Unless otherwise noted, consult Appendix I for the addresses of the colleges and universities listed in this section.

Semester and Academic Year

Business

State University of New York–Empire State College. *Program in Cyprus.* Nicosia. Semester and academic year. Business and technology in the Eastern

Mediterranean. Sophomores to graduate students and adults. Apply by June 15 for fall and academic year; November 30 for spring.

General Studies

International Student Exchange Program (ISEP). Fall and spring semesters. Direct reciprocal exchange between U.S. universities and Frederick Institute of Technology. Full curriculum options. Rolling admissions. Open only to students at ISEP-member institutions. Contact ISEP for list of members.

THE CZECH REPUBLIC

The Czech Republic may appear to be a ''new'' country due to the dissolution of the former Czechoslovakia, but a close inspection of the nation's history yields a somewhat different and fascinating picture. The name ''Czechoslovakia'' was born in 1918—when the Czechs and the Slovaks were placed by the Treaty of Versailles in a new state occupying territory that had long been part of the Austro-Hungarian Empire. These two peoples, each with their own language and traditions, continued to live in uneasy coexistence within this state until the 1992 separation. Although Czechs and Slovaks share common origins, they have distinct cultures and languages—Czechs have had traditionally Germanic affinities, while Slovaks lean towards Hungary. The 1992 split was in response to Slovak calls for self-determination.

Gothic and baroque buildings stand amid rows of stark gray apartment blocks in the Czech Republic, but the juxtapositions only start there. From Prague, the romantic city of a hundred spires in the heart of Bohemia, to Brno, capital of Moravia and site of painful defeats to Napoleon and Hitler, the country's colorful political history has left its mark. Signs of recent political upheavals are visible everywhere, manifest in the physical environs and in the people. Timid smiles stand in contrast to the weary faces that prevailed before the revolution in 1989. The people seem infused with a will to forge ahead as the country becomes once again a popular destination for international visitors.

But these are also challenging times. The country is experiencing a dramatic rise in inflation that is not being matched by wages. Czechs therefore find the cost of living exorbitant and increasing daily. In contrast, western tourists find the cost of living very cheap, and with the visa requirement removed, visitors from wealthier neighboring countries have begun to take advantage of bargain holidays and weekend breaks. Some come simply to buy large quantities of exquisite crystal.

On the weekends there is a mass exodus from the cities to the country. The beautiful scenery, lakes, mountains, wildlife, and a legacy of Victorian elegance in spa towns such as Karlsbad and Marienbad are strong reasons for leaving the bleak and depressing housing areas. Trains tend to be slower than the buses, but the metro in Prague is so clean and efficient that it puts most other subway systems to shame.

With its fairy-tale castle gazing down on the Vltava River flowing under the baroque statues on Charles Bridge, Prague has been called the most beautiful city in Europe. Steeped in history with Viennese-style squares, palaces, formal gardens, and street musicians, as well as a church where Mozart played and a library where Kafka worked (now the U.S. embassy), Prague was fortunate in emerging from both world wars virtually unscathed. The nation's numerous castles, which once guarded tiny principalities, are perhaps testament to the conflict and division that have characterized the area for centuries.

The people can be difficult to meet and get to know. After more than 40 years of oppression they are still very suspicious, but once the initial barriers are broken they can become good friends. More often than not, they will invite you to drink with them. They will be offended if you try to pay, however, so visitors should be considerate and try not to order too much.

—Sarah J. B. Eykyn, London, United Kingdom

Official name: Czech Republic. **Area:** 49,365 square miles (about the size of New York). **Population:** 10,298,731. **Population density:** 131 inhabitants per square kilometer. **Capital and largest city:** Prague (pop. 1,215,000). **Language:** Czech. **Religion:** Roman Catholic. **Currency:** Koruna. **Literacy rate:** 99%. **Average temperature:** Prague: June, 61°F; December, 31°F. **Average number of days with precipitation:** Prague: June, 12; December, 15.

TRAVEL

Holders of American passports do not need a visa to enter the Czech Republic, provided they stay for less than 30 days. However, travelers can easily apply for extensions within the country. For more information, contact the **Embassy of the Czech Republic**, 3900 Linnean Avenue NW, Washington, DC 20008; (202) 363-6315.

Getting Around

CSM offers comprehensive domestic air service. Travel by rail in the Czech Republic is inexpensive, and it's worth paying a little extra for express trains. **Inter-Rail** passes are valid in the country, but Eurailpasses aren't. The **European East Pass** can be used for travel in the Czech and Slovak Republics, Austria, Hungary, and Poland. Available in first class only, it costs $169 for 5 days of travel in 15 or $275 for 10 days in one month. In addition, there's a new **CzechoSlovak Flexipass**, also first-class, that costs $59 for 5 days of travel in 15. Both passes are available in the U.S. from Rail Europe (see page 62) or Council Travel (see pages xiii–xvi). **Buses** are faster than trains but charge slightly more. **Car** rental is very inexpensive and a good idea for visiting the country or Slovakia. Within Prague, use the convenient subway, local buses, and trams.

Eating and Sleeping

Because of the immense popularity of Prague, hotel rooms are scarce. However, there are many **youth hostels** in the Czech Republic. For more information, contact Hostelling International/American Youth Hostels (see page 54) or **KMC Club of Young Travelers**, Malostranské nábrezí 1, 11800 Prague 1-Malá Strana; (42) 2-538153; fax (42) 2-538858. A network of "**Junior Hotels**" is run by CKM (see "Especially for Students and Young People," below). Also check with CKM about lodging in **university dorms**. It's also fairly easy to rent a room with a **family**. If you want to make arrangements in advance, contact CEDOK (see "For Further Information," below).

Especially for Students and Young People

The Czech Republic's student/youth travel bureau and issuer of the International Student Identity Card is **CKM**, 12 Zitná Street, 12105 Prague 2; (42) 2-299941; fax (42) 2-2351297. In addition to providing typical travel services, CKM operates a network of "Junior Hotels."

For Further Information

Cedok, formerly the official tourist office of Czechoslovakia, has become a full-service travel agency and remains the best source of travel information on those countries.

In Prague, be sure to visit the **American Hospitality Center** at Malé náméstí 14 (phone: 268507) and check the message board for requests for English tutors, travel companions, and more.

A good guide for travel in the Czech Republic is *The Real Guide: Czechoslovakia* ($13.95). An excellent book to read in preparation for your trip is *Insight Guide: Czechoslovakia* ($19.95). For more information on *Real Guides* and *Insight Guides*, see page 57.

WORK

Getting a Job

To obtain employment in the Czech Republic, it is necessary to secure a long-stay permit, which can be applied for at the **Embassy of the Czech Republic** (see "Travel," above). For an application and more information, contact the embassy.

Internships/Traineeships

A program offered by a member of the Council on International Educational Exchange is listed below.

Association for International Practical Training. *IAESTE Trainee Program.* On-the-job training for undergraduate and graduate students in technical fields such as engineering, computer science, agriculture, architecture, mathematics, and the natural and physical sciences. See page 19 for more information.

Voluntary Service

CIEE places young people in voluntary-service **workcamps** in the Czech Republic organized by KMC, the Czech Youth Hostel Association, and INEX, a youth exchange organization in Prague. At these workcamps, groups of international volunteers get involved in various agricultural or conservation projects. Workcamps, which last two weeks, are scheduled during the summer vacation (July through September). Volunteers must be healthy, between the ages of 18 and 35, and able to do hard physical labor. In return for their service, they receive room and board. The applications of U.S. residents are processed by CIEE. For more information, contact the International Voluntary Service Department at CIEE.

STUDY

Persons considering study in the Czech Republic might want to check out the *AAASS Directory of Programs in Russian, Eurasian, and East European Stud-*

ies, which lists close to 75 academic programs in Russia, Eurasia, and Eastern Europe, including addresses and information on deadlines and costs. The directory also lists similar study programs in the U.S. and can be ordered prepaid from the **American Association for the Advancement of Slavic Studies**, Jordan Quad/Acacia, 125 Panama Street, Stanford, CA 94305-4130; (415) 723-9668. The price is $30 for nonmembers, $20 for members, plus $3 postage; you might be able to find it in libraries or study abroad offices.

Specific inquiries on studying abroad should be directed to the **Czech Ministry of Education, Youth, and Sport**, Karmelicka 7, 118 12 Praha 1, Czech Republic; fax (42) 2-5193790.

Study programs offered by CIEE-member institutions are listed below. Unless otherwise noted, consult Appendix I for the addresses of these colleges and universities.

Semester and Academic Year

Art and Architecture

North Carolina State University. *NCSU School of Design's Summer Study in Prague*. Offered in cooperation with Academy of Applied Arts in Prague and Czech University of Technology. Architecture, landscape architecture, urban design, illustration, film animation, drawing and painting, and poster design. Excursions and dormitory housing. Undergraduates, graduate students, teachers, and professionals. Apply by March 15. Contact: Summer Study in Prague, NCSU School of Design, PO Box 7701, Raleigh, NC 27695-7701; (919) 834-6533.

General Studies

Associated Colleges of the Midwest/Great Lakes College Association. Olomouc. Fall semester. Intensive language training, Czech studies, and field experiences. Dormitory housing with Czech students. Juniors and seniors. Apply by March 15.

American University. *Prague Semester*. Fall. Intensive Czech language, history, culture, and society. General studies or focus on film and media at FAMU Film School. Internships optional. Second-semester sophomores to seniors with 2.75 GPA. Apply by March 15. Contact: World Capitals Programs, American University, Dunblane House—Tenley Campus, Washington, DC 20016-8083; (202) 895-4900/4937.

Council on International Educational Exchange. *Cooperative East and Central European Studies Program at Charles University*. Prague. Fall and spring semesters. Undergraduates with 2.75 GPA and six semester-hours in economics, history, or other social science discipline. Apply by April 10 for fall; November 1 for spring. Contact University Programs Department.

New York University. *NYU in Prague*. Fall semester. Excursions to Poland, Austria, and Hungary. Undergraduates. Contact: NYU in Prague, FAS Summer Programs, 6 Washington Square North, New York, NY 10003; (212) 998-8170.

University of Pennsylvania. *Semester in Prague: Central European Studies*. Prague. Fall and spring semesters. Humanities, social sciences, contemporary issues, language study, and Jewish studies. Sophomores to seniors with 3.0 GPA. Apply by April 1 for fall; November 1 for spring.

Natural Sciences

World Learning/School for International Training. *College Semester Abroad*. Prague. Fall and spring semesters. Orientation, intensive language study, field-study seminar, and independent-study project. Homestays and excursions. Sophomores to graduate students with 2.5 GPA and previous coursework in environmental studies, ecology, biology, or related field. Apply by May 7 for fall; October 7 for spring. Contact: College Semester Abroad Admissions at (800) 336-1616.

Summer and Short-Term

General Studies

New York University. *NYU in Prague*. Five weeks in August and July. Offered in affiliation with Charles University in Prague. Undergraduate program in intensive Czech language, and Central European and Czech literature, culture, politics, and arts; graduate program in Central European politics, literature, and culture. Excursions to Poland, Austria, and Hungary. Undergraduates and graduates. Apply by April 15. Contact: NYU in Prague, FAS Summer Programs, 6 Washington Square North, Room 41, New York, NY 10003; (212) 998-8172.

University of Pennsylvania. *Penn-in-Prague*. Prague. Summer. Central European studies and Jewish studies. First-year college students to seniors. Apply by April 1.

International Relations

Ohio University. *Summer Program in Czech Republic*. Suchdol. June and July. Five-week program on economic, agricultural, and rural development issues surrounding changes in East Central Europe. Excursions. Undergraduates with 2.7 GPA. Apply by March 15.

Languages

Memphis State University. *International Language School at University of West Bohemia*. Pilsen. July. Three-week program in language (choice of Czech, German, or French), culture, current events, and TEFL (Teaching English as a Foreign Language). Excursions and residence hall housing. Undergraduates and graduate students. Apply by March 15. Contact: Dr. Charles Hall, Pilsen Summer School, Department of English, Memphis State University, Memphis, TN 38152; (901) 678-4496 or (901) 324-0377.

EXPLORING CZECH CULTURE

Readings

One of the most famous Czech books dating from the pre-communist era is Jaroslav Hašek's *Good Soldier Schwejk* (1921), which presents the absurdities of war and its bureaucratic machinery from the point of view of a common soldier who manages to survive its horrors through imagination and cunning. Franz Kafka is perhaps the most famous Czech author from this period. In novels such as *The Castle* and *The Trial*, he writes of paranoia and of the labyrinthian bureaucracy of Central Europe. Among other well-known authors of the pre-takeover period is Karel Capek, whose collection of short stories *Money and Other Stories* (1930) and novel *War with the Newts* (1937) are available in translation. Capek's play about the dangers of technology, *R.U.R.*, in which he coined the word "robot," is also widely available.

Since 1968, many emigrant and dissident Czechoslovakian writers have received attention in the West; Milan Kundera is probably the best known of this group. Kundera's *The Joke* (1969), a satire on Czechoslovakian politics, and the critically acclaimed *The Unbearable Lightness of Being* (1975), in which he attempts to overcome the failure of the Prague uprising in 1968 with a somewhat desperate philosophy of acceptance, are two of his best known works. Although Kundera has lived in Paris for many years, only his most recent novel, *Immortality* (1991), is set entirely outside of Czechoslovakia.

Other contemporary writers include Josef Skvorecky and Ivan Klima. Skvorecky's *The Engineer of Human Souls* (1984) and *Dvořák in Love* contrasts Communist Czechoslovakia with an emigrant community in Toronto. Klima's novel *Love and Garbage* is a semi-autobiographical work that takes place during the "normalization," when he was forbidden from writing and worked as a street sweeper. Ivan Klima's latest book is *Judge on Trial* (1993); this novel follows an idealistic judge whose own trial of conscience begins shortly after the Prague Spring of 1968. Bruce Chatwin's novel *Utz* takes place in the Jewish quarter of Prague and is the story of an avid porcelain collector.

Films

"For us, film is the most important of the arts!" V. I. Lenin's statement is often evoked when speaking about Eastern European filmmaking, and indeed much of the history of Czechoslovakian film is deeply intertwined with politics and the socialist agenda. *Closely Watched Trains* is one of the best known Czechoslovakian films; it won an Academy Award for Best Foreign Film in 1966. Directed by Jiri Menzel, it is the story of a young man working in a small town railroad station and his attempts to get sexually initiated. Two great films by Jan Nemac are *Diamonds of the Night* (1964), the story of two boys who escape from a Nazi transport train, and *A Report on the Party and the Guests* (1966), a political allegory in which a reluctant guest at a wedding party refuses to participate in the festivities.

Seventh Day, Eighth Night (1969), directed by Evald Schorm, is a black political farce about a village thrown into panic at the disappearance of the stationmaster. Two bored girls in search of decadence is the premise of Vera Chytilova's *Daisies*; the film, which attacks the conformity in a materialistic society, was banned for a time in Czechoslovakia. Jiri Menzel's *Capricious Summer* (1968) follows the sexual tension created in a sleepy town by the beautiful assistant of a wandering tightrope walker. Menzel also directed *My Sweet Little Village* (1985), the story of a small village and a mentally retarded worker who is forced to move to Prague.

In the U.S., Milos Forman is probably the best known Czech director. His film *Loves of a Blonde* is a funny, touching film about a young girl in a small Czech village. Another Forman masterpiece is his 1968 film, *Fireman's Ball*. The plot of this comedy revolves around the annual firemen's ball, where everything goes wrong. (Forty thousand firefighters quit their jobs in protest when this film was released!) Other good Czechoslovakian films include Jan Kadar's *Shop on Main Street* (1965), the story of a well-meaning carpenter who tries to shield an elderly Jewish woman during the Nazi invasion; and

Vojtech Jasny's *All My Good Countrymen* (1968), which is about seven friends during the rise of communism following World War II. Milan Kundera's novel *The Unbearable Lightness of Being* was adapted to film by Philip Kaufman.

DENMARK

Small is beautiful, say the Danes. Denmark, a constitutional monarchy, is the smallest and most densely populated of the Scandinavian countries. Although there have been periods—such as the Viking era and the 17th and 18th centuries—when Denmark was a major European power, the smallness of the country and its virtual lack of natural resources generally has been a steady guarantee against dreams of grandeur. Hitler walked over Denmark in 1944 and called it his "little canary." But Danish resistance to this insult, which included heroic efforts to save virtually all the Danish Jews headed for his extermination camps, expressed a Danish spirit and spunk that remains gigantic to this day.

Denmark serves as a geographic, cultural, and commercial bridge between the Continent and the rest of Scandinavia. Composed of the Jutland peninsula and 500 islands, Denmark is neatly surrounded by the sea and has a temperate, windy, rainy climate. There are no mountains or rivers but instead a changing scenery of fields, hills, forests, lakes, and small bucolic streams. Good beaches can be found almost everywhere on the coastline, which is about 450 miles long. Across its span of islands and inlets, sounds and seascapes, this tiny country sustains the illusion of space and quietude. It has a culture keenly devoted to design and beauty—urban blight is unknown, and few billboards mar the countryside. The red-roofed houses and carefully tended farms shelter one of the most courteous and sophisticated peoples in Europe.

Denmark became a full-fledged member of the North Atlantic Treaty Organization in 1949, and national consensus opened its borders to the European Economic Community in 1972. But with a current national deficit in the billions due to high unemployment and ever-higher taxes to pay for one of the most humane and generous social welfare systems in the world, there are good, objective reasons why the Danes should be pessimistic about their long-term economic future. Yet, as so often in the past, pragmatism, solidarity, and optimism prevail. With built-in cultural defenses and perspectives, Danes remain cheerful and relaxed—much more like Victor Borge than Hamlet!

Denmark is delicious pastries, great coffee, world-class design in home furnishings and urban architecture, people on bicycles, old manor houses, Tivoli (the original and, some say, still the best amusement park in the world), Legoland, Carlsberg and Tuborg beer, and multilayered sandwiches that are an aesthetic and gustatory delight. But it is much more, both for the gregarious and charming Danes who live there, and for visitors fortunate enough to become short-term guests. Indeed, surveys often rank Denmark first in the world for "quality of life."

For most travelers, Copenhagen is the gateway to Scandinavia. The airlines use it as a base from which flights go on to Stockholm, Oslo, and Helsinki. By car or train, you have to pass through the city unless you embark on a series of long ferry journies. Fortunately, the Danes honor this responsibility with gusto. You will always be made to feel welcome in this lovely city. Nearly every Dane speaks English readily and capably. Copenhagen resembles Paris with its cellar galleries and minuscule shops, its winding streets and pavements, its faded but durable charm. Twenty years ago, Copenhagen seemed exciting and risqué; today, most of the world's capitals have accelerated beyond it. But its appeal is unmistakable.

Not to visit the pastoral beauties of the rest of Denmark, however, is to miss much. Danes who live elsewhere describe it as "the real Denmark." Driving or taking the train to these places is easy and convenient. Modern ferries, bridges, and good roads connect all corners of the country. The island of Funen, for example, contains some of the lushest and most breathtaking countryside in the entire Nordic region. Verdant farmland also fills Jutland, the huge peninsula jutting north from Germany, where you will also find a profusion of sandy bathing beaches and dunes in recreational areas on each coast. Although the land is almost totally flat, most of the landscape is enhanced by gently undulating fields, bright in summer with the charlock, or wild mustard, unique to this part of the world. It is rare to find someone who has spent time in Denmark not recommending it enthusiastically to others.

—William W. Hoffa, Amherst, Massachusetts

Official Name: Kingdom of Denmark. **Size:** 16,633 square miles (about half the size of Maine). **Population:** 5,134,000. **Population density:** 308 inhabitants per square mile. **Capital and largest city:** Copenhagen (pop. 619,000). **Language:** Danish. **Religion:** Lutheran. **Per capita income:** US$15,200. **Currency:** Krone. **Literacy rate:** 99%. **Average daily high/low:** Copenhagen: January, 36°F/29°F; July, 75°F/55°F. **Average number of days with precipitation:** Copenhagen: June, 13; December, 17.

TRAVEL

U.S. citizens must have a passport to visit Denmark. However, a visa is not required for stays of up to 90 days (this period begins when you enter the Scandinavian region: Denmark, Finland, Iceland, Norway, and Sweden). For specific visa requirements, check with the **Royal Danish Embassy**, 3200 Whitehaven Street NW, Washington, DC 20008; (202) 234-4300.

Getting Around

Travelers flying Scandinavian Airlines (SAS) round-trip to the countries of Norway, Denmark, or Sweden are eligible for SAS's **Visit Scandinavia Fare**. The special plan allows the purchase of up to six discounted flight coupons for travel within the three countries. The coupons, which cost from $80 for one flight to $420 for six, must be purchased in the U.S. before departure and must be used within three months of arrival in Scandinavia. It can be used on any of the three Scandinavian airlines: Danair, Linjeflyg, and SAS (excluding flights to the Faroe Islands and Greenland). For more information, call SAS at (800) 221-2350.

Eurailpasses of all types are valid in Denmark. Eurailpass holders can take advantage of free service on most state-run ferry lines (including the line from

Helsingör to Helsingborg, Sweden). Those planning to travel extensively in Scandinavia should consider the following options:

- **The ScanRail Pass** is valid for travel on the state railway systems of Denmark, Finland, Norway, and Sweden on a certain number of days within a fixed period of time. For example, one may travel on any 14 days within one month for $475 first-class and $369 second-class. ScanRail also allows free passage on a number of ferry lines. For information and reservations, contact Rail Europe (see page 62) or Council Travel (see pages xiii–xvi).
- **The Nordturist Ticket** allows for 21 days of free travel on the state railway systems of the above-mentioned countries, including certain ferries. It's also good for a 50-percent discount on the Hirtshals-Hjörring private railway as well as other ferry lines and bus routes. This pass can only be bought in Scandinavia, and is a better buy than the ScanRail Pass. The cost for youths ages 12 to 25 traveling second-class is approximately US$250.

Bicyclists love Denmark for its flat terrain and bike paths. **Bicycles** can be rented at major train stations and tourist offices for under DK50 per day (US$7). Bikes can also be checked on trains as checked baggage for a small fee. For information on bicycle rental, pick up DSB's brochure *Take the Train—Rent a Bike*. Serious cyclists should contact the **Dansk Cyklist Forbund (Danish Cyclist Federation)** at Romersgade 7, 1362 Copenhagen K.

In Copenhagen, check out **USE IT** at Radhusstraede 13, DK-1466, Copenhagen K. A youth-oriented information service, USE IT distributes an excellent newspaper called *Playtime*, as well as a number of free brochures, provides a mail drop and free luggage storage for travelers, and puts hitchhikers in touch with people driving their way. The bulletin boards at USE IT are full of information and when the office is closed, there's a notice board outside.

Eating and Sleeping

There are over 100 **youth hostels** in Denmark. For more information, contact Hostelling International/American Youth Hostels (see page 54) or the national youth hostel organization, **Landsforeningen Danmarks Vandrerhjem**, Vesterbrogade 39, DK-1620 Copenhagen V; (45) 31-313612; fax (45) 31-313626. In addition, several Danish universities offer affordable **dormitory lodgings** to travelers. For more information, contact **Kilroy travels Denmark** (see "Especially for Students and Young People," below) or consult Campus Travel Service's *US and Worldwide Travel Accommodations Guide* (see page 54).

Especially for Students and Young People

Denmark's student travel agency and the organization that issues the International Student Identity Card is **Kilroy travels Denmark**, Skindergade 28, DK-1159 Copenhagen K. Kilroy provides a number of useful services for the student traveler, including bookings and information on transportation and accommodations. Branch offices are located in Aarhus, and Odense.

For Further Information

A number of publications geared to the student or budget traveler can be obtained from the **Danish Tourist Board**, 655 Third Avenue, New York, NY 10017; (212) 949-2333.

One of the best general guidebooks to Denmark and the entire Scandinavian region is Lonely Planet's *Scandinavian and Baltic Europe on a Shoestring*

($17.95). Also good is *The Real Guide: Scandinavia* ($14.95). An excellent book to read in preparation for your trip is *Insight Guide: Denmark* ($19.95). For more information on Lonely Planet, *Real Guides*, and *Insight Guides*, see pages 56–57.

WORK

At present, work permits for foreign guest workers are not being granted, with the exception of those foreigners possessing special training or skills not readily available in Denmark. In such cases, the employer applies for the work permit. Contact the Royal Danish Embassy (see "Travel," above) for further information. The **American-Scandinavian Foundation** (see "Study," below) can also assist Americans ages 21 to 30 with obtaining the requisite permit.

Internships/Traineeships

A program offered by a member of the Council on International Educational Exchange is listed below.

Association for International Practical Training. *IAESTE Trainee Program.* On-the-job training for undergraduate and graduate students in technical fields such as engineering, computer science, agriculture, architecture, mathematics, and the natural and physical sciences. See page 19 for more information.

Voluntary Service

CIEE places young people in Danish voluntary-service **workcamps** organized by Mellemfolkeligt Samvirke in Copenhagen. These workcamps, which bring together small groups of international volunteers, involve projects such as protecting the environment or collecting and shipping clothing and tools to the Third World. Volunteers must be 18 or over. The applications of U.S. residents are processed by CIEE. Contact the International Voluntary Service department at the CIEE's New York office for details.

For persons interested in longer-term voluntary service work, the "Year Abroad Program" sponsored by the **International Christian Youth Exchange** offers persons ages 18 to 30 opportunities in the fields of health care, education, the environment, construction, and more. See page 25 for more information.

STUDY

There are several sources of information on study programs for foreigners in Denmark. For a listing of English-language programs offered in Denmark during the academic year and summer, a good resource is *Study in Scandinavia*, published by the Exchange Division of the **American-Scandinavian Foundation**, 725 Park Avenue, New York, NY 10021; (212) 879-9779; fax (212) 249-3444. In addition, a useful pamphlet titled *Studying in Denmark*, as well as a fact sheet on higher education in Denmark published by the Ministry of Education, can be obtained from the Royal Danish Embassy (see "Travel," above) or from any Danish consulate.

The **Danish Cultural Institute** (Kultorvet 2, DK-1175 Copenhagen K) is a nonprofit institution receiving an annual grant from the Danish Ministry of

Culture. Its aim is to disseminate information about Denmark and improve cultural relations and international understanding. Among its activities are short-term courses and study tours on socio-cultural subjects, such as education for children and adults, libraries, social care, architecture, and design. For details, contact the Institute.

Academic programs sponsored by CIEE-member institutions are described below. Unless otherwise noted, consult Appendix I for the addresses of the colleges and universities listed in this section.

Semester and Academic Year

Communications

University of Wisconsin at Green Bay. Aalborg. Fall and spring semester. Study at the University of Aalborg. Media, culture and communications, international business economics, and graduate-sociological analysis. First-year college students to seniors. Apply by March 15 for fall; October 15 for spring.

General Studies

DIS, Denmark's International Study Program. Copenhagen. Semester and academic year. Affiliated with University of Copenhagen. Wide range of humanities and social sciences, in addition to marine science, ecology, architecture, graphic arts, international business, and landscape architecture. Juniors and seniors with 3.0 GPA. Apply through the more than 80 cooperating U.S. colleges and universities by contacting the study abroad office at your school or by calling (800) 247-3477 for catalog.

Scandinavian Seminar. *College Year in Denmark.* Individual placement in Danish folk colleges throughout Denmark. Danish language and liberal arts. Sophomores to graduate students and adults. Apply by April 15.

University of Wisconsin at Madison. *Semester or Academic Year at the University of Copenhagen.* Semester and academic year. Intensive Danish language, liberal arts, European medieval studies, and mass communications. Juniors to graduate students in good academic standing. Open to students at colleges and universities in Wisconsin and Wisconsin residents studying out of state. Apply by second Friday in February for fall, spring, and academic year.

International Relations

Scandinavian Seminar. *Semester Program on Nordic and Global Issues.* Helsingor and/or other locations. Fall and spring semester. International humanitarian organizations, global ecology, international conflict resolution, and sustainable economic development. Excursions. Sophomores to graduate students and adults. Apply by April 15 for fall; October 15 for spring.

Natural Sciences

DIS, Denmark's International Study Program. *Marine Environmental Studies.* Copenhagen. Fall semester. Affiliated with University of Copenhagen. Conservation, Danish language, ecology/environmental studies, marine biology, Russian language. Juniors and seniors with 3.0 GPA and previous coursework in biology. Apply through the more than 80 cooperating U.S.

colleges and universities by contacting the study-abroad office at your school or by calling (800) 247-3477 for catalog.

Summer and Short-Term

Art and Architecture

DIS, Denmark's International Study Program. *Architecture and Design Summer Semester*. Affiliated with University of Copenhagen. Architecture, graphic arts, industrial design, interior design, landscape architecture. Juniors and seniors with 3.0 GPA. Apply through one of the more than 80 cooperating U.S. colleges and universities by contacting the study-abroad office at your school or calling (800) 247-3477 for a catalog.

General Studies

DIS, Denmark's International Study Program. *Europe in Transition*. Copenhagen. Seven-week summer program. Affiliated with University of Copenhagen. Business, Danish language, economics, European Economic Community, international relations, military and political science, Scandinavian studies, and security issues. Juniors and seniors with 3.0 GPA. Apply through one of the more than 80 cooperating U.S. colleges and universities by contacting the study-abroad office at your school or calling (800) 247-3477 for a catalog.

Performing Arts

University of Pennsylvania. *Penn-in-Holstebro*. Summer. Study of methods of director Eugenio Barba. Apply by March 1.

EXPLORING DANISH CULTURE

Readings

Johannes Jensen, an outstanding author of the early 20th century, won the Nobel Prize for literature in 1944 for *The Long Journey* (1908–22). In this book, Jensen applied his interest in Darwinism, anthropology, and myth to the development of the human race from prehistoric times to the discovery of America. The best work of Martin Andersen Nexö, another well-respected Danish writer, is found in his poignant novels about the poverty and hunger he experienced while growing up as a shepherd boy and cobbler's apprentice. *Pelle the Conquerer* (1906–10), also a 1987 film, is about an immigrant farm worker; *Ditte* (1917–21), also a 1946 movie, tells the story of a working-class girl; and *Under the Open Sky: My Early Years* (1932–39) is a collection of Nexö's memoirs.

Ever since Klaus Rifbjerg published *Chronic Innocence* in 1958, he has arguably been the dominant Danish novelist. Jacob Paludan (*Birds Around the Light*) and Hans Kirk (*The Fisherman*) are other Danish writers worth looking up. Women authors in Denmark have enjoyed increased recognition since the 1970s; some pursue a feminist agenda, others seek to portray life as experienced by Danish women. In *Early Spring* (1985), Tove Ditlevsen depicts her life growing up in the working-class Vesterbro district of Copenhagen during the

1930s. *No Man's Land* (1988), edited by Annegret Heitmann, is a recent anthology of the country's modern women writers with a powerful Danish perspective.

Films

Gabriel Axel's *Babette's Feast* was named best foreign-language film of 1987 by the Academy of Motion Pictures Arts and Sciences. This poignant film is about an exiled French woman in a bleak Norwegian village who, when she wins the lottery, spends all the money to prepare an enormous Gallic feast for the entire town. Axel's latest film, *Christian* (1990), is about a young Danish criminal who finds love and happiness among warmhearted Arabs in Northern Africa. Another excellent Danish film is *Pelle the Conquerer* (1987), based on the novel by Martin Andersen Nexö. This epic movie, beautifully photographed and acted, is the story of a Swedish farm worker who travels to Denmark in search of a new wife for his son. This film, directed by Bille August, also won an Academy Award for best foreign-language film. *Best Intentions* (1992) is August's latest film.

Eddie Holm's Second Life (1985) is a black comedy from director Esben Hùilund Carlsen about a suicidal musician who is taken back through his life to discover what drove him to do it, while the intense dramatic tragedy *Katinka* (1988), written by Klaus Rifberg, is about a love affair between a farm foreman and the wife of the stationmaster. A smaller film, *Ladies on the Rocks* (1983), includes good performances from two women who take their cabaret act on the road.

ESTONIA

Gaining independence from the former Soviet Union in 1991 along with Latvia and Lithuania, Estonia is most often identified with the latter as one of the Baltic states. But this northerly nation has much more in common with its cousin across the gulf, Finland, with whose citizens Estonians are racially and linguistically related. Prior to World War I, thirsty Finns crossed the gulf to escape their country's dry laws. Today, Finns continue to pour in on the weekends, not to avoid dry laws but instead to beat the high cost of merry-making back home. For their part, the people of Estonia welcome their weekend guests, having had their TV antennas pointing north for years already.

Early Estonians shared a pagan religion similar to that of the Finns, but were forcibly Christianized by crusading Danes and Germans in the 12th century. By the 14th century the country was completely controlled by the Teutonic Knights, creating a social system in which a German nobility and merchant class reduced the native population to serfdom. Swedes swept in a century later and attempted to create an educational system, founding Tartu University in 1632. But they in turn were expelled by Peter the Great's armies in the Great Northern War of 1700–1721, firmly establishing Russian rule. Although Estonia enjoyed a few brief years of independence following World War I, it soon fell to the Soviet Union, the last of a centuries-long string of foreign rulers.

Slightly larger than Denmark, Estonia is mostly flat and heavily forested, with numerous lakes, extensive seashore, and hundreds of coastal islands. Lake Peipus, one of Europe's largest, almost entirely separates Estonia from Russia, providing a natural buffer that eastern invaders had to skirt. This geographical feature may be one reason why Estonians have historically looked to the West, in spite of their being equally anti-German. As a result of subjugation to various competing powers, Estonian towns and cities display a remarkable mix of styles, but by and large the German influence seems heaviest. Estonia's capital, Tallinn, is a beautiful medieval city fortified by the Teutonic Knights. A popular vacation destination for Russians who couldn't escape the confines of the Soviet Union, Tallinn has long been Estonia's Old World jewel. Tartu, reputedly Estonia's oldest city, is most famous for its university, which became the greatest repository for Estonian folk culture at a time when it was under siege.

Estonia's Russification began with the czars but continued under Stalin. Russians were transferred here after World War II to staff the factories of a land whose native population had severely dwindled. Forced industrialization marred historic towns and poisoned the countryside, giving rise to the environmental movement that sparked a peaceful revolution. The high point of this insurgence came with 1988's Singing Revolution, in which thousands of political protesters spontaneously joined in a banned Estonian song. In 1990, Estonian nationalists won a majority in the Estonian Supreme Soviet and ruled the existing constitution invalid. Full independence came soon after the attempted coup against Mikhail Gorbachev. In an effort to exclude resident Russians from parliamentary decisions, new citizenship laws included the ability to speak, read, and write Estonian and a waiting period of several years. Today, the status of resident Russians who make up 25 percent of Estonia's one million population remains undetermined.

Independent Estonia's first government, headed by Prime Minister Edgar Savisaar, collapsed under criticism of slowness in economic reform. The current government of Tiit Vähi has moved faster, but like other former Soviet republics, Estonia continues to have its economic woes and product shortages. Nevertheless, visitors to this reborn nation will find amenities better here than in any other. Tasty dishes of smoked fish and delicious beer can be had in any number of new restaurants, bars, and cafés opening up throughout Estonia's quaint medieval towns. And though they may run out of whatever's on the menu, you're sure to discover some pleasant improvisation. After a short while in Estonia, you'll see why it's so popular with the Finns.

—Tracey Lyme, Waterville, Maine

Official name: Republic of Estonia. **Area:** 17,413 square miles. **Population:** 1,581,000. **Population density:** 91 inhabitants per square mile. **Capital and largest city:** Tallinn (pop. 502,000). **Language:** Estonian (official), Russian. **Religion:** predominantly Evangelical Lutheran. **Currency:** Ruble.

TRAVEL

U.S. citizens need a passport to enter Estonia. Six-week visas are issued free of charge upon arrival. As the Baltic republics comprise a common visa zone, Estonian visas allow the bearer to enter Latvia and Lithuania. For more information, contact the **Consulate General of Estonia**, 630 Fifth Avenue, Suite 2415, New York, NY 10111; (212) 247-7634.

Getting Around

Domestic **air** transport is provided by the newly created Estonian Air, which also serves the other Baltic republics. Foreign tourists are charged several times what local residents pay for a ticket. To be sure of a seat, make your booking at Estonian Air's central office at 10 Vabaduse in Tallinn.

Rail service, frequent but slow, connects all major towns to Tallinn. Buses and long-distance coaches are inexpensive and reliable, but often quite crowded. It's also possible to rent a **car** from one of several local agents.

Eating and Sleeping

There are several **youth hostels** in Estonia. For more information, contact Hostelling International/American Youth Hostels (see page 54) or the **Estonian Youth Hostels Association**, Tallinn EE0001, Liivalaia 2; (7) 142-445853; fax (7) 142-445853. It's also easy to find **families** renting out rooms in their homes.

For Further Information

Good and relatively up-to-date information on travel in Estonia can be found in Lonely Planet's *Scandinavian and Baltic Europe on a Shoestring* ($17.95). For more information on Lonely Planet Publications, see page 56.

WORK

Internships/Traineeships

A program offered by a member of the Council on International Educational Exchange is listed below.

Association for International Practical Training. *IAESTE Trainee Program.* On-the-job training for undergraduate and graduate students in technical fields such as engineering, computer science, agriculture, architecture, mathematics, and the natural and physical sciences. See page 19 for more information.

FINLAND

Finland is a country for nature lovers. The best way to travel, and to admire its natural beauty, is to take one of the luxurious but fairly inexpensive ferries from Stockholm to Turku. You will travel past the Aland islands (which have self-rule but a common foreign policy with Finland) and through several archipelagos. In summer, the population multiplies due to the large number of summer residents and visitors. In June and July, Finns actually sleep less on the average than they do during the dark winters. The stillness of a Finnish summer night in the countryside is a remarkable experience. The summers are lush and filled with flowers. The natural beauty of Finland is more subtle than, for example, the spectacular Norwegian fjords. The Finnish beauty lies in its archipelagos, the light of the summer nights, its wildflowers, and the winding country roads that provide access to the beauty of the land.

You will find that the Finns are very interested in sports. Try to watch the Sunday evening sports hour on television to get a sense of the variety of sports played throughout the country. Almost all Finns engage in physical activities. For example, in addition to walking as a regular exercise, most people bike or swim in the summer and skate or ski in the winter. Finland is an excellent country for biking, and thanks to the excellent public transportation system, it is easy to venture into the interior of the country—to lake country—or to coastal towns such as Porvoo and Tammisaari.

Whether you are in a city or in a small town, take some time to notice Finnish architecture. The Jugend style in Helsinki and Tampere is especially appealing and very Finnish. Industrial arts and music are important in Finland; summer music festivals are popular and offer a flavor of everyday Finnish life. At this time of the year the cities are virtually empty during the weekends because people have taken off to the countryside. Leisure time is highly valued; everyone has at least one month of vacation. Finland is quite a wealthy country that values the welfare of its citizens. Therefore you will find virtually no poverty in Finland. Children are also very important in this culture, and you will see them everywhere. Thanks to the concern about the country's youth and equal opportunities, college students do not have to pay tuition.

To the traveler, Finland may seem very homogeneous, but if you take a closer look you will find differences between Finns from, for example, the eastern and the southern parts of Finland. The country has two official languages, Finnish and Swedish. Particularly in the south and in Helsinki you may meet Swedish-speaking Finns; the Aland islands are exclusively Swedish-speaking.

Finns are usually thought of as being extremely serious and not very outgoing. To some extent this is true, and if you want to get to know Finns, you might have to take the initiative. Asking Finns to dance might be the easiest way to start.

—Gunilla Holm, Kalamazoo, Michigan

Official Name: Republic of Finland. **Size:** 130,119 square miles (about the size of Montana). **Population:** 4,991,000. **Population density:** 38 inhabitants per square mile. **Capital and largest city:** Helsinki (pop. 490,000). **Language:** Finnish, Swedish. **Religion:** Lutheran. **Per capita income:** US$15,500. **Currency:** Markka. **Literacy rate:** 99%. **Average daily temperature:** Helsinki: June, 58°F; December, 26°F. **Average number of days with precipitation:** Helsinki: June, 13; December, 20.

TRAVEL

U.S. citizens need a passport to visit Finland. However, a visa is not required for a stay up to 90 days (this period begins when entering the Scandinavian region: Denmark, Finland, Iceland, Norway, and Sweden). For more information, check with the **Embassy of Finland**, 3216 New Mexico Avenue NW, Washington, DC 20016; (202) 363-2430; fax (202) 363-8233.

GETTING AROUND

It takes just over one hour to fly from Helsinki to Rovaniemi, on the Arctic Circle. If you plan to cover a lot of territory by plane, check with Finnair about their **Holiday Ticket**, which allows 15 days of unlimited economy travel throughout Finland for $300. The **Youth Holiday Ticket**, for people under 25, costs $250.

Finnish **rail** fares are among the least expensive in western Europe. Discounts of 20 percent are offered to groups of three or more adults traveling together, and discounts of 25 to 50 percent to groups of ten or more.

Eurailpasses of all types are valid for travel in Finland. Another option is the **Finnrailpass**, which entitles the holder to unlimited travel on all passenger trains throughout the country. A second-class pass costs $118 for eight days, $183 for 15 days, and $230 for 22 days. First-class passes are also available for $176, $274, and $345, respectively. The Finnrailpass can be purchased at rail stations in Finland, or in the U.S. from Rail Europe (see page 62) and Council Travel (see pages xiii–xvi). Those planning to travel extensively in Scandinavia should investigate these other options:

- **The ScanRail Pass** is valid for travel on the state railway systems of Denmark, Finland, Norway, and Sweden for a certain number of days within a fixed period of time. For example, you can travel on any 14 days within one month for $475 first-class and $369 second-class. ScanRail also allows free passage on a number of ferry lines. For information and reservations, contact Rail Europe (see page 62) or Council Travel (see pages xiii–xvi).
- **The Nordturist Ticket** allows for 21 days of free travel on the state railway systems of the above-mentioned countries, including certain ferries. It's also good for a 50-percent discount on the Hirtshals-Hjorring private railway as well as other ferry lines and bus routes. This pass can only be bought in Scandinavia, and is a better buy than the ScanRail Pass. The cost for youths ages 12 to 25 traveling second-class is approximately US$250.

The train system is good, but buses go to more places. In Lapland, the **bus** is the main form of transportation. The **Bussilomalippu pass** lets you travel up to 1000 km within a two-week period for FIM300 (US$50). You can buy this ticket at any bus station in Finland. Most bus lines offer student discounts for long-distance trips.

Eating and Sleeping

Finland has about 160 **youth hostels**. For more information, contact Hostelling International/American Youth Hostels (see page 54) or Finland's national youth hostel association, **Suomen Retkeilymajajärjestö**, Yrjönkatu 38 B 15, 00100 Helsinki; (358) 90-6940377; fax (358) 90-6931349.

Camping season starts in late May or early June. More than 200 campsites are registered with the Finnish Travel Association, which issues $15 vouchers, each good for an overnight stay. Contact the Camping Department, Mikonkatu 25, PB 776, 00100 Helsinki; (358) 90-170868; fax (358) 90-654358.

In the summer, many university dorms become **summer hotels**. However, they're not always a bargain. For more information on these and other possibilities, ask for a budget accommodation brochure from the Finnish Tourist Board (see "For Further Information," below). For **university housing**, also check Campus Travel Service's *US and Worldwide Travel Accommodations Guide* (see page 54).

Especially for Students and Young People

Finland's student/youth travel bureau and issuer of the International Student Identity Card is **Kilroy travels Finland,** Mannerheimintie 5C, 00100 Helsinki;

(358) 0-624101; fax (358) 0-651528. Kilroy also has branch offices in Oulu, Tampere, and Turku, all of which can provide travel information, and offers a variety of tours in Finland and abroad.

For Further Information

A number of publications geared to the student or budget traveler can be obtained from the **Finnish Tourist Board**, 655 Third Avenue, New York, NY 10017; (212) 949-2333. These include publications on camping, hiking, and youth hostels as well as maps and a calendar of events.

The best guide to Finland is Lonely Planet's *Finland: A Travel Survival Kit* ($15.95). Good guidebooks to the entire Scandinavian region include Lonely Planet's *Scandinavian and Baltic Europe on a Shoestring* ($17.95) and *The Real Guide: Scandinavia* ($14.95). An excellent book to read in preparation for your trip is *Insight Guide: Finland* ($19.95). For more information on Lonely Planet, *Real Guides*, and *Insight Guides*, see pages 56–57.

WORK

According to embassy personnel, it is very difficult for U.S. citizens to work in Finland. An offer of employment is required before you apply for a work permit. Contact the Embassy of Finland (see "Travel," above) for details. The **American-Scandinavian Foundation** (see "Study," below) can also assist Americans ages 21 to 30 with obtaining the requisite permit.

Anyone interested in living as an **au pair** in a Finnish family should contact the **Centre for International Mobility (CIMO)**, International Trainee Exchanges Unit, PO Box 343, 00531 Helsinki. The Centre provides information on au pair placements in Finland. In addition, the Centre's Finnish Family Program, similar to an au pair program, provides young people ages 17 to 23 with the opportunity to live with a Finnish family. Interested persons must be native speakers of English, French, or German.

Internships/Traineeships

Programs sponsored by members of the Council on International Educational Exchange are listed below.

Association for International Practical Training. *IAESTE Trainee Program* On-the-job training for undergraduate and graduate students in technical fields such as engineering, computer science, agriculture, architecture, mathematics, and the natural and physical sciences. See page 19 for more information.

Hospitality/Tourism Exchanges Program. On-the-job training for young people beginning a career in the hotel and food-service industries. Participants must have graduated or be currently enrolled in a university or vocational school and possess at least six months of training or experience in the chosen field. Training usually runs 6 to 18 months. In addition, the **American-Scandinavian Foundation** (see "Study," below) sponsors a program that provides summer training assignments for full-time students majoring in engineering, computer science, horticulture, agriculture, forestry, and chemistry, among others. The deadline for application is December 15.

The **Centre for International Mobility** (see above) also sponsors internship opportunities for students ages 18 to 30, with at least two years of study in their field. Placements are available from May to October in tourism and restaurant service, forestry, agriculture, horticulture, social services, language teaching, and commerce. In addition, graduates under 30 years of age may apply for longer-term placements (up to 18 months throughout the year) in their field of study. Some relevant work experience is required. The deadline for summer placements is March 31; other placements require applications be received at least three months prior to requested starting date of program.

AIESEC-US sponsors a reciprocal internship program for students in economics, business, finance, marketing, accounting, and computer science. See page 19 for more information.

Voluntary Service

One opportunity for voluntary service in Finland is the Year Abroad Program of the **International Christian Youth Exchange**. It offers persons ages 18 to 30 voluntary service opportunities in health, education, environment, construction, and more. See page 25 for more information.

STUDY

To acquaint yourself with Finland's educational system, read *An Introduction to Higher Education in Finland*, distributed by the cultural information officer at the Finnish Embassy (see "Travel," above). This guide also lists a number of valuable addresses, including those of foreign student advisers at major Finnish universities.

For a listing of English-language programs offered in Finland during the academic year and summer, a good resource is *Study in Scandanavia*, by the Exchange Division of the **American-Scandinavian Foundation**, 725 Park Avenue, New York, NY 10021; (212) 879-9779; fax (212) 249 3444. Available from the **Consulate General of Finland** are publications on adult education options in Finland and opportunities for Finnish-language study. They can be reached at 380 Madison Avenue, New York, NY 10017; (212) 573-6007.

Academic programs offered by CIEE-member institutions are described below. Unless otherwise noted, consult Appendix I for the addresses of the colleges and universities listed in this section.

Semester and Academic Year

General Studies

International Student Exchange Program (ISEP). Semester and academic year. Direct reciprocal exchanges between U.S. universities and institutions in Helsinki, Espoo, Joensuu, Jyvädkylä, Turku, Oulu, and Tampere. Full curriculum options. Rolling admissions. Open only to students at ISEP-member institutions. Contact ISEP for list of members.

Scandinavian Seminar. *College Year in Finland*. Academic year. Individual placement in Finnish folk colleges throughout Finland. Finnish language and liberal arts. Sophomores to graduate students and adults. Apply by April 15.

International Relations

Scandinavian Seminar. *Semester Program on Nordic and Global Issues*. Otava and/or other locations. Fall and spring semesters. Global environment, international conflict resolution, sustainable economic development, and international humanitarian organizations, from Nordic perspective. Sophomores to graduate students and adults. Apply by April 15 for fall; October 15 for spring.

FRANCE

For its relatively small size, France—affectionately referred to in the French press as *L'Hexagone*—is surprisingly diverse. Beautiful beaches line its Mediterranean coast; the French Alps have some of the best skiing in the world; the fertile soil of Bordeaux produces world-class wines; and the cool, rainy climate and dramatic rocky coasts of Brittany seem perfectly suited to its people's strong Celtic roots. This diversity in geography and climate are also reflected in the differing regional cultures.

In fact, as the 12-member European Community takes shape as a unified economic superstate, France is experiencing a burst of pride in regional culture. After more than 200 years of suppressing regional languages, the French government is setting up bilingual schools, notably in Provence and Brittany, to teach children the indigenous languages. Many provinces in France still exhibit the sway of their cultural ancestry. In Languedoc-Rousillon, there is a heavy Spanish influence that is reflected in the art, the architecture (such as the Moorish Palais des Rois de Majorque), and in the character of the inhabitants. A minority still speak Catalan and a large Catalonian literary center preserves this heritage in Perpignan.

In the south of France, or the "Midi," there is still abundant evidence that this country was once a Roman colony. Coliseums constructed by the Romans still stand in Nîmes and Arles, and are used today for bullfights, concerts, and other events; in Lyons there are the remains of a Roman theater where the martyrdom of a band of Christians marked the beginning of the Roman power in this region. It was also in this area that painters van Gogh and Cézanne rediscovered light in paintings and "impressionism" was born.

Paris nonetheless is still the center of French culture, although many other French cities play host to festivals and celebrations that can compete with those of the "city of light." For a large city, Paris is easy to get around. Taking the time to walk through its winding streets can often yield some of the city's lesser-known treasures. Any stroll through Paris seems to lead to a café, an essential part of French life, although the institution is threatened as people increasingly spend their evenings in front of the television. Parisian cafés such as the Café de la Paix, Les Deux Magots (a former Hemingway haunt), and the Café Le Flore, where for many years Jean-Paul Sartre and Simone de Beauvoir held court, are an essential part of the essence and image of Paris.

In the next few years, it will be interesting to see what changes come about in France as socialist President François Mitterand has to "cohabit" with the conservative Prime Minister Edouard Balladur. The new conservative government is now in charge of almost everything; and although he is a consummate politician, Mitterand's powers have effectively been reduced to overseeing foreign policy.

"France for the French" is the slogan of a right-wing movement in France called the National Front. They are protesting the influx of foreigners, mostly northern African people, coming into France and taking away jobs from native Gallic peoples. Although this movement has generated a lot of publicity from the press, it has gained comparatively few seats in recently held elections. This is in part due to the fact that the conservative party has adopted some of the movement's less extreme platforms, including stricter immigration laws.

France, although extremely proud of its technological developments, is still very much an agricultural nation; in fact, it is the largest agricultural nation in Europe. The French have a deep-rooted affection for their farmers, who have become a popular embodiment of the national image.

Visitors to France will find that they are amply rewarded by all it has to offer: the diversity and richness of its land and people, its 2,000 years of history and culture, its great cuisine and wine. It's no wonder France has been described as the country that defined "civilization."

—Jon D. Howard, New York, New York

Official name: French Republic. **Size:** 220,668 square miles (about the size of Texas). **Population:** 56,595,000. **Population density:** 256 inhabitants per square mile. **Capital and largest city:** Paris (pop. 2,152,000). **Language:** French. **Religion:** Roman Catholic. **Per capita income:** US$15,500. **Currency:** Franc. **Literacy rate:** 99%. **Average daily temperature:** Marseille: June, 69°F; December, 44°F. Paris: June, 63°F; December, 39°F. **Average number of days with precipitation:** Marseille: June, 4; December, 10. Paris: June, 12; December, 16.

TRAVEL

Americans going to France will need a passport, but a visa is not required for stays of up to three months. Students planning a stay of more than three months should see the special information under the "Study" heading later in this chapter. More information on French visa requirements is available from the visa section of the **French Consulate General**, 934 Fifth Avenue, New York, NY 10021; (212) 606-3688; fax (212) 606-3670. General information is available from **French Cultural Services**, 972 Fifth Avenue, New York, NY 10021; (212) 606-3680.

Getting Around

In addition to the Eurailpass, there are several other discount packages for **rail** travel throughout France:

- The **France Railpass** allows travel on any three days in one month. It costs $175 for first-class and $125 for second-class.
- The **France Rail 'n' Fly** package combines three days of rail travel with one day on Air Inter, France's domestic airline, to be used within one month. First-class travel for an adult costs $265; second class is $215.
- If you want to combine automobile excursions with train travel, the **France Rail 'n' Drive** package is a pretty good deal (compared with the regular France Railpass). It allows three days of train travel and three days of Avis car rental, for a total of six travel days within one month. For the car, you get your choice of economy, small, medium, and small automatic. With an

economy car, and traveling with a friend, the plan will cost each of you $189 for first class and $149 for second.

- Yet another option is the **France Fly, Rail 'n' Drive Pass**, which adds a day of air travel to the Rail 'n' Drive package above. Individual costs for two people with economy car are $275 for first class and $235 for second class.

All the above rail passes allow purchase of up to six additional rail days for $40 (first class) or $29 (second class). The Rail 'n' Fly and Fly, Rail 'n' Drive packages allow purchase of one extra flight day for $85. In addition, each package includes free rail transfer from Orly or Roissy–Charles de Gaulle airports to Paris and back, reduced rates on Seine River cruises, and a 50-percent discount on a private scenic railway from Nice to Digne.

For those traveling extensively in both France and the U.K., the **BritFrance Railpass** lets you take advantage of these two countries' rail networks in their entirety. The second-class youth pass (for those under 26) allows 5 days of travel over a 15-day period for $229, or 10 days of travel within one month for $349, and includes one round-trip Channel crossing via hovercraft. The BritFrance Railpass, as well as all the above-mentioned rail passes, can be purchased from Rail Europe (see page 62) or Council Travel (see pages xiii–xvi).

You can get a good deal on domestic **flights** with Air Inter's **France Pass**, which allows unlimited travel among 29 cities for any seven days within one month for $279. A smaller domestic airline, Air Littoral, offers the **See France Pass**, which offers seven consecutive days of air travel for $249 or ten consecutive days for $299. The See France Pass can be ordered by mail from Air Promotion Systems, 5777 West Century Boulevard, Suite 875, Los Angeles, CA 90045; (800) 677-4277.

Eating and Sleeping

France has more than 200 **youth hostels**. For more information, contact Hostelling International/American Youth Hostels (see page 54) or France's national youth hostel association, **Federation Unie des Auberges de Jeunesse**, 27 rue Pajol, 75018 Paris; (33) 1-46070001; fax (33) 1-46079310. In addition, several French universities offer affordable **dormitory lodgings** to travelers. For more information, contact one of France's student travel organizations (see "Especially for Students and Young People," below) or consult Campus Travel Service's *US and Worldwide Travel Accommodations Guide* (see page 54).

Especially for Students and Young People

CIEE/Council Travel operates travel offices in Paris, Lyon, Nice, Aix-en-Provence, and Montpellier:

- 22, rue des Pyramides 75001 Paris
- 16, rue de Vaugirard, 75006 Paris
- 36, quai Gailleton, 69002 Lyon
- 37bis, rue d'Angleterre, 06000 Nice
- 12, rue Victor Leydet, 13100 Aix-en-Provence
- 20, rue de l'Universite, 34000 Montpellier

These offices specialize in providing information and making arrangements for students and other budget travelers. They issue the International Student Identity Card, book discount train and plane tickets for students, and more.

Another organization that issues the International Student Identity Card is **OTU**, 6/8 rue Jean Calvin, 75005 Paris. OTU has 41 offices located throughout France. The *Paris Discount List*, with over 200 shops and restaurants, is available at the OTU office in Paris.

Useful youth services are also provided by *Accueil des Jeunes en France*, 119 rue St-Martin, 75004 Paris. This youth welcome service offers low-cost guaranteed accommodation in or near Paris (approximately $20 to $35 per person per night, bed and breakfast) in youth centers, student residences, and tourist hotels. It also provides discount air, bus, and train tickets. Accueil des Jeunes en France has four travel offices in Paris, including one at the Gare du Nord.

Students are a privileged class in France and are entitled to many discounts in museums, theaters, cinemas, and restaurants. International Student Identity Cardholders under 27 and youth under 25 may obtain discounts of up to 50 percent on flights within France on the domestic airline Air Inter. Your International Student Identity Card also entitles you to discounts on international bus lines, on domestic and international trains (up to 40 percent on off-peak travel), and on boats to Great Britain, Ireland, and Greece.

For Further Information

General travel information is available from the **French Government Tourist Office**, 628 Fifth Avenue, New York, NY 10020; (212) 757-1125. A good source of information for English speakers in France is the **American Library in Paris**, 10 rue du General Camou, Paris 75007; (33) 1-45514682. Its bulletin board advertises language courses and roommates, among other things. If you're in trouble, call the new **English-language help line** at 1-47238080.

For a comprehensive listing of low-cost accommodations, plus suggestions on what to do and see throughout France, get a copy of *Let's Go: France*. It's available for $16.95 in most bookstores and at Council Travel offices. *The Real Guide: France* ($12.95) is substantially larger and more detailed. In the same series, *The Real Guide: Paris* ($9.95) takes you through France's capital city neighborhood by neighborhood. An excellent book to read in preparation for your trip is *Insight Guide: France* ($19.95). For more information on *Let's Go, Real Guide*s, and *Insight Guide*s, see pages 56–57.

Going beyond the travel guide, *Paris Inside Out* ($12.95) is a good introduction for people seeking to settle in Paris for a longer term, whether to work, study, or just hang out. Its 30 chapters cover everything from finding an apartment to understanding social attitudes. For those seeking contact with Paris's large English-speaking community, *Paris-Anglophone* ($12.95) is a unique directory of English-language professional organizations and cultural activities. Both publications are available from Frank Books, 45 Newbury Street, Suite 305, Boston, MA 02116; (617) 536-0060; fax (617) 536-0068.

WORK

Getting a Job

In recent years a variety of new, quite stringent rules have gone into effect regarding working in France. In general, nonstudents will find it virtually impossible to find a job in France. With unemployment currently at unacceptably high levels, the government is anxious to discourage immigration.

Students seeking employment must follow some very specific regulations.

The best source of information on the subject is the French Cultural Services division of the French Consulate (see "Travel," above), which puts out a helpful information sheet, *Employment in France for Students*. Foreign students who come to France during the summer must do so under the aegis of an organization approved by the government.

CIEE can provide you with work authorization, which allows you to seek employment in France for up to three months anytime during the year. To qualify, you must be at least 18 years of age, a full-time college or university student with two years of college-level French, and be a U.S. citizen or permanent resident. The cost of the program is $160. Past participants have taught English in Paris, worked in the vineyards of Bordeaux, and served as lifeguards on the Côte d'Azur. Participants receive an orientation upon arrival, information on living and working in France, and assistance with seeking employment and accommodations. For details and an application form, contact CIEE's Work Exchanges Department, 205 East 42nd Street, New York, NY 10017.

Persons seeking a short-term job in France might be interested in *Emplois d'Été en France*, a do-it-yourself guide to job-hunting that is updated annually. Written in French, it can be ordered from CIEE for $16.95 plus $1.50 postage. An essential reference for the serious job hunter is *Working in France: The Ultimate Guide to Job Hunting and Career Success à la Française*, by Carol Pineau and Maureen Kelly. This guide provides you with the nuts and bolts of how to start a career in France; included are tips on resumé-writing, interviewing, and the French work culture, as well as tax and legal issues. Published by Frank Books, *Working in France* is also available from CIEE for $12.95 plus $1.50 for shipping.

Au Pair

Three organizations in France have earned solid reputations for au pair placements. These are listed in *Au Pair Work in France*, compiled by the French Cultural Services division of the French Consulate (see "Travel," above). You can write to the organizations directly for information on their particular programs: *L'Accueil Familial des Jeunes Etrangers*, 23 rue du Cherche-Midi, 75006 Paris; *Relations Internationales*, 20 rue de l'Exposition, 75007 Paris; and *Séjours Internationaux Linguistiques et Culturels*, 32 Rempart de l'Est, 16002 Angouleme, Cedex.

Farm Work

It is possible to find agricultural work such as picking grapes at harvest time without having to prearrange it. Your best bet is to approach farmers directly and offer your assistance. For a list of agricultural jobs available you also can write to **Nature et Progress**, c/o Michel Champy, Chez Roger Fransoret, Alan court Mancy, 51200 Epernay, France. **Maison des Jeunes et de la Culture** (25 rue Marat, Boite Postale 26, 11200 Lezignan, Corbieres) sets up work-camps during the grape harvest in the Languedoc section of France. The harvest lasts from 15 to 20 days beginning sometime in late September. Students over 16 years of age are eligible. All inquiries must be accompanied by an international postal reply coupon.

Teaching

The **French Government Teaching Assistantships in English** offers candidates the opportunity to teach English conversation in French secondary schools for an academic year. Most assignments are to provincial centers. "Strong preference in the competition is given to unmarried candidates under 30 years of age who plan careers in the teaching of French.'' Contact the **Institute of International Education**, U.S. Student Program Division, 809 United Nations Plaza, New York, NY 10017. Ask for their booklet, *Fulbright Grants and Other Grants for Graduate Study or Research Abroad* (1994–95), which describes the awards available.

Internships/Traineeships

Opportunities for internships in France include the following programs offered by CIEE-member institutions and organizations. In addition, Southwest Texas State University and Moorhead State University have internships open only to their own students. See Appendix I for the appropriate addresses where you can write for more information.

Association for International Practical Training. *IAESTE Trainee Program.* On-the-job training for undergraduate and graduate students in technical fields such as engineering, computer science, agriculture, architecture, mathematics, and the natural and physical sciences. See page 19 for more information.
Hospitality/Tourism Exchanges Program. On-the-job training for young people beginning a career in the hotel and food-service industries. Participants must have graduated or be enrolled in a university or vocational school and possess at least six months of training or experience in the chosen field. Training usually runs from 6 to 18 months.

Boston University. *Paris Internship Program.* Fall, spring, and summer. Sophomores through seniors; post-Baccalaureate students. 3.0 GPA in major and advisor's approval. Four semesters of college-level French with a grade of B minus or better. Intensive study of French followed by eight-week internship in areas such as arts administration, public relations, marketing, tourism, entertainment, human/health services, business, economics, politics. Apply by May 15 for fall; November 15 for spring. Contact: (617) 353-9888.

Syracuse University. *Internships at the Council of Europe in Strasbourg, France.* Undergraduates. Apply by March 1.

University of Louisville. *Work Exchange Program in Montpellier.* Summer. Sophomores to graduates. Minimum GPA of 2.75 and competion of one full academic year required. Apply by March 15. For more information, contact the International Center, Brodschi Hall, University of Louisville, Louisville, Kentucky 40292.

Voluntary Service

CIEE places young people in French voluntary-service **workcamps** organized by the following organizations:

- **Concordia** (in Paris) sponsors two- to three-week workcamps during the spring and summer. Projects take place all over France and generally involve construction, restoration work, conservation, or social work.
- **UNAREC** (in Paris) accepts volunteers for workcamps throughout France. Projects include restoring old houses and public buildings, creating playgrounds, maintaining river banks, and protecting sand dunes.

Volunteers must be 18 or older and speak French. The applications of U.S. residents are handled by CIEE. For more information, contact the International Voluntary Service Department at the CIEE.

In addition, two French organizations conduct workcamps for persons interested in volunteering to help restore historic buildings and monuments in various parts of France.

- **R.E.M.P. ART** (1, rue des Guillemites, 75004 Paris) organizes workcamps that last anywhere from a weekend to more than a month. An application fee is charged, and volunteers pay a daily fee (which varies according to location) to cover food and lodging expenses. Participants must be at least 14 years old.
- **Club du Vieux Manoir** (10, rue de la Cossonnerie, 75001 Paris) sponsors workcamps during spring vacation and from July 2 to September 30; a few operate year-round. During the summer, volunteers are required to stay at least 15 days, beginning on either the 2nd or 16th of the month. Camping facilities are provided at a cost of approximately $10 per day. Anyone over 15 years of age is eligible.

STUDY

A U.S. citizen who wishes to study at the undergraduate level in France for longer than 90 days must apply for a student visa at the French Consulate having jurisdiction over his or her place of residence. Consulates are located in Boston, Chicago, Houston, Los Angeles, Miami, New Orleans, New York, San Francisco, and Washington, DC. Contact the **French Consulate General** at 934 Fifth Avenue, New York, NY 10021; (212) 606-3688; for further information. Be sure to allow plenty of time, since applications received by mail take at least two weeks to be processed.

If you plan to study on your own in France, you should contact the Studies Office of **French Cultural Services** (see "Travel," above). This office handles the official process for applying to the first cycle (the first two years) of a French university. Applications are available from November 15 to January 15 of the year prior to studying. A high-school diploma and two years of university study are required. The Studies Office also supplies the booklet *Cours de français pour étudiants étrangers* that lists French language courses given at universities and institutions all over France. Although it is published in French, the booklet includes an English insert. Ask for the summer or the academic-year version. Other publications include *Studies in France*, which explains the basics of the French educational system. General information on fellowships and assistantships for graduates is also available.

Educational programs offered by CIEE-member institutions are described below. Consult Appendix I for the addresses of the colleges and universities listed in this section. In addition to the programs below, the American Graduate School of International Management North Carolina State University, University of California, Pepperdine University, State University of New York schools, and University of New Hampshire offer programs open to their own students only.

Semester and Academic Year

Art and Architecture

Northern Illinois University. *Painting and Drawing at Marchutz School of Art*. Aix-en-Provence. Semester and academic year. Studio art at beginning, intermediate, and advanced levels. Sophomores to seniors with 2.5 GPA. Apply by June 1 for fall and academic year; November 1 for spring. Contact: Foreign Study Office, Semester/Academic Year Programs, Northern Illinois University, Williston Hall 100, DeKalb, IL 60115-2854; (815) 753-0420/0304.

Business

Bentley College. *Bentley's Business Program in France*. Paris. Semester and academic year. Offered in association with Institut International du Commerce et de la Distribution. European Community, French culture, and other subjects. Excursions in France and to EC headquarters in Brussels. Juniors and seniors with 2.7 GPA. Apply by April 15 for fall and academic year; November 1 for spring.

Northern Illinois University. *Business, Management, and Economics*. Toulon. Semester and academic year. Offered in cooperation with Institute for American Universities and Université de Toulon. Sophomores to seniors with five semesters of college French and 2.5 GPA. Apply by June 1 for fall and academic year; November 1 for spring. Contact: Foreign Study Office, Semester/Academic Year Programs, Northern Illinois University, Williston Hall 100, DeKalb, IL 60115-2854; (815) 753-0420/0304.

University of Connecticut. *International Business Program*. Grenoble. Spring semester. Students with finance and marketing background. Apply by October 1.

University of Pennsylvania. *Semester in Lyon: Business and International Affairs*. Lyons. Fall and spring semesters. Sophomores to seniors with 3.0 GPA, introductory economics (micro and macro) and marketing, and four semesters of college French. Apply by February 15 for fall; October 15 for spring.

World Learning/School for International Training. *College Semester Abroad—International Business*. Toulouse. Fall and spring semesters. Intensive language, French life and culture, and international business seminar; internships available. Homestays. Sophomores to seniors with 2.5 GPA and two years of college French. Apply by May 7 for fall; October 7 for spring. Contact: College Semester Abroad Admissions at (800) 336-1616.

Economics

American University. *Paris Semester*. Spring. Economics, international relations, history, culture, French language. Internships with multinational organizations. Excursions. Second-semester sophomores to seniors with 2.75 GPA. Apply by October 15. Contact: World Capitals Programs, American University, Dunblane House—Tenley Campus, Washington, DC 20016-8083; (202) 895-4900/4937.

Education

State University of New York College at Cortland. *Cortland International Programs—Versailles*. Academic year. Elementary and secondary school teaching methods, and French language and culture at Université de Versailles. Dormitory housing. Juniors to graduate students with advanced French. Apply by February 15. Contact: Office of International Programs, SUNY College at Cortland, PO Box 2000, Cortland, NY 13045; (607) 753-2209.

French Language and Culture

Adventist Colleges Abroad. Collonges-sous-Salève. Fall, spring, and winter quarters and academic year. Undergraduates with 3.0 GPA in French and

2.5 overall. Open only to students at Adventist Colleges Abroad consortium institutions. Apply by March 15 for fall and academic year; November 1 for winter; January 15 for spring.

Boston University. Grenoble. Semester and academic year. Intensive language and cultural immersion program offering direct enrollment option at Université de Grenoble; instruction in French. Homestays. Sophomores to seniors with 3.0 GPA in major and one semester of French; five semesters for direct enrollment at Université de Grenoble. Apply by March 15 for fall and academic year; October 15 for spring.

Brethren Colleges Abroad. *University of Nancy.* Semester and academic year. Intensive language program with full range of academic curriculum available. English teaching work arranged upon request. Homestays and excursions. Juniors and seniors with 3.0 GPA and intermediate French. Apply by April 15 for fall and academic year; November 1 for spring.

University of Strasbourg. Semester and academic year. Intensive language program with full range of academic curriculum available. Excursions and study tours. Juniors and seniors with 3.0 GPA and two years of college French. Apply by April 15 for fall and academic year; November 1 for spring.

Macalester College. *PAAT (Paris, Aix, Avalon, and Toulon) French Program.* Spring semester. January orientation in Paris prior to study in Aix, Avignon, or Toulon. Sophomores to seniors with two years of college French. Apply by September 15.

Michigan State University. *French Language, Literature, and Culture in Paris.* Spring semester. Sophomores to seniors with two years of college French. Apply by November 30. Contact: Office of Overseas Study, 108 International Center, Michigan State University, East Lansing, MI 48824-1035; (517) 353-8920.

Ohio University. *Intensive French Abroad.* Tours. Spring semester (late March to early June). Advanced French language, culture, and literature. Undergraduates with beginning to intermediate French. Apply by December. Contact: Dr. William Wrage, Department of Modern Languages, 220 Ellis Hall, Ohio University, Athens, OH 45701; (614) 593-2765.

Polytechnicum-Université Catholique de Lille. *French Language and Culture.* Lille. Fall quarter (early October to mid-December), winter quarter (early January to late March), and spring quarter (mid-May to early July). Intensive French language at beginning and intermediate levels (advanced upon request).

Scripps College. *Scripps Program in Paris.* Semester and academic year. Study at University of Paris. Sophomores to seniors with B-minus average and four semesters of college French. Apply by February 5 for fall and academic year; September 25 for spring.

State University of New York College at Brockport. *Multi-Level French Language Immersion Program.* Tours. Fall and spring semesters. Homestays. Juniors and seniors with one year of college French and 2.5 GPA. Apply by February 15 for fall; October 15 for spring. Contact: Office of International Education, SUNY College at Brockport, Brockport, NY 14420; (716) 395-2119.

State University of New York College at Oswego. *French Language, Culture, Civilization Program at the Sorbonne, Paris.* Semester and academic year. French language, culture, civilization, and history; instruction in French. Excursions and housing in international student foyers. Juniors and seniors with two years of college French and 2.5 GPA. Apply by April 1 for fall and academic year; November 1 for spring. Contact: Office of International

Education, SUNY at Oswego, 102 Rich Hall, Oswego, NY 13126; (315) 341-2118.

Stetson University. Dijon. Semester and academic year. Sophomores to seniors with two years of French and 2.5 GPA (3.0 in major). Apply by March 1 for fall and academic year; October 15 for spring.

University of Massachusetts at Amherst. *French Studies in Rouen.* Academic year. Sophomores to seniors with one year of college French. Apply by March 1.

University of Nebraska—Lincoln. *Study at Université de Franche-Comté.* Besançon. Spring semester. French language, culture, and literature plus teaching French as a second language. Sophomores to seniors with four semesters of college French. Open only to students at member institutions of the Association of Big Eight Universities.

University of North Carolina at Chapel Hill. *UNC Year at Montpellier.* Academic year. Sophomores to graduate students with 2.7 GPA and two years of precollege French plus three semesters of college French. Apply by March 1.

University of Notre Dame. *International Study Program in Angers.* Academic year. Sophomores and juniors with two years of college French. Apply by December 1.

University of Oregon. *Intensive French Language Program.* Le Mans. Winter quarter (early January to mid-March). Intensive intermediate French language and culture at Université du Maine. Excursions and dormitory housing. Sophomores to seniors with four quarters of college French and 2.75 GPA. Apply by October 15.

University of Wisconsin at Milwaukee. *Study in Paris.* Paris. Spring semester. Offered in conjunction with the Urban Corridor Consortium. French language and culture. Sophomores to seniors with 3.0 GPA and three semesters of college French. Apply by October 1.

Whitworth College. *France Study Tour.* Paris. Spring semester every three years (next offered in 1995). French language, art, literature, and history. Sophomores to seniors with 2.5 GPA and one year of college French. Apply by April 1.

State University of New York College at New Paltz. *Study Abroad in France.* Besançon. Semester and academic year. French language, literature, and culture at University of Franche-Comté's Center for Applied Linguistics. Juniors and seniors with two years of college French. Rolling admissions. Contact: Office of International Education, HAB 33, SUNY College at New Paltz, New Paltz, NY 12561; (914) 257-3125.

University of Minnesota. *French in Montpellier.* Montpellier. Fall, winter, and spring quarters. Language and culture study; in spring quarter, literature and international relations courses available. Homestay and excursions. First-year college students to graduate students and adults with one year of college French and 2.5 GPA. Apply by July 1 for fall; October 15 for winter; January 15 for spring. Contact: The Global Campus, 106C Nicholson Hall, 216 Pillsbury Drive SE, University of Minnesota, Minneapolis, MN 55455-0138; (612) 625-3379.

General Studies

Alma College. *Program of Studies in France.* Paris. Semester and academic year. Culture, language, literature, history, and current events at Alliance Française; instruction in French. Internships available. Homestays and excursions. Sophomores to seniors with 2.5 GPA. Apply by June 15 for fall; October 15 for winter.

American Heritage Association. *Northwest Interinstitutional Council on Study Abroad—Avignon.* Fall, spring, and winter quarters. Sophomores to seniors with two semesters of French and 2.5 GPA. Apply by June 15 for fall; November 15 for winter; January 15 for spring. Contact: (800) 654-2051.

Beloit College. *French Seminar.* Rennes. Spring semester. Sophomores to graduate students with intermediate French and 2.5 GPA. Apply by November 1.

Brigham Young University. *BYU Paris Study Abroad.* Paris. Spring semester. First-year college students to seniors with one year of college French. Apply by February 1.

Brown University. *Brown in France.* Paris, Lyon, and Nice. Spring semester and academic year. Full enrollment in one of the following French universities: Université Lumière (Lyon II), Université Sophia Antipolis (Nice), La Sorbonne Panthéon (Paris I), La Sorbonne Nouvelle (Paris III), La Sorbonne (Paris IV), Institut d'Études Politiques (Sciences Po). Excursions. Internships available in spring Paris program. Sophomores to seniors in good academic standing and with six semesters of college French. Apply by February 1 for academic year; October 1 for spring.

Cornell University. *EDUCO.* Paris. Semester and academic year. Offered in conjunction with Duke University. Wide range of studies available at University of Paris I and VII; instruction in French. Homestays or apartment housing and excursions. Juniors and seniors with 3.0 GPA and four semesters of college French. Apply by February 15 for fall and academic year; October 15 for spring.

Council on International Educational Exchange. *Undergraduate Program at the University of Haute Bretagne.* Rennes. Semester and academic year. Excursions. Sophomores to seniors with 2.75 GPA overall, two years of college French, and 3.0 GPA in French. Apply by March 1 for fall and academic year; October 15 for spring. Contact University Programs Department.

Davidson College. *Davidson College Junior Year Abroad in Montpellier.* Academic year. Integrated program at University of Montpellier III. Juniors with two years of French and 2.75 GPA. Apply by February 1.

Hollins College. *Hollins Abroad.* Paris. Semester and academic year. French language, art, architecture, politics, economics, and history. Homestays and excursions. Juniors and seniors with intermediate French and 2.0 GPA. Apply by April 1 for fall and academic year; October 1 for spring. Contact: Hollins Abroad Office, PO Box 9597, Hollins College, Roanoke, VA 24020; (703) 362-6307.

Indiana University. *Overseas Study in Strasbourg.* Academic year. Indiana and Purdue University juniors and seniors with two years of French and 3.0 GPA. Apply by November 1.

International Student Exchange Program (ISEP). Academic year. Direct reciprocal exchange between U.S. institutions and institutions in Aix-en-Provence, Amiens, Angers, Besançon, Caen, Chambéry, Grenoble, Le Mans, Lyons, Montpellier, Nantes, Nice, Rennes, Saint-Étienne, Le Havre, and Lille. Full curriculum options. Rolling admissions. Open only to students at ISEP-member institutions. Contact ISEP for list of members.

James Madison University. *JMU Semester in Paris.* Fall and spring semesters. French art, language, civilization, theater, literature, politics, cuisine, and music. Sophomores to seniors with 2.8 GPA and intermediate French. Apply by November 15 for fall; February 1 for spring.

Marquette University. *Strasbourg Program.* Strasbourg. Spring semester. Offered in conjunction with St. Joseph's University, Philadelphia. French language, literature, religious studies, cultural anthropology, politics, and European Economic Community study; instruction in French. Brief homestays and dormitory housing. Sophomores to seniors with 3.0 GPA and four semesters of college French. Apply by November 1. Contact: Director, Strasbourg Program, Department of Foreign Languages and Literatures, Marquette University, Milwaukee, WI 53233; (414) 288-7063.

Middlebury College. *Junior Year Abroad*. Paris. Academic year. French language, literature, culture, and history. Juniors and seniors with five semesters of college French (or equivalent). Apply by January 31.

Graduate Program. Paris. Academic year. French language, literature, culture, and professional training. Graduate students with equivalent of B.A. in French. Apply by March 1. Contact: French School, Middlebury College, Middlebury, VT 05753; (802) 388-3711 ext. 5523.

New York University. *NYU in France*. Paris. Semester and academic year. Juniors to graduate students with three semesters of college French and 3.0 GPA. Apply by May 1 for fall and academic year; October 1 for spring. Contact: NYU in France, 19 University Place, Room 631, New York, NY 10003; (212) 998-8720.

Northern Illinois University. *French Studies in the South of France*.Aix-en-Provence, Toulon, or Avignon. Semester and academic year. Offered in cooperation with Institute for American Universities. Homestays. Sophomores to seniors with 2.5 GPA (and two years of college French for Avignon and Toulon). Apply by April 1 for fall and academic year; November 1 for spring. Contact: Foreign Study Office, Semester/Academic Year Programs, Northern Illinois University, Williston Hall 100, DeKalb, IL 60115-2854; (815) 753-0420/0304.

Portland State University. *Northwest Interinstitutional Council on Study Abroad—Avignon*. See listing under American Heritage Association.

Rosary College. *Rosary in Strasbourg*. Semester and academic year. Internships also available. Juniors and seniors with two years of college French. Rolling admissions on a space-available basis after April 1 for fall and academic year; November 1 for spring. Contact: Ann Charney, Director of Study Abroad, Rosary College, River Forest, IL 60305; (708) 524-6948.

Rutgers University. *Junior Year in France*. Tours (six weeks in Paris). Academic year. Juniors with two years of college French and French literature courses. Apply by March 1.

St. Lawrence University. *France Year Program*. Rouen (orientation in Paris). Academic year. Sophomores to seniors with 2.8 GPA and intermediate college French. Apply by February 20.

Skidmore College. *Skidmore Study Abroad in Paris*. Semester and academic year. French language and literature, art history, studio art, political science, history, sociology/anthropology, business, and economics. Internships available. Excursions and optional homestays. Juniors with 3.0 GPA and intermediate French for semester; intermediate to advanced for year program. Apply by February 15 for fall and academic year; October 15 for spring.

Southern Methodist University. *SMU in Paris*. Semester and academic year. French culture and language, art history, communications, and studio art. Excursions and homestays. Sophomores to seniors with one year of college French. Apply by March 15 for fall and academic year; October 15 for spring. Contact: Office of International Programs, SMU, 100 McFarlin Auditorium, Dallas, TX 75275-0391; (214) 768-2338.

State University of New York College at Brockport. *Paris Social Science Program*. Fall and spring semesters. Contemporary French society and language. Juniors and seniors with one year of college French and 2.5 GPA. Apply by February 15 for fall; November 1 for spring. Contact: Office of International Education, SUNY College at Brockport, Brockport, NY 14420; (716) 395-2119.

State University of New York College at Buffalo. *Program of French Language and Culture*. Grenoble. Semester and academic year. French language, literature, and civilization plus independent study; instruction in French. Study at University of Grenoble III. Excursions and homestays. Juniors to graduate students with four semesters of college French and 3.0 GPA. Apply by May 1 for fall and academic year; November 1 for spring. Contact: Study Abroad Coordinator, Office of International Education, SUNY College at Buffalo, 212 Talbert Hall, Box 601604, Buffalo, NY 14260-1604; (716) 645-3912.

State University of New York at Stony Brook. Paris. Fall semester and academic year. Juniors and seniors with two years of college French and 3.0 GPA. Apply by April 1. Contact: Dean for International Programs, SUNY at Stony Brook, NY 11794-2700; (516) 632-7030.

Syracuse University. *Syracuse in Strasbourg*. Fall and spring semesters. Sophomores to seniors with 3.0 GPA. Apply by March 15 for fall; October 15 for spring. Contact: (800) 235-3472.

Tufts University. *Tufts in Paris*. Academic year. Full university curriculum. Juniors with three years of college French and 3.0 GPA. Apply by February 1.

University of Colorado at Boulder. *Study Abroad in Bordeaux*. Academic year. Juniors and seniors with two years of college French and 2.75 GPA. Apply by March 1.

University of Connecticut. *Study Abroad Program in France*. Rouen and Paris. Academic year. Sophomores to seniors with two years of college French. Apply by February 15.

University of Kansas. *Exchange at the University of Franche-Comté*. Besançon and Paris. Spring semester and academic year. Sophomores with 3.0 GPA and four semesters of college French. Apply by March 15 for academic year; October 1 for spring.

University of Maryland. *Maryland in Nice*. Nice. Spring semester and academic year. Sophomores to seniors with 2.5 GPA and 12 semester-hours of college French. Apply by April 1 for academic year; October 15 for spring.

University of Minnesota. *Academic Year in France*. Montpellier. Academic year. Study at the Université Paul Valéry. Homestay, apartment, or dormitory housing. Sophomores to seniors and adults with 2.75 GPA and two years of college French with 3.0 GPA in French. Apply by April 1.

Integrated Semester in France. Montpellier. Spring semester. Study at the Université Paul Valéry. Homestay, apartment, or dormitory housing. Sophomores to seniors and adults with 2.75 GPA and two years of college French with 3.0 GPA in French. Apply by October 1.

University of North Carolina at Chapel Hill. *UNC Program to Lyons*. Academic year. Sophomores to seniors with 3.0 GPA and fluency in French. Apply by February 14.

University of Oregon. *Northwest Interinstitutional Council on Study Abroad—Avignon*. See listing under American Heritage Association.

University of Pennsylvania. *Reid Hall Programs in Paris*. Paris. Semester and academic year. Offered in conjunction with Columbia University. French language study, literature, humanities, film, social sciences, and women's studies. Sophomores to graduate students with 3.0 GPA and four semesters of college French. Apply by February 15 for fall and academic year; October 15 for spring.

University of Washington. *Northwest Interinstitutional Council on Study Abroad—Avignon.* See listing under American Heritage Association.

University of Wisconsin at Madison. *Academic Year in Aix-en-Provence.* Intensive pre-session in French language, literature, and civilization; year-long courses in liberal arts. Juniors to graduate students with five semesters of college French and in good academic standing. Open only to students at colleges and universities in Wisconsin and Wisconsin residents studying out of state. Apply by second Friday in November.

Washington State University. *Northwest Interinstitutional Council on Study Abroad—Avignon.* See listing under American Heritage Association.

Wesleyan University. *Wesleyan Program in Paris.* Semester and academic year. Sophomores to seniors with five semesters of college French and 3.0 GPA in French. Apply by March 10 for fall; October 10 for spring.

Western Washington University. *Northwest Interinstitutional Council on Study Abroad—Avignon.* See listing under American Heritage Association.

Whitworth College. Aix-en-Provence. Fall semester and academic year. Offered in conjunction with Université de Provence. French language and culture study; full curriculum. Sophomores to seniors with 2.5 GPA and two years of college French. Apply by February 1 for fall; October 1 for spring.

World Learning/School for International Training. *College Semester Abroad.* Toulouse. Fall and spring semesters. Intensive language study, interdisciplinary seminars on French life and culture, field-study methods seminar, and independent-study project. Homestays and excursions. Sophomores to seniors with 2.5 GPA and two years of college French. Apply by May 7 for fall; October 7 for spring. Contact: College Semester Abroad Admissions at (800) 336-1616.

International Relations

Syracuse University. *Certificate in European Studies.* Strasbourg. Semester and academic year. Political science, history, international relations, economics, communications, and cross-cultural understanding in relation to contemporary Europe after the Cold War, as well as French or German literature. Sophomores to seniors with introductory economics and international affairs and one year of modern European language at college level. Apply by March 15 for fall and academic year; October 15 for spring. Contact: (800) 235-3472.

Literature

State University of New York at Binghamton. *Mediterranean Studies Program.* Aix-en Provence. Spring semester. Literature and language. Juniors and seniors with five semesters of college French. Apply by October 15. Contact: Department of Romance Languages, SUNY at Binghamton, PO Box 6000, Binghamton, NY 13902-6000; (607) 777-2000.

Modern Culture and Media

Council on International Educational Exchange. *Critical Studies Program at University of Paris III.* Semester and academic year. Excursions. Juniors to graduate students with 3.0 GPA and two years of college French for academic year and fall semester: three years for spring semester. Apply by March 1 for fall and academic year; October 15 for spring. Contact: University Programs Department.

Summer and Short-Term

Art and Architecture

Rutgers University. *Summer Institute of Art History in Paris.* Undergraduates. Apply by March 1.

Tulane University. *Summer Abroad in Paris.* Five weeks in July and August. Art history, modern art, conversational French, French composers, and French opera. Excursions. High-school students to adults and nonstudents. Apply by April 15. Contact: Richard Marksbury, Tulane Summer School, 125 Gibson Hall, Tulane University, New Orleans, LA 70118-5698; (504) 865-5555.

University of Kansas. *Art and Design in Peyresq.* Tour through Belgium and France before stay in shepherd village. Summer. Undergraduates with 3.0 GPA. Apply by February 1.

University of Louisville. *Art History and French Language in Paris.* Four weeks in summer. Freshmen to graduate students with background in French. Apply by March 15.

Business

Bentley College. *Bentley's Summer Program Abroad in France.* Strasbourg. Summer. Offered in association with the European Institute of Advanced Business Studies. French language, French studies, and European business environment. Apartment housing and excursions. Sophomores to seniors with 2.7 GPA. Apply by April 1.

Monterey Institute of International Studies. *Summer Program in Rouen.* Six weeks in May and June. Offered in cooperation with Institut Formation Internationale. French language, culture, and business. Internships optional in July. Homestays and excursions. High-school students and up with intermediate to advanced French. Apply by March 1. Contact: Dr. Gisèle Kapuscinski, French Studies, Center for Language Services, MIIS, 425 Van Buren Street, Monterey, CA 93940; (408) 647-4115.

Ohio State University. *Summer Program in International Business.* Nantes. Five weeks in June and July. European history and civilization, European Economic Community, and European business and finance. Homestays and excursions. Undergraduates with 2.7 GPA and introductory micro and macro economics. Apply by March 15.

University of Pennsylvania. *Penn-in-Compiègne.* Summer. Language study and economics. Internships. Apply by March 1.

Culinary Arts

Michigan State University. *Culinary Arts.* Lyons. Summer. European food selection, marketing, preparation, and service systems. Juniors and seniors. Apply by April 15. Contact: Office of Overseas Study, 108 International Center, Michigan State University, East Lansing, MI 48824-1035; (517) 353-8920.

Film

University of Pennsylvania. *Penn-in-Cannes.* Summer. Perspective on film: survey of international cinema. Apply by February 1.

French Language and Culture

Adventist Colleges Abroad. Collonges-sous-Saleve. Summer. Six-week intensive courses at the advanced, intermediate, and beginning levels.

Excursions. High-school students, high-school graduates not enrolled in college, and college students with 2.5 GPA. Open only to students at Adventist Colleges Abroad consortium institutions.

Alma College. *Program of Studies in France*. Paris. Flexible enrollment period. Language courses plus special course in art and architecture at Alliance Française. Sophomores to seniors with 2.5 GPA. Apply by March 15.

Boston University. *Intensive French Language*. Fontenay. Intensive four-week summer program offering courses in second-semester French or advanced training in rapid and idiomatic French speech. Excursions and optional homestays. Sophomores to seniors and college graduates with successful completion of one semester (six for advanced class) of college French. Apply by April 1. *Intensive French Language and Liberal Arts*. Paris. Summer. Intensive six-week program offering academic options at intermediate and advanced levels; instruction in French. Excursions and dormitory housing. Sophomores to seniors with 3.0 GPA in major. Apply by April 1.

Council on International Educational Exchange. *France Today: Language and Culture at the Institut Catholique de Paris*. Co-sponsored with University of Wisconsin at Madison. Six-week summer program with intensive French language study and introduction to French culture. Excursions and dormitory housing. Sophomores to graduate students with 2.5 GPA. Apply by April 1. Contact University Programs Department.

Illinois State University. *Summer Program in French at University of Grenoble*. Eight-week program of French language and civilization. Dormitory housing and excursions. First-year college students to graduate students with one year of college French. Apply by March 15. Contact: Dr. George Petrossian, Department of Foreign Languages, Illinois State University, Normal, IL 61761-6901; (309) 438-3604 or 452-4902.

Indiana University. *Language Study in France*. Dijon. Summer. First-year college students to seniors with one year of college French and 2.8 GPA. Apply by mid-February.

Iowa State University. *Regents' Summer Study Program in Lyon*. Offered in conjunction with University of Iowa and University of Northern Iowa. Seven-week program in French language, civilization, history, and geography at Institut Catholique de Lyon. Homestays and excursions. Apply by February 1. Contact: Nelle Hutter, Department of Foreign Languages and Literatures, 300 Pearson Hall, Iowa State University, Ames, IA 50011.

Longwood College. *Summer Study Abroad at University of Toulouse*. Advanced French grammar and conversation as well as contemporary French culture. Dormitory housing and excursions. Sophomores to seniors with two semesters of college French with 3.0 GPA or three semesters with 2.0 GPA. Apply by February 14. Contact: Dr. John F. Reynolds, International Studies Program, Longwood College, Farmville, VA 23901; (804) 395-2172.

Miami University. *French in Dijon*. June. Five-week intensive French language and civilization program. Sophomores to graduate students with two years of college French. Apply by March 15.

Michigan State University. *French Language, Literature, and Culture in Tours*. Summer. Sophomores to seniors with two years of college French. Apply by April 15. Contact: Office of Overseas Study, 108 International Center, Michigan State University, East Lansing, MI 48824-1035; (517) 353-8920.

Rutgers University. *Cours d'été à Tours*. Summer. Undergraduates with one year of college French. Apply by January 15.

Southern Methodist University. *SMU in the South of France*. Boulouris. Six weeks from late May to early June. Intensive French language and culture, especially for intermediate to advanced levels. Excursions and homestays. Sophomores to seniors with one year of college French. Apply by March 1. Contact: Office of International Programs, Southern Methodist University, 100 McFarlin Auditorium, Dallas, TX 75275-0391; (214) 768-2338.

State University of New York College at New Paltz. *Summer Study in France*. Paris. Intensive French language, culture, and literature. High-school students to graduate students with one year of college French. Rolling admissions. Contact: Office of International Education, HAB 33, SUNY College at New Paltz, New Paltz, NY 12561; (914) 257-3125.

State University of New York College at Oswego. *French Language, Culture, Civilization Program in Paris and St. Malo*. Two weeks in Paris and last four weeks in St. Malo. French language, literature, and civilization; instruction in French. Homestays in St. Malo and excursions. Undergraduates with one year of college French and 2.5 GPA; qualified high-school students and graduate students also accommodated. Apply by April 1. Contact: Office of International Education, SUNY College at Oswego, 102 Rich Hall, Oswego, NY 13126; (315) 341-2118.

Syracuse University. *French Language and Culture*.Strasbourg. Six weeks in June and July. French language at all levels, and French society, culture, and cuisine. Internships available. Homestays and excursions. Undergraduates and graduate students. Apply by March 1. Contact: (800) 235-3472.

University of Alabama. *Academic Summer Program in France*. Touraine. Six weeks in July and August. French language at intermediate and advanced levels. Excursions and homestays. First-year college students to graduate students with two semesters of college French. Apply by March 1. Contact: (205) 348-5256.

University of Kansas. *Paris Orientation Program*. Mid to late September. Intensive language review appropriate for students enrolling directly in French universities. Sophomores to seniors with 3.0 GPA and four semesters of college French. Apply by July 1.

French Language and Culture in Paris, Picardy, Brittany, and Touraine. Undergraduates and advanced high-school students with two semesters of college French. Apply by February 1.

University of Kentucky. *Kentucky Institute for International Studies in Paris, France*. Paris. Summer. Language study. Excursions. First-year college students to graduate students and adults. Apply by March 1.

University of Michigan. *Summer Language Program in Saint-Malo*. Saint-Malo. Six weeks in summer. French language study. Homestays. First-year college students to seniors with two semesters of French. Apply by March 16.

University of New Hampshire. *Summer Study in Brest, France*. Brest. Four weeks in summer. French language study. High-school students to seniors with four years of French. Apply by April 15.

University of New Orleans. *Glories of France*. Montpellier. Four weeks in summer. Offered in conjunction with the *Cours intensif de français*. High-school students (with 3.25 GPA and two years of French) to graduate students. Apply by April 1.

University of North Carolina at Chapel Hill. *Paris Summer Program*. Paris. Four weeks in summer. Offered in conjunction with the University of Paris (the Sorbonne) and the University of North Carolina at Wilmington. French language and civilization. First-year college students to graduate students with two semesters of college French. Apply by March 15.

University of Toledo. *Study Abroad in France*. Paris, Montpellier. Four weeks in summer. French language, civilization, and culture. Sophomores to graduate students with three semesters of college French. Apply by February 28.

Villanova University. *Dijon/Paris Summer Program in France.* Dijon and Paris. From early July to mid-August in summer. Intensive French language study. First-year college students to seniors with 2.5 GPA and two semesters of college French. Apply by March 15.

General Studies

Louisiana State University. *LSU in Paris.* Summer. French language, culture, history, and art. Sophomores to seniors with 2.5 GPA and graduate students with 3.0 GPA. Apply by April 1.

New York University. *NYU in France.* Paris. Six weeks in July and August. Intensive French language, literature, and culture. High-school graduates, college undergraduates, and graduate students with 2.5 GPA. Apply by April 1. Contact: NYU in France, 19 University Place, Room 631, New York, NY 10003; (212) 998-8720.

University of South Carolina. *USC in Tours.* Tours. Summer. Intensive language study. First-year college students to graduate students with one year of college French. Apply by May 1.

International Relations

Syracuse University. *European Politics in Strasbourg.* June and Jul Lectures on the Council of Europe, European Parliament, and the Court of Human Rights, followed by internship program at the Council of Europe. Excursion to Geneva, Switzerland. Undergraduates and graduate students. Apply by March 1. Contact: (800) 235-3472.

EXPLORING FRENCH CULTURE

Readings

Some classics of French literature continue to provide a useful introduction to today's country. Although much has changed since the days of Balzac and Flaubert, reading the works of such influential authors can only add to your knowledge of French culture. Honoré de Balzac chronicled 19th-century France; his book *Old Goriot* (1835) deals with the decline of the French aristocracy and the rise of the bourgeoisie. From the same period is Gustave Flaubert's *Madame Bovary* (1857), about a woman who is unable to adapt to the provincial life she is forced to lead. *Germinal* (1885), by another French master of the pen, Émile Zola, depicts the miseries of urban life in the 1860s.

The 1930s saw the emergence of existentialism in France. Jean-Paul Sartre's *Nausea* (1938) is about a man who is disgusted with life and has no friends or family—a typical specimen of existential bliss. *The Age of Reason*, the first volume in Sartre's trilogy *The Roads to Freedom*, is set in the streets and cafés of 1938 Paris. Another existential landmark is Albert Camus's *The Plague* (1947), which chronicles the story of a town hit by an epidemic, often seen as an allegory for France under the German occupation.

During the 1940s and 1950s, the "new novel" emerged. New novelists saw themselves as inventors rather than transcribers of reality. They often portrayed characters without names, such as Nathalie Sarraute's *Portrait of a Man Unknown* (1948). And their stories were often timeless, such as Alain Robbe-Grillet's *The Erasers* (1953), which takes place within 24 hours, but not in any particular time in history.

Marguerite Duras's novel *The Lover* (1984) chronicles the end of France's colonial era. Set in Indochina, it is the story of a teenage girl and her wealthy Chinese lover. Colette is one of France's best known women writers; *The Collected Stories of Colette* includes 100 stories written between 1908 and 1945. For contemporary French fiction, read the works of Michel Butor (*Boomerang*, 1978), Philippe Sollers (*Paradise*, 1978), and the detective novels of Sebastien Japrisot, such as *The Lady in the Car with Glasses and a Gun*. France not only has produced its own great writers; it also has attracted expatriates of many nationalities writing in their own languages.

Films

Since the invention of the film projector in France by Louis and Auguste Lumière in 1885, French films have been among the world's best known. Jean Renoir (son of painter Pierre Auguste Renoir), perhaps one of the greatest filmmakers of all time, is best known for *Grand Illusion* (1937), which focuses on French prisoners of war and their cultured German commandant during World War I.

The French *Nouvelle Vague*, or "New Wave," has been an internationally influential film movement for the past 30 years. One of the most famous directors to come out of this movement is Jean-Luc Godard. His movie *Breathless* (1959) established the popular French film star Jean-Paul Belmondo. The film follows a Parisian hood (Belmondo), on the lam after stealing a car and killing a cop, and the American girl he meets. *Weekend* (1967) is Godard's diatribe against Western culture and materialism; it concerns an avaricious couple captured by cannibalistic guerrillas. Another leader of the French New Wave cinema, François Truffaut directed *The 400 Blows* (1959), the first in a series of semi-autobiographical films; in this film, his alter-ego is a youth who takes to a life of small-time crime.

Many original New Wave directors have continued to be vital and challenging filmmakers, such as Louis Malle with *Au Revoir les Enfants* (1987), the story of a Catholic boy's friendship with a Jewish boy who is hiding from the Nazis; and Agnes Varda with *Vagabond* (1985), an engrossing story of a young drifter. In addition, a number of recent French films such as Claude Berri's *Jean de Florette* and *Manon of the Spring* (both 1986) and Jean-Jacques Beineix's *Diva* (1982) and *Betty Blue* (1986) have gained large audiences in the United States.

The 1990 film of *Cyrano de Bergerac*, starring Gérard Depardieu and directed by Jean-Paul Rappeneau, was a great success in the United States. The 1992 Oscar winner for best foreign film was *Indochine*, directed by Régis Wargnier. This movie, set in the last years of French colonial rule in Vietnam, depicts Catherine Deneuve and her adopted Vietnamese daughter falling in love with the same French sailor.

GERMANY

October 3, 1990, marked the reunification of a country divided for 45 years into two entities: one with a communist government and centrally planned economy, the other with a democratic government and market economy. The destruction of the Berlin Wall was an emotionally charged symbol of the reunification of the German people and the German land. Germany, like its eastern and central European neighbors, is in the process of resituating itself within the political reordering of Europe.

Wonderful as the long-awaited reunification seemed at first, it has left a huge number of problems in its wake, especially in the social and economic spheres. Most poignant is the closing down of more than 50 percent of formerly GDR industry and the attendant steep rise in unemployment in the five new eastern German states. The western states, meanwhile, are struggling to absorb thousands of new citizens and incorporate another economic entity into their own system. This, and the generally slack world economy, recently has led to severe cutbacks in such major industry sectors as steel, car production, and tool manufacturing. Experts predict that it will take about a decade before the split will be overcome—economically, politically, and socially.

Fragmentation is not a new phenomenon to the Germans, however. Germany's location in the heart of Europe has made it a crossroads of cultures and has produced a variety of German peoples instead of a completely uniform nationality. German history shows the efforts of these different peoples to accommodate and adapt themselves to their geographical circumstances, struggling to achieve a common cultural identity, and to create a single political entity.

In fact, diversity may be the foremost characteristic of Germany. The nation encompasses a varied landscape that extends from the flat grasslands of the northern coast to the picturesque valleys of the Elbe and the Rhine, to the Black Forest and the Bavarian Alps in the south, or the Erzgebirge in the east. Linguistically, Germany is divided into the Low-German dialects of the north and the High-German dialects of the south. In terms of culture, language, and mentality, you will find great differences between Friesians, Westphalians, Berliners, Swabians, Saxons, and Bavarians—to name just a few of the German regional groups.

As a result of World War II and the division of Germany and its capital city, Berlin ceased to be the nation's predominant urban center. One consequence was that the traditional regional centers of Germany regained their importance. On the north coast are the seaports of Hamburg and Bremen, both rich in the traditions of the medieval Hanseatic merchant league. In western Germany there is Cologne, famous for its medieval city and cathedral; and Frankfurt, Germany's railway, communications, and banking center. In the south there's Stuttgart—the heart of the thriving high-tech state of Baden-Württemberg—and Munich, home of the Hofbrauhaus and capital of Bavaria. In the east are Leipzig and Dresden, the capital of Saxony, with its rich collection of museums and architectural gems.

In spite of all the reunification problems, Germany remains one of the leading exporting nations of the world, enjoys a fairly sound economy, and maintains a stable currency. However, although the unemployment rate in the western states has hovered around six to eight percent for most of the last decade, estimates for the next few years run much higher. An extensive welfare network provides a safety net for those out of work, but there is no denying the considerable frustration and unrest among the young, who increasingly face the possibility of joblessness after graduation. This is one of the factors that has given rise to the much televised outbreaks of violence against foreigners in both the eastern and western parts of Germany.

Except during summer vacation, Germans travel infrequently. Come July, however, millions of Germans depart for the beaches of Italy, Greece, and Spain. This exodus makes room for the foreign tourists who flock to Heidelberg, Neuschwanstein, and other romantic spots made famous in tourist brochures. Berlin is a popular destination, because of its historic importance and its reputation as one of Germany's liviest cities. The opening of the eastern parts has added a phenomenal amount of internal German east-west vehicular traffic, about which the foreign traveler should be warned.

Tourists will find getting around Germany fairly easy. Efficient public rail and bus services exist in east and west; hitchhiking is common among students (but not permitted on the autobahns). In addition, ride-sharing agencies can be found in any large city. If you lose your way, you'll soon find people willing to try their English on you. The language, people, culture, and history may be difficult to make sense of initially; however, a little effort to get tuned in will prove to be extremely rewarding.

—Kurt Gamerschlag, Bonn, Germany

Official name: Federal Republic of Germany. **Size:** 137,838 square miles (about the size of Montana). **Population:** 79,548,000. **Population density:** 577 inhabitants per square mile. **Capital and largest city:** Berlin (pop. 3,000,000). **Language:** German. **Religions:** Protestant and Roman Catholic. **Per capita income:** US$14,600. **Currency:** Deutsche Mark. **Literacy rate:** 99%. **Average daily temperature:** Berlin: June, 64°F; December, 34°F. Munich: June, 61°F; December, 31°F. **Average number of days with precipitation:** Berlin: June, 13; December, 15. Munich: June, 17; December 15.

TRAVEL

U.S. citizens need a passport but not a visa for stays of up to three months. For longer stays, check with the **Embassy of the Federal Republic of Germany**, 4645 Reservoir Road NW, Washington, DC 20007; (202) 298-4000; fax (202) 298-4249.

Getting Around

In addition to Eurail and Interrail passes, German Rail—known in Germany as Deutsche Bundesbahn (DB)—offers the **German Rail Pass,** which allows unlimited travel for any 5, 10, or 15 days within one month. Regular second-class passes cost $170 for 5 days, $268 for 10 days, and $348 for 15 days; first-class passes cost $250, $390, and $498, respectively. The second-class-only **German Rail Youth Pass**, for travelers under 26, costs $130 for 5 days, $178 for 10 days, and $218 for 15 days. These passes also allow you free travel on KD German Rhine Line steamers on the Rhine, Main, and Moselle rivers, as well as on selected bus lines. German Rail Passes *cannot* be purchased in Germany; they can be purchased in the U.S. through German Rail, 747 Third Avenue, New York, NY 10017; (212) 832-5210.

Under German Rail's **Bicycle at the Station** plan, passengers can rent a bicycle for DM8 per day (DM12 for nonpassengers) at more than 300 participating stations. Bikes may be dropped off at any other participating station. Most operate from April to October, but some operate year-round. Brochures listing rental stations can be obtained at German Rail offices.

Eating and Sleeping

There are over 600 **youth hostels** throughout Germany. For more information, contact Hostelling International/American Youth Hostels (see page 54) or Germany's national youth hostel association, **Deutsches Jugendherbergswerk**, Bismarkstrasse 8, Postfach 1455, D-4930 Detmold. For a list of independent hostels in Germany, contact **Independent Hostel Owners in Ireland, England, Malta, Scotland, Germany** (see page 161). In addition, several German universities offer affordable **dormitory lodgings** to travelers. For more information, contact one of Germany's student travel organizations (see "Especially for Students and Young People," below) or consult Campus Travel Service's *US and Worldwide Travel Accommodations Guide* (see page 54).

Especially for Students and Young People

Council Travel operates offices in Dusseldorf and Munich. Their addresses are:

- Graf-Adolph-Strasse 18, 4000 Dusseldorf 1; (49) 211-329088
- Adalbertstrasse 32, 8000 Munich 40; (49) 89-395022

The following German organizations also specialize in student travel; all of them issue the International Student Identity Card.

- **ARTU**, Hardenbergstrasse 9, 1000 Berlin 12; (49) 30-3100040
- **Reisedienst Deutscher Studentenschaften (RDS)**, Rentzelstrasse 16, 2000 Hamburg 13; (49) 40-9839
- **AStA-Reisen,** Pfaffenwaldring 45, 7000 Stuttgart 80; (49) 711-1310500
- **SRS**, Marienstrasse 25, D-1040 Berlin; (49) 372-2816741

All of the above organizations can arrange reduced-fare tickets for plane and train both within the country and from Germany to points in Europe and beyond. They can also provide information on all other student discounts available throughout Germany.

For Further Information

The best source for general tourist information is the **German National Tourist Office**, 122 East 42nd Street, 52nd Floor, New York, NY 10168-0072; (212) 661-7200; fax (212) 661-7174. General background information, as well as the free weekly newsletter *The Week in Germany*, are available from the **German Information Center**, 950 Third Avenue, New York, NY 10022; (212) 888-9840.

For basic budget-travel information, *Let's Go: Germany and Switzerland* ($16.95) is reliable. The best all-around guide to Germany, however, is *The Real Guide: Germany* ($13.95). *The Real Guide: Berlin* ($11.95) provides thorough coverage of Germany's most popular city. An excellent book to read in preparation for your trip is *Insight Guide: Germany* ($19.95). For more information on *Let's Go, Real Guide*s, and *Insight Guide*s, see pages 56–57.

WORK

Getting a Job

In almost all cases, it is necessary to obtain a work permit in order to get a job in Germany. U.S. citizens may apply at the local employment office after they enter the country. Students studying in Germany may work during the between-term period without a permit.

CIEE's Work in Germany Program is administered through its offices in New York and Bonn. The program enables you to work for a period of three months, from May 15 through October 15. Participants must be U.S. citizens at least 18 years of age, and full-time college or university students during the spring semester immediately preceding work in Germany. Participants must have a good working knowledge of the German language and are required to submit a language evaluation form which must be completed by a German language instructor. Past participants have worked in all types of jobs including farming in rural areas, hotel and restaurant work in tourist centers and large cities, and office and sales help all over the country. The cost of the program is $160. For details, contact CIEE's Work Abroad Department, 205 East 42nd Street, New York, NY 10017. Students who participate in the program receive overnight accommodations and an orientation from CIEE's Bonn office, which also provides information on living, working, and traveling in Germany.

CDS International offers both a Career Training Program and an Internship Program in the fields of business, engineering, or a technical field, as well as training in the hotel industry, or as a bilingual secretary. The Career Training Program is open to young professionals with degrees in any one of the above-mentioned areas. The program includes intensive language training, followed by a year to 18 months working in a German company. Participants should have at least one year of full-time experience in desired field of placement; trainees are responsible for finding their own jobs. The CDS Internship Program offers U.S. college seniors and recent graduates the opportunity to receive in-depth language training followed by a five-month paid internship with a German company. Applicants must be U.S. citizens and have a good knowledge of German for both programs. Details are available in the U.S. from CDS International, 330 Seventh Avenue, New York, NY 10001. For both programs, interested persons must have high intermediate competence in the German language.

Teaching

Teachers of German, as well as anyone else with a college degree and an interest in teaching German, may apply for a teaching assistantship in a German high school; participants will assist with the teaching of English, American Studies, and American Literature. Applicants should be under 30 years of age and unmarried. A stipend of DM 1,000 per month is provided. For more information, contact the **Institute of International Education**, U.S. Student Programs, 809 United Nations Plaza, New York, NY 10017. Ask for their booklet, *Fulbright and Other Grants for Graduate Study Abroad*.

Internships/Traineeships

Programs sponsored by member organizations of the Council on International Educational Exchange are listed below. In addition, Southwest Texas State University and Moorhead State University sponsor internship programs in Germany that are open only to their own students.

Association for International Practical Training. *IAESTE Trainee Program*. On-the-job training for undergraduate and graduate students in technical fields such as engineering, computer science, agriculture, architecture, mathematics, and the natural and physical sciences. See page 19 for more information.

Hospitality/Tourism Exchanges Program. On-the-job training for young people

beginning a career in the hotel and food-service industries. Participants must have graduated, or be currently enrolled in a university or vocational school and possess at least six months of training or experience in the chosen field. Training usually runs from 6 to 12 months. See address in Appendix I.
Ohio University. *The Consortium for Overseas Student Teaching.* Student teaching in local and independent schools. Sophomores to seniors attending Ohio University only. Contact: Wes Snyder, Center for Higher Education and International Programs, 129 McCracken Hall, Athens, OH 45701; (614) 593-4445; fax (614) 593-0569.

Carl Duisberg Sprachcolleg München sponsors a German language and traineeship program. Opportunities are available in economics, business, and engineering. Participants are required to complete an eight-week language course in business or technical German. Trainees are then placed in German companies for two to three months. For more information, contact Carl Duisberg Sprachcolleg, Collegleitung, Pfanderstr 6-10, D-8000 München 19, Germany.

Voluntary Service

CIEE places young people in German voluntary service **workcamps** organized by the following organizations:

- **Internationale Jugendgemeinschaftsdienste** in Bonn sponsors three- to four-week workcamps from the end of June to October. Workcamps are organized around historical-preservation projects, environmental-protection projects, and urban recreation activities. Volunteers must be over 18; knowledge of German is required for some workcamps.
- **Internationale Begegnung in Gemeinschaftsdiensten in Stuttgart** sponsors three-week workcamps, from June to September, that involve constructing hiking paths, renovation of youth centers, and forest conservation. Volunteers must be over 18.
- **Vereinigung Junger Freiwilliger** in Berlin sponsors three-week workcamps in July and August involving a range of ecological and restoration projects. Volunteers must be over 18.

The applications of U.S. residents for the workcamps of the organizations above are processed by CIEE. Contact the International Voluntary Service Department at the Council's New York office for details.

For persons interested in longer term voluntary service work, the **International Christian Youth Exchange**'s "Year Abroad Program" offers persons ages 18 to 30 voluntary-service opportunities in health, education, environment, construction, and more. See page 25 for more information.

In addition, **Goshen College** offers a study-service term that is open primarily to Goshen students; limited spaces are available to transient students.

STUDY

An excellent source of information on study and research in Germany is the **Deutscher Akademischer Austauschdienst (German Academic Exchange Service)**, at 950 Third Avenue, 19th Floor, New York, NY 10022;

(212) 758-3223. DAAD (its German acronym) not only distributes information but also administers academic grants and study programs both in the U.S. and in Germany. Ask for their brochures *Grants and Research Programs in German Studies*; *Goethe Institute—Language Courses*; *Summer Courses at German Universities*; and *Academic Studies in the Federal Republic of Germany*.

Educational programs offered by CIEE-member institutions are listed below. Unless otherwise noted, consult Appendix I for the addresses of these sponsoring institutions. In addition to the programs below, Pepperdine University, State University of New York schools, and University of Nebraska at Lincoln offer programs open only to their own students.

Semester and Academic Year

Art and Architecture

University of Nebraska—Lincoln. *University of Hannover—Architecture Exchange*. Hannover. Semester and academic year. Building construction, city planning, rural planning, structural design, architecture and planning theory, physics and history. Dormitory or apartment housing. Fifth-year students and graduate students at member institutions of the Association of Big Eight Universities. Apply by March 1 for fall and academic year; October 1 for spring.

Business

State University of New York College at Cortland. *Fachhochschule, Münster*. Spring quarter (early March to mid-July; and academic year). Business, economics, and intensive German language; instruction in German at Fachhochschule Münster. Dormitory housing. Juniors to graduate students with three years of college German and background in business or economics. Apply by March 7 for academic year; November 1 for spring. Contact: Office of International Programs, SUNY College at Cortland, PO Box 2000, Cortland, NY 13045; (607) 753-2209.

Education

State University of New York College at Cortland. *Deutsche Sporthochschule*. Cologne. Spring semester. Physical education, sports, and recreation. Dormitory housing. Juniors and seniors with one semester of college German and 2.5 GPA in physical education major. Apply by October 15. Contact: Office of International Programs, SUNY College at Cortland, PO Box 2000, Cortland, NY 13045; (607) 753-2209.

Engineering

Michigan State University. *Engineering in Aachen*. Spring semester. Mechanical engineering at Technical University of Aachen with option to research and explore German industrial activities. Juniors and seniors with mechanical engineering background. Apply by November 30. Contact: Office of Overseas Study, 108 International Center, Michigan State University, East Lansing, MI 48824-1035; (517) 353-8920.

General Studies

American Heritage Association. *Northwest Interinstitutional Council on Study Abroad—Cologne*. Fall and spring quarters. Sophomores to seniors; no language requirement for fall program, two quarters or one semester of college German required for spring. Apply by June 1 for fall; January 15 for spring. Contact: (800) 654-2051.

Antioch University. *Antioch in Tübingen.* Semester and academic year. Intensive language courses at Goethe Institute prepare students for direct enrollment in Eberhard Karls Universität. Housing with German students. Juniors and seniors with two years of German. Apply by February 1. Contact: (800) 874-7986.

Beaver College. *University of Potsdam.* Semester and academic year. Full German language immersion and integration into academic courses. Juniors and seniors with knowledge of German and 3.0 GPA. Apply by April 20 for fall and academic year; October 15 for spring.

Beloit College. *German Seminar.* Hamburg. Fall semester. Homestays. Sophomores to graduate students with intermediate German and 2.5 GPA. Apply by April 1.

Brethren Colleges Abroad. Marburg University. Semester and academic year. Intensive language program; full university curriculum open to qualified students. Study tours. Juniors and seniors with two years of college German and 3.0 GPA. Apply by April 15 for fall and academic year; November 1 for spring.

Brown University. *Brown in Germany.* Tübingen and Rostock. Spring semester and academic year. Full enrollment at University of Tübingen with wide variety of disciplines available. Dormitory or apartment housing. Sophomores to seniors in good academic standing and with five semesters of college German. Apply by March 1 for academic year; October 15 for spring.

Cornell University. *Cornell Abroad in Germany.* Hamburg. Semester and academic year. Wide range of studies available at University of Hamburg with instruction primarily in German; internships available. Excursions. Juniors and seniors with 3.0 GPA and four semesters of college German. Apply by February 15 for fall and academic year; October 15 for spring.

Davidson College. *Davidson College Junior Year Abroad in Würzburg.* Academic year. Integrated program at University of Würzburg. Juniors with two years of German and 2.75 GPA. Apply by February 1.

Indiana University. *Overseas Study in Hamburg.* Academic year. Indiana, Purdue, and Ohio State University juniors and seniors with two years of German and 3.0 GPA. Apply by November 1.

International Student Exchange Program (ISEP). Semester and academic year. Direct reciprocal exchange between U.S. universities and institutions in Braunschweig, Eichstät, Geissen, Kassel, Marburg, and Trier. Full curriculum options. Rolling admissions. Open only to students at ISEP-member institutions. Contact ISEP for list of members.

Kalamazoo College. *Kalamazoo in Erlangen.* Fall semester and academic year. University-integrated program. Juniors and seniors with 2 years of college German and 2.75 GPA. Apply by March 15.

Lewis and Clark College. *Year of Study in Munich.* Academic year. Offered in cooperation with Reed College and Willamette University. Intensive academic and cultural orientation in preparation for direct enrollment in University of Munich. Liberal arts and German language; instruction in German. Juniors and seniors with 3.0 GPA and two years of college German. Apply by February 1.

Loyola Marymount University. Bonn. Semester and academic year. Business, liberal arts, fine and communication arts, and science and engineering. Internships and excursions. Sophomores to seniors with 2.8 GPA. Apply by March 30 for fall and academic year; November 15 for spring.

Millersville University. *Junior Year in Marburg*. Study at Phillips University. Juniors with two years of college German and 2.4 GPA. Apply by February 15.
Portland State University. *Baden-Württemberg Program*. Academic year. Juniors to graduate students and teachers with two years of college German. Apply by January 31.
Northwest Interinstitutional Council on Study Abroad—Cologne. See listing under American Heritage Association.
Rosary College. *Rosary in Heidelberg*. Semester and academic year. Full range of academic courses at University of Heidelberg and/or its institutes; instruction in German. Juniors and seniors with two years of college German and 3.0 GPA. Apply by April 1 for fall and academic year; November 1 for spring. Contact: Ann Charney, Director of Study Abroad, Rosary College, River Forest, IL 60305; (708) 524-6948.
Rutgers University. *Junior Year in Germany*. Constance. Academic year. Juniors with two years of college German, 3.0 GPA, and German literature courses. Apply by March 1.
Scripps College. *Scripps Program in Heidelberg*. Semester and academic year. Study at University of Heidelberg. Sophomores to seniors with four semesters of college German and B-minus average. Apply by February 1 for fall and academic year; September 25 for spring.
State University of New York College at Cortland. *Schiller International University*. Heidelberg. Fall and spring semesters. Humanities, social sciences, and business administration. Excursions and dormitory housing. Sophomores to seniors with one semester of college German and 2.5 GPA. Apply by March 7 for fall; October 15 for spring. Contact: Office of International Programs, SUNY College at Cortland, PO Box 2000, Cortland, NY 13045; (607) 753-2209.
State University of New York College at Oneonta. *German Language and Literature Program*. Würzburg. Semester and academic year. Regular liberal arts and German language and literature courses at Bayerische Julius-Maximilians University; instruction in German. Juniors to graduate students with ability to understand lectures in German. Rolling admissions. Contact: International Education Office, Netzer Building 332C, SUNY College at Oneonta, Oneonta, NY 13820-4015; (607) 436-3369.
State University of New York College at Oswego. *Georg-August Universität in Göttingen*. Academic year. Juniors and seniors with fluent German. Apply by April 1. Contact: International Education, 102 Rich Hall, SUNY College at Oswego, Oswego, NY 13126; (315) 341-2118.
State University of New York at Stony Brook. Tübingen. Academic year. Sophomores to graduate students with two years of college German and 3.0 GPA. Apply by April 1. Contact: Dean for International Programs, SUNY at Stony Brook, Stony Brook, NY 11794-2700; (516) 632-7030.
Stetson University. Freiburg. Semester and academic year. Sophomores to seniors with two years of German and 2.5 GPA (3.0 in major). Apply by March 1 for fall and academic year; October 15 for spring.
Syracuse University. *Syracuse in Germany*. Marburg. Spring semester and academic year. Exchange program with Philipps Universität. Juniors and seniors with two years of college German and 3.0 GPA. Apply by March 15 for academic year; October 15 for spring. Contact: (800) 235-3472.
Tufts University. *Tufts in Tübingen*. Spring semester and academic year. Full university curriculum, German language, and German studies. Juniors and seniors with two years of college German and 3.0 GPA. Apply by February 1.

University of Colorado at Boulder. *Academic Year in Regensbourg.* Juniors and seniors with four semesters of college German and 2.75 GPA. Apply by March 1.

University of Massachusetts at Amherst. *Freiburg/Baden-Württemberg Exchange.* Academic year at Freiburg, Stuttgart, Konstanz, Heidelberg, and five other Baden-Württemberg universities. Juniors to graduate students with 3.0 GPA and fluency in German. Apply by March 1.

University of Nebraska—Lincoln. *Bayreuth University Exchange.* Bayreuth. Semester and academic year. German language and literature, business, natural sciences, law, computer science, geography, African studies, and sports economics; instruction in German. Dormitory housing. Sophomores to graduate students with four semesters of college German and 3.0 GPA. Open only to students at member institutions of the Association of Big Eight Universities. Apply by March 1 for academic year; October 1 for spring.

University of North Carolina at Chapel Hill. *UNC Program to Berlin.* Academic year. Sophomores to seniors with 3.0 GPA and fluency in German. Apply by February 14.

UNC Program to Göttingen. Academic year. Sophomores to seniors with 3.0 GPA and fluency in German. Apply by February 14.

UNC in Tübingen. Academic year. Sophomores to seniors with 3.0 GPA and two years of college German. Apply by February 14.

University of Oregon. *Northwest Interinstitutional Council on Study Abroad—Cologne.* See listing under American Heritage Association.

OSSHE—Baden-Württemberg Universities Exchange. Tübingen, Stuttgart, Mannheim, Konstanz, Hohenheim, Freiburg, Karlsruhe, or Ulm. Academic year. Students with two years of college German and 3.0 GPA. Apply by January 31.

University of Washington. *Northwest Interinstitutional Council on Study Abroad—Cologne.* See listing under American Heritage Association.

University of Wisconsin at Madison. *Academic Year at Rheinische Friedrich Wilhelms University.* Bonn. Liberal arts, business, German-language study, and natural sciences. Two-month business internship option. Juniors and seniors with five semesters of college German and in good academic standing. Open only to students at higher education institutions in Wisconsin or Wisconsin residents studying outside the state. Apply by second Friday in November.

Bonn Intensive Program at Rheinische Friedrich Wilhelms University. Bonn. Academic year. Semester-long intensive German-language study, followed by courses in liberal arts, business, German language, and natural sciences. Juniors and seniors with two semesters of college German and in good academic standing. Open only to students at higher education institutions in Wisconsin or Wisconsin residents studying outside the state. Apply by second Friday in February.

Academic Year Exchange in Frankfurt. Frankfurt. Humanities, social and physical sciences. Juniors to graduate students with five semesters of college German and in good academic standing. Open only to students at higher education institutions in Wisconsin or Wisconsin residents studying outside the state. Apply by second Friday in February.

Academic Year at Albert-Ludwigs University. Freiburg. German language study, humanities, social and natural sciences. Juniors and seniors in good academic standing and with five semesters of college German. Open only to students at higher education institutions in Wisconsin or Wisconsin residents studying outside the state. Apply by second Friday in November.

Academic Year at Giessen. Giessen. German-language study, humanities, social sciences and natural sciences. Juniors to graduate students in good academic standing and with five semesters of college German. Open only to students at higher education institutions in Wisconsin or Wisconsin residents studying outside the state. Apply by second Friday in February.

University of Wisconsin at Green Bay. *Kassel University Exchange*. Kassel. Semester and academic year. German language and culture. First-year college students to seniors with proficiency in German. Apply by March 15 for fall and academic year; November 15 for spring.

Washington State University. *Northwest Interinstitutional Council on Study Abroad—Cologne*. See listing under American Heritage Association.

Wayne State University. *Junior Year in Freiburg*. Academic year at Albert-Ludwigs University. Offered in conjunction with Michigan State University, University of Michigan, and University of Wisconsin. Juniors with 3.0 GPA and four semesters of college German. Seniors accepted on space-available basis. Apply by April 1.

Junior Year in Munich. Ludwig-Maximilians University. Academic year. Juniors with 3.0 GPA and four semesters of college German. Seniors accepted on space-available basis. Apply by April 1.

Wesleyan University. *Wesleyan University Program in Germany*. Regensburg. Spring semester. Preparatory language course plus spring semester at the University of Regensburg, where regular classes are supplemented by program tutorials. Sophomores to seniors with three semesters of German and 3.0 average in German. Apply by November 1.

Western Washington University. *Northwest Interinstitutional Council on Study Abroad—Cologne*. See listing under American Heritage Association.

World Learning/School for International Training. *College Semester Abroad*. Berlin. Fall and spring semesters. Intensive language, interdisciplinary seminar, field-study methods seminar, independent-study project. Homestays and excursions. Sophomores to seniors with 2.5 GPA. Apply by May 7 for fall; October 7 for spring. Contact: College Semester Abroad Admissions at (800) 336-1616.

German Language and Culture

Alma College. *Program of Studies in Germany*. Kassel. Semester and academic year. German language, literature, culture, and current events; instruction in German. Homestays and excursions. Sophomores to seniors with 2.5 GPA. Apply by June 15 for fall; October 15 for winter.

Colorado College. *German Semester in Lüneburg*. Spring semester. Intensive German language, literature, history, and politics; instruction in German. Homestays and excursions. Juniors and seniors with B average and two years of college German. Apply by April 15. Contact: Professor Aimin Wishard, Colorado College, Colorado Springs, CO 80903; (719) 389-6520.

Heidelberg College. *American Junior Year at Heidelberg*. Semester and academic year. German language and other subjects. Dormitory housing and excursions. Juniors and seniors with two years of college German (or equivalent). Apply by April 15 for fall and academic year; October 15 for spring. Contact: Dr. Raymond Wise, Registrar, Heidelberg College, 310 East Market Street, Tiffin, OH 44883; (419) 448-2090/2000.

Kalamazoo College. *Kalamazoo in Münster*. Fall and winter quarters (September 15 to February 15). Juniors and seniors with 15 quarter-hours of German and 2.5 GPA. Apply by March 15.

Middlebury College. *German School Abroad.* Mainz. Semester and academic year. Humanities, social sciences, German language, and German studies. Juniors to graduate students fluent in German. Rolling admissions. Contact: German School, Middlebury College, Middlebury, VT 05753; (802) 388-3711, ext. 5529.

Portland State University. *Spring Intensive Language Program.* Tübingen. Spring quarter. First-year college students to graduate students with two quarters of German and 2.5 GPA. Limited to students of Oregon State System of Higher Education. Apply by January 31.

University of Kansas. *Academic Year in Bonn.* Bonn. Academic year. German language and culture. Five-week orientation. Juniors and seniors with 3.0 GPA and two years of college German. Apply by February 15.

Semester Program in Berlin. Fall. One year at college German required. Apply by February 12.

University of Oregon. *OSSHE—Intensive German Language Program.* Tübingen. Spring semester. Sophomores to graduate students with two quarters of college German and 2.5 GPA. Apply by January 31.

World Learning/School for International Training. *College Semester Abroad—German Language Immersion.* Tübingen. Fall and spring semesters. Intensive language immersion, life and culture seminar. Homestays and excursions. Sophomores to seniors with 2.5 GPA. Apply by May 7 for fall; October 7 for spring. Contact: College Semester Abroad Admissions at (800) 336-1616.

Summer and Short-Term

Art and Architecture

Syracuse University. *The Making of Romanesque Art in Central Germany: The Use of Art for the Game of Power.* Berlin, Schierke, Hildesheim, Cologne, Worms, Aachen, and Frankfurt. Eighteen days in August. Development of various phases of Romanesque art, architectural monuments, sculpture, and objects. Undergraduates and graduates. Apply by March 1. Contact: (800) 235-3472.

General Studies

Loyola Marymount University. Bonn. Summer. Courses available in business, liberal arts, fine and communication arts, and science and engineering. Excursions. Sophomores to seniors and high-school graduates not enrolled in college with 2.8 GPA. Rolling admissions.

University of Kentucky. *Kentucky Institute for International Studies in Munich.* First-year college students to graduate students and adults. Apply by March 1.

German Language and Culture

Alma College. *Program of Studies in Germany.* Four- to eleven-week programs in summer. Instruction in German. Homestays and excursions. Sophomores to seniors with 2.5 GPA. Apply by March 15.

Illinois State University. *Summer Program in Germany.* Bonn. Six-week program in summer. German language, literature, and culture. Dormitory housing. First-year students to graduate students with intermediate German.

Apply by March 12. Contact: Dr. David J. Parent, 4300 Foreign Language Department, Illinois State University, Normal, IL 61761; (309) 438-7192.

International Student Exchange Program (ISEP). Rostock. Three-week program in June and July. Offered in cooperation with Northwestern State University of Louisiana. Intensive German language and culture for beginning to advanced students of German. Sophomores to graduate students with 2.5 GPA. Apply by March 1.

Miami University. Heidelberg and Berlin. Summer. Intensive German. Homestays and excursions. High-school graduates and up with one year college of German. Apply by February 15.

Michigan State University. *German Language Program in Mayen.* Summer. Juniors and seniors with two years of college German. Apply by April 15. Contact: Office of Overseas Study, 108 International Center, Michigan State University, East Lansing, MI 48824-1035; (517) 353-8920.

Northern Arizona University. *German Intensive Language Program.* Tübingen. April to July. Offered in cooperation with Eberhard-Karls-Universität. Sophomores (with 2.5 GPA) to graduate students with one semester of German. Apply by November 15.

Rutgers University. *Summer in Constance.* Mid-July to late August. High-school seniors to college seniors. Contact: Department of Germanic Languages, 64 College Avenue, Rutgers University, New Brunswick, NJ 08903; (908) 932-7201.

State University of New York College at New Paltz. *Summer Study in Germany.* Hamburg and Stade. Six weeks in summer. Intensive German language and civilization program. Excursions. High-school students to graduate students with one year of college German. Rolling admissions. Contact: Office of International Education, HAB 33, SUNY College at New Paltz, New Paltz, NY 12561; (914) 257-3125.

State University of New York College at Oneonta. *German and European Studies.* Würzburg. Summer. Ten-week program in German history, music, sciences, law, philosophy, and political science. Dormitory housing with German students. Sophomores to seniors. Rolling admissions. Contact: International Education Office, Netzer Building 332C, SUNY at Oneonta, Oneonta, NY 13820-4015; (607) 436-3369.

University of Alabama. *Alabama in Germany.* Weingarten, Munich, and Berlin. Summer. Excursions. Freshmen to graduate students with two semesters of college German. Apply by March 1. Contact: (205) 348-5256.

University of Colorado at Boulder. *Study Abroad in Kassel.* Summer. Intensive German language at all levels. Undergraduates with 2.75 GPA. Apply by March 1.

University of Louisville. *Unified Germany in a United Europe.* Mainz. Political science and sociology. Excursions. Freshmen to graduate students. Apply by March 15.

University of Maryland. *Summer in Kassel.* Sophomores to seniors with two years of college German with 3.0 GPA in German. Apply by March 15.

University of Nebraska at Lincoln. *Language and Culture in Germany.* Köln and Schwäbisch Hall. Winter break. Intensive study of German language and culture. Family visits and excursions. High-school graduates, college undergraduates, graduate students and adults with three semesters of German language. Apply by October 1.

University of North Carolina at Chapel Hill. *Munich Summer Program.* Munich. Four weeks in summer. German language and culture study.

Undergraduates to graduate students with two semesters of college German. Apply by March 15.

University of Pennsylvania. *Penn-in-Freiburg*. For students interested in German language studies. One year of German required. Apply by April 1.

University of South Carolina. *USC Summer Study in Lichtenfels*. Lichtenfels. Four weeks in summer. German language and culture study. Sophomores to seniors with two semesters of college German. Apply by January 15.

University of Utah. *Kiel German Language Program*. Christian-Albrechts University. Six weeks in summer. Undergraduates, graduate students, and others with 2.0 GPA and recommended one or two quarters of college German. Apply by March 1.

University of Washington. *Summer in Munich*. Munich. Summer. German-language study, culture. Sophomores to seniors with one year of college German. Apply by May 15.

Villanova University. *Freiburg Summer Program in Germany*. Frieburg. From early July to late August. Intensive German language study. Freshmen to seniors with 2.5 GPA and one year of college German. Apply by March 15.

Social Work

University of Louisville. *Social Work in Munich*. Two weeks during spring semester. Munich. Exchange program with the Katholische Stiftungsfachhochschule. Graduate students and social-work professionals. Apply by January 30.

EXPLORING GERMAN CULTURE

Readings

Until recently, postwar German literature has been divided into two camps—East and West. However, on both sides of the Iron Curtain similar themes were explored, and together the two bodies of work offer insight into Germany's fascinating political and historical background.

The legacy of World War II is a theme that pervaded West German writing. Thomas Mann's *Mario and the Magician* is a 40-page novelette dealing with the rise of Nazi Germany. One of the pioneers of postwar German literature, Heinrich Böll, is the author of *The Bread of Those Early Years*, the story of love transforming a cynic in a post–World War II Rhineland town. Günter Grass, a prolific writer, continues to write about the problems and guilt caused by the war. *The Tin Drum* is one of his finest works; along with *Cat and Mouse* and *Dog Years*, it forms the well-known *Danzig Trilogy*. Siegfried Lenz, another critical, politically oriented writer of Grass's generation, is the author of *The German Lesson* (1986) and *Homeland Museum* (1978). Botho Strauss's novels and plays, such as *A Rumour* and *The Young Man* (1989), reflect modern German concerns with establishing identity by looking back at German history, particularly to World War II.

Peter Schneider, who lived in West Berlin, is the author of *Knife in the Head* and *The Wall Jumper* (1985), which deal with the tensions of life in this West German island in the middle of East Germany during the Cold War era. A more current novel about Berlin and the symbolic division that, until recently, it represented is Ian Walker's *Zoo Station* (1987). Littered with ultra-hip references to underground dance clubs, Engels, and black-market Levi's, Walker's rambling prose chronicles the two Berlins, "where two systems of life and thought wage war."

Franz Xavier Kroetz depicts the lower depths of Bavarian society in books like *Agnes Bernauer* and *Maria Magdalena*, the story of a single working-class woman and the problems she encounters when she discovers that she is pregnant. Gabriele Wohmann writes about women trying to find themselves in an atmosphere of modern urban angst. In *Serious Intention*, for instance, a woman, in recounting her life during a sickness, deals with problems of women in modern Germany and the conflicts between the generations. Walter Abish, a noteworthy modern German-American writer, recently treated the same subject with surprising insight in *How German Is It* (1980).

Like their Western counterparts, East German writers also have a strong political streak. After World War II, they had to confront not only the legacy of the war but also a new political system and way of life. In *A Model Childhood* (1980), Christa Wolf writes about her childhood in Nazi Germany and coming to terms with it in later life. *Cassandra* (1984), perhaps her most widely read book, is a very personal and searching look at the complexities of life in East Germany.

Other modern writers from the eastern sector include Ulrich Plensdorf, who used a famous work by Goethe (*The Sorrows of Young Werther*) as the basis for a novel dealing with the problems of life in East Germany in the 1970s, *The New Sorrows of Young Werther* (1978). In a similar vein, *Sleepless Days*, by Jurek Becker, describes the monotony of living in an authoritarian society. Herman Kant, whose novels were published mostly in the 1960s and 1970s (*The Assembly Hall* among them), was another critic of life in East Germany, although he believed in the principles on which the government and economy were organized.

Films

Early German filmmaking is best represented by the films made between the two world wars, pictures known for their production values and high technical quality. Many of the themes in such films as *Die Niebeulungen*, by Fritz Lang, *The Student of Prague*, by Henrik Galeen, and *The Cabinet of Dr. Caligari*, by Robert Wiene, call upon German folklore and tradition. Later films of this period delved into subjects associated with modern urban life: crime, graft, and seduction are the focus of G. W. Pabst's *The Threepenny Opera* (1931); sexual intrigue characterized Josef Von Sternberg's *The Blue Angel* (1930) and Pabst's *Pandora's Box* (1929); and the life of a pathological child murderer and mob justice was the subject of Lang's *M* (1931).

R. W. Fassbinder's *The Marriage of Maria Braun* (1979) was an extended metaphor for postwar Germany. He linked contemporary Germany with German history in *Berlin Alexanderplatz* (1979) and *Lili Marlene* (1980). This preoccupation with German history and tradition and Germany's peculiar relationship with the U.S. is also found in the films of Hans Jurgen Syberberg, which include *Our Hitler*, *Parsifal*, and *Ludwig the Mad Bavarian King*. Similar themes pervade Wim Wenders's work: *Wings of Desire* (1988), a love story under the big top, and *The American Friend* (1977), loosely based on a psychological thriller by Patricia Highsmith.

Other German films of note include Volker Schlöndorff's *The Tin Drum* (1979), the story of a boy who refuses to grow physically while the Nazis take power, and *The Lost Honor of Katherine Blum* (1975), a film based on a Heinrich Böll novel. Ulrike Ottinger's *Ticket of No Return*, an investigation into female identity, is also worth viewing. *The Nasty Girl* (1989), directed by Michael Verhoeven, is an award-winning black comedy with a misleading English translation as a title. Based on a true story, the plot revolves around a young student attempting to write an essay about the Nazis who quickly becomes an object of scorn for townspeople with a surprising amount to conceal. The film offers a fascinating glimpse of today's Germany, moving forward but still trying to deal with its past.

GREECE

The land of ancient Greece has little in common with the country of today. The arid, hilly land that gave birth to many seminal Western philosophers is now often seen as a yearlong party by youthful visitors from around the globe in search of sunny beaches and cheap beer. This superficial image does little justice to Greece's multifaceted culture. Absorbing both European and Middle Eastern influences, Greece's seemingly effortless Mediterranean lifestyle belies the complexity of its history and the character of its people. To view Greece as little more than a global soirée is to overlook the rich culture and fascinating past of a group of islands whose contributions to Western culture have spread far beyond its water-bound boundaries. Like Plato's analogy of the Cave, Greece's tourist-forged images are merely shadows of its deeper identity.

Greece was ruled by Turkey for much of the Middle Ages, until the allied navies of Britain, France, and Russia helped Greece regain independence—keeping, however, a few fingers on the proverbial political steering wheel. The 20th century for Greece was tragically littered with uprisings, coups, and a debilitating civil war between the Communists (who formed the core of wartime resistance against the Germans during WWII) and the Western-backed right-wing ''government'' forces. A coup in 1967 instituted a military dictatorship that lasted until 1974. For the last decade or so, Greece has experienced relative democratic stability and economic growth, due in part to its healthy tourist economy and its EC membership.

Greece is truly a country of natural beauty. Its beaches and mountains will fulfill anyone's postcard-photo expectations; the only problem might lie in finding an alcove that hasn't already been ''discovered.'' Culturally, Greece is an interesting mélange of influences—ancient and modern, Middle Eastern and European. Although some Greeks are slightly embittered by the never-ending stream of tourists, the simple courtesy of learning a few words in Greek will soften even the toughest: ''Please'' is *parakaló*. ''Thank you'' is *efharistó*.

The treasures of its ancient civilization are often overlooked by tired travelers eager for a place to set down their bags, but should be seen at all costs. The Acropolis in Athens, the Parthenon, the isle of Lesbos, Mount Olympus: Your knowledge of and curiosity about Greek history and mythology will help shape your itinerary. Museums, local artisans, archeological wonders—these things make Greece fascinating. Renting a moped and whizzing along hilly roads, passing every once in a while through the musky stench of rotting olives (a scent unlike anything else in this world); swimming through clear warm water without another being in sight; or sitting at a small café on the oceanside munching on feta cheese and fresh bread: To be sure, the other pleasures of Greece are not to be ignored.

—Nicole Ellison, Los Angeles, California

Official name: Hellenic Republic. **Size:** 51,146 square miles (about the size of Arkansas). **Population:** 10,042,000. **Population density:** 196 inhabitants per square mile. **Capital and largest city:** Athens (pop. 3,016,457). **Language:** Greek. **Religion:** Greek Orthodox. **Per capita income:** US$7,650. **Currency:** Drachma. **Literacy rate:** 92%. **Average daily temperature:** Athens: June, 76°F; December, 52°F. **Average number of days with precipitation:** Athens: June, 4; December, 15.

TRAVEL

A passport is required for U.S. citizens visiting Greece. However, a visa is not required for stays up to three months. For more information, contact the **Greek Embassy**, 2221 Massachusetts Avenue NW, Washington, DC 20008; (202) 939-5800. There are also Greek Consulates General in Atlanta, Boston, Chicago, Houston, New Orleans, New York, and San Francisco.

Getting Around

Ferries shuttle between the islands, always jammed with young vacationers. Eurail and Interrail passes may be used on Greek trains and many ferries. In addition, Rail Europe offers a **Greek Railpass**, which allows 5 days of first-class travel in 15 for $70, or 10 days in one month for $125. Second-class passes cost $62 and $99, respectively. You might also be interested in asking about the **Greek Rail 'n' Drive Pass**, which allows 5 days of rail travel and 2 days of car rental within 15 days. For two travelers driving an economy car in the high season, for example, the cost would be $129 per person. Both passes are available through Rail Europe (see page 62) or Council Travel (see pages xiii–xvi).

Greece offers outstanding opportunities for **hiking** and mountaineering. *Greece on Foot: Mountain Treks, Island Trails* is available for $10.95 from The Mountaineers Books. Lonely Planet publishes *Trekking in Greece* ($15.95). For more information on The Mountaineers and Lonely Planet, see pages 56–57.

Eating and Sleeping

There are a number of **youth hostels** scattered about the Greek islands. For information, contact Hostelling International/American Youth Hostels (see page 54) or the **Greek Youth Hostels Association**, 4 Dragatsaniou Street, Athens 105 59; (30) 1-3234107; fax (30) 1-3237590.

Especially for Students and Young People

A student travel organization active in Greece is **Usit,** 1 Filellinon Street Syntagma Square, 105 57 Athens; (30) 1-3241884; fax (30) 1-3225974. Usit also has an office in Salonika. Both offices offer student/youth discounts on ferries, international flights, and international train tickets.

For Further Information

A good source of general travel information is the **Greek National Tourist Organization**, 645 Fifth Avenue, Fifth Floor, New York, NY 10022; (212) 421-5777.

Budget travelers will want to take along *Greece: A Travel Survival Kit*, available for $15.95 from Lonely Planet Publications. However, island hoppers will find *Cadogan Guides' Greek Islands* ($16.95) an all-around better guide. Also good is *The Real Guide: Greece* ($18). An excellent book to read in preparation for your trip is *Insight Guide: Greece* ($19.95). For more information on Lonely Planet, *Cadogan Guides, Real Guides*, and *Insight Guides*, see pages 56–57.

WORK

Job opportunities are scarce, and the Greek government tries to limit employment to Greek citizens and visitors from the European Community (EC). A work permit is mandatory and is granted for specialized work only; contact the **Ministry of Labor**, 40 Pireos Street, 10437 Athens. Foreign firms located in Greece are allowed to secure work permits for their foreign employees. For $40, you can get a list of American firms and subsidiaries operating in Greece from **The American Hellenic Chamber of Commerce**, 17 Valaoritou Street, 10671 Athens. They can provide advice on how to get a short- or long-term position in Greece.

Internships/Traineeships

A program offered by a member of the Council on International Educational Exchange is listed below.

Association for International Practical Training. *IAESTE Trainee Program.* On-the-job training for undergraduate and graduate students in technical fields such as engineering, computer science, agriculture, architecture, mathematics, and the natural and physical sciences. See page 19 for more information.

In addition, the **American Farm School/Summer Work Activities Program** sponsors a program on the farm in Thessaloniki for eight weeks during the summer. Participants bale hay, harvest crops, milk cows, and do other various types of farm work. For more information contact the American Farm School, 1133 Broadway at 26th Street, New York, NY 10010.

STUDY

Contact the **Office of Press Information** of the Greek Embassy (see "Travel," above) for their fact sheets on summer and academic year study in Greece.

The study programs offered by CIEE-member institutions are listed below. Unless otherwise noted, consult Appendix I for the addresses of the colleges and universities listed in this section.

Semester and Academic Year

Archaeology and Classical Studies

Beaver College. *Classical, Byzantine, and Modern Greek Studies.* Athens. Semester and academic year. Co-curricular field-study trips to northern Greece and the Peloponnesus. Juniors and seniors with 3.0 GPA. Apply by April 20 for fall and academic year; October 15 for spring.

Business

State University of New York—Empire State College. *Athens: Business Studies*. Semester and academic year. Individually designed study programs in business and the European Community, supervised by U.S. and Greek faculty at most institutions in Athens. Sophomores to graduate students. Apply by June 1 for fall and academic year; November 15 for spring.

General Studies

Brethren Colleges Abroad. University of La Verne in Athens. Semester and academic year. Full range of academic curriculum. Excursions and study tours. English teaching work arranged upon request. Sophomores to graduate students (in business and management studies) with 2.8 GPA. Apply by April 15 for fall and academic year; November 1 for spring.

Portland State University. *PSU in Athens*. Fall and spring quarters. Offered in conjunction with Central Washington University and Western Washington University. History, political science, art history, and modern Greek. Excursions. First-year college students to graduate students with 2.5 GPA. Apply by July 15 for fall; August 25 for spring.

Western Washington University. *Study in Greece*. Athens Centre. Fall and spring quarters. Offered in conjunction with Central Washington University and Portland State University. History, political science, art history, and modern Greek. Apartment housing and field trips. First-year college students to graduate students with 2.5 GPA. Apply by August 1 for fall; March 1 for spring. Contact: (800) 426-1349.

World Learning/School for International Training. *College Semester Abroad—Island Culture and Environment*. Thessaloniki; and Mytilene, Lesbos. Fall and spring semesters. Intensive language, island culture and environment seminar, field-study methods seminar, and independent-study project. Homestays and excursions. Sophomores to seniors with 2.5 GPA. Apply by May 7 for fall; October 7 for spring. Contact: College Semester Abroad Admissions, (800) 336-1616.

Summer and Short-Term

Archaeology and Classical Studies

Adventist Colleges Abroad. Athens. Six-week intensive summer course in intermediate New Testament Greek or Biblical archaeology. Excursions. Sophomores to seniors with 2.5 overall GPA and one year of beginning New Testament Greek (2.5 GPA). Apply by March 25.

Boston University. *Ancient Greece*. Various cities. Summer. In-depth introduction to political and cultural history of ancient Greece with visits to major sites including Delphi and Olympia. Sophomores to college graduates in good academic standing. Apply by April 1.

Archaeological Field School. Nikopolis. Summer. Multidisciplinary archaeological survey project; use of advanced technology. Sophomores to seniors, college graduates, and graduate students in good academic standing. Apply by April 1.

Southern Illinois University at Carbondale. *Travel Study Program to Greece and Egypt.* Summer. Seminars on ancient Greek experience. High-school graduates to college graduates and adults with college background. Apply by April 1.
State University of New York College at Brockport. *Greek Mythology.* Instruction at relevant sites such as Crete, Athens, and Philopapas. Summer. Undergraduates and graduates. Apply by March 15. Contact: Office of International Education, SUNY College at Brockport, Brockport, NY 14420; (716) 395-2119.

Art and Architecture

Syracuse University. *Summer in the Aegean: An Exploration of Classical and Vernacular Greek Architecture.* Greek islands, Athens, and the Peloponnese. Site visits. Undergraduates and graduate students. Apply by March 1. Contact: (800) 235-3472.

General Studies

University of North Carolina at Chapel Hill. *UNC Summer Program to Greece.* Excursions to various cities. Sophomores to graduate students.

EXPLORING GREEK CULTURE

Readings

Greek literature is divided into two very distinct categories: ancient and modern. Among Greece's modern bards, Nikos Kazantzakis has been the most celebrated. His most famous novels are *Zorba the Greek* (1946) and *The Last Temptation of Christ* (1971). *Zorba* is a masterful character study of an exuberant, larger-than-life Greek man and his relationship with a British intellectual who is visiting the country, while the controversial *Temptation* casts Jesus Christ in a very human role, in which he doubts his destiny as savior and wishes to lead an ordinary life. Other books by Kazantzakis deal more explicitly with life in Greece. *The Fratricides* (1964) is about a priest who tries to mediate between the Communists and the Loyalists during the Greek civil wars of the 1940s; *The Greek Passion* (1954) is a reenactment of Christ's crucifixion in a Greek village; and *Freedom or Death* (1956) focuses on events during the Cretan Revolt of 1889.

In recent years, women have been making their mark on contemporary Greek literature. The most prominent female author Greece has produced is Dido Sotiriou. Her *Farewell Anatolia* is considered a classic in Greece; it retraces the traumatic end of Greek life in Asia Minor from 1912 to 1922. *The New Moon with the Old Moon in Her Arms* (1990), by Ursule Molinaro, is a story of a young poet in ancient Athens who observes the Moon Goddess Circe's decline in popularity and predicts a similar fate for mortal women in Greek society. Sheelagh Kanelli, a British woman who has spent much of her adult life in Greece, reconstructs events leading up to a catastrophe in a small Greek village in her brief but vivid novel *Nets* (1985).

Other recent releases from Greece include the best-seller *Achilles' Fiancée*, by Alki Zei; *The History of a Vendetta*, by Yiorgo Yatromanolakis, a magic-realist novel about two families who unravel a murder in a Cretan village; and Petros Haris's collection of short stories set in Athens during the German occupation of 1940–44, *The Longest Night: Chronicle of a Dead City*.

Films

Greek cinema reached an all-time high in the 1960s and early '70s when both attendance and production peaked. The greatest films of this period were the film adaptation of Nikos Kazantzakis's *Zorba the Greek* (1964), Costa-Gavras's screen version of the novel Z (1968), and *Never on Sunday* (1959). Written and directed by Jules Dassin, *Never on Sunday* recasts the Pygmalion theme with an American scholar who becomes infatuated with a Greek prostitute.

The Greek film industry again experienced a comeback beginning in the mid-'80s when flagging cinema funding was increased. The 1984 film *The Price of Love*, by Tonia Marketaki, takes place at the turn of the century on Corfu and tells the story of a daughter who spoils her mother's dreams of a respectable marriage by moving in with her lover. Many films from this period explore the nation's feelings of devastation and pain over the scarring civil war between the Communists and democratic forces that broke out immediately after the Second World War. The most moving film of this genre would probably be Pandelis Voulgaris's *Stone Years*, which focuses on the love story of a couple suspected of Communist sympathies who are reunited only after 20 years. The winner of almost all the Thessaloniki Film Festival awards in 1988, *In the Shadow of Fear*, by George Karapidis, is an excellently produced Kafka-esque thriller about a mysterious composer who flees unknown pursuers. Athens-bound explores may want to check out *Quiet Days in August*, by director Pandelis Voulgaris, or George Tsemberopoulos's *Take Care*, both offering unusual glimpses of Athenian life.

HUNGARY

With the rest of Eastern Europe, Hungary forges ahead in its economic and political transformation geared toward integration into the European Community by the year 2000. The continuing modernization and privatization of the economy have put strains on Hungarian society. The consequent economic pressures, resulting in rising unemployment coupled with Hungary's willingness to accept refugees from the wars in the former Yugoslavia, have led to increased instances of racism in the streets and the emergence of a rightist-nationalist polity. However, the progressive elements in Hungarian society are a source of stability in the changing times and have served as the country's backbone in the early years of post-communist democracy.

Budapest, home to 20 percent of Hungary's population, is the thriving center of Hungarian cultural, political, and economic activity. Its markets overflow with produce, including a wide variety of paprika, kolbasz, cheeses, and meat products from the countryside. A number of building projects, including the construction of a new subway line, have begun in Budapest in preparation for the 1996 World Expo, jointly hosted with Vienna. The cooperation with Austria in co-sponsoring the Expo reflects the historical ties between Austria and Hungary, dating back to the Hapsburg Monarchy, which became notable for Austrian investment in Hungary in the 1970s and '80s.

Hungary emerged from the fall of communism in 1989 in better shape than its neighbors, primarily because of a history of economic reforms dating back to the New Economic Mechanism in 1968. The allocations for small-scale privatization seen in the 1970s and '80s coupled with increased Western investment and lending provided the economic fix for "goulash communism." These factors have served Hungary well in the political transition, and Hungarians credit them with the success of reform. The younger, educated class benefitted most from goulash Communism, as it included a loosening of travel restrictions to the West and greater interaction with foreigners.

Today's politics often revolve around the international situation, since Hungary borders Serbia on the south. The presence of over 500,000 Hungarians in Serbia, two million in Transylvania, and 600,000 in Slovakia as a result of the post–World War I Treaty of Trianon—which stripped Hungary of two-thirds of its territory—continues to play a leading role in Hungarian politics and to fuel the popularity of the Hungarian right. Media reports abound with discussion of the Hungarians in neighboring countries, which were once part of a greater Hungary.

No visit to Hungary should go without excursions to the Great Plain, home of the Hungarian *csikos* (horsemen); Lake Balaton, the largest freshwater lake in Europe; the wine centers in Eger and Tokaj; and the historic university towns of Szeged, Debrecen, Pécs, Miskolc, and Györ. It is in the cities outside of Budapest and the outlying countryside where visitors best experience Hungarian culture and traditions.

—John Meyers, New York, New York

Official name: Republic of Hungary. **Area:** 35,919 square miles (about the size of Indiana). **Population:** 10,588,000. **Population density:** 294 inhabitants per square mile. **Capital and largest city:** Budapest (pop. 2,016,000). **Language:** Magyar. **Religion:** Roman Catholic, Protestant. **Per capita income:** US$5,800. **Currency:** Forint. **Literacy rate:** 98%. **Average daily temperature:** Budapest: June, 68°F; December, 35°F. **Average number of days with precipitation:** Budapest: June, 13; December, 13.

TRAVEL

Holders of a U.S. passport can stay in Hungary for up to 90 days without a visa. If you wish to stay for more than 90 days, you must report to the local police authority in Hungary for the proper documentation. For further information, contact the **Embassy of the Republic of Hungary**, 3910 Shoemaker Street NW, Washington, DC 20008, (202) 362-6737.

Getting Around

Whether you're traveling by bus, train, or car, the quickest route between any two points in the country will probably be through Budapest, the hub of the nation's transportation system. Hungarian **trains** are inexpensive, clean, and reliable. Eurail and InterRail passes are valid in Hungary, and the **European East Pass** is valid in Hungary, as well as the Czech and Slovak Republics, Poland, and Austria. Available in first class only, rail travel on any 5 days within a 15-day period is $169, and any 10 days within one month is $275. A new Hungarian Flexipass (first class) gives you 5 days of travel in 15 for $39 or 10 days of travel in one month for $59. Contact Rail Europe (see page 62) or Council Travel (see pages xiii–xvi).

Bus service is also cheap but slower and more crowded than the train. One of the most enjoyable ways to travel (and the most expensive) is on the Danube **hydrofoils** between Vienna and Budapest. You can get information on **cycling** from IBUSZ offices (see "For Further Information," below) as well as local Tourinform offices or by writing to the **Hungarian Cycling Federation**, Szabó J. u. 3., Budapest 1146.

Eating and Sleeping

Accommodations are easy to find and inexpensive. There are a number of **youth hostels** in Hungary. For more information, contact Hostelling International/American Youth Hostels (see page 54) or EXPRESS Travel (see "Especially for Students and Young People," below). **IBUSZ**, the Hungarian national travel agency, with offices in city centers throughout the country, will reserve rooms in hotels or private homes. In Budapest, the main IBUSZ office is located on the Pest side of the Danube near the Hotel Continental. For IBUSZ's U.S. address, see "For Further Information," below.

Especially for Students and Young People

Hungary's youth/student travel bureau and issuer of the International Student Identity Card is **EXPRESS**, Szabadság Tér 16, 1395 Budapest 5; (36) 1-530660; fax (36) 1-1531715. EXPRESS has 35 office sites and operates 32 hostels and hotels around the country. Vouchers for accommodations at EXPRESS hostels and hotels are available through Council Travel offices.

For Further Information

For general tourist information, contact Hungary's official travel agency, **IBUSZ**, 1 Parker Plaza, Suite 1104, Fort Lee, NJ 07024; (201) 592-8585. IBUSZ also has a midwest office at 233 North Michigan Avenue, Suite 1308, Chicago, IL 60601; (312) 819-3510. Their catalog includes information on tours, hotels, car rentals, and travel packages.

The Real Guide: Hungary ($12.95) is an invaluble source of information on independent travel on a budget in Hungary. An excellent book to read in preparation for your trip is *Insight Guide: Hungary* ($19.95). For more information on *Real Guide*s and *Insight Guide*s, see pages 56–57.

WORK

It is possible to work for a company in Hungary that is partially or totally foreign-owned. To get a regular paid job, you will need to obtain a work permit, which is secured with proof of employment in Hungary. Contact the Embassy of the Republic of Hungary (see "Travel," above) for specific regulations on the subject. As an alternative to regular employment, you might be interested in a trainee program or participation in a workcamp.

If you're interested in **teaching** in Hungary, **Beloit College** sponsors "Teach Hungary," a placement service that matches qualified college graduates with Hungarian primary and secondary schools to teach English as a Foreign Language (TEFL). Some TEFL experience is required. Teachers are required to teach for the full academic year, which runs from September 1 through mid-June; participants have the option to stay longer, if desired. For more information, contact Lesley Davis, Beloit College, Box 242, 700 College Street, Beloit, WI 53511; (608) 363-2619.

Internships/Traineeships

Programs offered by members of the Council on International Educational Exchange are described below.

Association for International Practical Training. *IAESTE Trainee Program.* On-the-job training for undergraduate and graduate students in technical fields such as engineering, computer science, agriculture, architecture, mathematics, and the physical and natural sciences. See page 19 for more information. *Hospitality/Tourism Exchanges Program.* On-the-job training for young people beginning a career in the hotel and food-service industries. Participants must have graduated from a university or vocational school and possess at least six months of training or experience in the chosen field. Training usually runs from 6 to 18 months.

State University of New York College at Brockport. *Internships in Hungary.* Various sites in and around Budapest. Fall and spring semesters. Placement with Hungarian businesses and governmental organizations. Juniors to graduate students with 2.5 GPA (3.0 in major). Apply by April 1 for fall; November 1 for spring. Contact: Office of International Education; SUNY College at Brockport, Brockport, NY 14470; (716) 395-2119.

Voluntary Service

CIEE places young people in voluntary-service **workcamps** in Hungary organized by **UNIO** in Budapest. At these workcamps, groups of volunteers from different countries work on a variety of restoration and environmental projects. Volunteers must be 18 years of age or older; room and board are provided. The applications of U.S. residents are processed by CIEE. For more information, contact CIEE's International Voluntary Service Department.

STUDY

Persons considering study in Hungary might want to check out the *AAASS Directory of Programs in Russian, Eurasian, and East European Studies*, which lists close to 75 academic programs in Russia, Eurasia, and Eastern Europe, including addresses and information on deadlines and costs. The directory also lists similar study programs in the U.S. and can be ordered prepaid from the **American Association for the Advancement of Slavic Studies**, Jordan Quad/Acacia, 125 Panama Street, Stanford, CA 94305-4130; (415) 723-9668. The price is $30 for nonmembers, $20 for members, plus $3 postage; you might be able to find it in libraries or study-abroad offices.

The following educational programs are offered by CIEE-member institutions. Unless otherwise noted, consult Appendix I for the addresses where you can write for further information.

Semester and Academic Year

General Studies

American University. *Budapest Semester.* Spring semester. Politics, economics, history, and Hungarian language; internships optional. Two-week field trip to

Russia. Second-semester sophomores to seniors with 2.75 GPA. Apply by October 15. Contact: World Capitals Programs, American University, Dunblane House—Tenley Campus, Washington, DC 20016-8083; (202) 895-4900/4937.

Beaver College. *The Program in European Transition at the Center for European Studies.* Berzsenyi College in Szombathely. Semester and academic year. Political science and Hungarian language. Excursions. Juniors and seniors with 3.0 GPA. Apply by April 20 for fall and academic year; October 15 for spring.

Beloit College. *Hungary Exchange Program.* Eotvos Kollegium in Budapest. Spring semester. Hungarian language, literature, and history. Housing with Hungarian students. Sophomores to graduate students with 3.0 GPA. Apply by November 1.

Council on International Educational Exchange. *Cooperative East and Central European Studies Program at the Budapest University of Economic Sciences.* Fall and spring semesters. Internships available in such fields as business, environmental science, law, public administration, and English. Undergraduates with 2.75 GPA and six semester-hours in economics, history, or other social science discipline. Apply by April 10 for fall; November 1 for spring. Contact University Programs Department.

International Student Exchange Program (ISEP). Budapest. Semester and academic year. Direct reciprocal exchange between U.S. institutions and Janus Pannonius University, Lajos Kossuth University, and Technical University of Budapest. Full curriculum options. Rolling admissions. Open only to students at ISEP-member institutions. Contact ISEP for list of members.

Portland State University. Szeged. Semester and academic year. Hungarian language and culture at Joszef Attila University. Sophomores to seniors in good academic standing.

Trinity University. *Transformation of Central Europe.* Budapest. Fall semester. Offered in cooperation with Associated Colleges of the South and Millsaps College. Political and economic transformation of Central Europe, Central European culture, history, art, architecture, drama and film, and Hungarian language. Excursions to Austria, Czech Republic, and Poland. Sophomores to seniors in good academic standing. Apply by April 15. Contact: Dr. Karl Markgraf, Millsaps College, Jackson, MS 39210; (601) 974-1317.

University of Massachusetts at Amherst. *Exchange with Janus Pannonius University.* Pécs. Fall and spring semesters. Sophomores to seniors with 3.0 GPA. Apply by March 15 for fall; October 15 for spring.

University of Wisconsin at Madison. *Semester or Academic Year in Budapest.* Fall semester and academic year. Hungarian language, history, politics, and economics. Juniors to graduate students with a 2.75 GPA. Apply by February 15.

Summer and Short-Term

Archaeology and Classical Studies

North Carolina State University. *Summer Program in Environment and Archaeology.* Keszthely. June to August. Eight-week program offered in cooperation with Pannon University of Agriculture, Keszthely; Balaton Museum of Natural History, Keszthely; and National Institute of Archaeology, Budapest. Multi-disciplinary field school in archaeology and ecology of Pannonian Hungary: land use and technology on Northern Frontier of Roman Empire. Sophomores to graduate students. Apply by April 1.

Business

Ohio University. *Institute for Global Competitiveness.* Pécs. Six weeks in summer. Business administration with internship with Hungarian company. Excursions. Undergraduates. Apply by January 1. Contact: R. C. Scamehorn, 214 Copeland Hall, Ohio University, Athens, OH 45701; (614) 593-2025.

General Studies

International Student Exchange Program (ISEP). Budapest. Summer. Direct reciprocal exchange between U.S. institutions and Janus Pannonius University and Technical University of Budapest. Full curriculum options. Rolling admissions. Open only to students at ISEP-member institutions. Contact ISEP for list of members.
University of Massachusetts at Amherst. *Exchange with Janus Pannonius University.* Pécs. Sophomores to seniors with 3.0 GPA. Apply by March 15.

EXPLORING HUNGARIAN CULTURE

Readings

Modern Hungarian literature can be traced directly to the founding of the turn-of-the-century periodical *Nyugat* (West) by Hungary's leading writers in 1908. Zsigmond Moricz, the first Hungarian writer to demystify Hungarian peasant life, is one of the most significant prose writers in Hungarian literature (*Be Faithful unto Death*, 1962; *The Torch*, 1931). Moricz's studies inspired a new generation of writers intrigued by Hungarian peasant life. The *falukutatok*, or village sociographers, as they were known, addressed everyday life in rural Hungary. Gyula Illyés's *People of the Puszta* is an unromantic close-up view of village life and customs. However, Illyés is probably best known for his condemnation of the totalitarian state in his poem "One Sentence on Tyranny," which infused the 1956 revolutionary movement. T. Kabdebo and P. Tabori's *A Tribute to Gyula Illyés* contains selected poems and prose by Illyés.

Contemporary Hungarian literature is best noted in the works of Gyorgy Konrad, whose widely acclaimed *The Case Worker* (1974) gave voice to Hungary's suffering voiceless. Konrad, widely translated in the West, also wrote *The Loser* (1982), *The City Builder* (1987), and most recently, *Feast in the Garden* (1992). Peter Esterhazy's *Helping Verbs of the Heart* (1991) introduces Western readers to one of Hungary's leading contemporary prose writers. The prose of Hungary's writer-president, Arpad Goncz, can be found in his *Plays and Other Writings* (1990).

Films

The Hungarian film industry, always turning out a stream of critically acclaimed and politically relevant productions, has been the envy of Eastern Europe since World War II. One of the defining greats of Hungarian film is director István Szabó. His latest picture, *Sweet Emma, Darling Böbe* (1992), is an intimate story of two country girls trying to survive as teachers in post-Communist Budapest. *Mephisto*, which won the Academy Award for best foreign film in 1981, is a stylish, political drama about an actor in 1920s Germany who sells himself when the Nazis come to power. *Mephisto* is part of a trilogy completed by *Colonel Redl* (1984) and *Hanussen* (1988), both nominated for Academy Awards. *Redl* chronicles the ascent of a homosexual soldier of ordinary background to high military station, and his eventual suicidal death as a spy, while *Hanussen* is an intriguing tale of an Austrian World War I soldier, who becomes a clairvoyant and a pawn of the Nazis after he is shot in the head. Szabó's recent English-language film, *Meeting Venus* (1990), starring Glenn Close, was not as popular with the critics. Nonetheless, it is a thought-provoking comedy about a married Hungarian conductor who has an affair with the principal singer.

Another celebrated Hungarian director is Márta Mézároz. The winner of a special jury prize at Cannes in 1984, *Diary for My Children* (1982) is a gripping picture about three generations of a Hungarian family as seen through the eyes of an orphan who returns to Budapest after World War II. The sequel, *Diary for My Loves* (1987), concentrates on a young Hungarian woman who travels to Stalinist Moscow to become a filmmaker and to find her father. Respected director Miklós Jancsó's latest releases are *God Walks Backwards* (1991) and *The Blue Danube Waltz* (1992), a strong and honest movie based on the events surrounding a political assassination.

Other noteworthy films of Hungary include *The Revolt of Job* (1983), a touching film told from the viewpoint of a young Christian orphan taken in by a Jewish couple who fear the Nazis; *The Princess* (1982), a documentary-style movie about a teenager who discovers, after moving to Budapest, that life is tougher than she imagined; and the story of the incestuous love of a peasant step-brother and -sister, *Forbidden Relations* (1983).

ICELAND

Viewed from any angle, Iceland is a natural and cultural phenomenon and a terrific place to visit. The average life span of Icelandic women is the longest in the world, and that of Icelandic men is the second longest. The country's popular female president Vidis Finnbogadottir was swept into office for a third term in the summer of 1988. In social legislation Iceland has followed the example of the other Nordic countries: there is universal health insurance and an old-age pension plan. The streets are safe, and there is almost no violent crime. The water is among the purest in the world, and stunning, unspoiled nature dominates everywhere. Geothermal sources yield hot water year-round for 85 percent of all local homes. Beauty, strength, longevity, political enlightment, and a clean environment—what more could one ask!

Iceland has existed precariously for centuries, perched atop the Mid-Atlantic geological fault line. It is often called "the land of fire and ice" because volcanic eruptions have occured with great regularity over the centuries, and a full 11.5 percent of the island is covered with glaciers—including one called Vatnajokull, which—exclusive of Antarctica and Greenland—is the largest ice cap in the world. But due to the tempering influence of the Gulf Stream, Iceland enjoys a surprisingly moderate climate given that its northern tip crosses the Arctic Circle. Winters are mild, though stormy and humid, with the January temperature in Reykjavik averaging roughly the same as in Copenhagen (a lot milder than Chicago); summers are cool and can be rainy..But in June, July, and August, days and even weeks of crisp, gloriously sunny weather are not uncommon. Whatever the weather, the stark and beautiful landscape of Iceland is pure, dramatic, and utterly unforgettable for most visitors.

Iceland was for centuries the farthest outpost of Scandinavian Viking culture and for centuries the most Western extension of Christianity. The quarter of a million Icelanders living today on this large mid-Atlantic island are mainly the descendents of settlers who arrived from Norway from A.D. 879 to 950 with their families, slaves, sheep, and horses. Iceland has succeeded in preserving many of the rural values of its earliest Norwegian inhabitants, as well as their language—modern Icelandic is essentially old Norse. The Icelandic Commonwealth came under the Norwegian Crown in 1262, then was ruled by Denmark from 1814. Although Iceland became independent in 1918, it recognized the King of Denmark as a titular head of state until 1944, when Iceland declared itself a republic. Its Althing, or parliament, established in 930, is one of the oldest national legislative assemblies in the world. Bravely and against many environmental and cultural odds, Iceland has evolved into an independent culture that is thoroughly modern, humane, vigorous, and technologically advanced.

Over the past half-century, Icelanders have increasingly gravitated to the larger cities and towns along the coast. The Greater Reykjavik area, with well over 120,000 inhabitants, now contains nearly half the nation's population. Fewer than 20 percent of Icelanders live in rural areas. Iceland is self-supporting in fish, meat, and dairy products, as well as in a few other areas. However, the economy is still so one-sided that foreign trade per capita is greater than in any other country. Fish products account for some 75 percent of all exports, while industry contributes 20 to 25 percent of the total.

Educational and cultural standards have been high from the earliest times. All young people learn both Danish and English; those going to university studies are likely to master two or three additional languages. More books per capita are published in Iceland than in any other country.

Because it has a special history, beauty, and tranquility, and because its tourist and transportation industries are modern and efficient, Iceland is rapidly becoming more popular among Europeans and Americans who spend their lives in big cities, and who seek a place with real wilderness and space for adventurous hiking, fishing, bird-watching, horse-trekking, camping, or just roaming and getting away form it all. You can wander up mountains, over sands and rivers, even catch a trout, and in the evening be able to relax in a hot spring. Once you've had this invigorating experience, it's likely you'll want to return again and again.

—William W. Hoffa, Amherst, Massachusetts

Official name: Republic of Iceland. **Size:** 39,769 square miles (about the size of Virginia). **Population:** 259,000. **Population density:** 6 inhabitants per square mile. **Capital and largest city:** Reykjavik (pop. 97,000). **Language:** Icelandic. **Religion:** Lutheran. **Per capita income:** US$16,300. **Currency:** Kronur. **Literacy rate:** 99%. **Average daily temperature:** Reykjavik: June, 49°F; December, 34°F. **Average number of days with precipitation:** Reykjavik: June, 15; December, 20.

TRAVEL

U.S. citizens need a passport to visit Iceland. A visa is not required for stays of up to three months. For specific requirements, check with the **Embassy of**

Iceland, 2022 Connecticut Avenue NW, Washington, DC 20008; (202) 265-6653.

Getting Around

Iceland has no railroads, but its **bus** network reaches even the most isolated communities. While bus transportation is the best way to see Iceland, it can be quite slow. In the winter, many roads are impassable. For twice the cost of a bus ticket, you can fly point to point within Iceland. Iceland's domestic **airlines** are Icelandair, Norlandair, and East Air. All three airlines sell the **Air Rover Pass** good for a certain number of flights within 30 days. A five-flight pass, for example, costs US$290. Icelandair and East Air also have a **Fly As You Please Pass** that allows unlimited flight for 30 days for US$393. These passes can be purchased in Iceland or in the U.S. through Icelandair, (212) 967-8888.

The **Omnibus Passport** is a special discount bus ticket, valid for unlimited travel on all scheduled bus routes in Iceland within specified time limits ranging from one to four weeks. The one-week pass costs ISK13,000 (US$225) and four weeks cost ISK24,500 (US$425). Stopovers can be made anywhere and as often as you like. The **Full Circle Passport** allows unlimited travel on Iceland's main road (the ring-road) for ISK11,000 (US$200); there is no time limit, but you have to maintain a continuous direction around the island. They can be purchased from airlines and travel agencies in the U.S. or in Iceland.

There are several rental **car** agencies in Iceland. Cars can be rented from about ISK2,650 (US$50) per day. Hitchhiking can be fairly easy but traffic is sometimes sparse. Be prepared for rain and cold weather.

Eating and Sleeping

There are more than 20 **youth hostels** in Iceland. For more information, contact Hostelling International/American Youth Hostels (see page 54) or the national youth hostel organization, **Bandalag Islenskra Farfugla**, Sundlaugavegur 34, PO Box 1045, 121 Reykjavík; (354) 1-9138110; fax (354) 1-91679201. **EDDA Hotels**, run by the Iceland Tourist Bureau, offer bed-and-breakfast as well as sleeping-bag accommodations at fairly low prices. Some **farms** that cater to travelers also allow you to bring your sleeping bag; contact Icelandic Farm Holidays, Baendahöllin at Hagatorg, IS-107 Reykjavik; (354) 1-623640; fax (354) 1-623644. In fact, many lodgings, from summer hotels to guest houses, offer cheaper lodgings for those with sleeping bags—so be sure to take yours along.

Especially for Students and Young People

Iceland's student travel agency and issuer of the International Student Identity Card is **Icelandic Student Travel**, University Student Center, v/Hringbraut, IS-101 Reykjavik; (354) 1-615656; fax (354) 1-19113. In addition to providing discount student travel services, Icelandic Student Travel offers a number of outdoor adventure programs.

For Further Information

General tourist information is available from the **Iceland Tourist Board**, 655 Third Avenue, New York, NY 10017; (212) 949-2333; fax (212) 983-5260.

The best guide to Iceland is *Iceland, Greenland, and the Faroe Islands: A Travel Survival Kit*, available for $14.95 from Lonely Planet Publications. Good guidebooks to the entire Scandinavian region include Lonely Planet's

Scandinavian and Baltic Europe on a Shoestring ($17.95) and *The Real Guide: Scandinavia* ($14.95). An excellent book to read in preparation for your trip is *Insight Guide: Iceland* ($19.95). For more information on Lonely Planet, *Real Guides*, and *Insight Guides*, see pages 56–57.

WORK

In order to work in Iceland, it is necessary to obtain a work permit. The **American-Scandinavian Foundation** (see "Study," below) can assist Americans ages 21 to 30 with obtaining the requisite permit.

Internships/Traineeships

A program offered by a member of the Council on International Educational Exchange is listed below.

Association for International Practical Training. *IAESTE Trainee Program.* On-the-job training for undergraduate and graduate students in technical fields such as engineering, computer science, agriculture, architecture, mathematics, and the physical and natural sciences. See page 19 for more information.

Voluntary Service

Voluntary-service work can be arranged through the Year Abroad Program sponsored by the **International Christian Youth Exchange**. The program offers persons ages 18 to 30 voluntary-service opportunities in the fields of health care, education, the environment, construction, and more. See page 25 for more information.

STUDY

For general information on Iceland's educational system, ask the **Ministry of Education** (Solvholsgotu 4, 150 Reykjavik) for their brochure *Education in Iceland*. A good listing of English language programs offered in Iceland during the academic year and summer is *Study in Scandinavia*, a free publication by the Exchange Division of the **American Scandinavian Foundation**, 725 Park Avenue, New York, NY 10021; (212) 879-9779; fax (212) 249-3444.

EXPLORING ICELANDIC CULTURE

Readings

Iceland's greatest contributions to world literature are the medieval sagas. These sweeping epic stories unfold colorful, bloody, and romantic tales of heroes and heroines, kings, and fearsome monsters. The Icelandic people are very proud of this literary achievement, and the sagas still play an important role in the nation's psyche. The most readable of the sagas are *Ladela Saga, Ngáls Saga*, and *Egil's Saga*, all of which can be found in English translation.

Modern Iceland's most important literary figure is Hálldór Laxness. The first to deviate, and even criticize, the nation's traditional love of pastoral poetry, Laxness was responsible for bringing Iceland's literature into the 20th century. Laxness, who won the Nobel Prize for literature in 1955, is widely praised for his powerful novels about Icelanders. His finest works are considered *Fish Can Sing (Salka Valka)*, *Independent People*, *World Light*, and *Iceland's Bell*. *Fish Can Sing* (1933) is about the transitions a simple fishing village goes through when faced with a sophisticated world. *Independent People* (1935) highlights the author's most famous character, Bjartur of Summerhouses, a peasant hero who has come to represent the archetypal Icelander, and *World Light* (1940) is about a poet who struggles to come to grips with his role and his genius. The celebrated *Iceland's Bell* (1946) is a historical novel of three parts that takes place in the 18th century.

Another prominent Icelandic prose writer is Gunnar Gunnarsson. Gunnarsson's novels focus on the Icelandic people and their culture, and often dwell on the theme that human isolation can be overcome with faith and courage. His works have been widely translated and include *The Black Cliffs* (1929) and *The Good Shepherd* (1910), the latter of which is about the life of a shepherd and his dog in the lonely and rugged mountains of Iceland.

IRELAND

In Ireland, a small island on the far western edge of Europe, no point is more than 150 miles from the sea. Its population (3,489,000) is a little larger than that of the borough of Brooklyn in New York City. Nevertheless, people of Irish ancestry are scattered all over the world. There are about 40 million of them in the United States alone. They share an ancestry famous, and sometimes infamous, for its myths. While some of the preconceptions bandied about when the name of this small island crops up in conversation are misguided, some of the stories are true. A visit to Ireland will provide the traveler with palpable and contemporary insights into a centuries-old culture and a country with a relaxed and easy pace of life. The native love of conversation will be immediately evident, though sometimes to the detriment of getting things done.

While many of its cities are beautiful historical treasures, the greatest attractions of Ireland are predominantly rural. The rugged scenery of County Donegal in the northwest and County Kerry in the southwest is especially spectacular. While Ireland's economy is modern and the country has been a member of the European Community since 1973, the industrialized world has made surprisingly few inroads into the fabric of the countryside. This will certainly strike anyone who travels there from England; the land is remarkably unspoiled. There are no abandoned steel mills or coal mines. A lack of natural resources and perhaps an insular outlook caused by the Great Famine of the 1840s allowed Ireland to leapfrog the Industrial Revolution. The environment is remarkably clean and ideal for a biking or walking vacation. The cities are very compact and usually can be traversed in an afternoon.

There are many traces of ancient cultures, some of them long dead, scattered over the landscape. Remains such as Newgrange in County Meath or the clifftop fortress of Dun Aenghus in County Galway give evidence of a strong civilization in place long before the coming of St. Patrick and Christianity. Burial mounds and toppled Celtic crosses dot the lush green countryside. Some of the crosses have Christian symbols on one side and pagan ones on the other—an early Irish example of hedging your bets.

Visitors to Ireland are likely to be participants or witnesses to at least one earnest discussion on a political, social, or economic theme each day. The Irish are very politicized, and history weighs heavily on people. The economy has been in a slump, with unemployment in the early 1990s the highest ever. This is one of the reasons that emigration is a fact of life in this country, and thousands depart its shores each year for the U.S. or Britain. These topics provide endless fuel for debate, and that debate will most likely be held in the most Irish of institutions: the pub. A traveler won't spend long in Ireland without realizing that the pub plays an important role in the country's social life. It is the center of an evening's entertainment, whether for a conversation or a live music session. The Irish pubs are not necessarily the same as American bars. Pubs are usually comfortable and pleasant places, and to miss out on them is to miss out on a large part of the Irish experience.

Ireland has always had a strong reputation in the arts. Irish writers such as James Joyce and Samuel Beckett are well known around the world. That artistic tradition continues to today, and has been expanded and modernized to include many young bands trying to emulate the success of U2 and Sinéad O'Connor. Many of the voices raised nowadays are of protest at Ireland's headlong rush to become increasingly integrated with the rest of Europe. However, this is not the only reason for change in Ireland. Many of its rigid social and economic bonds are loosening, heralding a new phase in its long history.

—Allister O'Brien, New York, New York

Official name: Republic of Ireland. **Area:** 27,137 square miles (about the size of West Virginia). **Population:** 3,489,000. **Population density:** 128 inhabitants per square mile. **Capital and largest city:** Dublin (pop. 502,000). **Language:** English, Irish Gaelic. **Religion:** Roman Catholic. **Per capita income:** US$9,690. **Currency:** Irish pound (punt). **Literacy rate:** 99%. **Average daily temperature:** Dublin, June, 57°F, December, 42°F. **Average number of days with precipitation:** Dublin: June, 11; December, 14.

TRAVEL

U.S. citizens need a passport, but a visa is not required for tourists staying up to 90 days. Visitors may be required to produce an onward/return ticket or proof of sufficient funds for length of stay. For further information, consult the **Embassy of Ireland**, 2234 Massachusetts Avenue NW, Washington, DC 20008; (202) 462-3939. Ireland also has Consulates General in Boston, Chicago, San Francisco, and New York.

Getting Around

Eurail and InterRail passholders receive free **boat** passage between France and Rosslare in southeastern Ireland. Ferries also link Ireland with several ports in Wales and England, with easy connections to cities around Britain. Discounts on ferries between Ireland and ports in France and Britain are available to holders of the **International Student Identity Card** on Irish ferries. Within Ireland, cardholders receive a discount of up to 10 percent on Aer Arann flights between Galway and the Aran Islands.

Trains connect the cities of Ireland to Dublin, but the other cities are not well connected with one another. **Buses** fill in the gaps in rail service. Eurailpasses are valid on trains and some buses in Ireland, and students can save up to 50 percent on rail and bus travel in Ireland if they have an International Student Identity Card with the **Travelsave stamp** (see "Especially for Students and Young People" below).

The **Rambler Pass** system offers a number of options for rail and bus travel throughout Ireland. A student/youth Rambler Pass, good for unlimited combined rail and bus travel within Ireland, is available for anyone between 14 and 26. Student/youth Rambler Passes for 8 days of travel within a 15-day period cost $130.50; passes valid for 15 days of travel in a 30-day period cost $180; and passes good for 30 consecutive days of travel cost $270. Rambler Passes can be purchased in the U.S. or in Ireland. In the U.S. the Rambler Pass is available from CIE Tours International, 108 Ridgedale Avenue, PO Box 2355 Morristown, NJ 07962-2355; (800) 243-8687.

A new pass introduced by Britrail allows unlimited travel on trains in Ireland as well as in the U.K. The **BritIreland Pass** gives you 5 days of standard train travel in 15 days for $269 or 10 days of travel in one month for $419. The pass also includes sea passage. For more information, contact Council Travel (see pages xiii–xvi) or BritRail, 1500 Broadway, New York, NY 20036; (212) 575-2667.

Car rental is generally inexpensive. If standing in the rain doesn't deter you, hitching in Ireland, especially in rural areas, is often the best way to get around. People will generally stop and be interested in tales of your travels.

One of the most popular ways to see Ireland is by **bicycle**. Renting a bike in Ireland is easy, and you usually have a choice of racing, touring, or mountain bikes. The rental rate for a mountain bike is about US$40 per week.

Eating and Sleeping

There are a number of **youth hostels** in Ireland, and buying your hostel card in Ireland is less expensive than in the U.S. For more information on hostels, contact Hostelling International/American Youth Hostels (see page 54) or **An Oige**, Irish Youth Hostel Association, 61 Mountjoy Street, Dublin 7; (353) 1-304555; fax (353) 1-305808. For a listing of independent hostels in Ireland, contact **Independent Hostel Owners in Ireland, England, Malta, Scotland, Germany**, Information Office, Dooey Hostel, Glencolumkille, Co. Donegal; (353) 73-30130.

Usit, Ireland's student and youth travel organization (see "Especially for Students and Young People," below), operates three high-quality accommodations centers in Ireland geared toward budget travelers. The three centers, in Dublin, Cork, and Galway, offer bed and continental breakfast from IR£10. For long-term summer stays, check out Usit's apartment accommodations at University College Dublin.

Several Irish universities offer affordable **dormitory lodgings** to travelers. For more information, consult Campus Travel Service's *US and Worldwide Travel Accommodations Guide* (see page 54).

Bed and breakfasts are also an option. Open vouchers, good for accommodation in approved Bed and Breakfasts, can be bought for around US$20 per night. Contact the Irish Tourist Board (see "For Further Information," below).

Especially for Students and Young People

Any information that you might need about Ireland is available from **Usit**, 19 Aston Quay, Dublin 2; (353) 1-6778117; fax (353) 1-6778098. In addition to the Dublin locations, Usit has offices in downtown Belfast, Cork, Derry,

Limerick, and Waterford, with campus travel shops at University College Dublin, University College Cork, University College Galway, Dublin City University, and University of Ulster at Coleraine and Jordanstown. Usit offices will affix the **Travelsave stamp** to your International Student Identity Card for IR £7 (about US $10); this stamp entitles you to up to 50 percent off train and bus tickets for travel within Ireland.

Museums in Ireland are free to everyone. Holders of the International Student Identity Card can take advantage of the Student Theatre Stand-By Scheme, which makes available reduced-rate theater tickets 15 minutes before the performance. A broad range of other discounts are available as well. Check with Usit for more information.

For Further Information

General tourist information is available from the **Irish Tourist Board**, 757 Third Avenue, New York, NY 10017; (212) 371-9052; fax (212) 418-0800. In addition, persons interested in visiting Northern Ireland can get information from the **Northern Ireland Tourist Board**, 276 5th Avenue, Suite 500, New York, NY 10001.

Basic budget-travel information can be found in *Let's Go: Britain and Ireland* ($16.95). For more detail, however, *The Real Guide: Ireland* ($17) is a better book. An excellent book to read in preparation for your trip is *Insight Guide: Ireland* ($19.95). For more information on *Let's Go, Real Guide*s, and *Insight Guide*s, see pages 56–57.

WORK

Getting a Job

To work in Ireland, you must be in the country when applying for a job. Application for a work permit should be made by the prospective employer on your behalf. As with most Western European countries, preference is given to Irish citizens, then to members of the EC. For further information, contact the Embassy of Ireland (see "Travel," above).

CIEE will help you secure a work permit for up to four months any time of the year in Ireland. Full-time college or university students who are at least 18 years of age and permanent residents or citizens of the U.S. are eligible. Once you're in Ireland, the Usit office in Dublin will advise you on the current job situation. There is an $160 fee, which includes one night's accommodation and breakfast. Contact CIEE's Work Abroad Department for more information.

Internships/Traineeships

Programs sponsored by members of the Council on International Educational Exchange are listed below.

Association for International Practical Training. *IAESTE Trainee Program.* On-the-job training for undergraduate and graduate students in technical fields such as engineering, computer science, agriculture, architecture, mathematics, and the physical and natural sciences. See page 19 for more information.
Hospitality/Tourism Exchanges Program. On-the-job training for young people beginning a career in the hotel and food-service industries. Participants must have graduated from, or be enrolled in, a university or vocational school and possess at least six months of training or experience in the chosen field.

Training usually runs from 6 to 18 months. Consult Appendix I for the address of the sponsoring institution.

Beaver College. *Parliamentary Internship Program*. Dublin. Fall and spring semester. In cooperation with Institute of Public Administration. Students take three courses plus the internship as an aide to a member of Irish Parliament. Juniors and seniors with 3.2 GPA. Apply by April 20 for fall; October 15 for spring.

State University of New York College at Cortland. *Internships in Dublin*. Fall, spring, and summer. Opportunities in many types of organizations, from the Irish Parliament to financial institutions to the communications industry and business. Apply by March 15 for fall; September 1 for spring; February 1 for summer. Contact: Office of International Programs, SUNY College at Cortland, PO Box 2000, Cortland, NY 13045; (607) 753-2209.

STUDY

The **Consulate General of Ireland** distributes an information sheet on Irish universities and other institutions of higher education in Ireland. Its address is 515 Madison Avenue, New York, NY 10022; (212) 319-2555. Usit recommends that students who are planning to study in Ireland contact the **Central Applications Office**, Tower House, Eglinton Street, Galway, Ireland.

The **Irish Tourist Board** (see "For Further Information," above) publishes a pamphlet entitled *Study Abroad—Ireland*, which lists a number of academic year and semester programs, as well as study tours, summer schools, and high-school programs.

On behalf of Usit, **CIEE** administers the "Encounter Ireland" program, six weeks of Irish studies for college credit. This summer course (June 23 to August 4) is run in association with Trinity College, Dublin, and covers Irish literature, history, politics, social and cultural studies, and the visual arts. It carries a maximum of six credits. Costs of the program include tuition, field trips, theater tickets, cultural activities, homestay accommodation, and transportation from New York. Students should be enrolled full-time at an accredited U.S. college or university. The application deadline is May 28. Usit also offers a number of other summer study programs.

Following are the study programs offered by CIEE-member institutions. Unless otherwise noted, consult Appendix I for the addresses of the sponsoring institutions. In addition to the programs listed below, University of Notre Dame offers programs open only to its own students.

Semester and Academic Year

Business

Beaver College. *University of Limerick*. Semester and academic year. Business and management studies. Juniors and seniors with 3.0 GPA. Apply by April 20 for fall and academic year; October 15 for spring.

Education

Beaver College. *Mary Immaculate College*. Limerick. Academic year. Educational studies with practice teaching. Juniors and seniors with 3.0 GPA. Apply by April 1.

University of Wisconsin at River Falls. *Overseas Practice Teaching*. Various sites. Fall and spring semesters. Individualized student-teaching experience. Seniors with preparatory education courses. Apply three months before desired teaching time. Contact: Carol LeBreck, Coordinator, Karges Center, UW at River Falls, River Falls, WI 54022; (715) 425-3778/3705.

Engineering

Beaver College. *University of Limerick*. Semester and academic year. Juniors and seniors with 3.0 GPA. Apply by April 20 for fall and academic year; October 15 for spring.

General Studies

Beaver College. *Mary Immaculate College*. Limerick. Semester and academic year. Juniors and seniors with 3.0 GPA. Apply by April 20 for fall and academic year; October 15 for spring.
St. Patrick's College. Maynooth. Academic year. Juniors and seniors with 3.1 GPA. Apply by April 20.
Trinity College. Dublin. Academic year. Juniors and seniors with 3.0 GPA. Apply by March 1 for English study; April 1 for all other studies.
University College. Cork. Semester and academic year. Juniors and seniors with 3.0 GPA. Apply by April 20 for fall and academic year; October 15 for spring.
University College. Dublin. Semester and academic year. Juniors and seniors with 3.0 GPA. Apply by April 20 for fall and academic year; October 15 for spring.
University College. Galway. Semester and academic year. Juniors and seniors with 3.0 GPA. Apply by April 20 for fall and academic year; October 15 for spring.
University of Limerick. Semester and academic year. Juniors and seniors with 3.0 GPA. Apply by April 20 for fall and academic year; October 15 for spring.
Butler University. *Trinity College, Dublin*. Academic year. Fully integrated program with study possible in most arts and sciences disciplines. Juniors and seniors with 3.0 GPA and previous study in field of interest. Apply by January 1.
University College, Cork. Semester and academic year. Fully integrated program with study possible in most arts and sciences disciplines; emphasis on Irish Studies and Gaelic language. Juniors and seniors with 3.0 GPA and previous study in field of interest. Apply by April 15 for fall and academic year; October 15 for spring.
University College, Galway. Semester and academic year. Fully integrated program with study possible in all arts and sciences disciplines. Juniors and seniors with 3.0 GPA and previous study in field of interest. Apply by April 15 for fall and academic year; October 15 for spring.
University of Limerick. Fall term, spring, summer, or academic year. Fully integrated program with study possible in all arts and sciences disciplines plus business, marketing, and management. Juniors and seniors with 3.0 GPA and previous study in field of interest. Apply by April 15 for fall and academic year; October 15 for spring.
Contact: Institute for Study Abroad, Butler University, 4600 Sunset Avenue, Indianapolis, IN 46208-3485; (800) 858-0229.
Marymount College, Tarrytown. *Trinity College*. Dublin. Academic year. Courses available in most major disciplines. Juniors and seniors with 3.3 GPA. Rolling admissions.

University College, Dublin. Academic year. Courses available in most major disciplines. Juniors and seniors with 3.3 GPA. Rolling admissions.
Rutgers University. *Study Abroad in Ireland*. University College, Dublin. Academic year. Juniors with 3.0 GPA. Apply by February 1.
State University of New York at Cortland. *University College Cork*. Cork. Fall and spring semesters. Irish/Celtic studies, Irish language, humanities, social science, and music. Apartment housing. Juniors and seniors with 3.0 GPA. Apply by March 7 for fall; October 15 for spring. Contact: Office of International Programs, SUNY at Cortland, PO Box 2000, Cortland, NY 13045; (607) 753-2209.
State University of New York at Oneonta. *Dublin Program*. Semester and academic year. Regular liberal arts and education classes at St. Patrick's College (participation/observation possible for education students). Dormitory housing. Sophomores to seniors. Rolling admissions. Contact: International Education Office, Netzer Building 332C, SUNY at Oneonta, Oneonta, NY 13820-4015; (607) 436-3369.

International Relations

World Learning/School for International Training. *College Semester Abroad*. Dublin and Northern Ireland. Fall and spring semesters. Peace and conflict studies. Peace-studies seminar, field-study methods, and independent-study project. Excursions and homestays. Sophomores to graduate students with 2.5 GPA. Apply by May 7 for fall; October 7 for spring. Contact: College Semester Abroad Admissions, (800) 336-1616.

Literature

Michigan State University. *English Literature in Dublin*. Spring semester. History, literature, and culture. Excursions. Sophomores to graduate students. Apply by November 30. Contact: Office of Overseas Study, 108 International Center, Michigan State University, East Lansing, MI 48824-1035; (517) 353-8920.

Performing Arts

Beaver College. *Drama at Trinity College*. Dublin. Academic year. Juniors and seniors with 3.0 GPA. Apply by April 1.

Summer and Short-Term

General Studies

Shoreline Community College. *Dublin Experience*. Four weeks in July. Humanities and social sciences at Trinity University. Excursions and dormitory housing. First-year college students, sophomores, and adults. Apply by April 1. Contact: Coordinator, Study Abroad Programs, Shoreline Community College, 16101 Greenwood Avenue North, Seattle, WA 98133; (206) 546-4602.
State University of New York College at Cortland. *University College Cork*. Cork. Summer. Irish studies: history, literature, music, folklore, art, geography, and others. Excursions and dormitory housing. Sophomores to seniors with 2.5 GPA. Apply by April 1. Contact: Office of International Programs, SUNY College at Cortland, PO Box 2000, Cortland, NY 13045; (607) 753-2209.
State University of New York College at Oneonta. *Irish Intersession*. Galway, Tralee, Cork, and Dublin. Two weeks in January. Irish studies. First-year college students to graduate students and continuing-education students.

Rolling admissions. Contact: International Education Office, Netzer Building 332C, SUNY College at Oneonta, Oneonta, NY 13820-4015; (607) 436-3369.
University of Kentucky. *Cooperative Center for Study*. Dublin. Summer. First-year college students to graduate students and adults. Apply by March 22.
University of Toledo. *Study Abroad in Ireland*. Cork. Two weeks in June. Education, history, structure, children's literature, folklore, and traditions. Sophomores to graduate students. Apply by February 28.
Villanova University. *Summer Program in Galway*. Galway. Mid-June to late July. First-year college students to seniors with 2.5 GPA. Apply by March 15.

EXPLORING IRISH CULTURE

Readings

The great shadow of James Joyce falls across Irish literature, sometimes obscuring other important figures. Joyce's *Ulysses* (1922) is, however, the central text of modern literature and its influence stretches far beyond the borders of Ireland. It is both a comic masterpiece and a profound exploration of the human psyche in its strengths and weaknesses. Other works, particularly *Dubliners* (1914) and *Portrait of the Artist as a Young Man* (1916), may offer a less daunting introduction to the Irish master.

Characteristic of much Irish literature is a great capacity for verbal wit and linguistic inventiveness. One of the Irish greats, Oscar Wilde, richly imbued his writing with inversion and comic paradox in *The Importance of Being Earnest* (1895). A flamboyant character himself, Wilde powerfully explores the joys as well as the consequences of pursuing a frivolous life of sensual pleasure in his classic novel, *The Picture of Dorian Gray* (1891). Another Irish writer with a highly developed ear for language and the ability to exploit its comic potential is playwright J. M. Synge. His *Playboy of the Western World* (1907) is a rich comedy precisely capturing the cadence of Irish speech while unromantically depicting the peasants of western Ireland.

Of the contemporary Irish playwrights, Hugh Leonard and Brian Friel have received the most enthusiastic praise. Leonard's *Da* describes how a son, returning to Ireland for the funeral of his father, comes to terms with their relationship. Brian Friel's acclaimed works include *Philadelphia, Here I Come*, which evokes the rural Ireland of the 1950s on the eve of an only son's emigration to the U.S., and the recent London and Broadway hit, *Dancing at Lughnasa*, in which a family of young women struggles to make ends meet while awaiting the mysterious return of their missionary father.

Witty and poetic literature also abounds in modern Irish novels. Christopher Nolan writes about his life with cerebral palsy in *Under the Eye of the Clock* (1987). In Nolan's first work, *Damburst of Dreams*, he releases the poetic outpourings that had built up before he had a means to communicate. John McGahern, another contemporary writer, comically depicts a Dubliner whose formula porn stories begin to happen in real life in *The Pornographer* (1979). In *Borstal Boy*, author Brendan Behan portrays the mannerisms and humor of Dublin in a British reform school. Also fascinating is literary editor of *The Irish Times* John Banville's *Book of Evidence*. Based on a true story, *Evidence* is the testimony of a ruthless, upper-class Anglo-Irish murderer. Another contemporary Irish prose writer of note is Roddy Doyle, author of the novel *The Commitments*, which formed the basis for the 1991 hit movie of the same name. *The Commitments* is the first of a three-part series by Doyle about a north Dublin working-class family; the trilogy is completed by *The Snapper* and *The Van*.

Films

The first films made in Ireland were travelogue/documentaries, followed by historical dramas with nationalist themes intended to stir a populace long since disgruntled with British rule—*Rory O'More* (1911), *Ireland the Oppressed* (1913), and *Ireland a Nation* (1914).

Ireland's rugged landscapes and modest production costs attracted Francis Ford Coppola to Ireland to make his first feature, *Dementia 13*, in 1963; and the Wicklow hills provided the setting for Robert Altman's psychodrama *Images* in 1972. With greater authenticity than previously seen, the pastoral romance had made a comeback two years earlier in David Lean's *Ryan's Daughter* (1970), starring Robert Mitchum. Another aspect of Irish culture, that of the illegal distilling of alcohol, was dealt with in a feature by independent filmmaker Bob Quinn, in *Poitin* (1978).

The 1980s brought a new era of Irish films, portraying a modern Ireland that encompassed a broad range of issues: unemployment and dream fulfillment in Peter Ormrod's *Eat the Peach* (1986); organized crime in the taut urban thriller *The Courier* (1988), starring Gabriel Byrne; and nontraditional sexual liaisons in Joe Comerford's *Reefer and the Model* (1988). Gaelic culture was addressed more directly than ever before in independent productions like Bob Quinn's *Budawanny* (1986), a daring tale of a priest's romance with his housekeeper. Anglo-Irish literature continued to provide a rich source of cinematic inspiration in John Huston's elegiac last film, *The Dead* (1987), based on the story from Joyce's *Dubliners*.

The quality of Irish films continues to improve in the 1990s, as does the critical and commercial acclaim accorded to films as diverse as Jim Sheridan's *My Left Foot* (1990), for which Daniel Day-Lewis won an Oscar for best actor; Alan Parker's *The Commitments* (1991), a rapid-paced story of no-future teenagers trying to start a Dublin soul band; and Neil Jordan's *The Crying Game* (1992), set in Belfast and London and bringing a new twist to the old formulaic terrorism. All point to a bright future for an industry that has emerged from the doldrums and entered the mainstream without losing the qualities that make Ireland unique.

ITALY

Italy's character is attributable more to the tastes and traditions of its diverse provinces than to a strong sense of national identity. Natural barriers—both mountains and seas—and the lack of national unity from the fall of the Roman Empire until the establishment of Italy as a nation-state in 1861 have encouraged deep-rooted regional identities. This regionalism is reflected in distinctive architectural, gastronomic, and linguistic styles, a host of political parties, and 16 highly competitive soccer teams—all of which contribute to Italy's flavor and charm.

At the heart of the Italian culture is a tremendous respect for history and tradition coupled with the innovation and dynamism of an advanced and modern society. However, the antique and the avant-garde, the rustic and the cosmopolitan coexist with little sense of continuity. In the Northern provinces, fast-food restaurants, designer department stores, and Fortune 500 companies flourish amidst Etruscan ruins, Renaissance palaces, and Gothic cathedrals. One of the most productive regions in the European Community, northern Italy is almost entirely responsible for a rapidly growing GNP that has recently surpassed that of Great Britain. By contrast, the South—il Mezzogiorno—a testament to Italy's rural tradition of artisan craftsmanship and strict Catholic values, has been unable to sustain itself economically. Likened to a Third World country, il Mezzogiorno has an unemployment rate of 20 percent and a level of production one-third that of the North.

The Italian central government has been unable to reconcile these cultural and economic schisms. The fact that Italy has seen more than 50 different governments since the Second World War may be attributed to the lack of political consensus in a multiparty arena and seen as a symptom—or cause—of a widespread sense of disillusionment and apathy of the populace. Instead, Italy's principal political powers, the Christian Democrats, the Socialists, and the Democratic Party of the Left (formerly the Communist party), often exert their power through other institutions such as Italy's TV stations, newspapers, and large corporations.

However, if one were to ascribe a national trait to the Italian people, it would be the innate ability to live life to its fullest. Great emphasis is given to ritual, tradition, and simple pleasures. Both young and old take their *passeggiata*, or daily evening stroll, old men congregate in the town piazzas for a *vino santo* and a discussion of the latest soccer scores, and paramount importance is placed on the preparation, presentation, and consumption of food—regarded not merely as sustenance for the body but also as medicine for the soul.

The traveler to Italy may find its people stubborn and opinionated, but generally warm and receptive to foreigners, particularly Americans, as the Italian youth continues to be obsessed with American pop culture. Italians are always eager to interact and are quick to help foreigners with their language in exchange for a few lessons in English slang; a feeble attempt at speaking a few words in Italian is much appreciated. Italy has always welcomed visitors, and visitors have gladly journeyed there, remembering always to toss a coin in the Roman "Trevi Fountain" to ensure their speedy return.

—Christina Bennett, New York, New York

Official name: Italian Republic. **Size:** 116,303 square miles (slightly larger than Arizona). **Population;** 57,772,000. **Population density:** 496 inhabitants per square mile. **Capital and largest city:** Rome (pop. 2,800,000). **Language:** Italian. **Religion:** Roman Catholic. **Per capita income:** US$14,600. **Currency:** Lira. **Literacy rate;** 98%. **Average daily temperature:** Rome: June, 71°F; December, 49°F. **Average number of days with precipitation:** Rome: June, 2; December, 10.

TRAVEL

U.S. citizens will need a passport, but a visa is not required for tourist stays of up to three months. For further information, check with the **Italian Embassy**, 1601 Fuller Street NW, Washington, DC 20009; (202) 328-5500.

Getting Around

Italy has a modern **railroad** network, and travel on Italian trains is still relatively inexpensive. Eurailpasses are valid for use on the Italian rail network. **Buses** also provide intercity transport and, for short trips in mountainous regions, a bus may be faster than the train, which often takes a more circuitous route. Another option is to rent a **car**. Although most of the pre-Fiat city streets are too narrow for cars, Italian roads are generally good and the comprehensive high-speed expressway, or *autostrada*, network runs the length of the country.

Italian State Railways offers three railpasses. The **BTLC Railpass** is good for unlimited travel on Intercity, Eurocity, and Rapido trains without surcharges or seat reservation fees (except for the new, first-class only, express TR450 trains). The second-class pass costs $152 for 8 days, $190 for 15 days, $220 for 21 days, and $264 for 30 days. First-class BTLC passes cost $226 for 8 days, $284 for 15 days, $330 for 21 days, and $396 for 30 days.

The **Italian Flexi Railcard (IFR)** is a flexible railpass that offers the same supplement exemptions as the BTLC. A second-class IFR allows 4 days of travel in 9 days for $116, 8 days in 21 for $164, or 12 days in 30 for $210. The first-class IFR for the same periods costs $170, $250, or $314, respectively.

The **Italian Kilometric Ticket (KLM)**, good for two months, is valid for 20 trips up to a total of 3,000 kilometers (1,875 miles). The KLM is valid on all regular trains; travel in Intercity, Eurocity, Rapido, and TR450 trains is possible with supplemental charges. The KLM may also be used by several people traveling together by multiplying the mileage by the number of travel companions. A second-class KLM costs $156; first class costs $264.

These railpasses can be purchased from Italian State Railways' U.S. representative, **CIT Tours**, 342 Madison Avenue, Suite 207, New York, NY 10173; (800) 248-8687; fax (212) 697-1394. An additional $10 administrative fee is charged by CIT for each pass.

Throughout Italy, except on some express trains, **bicycles** may be taken as checked baggage. You pay an extra charge based on weight and distance traveled. For information on hiking Italy's Alps, contact the **Touring Club Italiano**, Corso Italia 10, 20122 Milan; (39) 2-85261; fax (30) 2-8526362. The **Club Alpino Italiano** operates about 600 huts in the mountains; for information, contact the club at Via Ugo Foscolo 3, 20122 Milan; (39) 2-72023085.

Eating and Sleeping

There are more than 50 **youth hostels** in Italy. For more information, contact Hostelling International/American Youth Hostels (see page 54) or **Associazione Italiana Alberghi per la Gioventù**, Via Cavour 44, 00184 Rome; (39) 6-4871152; fax (39) 6-4880492.

Students can also take advantage of an extensive **student hostel** network. For more information, obtain the *Guide for Foreign Students* from the Italian Ministry of Education, Viale Trastevere, 00153 Rome.

Camping is very popular in Italy, with over 1,700 official campsites. For a list of site locations, contact the Italian Government Travel Office (see "For Further Information," below). The Italian Government Travel Office can also provide information on convents, monasteries, and other religious institutions that offer lodgings.

Especially for Students

Centro Turistico Studentesco e Giovanile (CTS) is Italy's main student travel bureau, with offices around Rome and in 70 other Italian cities. You can contact them at CTS Centro Turistico Studentesco, Via Nazionale, 66, 00186 Rome; (39) 6-46791. CTS can arrange low-cost accommodations and travel.

For Further Information

Italia—General Information for Travelers, which covers everything you need to know about travel in the country, is available free from the **Italian Government Travel Office**, 630 Fifth Avenue, Suite 1565, New York, NY 10111; (212) 245-4822. Also available are maps and hotel lists.

For basic budget-travel information, *Let's Go: Italy* ($16.99) is always dependable. For more detail, however, *The Real Guide: Italy* ($13.95), is an all-around better book. The excellent *Cadogan Guide*s series offers several highly detailed regional guides to Italy, including *Northwest Italy, Italian Islands, Rome, Venice, Sicily*, and *Tuscany, Umbria and the Marches*. An excellent book to read in preparation for your trip is *Insight Guide: Italy* ($19.95). For more information on Lonely Planet, *Real Guide*s, *Cadogan Guide*s, and *Insight Guide*s, see pages 56–57.

WORK

In Italy, laws regulating work by foreigners are very strict. The Italian Ministry for Home Affairs must first grant the prospective employee a residence permit for work purposes. When the permit has been issued, the employer must provide a certified declaration that no nationals in the area are able to perform the work in question. For more information contact the **Embassy of Italy**, Commerical Affairs Division, 1601 Fuller Street NW, Washington, DC 20009; (202) 328-5500.

American teachers interested in teaching in Italy should write for the booklet *Schools for English-Speaking Students in Italy*. It is available from the **Italian Cultural Institute** (see "Study," below).

Internships/Traineeships

A program offered by a member of the Council on International Educational Exchange is listed below.

Association for International Practical Training. *IAESTE Trainee Program*. On-the-job training for undergraduate and graduate students in technical fields such as engineering, computer science, agriculture, architecture, mathematics, and the natural and physical sciences. See page 19 for more information.

Voluntary Service

For persons interested in voluntary-service work, the Year Abroad Program sponsored by the **International Christian Youth Exchange** offers persons ages 18 to 30 voluntary-service opportunities in the fields of health care, education, the environment, construction, and more. See page 25 for more information.

STUDY

There are numerous schools and academies throughout Italy, particularly in Florence, that specialize in instruction of foreigners in art, language, and history. *Schools for Foreigners in Italy*, a directory of Italian schools offering programs for foreign students, is available from the **Italian Cultural Institute**, 686 Park Avenue, New York, NY 10021; (212) 879-4242. *The Italian Educational System: A Brief Outline* is available from the same source.

Following are the educational programs offered by CIEE-member institutions. Unless otherwise noted, consult Appendix I for the address of the colleges and universities listed in this section. In addition to those listed below, Pepperdine University and University of Pennsylvania offer programs open only to their own students.

Semester and Academic Year

Archaeology and Classical Studies

Stanford University. *Intercollegiate Center for Classical Studies in Rome*. Fall and spring semesters. Juniors and seniors with classical studies major and 3.0 GPA. Apply by March 15 for fall; October 15 for spring.

Art and Architecture

Eckerd College. *Eckerd in Florence*. Spring semester. Drawing, etching, and watercolor, as well as Italian language and culture. Homestays and excursions. Sophomores to seniors with 2.75 GPA. Apply by November 15.

General Studies

American Heritage Association. *Northwest Interinstitutional Council on Study Abroad—Siena*. Fall, winter, and spring quarters. Sophomores to seniors with 2.5 GPA. Apply by June 15 for fall; November 1 for winter; January 15 for spring.

Study in Macerata, Italy. Fall, winter, and spring quarters. Offered in conjunction with Portland State University and Western Washington University. Study at Università di Macerata. Excursions and homestays. Sophomores to seniors in good academic standing. Apply by July 15 for fall; November 15 for winter; February 1 for spring. Contact: (800) 654-2051.

American University. Rome. Semester and academic year. Orientation in Siena. Italian language, literature, history, culture, theater, political science, and society. Excursions. Sophomores to seniors with 2.75 GPA. Apply by March 15 for fall and academic year; October 15 for spring. Contact: World Capitals Programs, American University, Dunblane House—Tenley Campus, Washington, DC 20016-8083; (202) 895-4900/4937.

Associated Colleges of the Midwest. *ACM Florence Program*. Courses in art history, language, and other social sciences and humanities. Sophomores to seniors with 2.75 GPA; some Italian recommended. Apply by March 15.

Boston University. Padova. Semester and academic year. Intensive language and cultural immersion program offering direct enrollment in Università degli Studi di Padova; instruction in Italian. Homestays or dormitory housing. Sophomores to seniors with 3.0 GPA in major; four semesters of college Italian for advanced course and direct enrollment. Apply by March 15 for fall and academic year; October 15 for spring.

Brown University. *Brown in Italy*. Academic year. Two-month orientation courses in preparation for direct enrollment at University of Bologna; full range of academic curriculum. Excursions and furnished apartment housing. Juniors in good academic standing and with one year of college Italian. Apply by February 15.

Drake University. Florence. Semester and academic year. Offered in affiliation with Institute of Italian Studies. Humanities as well as Italian language, art and architecture, communications, and international business. Excursions. Rolling admissions; final deadline July 1. Contact: Institute of Italian Studies, PO Box 23007, Des Moines, IA 50325-9406; (515) 225-2998; fax (515) 225-0196.

Gonzaga University. *Gonzaga in Florence.* Academic year. Liberal arts and business administration curriculum. Juniors with 2.8 GPA. Apply by April 1.

Hiram College. Rome. Academic year, and fall, winter, and spring quarters. Study at John Cabot University. Sophomores to seniors with 2.5 GPA.

Indiana University. *Cooperative Studies Program.* Bologna. Academic year. Offered by consortium of Cornell University, Indiana University, Northwestern University, University of Minnesota, University of North Carolina, University of Pennsylvania, and University of Wisconsin. Direct enrollment in University of Bologna. Juniors and seniors with two years of Italian and 3.0 GPA. Apply by January 15.

International Student Exchange Program (ISEP). Semester and academic year. Direct reciprocal exchange between U.S. universities and institutions in Pavia, Rome, and Urbino. Full curriculum options. Rolling admissions. Open only to students at ISEP-member institutions. Contact ISEP for list of members.

James Madison University. *JMU Semester in Florence.* Fall and spring semesters. Italian art, film, literature, language, civilization, music, and politics. Sophomores to seniors with 2.8 GPA. Apply by November 15 for fall; February 1 for spring.

Kent State University. Florence. Fall semester. Fine and liberal arts and Italian language. Sophomores to seniors with 2.5 GPA. Rolling admissions.

Middlebury College. *Middlebury in Italy.* Florence. Academic year. Art history, film, history, Italian language, Italian studies, and literature; instruction in Italian. Juniors to graduate students with five semesters of college Italian. Apply by March 1. Contact: Dean, Italian School, Middlebury College, Middlebury, VT 05753; (802) 388-3711, ext. 5543.

Pitzer College. *Pitzer in Parma.* Semester and academic year. Intensive language instruction, core seminar, independent-study project, and regular or special university courses for students with appropriate language skills. Study at University of Parma. Homestays and excursions. Sophomores to seniors. Apply by May 15 for fall and academic year; October 15 for spring.

Portland State University. *Northwest Interinstitutional Council on Study Abroad—Siena.* See listing under American Heritage Association.

Study in Macerata, Italy. See listing under American Heritage Association.

Rutgers University. *Junior Year in Italy.* Florence. Academic year. Juniors with two years of college Italian. Apply by March 1. Contact: Study Abroad Office, Milledoler Hall, Rutgers University, New Brunswick, NJ 08903; (908) 932-7787.

State University of New York College at Buffalo. Siena, Italy. Fall and spring semesters. Offered in cooperation with State University of New York at Geneseo. Italian art, architecture, language, culture, and history. Excursions and homestays. Sophomores to seniors with 2.5 GPA and one semester of college Italian. Apply by April 1 for fall; October 15 for spring. Contact: Office of International Education, GC 416, SUNY College at Buffalo, 1300 Elmwood Avenue, Buffalo, NY 14222-1095; (716) 878-4620.

State University of New York College at New Paltz. *Academic Year in Italy.* Urbino. Regular university courses at University of Urbino. Juniors and seniors with two years of college Italian. Rolling admissions. Contact: Office of International Education, HAB 33, SUNY College at New Paltz, New Paltz, NY 12561; (914) 257-3125.

State University of New York at Stony Brook. *Stony Brook in Rome.* Academic year. Humanities and social sciences. Excursions. Juniors and seniors with two years of college Italian. Apply by March 15. Contact: Dean for International Programs, SUNY, Stony Brook, NY 11794-2700; (516) 632-7030.

Syracuse University. *Syracuse in Florence.* Semester and academic year. Sophomores to graduate students with 3.0 GPA. Apply by March 15 for fall and academic year; October 15 for spring. Contact: (800) 235-3472.

Trinity College. *Trinity College/Rome Campus.* Fall and spring semester. Sophomores to seniors. Apply by March 15 for fall; October 15 for spring. Contact: Trinity College/Rome Campus, Hartford, CT 06106-3100; (203) 297-2436.

University of Connecticut. *Study Abroad Program in Florence.* Academic year. Sophomores to graduate students with one year of college Italian. Apply by April 1.

University of Michigan. *Academic Year or Semester in Florence.* Florence. Semester and academic year. Sophomores to seniors. Apply by late February.

University of North Carolina at Chapel Hill. *Cooperative Studies to Bologna.* Academic year. Sophomores to seniors with 3.0 GPA and fluency in Italian. Open only to North Carolina residents. Apply by February 14.

University of Oregon. *Northwest Interinstitutional Council on Study Abroad—Siena.* See listing under American Heritage Association.

University of Washington. *Northwest Interinstitutional Council on Study Abroad—Siena.* See listing under American Heritage Association.

University of Wisconsin at Madison. *Academic Year at the University of Bologna.* See listing under **Indiana University**.

Academic Year or Semester in Florence. See listing under **University of Michigan**.

Washington State University. *Northwest Interinstitutional Council on Study Abroad—Siena.* See listing under American Heritage Association.

Western Washington University. *Northwest Interinstitutional Council on Study Abroad—Siena.* See listing under American Heritage Association.

Study in Macerata, Italy. See listing under American Heritage Association.

Italian Language and Culture

University of North Carolina at Chapel Hill. *UNC Program of Siena.* Semester and academic year. Sophomores to seniors. Apply by February 14 for fall and academic year; October 15 for spring.

University of Massachusetts at Amherst. *Semester in Siena.* Spring semester. Sophomores to seniors with two semesters of college Italian. Apply by October 15.

Performing Arts

Whitworth College. Rome. Semester and academic year. Offered in conjunction with the American University of Rome. Music study, Italian language and culture. Second-semester sophomores to seniors with 3.0 GPA. Audition tape required. Apply by June 1 for fall and academic year; November 1 for spring.

Summer and Short-Term

Anthropology

University of New Orleans. *UNO/UF Field School in Anthropology*. Merano. Four weeks in summer. Offered in conjunction with the University of Florida. Cultural anthropology/ethnology, historical and contemporary cultural ecology of Tirolean Alpine region. Undergraduates, graduates, and adults with introductory course in anthropology. Apply by April 15.

Archaeology and Classical Studies

Michigan State University. *Prehistoric Archaeology in Italy*. Siena. Summer. Sophomores to graduate students. Apply by April 15. Contact: Office of Overseas Study, 108 International Center, Michigan State University, East Lansing, MI 48824-1035; (517) 353-8920.

Art and Architecture

Ball State University. *ArkItalia: Architecture, Planning, and Landscape in Italy's Historic Centers*. Florence, Rome, Perugia, plus day trips to other cities. Four weeks in summer. Sophomores to graduate students with 2.5 GPA. Apply by April 1. Contact: Field Studies Director, College of Architecture and Planning, Ball State University, Muncie, IN 47306; (317) 285-1900.

Drake University. Florence. Summer. Offered in affiliation with Institute of Italian Studies. Art and architecture as well as humanities, Italian language, communications, and international business. Excursions. Rolling admissions; final deadline May 1. Contact: Institute of Italian Studies, PO Box 23007, Des Moines, IA 50325-9406: (515) 225-2998; fax (515) 225-0196.

Flagler College. *Study in Italy*. Fano (near Urbino). Four weeks in May. Drawing, art history, and Italian language and culture. Excursions. Sophomores to seniors with 2.5 GPA. Apply by November 15. Contact: Mr. Robert Hall, Art Department, Flagler College, PO Box 1027, St. Augustine, FL 32085-1027; (904) 829-6481 ext. 214 or 222.

Ohio University. *Art History in Italy*. Rome and Florence. Five weeks in summer. Renaissance art and society. Undergraduates. Apply by March 1. Contact: Professor Marilyn Bradshaw, School of Art, Siegfried Hall, Ohio University, Athens, OH 45701; (614) 593-4282.

State University of New York College at Brockport. *Ceramics and Art History*. National Institute of Ceramic Art at Faenza. Summer. Hotel accommodations. Juniors to graduate students with 2.5 GPA. Apply by April 15. Contact: Office of International Education, SUNY College at Brockport, Brockport, NY 14420; (716) 395-2119.

State University of New York College at New Paltz. *Art History Abroad*. Various locations. Summer. On-site study of specific topic in art history, such as Roman wall painting, Romanesque architecture, and art in the Age of Augustus. High-school students to graduate students. Rolling admissions. Contact: Office of International Education, HAB 33, SUNY College at New Paltz, New Paltz, NY 12561; (914) 257-3125.

Syracuse University. *Architecture in Florence*. Summer. Undergraduates with three years of architectural design, and graduate students with two years. Apply by March 1.

Pre-Architecture in Florence. Summer. Undergraduates. Apply by March 1.

Visual Arts in Florence. Summer. Excursions. Sophomores to graduate students and professionals. Apply by March 1. Contact: (800) 235-3472.

University of Colorado at Boulder. *Art History in Italy*. Summer. Classroom instruction plus site visits. Sophomores to graduate students with 2.75 GPA and some knowledge of fine arts. Applications accepted from late November until program fills.
University of Oregon. *Architecture Studio in Rome*. Summer. Architecture majors only. Apply by April 1.

Education

Syracuse University. *Seminar in Italy: Inclusive Education*. Florence, Rome, and Parma. May and June. Observation of Italy's integrated educational programs for children with disabilities; lectures on Italian philosophy of education and implementation of educational policy; art and architecture on weekends. Undergraduates and graduate students. Apply by March 1. Contact: (800) 235-3472.

General Studies

American Heritage Association. *Cultural Summer Program in Macerata*. Offered in conjunction with Portland State University and Western Washington University. Italian culture and history at Università di Macerata. Excursions and homestays. Sophomores to seniors in good academic standing. Apply by April 15.
Michigan State University. *Social Science in Rome*. Summer. Politics, economics, educational systems, and culture of Italy. Undergraduates. Apply by April 15. Contact: Office of Overseas Study, 108 International Center, Michigan State University, East Lansing, MI 48824-1035; (517) 353-8920.
Portland State University. *Cultural Summer Program in Macerata*. See listing under American Heritage Association.
Southern Methodist University. *SMU in Italy*. One week in Tuscany, four weeks in Rome. Summer. Italian culture, politics, history, art history, and studio art. Sophomores to seniors. Apply by March 1. Contact: Office of International Programs, SMU, 100 McFarlin Auditorium, Dallas, TX 75275-0391; (214) 768-2338.
State University of New York at New Paltz. *Summer Study in Italy*. Urbino. Italian language, art history, literature, film, and culture. High-school students to graduate students. Rolling admissions. Contact: Office of International Education, HAB 33, SUNY at New Paltz, New Paltz, NY 12561; (914) 257-3125.
Syracuse University. *Humanism and the Arts in Renaissance Italy*. Florence. Summer. Excursions. Sophomores to graduate students and professionals. Apply by March 1. Contact: (800) 235-3472.
Trinity College. *Trinity College/Rome Campus*. Summer. Sophomores to seniors. Contact: Trinity College/Rome Campus, Hartford, CT 06106-3100; (203) 297-2436.
University of Alabama. *Alabama in Italy*. Florence. Five weeks in May and June. Italian language, culture, literature, and art. Excursions. Undergraduates and graduates. Apply by March 1. Contact: (205) 348-5256.
University of Hartford. *Landmarks, Legends, and Life of Early Italy*. Rome, Florence, Venice. Three weeks during winter interim. All interested individuals.
University of Louisville. *Art, Language, History, and Culture in Perugia*. Perugia. Summer. First-year college students to graduate students. Apply by April 1.

University of Michigan. *Summer Study Abroad in Florence.* Florence. Six weeks in summer. First-year college students to seniors. Apply by March 1.

Villanova University. *Rosemont Summer Program in Siena.* Siena. Art history, urban history, and studio arts. Late May to late June. First-year college students to seniors with 2.5 GPA. Apply by February 26.

Urbino/Florence Summer Program in Italy. Urbino and Florence. July to mid-August. Intensive Italian-language study at the Università degli Studi di Urbino and at the Scuola Leonardo da Vinci in Florence. First-year college students to seniors with 2.5 GPA. Apply by March 15.

Western Washington University. *Cultural Summer Program in Macerata.* See listing under American Heritage Association.

World Learning/School for International Training. *College Semester Abroad.* Siena. Fall and spring semesters. Intensive language, life and culture seminar, field-study methods seminar, independent-study project. Homestays and excursions. Sophomores to seniors with 2.5 GPA. Apply by May 7 for fall; October 7 for spring. Contact: College Semester Abroad Admissions, (800) 336-1616.

History

Michigan State University. *History in Rome.* Summer. Italian language, and Medieval and Renaissance studies. Sophomores to graduate students. Apply by April 15. Contact: Office of Overseas Study, 108 International Center, Michigan State University, East Lansing, MI 48824-1035; (517) 353-8920.

Interior Design

Syracuse University. *Environmental Design in Florence.* June. Harmonious development of Italian interior program with street, square, and city; sketching for interior designers; and environmental design studio. Site visits. Undergraduates and graduates. Apply by March 1. Contact: (800) 235-3472.

Italian Language and Culture

Adventist Colleges Abroad. Florence. Summer. Six-week intensive course at advanced, intermediate, and beginning levels. Excursions. High-school students, high-school graduates not enrolled in college, and college students with 2.5 GPA. Open only to students at Adventist Colleges Abroad consortium institutions. Apply by March 25.

Boston University. *Summer Program in Padova.* Intensive six-week language and cultural immersion with academic options available at intermediate and advanced levels; instruction in Italian. Excursions. Sophomores to seniors with 3.0 GPA in major. Apply by April 1.

Indiana University. *Overseas Study in Florence.* Summer. Italian language and culture; studio art also offered. Freshmen to graduate students with 2.8 GPA. Apply by February 5.

Michigan State University. *Italian Language, Literature, and Culture in Florence.* Summer. Undergraduate and graduate students. Apply by April 15. Contact: Office of Overseas Study, 108 International Center, Michigan State University, East Lansing, MI 48824-1035; (517) 353-8920.

Ramapo College of New Jersey. *Summer Study in Italy.* Urbino. Early July to mid-August. Intensive Italian-language and economic, social, and cultural aspects of Italy. Dormitory housing. Sophomores to seniors. Apply by April 1. Contact: Study Abroad Office, Ramapo College of New Jersey, 505 Ramapo Valley Road, Room D-204, Mahwah, NJ 07430-9926; (201) 529-7463.

Rosary College. *Rosary in Florence*. Summer. Italian language with emphasis on Italian literature, history, and art history. Sophomores to seniors and nonstudents interested in Italian culture. Apply by April 1. Contact: Ann Charney, Director of Study Abroad, Rosary College, River Forest, IL 60305; (708) 524-6948.

Rutgers University. *Summer Program in Italy*. Urbino. Summer. Italian language (at all levels), literature, and art of Italian Renaissance. Excursions. Undergraduates, graduates, and teachers. Apply by April 30. Contact: Department of Italian, Rutgers University, New Brunswick, NJ 08903; (908) 932-7031/7536.

State University of New York College at Oswego. Altomonte, Italy. July. Six-week program in Italian language, art, and civilization. Excursions. Undergraduates. Apply by April 1. Contact: International Education, 102 Rich Hall, SUNY College at Oswego, Oswego, NY 13126; (315) 341-2118.

State University of New York at Stony Brook. *Summer Study in Rome*. Late June to late July. Italian language, literature, art history, culture, and civilization. Excursions. First-year college students to adults. Apply by March 15. Contact: Dean for International Programs, SUNY, Stony Brook, NY 11794-2700; (516) 632-7030.

Syracuse University. *Italian Language and Culture*. Florence. Excursions. Sophomores to graduate students and professionals. Apply by March 1. Contact: (800) 235-3472.

University of Kentucky. *Kentucky Institute for International Studies in Florence, Italy*. Florence. Summer. Language study. Excursions. First-year college students to graduate students and adults. Apply by March 1.

University of Oregon. *Intensive Italian Program in Perugia*. Six weeks in summer. First-year college students to graduate students. Apply by April 1.

University of Pennsylvania. *Penn/Bryn Mawr Italian Studies Summer Institute in Florence*. For students interested in Italian language and culture. Apply by March 15.

University of Pittsburgh. *Summer Program in Italy*. Feltre. Summer. Italian language and culture study. Excursions. Sophomores to seniors. Apply by March 15.

University of Utah. *Siena, Italy—Language Program*. Dante Alighieri Institute. Four weeks in summer. Undergraduates, graduate students, and others with 2.0 GPA and recommended one or two quarters of college Italian. Apply by March 1.

Performing Arts

State University of New York College at New Paltz. *Dance in Italy*. Urbino. Summer. Intensive workshop in modern dance, including daily technique class, development of performance skills, and on-site performance. High-school students to graduate students with prior dance experience. Rolling admissions. Contact: Office of International Education, HAB 33, SUNY at New Paltz, New Paltz, NY 12561; (914) 257-3125.

EXPLORING ITALIAN CULTURE

Readings

The generation of writers growing up during and after the fascist years of WWII developed a socially conscious literature in opposition to the regime.

Particularly touching as well as fascinating is Carlo Levi's *Christ Stopped at Eboli* (1946), the author's account of his exile in a forgotten southern village and the strange sort of existence of the poverty-stricken inhabitants. Cesare Pavese's works are almost always concerned with the traumas incurred by Italy's transition from an agrarian society to an industrial one. His work *The Moon and the Bonfire* (1968) is about the narrator's quest for the truth about both his past and future possibilities in a village in his native Piedmont. Giorgio Bassani's *Garden of the Finzi-Continis* tells the poignant story of a wealthy Italian Jewish family in 1938 that watch their world slowly collapse around them, tragically ending in their abduction for the concentration camps. Alberto Moravia, a writer and part of the morally conscious neorealist movement, often focuses on social alienation and the power of sex and money: *The Conformist* (1951), *The Women of Rome* (1947), and *Roman Tales* (1954) are among his best.

Natalia Ginzburg is probably the most widely read of Italian women writers. A liberal politician who sits in the Senate in Rome, she has written several short stories and books. *Family Sayings* (1986) tenderly portrays family life in Northern Italy, a common theme of this author. First published in 1906, *A Woman* (1980), by Sibilla Aleramo, is considered a classic in Italy; it is the story of a girl who breaks away from her beloved father and forges her own life.

The contemporary Sicilian writer Leonard Sciascia is said to have redefined the historical novel. Through Sciascia's passionate and continual examination of Sicilian subjects in such books as *Mafia Vendetta (Il giorno della civetta)*, he created a "metaphor of the modern world" out of his native island. Another acclaimed author from Sicily is Giuseppe Tomasi di Lampedusa, whose well-known novel *The Leopard* (1958) recounts the dramatic transition from Bourbon to Piedmontese rule by way of an intriguing family saga, and includes some well-written descriptions of the Sicilian landscape.

Italo Calvino is commonly considered the greatest of contemporary Italian authors. Filled with magic-realist touches and intellectual musings, his books *Marcovaldo, Invisible Cities*, and *Italian Folktales* (1988) are all excellent choices. Umberto Eco is the most recent entrant on the Italian literary scene: his best-selling novel *The Name of the Rose* (1983)—also a 1986 movie—is an allusive, tightly plotted medieval mystery, whereas the heavier but critically acclaimed *Foucault's Pendulum* (1989) takes place in modern times.

The Italians (1964), by Luigi Barzini, is widely regarded as the definitive portrait of the Italian character. The Italian sociologist touches upon many aspects of Italian life: its virtues, vices, and charms.

Films

The fall of Mussolini and Fascism at the end of the Second World War meant the reinvigoration of the Italian film industry in the form of the neorealism movement. Some of the most acclaimed films from this era are Roberto Rossellini's *Open City* (1945), about a underground worker movement in Rome during the Nazi occupation; Academy Award–winning *The Bicycle Thief* (1949), by director Vittorio de Sica, about a man robbed of the bicycle he depends on for his livelihood; and Luchino Visconti's unofficial remake of *The Postman Always Rings Twice*: the powerful melodrama *Ossessione* (1942).

Visconti, as well as Federico Fellini and Michelangelo Antonioni, went on to direct some of the most unforgettable films of the post-neorealist Italian cinema. Visconti's adaptation of the novel *The Leopard* (1963) is a technically brilliant rendering of an elaborate and complex family saga. Fellini's most famous picture, and probably his most straightforward, is *La Dolce Vita* (1960), in which actor Marcello Mastroianni sees his decadent life as a journalist in Rome as shallow but cannot change. Two of his most deserving Academy Award–winners are *Nights of Cabiria* (1957), about a hopeless Roman prostitute who has dreams of romance and grandeur, and *La Strada* (1954), the story of a simpleminded peasant girl sold to a circus strongman who mistreats her. Antonioni's most accessible film is probably his English-language hit, *Blow-Up* (1966), about a fashion photographer who thinks he sees a murder in trendy, swinging London.

Another notable postwar Italian filmmaker is Lina Wertmuller, who often explores the dynamics of sexual politics. Wertmuller's slightly disturbing *Swept Away* (1975) explores a reversal of power and sex roles on a desert island, and *Seven Beauties* (1976) is about the survival of an incorrigible casanova through the horrors of World War II. Bernardo Bertolucci has concentrated on the darker side of Italian life, both past and present, in such films as *The Conformist* (1969) and his epic saga *1900* (1976).

In the late 1970s and '80s, the Taviani brothers, Paolo and Vittorio, entered the scene with a series of well-received movies. Two of their finest are *The Night of the Shooting Stars* (1982), an extraordinarily touching story of a community of Tuscan villagers right before their rescue by the Americans during World War II, and *Padre Padrone* (1977), based on an autobiographical book by Gavino Ledda about a peasant boy in rural Sardinia who is abused by his tyrannical father.

The Italian film industry continues to produce a variety of films that are well received around the world. Giuseppe Tornatore's Academy Award–winning *Cinema Paradiso* (1989) is about a young Italian boy coming of age. Made by the same people and also earning an Academy Award is *Mediterraneo* (1991), a playful film by Gabrielle Salvatore about several Italian soldiers who get stranded on a remote Greek island. *The Icicle Thief* (1990), a satire borrowing liberally from de Sica's masterpiece, is another recent release from "Italy's Woody Allen," Maurizio Nichetti. Nichetti's latest picture, *Volere Volare* (1993), is a slapstick love story that eventually turns into a "Who Framed Roger Rabbit" take-off when Nichetti discovers that one of his hands has turned into a glowing animated cartoon hand.

The highest-grossing film in recent years, and actually in the history of Italian cinema, was *Johnny Stecchino* (1992). This film stars the triply talented Roberto Begnini, who also directed and wrote it. *Stecchino* is a rollicking comedy of mistaken identity about a bus driver for a mental institution who is taken for a convicted mafioso.

LUXEMBOURG

Founded in A.D. 963, the Grand Duchy of Luxembourg is one of the oldest nations in Europe. Yet, for much of its history it was a highly fortified no-man's-land between the major families and countries of Europe, who were almost constantly at war with each other until the late 20th century. Luxembourg has been called the "Gibraltar of the North" for the many castles and fortresses that dot its landscape. Its name comes from the word *Lucinburhuc*, or "small fortress."

Luxembourg was a major battleground most recently during World War II; the Battle of the Bulge was fought in the Ardennes Forest, which covers the north. Luxembourg City was liberated by American troops in 1944, only to be recaptured and subsequently reliberated. American and German tanks and weapons still stand as memorials to the battles fought in Luxembourg. Do not be surprised if you round a corner and find a Sherman tank or a German 88 staring you in the face—they are part of the landscape now.

Although the Grand Duchy once comprised an area some three hundred times larger than it does today, its occupation by a succession of Burgundians, Spaniards, Austrians, French, and Germans from 1448 to 1815 led to a reduction of the country's size and importance. Its importance seems to be rising again, however, as its central location and strict bank secrecy laws have made it an important part of the emerging European Community. Today, medieval walls and spires share the skyline with modern office complexes in Luxembourg City. Strikingly poised on two sides of the gorge formed by the Alzette River, this small city is home to a great deal of international business and the European Courts of Justice.

Most Luxembourgers speak German, French, and Luxembourgish, a Middle-High German dialect similar to Dutch and German but unintelligible to native speakers of either. Their unique language has contributed to the strong sense of identity Luxembourgers have maintained. Because of the country's small size and the stubbornly rural atmosphere outside its capital, Luxembourg provides a pocket of relative peace and tranquility for those seeking to escape the tourist crush in the cities of its much more populous neighbors.

—Marta Escovar, Austin, Texas

Official name: Grand Duchy of Luxembourg. **Size:** 998 square miles (smaller than Rhode Island). **Population:** 388,000. **Population density:** 388 inhabitants per square mile. **Capital and largest city:** Luxembourg (pop. 86,000). **Language:** Luxembourgish, French, German. **Religion:** Roman Catholic. **Per capita income:** US$18,000. **Currency:** Luxembourg franc. **Literacy rate:** 100%. **Average daily temperature:** Luxembourg: June, 60°F; December, 34°F. **Average number of days with precipitation:** Luxembourg: June, 14; December, 20.

TRAVEL

U.S. citizens will need a passport but not a visa for stays of up to three months. Travelers must be in possession of sufficient funds and onward or return ticket. For further information, check with the **Embassy of Luxembourg**, 2200 Massachusetts Avenue NW, Washington, DC 20008; (202) 265-4171.

Getting Around

Most travelers to Luxembourg will also want to visit neighboring countries. Eurailpasses, of course, are a good option for multi-country train travel. Those planning to spend most of their time in Luxembourg, Belgium, and the Netherlands would do well to inquire into the **Benelux Tourrail Pass**, which allows 5 days of travel throughout the three countries during a 17-day period. Youths under 26 pay $92 for second class. The Benelux Tourrail Pass can be purchased from Rail Europe (see page 00) or Council Travel (see pages 00–00).

Luxembourg's train and bus networks operate in tandem, with buses serving just about every location. You can purchase a **Network ticket** good for one day of unlimited use of the entire public transportation system for 120F (US $20). Network tickets good for a month cost 1200F ($205).

Bicycling is encouraged in Luxembourg. In fact, if you take your bike on the train you can receive a reduction of 18F ($0.50) on your ticket, although you have to pay 30F ($1) for the bike. **Note:** Bikes are permitted only when there is sufficient room on board. You can get information on cycling routes and bike rental from the Luxembourg National Tourist Office (see "For Further Information," below).

Eating and Sleeping

There are a number of **youth hostels** in Luxembourg. For more information, contact Hostelling International/American Youth Hostels (see page 54) or Luxembourg's national youth hostel organization, **Centrale des Auberges de Jeunesse Luxembourgeoises**, 18 Place d'Armes, L-1136 Luxembourg; (352) 225588; fax (352) 463987. This organization also sells BIJ train tickets, with reductions of up to 40 percent off regular prices, as well as distributing general travel information and arranging accommodations, tours, and outdoor activities. Information on camping can be obtained from the Luxembourg National Tourist Office (see "For Further Information," below).

Especially for Students and Young People

Holders of the International Student Identity Card are entitled to a 50-percent discount at most museums. For further information on student discounts, contact Centrale des Auberges de Jeunesse Luxembourgeoises (see "Eating and Sleeping," above) or **Voyages Sotour-Tourisme des Jeunes**, 15 Place du Theatre, L-2010 Luxembourg; (352) 461514.

For Further Information

For general travel information, contact the **Luxembourg Tourist Office**, 801 Second Avenue, New York, NY 10017; (212) 370-9850.

The best travel guide to Luxembourg and surrounding countries is *The Real Guide: Holland, Belgium, and Luxembourg* ($16). For more information on *Real Guides*, see page 57.

WORK

In order to secure employment in Luxembourg, you must obtain a work permit and an authorization of temporary residence. In order to secure a work permit, you must be offered a position by an employer based in Luxembourg, who is responsible for proving that the job description makes it necessary to recruit outside the EC job market. A good working knowledge of French and/or German is often required.

Internships/Traineeships

A program offered by a member of the Council on International Educational Exchange is listed below.

Association for International Practical Training. *IAESTE Trainee Program.* On-the-job training for undergraduate and graduate students in technical fields such as engineering, computer science, agriculture, architecture, mathematics, and the natural and physical sciences. See page 19 for more information.

STUDY

A program offered by a CIEE-member institution is listed below. Consult Appendix I for the address to write for more information.

Semester and Academic Year

General Studies

Miami University. Semester and academic year. European studies with French or German language at John E. Dolibois European Center. Field trips. First-year to juniors with 2.5 GPA. Apply by January 24.

MALTA

The small nation of Malta—comprised of the islands of Malta, Gozo, and Comino—is strategically located in the heart of the Mediterranean Sea, where a blend of Eastern mysticism and Western pragmatism shapes daily life. The Phoenicians, Carthaginians, Greeks, Romans, Byzantines, Arabs, Normans, the Knights of St. John, the French, and the British have all left their mark on the islands. Today the southern Italian influence is most obvious in the Maltese people, their food (lots of pasta), and their churches. Arabic influences are apparent in the architecture, the narrow winding streets of Valletta, and the language: Maltese is closely related to Arabic, but also includes elements of languages from the many different countries that once dominated these small islands.

The relics of colonial Britain can be seen everywhere—nearly everyone speaks English as well as Maltese. Under British control in World War II, its populace earned Britain's George Cross for refusing to surrender under a devastating Axis bombardment. The George Cross now appears on the flag of Malta, which became an independent nation in 1964 after 150 years of British rule. The abundance of British pubs and restaurants serving fish and chips around Silema and St. Julians make it a popular destination for British vacationers.

Malta is only 19 miles long and 7 miles wide, but once you escape the crowded coast, the island is relatively unspoiled. The shores of Malta have provided a safe haven for many passing ships during winter storms; they also have been the scene of some famous shipwrecks—most notably St. Paul on his way to Rome. Religion has also left an imprint in the culture; most Maltese are Roman Catholic, and each village has an impressive Catholic church and celebrates the feast day of its patron saint. Religious icons can be found everywhere, often adorned with multicolored lights.

Valletta, the capital of Malta, is an 18th-century fortress city famous for its lace-making and silversmithing. Its palaces, churches, museums, and the imposing St. John's Cathedral are worth visiting, as is the Grand Harbour. Valletta can be explored on foot, but the rest of the island can be reached on the green buses that depart from the city gate terminus in Floriana. Take a bus to Mdina, the ancient capital city, and get a feel of what Malta was like before the advent of the car. Cars are not allowed inside this walled medieval city, where the inhabitants still live behind huge carved wooden doors.

The neighboring islands of Comino and Gozo can only be reached by ferry. Comino is a small, dry island with two hotels and no cars; Gozo is half the size of Malta and much greener.

The Maltese are an incredibly outgoing and friendly people. All that's needed to experience the real Malta is to leave behind the hotel complexes of Silema and St. Pauls and head for the smaller towns and fishing villages.

—Wendy Tabuteau, London, United Kingdom

Official name: Republic of Malta. **Size:** 122 square miles (about one-fifth the size of Rhode Island). **Population:** 354,000. **Population density:** 2,901 inhabitants per square mile. **Capital:** Valletta. **Largest city:** Birkirkara (pop. 21,000). **Language:** Maltese, English (both official). **Religion:** Roman Catholic. **Per capita income:** US$6,564. **Currency:** Maltese Lera. **Literacy rate:** 90%. **Average daily high/low:** Valletta: January 59°F/31°F; July, 84°F/72°F. **Average days with precipitation:** Valletta: January, 13; July, 1.

TRAVEL

A passport is required for U.S. citizens traveling to Malta, but a visa is not required for stays of up to three months. For specific requirements, check with the **Embassy of Malta**, 2017 Connecticut Avenue NW, Washington, DC 20008; (202) 462-3611; fax (202) 387-5470.

Getting Around

Ferries link Valletta with several cities of southern Italy; smaller ferries connect Malta to the outer islands of Gozo and Comino, both of which are more rural and relaxed than the crowded, bustling main island for which the entire country is named.

Buses serving all parts of the island of Malta provide an inexpensive way of getting around. Mopeds, which can be rented at various locations around the island, are another popular means of travel.

Eating and Sleeping

There are several **youth hostels** on the islands of Malta, although none are full members of Hostelling International. For more information, contact NSTS—Student and Youth Travel (see "Especially for Students and Young People," below) or the **Malta Youth Hostels Association**, 17 Triq Tal-Borg, Pawla, PLA 06; (356) 239361. Also contact **Independent Hostel Owners in Ireland, England, Malta, Scotland, Germany** (see page 161).

Especially for Students and Young People

Malta's student travel organization and issuer of the International Student Identity Card is **NSTS—Student and Youth Travel**, 220 St. Paul Street,

Valletta; (356) 244983; fax (356) 230330. With offices on Malta and Gozo, NSTS provides information on travel and accommodations throughout the country, offers student tours and cruises, operates a student accommodations center, and runs a water-sports facility. Students with the International Student Identity Card will receive discounts on all of these NSTS services. Other discounts for cardholders include free entrance to all government museums and discounts at a number of retail stores. NSTS organizes many social activities for visiting young people from June to September—contact them for details.

Many inexpensive guesthouses on Malta are suitable for students. Contact NSTS for further information on places to stay (NSTS requests people writing for information enclose two international postal reply coupons). The International Youth Card is good for discounts on tours, excursions and cruises around the island, recreational facilities, restaurants, and accommodations.

For Further Information

Lonely Planet's *Mediterranean Europe on a Shoestring* ($24.95) has an informative chapter on Malta. For a better introduction to the country, read *Insight Guide: Malta* ($19.95). For more information on Lonely Planet and *Insight Guides*, see pages 56–57.

WORK

In order to work in Malta, foreigners must secure a job offer prior to going to the country. The prospective employer then applies for the work permit on your behalf. Opportunities are usually only available in specialized fields. For further information contact the Administrative Secretary, **Immigration and Nationality Branch**, Auberge de Castille, Valletta, Malta.

Internships/Traineeships

A program offered by a member of the Council on International Educational Exchange is listed below.

Association for International Practical Training. *IAESTE Trainee Program.* On-the-job training for undergraduate and graduate students in technical fields such as engineering, computer science, agriculture, architecture, mathematics, and the physical and natural sciences. See page 19 for more information.

STUDY

A program offered by a CIEE-member institution is listed below. Consult Appendix I for the address to write for more information.

Semester and Academic Year

General Studies

International Student Exchange Program (ISEP). Semester and academic year. Direct reciprocal exchange between U.S. universities and University of

Malta. Full curriculum options. Rolling admissions. Open only to students at ISEP-member institutions. Contact ISEP for list of members.

THE NETHERLANDS

The Netherlands' proximity to the North Sea, and the fact that much of the country lies below sea level, shape the character of the country. The Dutch have long been sailors and vigorous entrepreneurs, inspiring an outward-looking society that takes pride in welcoming and assimilating foreigners. But although the sea is a door opening outwards, it is also a source of potential catastrophe. The successful battle to keep the water at bay has brought to the society a strong sense of community, which in turn is the foundation for one of the strongest welfare states in the world. The Dutch pay very high taxes and social premiums; their expectations of government services are accordingly much higher than in most countries. The Delta Project, an elaborate system of dikes and dams designed to protect the low-lying coastline, was publicly financed. Similarly, virtually all education, including religious schools, is state sponsored. By American standards, health care, public transportation, the arts, sports, and social services are all heavily subsidized.

Discussing national or international political issues is a daily pastime for the Dutch, either among family members, with co-workers during the morning coffee break, or with friends in one of the country's pubs and bars. American visitors are encouraged to be well informed about their country's foreign policy, as the topic is likely to come up sooner or later. Such discussion will be in English, which most Dutch speak quite well. (In comparing political systems, it is helpful to know that the Dutch word *liberaal* does not translate into "liberal" in English. *Liberaal* refers to laissez-faire economic policy, and the Dutch *liberalen* are considered conservatives, though many do share the American "liberal" views on issues like abortion, gay rights, and so on.)

Current challenges facing Dutch society include the maintenance of its welfare system, which has become a heavy burden for the lackluster national economy since the 1980s. Another challenge is assimilating the growing numbers of ethnic peoples into Dutch society. Since the early 1960s, the Netherlands, like many northern European countries, has become a magnet for migrant workers from the Mediterranean region. In addition, many people from former Dutch colonies like Suriname and Indonesia have emigrated to the Netherlands. Refugees from all over the world have sought and been granted political asylum there. As a result, the country known for its tolerance now has the difficult task of finding solutions for the problems this influx of newcomers has created.

—Angelique Dietz, Northfield, Minnesota

Official name: Kingdom of the Netherlands. **Size:** 15,770 square miles (about twice the size of New Jersey). **Population:** 15,022,000. **Population density:** 952 inhabitants per square mile. **Capital and largest city:** Amsterdam (pop. 694,000). **Language:** Dutch. **Religion:** Roman Catholic, Dutch Reformed. **Per capita income:** US$14,600. **Currency:** Guilder. **Literacy rate:** 99%. **Average daily temperature:** Amsterdam: June, 60°F; December, 37°F. **Average number of days with precipitation:** Amsterdam: June, 14; December, 21.

TRAVEL

U.S. citizens will need a passport, but a visa is not required for stays of up to 90 days. For further information, check with **Embassy of the Netherlands**, 4200 Linnean Avenue NW, Washington, DC 20008; (202) 328-4800. You can also contact the nearest **Dutch Consulate General** in Chicago, Houston, Los Angeles, or New York.

Getting Around

Holland's **railway** system is an efficient network providing excellent service to all parts of the country, of which Eurailpass holders may take full advantage. Other than beautiful Friesland in the north, most points of interest are between Amsterdam and Rotterdam. To use Holland's public transportation system, which includes buses, trams, and the underground, you must purchase a *strippenkaart*, a zone card accepted universally instead of cash (you can't use coins). The card is also valid for second-class rail travel within the city limits of Amsterdam, Rotterdam, The Hague, Utrecht, and Zoetermeer. **Strippenkaarts** are sold in railway stations, transportation offices, post offices, and tobacconists.

Those planning to spend most of their time in the Netherlands, Belgium, and Luxembourg should ask about the **Benelux Tourrail Pass**, which allows 5 days of travel throughout the three countries during a 17-day period. Youths under 26 pay $92 for second class. The Benelux Tourrail Pass can be purchased from Rail Europe (see page 62) or Council Travel (see pages xiii–xvi).

There are two other rail pass options for those who wish to remain in the Netherlands. However, because the major points of interest require only short journeys, think carefully before investing in either. **Domino tickets** allow 3, 5, or 10 days of train travel in one month. Second-class for youths under 26 are $45, $76, and $151, respectively. The **Railrover ticket** allows seven consecutive days of travel for $134 (first class) and $89 (second class). For an additional charge of $16, you can receive unlimited use of all public buses, trams, and subways with the Railrover ticket. Domino and Railrover tickets can be purchased in the U.S. from the Netherlands Board of Tourism (see "For Further Information," below).

The flat lowlands of the country are probably best seen by **bicycle**. Most streets and highways have separate bike lanes. Bicycle rental agencies are plentiful and include most train stations. There is an extra charge for carrying bikes on trains that varies depending on distance, season, and day.

Eating and Sleeping

There are about 40 **youth hostels** in the Netherlands. For more information, contact Hostelling International/American Youth Hostels (see page 54) or the national youth hostel organization, **Stitching Nederlandse Jeugdherberg Centrale (NJHC)**, Prof Tulpplein 4, 1018 GX Amsterdam; (31) 20-5513155; fax (31) 20-6234986.

In addition, several Dutch universities offer affordable **dormitory lodgings** to travelers. For more information, contact NBBS (see "Especially for Students and Young People," below) or consult Campus Travel Service's *US and Worldwide Travel Accommodations Guide* (see page 54). VVV tourist offices (look for the blue triangular sign) can always book accommodations for you and can often find less-expensive rooms in private homes.

Especially for Students and Young People

Holland's student and youth travel bureau and issuer of the International Student Identity Card is **NBBS**, Schipholweg 101, 2316 XC Leiden; (31) 7-253333; fax (31) 7-226475. NBBS has 25 offices around the country, including one at 17 Dam Square, in Amsterdam. NBBS can provide travel information and student discounts on international travel by plane or train. NBBS also offers tours of Amsterdam and bicycle tours of the Netherlands.

For Further Information

For general travel information, contact the **Netherlands Board of Tourism**, 355 Lexington Avenue, New York, NY 10017; (212) 370-7367. The Netherlands Board of Tourism also has a midwest office at 225 North Michigan Avenue, Suite 326, Chicago, IL 60601; (312) 819-0300; fax (312) 819-1740.

The best guide to the Netherlands and surrounding countries is *The Real Guide: Holland, Belgium, and Luxembourg* ($16). *The Real Guide: Amsterdam* ($9.95) takes an in-depth look at the Netherlands' most vital city. An excellent book to read in preparation for your trip is *Insight Guide: Netherlands* ($19.95). For more information on *Real Guides* and *Insight Guides*, see pages 56–57.

WORK

A work permit is required, but it is difficult to obtain because there are very few positions open to students. Contact the Embassy of the Netherlands (see "Travel," above), for further information.

Internships/Traineeships

Programs offered by members of the Council on International Educational Exchange are listed below.

Association for International Practical Training. *IAESTE Trainee Program*. On-the-job training for undergraduate and graduate students in technical fields such as engineering, computer science, agriculture, architecture, mathematics, and the physical and natural sciences. See page 19 for more information.
Hospitality/Tourism Exchanges Program. On-the-job training for young people beginning a career in the hotel and food-service industries. Participants must have graduated or be currently enrolled in a university or vocational school and possess at least six months of training or experience in the chosen field. Training usually runs from 6 to 18 months. Consult Appendix I for the address where you can write for more information.

Ohio University. *The Consortium for Overseas Student Teaching*. Student teaching in local and independent schools. Quarter. Sophomores to juniors attending Ohio University only. Contact: Wes Snyder, Center for Higher Education and International Programs, 129 McCracken Hall, Athens, OH 45701; (614) 593-4445; fax (614) 593-0569.

Voluntary Service

CIEE places young people in voluntary-service **workcamps** in the Netherlands organized by SIW International Voluntary Projects in Utrecht. Projects include construction work, forest management, and a variety of social projects. Volunteers work in groups of 10 to 15 people for about three weeks during the summer. Room and board are provided, although no wages are paid. Applicants must be between the ages of 18 and 30. The applications of U.S. residents are processed by CIEE. For more information, contact the International Voluntary Service Department at CIEE.

STUDY

Information on higher education, international courses, and scholarships available to foreign students in the Netherlands is available from the **Netherlands Organisation for International Cooperation in Higher Education (NUFFIC)**. Write to NUFFIC, Information Department, PO Box 90734, 2509 LS The Hague, Netherlands. Information is also available through the Press and Cultural Sections of the Netherlands Consulate General in New York, San Francisco, Los Angeles, Houston, and Chicago, as well as the Embassy in Washington, DC. In addition to providing information and assistance to foreigners who want to study the Netherlands, the **Foreign Student Service (FSS)** also issues two helpful booklets. *Vademecum: A Concise Guide to Studying in the Netherlands for Foreign Students*, which lists study possibilities for foreigners at Dutch universities and colleges of professional education, is available for US$7 (postage inclusive), and *Non-University Dutch Language Courses* is available for US$4, both from the FSS, Oranje Nassaulaan 5, 1075 AH Amsterdam; (31) 20-6715915.

Following are the educational programs offered by CIEE-member institutions. Unless otherwise noted, consult Appendix I for the addresses of colleges and universities listed in this section. In addition to the programs below, the University of Oregon offers a program open only to its own students.

Semester and Academic Year

Business

University of Connecticut. *Study Abroad Program in Maastricht*. Fall semester. International business and economics. Juniors and seniors with 2.75 GPA. Apply by February 15.

Film

University of Amsterdam. *Film and Television Studies*. Amsterdam. Semester (for non-master's degree candidates) and academic year (for degree candidates). English-language program leading to M.A. in film and television studies. Seniors (on a semester basis) and graduate students in good academic standing. Apply by June 1. Contact: Professor Thomas Elsaesser, Filmen Televisiewetenschap, Nieuwe Doelenstraat 16, University of Amsterdam, 1012 CP Amsterdam, The Netherlands; (31-20) 5252980.

General Studies

International Student Exchange Program (ISEP). Semester and academic year. Direct reciprocal exchange between U.S. universities and institutions in Amsterdam, Groningen, Leiden, Nijmegen, Tilburg, and Utrecht. Full curriculum options in Dutch; special programs available in English. Rolling admissions. Open only to students at ISEP-member institutions. Contact ISEP for list of members.

University of Amsterdam. *ACCESS: Amsterdam Center for Comparative European Social Sciences.* Fall, winter, and spring quarters, and academic year. Ethnicity and nationalism, environmental movements, discourse, economics, sociology, political philosophy, sex and gender studies, communications, and other disciplines. Juniors to graduate students with 3.0 GPA. Apply by May 15 for undergraduates; April 15 for graduate students. Contact: Christel van Rooy, ACCESS, University of Amsterdam, Oudezijds Achterburgwal 237, 1012 DL Amsterdam, The Netherlands; (31-20) 5254702.

Discourse and Argumentation Studies at Amsterdam. Fall, winter, and spring quarters, and academic year. Theoretical and methodological basis in discourse analysis and argumentation theory: use of language for informative and argumentative purposes in variety of contexts. Juniors to graduate students. Apply three months before projected start of studies. Contact: DASA, Instituut voor Neerlandistick, University of Amsterdam, Spuistraat 134, 1012 VB Amsterdam, The Netherlands, (31-20) 5254716.

University of Nebraska—Lincoln. *University of Amsterdam Exchange.* Amsterdam. Spring semester and academic year. European studies, social studies, Dutch language, law, and international relations. Juniors to graduate students in good standing at member institutions of the Association of Big Eight Universities. Apply by March 15 for academic year; October 1 for spring semester.

University of Wisconsin at Madison. *University of Utrecht Exchange.* Semester and academic year. Dutch language, European economics, politics, literature, business administration, and liberal arts. Juniors to graduate students in good academic standing. Open only to students at higher education institutions in Wisconson or Wisconsin residents studying outside the state. Apply by second Friday in February.

Webster University. *Study Abroad in Leiden.* Quarter, semester, and academic year. High-school graduates to graduate students. Apply four months before projected start of study. Contact: (800) 753-6765.

Lesbian, Gay, and Bisexual Studies

World Learning/School for International Training. *College Semester Abroad.* Amsterdam and Utrecht. Fall and spring semesters. Intensive language, life, and culture seminar; lesbian, gay, and bisexual studies seminar; field-study methods seminar; and independent study project. Homestays. Sophomores to seniors with 2.5 GPA. Apply by May 7 for fall; October 7 for spring. Contact: College Semester Abroad Admissions at (800) 336-1616.

Law

University of Amsterdam. *Amsterdam Law Program.* Spring semester. Legal theory, legal specializations, and Dutch, European, and international law. Advanced law students and law graduates. Contact: Committee on Foreign Relations of the Faculty of Law, University of Amsterdam, PO Box 1030, 1000 BA Amsterdam, The Netherlands.

Political Science

Indiana University. *University of Leiden.* Fall semester. Public policy and administration program of study. Purdue and Indiana University juniors and seniors with 3.0 GPA. Apply by February 1.

Erasmus University. Rotterdam. Spring semester. Public policy and administration program of study. Purdue and Indiana University juniors and seniors with 3.0 GPA. Apply by October 1.

Summer and Short-Term

General Studies

University of Amsterdam. *Amsterdam Summer University (ASU)*. Late July to early September. Wide variety of arts and sciences disciplines. Evening cultural program and hotel/apartment housing. Freshmen to graduate students and professionals. Apply by June 1. Contact: Amsterdam Summer University, Box 53066, 1007 RB Amsterdam, The Netherlands; (31-20) 6200225.
Webster University. *Study Abroad in Leiden*. Summer. High-school graduates to graduate students. Apply four months ahead. Contact: (800) 753-6765.

Health and Medicine

University of Amsterdam. *Amsterdam International Medical Summer School (AIMSS)*. Mid-July to mid-August. Recent advances in most medical fields, such as cardiovascular disease, neuroscience, immunology, health care, and endocrinology. Advanced undergraduate medical students. Contact: AIMSS, Office of International Affairs, Faculty of Medicine at University of Amsterdam, Academic Medical Center, Meibergdreef 15, 1105 AZ Amsterdam, The Netherlands; (31-20) 5664646.

Political Science

University of Alabama. *Alabama in the Netherlands*. Groningen. Economics and politics at Hanse Polytechnic. Undergraduates, graduate students, and adults with 2.5 GPA. Apply by April 1.

EXPLORING DUTCH CULTURE

Readings

Much recent Dutch literature seems to focus on World War II and its effects. Anne Frank's *The Diary of a Young Girl* is probably among the most revealing documentation of the plight of Amsterdam's Jews. Other books about Jewish children's experiences of the war include *Etty: An Interrupted Life*, by Etty Hillesium, and Jona Oberski's *Childhood*. Marga Minco has published *The Glass Bridge* (1989) and *An Empty House* (1990), a popular drama about the experiences of a Dutch Jewish woman during the same period. A novel that deals with World War II and its emotional effects is Harry Mulisch's *The Assault*. This novel was the first by this prominent Dutch writer to be translated into English and it revolves around the sole young survivor of a family slaughtered in a Nazi vendetta massacre and his attempt to come to terms with it many years later. Mulisch's most recent novel, *Last Call*, is set in contemporary Amsterdam and explores the link between illusion and reality.

Another prolific Dutch writer is Janwillem Van de Wetering. His novel *The Streetbird* is a murder mystery set in the red-light district of Amsterdam. *Corpse on the Dike* and *Hard Rain* are other Holland-based offbeat detective tales by this quirky, humorous novelist. Another contemporary Dutch novelist is Jan Wolkers; his novel *Turkish Delights*, a semi-autobiographical book about marital turbulence and infidelity set in Amsterdam in the 1970s, was made into a successful film by Paul Verhoeven in 1974.

Film

Paul Verhoeven is perhaps the Netherlands' most famous filmmaker. He has had a number of successful American films, including the hits *Robocop, Total Recall*, and *Basic Instinct. The Fourth Man* (1984) is a film Verhoeven made before coming to America; it is a black comedy about a gay novelist who seduces a widow in order to get close to her boyfriend. Three young men are involved with a mobile-kitchen sex kitten in *Spetters*, a Verhoeven film from 1980.

George Sluizer has had some success outside the Netherlands with *The Vanishing* (1991), the story of a man who, after three years of obsession with his girlfriend's disappearance, confronts her kidnapper. Sluizer directed both the European and American versions. He also directed the critically acclaimed *Utz*, based on the novel by Bruce Chatwin.

Abel (1985) is a witty black farce on family life from writer/director Alex Van Warmerdam. Dick Maas wrote and directed *Amsterdamned* (1988), about a cop investigating the murder of a prostitute in a canal. A lawyer defends three women who claim that their gratuitous act of murder is the result of masculine oppression in the stylish *A Question of Silence* (1982), written and directed by Marleen Gorris. In Fons Rademakers's *The Assault* (1986 Oscar winner for best foreign film), a man is forced to confront the memory of his family's murder by Nazis during his childhood.

NORWAY

A long Atlantic coastline punctuated by innumerable fjords, mountainous terrain, and a climate warmed by the Gulf Stream characterize the natural conditions of Scandinavia's westernmost nation. Norway offers a landscape that resembles—and often surpasses—that of Switzerland, with its small towns nestling among peaks and beside lakes, its chalets and tumbling streams, and its superb rail network. As in Switzerland, too, the mountain landscape offers beauty and peace, encourages sports and outdoor recreation, but takes its toll in increasing the costs of commerce and communications.

For most visitors, the fjords constitute Norway's claim to a unique place in the world's geography. Their mirror-still waters, the rearing height of the rocky sides veined with waterfalls and studded with enormous boulders—all radiate a majesty and a tranquility that encroaching civilization has not yet contrived to spoil.

For most of its long history, Norway was a nation of subsistence farmers and woodsmen, fishermen, and sailors. Between approximately A.D. 700 and 1000, profiting from their superior nautical technology and extensive coastline, Norwegian Vikings exerted great power. These bold and rapacious adventurers roved the seas as far as North America, striking fear into the hearts of more settled peoples. Their aggressive expansion finally was muffled by the pacifying forces of Christianity in about the year 1000.

For centuries Norway was ruled by its more populous neighbors, Denmark and later, Sweden. Throughout the 19th century a wave of ardent Norwegian nationalist fervor grew, leading to independence from Sweden in 1905. A Danish prince became the first king of Norway and his son, Olav V, remained on the throne until his death in 1990, a beloved symbol of national unity and independence.

Following the example of its richer and more innovative neighbors, Sweden and Denmark, Norway also enacted substantial social welfare legislation. Norwegians are proud of their legal and educational systems, designed to give everyone an equal chance in life. Its people have a passionate concern for individual independence, the equitable distribution of wealth, and outdoor life. Since the discovery and development of offshore oil, Norwegians have struggled to preserve their natural environment and the traditional sources of income it provides—fishing, forestry, and farming. Indeed, Norway's protection of its natural heritage, which includes a humble respect for the powers of nature, offers an ecological model for the world to follow. While Norway initially shied away from membership in the EC, it is now applying to join.

Oil revenues brought sudden wealth to the country during the 1970s and early '80s, along with increased urbanization, industrialization, and social benefits for its four million citizens. But revenues from this source dropped sharply during the mid-1980s, resulting in inflation and deficit spending. Norway has thus become an expensive country for both Norwegians and visitors. But for your money, you will be well looked after. Hotels and homes are clean and well ordered. Norwegians are justly proud of "The Solid Standard" in all goods and services.

As a traditionally rural people, Norwegians are wonderfully hospitable, even in sophisticated and up-to-date Oslo, with its many museums, shops, restaurants, and parks. Manners are relaxed and dress is largely casual throughout the country. As an old "folk culture," Norway has more than its share of tales and legends, arts and crafts, all now in full flourish.

—William W. Hoffa, Amherst, Massachusetts

Official name: Kingdom of Norway. **Size:** 125,181 square miles (about the size of New Mexico). **Population:** 4,273,000. **Population density:** 34 inhabitants per square mile. **Capital and largest city:** Oslo (pop. 461,000). **Language:** Norwegian. **Religion:** Lutheran. **Per capita income:** US$17,400. **Currency:** Kroner. **Literacy rate:** 99%. **Average daily temperature:** Oslo: June, 57°F; December 25°F. **Average number of days with precipitation:** Oslo: June, 13; December, 17.

TRAVEL

A passport is required for U.S. citizens visiting Norway. However, a visa is not required for stays of up to 90 days, a period that begins as soon as one enters the Scandinavian region (Denmark, Finland, Iceland, Norway, and Sweden). For specific requirements, check with the **Royal Norwegian Embassy**, 2720 34th Street NW, Washington, DC 20008; (202) 333-6000.

Getting Around

Travelers flying Scandinavian Airlines (SAS) round-trip to the Scandinavian countries of Norway, Denmark, or Sweden are eligible for SAS's **Visit Scandi-**

navia fare. The special plan allows the purchase of up to six discounted flight coupons for travel within the three countries. The coupons, which cost from $80 for one flight to $420 for six, must be purchased in the U.S. before departure and must be used within three months of arrival in Scandinavia. It can be used on any of the three Scandinavian airlines: Danair, Linjeflyg, and SAS (excluding flights to the Faroe Islands and Greenland). For more information, call SAS at (800) 221-2350.

Another airline, Braathens SAFE, offers **Visit Norway Passes**, which are discount tickets for individual flights. Short flights cost $66 and long flights cost $132. Contact STC Tour Consultants, 8939 Sepulveda Boulevard, Suite 220, Los Angeles, CA 90045; (800) 272-2626.

Norway has five major **railroad** lines, branching out from Oslo to cities such as Bergen, Trondheim, and Bodø, north of the Arctic Circle. The 200-mile Bergen Line, connecting Oslo to Bergen in a six-hour journey, is one of the world's most spectacular railway routes, reaching heights of over 1,300 meters. Discount tickets are sold for trains that depart at low-traffic times (marked by green dots on the timetable).

Eurailpasses of all types are valid in Norway. Those planning to travel extensively in Scandinavia should also consider the following options:

- **The Scanrail Pass** is valid for travel on the state railway systems of Norway, Denmark, Finland, and Sweden on a certain number of days within a fixed period. For example, one may travel on any of 14 days within one month for $475 first class or $369 second class. Scanrail also allows free or discounted passage on a number of ferry lines. The Scanrail Pass can be purchased through Rail Europe (see page 62) or Council Travel (see pages xiii–xvi).
- **The Nordturist Pass** allows for 21 days of free travel on the state railway systems of the four above-mentioned countries, including certain ferries. It's also good for a 50-percent discount on other ferry lines and bus routes. This pass can only be bought in Scandinavia, and is a better buy than the ScanRail Pass. The cost for youths ages 12 to 25 traveling second-class is approximately US$250.

If you have the time you may also want to investigate the legendary coastal **steamers** that link towns along the coast from Bergen to Kirkenes, near the Russian border. Auto touring can also be a pleasant experience.

Since so much of Norway is mountainous wilderness, hiking and biking are favorite pastimes for both Norwegians and tourists. **Bicycles** can be rented virtually anywhere. Of course, all sorts of outdoor sports are available in Norway, including sailing, rafting, summer skiing, and dogsledding.

Eating and Sleeping

For low-priced accommodations, look for the words *pensjon* or *pensjonat* (pension) in the hotel name. There are also some 90 **youth hostels** throughout Norway. For more information, contact Hostelling International/American Youth Hostels (see page 54) or the national youth hostel organization, **Norske Vandrerhjem**, Dronningensgate 26, N-0154 Oslo; (47) 2-22421410; fax (47) 2-22424476. For information on camping and low-cost lodging for bikers and hikers, contact the **Norwegian Tourist Board** (see "For Further Information," below).

In addition, several Norwegian universities offer affordable **dormitory lodgings** to travelers. For more information, contact **Kilroy travels Norway** (see

"Especially for Students and Young People," below) or consult Campus Travel Service's *US and Worldwide Travel Accommodations Guide* (see page 54).

Especially for Students and Young People

Norway's student travel bureau and issuer of the International Student Identity Card is **Kilroy travels Norway**, Box 54, Blindern, 0313 Oslo 3; (47) 2-453200; fax (47) 2-453239. It also has offices in As, Bergen, Stavanger, and Tromsö, all good sources of information on student discounts.

For Further Information

A number of detailed publications including information on camping, hiking, and youth hostels, as well as maps and a calendar of events can be obtained from the **Norwegian Tourist Board**, 655 Third Avenue, New York, NY 10017; (212) 949-2333; fax (212) 983-5260.

One of the best general guidebooks to Denmark and the entire Scandinavian region is Lonely Planet's *Scandinavian and Baltic Europe on a Shoestring* ($17.95). Also good is *The Real Guide: Scandinavia* ($14.95). An excellent book to read in preparation for your trip is *Insight Guide: Norway* ($19.95). For more information on Lonely Planet, *Real Guide*s, and *Insight Guide*s, see pages 56–57.

WORK

Getting a Job

Foreigners may not work in Norway without obtaining a work permit before entering the country. For those interested in **summer employment**, a work permit can be issued for a maximum of three months between May 15 and October 15. To get a permit, a written offer of employment from the prospective employer is required, along with a recommendation from the Norwegian local employment service and the police (procured by the employer). Recommendations are granted only after an effort has been made to have the position filled by a Norwegian national. Generally, work permits are issued only to a specific few: aliens with long-standing and special ties to Norway, scientists, performing artists and musicians, trainees admitted under agreement with other countries, and young people who enter Norway sponsored by any of the youth exchange programs of the Norwegian Foundation for Youth Exchange (see "Farm Work," below). For further information contact the **Norwegian Information Service in the United States**, 825 Third Avenue, New York, NY 10022; (212) 421-7333. The **American-Scandinavian Foundation** (see "Study," below) can also assist Americans ages 21 to 30 with obtaining the requisite permit.

Farm Work

Atlantis—Norwegian Foundation for Youth Exchange (Rolf Hofmosgate 18, 0655 OSLO 6; tel: 47-22-670043). Atlantis will place young people 18 to 30 years of age as working guests or au pairs in Norwegian families. Chores might include haymaking, weeding, milking, picking fruit, or feeding cattle as well as normal housework and childcare. Free-time activities include walking tours in the mountains and forests, swimming, fishing, boating, and excursions to famous Norwegian sights. Placement occurs year-round, with a minimum placement of 4 weeks and a maximum of 12 weeks. Applicants must be between the ages of 18 and 30. Participants receive room and board and approximately $76 per week in pocket money. The registration fee is approximately $127. Enclose two international postal reply coupons when writing for information.

Internships/Traineeships

A program offered by a member of the Council on International Educational Exchange is described below.

Association for International Practical Training. *IAESTE Trainee Program.* On-the-job training for undergraduate and graduate students in technical fields such as engineering, computer science, agriculture, architecture, mathematics, and the natural and physical sciences. See page 19 for more information.

Voluntary Service

For persons interested in voluntary-service work, the Year Abroad Program sponsored by the **International Christian Youth Exchange** offers persons ages 18 to 30 voluntary-service opportunities in the fields of health care, education, the environment, construction, and more. See page 25 for more information.

STUDY

The **Norwegian Information Service** distributes several publications of interest, including *The Norwegian Educational System* and *Admission Requirements for Foreign Students to Universities, University Colleges, and Regional Colleges in Norway*. It also publishes a list of grants for U.S. citizens who wish to study in Norway. The service can be contacted at 825 Third Avenue, 38th Floor, New York, NY 10022; (212) 421-7333.

For a listing of English-language programs offered in Norway during the academic year and summer, a good resource is *Study in Scandinavia*, published by the Exchange Division of the **American-Scandinavian Foundation**, 725 Park Avenue, New York, NY 10021; (212) 879-9779; fax (212) 249-3444.

Following are the study-abroad programs offered by the institutions that are members of the Council on International Educational Exchange. Unless otherwise noted, consult Appendix I for the addresses of the colleges and universities listed in this section.

Semester and Academic Year

General Studies

Scandinavian Seminar. *College Year in Norway.* Individual placement in Norwegian folk colleges throughout Norway. Norwegian language and liberal arts. Sophomores to graduate students and adults. Apply by April 15.

University of Wisconsin at Madison. *Academic Year at the University of Tromsø.* Tromsø. Norwegian and Sami (Lapp) culture and language study, literature, social sciences, health studies, mathematics, science, and law.

Juniors to graduate students in good academic standing and with four semesters of college Norwegian. Apply by second Friday in February. Open only to students studying at colleges and universities in Wisconsin and Wisconsin residents studying outside the state.

International Relations

Scandinavian Seminar. *Semester Program on Nordic and Global Issues.* Kleppe and/or other locations. Fall and spring semesters. International humanitarian organizations, global ecology, international conflict resolution, and sustainable economic development. Excursions. Sophomores to graduate students and adults. Apply by April 15 for fall; October 15 for spring.

EXPLORING NORWEGIAN CULTURE

Readings

Perhaps Norway's greatest literary figure is Henrik Ibsen, one of the fathers of modern drama. Some of his most famous plays are *A Doll's House, Hedda Gabler*, and *Ghosts*. *The Wild Duck* (1884) is generally considered his dramatic masterpiece; its theme is that the lie is necessary for survival in the modern world. Ibsen's long dramatic poem *Peer Gynt* has also been highly influential; here, the central theme is the search for self amid moral chaos.

Knut Hamsun won the Nobel Prize for literature in 1920. His major work is *The Growth of the Soil* (1917), a moving celebration of traditional values that follows a family's struggles in the Norwegian wilderness. Some of his other novels are *Mysteries, Pan*, and *Victoria*. In 1928, Sigrid Undset was awarded the Nobel Prize for literature. Her historical trilogy *Kristin Lavransdatter* (1920–22) is generally considered her masterpiece as well as one of the great works of Norwegian literature.

Bjorg Vik is perhaps Norway's best known feminist writer. A collection of her short stories, *Aquarium of Women*, is available in English. Cora Sandel's *Alberta* trilogy (*Alberta and Jacob, Alberta and Freedom*, and *Alberta Alone*) is a pivotal work in modern Norwegian literature; it follows a young woman's attempt to prove herself in a hostile environment.

POLAND

Everywhere in Poland you can see evidence of the nation's fascinating history and the profound changes shaping the future of the country. You can explore the medieval walled city of Cracow, where Copernicus taught, or visit the Gdańsk shipyards, where Lech Walesa started Solidarity. You can see the most sacred icon of Catholic Poland, the Black Madonna at Częstochowa, or visit Auschwitz, a symbol of Nazi atrocities still fresh in many Poles' memories.

With the exception of the extreme south, Poland is a flat plain that stretches on into Germany to the west and Lithuania, Belarus, and Ukraine to the east. Its geography helps explain why the history of Poland has been one of repeated invasions: Germans, Russians, Tartars, Turks, Swedes, even Genghis Khan, all have taken advantage of Poland's lack of natural obstacles at one time or another. And yet, for a brief period in the 16th and 17th centuries, Poland rose to become a leading European power. Polish kings were even credited with saving Western Europe in 1683 by turning back the invading Turks outside the gates of Vienna. Eventually, however, Poland lost its independence—partitioned by Russia, Prussia, and Austria in 1795—and did not regain it until 1918. Twenty years later, the Nazis again made Poland an occupied territory; by the time the Second World War ended in 1945, six million Poles had been killed and the country lay in ruins. Poland officially regained its independence after the war, but until recently remained under the influence of its "friendly" local superpower, the Soviet Union.

But Polish history is not just the history of military invasions and bitter defeats. Poles are proud of their contributions to science, literature, and the arts, and point to Copernicus, Madame Curie, Chopin, three Nobel Prize–winning authors, and other notables in many fields. Two Polish generals, Pulaski and Kosciusko, played vital roles in helping Americans win their own struggle for independence.

Today, Poland seems to be a country wracked with crises. The political and economic system imposed in 1945 has failed, and the fundamental reforms currently underway won't revitalize the country overnight. In 1989 the country witnessed the swearing in of Eastern Europe's first noncommunist prime minister in 40 years, Tadeusz Mazowiecki, the editor of Solidarity's newspaper. In 1990 Lech Walesa, former leader of Solidarity, was elected President. Poland's first female prime minister, Hanna Suchocka, was elected during the summer of 1992 after the government changed hands three times. The radical reforms that have been enacted to bring Poland toward a free-market economy have drawn protests from unions, farmers, and miners. Some of the changes enacted by the government—such as eliminating subsidies, freezing wages, and devaluating the currency—have been unpopular because they have caused unemployment and a recession.

In spite of improved East-West relations, Poland does not receive many visitors from the United States. Few Poles speak English, and a trip there will require some initiative and preparation. However, Americans who do travel to Poland will find the people especially friendly. Perhaps it's the mixture of fascination and admiration (and a bit of jealousy) with which they look at the United States. Or perhaps it's the ethnic tie to eight million Polish-Americans. Whatever the reason, a visit to Poland is sure to be an interesting one.

—Jan Rudomina, New York, New York

Official name: Republic of Poland. **Area:** 120,727 square miles (about the size of New Mexico). **Population:** 37,799,000. **Population density:** 313 inhabitants per square mile. **Capital and largest city:** Warsaw (pop. 1,600,000). **Language:** Polish. **Religion:** Roman Catholic. **Per capita income:** US$4,200. **Currency:** Zloty. **Literacy rate:** 98%. **Average daily temperature:** Warsaw: June, 63°F; December, 33°F. **Average number of days with precipitation:** Warsaw: June, 13; December, 16.

TRAVEL

U.S. citizens traveling to Poland will need a passport, but a visa is not required for stays of up to 90 days. For more information, check with the **Embassy of**

the Republic of Poland, 2640 16th Street NW, Washington, DC 20009; (202) 234-3800.

Getting Around

Travel by **train** in Poland is inexpensive, and the rail network serves almost every town. But be forewarned: ticket lines are long and trains can be slow, crowded, and uncomfortable. It's always advisable to make reservations at least a day in advance. Try to use express trains whenever possible—they make very few stops. Eurailpasses are not valid in Poland, but the **European East Pass** is valid for travel in Poland as well as the Czech and Slovak republics, Austria, and Hungary. Available in first class only, rail travel on any five days within a 15-day period costs $169, and any 10 days within one month costs $275. A new **Polrail Pass** gives travelers unlimited use of the entire national rail network for various numbers of consecutive days. The **Junior Polrail Pass** (for travelers under 26) costs $39 for 8 days, $45 for 15 days, $51 for 21 days, and $57 for one month. These prices are for first-class travel; fares are even lower for second class. Both the European East Pass and the Polrail Pass can be purchased from Rail Europe (see page 62) or Council Travel (see pages xiii–xvi).

Buses are slow and crowded—even more so than the trains. Again, book in advance. Fares on the nation's bus system are about the same as for the train. Faster and more comfortable travel is available on the national airline, LOT, which serves a number of Polish cities.

Eating and Sleeping

Poland has more than 150 **youth hostels**. For more information, contact Hostelling International/American Youth Hostels (see page 54) or the national youth hostel association, **Polskie Towarzystwo Schronisk Mlodziezowych**, ul. Chocimska 28, 00-791 Warsaw; (48) 2-498128; fax (48) 2-498354. ALMATUR (see "Especially for Students and Young People," below) operates low-cost **student hotels** in 20 cities during the summer.

Especially for Students and Young People

Poland's student/youth travel agency and issuer of the International Student Identity Card is **ALMATUR**, Kopernik 15, 00-359 Warsaw; (48) 22-265381; fax (48) 22-262353. ALMATUR has offices throughout Poland.

For Further Information

The best source for general information is **Orbis Polish Travel Bureau**, 342 Madison Avenue, New York, NY 10173; (212) 867-5011.

The best budget-travel guide to Poland is Lonely Planet's *Poland: A Travel Survival Kit* ($16.95). Also good is *The Real Guide: Poland* ($13.95). An excellent book to read in preparation for your trip is *Insight Guide: Poland* ($19.95). For more information on Lonely Planet, *Real Guides*, and *Insight Guides*, see pages 56–57.

WORK

Foreigners are not allowed regular employment in Poland. As an alternative, you might be interested in a trainee program or a workcamp.

Internships/Traineeships

A program offered by a member of the Council on International Educational Exchange is listed below.

Association for International Practical Training. *IAESTE Trainee Program.* On-the-job training for undergraduate and graduate students in technical fields such as engineering, computer science, agriculture, architecture, mathematics, and the natural and physical sciences. See page 19 for more information.

Voluntary Service

CIEE places young people in voluntary-service **workcamps** in Poland organized by the Foundation for International Youth Exchange in Warsaw. At these workcamps, groups of volunteers from various countries are involved in construction, maintenance work, gardening, or archaeological excavations. Volunteers must be at least 18 years old. Room and board are provided by the camp. The applications of U.S. residents are processed by CIEE. For more information, contact the International Voluntary Service Department at CIEE.

Global Volunteers sponsors a three-week service program in Poland. Participants live in rural villages and teach English in local schools, camps, and at a retreat center. Opportunities are available in elementary and secondary schools as well as universities. For more information, contact Global Volunteers, 375 East Little Canada Road, St. Paul, MN 55117; (612) 482-1074.

STUDY

For information on scholarships, grants, and study programs administered by the **Kosciuszko Foundation**, write to 15 East 65th Street, New York, NY 10021; (212) 734-2310. Most of the scholarships are for graduate study only, but the foundation does administer an academic-year and summer program for undergraduates at the University of Cracow for which grants are available. The deadline for all scholarships and the year program is January 15, and March 31 for the summer program.

Persons considering study in Poland might want to check out the *AAASS Directory of Programs in Russian, Eurasian, and East European Studies*, which lists close to 75 academic programs in Russia, Eurasia, and Eastern Europe, including addresses and information on deadlines and costs. The directory also lists similar study programs in the U.S. and can be ordered prepaid from the **American Association for the Advancement of Slavic Studies**, Jordan Quad/Acacia, 125 Panama Street, Stanford, CA 94305-4130; (415) 723-9668. The price is $30 for nonmembers, $20 for members, plus $3 postage; you might be able to find it in libraries or study-abroad offices.

For those seriously considering direct enrollment in a Polish university, a five-part guide book on the higher educational system of Poland written by the Ministry of National Education can be requested from the Polish Embassy (see "Travel," above).

The following are the educational programs offered by CIEE-member institutions. Unless otherwise noted, consult Appendix I for the addresses of the colleges and universities listed in this section.

Semester and Academic Year

General Studies

American University. *Poland Semester.* Poznan. Fall and spring semesters. Polish language and liberal arts courses. Second-semester sophomores to seniors with 2.75 GPA. Apply by March 15 for fall; October 15 for spring. Contact: World Capitals Programs, American University, Dunblane House—Tenley Campus, Washington, DC 20016-8083; (202) 895-4900/4937.

Brown University. *Brown in Poland.* Spring semester and academic year. Study at Adam Michiewicz University's Institute of England. Dormitory housing with Polish students. Apply by March 1 for academic year; October 1 for spring.

Council on International Educational Exchange. *Cooperative East and Central European Studies Program at the Warsaw School of Economics.* Fall and spring semesters. Undergraduates with 2.75 GPA and six semester-hours in economics, history, or other social-science discipline. Apply by April 10 for fall; November 1 for spring. Contact: University Programs Department.

State University of New York at Stony Brook. Warsaw and Wroclaw. Fall semester and academic year. Juniors and seniors with one year of Polish or Russian and 3.0 GPA. Apply by April 1. Contact: Dean for International Programs, SUNY at Stony Brook, Stony Brook, NY 11794-2700; (516) 632-7030.

Polish Language and Culture

University of Massachusetts at Amherst. Poznan. Semester and academic year. Sophomores to graduate students with 3.0 GPA. Apply by January 29 for fall and academic year; September 19 for spring.

Summer and Short-Term

Agriculture

Michigan State University. *Food and Agricultural Systems in Poland.* Gdańsk, Warsaw, and Cracow. Summer. Juniors to graduate students. Apply by April 15. Contact: Office of Overseas Study, 108 International Center, Michigan State University, East Lansing, MI 48824-1035; (517) 353-8920.

Economics

University of Pennsylvania. *Penn in Warsaw.* Summer. Political and economic system of Poland, Polish history and culture, and conditions for doing business with socialist countries. Apply by March 1.

General Studies

University of Wisconsin at Milwaukee. *Summer in Poland.* Lublin. Polish history, literature, theater, and music. Sophomores to seniors. Apply by April 15.

Polish Language and Culture

State University of New York College at Buffalo. *Summer Program of Polish Culture and Language.* Cracow. Six weeks in July and August. Polish history, contemporary social and economic problems, politics, theater and film, litera-

ture, religion, music and art, landscape, and language (at all levels). Study at Jageillonian University. Excursions and dormitory housing. Undergraduates to graduate students. Apply by April 15. Contact: Study-Abroad Coordinator, Office of International Education, SUNY College at Buffalo, 212 Talbert Hall, Box 601604, Buffalo, NY 14260-1604; (716) 645-3912.
University of Connecticut. *Summer Program in Poland.* Cracow. Undergraduates. Apply by March 15.
University of Massachusetts at Amherst. Poznan. Summer. Sophomores to graduate students with 3.0 GPA. Apply by January 29.

EXPLORING POLISH CULTURE

Readings

Tadeusz Konwicki has been one of Poland's foremost writers since the fifties. *A Minor Apocalypse* follows a man who has promised to set himself on fire in front of Party headquarters; his *The Polish Complex* takes an often elusive look at contemporary Polish life.

Jerzy Kosinski was a Polish-born novelist who wrote in English. His book *The Painted Bird* is the story of a child's nightmarish experiences separated from his parents and hiding from the Nazis in the Polish countryside during World War II. Kosinski also wrote the screenplay based on his own novel *Being There*, which starred Peter Sellers as Chance the Gardener, an illiterate, childlike 50-year-old man believed a profound genius by the rich and powerful people he meets.

The Captive Mind and *The Issa Valley* are two works that have been translated into English from Polish poet and novelist Czeslaw Milosz, who won the Nobel Prize for literature in 1980. Describing the effects of Communist repression on cultural life, *The Captive Mind* analyzes why so many artists and intellectuals sold out to it after 1945. *The Issa Valley* is an semi-autobiographical novel of a boy growing up in the Lithuanian countryside. Louis Begley was nominated for a National Book Award in 1991 for his work, *Wartime Lies*, about a Jewish boy and his aunt trying to survive during the Nazi occupation of Poland.

Film

One of the best-known Polish film directors is Roman Polanski, whose most famous Polish-language film in the United States is *Knife in the Water* (1962), a melodrama about a young couple who pick up a student hitchhiker and ask him to spend the weekend on their yacht. He has also made a number of English-language films, including *Chinatown* (1974), *Tess* (1980), and *Rosemary's Baby* (1968). Another internationally known Polish film director is Andrzej Wajda. He directed a trilogy of films about Polish resistance to the Nazis during World War II, entitled *A Generation* (1954), *Kanal* (1956), also known as *They Loved Life*, and *Ashes and Diamonds* (1958).

Set during the 1930s, the satiric *Baritone* (1984), directed by Janusz Zaorski, concerns a famous opera singer who returns home after 25 years, then loses his voice before a celebratory concert. In *The Contract* (1980), writer/director Krzysztof Zanussi takes a satiric look at Polish high life. Zanussi also directed the satiric *Camouflage* (1977), about an arrogant professor who challenges a teaching assistant. A singer is arrested, interrogated, and tortured by secret police in Ryszard Bugajski's harrowing *Interrogation* (1982). Polish emigré Jerzy Skolimowski wrote and directed the British-produced *Moonlighting* (1982), about four Polish men sent to London to renovate a wealthy man's apartment just before martial law is imposed in their homeland.

Some prominent Polish film directors of recent years include Agnieszka Holland, who made such films as *Europa Europa* (1992), the story of a Polish-Jewish boy's escape from the Nazis, and *Olivier Olivier* (1993), in which a family falls apart following the disappearance of their young son until they believe he has been found six years later. Krzysztof Kieslowski directed *The Double Life of Veronique* (1992), which focuses on the parallel lives of two women, Veronique and Veronika (both played by Irène Jacob), one living in France, the other in Poland.

PORTUGAL

Portugal is a treasure house of history. The Portuguese, proud of their rich cultural heritage, have preserved their past and delight in sharing it with visitors. Portugal was once a great seafaring kingdom that spanned the globe—Magellan and Vasco da Gama are two of the many Portuguese explorers who ventured to discover new lands and seas. Portugal now survives on manufacturing, farming, wine production, tourism, and the income sent home by a large population of Portuguese workers in the wealthier countries of Europe.

Throughout Portugal you can find reminders of the country's glorious past, such as royal castles, ancient monuments, and antique *azulejos* (tiles) on walls and buildings. The past of a once-powerful empire is still remembered nostalgically by the people of a country that is now one of the poorest in Europe. Consequently, many people, especially from the countryside, have sought work in other countries, such as France, Germany, and Spain. The mournful themes of a seafaring past and a bleak present are heard throughout the land in *fados*, a singing style that is often compared to the blues. But the nostalgia and melancholy associated with the people of Portugal have not changed their genuine hospitality and their gentleness. The country's many festivals or *festas*, both religious and secular, provide an excellent opportunity to meet the Portuguese people and share their food, wine, and folklore.

Lisbon offers the visitor a change of pace from life in larger European capitals. Its relatively small size encourages its discovery on foot. In this city, as in many others throughout Portugal, the architecture proves to be a feast for the eyes. Ceramic tile walls, orange tile roofs, and mosaic sidewalks add structural texture to the pastel stucco buildings.

Portugal was the last European power to hang on to a large colonial empire in Africa. After a successful revolution overthrew Portugal's 50-year military regime in 1974 and installed the current democratic government, Portugal finally granted independence to Mozambique, Angola, and its other African colonies. Today, all its formal colonies are gone, with the exception of the tiny enclave of Macao, due to be ceded to China at the end of the century. Yet both the nation's warm people and fascinating points of interest constantly remind visitors of the nation's past greatness—and by implication, its future potential.

—Sandra L. Fontes, Providence, Rhode Island

Official name: Republic of Portugal. **Size:** 36,390 square miles (about the size of Kentucky). **Population:** 10,387,000. **Population density:** 285 inhabitants per square mile. **Capital and largest city:** Lisbon (pop. 2,000,000). **Language:** Portuguese. **Religion:** Roman Catholic. **Per capita income:** US$5,580. **Currency:** Escudo. **Literacy rate:** 83%. **Average daily temperature:** Lisbon: June, 68°F; December, 53°F. **Average number of days with precipitation:** Lisbon: June, 5; December, 15.

TRAVEL

Americans will need a valid passport, but a visa is not required for visits of up to 60 days. This period may be extended twice while in the country for a total of six months. For more information, contact the **Embassy of Portugal**, 2125 Kalorama Road NW, Washington, DC 20008; (202) 328-8610.

Getting Around

Portugal is still one of the least expensive countries to visit in Europe and is well worth considering when you plan your itinerary.

Except for express trains between Lisbon and Oporto and between Lisbon and the Algarve, **train** travel in Portugal is slow. The Intercity **buses** are faster and more comfortable, although usually a little more expensive than the train. Eurailpasses are valid throughout Portugal. In addition, Rail Europe offers a first-class **Portuguese Railpass**, which allows unlimited rail travel for 4 days in 15 for $95 or 7 days in 21 for $145. The **Portuguese Rail 'n' Drive Pass** allows 3 rail days and 3 days of car rental within 15 days. For two adults driving an economy car, the pass costs $135 per person. Both the Portuguese Railpass and the Rail 'n' Drive Pass must be purchased in the U.S. For more information, contact Rail Europe (see page 62) or Council Travel (see pages xiii–xvi).

Within Portugal, you can buy an unlimited train pass called the **Tourist Ticket**. The Tourist Ticket costs 15,200 escudos (US $88) for 7 days; 24,200 (US $140) for 14 days; and 34,600 (US $200) for 21 days. Portugal also issues a variety of **Social Passes** that allow unlimited use of various urban public transportation systems by the month. For information on these and other Portugese transportation packages, contact the **Portuguese National Tourist Office** (see "For Further Information," below).

Eating and Sleeping

There are over 20 **youth hostels** in Portugal. For more information, contact Hostelling International/American Youth Hostels (see page 54) or the **Portuguese Youth Hostel Association**, Av. Duque D'Avila 137, 1000 Lisbon; (351) 1-3559081; fax (351) 1-3528621. The organization also offers a variety of low-cost **tours** and outdoor programs in mainland Portugal as well as in the Azores and Madeira. For a map listing **campsites** throughout the country, contact the Portuguese National Tourist Office (see "For Further Information," below).

Especially for Students and Young People

Portugal has two student-travel organizations, the larger, with six offices including branches in Albufeira, Coimbra, and Porto, is **TAGUS Youth Travel**, Praça de Londres 9B, 1000 Lisbon; (351) 1-8484957; fax (351) 1-1532715. The second is **ATEJ**, Rua Joaquím Antonio de Aguiar 255, 4300 Porto; (351) 02-568542; fax (351) 2-381435. Both organizations provide travel information, sell discounted train, bus, and plane tickets for students, and operate sightseeing tours. Both also provide a list of stores offering discounts to youth and students.

For Further Information

General tourist information is available from the **Portuguese National Tourist Office**, 590 Fifth Avenue, New York, NY 10036-4704; (212) 354-4403; fax (212) 764-6137.

For basic budget-travel information, *Let's Go: Spain and Portugal* ($16.95), is always dependable. Also good is *The Real Guide: Portugal* ($10.95). The best all-around guide, however, is *Cadogan Guides'* Portugal ($16.95). An excellent book to read in preparation for your trip is *Insight Guide: Portugal* ($19.95). For more information on *Let's Go, Real Guide*s, *Cadogan Guides*, and *Insight Guide*s, see pages 56–57.

WORK

For regular employment in Portugal, which is very difficult for a U.S. citizen to obtain, it is necessary to have a work permit, which is obtained by the employer. After application for the permit is approved by the Ministry of Labor, the employee must get the appropriate visa from the **Portuguese Consulate**, 630 Fifth Avenue, Suite 655, New York, NY 10111.

Internships/Traineeships

A program offered by a member of the Council on International Educational Exchange is listed below.

Association for International Practical Training. *IAESTE Trainee Program.* On-the-job training for undergraduate and graduate students in technical fields such as engineering, computer sciences, agriculture, architecture, mathematics, and the natural and physical sciences. See page 19 for more information.

STUDY

The Cultural Counsellor at the Embassy of Portugal (see "Travel," above) distributes several fact sheets, including *Information on Study in Portugal, Higher Education in Portugal*, a list of universities and general information, and *Cultural News*, a newsletter that often lists contacts for scholarships and awards.

The following are educational programs offered by CIEE-member institutions. Unless otherwise noted, consult Appendix I for the addresses of the colleges and universities listed.

Semester and Academic Year

General Studies

University of Wisconsin at Madison. *Academic Year in Portugal.* Coimbra. Academic year. Humanities and social sciences plus Portuguese language and culture. Juniors and seniors in good academic standing and with two semesters of college Portuguese. Apply by second Friday in February.

Summer and Short-Term

Economics

University of Pennsylvania. *Penn-in-Lisbon.* Summer. For students interested in economics and international relations. Apply by April 1.

EXPLORING PORTUGUESE CULTURE

Readings

For many years, Portuguese writing was limited by the controlling regime of Antonio de Oliveira Salazar, whose 40-year dictatorship ended in 1974. Much of the literature written immediately after 1974 can be seen as a reaction—direct or indirect—to the repression of this period. José Cardoso Pires's mystery novel, *Ballad of Dogs' Beach*, analyzes the fear that gripped the nation during the Salazar regime. *The Promise*, by Bernando Santereno, also deals with the repression and censorship of this period.

Women novelists have recently brought a new voice to Portuguese literature. A collage of stories, letters, and poems, *New Portuguese Letters: The Three Marias*, by Maria Isabel Barreno, Maria Teresa Horta, and Maria Velho de Costa, is a modern feminist parable based on a 17th-century collection of letters. This book became a cause célèbre when it was published in 1972 because its authors were put to trial by the state. *Lemon Verbena* is a novel by one of these authors, Velho de Costa, that explores the role of women in a repressive society.

A couple of other modern Portuguese writers are worthy of note. José Saramago came to the fore in the 1980s. His *Memorial of the Convent* (1982) is about the building of a magnificent convent and, like his other novels, combines an acute observation of reality with flights of poetic fancy. Jorge de Sena's collection of well-crafted stories, *By the Rivers of Babylon and Other Stories*, was written between 1946 and 1964; many of the pieces involve Portuguese historical figures. His 1978 novel, *Signs of Fire*, concerns the effects of the Spanish Civil War on Portugal.

ROMANIA

Count Dracula may be Romania's most famous personage, but there is much more to explore in this country beyond his myth. While relatively small in size, Romania is a country with a long history and a great diversity of natural and cultural assets. The name Romania is a symbol of the importance of the Roman influence on this country's history and national language, but it belies the influence many other groups have exerted; the Turks, Goths, Slavs, Bulgars, Hungarians, and Russians have also left their mark. Like many other countries in Eastern Europe, Romania as a nation-state is a young country whose boundaries have been drawn and redrawn over the centuries. In fact, the name Romania did not come into being until 1862, following the 1859 unification of the principalities of Moldavia and Walachia.

Transylvania is but one of the regions that make up the country, although it seems to be the most popular destination for American travelers. It is a fertile area covered by forests, hills, and farms, a rich landscape that is home to countless imposing feudal castles and fortified towns. It was here that the real Vlad Dracula, who was not a count but a prince, was born. His birthplace in the city of Sighişoara is now a restaurant popular with tourists. Castle Dracula, located near the city of Braşov, has been acclaimed by tourists as the definitive lair for the much-feared prince known as The Impaler. This name suggests cruelty, and rightly so; the prince had a penchant for maiming, torturing, and impaling victims on stakes, sometimes hundreds at a time. Although the sight of blood pleased him, the historical record offers no evidence to suggest Vlad Dracula was a vampire. Nonetheless, the popular literary character borrows much from the historical figure and the dramatic beauty of Transylvania.

Transylvania is surrounded by the Carpathian Mountains, an area enshrined in mystery and steeped in folk tradition. The townsfolk of this region live much as their ancestors did, and their limited contact with the outside world allows them to preserve their peasant traditions. The majestic beauty of the Carpathian region marks a sharp contrast with the tranquil meadows of the Danube Delta, where sumptuous forests and a temperate climate have attracted settlers throughout the years. The Black Sea is the final destination for the Danube River and for travelers seeking its sandy shoreline and the therapeutic benefits of its spas and beach resorts. Health resorts and mineral springs, however, are to be found throughout the country, just as appealing today as they were when the Romans used them.

Precious treasures of art and architecture from the Roman and Byzantine periods can be found in Moldavia, an area famous for its famous painted churches. Bukovina, a region in the north of Moldavia, is particularly renowned for its monasteries and citadels. Moldavia gave birth to a particular style of art that blends folk tradition with Byzantine and Gothic influences. The serene frescoes on the walls complement the gentle hills and placid lakes of this part of the country and mark a prominent educational achievement of the Middle Ages. Tales, legends, historical events, and, of course, stories from the Bible, were painted on the façades, exposing the masses to art and history before books were printed.

Romanian, a language derived from Latin, is the country's official language, and has more in common with Spanish, French, and Portuguese than with German, Hungarian, and the other languages spoken by the many ethnic-minority groups that make up today's Romania. The Latin influence also shows in the character of Romania's capital, Bucharest, although much of its beauty was stripped away by the communist regime. Parts of Bucharest still retain the charm of café-lined boulevards, parks, garden restaurants, and neoclassical architecture. Unfortunately, both for the people of Romania and for its visitors, historic neighborhoods were supplanted by concrete-box housing projects and socialist architectural nightmares, all at the whim of the communist leaders.

The communist chapter of Romania's history seems closed now: The regime came to a violent end in December 1989, when Nicolae Ceausescu was overthrown and executed along with his wife. The May 1990 election was won by Ion Iliescu, who had ties to the former regime but led the National Salvation Front against Ceausescu. The new government made some democratic reforms and produced a new constitution. But the government also has been criticized for forcibly repressing the opposition and restricting civil rights. While it seems that Romania is intent on leaving behind the legacy of social and economic controls of the communist years, there is no consensus on the appropriate pace of reform or the specific course of action. These uncertainties, fueled by the rivalries between pro- and anti-government forces, are preventing the country from making some definite steps toward market reform and a democratic state.

—Fabio Negretti, Florence, Italy

Official name: Romania. **Area:** 91,699 square miles. **Population:** 23,397,000. **Population density:** 255 inhabitants per square mile. **Capital and largest city:** Bucharest (pop. 2,036,000). **Language:** Romanian (official), Hungarian, German. **Religion:** Orthodox, Roman Catholic. **Per capita income:** US$3,000. **Currency:** Lei. **Literacy rate:** 96%. **Average daily high/low:** Bucharest: January, 34°F/19°F; June, 81°F/57°F. **Average number of days with precipitation:** Bucharest: January, 11; June, 12.

TRAVEL

A visa is required for U.S. citizens to visit Romania. Tourust visas valid for 60 days cost $31; multiple-entry visas cost $68. You can obtain tourist and transit visas in the U.S. or upon arrival. For more information, contact the **Embassy of Romania**, 1607 23rd Street NW, Washington, DC 20008; (202) 232-4747; fax (202) 232-4748.

Getting Around

Train service comes in three types, the fastest two known as *rapid* and *accelerat*. For comfort and security, ride in first class; you'll meet more students in second class, however. Romanian trains are known for incidents of theft. **Buses** are much cheaper than trains, but overcrowded. Flying, more expensive but still affordable, is another option.

For Further Information

General tourist information can be obtained from the **Romanian National Tourist Office**, 342 Madison Avenue, New York, NY 10173; (212) 697-6971. A comprehensive travel guide to Romania, the *Companion Guide to Romania*, is available for $14.95 from Hippocrene Books, Attn: Order Department, 171 Madison Avenue, New York, NY 10016; (718) 454-2366. Lonely Planet's *Eastern Europe on a Shoestring* ($21.95) also contains a good chapter on Romania. For more information on Lonely Planet publications, see page 56.

WORK

In order to work in Romania, it is necessary to obtain a work permit. The job must be secured before entering Romania. For more information, contact the

Ministry of Labor and Social Protection, Demetriu Dobrescu, #2, Sector 1, Bucharest.

Internships/Traineeships

A program sponsored by a member of the Council on International Educational Exchange is listed below.

Association for International Practical Training. *IAESTE Trainee Program.* On-the-job training for undergraduate and graduate students in technical fields such as engineering, computer science, agriculture, architecture, and the natural and physical sciences. See page 19 for more information.

STUDY

Below is an academic program sponsored by a CIEE-member institution. Consult Appendix I for the contact address and phone.

Summer and Short-Term

Political Science

University of Louisville. *The Political and Economic Reconstruction of Eastern Europe.* Costaneşti, Bucureşti. Three weeks in summer. First-year college students to graduate students and adults. Apply by April 1.

RUSSIA

Out of the fallen empire of the USSR a rising star, Russia, is born. While the British and Ottoman empires whittled down slowly in size and power, the USSR went out with a bang, in two strokes. First came the botched 1991 August coup that destroyed the legitimacy of the Soviet communists, followed by the real coup of December 1991, masterminded by the current president of Russia, Boris Yeltsin. He cajoled the presidents of several other Soviet republics to create the illusion of a new and lasting entity, the Commonwealth of Independent States (CIS), and put to rest the faltering Union of Soviet Socialist Republics forever—or so it now seems. While the CIS may quickly go the way of the USSR, the nation of Russia is most likely going to be around for a while.

Visitors to this fledgling modern country and ancient land should leave guidebooks at home unless they happen to be recent editions. The traveler's experience is something completely different from what it was when the lands were Soviet. Cities have been renamed, as have streets, subway stops, parks, rivers, and squares. And renaming is just the beginning: Gone are the ubiquitous lines bending around buildings like serpents, and the endless search for a decent roll of toilet paper. Gone are the surly waiters and meals of grisly meat and canned peas. The fleet of Hungarian buses that comprise Russia's entire bus inventory is dwindling, making the buses run infrequently and unbearably crowded. Now that the Russians are no longer buying from the Hungarians at Eastern-Bloc prices, they can no longer afford replacements. The Soviet-built metros in Moscow and St. Petersburg, however, are still a marvelous source of transportation and entertainment—some of the most amazing relics of Soviet esthetics can be found in the interiors of the metro stations.

But what does the new Russia have to offer its steady stream of foreign guests? There must be something appealing about it, as a sizable group of young people from the U.S. have made Moscow their home away from home. Like Hemingway's Paris, Moscow in the '90s has become a haven for the young and adventurous. Perhaps the frontier quality—a kind of primitive anything goes, "stake it and make it" feeling in the air—attracts the young and daring. This, combined with Russia's rich history and culture, are enough to entice anyone with a curious spirit to this region of the world. From the wooden Orthodox churches of Kizhi to the grand cathedrals covered with icons and frescoes in the Moscow Kremlin, from the stately neoclassical pastel-colored buildings that line the embankment of the Neva River in St. Petersburg to the mesmerizing rows of tea plants covering the green hills above Sochi, almost anyone can find something of interest in the country's vast array of cultural and natural treasures. For the specialist and the general tourist alike, now is an especially exciting time to visit this enigmatic country in the process of fundamental change.

The profound political thaw that began under Gorbachev, and has done somersaults under Yeltsin, provides the visitor with a wide selection of cultural offerings, such as art exhibits of the works of great masters considered too "bourgeois" during the Soviet period and new avant-garde renditions of Russian classical theater. In addition to the still-breathtaking precision of productions of old favorites like the Bolshoi Ballet in Moscow and the Mariynskiy (formerly Kirov) Opera, the visitor can explore the rock music scene, once an obscure movement of some dissident teenagers and now a national obsession.

Yet the country remains as enigmatic as ever. Not even the gypsies dressed in colorful garb, who approach foreigners in the cities claiming to tell fortunes for a small hard-currency fee, can read the future of Russia. Not even the scholars of the former Soviet Union, none of whom predicted the August coup or the Soviet Union's quick demise, knew how to read the tea leaves. And questions remain. Will Russia "democratize" and "marketize," as many Western countries are hoping? What groups will rise to power? Will the new society find a structure or will Russia hobble along in chaotic style for years to come? One cannot find the answers to these questions on a trip to Russia, but all travelers will come back far more informed and with a sense of having seen history in the making.

In spite of all the uncertainty, the most compelling thing about Russia is that which endures regardless of the political era. Among the timeless qualities of the Russian people are their warm hospitality, their ironic sense of humor, and their boundless faith—which has seen them through the best and worst of times.

—Julie Raskin, New York, New York

Official name: Russia. **Area:** 6,592,800 square miles (76 percent of the former USSR). **Population:** 148,542,000. **Population density:** 22 inhabitants per square mile. **Capital and largest city:** Moscow (pop. 8,800,000). **Language:** Russian (official), Ukrainian, Byelorussian, Georgian, Armenian, many others. **Religion:** Russian Orthodox, nonreligious. **Per capita income:** US$3,000. **Currency:** Ruble. **Literacy rate:** 99%. **Average daily temperature:** Moscow: June, 62°F; December, 20°F. **Average number of days with precipitation:** Moscow: June, 12; December, 23.

TRAVEL

At press time, the consular offices of various former Soviet states comprising the Commonwealth of Independent States continue to be represented by the Embassy of the Russian Federation. Visas continue to be issued jointly for travel among these various countries. U.S. citizens need a passport and a visa to enter Russia and other member countries of the Commonwealth of Independent States.

Obtaining a visa for independent travel in Russia can be difficult without going through various official channels, which can run up your expenses. Your best bet may be to go as part of a group tour from which you can later separate. Or you may want to take part in a homestay program. To obtain a tourist visa to Russia, you must plan a substantial amount of your itinerary ahead of time: you will be required to provide proof of confirmed arrival and departure dates, as well as to describe your itinerary. However, it is possible to change your itinerary and extend your stay once in Russia.

The official travel agency of Russia is **Intourist,** 630 Fifth Avenue, Suite 868, New York, NY 10111; (212) 757-3884; fax (212) 459-0031. Unless you have an invitation from either an individual or an organization in Russia, you'll have to make your travel arrangements directly through Intourist or an Intourist-approved travel agency. **Note:** Intourist accommodations are not cheap. Since Russians like Western visitors, you may be able to win a certain amount of independence by arranging an official invitation from any number of Russian organizations; see if anyone at your school has contacts in Russia that could be of help.

Once you have made your plans, you must submit a visa application form, which ought to be provided by your travel agent. Otherwise, they are available from the **Embassy of the Russian Federation**, Consular Division, 1825 Phelps Place NW, Washington, DC 20008; (202) 939-8907; fax (202) 483-7579.

When you submit the visa application form, you must also provide the following:

- photocopies of pages 2 and 3 of your U.S. passport, which should be valid at least one month after the date of departure from Russia or the CIS (do *not* send your original passport)
- three identical 1½ × 1¾–inch photographs made on matte (nonglossy) paper with a white background and taken during the last 12 months
- photocopies of all telexes from organizations in Russia confirming your travel reservations (receiving organizations must be registered with the Ministry of Foreign Affairs and assigned a special index; this index and a reference number must be included in each telex)
- a cover letter from your travel agency including your name, passport number and expiration date, dates and points of arrival in and departure from the CIS, means of transportation, cities to be visited, your confirmation number, and the index and reference number of receiving organizations
- if applying by mail, a return envelope or prepaid airbill
- a money order for the processing fee: $20 for two-week processing, $30 for one week, or $60 for three days

If traveling through Russia en route to another country, such as China, you should obtain a transit visa, which is less expensive than a tourist visa. To get a transit visa, you must start your trip from a country that borders the former USSR and exit into a different nation. Transit visas used to be available only through consulates in neighboring countries, but are now available in the U.S. through the Consular Division of the Russian Embassy.

Getting Around

In major cities like Moscow and St. Petersburg, you can get around on the **metro** system. Otherwise, the options are buses and trams. Rail Europe has a new **Russian Flexipass,** which allows 4 days of rail travel in a 15-day period for $298 (first class) or $198 (second class). Additional rail days may be purchased for $65 or $45, respectively. For more information, contact Rail Europe (see page 62) or Council Travel (see pages xiii–xvi).

Those who want to see Russia from one end to the other can travel the legendary **Trans-Siberian Railroad**, one of the longest and most famous railways in the world. Council Travel offices can arrange a tour that includes a train journey from Beijing to St. Petersburg with several days of sightseeing in Irkutsk, Moscow, and St. Petersburg. However, most travelers who make this train trip on their own start from Budapest, which is the cheapest place to book passage and obtain visas. From Moscow you can ride the Trans-Siberian Express to Beijing (through either Mongolia or Manchuria) or to the Russian city of Nakhodka, where you can get a ferry to Japan. Many travelers make the journey across Russia on the less-expensive transit visa (see "Travel," above). With a transit visa, you can leave the train for up to three days in any city en route, as long as you have the proper connecting train tickets. For a look at one traveler's alternative route across Russia, read Mark Jenkins's *Off the Map: Biking Across Siberia*.

Money Matters

There is no mandatory currency-exchange requirement in Russia. However, travelers are prohibited from taking rubles in or out of the country. When you enter Russia, you'll be given a currency declaration form on which each exchange transaction will be entered during your stay. You must keep this form, together with all receipts from transactions involving the spending or exchange of money, since they will be checked and the form turned in to a customs agent on departure. You cannot reconvert rubles not recorded on this form. Hard-currency shops accept dollars.

Organized Tours

Council Travel offices can book you on several types of organized tours ranging from kayaking an untamed river to crossing the country on the Trans-Siberian Express. Other organizations that specialize in travel to Russia and former Soviet republics are listed in Intourist's *Guide to Travel in the Commonwealth of Independent States*.

Eating and Sleeping

Those on group tours will have accommodations arranged by Intourist or Sputnik (see "Especially for Students and Young People," below). Russia has no members of Hostelling International. For a list of independent hostels, contact **Russian Youth Hostels and Tourism**, 409 North Pacific Coast Highway, #106, Suite 309, Redondo Beach, CA 90277.

Especially for Students and Young People

Russia's student travel bureau is **SPUTNIK**, 15 Kosygin Street, 117946 Moscow: (7) 95-9398586; fax (7) 95-9382056. It can arrange travel programs for single travelers and groups.

For Further Information

Contact the New York office of **Intourist** (see "Travel," above) for general travel information as well as specific information about tours and travel agents in the United States authorized to work with Intourist.

Few countries outdate their travel guidebooks as quickly as Russia. One of the most recent guides is the *Language and Travel Guide to Russia*. It's available for $14.95 from Hippocrene Books, Attn: Order Department, 171 Madison Avenue, New York, NY 10016; (718) 454-2366. Another relatively up-to-date guide is *Fodor's Russia and the Baltic Countries* ($18). Those traveling from Russia to former Soviet Central Asia may want to read *Samarkand and Bukhara*, a guide to the ancient capitals of this region. It's one of the *Travel to Landmarks* series distributed by St. Martin's Press. An excellent introduction to the new Russia can be found in *Insight Guide: Eastern Europe* and *Insight Guide: Russia* (both $19.95). For more information on *Insight Guides*, see page 57.

Surviving Together, a journal published by ISAR (Institute for Soviet-American Relations, 1608 New Hampshire Avenue NW, Washington, DC 20009) offers information on teaching positions in the former Soviet republics. A yearly subscription is $25 and can be ordered from the address above; single copies can be purchased for $8 each. Also available is the *Handbook of Organizations Involved in Soviet-American Relations* (available for $15 from the address above), which lists organizations involved with the former Soviet republics.

WORK

Internships/Traineeships

Programs offered by members of the Council on International Educational Exchange are listed below.

Association for International Practical Training. *IAESTE Trainee Program*. On-the-job training for undergraduate and graduate students in technical fields such as engineering, computer science, agriculture, architecture, mathematics, and the natural and physical sciences. See page 19 for more information.

Boston University. *Moscow Internship Program*. Intensive Russian-language study, an elective course, and an eight-week internship. Fall and spring semesters; summer. Sophomores to post-Baccalaureate students. Regular semester program students are required to have completed at least six semesters of college-level Russian; extended semester program requires completion of four semesters of college-level Russian. Apply by March 15 for the summer and fall; October 15 for the spring. Contact: (617) 353-9888.

Voluntary Service

CIEE places young people in voluntary-service **workcamps** in Russia organized by a variety of youth organizations. At these workcamps, groups of volunteers from different countries work on archaeological, environmental, and renovation projects of various types. Volunteers receive room and board in return for their labor. The applications of U.S. residents are processed by CIEE. For more information contact the International Voluntary Service Department at CIEE.

In addition, **AFS Intercultural Programs** sponsors a Global-Service Program that enables adults to do community service work in Russia. Service projects are arranged individually according to the participant's interests or expertise. There are also projects for teachers, volunteers interested in sharing information on AIDS, as well as those interested in doing outdoor work such as historic preservation. Projects run from three to seven weeks. The program is open to all interested persons at least 19 years old. For more information, contact AFS Intercultural Programs, 313 East 43rd Street, New York, NY 10017; (800) 237-4636.

Global Volunteers (375 East Little Canada Road, St. Paul, MN 55117; [612] 482-1074) sponsors a three-week service program in Russia. Participants teach English and government administration, provide agribusiness consultation, demonstrate home gardening, develop planning and problem-solving capabilities, and instruct tradesmen in construction. Also sponsored by Global Volunteers are Free Enterprise Institutes, which run from two to three weeks and are concerned with educating the people of the former Soviet republics about American business methods. Topics include business management, marketing and sales, and finance.

STUDY

Persons considering study in the Russia might want to check out the *AAASS Directory of Programs in Russian, Eurasian, and East European Studies*, which lists close to 75 academic programs in Russia, Eurasia, and Eastern Europe, including addresses and information on deadlines and costs. The directory also lists similar study programs in the U.S. and can be ordered prepaid from the **American Association for the Advancement of Slavic Studies**, Jordan Quad/Acacia, 125 Panama Street, Stanford, CA 94305-4130; (415) 723-9668. The price is $30 for nonmembers, $20 for members, plus $3 postage; you might be able to find it in libraries or study-abroad offices.

Educational programs offered CIEE-member institutions are listed below. Unless otherwise noted, consult Appendix I for the addresses of the colleges and universities that sponsor these programs. In addition to those listed below, California State University at Sacramento and Pepperdine University offer programs open only to their own students.

Semester and Academic Year

Business

State University of New York College at Brockport. *Business Internship Abroad*. Moscow. Fall and spring semesters. Russian language and Russian business, economics, or politics with business internship. Visits to factories, cooperatives, joint ventures, banks and exchanges, and meetings with Russian entrepreneurs. Excursions and dormitory housing. Juniors and seniors with one semester of college Russian. Apply by March 15 for fall; October 15 for spring. Contact: Office of International Education, SUNY College at Brockport, Brockport, NY 14420; (716) 395-2119.

General Studies

American University. *Moscow Semester*. Fall. Political science, Russian language and culture; seminars taught by professionals from the media and the political, economic, and social fields. Excursions. Second-semester sophomores to graduate students with 2.75 GPA. Apply by April 30. Contact: World Capitals Programs, Dunblane House—Tenley Campus, Washington, DC 20016-8083; (202) 895-4900/4937.

Associated Colleges of the Midwest. *Semester in Russia*. Krasnodar. Fall. Juniors and seniors with two years of college Russian. Apply by March 15.

Council on International Educational Exchange. *Social Sciences Program for Advanced Students of Russian at St. Petersburg University and the Russian Academy of Sciences*. Fall and spring semesters. Graduate students with three years of college Russian. Applicants must have a degree in the social sciences or be enrolled in a graduate degree program in the social sciences or in Slavic languages and literatures. Financial aid available through U.S. Department of State. Apply by March 1 for fall; October 1 for spring. Contact: University Programs Department.

Middlebury College. *Middlebury in Russia*. Moscow. Fall semester (for undergraduates) and academic year (for graduate students). Russian civilization, language, literature, and Russian studies; instruction in Russian. Juniors and graduate students with Russian language and area studies. Apply by March 15. Contact: Professor Thomas Beyer, Russian School, Middlebury College, Middlebury, VT 05753; (802) 388-3711.

State University of New York at Brockport. *Russian Area Studies Abroad*. Moscow. Fall and spring semesters. Russian language, history, culture, political science, and economics at the Plekhanov Economic Academy. Juniors and seniors with one semester of college Russian. Excursions and dormitory housing. Apply by March 15 for fall; October 15 for spring. Contact: Office of International Education, SUNY at Brockport, Brockport, NY 14420; (716) 395-2119.

Stetson University. *Semester in Moscow*. Fall and spring semesters. Study at Moscow State University; instruction in Russian. Sophomores to seniors with 2.5 GPA and two years of college Russian. Apply by March 1 for fall; October 15 for spring.

Tufts University. *Tufts in Moscow*. Semester and academic year. Juniors and seniors with three years of college Russian. Apply by February 1 for fall and academic year; October 15 for spring.

University of Wisconsin at Madison. *Semester or Academic Year in Moscow*. Moscow. Semester and academic year. Russian language and culture study at Moscow State University. Juniors to graduate students with six semesters of college Russian. Open only to students at accredited institutions of higher education in Wisconsin and Wisconsin residents at universities in other states. Apply by second Friday in November for fall, spring, and academic year.

Russian Language and Culture

Council on International Educational Exchange. *Cooperative Russian Language Program at St. Petersburg University and the St. Petersburg Gornyi Institut*. Academic year at St. Petersburg University; semester at St. Petersburg

University or St. Petersburg Gornyi Institut. Undergraduates and graduate students with three years of college Russian for academic year; two years for semester. Apply by March 1 for fall; October 1 for spring. Contact University Programs Department.

State University of New York College at Buffalo. *Program of Russian Language and Culture.* Tver. Semester and academic year. Russian history, culture, literature, and intensive language. Sophomores to graduate students with one year of college Russian and 2.5 GPA. Apply by May 1 for fall and academic year; November 1 for spring. Contact: Study Abroad Coordinator, Office of International Education, SUNY College at Buffalo, 212 Talbert Hall, Box 601604, Buffalo, NY 14260-1604; (716) 645-3912.

University of Illinois at Urbana-Champaign. *Semester in St. Petersburg.* Fall and spring semesters. Language, literature, culture, civilization, and independent study. Sophomores to graduate students with 3.0 GPA and one year of Russian. Apply by April 1 for fall; October 1 for spring.

University of Massachusetts at Amherst. St. Petersburg State Technical University. Fall semester. Students with three years of Russian. Apply by March 15.

University of Minnesota. *Russian in St. Petersburg.* Spring quarter. Study at the Herzen Pedagogical University. Russian language and culture. Excursions. Homestay or dormitory housing. First-years to seniors with 2.5 GPA and five quarters (three semesters) of Russian with 3.0 GPA in Russian. Apply by January 15.

University of North Carolina at Chapel Hill. *Rostov-on-Don, Russia.* Fall and spring semesters. Russian-language study. Excursions. First-year college students to graduate students with four semesters of college Russian. Apply by February 14 for fall; October 1 for spring.

World Learning/School for International Training. *College Semester Abroad.* St. Petersburg. Fall and spring semesters. Intensive language, life and culture seminar, field-study methods seminar, independent-study project. Excursions and homestays. Sophomores to seniors with 2.5 GPA and two years of college Russian. Apply by May 7 for fall; October 7 for spring. Contact: College Semester Abroad Admissions, (800) 336-1616.

College Semester Abroad. Volgograd. Fall and spring semesters. Intensive language study and life and culture seminar. Excursions and homestays. Sophomores to seniors with 2.5 GPA. Apply by May 7 for fall; October 7 for spring. Contact: College Semester Abroad Admissions, (800) 336-1616.

Summer and Short-Term

Business

Council on International Educational Exchange. *Moscow Summer Business Program at the Russian Economics Academy.* Juniors to graduate students with business or economics background. Apply by March 15. Contact University Programs Department.

Monterey Institute of International Studies. Moscow. Six weeks in May and June. Offered in cooperation with Diplomatic Academy of the Russian Foreign Ministry. Advanced Russian language, culture, and business. Internships available in July. Academy residence housing and excursions. Juniors to graduate students with advanced Russian. Contact: Dean Jon M. Strolle,

Language Studies, MIIS, 425 Van Buren Street, Monterey, CA 93940; (408) 647-4185.

State University of New York College at Brockport. *Business Internship Abroad*. Moscow. Summer. Study of Russian language and Russian business, economics, or politics with business internship. Visits to factories, cooperatives, joint ventures, banks and exchanges, and meetings with Russian entrepreneurs. Excursions and dormitory housing. Juniors and seniors with one semester of college Russian. Apply by March 15. Contact: Office of International Education, SUNY College at Brockport, Brockport, NY 14420; (716) 395-2119.

University of Nebraska—Lincoln. *Business in Russia*. Moscow (International Business School) and St. Petersburg. Three weeks in summer. Business and economics, with Russian civilization. Visits to business firms and cultural excursions. Sophomores to seniors with one year of economics. Apply by February 1.

Economics

Eastern Michigan University. *Labor Studies in Moscow*. Summer. One-month residential seminar on trade unions and changing economy of Russia. Undergraduates with 2.5 GPA. Apply by March 1.

General Studies

Syracuse University. *Moscow and St. Petersburg: The Tale of Two Cities*. Five weeks in May and June. Interdisciplinary program on architecture and urban geography. Excursions. Undergraduates and graduate students. Apply by March 1. Contact: (800) 235-3472.

Performing Arts

New York University. *Circle Summer Sessions in Moscow*. Four-week study program at Shepkin Theater School. Auditions required. Contact: Circle in the Square Theater School, (212) 307-2732.

Political Science

State University of New York at Brockport. *Russia: Political Economy of the Contemporary Russian State*. Moscow and St. Petersburg. Three weeks in June. Russian history, economics, and politics. Dormitory housing and excursions. Juniors and seniors with 2.5 GPA. Apply by April 1. Contact: Office of International Education, SUNY at Brockport, Brockport, NY 14420; (716) 395-2119.

Russian Language and Culture

Boston University. *Intensive Russian Language*. St. Petersburg. Intensive four-week summer program offering fourth-, fifth-, and sixth-semester Russian. Sophomores to seniors and college graduates with successful completion of three to five semesters of college Russian. Apply by March 15.

Council on International Educational Exchange. *Cooperative Russian Language Program at St. Petersburg University and the St. Petersburg Gornyi Institute*. Summer. Sophomores to graduate students with two years of Russian. Apply by April 1. Contact: University Programs Department.

Cooperative Russian Language Program in the Natural Sciences at Novosibirsk State University. Summer. First-year college students to graduate students with one year of college Russian. Apply by January 20. Contact: University Programs Department.

Cooperative Russian Language Program in the Social Sciences at Novosibirsk State University. Summer. First-year college students to graduate students with three to five semesters of college Russian. Apply by April 1. Contact: University Programs Department.

Russian Language for Research Program at St. Petersburg University and the Russian Academy of Sciences. Summer. Graduate students with four semesters of college Russian. Apply by March 1. Contact: University Programs Department.

Cornell University. *Colgate and Cornell Study Program in Moscow.* Fall semester. Russian language, culture, and politics. Excursions and homestays. Sophomores to seniors with four semesters of college Russian and 3.0 GPA.

Illinois State University. *Summer Program in Russia.* Vladimir. Four-week intensive Russian-language program with courses in Russian art, history, music, and literature at Vladimir Pedagogical University. Homestays and excursions. Sophomores to seniors with one year of college Russian and 2.5 GPA. Apply by March 1. Contact: Dr. Mark Kaiser, Illinois State University, 4300 Foreign Languages Department, Normal, IL 61761; (309) 438-7856.

Indiana University. *Overseas Study in St. Petersburg.* Summer. Undergraduates with one year of Russian and 3.0 GPA. Apply by February 6.

Miami University. Moscow and St. Petersberg. Summer. Language-study tour. Freshmen to adults with college education. Apply by April 1.

State University of New York College at Buffalo. *Program of Russian Language and Culture.* Tver. Summer. Russian history, culture, literature, and intensive language. Sophomores to graduate students with one year of college Russian and 2.5 GPA. Apply by April 15. Contact: Study-Abroad Coordinator, Office of International Education, SUNY College at Buffalo, 212 Talbert Hall, Box 601604, Buffalo, NY 14260-1604; (716) 645-3912.

State University of New York at New Paltz. *Summer Study in Russia.* Various locations. Eight-week intensive language program. Excursions. High-school students to graduate students with one year of college Russian. Rolling admissions. Contact: Office of International Education, HAB 33, SUNY New Paltz, New Paltz, NY 12561; (914) 257-3125.

University of Alabama. *Study Tour of the Former Soviet Union.* Russia, Ukraine, and Georgia. Three weeks in May. Undergraduates and graduate students. Apply by March 15.

University of Illinois at Urbana-Champaign. *Summer in St. Petersburg.* Language, literature, civilization, culture, and independent study. Sophomores to graduate students with 3.0 GPA and one year of Russian. Apply by March 1.

University of Nebraska—Lincoln. *Russian Language and Civilization.* St. Petersburg. Four weeks in summer. Intensive Russian language and culture at University of St. Petersburg. Homestays and excursions. Sophomores to seniors with one year of Russian. Apply by February 1.

University of North Carolina at Chapel Hill. *Rostov-on-Don, Russia.* Six weeks in summer. Russian-language study. Excursions. Freshmen to graduate students. Apply by March 15.

Washington State University. *Intensive Russian Language Program.* Vladivostok. Mid-July to mid-August. Juniors to graduate students and adults with one and a half to two years of Russian. Apply by April 15.

EXPLORING RUSSIAN CULTURE

Readings

In the past decade, literary works previously considered "inappropriate" for publication are now being read by Russians. Some of these literary works have already received wide acclaim in the West, such as Boris Pasternak's *Doctor Zhivago* (1959), which chronicles the period of the Revolution, the proletariat upheaval and the communist secession; Alexander Solzhenitsyn's *Gulag Archipelago*; Evgeny Zamyatin's *We* (1983); and Andrei Platonov's *The Foundation Pit*. Other authors are being published for the first time in both Russia and the West. Anatoly Rybakov's *Children of the Arbat* (1988), which tells the story of a group of young adults in Moscow at the onset of the Second World War, and *Life and Fate* (1987), by Vasily Grossman, are stellar examples. One of the best known of contemporary Soviet writers is Tatyana Tolstaya, the great-grandniece of Leo Tolstoy. Her collection of short stories, *On the Golden Porch*, was translated into English in 1989.

Nikolay Gogol's works had an enormous impact on Russian society, in part because he was a Ukrainian by birth and saw Russian society as an outsider. *The Inspector General*, his satirical comedy written in the 1830s, is still eminently readable. Fyodor Dostoyevsky is another strong force in Russian literature: his intellectual, moody novels are considered by many to be among the best ever written. Many of the settings, characterizations, symbols, and attitudes found in his two major works, *Crime and Punishment* and *The Brothers Karamazov*, endure in the country today.

Hedrick Smith's 1983 collection of essays, *The Russians*, which has been recently updated, consists of reworked pieces from the years he spent in the Soviet Union as a correspondent for the *New York Times*. Another good book along these lines is *Russia: Broken Idols, Solemn Dreams*, by Pulitzer Prize–winning journalist David Shipler. Paul Theroux's *The Great Railway Bazaar* is recommended by many: In this work, Theroux travels the Trans-Siberian Express. *Where Nights Are Longest* (1983) is a travel memoir by author Colin Thubron, who traveled by car thousands of miles throughout most of western Russia.

Films

The cinema has been an integral part of modern Russian culture. Consistent with the ideas of industrialization, mass culture, and modernity associated with the Russian Revolution, film was idealized as the art form of the proletariat. Montage-style film editing is the hallmark of Sergei Eisenstein's *The Battleship Potemkin* (1925), about the 1905 Revolution; *October* (1928), a film about Russia's October Revolution; as well as Dziga Vertov's *Man with a Movie Camera* (1929). In addition to their then-revolutionary technique, these films took an aggressive, confrontational look at the intricacies of class difference, revolution, and the role of cinema.

The position of women in Soviet society is examined in *Several Interviews on Personal Problems* (1979), directed by Lana Gogoberidze; interspersed with interviews is the story of a journalist who attempts to solve other people's problems but cannot manage her own. In *The Swimmer* (1981), written and directed by Irakli Kvirikadze, a man invades a film set to tell about his father and grandfather, famous swimmers cheated of success. In *Trial on the Road* (1985), directed by Alexei Gherman, a former Red Army soldier fighting for the Germans in Russia deserts to fight for the partisans.

A multitude of recent films probing historical questions, the malaise of Soviet youth, the meaning of glasnost, and a range of social problems have received international attention. Typical of this trend is Vassili Pitchul's film, *Little Vera* (1988), a witty look at the bleak prospects for Soviet youth. *Moscow Does Not Believe in Tears*, Vladimir Menshov's 1980 film, is the funny, charming story of three provincial young women who travel to Moscow in search of husbands. *Freeze, Die, Come to Life* (1990), the story of a young boy growing up in Siberia during World War II, is also worth seeing. A Mongolian herdsman saves a Russian truck driver after a crash in *Urga* (1991), a delightful clash-of-cultures fable from director Nikita Mikhalkov.

SLOVAKIA

An agrarian state that still clings to its peasant traditions, Slovakia has finally emerged from the grip of outside control that has characterized its history. On July 17, 1992, Slovakia declared sovereignty, and January 1, 1993, marked the dissolution of Czechoslovakia. Slovakia itself has never been an independent state, unless being a Nazi protectorate in World War II is considered being "independent." In addition to Germany, Hungary and the former USSR and its provinces have held power over this land through the centuries—parts of Slovakia are very much an extension of Hungary while some towns, particularly in the far east, are typically Ukrainian. The most recent struggle for independence was waged against the power of the Czech-controlled government of Prague, which most Slovaks considered far removed from their concerns and impervious to their needs.

In the end, the distinctions between Slovakia and the Czech Republic superseded the qualities they share. During the years of Austrian rule over the Czech provinces of Moravia and Bohemia, industrialization was emphasized over agriculture. But during that time Slovakia was part of Hungary, retaining an agrarian character and economy. Although agriculture is giving way to the development of industries in Slovakia today, the peasant way of life and its mores remain the keystone of Slovak cultural life. This character and regional differences have been protected and perpetuated in part by the impenetrability of the mountainous landscape of the country; Slovakia has some of Europe's highest mountains outside the Alps. These barriers have also played an obvious role in preventing the introduction of industrialization to many regions of Slovakia.

However, the mountains have graced the country with dramatic landscapes and a geographical diversity to satisfy the cravings of most nature enthusiasts. From the vineyards of the rolling hills at the foot of the Little Carpathians, the sheer magnificence of the Tatra or Fatra mountain ranges, and the valleys in between, Slovakia's beauty is virtually unspoiled. Medieval towns in East Slovakia are preserved jewels rarely visited by tourists. More than 200 castles and castle ruins are also perched on hills and mountains throughout the country, providing a doorway to the past and memorials to the many cultures that have settled in Slovakia at one point or another.

Bratislava, the nation's capital, has been described as the home of a hundred decaying towers when compared to the beauty of the hundred spires of Prague. Its industrial skyline and stark apartment blocks stand in contrast to the historic center of a town that was the capital of Hungary for three centuries. But

Bratislava's location on the banks of the Danube River and right next to the Austrian and Hungarian borders make it a convenient base for exploring the neighboring countries and the Carpathian Mountains, which slope downward to meet the river here. Many outstanding castles wait to be explored along the Danube, such as Bratislava Castle and Devin Castle—former frontier posts of the Roman Empire. In many ways the past is alive in Slovakia, but it does not block the path Slovaks have chosen for their country. Instead, history provides the impetus for the reclaiming of the nation.

—Natalia Donato, Boise, Idaho

Area: 30,468 square miles. **Population:** 5,287,000. **Population density:** 108 inhabitants per square kilometer. **Capital and largest city:** Bratislava (pop. 440,000). **Language:** Slovak. **Religion:** Roman Catholic. **Currency:** Koruna. **Literacy rate:** 99%.

TRAVEL

Holders of American passports do not need a visa to enter Slovakia, provided they stay for less than 30 days. However, travelers can easily apply for extensions within the country. For more information, contact the **Embassy of Slovakia**, 3900 Linnean Avenue NW, Washington, DC 20008; (202) 363-6315.

Getting Around

Interrail passes are valid in the country, but Eurailpasses are not. The recently introduced **European East Pass** can be used for travel in the Czech and Slovak Republics, Austria, Hungary, and Poland. Available in first class only, it costs $169 for five days of travel in 15 or $275 for 10 days in one month. In addition, there's a new **CzechoSlovak Flexipass**, also first-class, that costs $59 for five days of travel in 15. Both passes are available in the U.S. from Rail Europe (see page 62) or Council Travel (see pages xiii–xvi). From Bratislava, there is international bus service to the Czech Republic, Austria, and Hungary. There is also boat service along the Danube to Vienna.

Eating and Sleeping

There are plenty of low-cost lodgings around Bratislava. To book special **student accommodations**, contact CKM (see "Especially for Students and Young People," below). You can book rooms with **families** through the central office of Cedok (see "Meeting the People," below) at Jesenského 5 or at Bratislava Information Service (BIS), Laurinská 1.

Especially for Students and Young People

CKM, the student travel bureau of the Czech and Slovak Republics, has an office in Bratislava at Hviezdoslavovo nám 16. (For CKM's main office, see page 94). CKM can book inexpensive student lodgings and provide student travel services.

For Further Information

Cedok, formerly the official tourist office of Czechoslovakia, has become a full-service travel agency and remains the best source of travel information on those countries.

A good guide for travel in Slovakia is *The Real Guide: Czechoslovakia* ($13.95). An excellent book to read in preparation for your trip is *Insight Guide: Czechoslovakia* ($19.95). For more information on Lonely Planet and *Insight Guides*, see pages 56–57.

WORK

In order to work in Slovakia, it is necessary to obtain a work permit before going to the country for most types of jobs. For more information, contact the **Ministry of Labor in Slovakia**, Ministerstva Prace, Socialnych, Veci a Rodiny S.R., Spitalska 4, 81643.

Internships/Traineeships

The following program is sponsored by a member of the Council on International Educational Exchange.

Association for International Practical Training. *IAESTE Trainee Program.* On-the-job training for undergraduate and graduate students in technical fields such as engineering, computer science, agriculture, architecture, and mathematics. See page 19 for more information.

SLOVENIA

The first region to break away from the former Yugoslavia as an independent country, Slovenia has moved decisively to become a part of the new Europe. Historic, cultural, and economic links with Austria and Hungary have contributed to a spirit of renewal and a focus on the future. Snuggled close to Austria, all of Slovenia is within an easy afternoon's automobile drive from Austria, Italy, or Hungary.

Long a tourist destination for Europeans, Slovenia offers the ambiance of Western European resorts at considerably lower prices and with less crowding. The variety in this small country is astounding: rugged alpine villages contrast with Portoroz's sophisticated waterfront casino, scholarly tours of Roman ruins are conducted next to "clothes optional" beaches. The often unpublicized Slovenian health resorts blend ancient traditions, magnificent settings, and modern entertainment.

Lively discussion is the way of life in Slovenia. Slovene students and business people alike bring a no-nonsense perspective and rich insights to any negotiation or debate. Keep an open mind and be prepared to defend your ideas with reasoned arguments and logic—many Western assumptions are not automatically accepted as starting points. An evening devoted to talking and exploring wide-ranging topics is virtually guaranteed to produce fresh insights on the complexities of the world in general and the Balkans in particular.

Slovenia's 90-member Parliament elected a coalition government in January 1993. Key members of the Cabinet are all former Communists whose platform is almost identical to that of the Slovenian leadership of the time when the republic was part of Yugoslavia.

A bit of time spent reading some history of the region will pay off in many ways during a visit to Slovenia. This is particularly true in the mountains, off the beaten path. While the tourist centers are usually staffed by sophisticated personnel common in Europe, small shop owners and villagers retain an eagerness to talk with visitors who express a genuine interest in their community.

Slovenia offers a fascinating kaleidoscope of scenery, ideas, and perspectives. The recent strife in the neighboring sections of the former Yugoslavia is but the latest chapter in the region's turbulent history. The ebb and flow of empires over the past 75 years have swept the society and economy, leaving tough, adaptive survivors. Although formerly part of Yugoslavia, Slovenia does not suffer from the ethnic infighting currently characterizing the region. The excitement of a new country being shaped by dynamic social changes, pragmatic reasoning, and action brings the thoughtful traveler back repeatedly.

—Bill Peirce, Forestdale, Massachusetts

Official name: Slovenia. **Area:** 7,819 square miles. **Population:** 1,974,000. **Population density:** 252 inhabitants per square mile. **Capital and largest city:** Ljubljana (pop. 330,000). **Language:** Slovenian. **Religion:** Roman Catholic. **Currency:** Tolar. **Literacy rate:** 90%.

TRAVEL

U.S. citizens need a passport and a visa to enter Slovenia. Multiple-entry visas are issued in the U.S. or upon arrival free of charge. For more information, contact the **Embassy of the Republic of Slovenia**, 1300 Nineteenth Street NW, Washington, DC 20036; (202) 828-1650; fax (202) 828-1654.

Getting Around

Ljubljana is the transportation hub of Slovenia. Just 40 kilometers from Austria, it is a major intersection of north-south and east-west rail lines. Other than **rail** travel, most transportation in Slovenia is by **bus**.

Eating and Sleeping

There are several **youth hostels** in Slovenia. For more information, contact Hostelling International/American Youth Hostels (see page 54) or the **Youth Holiday Association of Slovenia**, Parmova 33, 61000 Ljubljana; (38) 61-312150; fax (38) 61-121107. During the summer, students can find inexpensive **dormitory accommodations** at Studenski Domovi, C. 27, Aprila 31, Ljubljana 61000; (38) 61-23735. Other low-cost accommodations can be booked by the **Ljubljana Tourist Information Center** at Slovenska 35.

For Further Information

At press time, there was no single guide to Slovenia on the market. However, Lonely Planet's recently published *Mediterranean Europe on a Shoestring* ($24.95) has a good chapter on travel in Slovenia and other former Yugoslavian states. For more information on Lonely Planet Publications, see page 56.

WORK

Internships/Traineeships

A program sponsored by a member of the Council on International Educational Exchange is listed below.

Association for International Practical Training. *IAESTE Trainee Program.* On-the-job training for undergraduate and graduate students in technical fields such as engineering, computer science, agriculture, architecture, and mathematics. See page 19 for more information.

Voluntary Service

CIEE places young people in voluntary-service **workcamps** in Slovenia organized by MOST, a small nonprofit service organization in Ljubljana. At these workcamps, groups of volunteers from various countries work together on projects that involve reforestation efforts, recreation for people with muscular diseases, and conservation of historical sites. Volunteers must be at least 18 years old. Room and board are provided by the camp. The applications of U.S. residents are processed by CIEE. For further information, contact the International Voluntary Service Department at CIEE.

SPAIN

Merely mentioning Spain conjures up familiar images, even among those who have never been there: images of spirited bullfights, crowded tapas bars, passionate flamenco dancers, sun-drenched castles, colorful Easter processions. This is the Spain, exotic and romantic, that can draw more than 50 million visitors a year to a country of 36 million people. Those who arrive in search of Don Quixote's Spain will find enough of it to satisfy their romantic expectations: from the Altamira cave paintings in Asturias, to the Roman aqueduct in Segovia, the Moorish Alhambra Palace in Granada, the medieval walls of Avila, and the Royal Palace in Madrid, the remains of Spain's rich and glorious past are easy to locate.

However, most visitors will also be struck by the ways that many of today's images differ from those featured in the travel brochures. The tradition-bound Spain that for centuries asserted its uniqueness by proudly declaring that "Europe ends at the Pyreness" has in recent years transformed itself into one of Europe's most dynamic and rapidly changing countries.

The population of Madrid, the thriving capital, has grown to nearly five million. The city is renowned for the variety and energy of its nightlife, especially during the spring and summer when Madrileños young and old follow an evening at the theater or a restaurant with a stop at one of the many sidewalk cafés. Within the modern, cosmopolitan Madrid can still be found the more traditional Spanish city with its bullring, Rastro flea market, Prado art museum, and old quarter around the Plaza Mayor. A word of caution: Madrid's heady plunge into modernity has made it one of Europe's most expensive capitals.

The change in Spain has not been confined to Madrid. Barcelona, Madrid's longtime commercial and cultural rival on the Mediterranean coast, thrives as a center of trade and industry and the focus of a resurgent Catalan language and culture. Outside the major cities, television, improved transportation, and economic growth have spread modern consumer culture into traditionally isolated areas.

Much of Spain's continuing transformation can be traced to the emergence of democracy in 1976 after nearly 40 years of military dictatorship under General Francisco Franco. Today Spain is a constitutional monarchy. Its king, Juan Carlos I, officially has little political authority under the terms of the 1978 Constitution; however, he is generally credited with having saved the young democracy in 1981 when he energetically intervened to help put down an attempted coup by dissatisfied military officers. Now regarded as a stable Western-style democracy, Spain officially ended its many years of political isolation from Europe when it joined NATO and the European Community in 1986. International attention focused on Spain in 1992 as the country hosted the summer Olympics in Barcelona and the World's Fair in Seville. The year also marked the 500th anniversary of Columbus's voyage to the Americas.

—Michael Vande Berg, Kalamazoo, Michigan

Official name: Kingdom of Spain. **Size:** 194,896 square miles (about three-fourths the size of Texas). **Population:** 39,384,000. **Population density:** 202 inhabitants per square mile. **Capital and largest city:** Madrid (pop. 4,500,000). **Language:** Spanish, Catalan, Basque, Galician. **Religion:** Roman Catholic. **Per capita income:** US$11,100. **Currency:** Peseta. **Literacy rate:** 97%. **Average daily temperature:** Barcelona: June, 71°F; December, 51°F. Madrid: June, 69°F; December, 42°F. **Average number of days with precipitation:** Barcelona: June, 6; December, 6. Madrid: June, 5; December 10.

TRAVEL

A passport is required for U.S. citizens going to Spain, but a visa is not required for tourists staying up to three months. Extensions may be applied for at immigration offices in Spain. For specific regulations, check with the **Spanish Embassy**, 2700 19th Street NW, Washington, DC 20009; (202) 265-0190.

Getting Around

If you're traveling to Spain by **rail**, you'll have to change trains at the French border, since most of Spain's railroads are a different gauge than those in the rest of Europe. Travelers with Eurailpasses are required to make advance reservations for all long-distance trains and pay supplements on *talgo* (express) trains. The **Spain Flexipass** allows a variable number of travel days within one month. Three days cost $180 first class and $140 second class; 5 days cost $280 first class and $220 second class; and 10 days costs $480 first class and $340 second class. The **Spain Rail 'n' Drive Pass** allows three days of rail travel and three car rental days within one month. The cost for two adults driving an economy car is $315 first class or $275 second class per person. Like all Eurailpasses, the above passes must be purchased in the U.S.; for more information, contact Rail Europe (see page 62) or Council Travel (see pages xiii–xvi).

A number of **bus** companies also provide intercity service in Spain, which costs about the same or even more than the train. However, along the Cantabrican coast and in the southern region of Spain, buses fill in the gaps in the national rail network, providing more direct and convenient service than that available by rail.

Iberia Airlines' **Visit Spain Pass** provides coupons for four consecutive flights in Spain (which means you must always depart from the city in which you most recently arrived). Valid for 60 days, the Visit Spain Pass costs $249 from October 1 through June 14 and $299 from June 15 through September 30. One round-trip flight to the Canary Islands costs $50 extra. You must purchase the Visit Spain Pass in the U.S. in conjunction with a transatlantic flight to Spain (it's available through most major airlines), and travel within Spain is limited to Iberian and Aviaco airlines.

Passenger **boats** link the Spain's Mediterranean ports with the famed Balearic islands of Mallorca, Menorca, and Ibiza. Before hopping on a boat, however, check the airfare; in many cases, flying is actually cheaper. Ferries also link Mediterranean ports with North Africa.

Bicycling is enjoyable but difficult because rough pavement characterizes most Spanish secondary roads, and mountains crisscross the country. However, bikes may be carried on trains as baggage at no extra charge.

Spain also offers some of Europe's best **hiking**, with an unusual and highly varied terrain. A good guide is *Trekking in Spain*, available for $11.95 from Lonely Planet Publications (for ordering information, see page 56).

Eating and Sleeping

In addition to a wide variety of hotels and pensions, Spain has more than 100 **youth hostels**. For more information, contact Hostelling International/American Youth Hostels (see page 54) or the national youth hostel organization, **Red Española de Albergues Juveniles**, José Ortega y Gasset 71, 28006 Madrid; (34) 1-3477700; fax (34) 1-4018160. Spain also has scores of excellent campsites, which can be found along the coasts, on the islands, and in scenic inland areas.

In addition, several Spanish universities offer affordable **dormitory lodgings** to travelers. For more information, contact TIVE (see below) or consult Campus Travel Service's *US and Worldwide Travel Accommodations Guide* (see page 54).

Especially for Students and Young People

Spain's student travel bureau is **TIVE**, José Ortega y Gasset 71, 28006 Madrid; (34) 1-3477700; fax (34) 1-4022194. You can find information on travel, accommodations, and student discounts at its offices in Madrid and 30 other Spanish cities.

For Further Information

General tourist information is available from the **Tourist Office of Spain**, 665 Fifth Avenue, New York, NY 10022; (212) 759-8822. Every city of Spain has its own tourist office where you can get maps, brochures, and help finding accommodations.

For basic budget-travel information, *Let's Go: Spain and Portugal* ($16.95) is always dependable. *The Real Guide: Spain* ($12.95) is also good. For depth of detail, however, *Cadogan Guides' Spain* ($17.95) is probably the best guide around. Two excellent books to read in preparation for your trip are *Insight Guide: Spain* and *Insight Guide: Southern Spain* (both $19.95). For more information on *Let's Go, Real Guides*, *Cadogan Guides*, and *Insight Guides*, see pages 56–57.

A helpful guide for those planning to spend some time working or studying in Madrid is *Madrid Inside Out*, available for $12.95 from Frank Books, 45 Newbury Street, Suite 305, Boston, MA 02116; (617) 536-0060; fax (617) 536-0068.

WORK

Getting a Job

In most cases it is necessary to secure a job offer and a work permit before departure. After receiving a job offer, you must contact the nearest Spanish consulate or embassy and apply for permission to work. If permission is granted, it is then the employer's responsibility to apply for a work permit from the Spanish Ministry of Labor on your behalf. According to the Spanish authorities, employers may obtain a work permit for a U.S. citizen only if there are no Spanish applicants for the job. Work permits issued by the Ministry of Labor generally take between one and seven months to process. For more information, contact the Embassy of Spain (see "Travel," above). For those interested in teaching English, however, a permit is not usually required.

Internships/Traineeships

A program sponsored by a member organization of the Council on International Educational Exchange is listed below. In addition, Southwest Texas State University and Moorhead State University sponsor programs open only to their own students.

Association for International Practical Training. *IAESTE Trainee Program*. On-the-job training for undergraduate and graduate students in technical fields such as engineering, computer science, agriculture, architecture, mathematics, and the physical and natural sciences. See page 19 for more information.

Boston University. *Madrid Internship Program*. Fall, spring, and summer. Semester program offers twelve credits of course work plus a four-credit internship in one of the following areas: business, economics, international organizations, journalism, public relations, marketing. Summer program offers a four-credit course plus the four-credit internship. Sophomores to seniors with 3.0 GPA in major, five semesters of college Spanish (with a minimum grade of B minus). Apply by March 15 for fall and summer; October 15 for spring. Contact: (617) 353-9888.

Voluntary Service

CIEE places young people in voluntary-service **workcamps** in Spain that are organized by Servicio Voluntario Internacional, a division of the Ministry of Youth in Madrid. At these summer workcamps, groups of international volunteers work on a variety of projects involving archaeology, forestry, and social work. Applicants must be between 18 and 26 years of age and have some knowledge of Spanish. The average length of service is 15 to 20 days. The applications of U.S. residents are processed by CIEE. For more information, contact CIEE's International Voluntary Service Department.

For persons interested in longer-term voluntary-service work, the Year Abroad Program sponsored by the **International Christian Youth Exchange** offers persons ages 18 to 30 opportunities in the fields of health care, education, the environment, construction, and more. See page 25 for more information.

STUDY

For information on studying in Spain, contact the **Education Office** of the Spanish Embassy or a consulate in your region. They have a few fact sheets, including a book of Spanish language programs entitled *Cursos de Lengua y Cultura para Extranjeros en España*, as well as information for those who want to enroll directly in a Spanish university, taken from the directory *Higher Education in the European Community*. The address is 1350 Connecticut Avenue NW, Washington, DC 20036; (202) 452-0005.

Study programs offered by CIEE-member institutions are described below. Unless otherwise noted, consult Appendix I for the addresses of the colleges and universities listed in this section. In addition to the programs below, Pepperdine University, University of Notre Dame, and University of Wisconsin system schools offer study-abroad programs open only to their own students.

Semester and Academic Year

Business

Council on International Educational Exchange. *Business and Society Program at the University of Seville*. Semester and academic year. Sophomores to graduate students (not for graduate credit) with advanced Spanish, 2.75 GPA, and previous study in business or economics. Apply by April 1 for fall and academic year; October 15 for spring. Contact University Programs Department.

World Learning/School for International Training. *College Semester Abroad*. Granada. Fall and spring semesters. Intensive language study, international business seminar and internship. Homestays and excursions. Sophomores to seniors with 2.5 GPA and two years of college Spanish. Apply by May 7 for fall; October 7 for spring. Contact: College Semester Abroad Admissions, (800) 336-1616.

General Studies

Alma College. *Program of Studies in Spain*. Madrid or Segovia. In Segovia, language, literature, culture, and art history; instruction in Spanish. In Madrid, intensive Spanish. Homestays and excursions. Sophomores to seniors with 2.5 GPA; two years of Spanish required for Segovia program. Apply by June 15 for fall; October 15 for winter.

American Heritage Association. Barcelona. Fall, winter, and spring quarters. Social sciences and Spanish language at Institute for Social and International Studies. Sophomores to seniors with 3.0 GPA. Apply by July 1 for fall; November 1 for winter; February 1 for spring.

Brethren Colleges Abroad. University of Barcelona. Semester and academic year. Full range of academic curriculum available plus intensive language study. Excursions. Juniors and seniors with 3.0 GPA and two years of college Spanish. Apply by April 15 for fall and academic year; November 1 for spring.

Cornell University. *Cornell Abroad at University of Seville.* Semester and academic year. Offered in conjunction with University of Michigan. Wide range of studies available; instruction in Spanish. Excursions. Juniors to seniors with 3.0 GPA and four semesters of college Spanish. Apply by February 15 for fall and academic year; October 15 for spring.

Council on International Educational Exchange. *Liberal Arts Program at the University of Seville and the Universidad Internacional Menéndez.* Pelayo, Seville. Semester and academic year. Sophomores to graduate students (not for graduate credit) with five semesters of college Spanish. Apply by April 1 for fall and academic year; October 15 for spring. Contact University Programs Department.

Indiana University. *Overseas Study in Madrid.* Academic year. Study at University of Madrid. Indiana, Purdue, and University of Wisconsin juniors and seniors with two years of Spanish and 3.0 GPA. Apply by November 1.

International Student Exchange Program (ISEP). Academic year. Direct reciprocal exchange between U.S. universities and institutions in Madrid and Santiago de Compostela. Full curriculum options. Rolling admissions. Open only to students at ISEP-member institutions. Contact ISEP for list of members.

Iowa State University. *ISU/Valladolid Exchange.* Semester and academic year. Spanish language and culture. Sophomores to graduate students with 3.0 GPA and two years of college Spanish. Apply by March 25. Contact: Department of Foreign Languages and Literature, 300 Pearson, Iowa State University, Ames, IA 50011.

James Madison University. *JMU Semester in Salamanca.* Fall and spring semesters. Spanish art, civilization, politics, economics, history, language, and literature. Homestays and excursions. Sophomores to seniors with 2.8 GPA and intermediate Spanish. Apply by November 15 for fall; February 1 for spring.

Longwood College. *Hispanic Studies Program at the University of Valencia.* Spring semester and academic year. Offered in cooperation with University of Virginia. Spanish language, literature, history, economics, and culture; instruction in Spanish. Homestays and excursions. Juniors with four semesters of college Spanish (or equivalent) and 2.5 GPA. Apply by February 14. Contact: Dr. John F. Reynolds, International Studies Program, Longwood College, Farmville, VA 23901; (804) 395-2172.

Marquette University. *Marquette in Madrid.* Semester and academic year. Full arts and sciences curriculum at Universidad Complutense de Madrid. Homestays. Sophomores to seniors with 3.0 GPA and above intermediate Spanish. Apply by March 15 for fall and academic year; November 30 for spring. Contact: Director, Madrid Study Center, Marquette University, Milwaukee, WI 53233; (414) 288-6832.

Middlebury College. *Junior Year Abroad.* Madrid. Semester and academic year. Language, literature, culture, history, economics; instruction in Spanish. Juniors with five semesters of college Spanish. Apply by March 1 for fall, spring, and academic year.

Graduate Program. Madrid. Academic year. Language, literature, culture, professional training; instruction in Spanish. Graduate students with graduate Spanish. Rolling admissions. Contact: Spanish School, Middlebury College, Middlebury, VT 05753; (802) 388-3711, ext. 5538.

New York University. *NYU in Spain.* Madrid. Semester and academic year. Undergraduate and graduate program in Hispanic literature and civilization. Juniors with intermediate Spanish and 3.0 GPA; graduate students with Spanish major. Apply by May for fall and academic year; November for spring. Contact: NYU in Spain, 19 University Place, Room 409, New York, NY 10003; (212) 998-8760.

Northern Arizona University. *Study Abroad in Spain*. Granada. Fall and spring semesters. Spanish language, history, literature, art, music, politics, and economics. Homestays. Sophomores to seniors with two years of Spanish. Apply by April 1 for fall; November 1 for spring.

Northern Illinois University. *Academic Internships in Madrid*. Fall and spring semesters. Internship plus two courses. Sophomores to seniors with 3.0 GPA. Apply by April 4 for fall; November 1 for spring.

Spanish Studies. Segovia. Semester and academic year. Sophomores to seniors with five semesters of college Spanish. Apply by June 1 for fall and academic year; November 1 for spring. Contact: Foreign Study Office, Semester/Academic Year Programs, Northern Illinois University, Williston Hall 100, DeKalb, IL 60115-2854; (815) 753-0420/0304.

Ohio State University. *The Toledo Program*. Toledo. Semester and academic year. Anthropology and archaeology, art history, history, interdisciplinary studies, Spanish linguistics, Spanish and Latin American literature, philosophy, political science, and Spanish language; instruction in Spanish. Excursions and optional homestays. Undergraduates and graduates with 2.7 GPA and two years of college Spanish. Apply by June 1 for fall and academic year.

Portland State University. Barcelona. See listing under American Heritage Association.

Rutgers University. *Junior Year in Spain*. Valencia. Academic year. Juniors with two years of college Spanish and 3.0 GPA. Apply by March 1. Contact: Department of Spanish and Portuguese, Rutgers University, 105 George Street, New Brunswick, NJ 08093; (908) 932-9323.

St. Lawrence University. *Spain Year Program*. Madrid (orientation in Salamanca). Academic year. One-month village homestay. Sophomores to seniors with intermediate college Spanish and 2.8 GPA. Apply by February 20.

Skidmore College. *Skidmore Study Abroad in Madrid*. Semester and academic year. Spanish language and literature, art history, political science, history, business, economics, philosophy, and psychology. Excursions and optional homestays. Juniors with 3.0 GPA and intermediate Spanish for semester program; intermediate to advanced for year. Apply by February 15 for fall and academic year; October 15 for spring.

Southern Methodist University. *SMU in Spain*. Madrid. Semester and academic year. Culture and civilization, language, art history, history, and political science. Homestays and excursions. Sophomores to seniors with one year of college Spanish. Apply by March 15 for fall and academic year; October 15 for spring. Contact: Office of International Programs, SMU, 100 McFarlin Auditorium, Dallas, TX 75275-0391; (214) 768-2338.

State University of New York College at Cortland. *University of Salamanca*. Semester and academic year. Humanities, social sciences, and Spanish language and literature. Homestays. Sophomores to seniors with two years of college Spanish and 2.5 GPA. Apply by March 7 for fall and academic year; October 15 for spring. Contact: Office of International Programs, SUNY College at Cortland, PO Box 2000, Cortland, NY 13045; (607) 753-2209.

State University of New York College at Oswego. *Oswego Barcelona Program*. Semester and academic year. Hispanic studies at University of Barcelona. Sophomores to graduate students with 2.5 GPA and intermediate Spanish. Apply by April 1 for fall and academic year; November 1 for spring. Contact:

International Education, 102 Rich Hall, SUNY College at Oswego, Oswego, NY 13126; (315) 341-2118.

Syracuse University. *Syracuse in Madrid.* Fall and spring semesters. Sophomores to seniors with 3.0 GPA. Apply by March 15 for fall; October 15 for spring. Contact: (800) 235-3472.

Tufts University. *Tufts in Madrid.* Academic year. Full university curriculum, advanced Spanish language, and Spanish studies. Juniors with three years of college Spanish and 3.0 GPA. Apply by February 1.

University of Connecticut. *Study Abroad Program at University of Granada.* Fall and spring semesters. Sophomores to seniors with five semesters of college Spanish. Apply by March 15 for fall; October 15 for spring.

University of Kansas. *Semester in Spain.* Santiago de Compostela. Semester and academic year. Spanish language, literature, and culture. Sophomores to seniors with five semesters of college Spanish. Apply by March 1 for fall and academic year; October 1 for spring.

University of Michigan. *Academic Year in Seville.* Seville. Spring semester and academic year. Offered in conjunction with Cornell University. Homestay. Juniors and seniors with two years of college Spanish. Apply by late January.

University of Minnesota. *International Program in Toledo: Spanish Language, Latin American, and European Studies.* Toledo. Semester and academic year. Language and linguistics, anthropology, art history, culture, economics, geography, interdisciplinary studies, and political science. Two years of college Spanish required. Apply by July 15 for fall; November 15 for spring. Contact: The Global Campus, 106C Nicholson Hall, 216 Pillsbury Drive SE, University of Minnesota, Minneapolis, MN 55455-0138; (612) 625-3379.

University of North Carolina at Chapel Hill. *NC Year at Seville.* Seville. Semester and academic year. Juniors and seniors with 2.5 GPA and two years of college Spanish. Apply by March 15 for fall and academic year; October 15 for spring.

University of Wisconsin at Madison. *Academic Year in Madrid.* Spanish language, literature, and liberal arts. Juniors and seniors in good academic standing and with five semesters of Spanish. Open to students at Indiana and Purdue universities, and to students at higher education institutions in Wisconsin (as well as Wisconsin residents studying outside the state). Apply by second Friday in November.

University of Wisconsin at Platteville. *Seville Study Center.* Seville. Semester and academic year. Study at Spanish-American Institute. Spanish language and literature, liberal arts, and international business. Sophomores to seniors with 2.5 GPA. Apply by April 30 for fall and academic year; October 20 for spring.

World Learning/School for International Training. *College Semester Abroad.* Granada. Fall and spring semesters. Intensive language study, life and culture seminar, village visit, field-study methods seminar, independent-study project. Homestays and excursions. Sophomores to seniors with 2.5 GPA and two years of college Spanish. Apply by May 7 for fall; October 7 for spring. Contact: College Semester Abroad Admissions, (800) 336-1616.

International Relations

American University. *Madrid Semester.* Spring semester. Spanish politics, economics, and foreign policy. Internships with multinational organizations. Juniors and seniors with two years of college Spanish and 2.75 GPA. Apply by October 15. Contact: World Capitals Programs, American University, Dunblane House—Tenley Campus, Washington, DC 20016-8083; (202) 895-4900/4937.

Spanish Language and Culture

Adventist Colleges Abroad. Sagunto. Fall, spring, and winter quarters and academic year. Undergraduates with 3.0 GPA in Spanish and 2.5 overall. Open only to students at Adventist Colleges Abroad consortium institutions. Apply by March 15 for fall and academic year; November 1 for winter; January 15 for spring.

Boston University. Madrid. Semester and academic year. Intensive language and cultural immersion program at Instituto Internacional en España; direct enrollment at Universidad Autónoma de Madrid and/or internships for qualified students. Homestays. Sophomores to seniors with 3.0 GPA in major and one semester of college Spanish; five semesters for advanced course. Apply by March 15 for fall and academic year; October 15 for spring.

Council on International Educational Exchange. *Language and Area Studies Program at the University of Alicante.* Semester and academic year. Sophomores to graduate students (not for graduate credit). Apply by April 1 for fall and academic year; October 15 for spring. Contact University Programs Department.

Language and Society Program at the Universidad Internacional Menéndez. Pelayo, Seville. Fall and spring semesters. Sophomores to graduate students (not for graduate credit) with three to four semesters of college Spanish and 2.75 GPA. Apply by April 1 for fall; October 15 for spring. Contact University Programs Department.

Davidson College. *Spring Semester in Spain.* Madrid. Offered in odd-numbered years only. First-year college students to juniors with intermediate Spanish with 2.75 GPA. Apply by October 1.

Heidelberg College. Seville. Semester and academic year. Offered in affiliation with Center for Cross-Cultural Study. Sophomores to graduate students with intermediate college Spanish and 3.0 GPA. Apply by May 15 for fall and academic year; November 15 for spring. Contact: Center for Cross-Cultural Study, Department C, 219 Strong Street, Amherst, MA 01002; (413) 549-4543.

Michigan State University. *Spanish Language, Literature, and Culture in Cáceres.* Spring semester. Sophomores to seniors with two years of Spanish. Apply by November 30. Contact: Office of Overseas Study, 108 International Center, Michigan State University, East Lansing, MI 48824-1035; (517) 353-8920.

North Carolina State University. *Semester in Spain.* Santander. Fall semester. Sophomores to graduate students with four semesters of Spanish and 2.5 GPA overall and in Spanish. Apply by March 1.

State University of New York College at New Paltz. *Semester Study in Spain.* Oviedo. Fall and spring semesters. Spanish language and civilization at University of Oviedo. Juniors and seniors with two years of college Spanish. Rolling admissions.

Study Abroad in Spain. Seville. Semester and academic year. Spanish language and civilization at University of Seville in courses specially designed for foreign students. Juniors and seniors with two years of college Spanish. Rolling admissions.

Contact: Office of International Education, HAB 33, SUNY College at New Paltz, New Paltz, NY 12561; (914) 257-3125.

Stetson University. Madrid. Semester and academic year. Sophomores to seniors with 2.5 GPA (3.0 in major). Apply by March 1 for fall and academic year; October 15 for spring.

University of Massachusetts at Amherst. Oviedo. Semester and academic year. Students with 2.75 GPA and four semesters of college Spanish. Apply by April 1 for fall and academic year; November 1 for spring.
University of Oregon. *Study in Seville.* Winter and spring quarters. Sophomores to seniors with two years of college Spanish and 3.0 GPA. Apply by May 1.
University of Toledo. *Study Abroad in Spain.* Toledo. Fall semester. Offered in conjunction with the José Ortega y Gasset Foundation. Spanish language and liberal arts. Sophomores to graduate students with three semesters of college Spanish. Apply by February 28.
University of Wisconsin at Green Bay. León. Fall semester and academic year. Study at the University of León. Spanish language and culture study. First-year college students to seniors with proficiency in Spanish. Apply by March 15.
Wesleyan University. *Vassar-Wesleyan-Colgate Program in Spain.* Santiago de Compostela, Madrid. Semester and academic year. Sophomores to seniors with four semesters of college Spanish and 3.0 average in Spanish. Apply by March 1 for fall or academic year; October 1 for spring.
Whitworth College. Seville. Semester and academic year. Offered in conjunction with the Center for Cross-Cultural Study. Spanish language, culture, and literature. Juniors and seniors with 2.5 GPA and two years of college Spanish. Apply by February 1 for fall; October 1 for spring.
World Learning/School for International Training. *College Semester Abroad—Language Immersion.* Granada. Fall and spring semesters. Intensive language and culture. Homestays and excursions. Sophomores to seniors with 2.5 GPA. Apply by May 7 for fall; October 7 for spring. Contact: College Semester Abroad Admissions, (800) 336-1616.

Summer and Short-Term

Education

University of Minnesota. *Summer Program for Teachers.* Madrid. Five weeks in summer. Graduate students and teachers with intermediate Spanish (as defined by ACTFL guidelines). All participants receive partial King Juan Carlos Fellowships. Apply by April 15. Contact: The Global Campus, 106C Nicholson Hall, 216 Pillsbury Drive SE, University of Minnesota, Minneapolis, MN 55455-0138; (612) 625-3379.

General Studies

Alma College. *Program of Studies in Spain.* Madrid or Segovia. Six-week summer program in Segovia; flexible enrollment period for Madrid. History, art, literature and other humanities in Segovia; intensive Spanish in Madrid. Homestays and excursions. Sophomores to seniors with 2.5 GPA; one year of Spanish required for Segovia program. Apply by March 15.
American Heritage Association. Barcelona. Summer. Social sciences and Spanish language at Institute for Social and International Studies. Sophomores to seniors with 3.0 GPA. Apply by May 1. Contact: (800) 654-2051.
New York University. *NYU in Spain.* Salamanca. Four weeks in July. Undergraduate and graduate programs in intermediate and advanced Spanish language, and contemporary Spanish culture and literature. Excursions.

Undergraduates with elementary Spanish; graduate students with Spanish major or equivalent. Apply by May. Contact: NYU in Spain, 19 University Place, Room 409, New York, NY 10003; (212) 998-8760.

Ohio State University. *The Toledo Program.* Toledo. Six weeks in summer. Anthropology and archaeology, art history, history, interdisciplinary studies, Spanish linguistics, Spanish and Latin American literature, philosophy, political science, and Spanish language; instruction in Spanish. Excursions and optional homestays. Undergraduates and graduates with 2.7 GPA and two years of college Spanish. Apply by April 1.

Portland State University. See listing under American Heritage Association.

Rollins College. *Verano Español.* Madrid. Summer. High-school graduates, college students, and teachers with two years of college Spanish. Apply by March 15.

University of Minnesota. *International Program in Toledo: Spanish Language, Latin American, and European Studies.* Toledo. Summer. Language and linguistics, anthropology, art history, culture, economics, geography, interdisciplinary studies, and political science. One year of college Spanish required. Apply by April 15. Contact: The Global Campus, 106C Nicholson Hall, 216 Pillsbury Drive SE, University of Minnesota, Minneapolis, MN 55455-0138; (612) 625-3379.

University of Wisconsin at Platteville. *Summer Session in Seville.* Seville. Summer. Spanish language study, culture, and history. Field trips, a Spanish intercambio partner, and homestay. Sophomores to seniors with 2.0 GPA and one year of college Spanish. Apply by April 1.

Political Science

Syracuse University. *The Story of Spain: Hispanic Political Narratives.* Madrid, Cordoba, Granada, Barcelona, and San Sebastian. Four weeks in June. Study tour on forces of integration and fragmentation in Spain from political, historical, and sociological standpoint. Undergraduates and graduates. Apply by March 1. Contact: (800) 235-3472.

Spanish Language and Culture

Adventist Colleges Abroad. Sagunto. Six-week intensive summer course at advanced, intermediate, and beginning levels. Excursions. High-school students, high-school graduates not enrolled in college, and college students with 2.5 GPA. Open only to students of Adventist Colleges Abroad consortium institutions. Apply by March 25.

Boston University. Madrid. Summer. Intensive six-week language and cultural immersion program at International Institute in Spain for intermediate and advanced levels. Excursions and homestays. Sophomores to seniors with 3.0 GPA in major and two semesters of college Spanish. Apply by April 1.

Central Washington University. La Coruña. Four-week summer program. Sophomores to seniors and teachers with one year of Spanish. Apply by June 15.

Council on International Educational Exchange. *The Spanish Mediterranean: Language & Area Studies at the University of Alicante.* Summer. First-year college students (with one semester college study) to graduate students with 2.5 GPA. Apply by March 15. Contact University Programs Department.

Indiana University. *Summer Study in Salamanca.* Undergraduates with 3.0 GPA and five semesters of college Spanish. Apply by February 15.

Iowa State University. *ISU/Iowa Regents' Program in Spain*. Valladolid. Summer. Offered in conjunction with University of Iowa and University of Northern Iowa. Total immersion in Spanish language and culture. Sophomores to graduate students with two years of college Spanish. Apply by March 1. Contact: Department of Foreign Languages and Literature, 300 Pearson Hall, Iowa State University, Ames, IA 50011.

Longwood College. *Summer Study Abroad Program at Institute of Spanish Studies*. Valencia. July. Four-week program in Spanish language, history, literature, and civilization. Homestays and excursions. Juniors, seniors, and Spanish teachers with one year of college Spanish and 2.5 GPA. Apply by February 14. Contact: Dr. John F. Reynolds, International Studies Program, Longwood College, Farmville, VA 23901; (804) 392-2172.

Louisiana State University. *LSU in Spain*. Salamanca. June to early July. Six-week program in Spanish language and literature. Excursions and homestays. Sophomores to seniors with 2.5 GPA (graduate students with 3.0 GPA) and one year of college Spanish. Apply by March 15.

Michigan State University. *Spanish Language, Literature, and Culture in Denia*. Summer. Sophomores to seniors with two years of college Spanish. Apply by April 15. Contact: Office of Overseas Study, 108 International Center, Michigan State University, East Lansing, MI 48824-1035; (517) 353-8920.

Rutgers University. *Summer Study Spain*. Five-week program from late June to early August. Excursions and dormitory housing. High-school graduates, college undergraduates, and graduate students with equivalent of intermediate-level college Spanish. Apply by March 1. Contact: Department of Spanish and Portuguese, Rutgers University, 105 George Street, New Brunswick, NJ 08903; (908) 932-9323.

State University of New York at Buffalo. *Programa de Estudios Hispanicos*. Salamanca. Five weeks in June and July. Co-sponsored by State University of New York College at Buffalo and offered in cooperation with University of Salamanca. Spanish culture and intensive language. Excursions and homestays. Sophomores to graduate students with one year of college Spanish. Apply by April 15. Contact: Study Abroad Coordinator, Office of International Education, SUNY at Buffalo, 212 Talbert Hall, Box 601604, Buffalo, NY 14260-1604; (716) 645-3912.

State University of New York College at New Paltz. *Summer Study in Spain*. Oviedo. Intensive Spanish language at all levels. Excursions. High-school students to graduate students. Rolling admissions. Contact: Office of International Education, HAB 33, SUNY College at New Paltz, New Paltz, NY 12561; (914) 257-3125.

State University of New York College at Oswego. *Spanish Language, Culture, Civilization Program in Madrid*. Six weeks in summer. Instruction in Spanish. Excursions. Undergraduates (and qualified high-school students and graduate students) with one year of college Spanish and 2.5 GPA. Apply by April 1. Contact: Office of International Education, SUNY at Oswego, 102 Rich Hall, Oswego, NY 13126; (315) 341-2118.

Syracuse University. *Summer in Spain: A Cultural, Linguistic, and Historical Journey*. Madrid, Cordoba, Sevilla, Trujillo, Toledo, and Cáceres. Six weeks in June and July. Spanish language at all levels, and prehistoric and cultural anthropology of Spain and its region. Undergraduates and graduate students. Apply by March 1. Contact: (800) 235-3472.

University of Alabama. *Alabama in Spain*. Valencia. Summer. Spanish language, civilization, and culture. Excursions. First-year college students to

graduate students with two semesters of college Spanish. Apply by March 1. Contact: (205) 348-5256.
University of Kansas. Barcelona. Undergraduates with two semesters of college Spanish. Apply by February 15.
University of Kentucky. *Kentucky Institute for International Studies in Madrid, Spain*. Madrid. Summer. Language study. Excursions. First-year college students to graduate students and adults. Apply by March 1.
Kentucky Institute for International Studies in Soria, Spain. Soria. Summer. Language study. Excursions. First-year college students to graduate students and adults. Apply by March 1.
University of Louisville. *Spanish Language and Culture in Segovia*. Segovia. Summer. Undergraduates to graduate students with background in Spanish. Apply by April 30. Offered in alternate years.
University of Maryland. *Summer in Madrid*. Madrid. Sophomores to seniors with 3.0 GPA and two years of college Spanish. Apply by March 1.
University of Massachusetts at Amherst. *Summer Program in Spain*. Salamanca. Juniors to graduate students with three years of college Spanish. Apply by April 6.
University of Michigan. *Summer Language Study in Salamanca*. Salamanca and Madrid. Six weeks in summer. First-year college students to seniors. Apply by March 1.
University of Minnesota. *Quincentennial Summer Program for Teachers of Spanish*. Open to graduate students and teachers with intermediate Spanish proficiency as defined by ACTFL guidelines. Apply by April 15.
International Program in Toledo. Toledo. Summer. First-year college students to graduate students and adults with one year of college Spanish. Apply by April 15.
University of Pennsylvania. *Penn-in-Alicante*. Provides an intensive introduction to the many facets of the Spanish language and culture. Apply by April 1.
University of Rhode Island. *URI Summer Study Program*. Salamanca. Five weeks in summer. Intensive language study, literature, and culture. Freshmen to graduate students with one year of college Spanish. Apply by May 1.
University of Toledo. *Study Abroad in Spain*. Toledo. Six weeks in summer. Spanish language study and liberal arts. Sophomores to graduate students with three semesters of college Spanish. Apply by February 28.
University of Tulsa. *Summer Immersion Program*. Málaga. Mid-May to late June. Spanish language and culture. First-year college students to seniors with one year of college Spanish and 2.5 GPA in Spanish. Apply by March 15.
University of Utah. *Salamanca Spanish Language Program*. University of Salamanca. Four weeks of Spanish language study preceded by two weeks of travel study in Europe. Undergraduates, graduate students, and others with 2.0 GPA and recommended one or two quarters of college Spanish. Apply by March 1.
University System of Georgia. *Salamanca, Spain*. Salamanca. Seven weeks in summer. Total immersion program. Excursions, homestays. Undergraduates to graduate students with 2.5 GPA overall and three semesters or quarters in college Spanish with 3.0 GPA in Spanish. Apply by April 1.
Villanova University. *Villanova Cádiz Summer Program in Spain*. Cádiz. Late June to early August. Intensive Spanish language study. First-years to seniors with 2.5 GPA and one year of college Spanish. Apply by March 15.

EXPLORING SPANISH CULTURE

Readings

Miguel de Cervantes's *Don Quixote de la Mancha* (Part I, 1605; Part II, 1615) is considered one of the world's greatest novels. *The Portable Cervantes* (1951) is an anthology of the works of this legendary literary figure including an abridged version of *Don Quixote*.

Federico García Lorca is the leading playwright of 20th-century Spain. *Blood Wedding* (1933) deals with love that defies village tradition and leads to an inescapable tragic end. *The House of Bernarda Alba* (1936) tells of the conflict between a domineering mother and her five daughters, who find themselves imprisoned by Spanish traditions and beliefs.

Awarded the 1989 Nobel Prize for Literature, Camilo José Cela is one of the preeminent Spanish writers of the 20th century. His book *The Hive*, depicting the suffering of the post–Civil War nation and its disillusioned people, was banned upon publication in 1951. Life in Madrid is portrayed as brutal, hungry, and senseless. In *Journey to the Alcarria* (1948), Cela draws upon personal experience in writing about travels through the rural countryside northeast of Madrid.

More recent views of Spain are presented by a variety of contemporary authors. José María Gironella's trilogy takes place during the time of the Spanish Civil War. These three novels, which explore the experiences of a middle-class family, are *The Cypresses Believe in God* (1955), *One Million Dead* (1963), and *Peace After War* (1969). *The Heliotrope Wall and Other Stories* (1961), by Ana María Matute, is a collection of her best stories, in which the theme of a rural childhood in Spain is rendered in the style that has become known as "magical realism." In *The Countryside of Nijar* (1960), Juan Goytisolo writes two novels of travels to Andalusia, and in his *Forbidden Territory: Memoirs, 1931–1956*, a victim of the Franco regime fights his way out of a cultural and intellectual wasteland. *Marks of Identity* (1966) is Goytisolo's autobiography. *Five Hours with Mario* (1966), by Miguel Delibes, is the story of the troubled marriage of a politically active novelist and his comfortably middle-class Francoist wife. In Juan Benet's *Return to Region* (1967), the mythical Region represents all that is paradoxical and mysterious about Spain. Finally, Carmen Martin Gaite's *The Back Room* (1983) provides a portrait of the lives of women in Spain.

Those interested in general background reading on Spain should pick up James Michener's *Iberia* (1968), a comprehensive travelogue and interpretation of Spanish culture, history, art, and politics; or *Spain* (1979), another excellent descriptive essay on Spain by Jan Morris. *The Spanish Temper* (1989), by V. S. Pritchett, is a concise analysis of the Spanish character.

Films

Films celebrating nationalism, patriotism, and national heroics were the norm until filmmakers such as Juan Antonio Bardem, with *Death of a Cyclist* (1955) and *Calle Mayor* (1956), and Luís Buñuel, in *Viridiana* (1961) and *Tristana* (1970), began obliquely to criticize Spanish society and government.

Only since Franco's death in 1976 have filmmakers been free to delve into themes of Spanish society and government without fear of censorship. Among the best known of these contemporary filmmakers of Spain is Carlos Saura, whose films range from the *Garden of Delights* (1970), a satire of Spanish society and human venality, to *Blood Wedding* (1981), a filmed version of

Lorca's play without any dialogue—only music and flamenco ballet. Saura's latest film, *Ay Carmela!* (1990), is a comic tragedy about a vaudeville act recruited to entertain Fascist troops during the Civil War.

It is significant that the most popular Spanish director today, Pedro Almodóvar, shuns the traditional historical and political subjects and prefers more up-to-date material like the changing Spanish social and sexual norms. Almodóvar is known for his outrageous and comically melodramatic plot lines and characters. Representative of this style is the film *Law of Desire* (1987), in which a glamorous gay film director is pursued by a male would-be lover. Almodóvar's other films include *High Heels* (1991), about a singer who rekindles a relationship with a former lover who is now married to her daughter; the more mainstream *Women on the Verge of a Nervous Breakdown* (1988), which was nominated for an Oscar for best foreign film; and *Matador* (1986), a black comedy that chronicles the plight of a retired bullfighter who passes his time appearing in snuff films.

SWEDEN

Sweden, the largest, most populous, and most industrialized of the Scandinavian nations, is also a land of forests, farms, and lakes. Frequently cited as the model social welfare state, this constitutional monarchy enjoys one of the highest standards of living in the world. It is highly regarded as a leader in urban design, economic planning, and social engineering. As a country and as an economy, Sweden functions as well as any in the world.

Because of its size, resources, geography, and traditionally strong monarchy, Sweden has almost always been in a position of relative political and economic dominance compared to the other Scandinavian countries. Only Denmark, during periods in the 16th and 17th centuries, has threatened this hegemony. Three hundred years ago, Sweden was regarded as warlike, and Swedish armies rampaged abroad. But the glamour of foreign exploits and a Nordic empire greatly diminished throughout the 18th century. By the beginning of the 19th century, it had lost all of its Baltic possessions, including Finland. In 1905 Norway declared its independence, establishing Swedish borders where they are today. Since the early 19th century, Sweden has pursued a neutral foreign policy, which kept it out of both world wars. Instead, Sweden has been a major force for international peace and disarmament, working both unilaterally and within the framework of the United Nations. It frequently serves as a mediator of international conflicts.

Parliamentary democracy combined with the rise of industrialism in the late 19th century to establish "the middle way" of the modern Swedish welfare state—a blend of humane social justice, equitable wealth distribution, respect for individual liberties, and a degree of economic planning between labor and industry. Swedish efficiency, energy, and organization created major triumphs during the 1950s and 1960s. Ninety-three percent of Swedish corporations are privately owned and nearly half of its production is exported to foreign markets. Over the past decade Sweden has become a world leader in electronics and high technology. Sweden is also known as a pioneer in "workplace democracy."

This affluent society, however, has been shaken somewhat by the same economic crisis that has struck the rest of Western Europe. Additionally, Swedes have begun to question the degree to which the government's social policy should be involved in all aspects of life, cradle-to-grave, as well as the huge tax burden necessary to finance such involvement. One finds, especially among young Swedes, an increasing skepticism about the ability of the politicians and social experts to solve all human problems through national policies, however well intentioned. The debate rages over how to find a new "middle way" that will balance fundamental social benefits and securities against private freedoms and responsibilities.

Sweden offers some of the best urban sophistication (especially in Stockholm, the most urbane and opulent of the Nordic capitals), along with the rural charm of an old and rustic countryside with its villages, customs, and crafts largely intact, plus spacious tracts of some of the last true wilderness remaining in Europe. Moreover, travel from one corner to another is made possible by convenient air routes, extensive railways, modern and safe highways—or, for the recreational tourist, boating canals and biking, hiking, and skiing trails. Visitors will find a welcome everywhere, as well as the engaging informality and cheerful efficiency that are the envy of many nations.

—*William W. Hoffa, Amherst, Massachusetts*

Official name: Kingdom of Sweden. **Size:** 173,731 square miles (slightly larger than California). **Population:** 8,564,000. **Population density:** 49 inhabitants per square mile. **Capital and largest city:** Stockholm (pop. 672,000). **Language:** Swedish. **Religion:** Lutheran. **Per capita income:** US$16,200. **Currency:** Krona. **Literacy rate:** 99%. **Average daily temperature:** Stockholm, June 59°; December, 32°. **Average number of days with precipitation:** June, 11; December, 15.

TRAVEL

U.S. citizens traveling to Sweden will need a passport. Visas are not required for stays of up to three months, a period that begins as soon as one enters the Scandinavian region (Sweden, Norway, and Denmark). For specific requirements, check with the **Embassy of Sweden**, 600 New Hampshire Avenue NW, Washington, DC 20037; (202) 944-5600.

Getting Around

Travelers flying Scandinavian Airlines (SAS) round-trip to the Scandinavian countries of Norway, Denmark, or Sweden are eligible for SAS's **Visit Scandinavia fare**. The special plan allows the purchase of up to six discounted flight coupons for travel within the three countries. The coupons, which cost from $80 for one flight to $420 for six, must be purchased in the U.S. before departure and must be used within three months of arrival in Scandinavia. They can be used on any of the three Scandinavian airlines: Danair, Linjeflyg, and SAS (excluding flights to the Faroe Islands and Greenland). For more information, call SAS at (800) 221-2350.

The Swedish rail network serves all of southern Sweden and much of the north, crossing even the Arctic Circle. **Trains** are expensive, however. If you can, take advantage of "red departure" tickets, half-price one-way fares valid during certain hours. Eurialpasses of all types are valid throughout Sweden.

Those planning to travel extensively in Scandinavia should consider the following options:

- The **ScanRail Pass** is valid for travel on the state railway systems of Denmark, Finland, Norway, and Sweden on a certain number of days within a fixed period of time. For example, one may travel on any 14 days within one month for $475 first class and $369 second class. For information and reservations, contact Rail Europe (see page 62) or Council Travel (see pages xiii–xvi).
- The **Nordturist Ticket** allows for 21 days of free travel on the state railway systems of the above-mentioned countries, including certain ferries. It's also good for a 50-percent discount on the Hirtshals-Hjörring private railway as well as other ferry lines and bus routes. This pass can only be bought in Scandinavia, and is a better buy than the ScanRail Pass. The cost for youths ages 12 to 25 traveling second-class is approximately US$250.

Sweden also has an extensive **ferry** system, but these luxurious boats are expensive. An inexpensive travel alternative is the **bus**. On Fridays and Sundays Swebus offers special weekend express service. The trip from Stockholm to Göteborg, for example, costs around $20. For more information, call Swebus at (46) 31-103800. To visit the countryside in the far north, you'll have to leave the trains behind and connect with a postal bus; call Postens Diligenstrafik at (46) 90-150690.

Eating and Sleeping

Sweden has around 300 **youth hostels**. For more information, contact Hostelling International/American Youth Hostels (see page 54), or the Sweden's national youth hostel organization, **Svenska Turisföreningen**, Box 25, Drottninggatan 31-33, 10120 Stockholm; (46) 8-7903100; fax (46) 8-201332. There are also more than 700 government-approved **campsites** throughout Sweden. In the summer, many student residence halls open their doors to travelers. More information on camping, student residence halls, and other low-cost options, is available in *Budget Accommodation in Sweden*, available from the Swedish Tourist Board (see "For Further Information," below). Also consult Campus Travel Service's *US and Worldwide Travel Accommodations Guide* (see page 54).

Especially for Students and Young People

Sweden's student travel bureau is **Kilroy travels Sweden**, Kungsgatan 4, Box 7144, S-103 87 Stockholm; (46) 8-234515. Holders of the International Student Identity Card get discounts on plane and train travel from Sweden to destinations around the world.

For Further Information

General tourist information can be obtained from the **Swedish Tourist Board**, 655 Third Avenue, New York, NY 10017; (212) 949-2333; fax (212) 983-5260.

One of the best general guidebooks to Sweden and the entire Scandinavian region is Lonely Planet's *Scandinavian and Baltic Europe on a Shoestring* ($17.95). Also good is *The Real Guide: Scandinavia* ($14.95). An excellent book to read in preparation for your trip is *Insight Guide: Sweden* ($19.95).

For more information on Lonely Planet, *Real Guides*, and *Insight Guides*, see pages 56–57.

WORK

In order to work full-time in Sweden you will need to obtain a work permit before entering the country. To be eligible for a permit, you must show written proof that your job and accommodations in Sweden have already been arranged. For more information, contact the **Swedish Consulate General** (One Dag Hammarskjold Plaza, New York, NY 10017-2201) for a copy of *Employment and Residency in Sweden*. The **American-Scandinavian Foundation** (see "Study," below) can also assist Americans ages 21 to 30 with obtaining the requisite permit.

Internships/Traineeships

A program offered by a member of the Council on International Educational Exchange is listed below.

Association for International Practical Training. *IAESTE Trainee Program*. On-the-job training for undergraduate and graduate students in technical fields such as engineering, computer science, agriculture, architecture, mathematics, and the natural and physical sciences. See page 19 for more information.

STUDY

The **Swedish Information Service** distributes a number of brochures including *Studying in Sweden*, containing a wealth of introductory information about undergraduate studies, preparatory Swedish language courses, and postgraduate studies; *Swedish Higher Education*, which lists programs and courses offered in English by Swedish universities and colleges; and *Summer Opportunities in Sweden*. Ask for their *Fact Sheets on Sweden* order form to access short information forms on everything from education to Swedish foreign policy and social issues. The service can be contacted at One Dag Hammarskjold Plaza, New York, NY 10017-2201; (212) 751-5900. The Exchange Division of the **American Scandinavian Foundation** publishes *Study in Scandinavia*, which also includes a listing of English-language programs offered in Sweden during the academic year and summer. Contact them at 725 Park Avenue, New York, NY 10021; (212) 879-9779; fax (212) 249-3444.

Following are the study programs offered by CIEE-member institutions. Unless otherwise noted, consult Appendix I for the addresses of the colleges and universities listed in this section.

Semester and Academic Year

General Studies

International Student Exchange Program (ISEP). Semester and academic year. Direct reciprocal exchange between U.S. universities and Luleana and

Växjö universities. Full curriculum options. Rolling admissions. Open only to students at ISEP-member institutions. Contact ISEP for list of members.
Scandinavian Seminar. *College Year in Sweden.* Individual placement in Swedish folk colleges throughout Sweden. Swedish language and liberal arts. Sophomores to graduate students and adults. Apply by April 15.
University of Oregon. *University of Oregon—Uppsala University Exchange.* Fall semester and academic year. Juniors and seniors with two years of college Swedish and 2.75 GPA. Apply by March 1.
University of Wisconsin at Madison. *Academic Year at University of Linköping.* Scandinavian language, literature, politics, history, business, and engineering. Juniors to graduate students in good academic standing and with five semesters of college Swedish. Open only to students at higher education institutions in Wisconsin and Wisconsin residents studying outside the state. Apply by second Friday in February.

International Relations

Scandinavian Seminar. *Semester Program on Nordic and Global Issues.* Mariefred (fall), Trosa (spring). Swedish language, global ecology, international conflict resolution, international humanitarian organizations, and sustainable economic development, from Nordic perspective. Excursions. Sophomores to graduate students and adults. Apply by April 15 for fall; October 15 for spring.

Summer and Short-Term

Marketing and Public Relations

Michigan State University. *Packaging in Sweden.* Lund. Summer. Juniors and seniors. Apply by April 15. Contact: Office of Overseas Study, 108 International Center, Michigan State University, East Lansing, MI 48824-1035; (517) 353-8920.

EXPLORING SWEDISH CULTURE

Reading

Perhaps Sweden's most famous writer, August Strindberg is one of the fathers of modern drama and author of the plays *Miss Julie* and *The Father*. Sexual conflict and the roles of the sexes both in and outside of marriage are the themes of both these works. Romantic poet Carl Verner von Heidenstam won the Nobel Prize for literature in 1916. His collections *Poems* and *New Poems* have a rare intensity for Swedish literature.

Pär Lagerkvist was a novelist, poet, and dramatist who won the Nobel Prize for literature in 1951. His novels *The Hangman*, *The Dwarf*, and *Barabbas* illustrate the conflict in man's dichotomy of good and evil. In 1974, two Swedes shared the Nobel Prize for literature: Harry Edmund Martinson and Eyvind Johnson. Martinson's most famous novel, *The Road*, describes the life of an outcast. Johnson was a novelist who wrote a series of semi-autobiographical works focusing on his early years in northern Sweden, including *1914*.

P. C. Jersild's novel on the experiences of a bodiless human brain floating in liquid called *A Living Soul* has given him an international reputation as an entertaining, provocative author. Stig Dagerman's collection of intense short stories, *The Games of the Night*, includes some of his best work. *Short Stories*, a stylish collection of twenty-six from Hjalmar Söerberg, are set on the streets of Stockholm.

Films

Swedish film is closely related to Swedish theater. Many filmmakers, including Ingmar Bergman, have worked regularly in the theater, and many traditional themes of Swedish theater have been explored in their movies. Bergman films include *The Seventh Seal* (1956), about a knight returning from the crusades who attempts to stave off death with a game of chess; *Wild Strawberries* (1957), in which an elderly professor reflects upon the disappointments in his life; and *Fanny and Alexander* (1983), which won an Oscar for best foreign film and takes place at a turn-of-the-century family gathering.

Oscar-winner Arne Sucksdorff wrote and directed *The Great Adventure* (1953), which follows two boys on a farm during the course of the four seasons. In Bo Widerberg's *Elvira Madigan* (1967), a married army officer runs away with a tightrope dancer. In the entertaining *Montenegro* (1981), directed by Dusan Makavejev, a bored housewife takes a lover and then murders him. Writer/director Bo Widerberg made *The Man from Majorca* (1984), a stylish suspense film about two policemen attempting to uncover a political sex-scandal. *My Life as a Dog* (1985), directed by Lasse Halstrom, is a charming tale of a young boy learning to cope with his mother's illness, and his own propensity for getting in trouble, while staying with relatives in the idyllic Swedish countryside.

The Emigrants (1971) and its sequel *The New Land* (1972), both written and directed by Jan Troell, follow a 19th-century farmer and his family as they settle in the United States—a fascinating outsider's depiction of the U.S. In *The Ox* (1992), director Sven Nykvist takes the other side of the tale told in *The Emigrants* and *The New Land*: He follows the peasants and farmers who did not join the exodus to America in the 1860s, risking starvation in the harsh winter conditions.

SWITZERLAND

Switzerland is a land of exceptional natural beauty—mountain peaks, Alpine skiing resorts, and quaint villages alternate with green well-kept meadows. But there is another Switzerland as well: the land of modern banks and investment houses connected with other world financial capitals via computers and satellites; of highly efficient rail, highway and air networks; of cities with a healthy blend of old-world charm and high-tech convenience. Where else in the world can one walk into a 24-hour banking center to change currencies, make account transfers, and buy gold bullion and coins—all at the push of a button?

It is difficult to find any evidence of poverty in Switzerland. Although Switzerland has encountered many of the same economic problems facing other European countries, the Swiss unemployment rate is still lower than in almost any other modern industrial nation, and the Swiss per capita income is one of the highest in the world.

Switzerland currently is faced with the task of defining its role in the new

Europe. Does it join its neighbors and become a full member of the European Community? Or does Switzerland go it alone, hoping to preserve its role as an independent and neutral country in the heart of Europe? Switzerland's role in Europe won't be decided easily. As the world's oldest democracy (the Swiss just celebrated 700 years of democratic rule), Switzerland relies on a time-consuming system of referendums, used to decide everything from plans for a new highway to the need for a large, well-armed military.

Over the last century, the Swiss have been able to transform a poor federation of small agricultural cantons into one of the world's wealthiest and most stable countries. The major industries in Switzerland are tourism, watchmaking, chemicals, banking, and agriculture. Much of the unskilled labor is provided by foreigners who are allowed to work in Switzerland for limited periods of time.

The young Swiss who have grown up in this idyllic land seem to live a charmed life. Fluent in many languages, they benefit from Switzerland's role as the crossroads of Europe. They eat French food, wear Italian clothes, drive German cars, and are fed a steady diet of American and British rock music and television via cable and satellite broadcast. This "good life" also has its downside: drug abuse is relatively widespread in Switzerland's cities.

There is no "Swiss" language. Depending on the region of the country, people in Switzerland speak French, German, or Italian (in some of the mountain regions, people speak a Latin-based language called Romansch). Most young Swiss also speak fluent English.

—Randy Epping, Zurich, Switzerland

Official name: Swiss Confederation. **Size:** 15,941 square miles (about the size of Massachusetts, Rhode Island and Connecticut combined). **Population:** 6,783,000. **Population density:** 425 inhabitants per square mile. **Capital:** Bern (pop. 135,000). **Largest city:** Zurich (pop. 342,000). **Language:** German, French, Italian. **Religion:** Roman Catholic, Protestant. **Per capita income:** US$18,700. **Currency:** Swiss franc. **Literacy rate:** 99%. **Average daily temperature:** Geneva: June, 64°F; December, 36°F. **Average number of days with precipitation:** Geneva: June, 11; December 10.

TRAVEL

U.S. citizens need a passport for travel to Switzerland. A visa is not required for stays of up to three months. For specific requirements, check with the **Embassy of Switzerland**, 2900 Cathedral Avenue NW, Washington, DC 20008; (202) 745-7900; fax (202) 387-2564.

Getting Around

Switzerland has an excellent national railway network connecting government and private lines. Eurail and InterRail passes are valid only on the government railroads. Travel by **train** is quite expensive in Switzerland, but the **Half-Fare Travel Card** gives a 50-percent reduction on all trips on both government and private railways in Switzerland. The card costs 150 Swiss francs (US $100) for one year or 85 francs ($58) for one month.

Rail Europe sells three other passes good for unlimited travel on public and selected private railroads, as well as lake steamers, city transportation, and postal buses. It also gives 25-percent discounts on most mountain cable lines, including those up Jungfrau, Matterhorn, and Pilatus. For second-class travel, the **Swiss Pass** costs $186 for 8 days, $214 for 15 days, and $296 for one month. First-class Swiss Passes cost $266, $312, and $430, respectively. The **Swiss Flexipass** is valid for any 3 days in a 15-day period. It costs $148 second class and $222 first class. The **Swiss Rail 'n' Drive Pass** gives you three days of rail travel and three days of car rental over a one-month period. The cost for two people in an economy car is $285 second class or $359 first class, per person. For more information, contact Rail Europe (see page 00) or Council Travel (see pages 00–00).

One of the most spectacular ways to see Switzerland's natural beauty is to hike its alpine trails. *Berghotels* or *auberges de montagne* are rustic mountain **guesthouses** that provide hikers with food and a place to stay in scenic spots far from the nearest road or railway. For more information, pick up a copy of *Walking Switzerland the Swiss Way*, by Marcia and Philip Lieberman, available for $12.95 from The Mountaineers Books (for ordering information, see page 57).

Eating and Sleeping

This small country has more than 100 **youth hostels**. For more information, contact Hostelling International/American Youth Hostels (see page 54) or Switzerland's national youth hostel organization, **Schweizer Jugendherbergen**, Postfach, 3001 Bern; (41) 31-3025503; fax (41) 31-3016671.

In addition, several Swiss universities offer affordable **dormitory lodgings** to travelers. For more information, contact SSR Reisen (see "Especially for Students and Young People," below) or consult Campus Travel Service's *US and Worldwide Travel Accommodations Guide* (see page 54).

Especially for Students and Young People

Switzerland's student travel bureau and issuer of the International Student Identity Card is **SSR-Reisen**, Bäckerstrasse 52, CH-8026 Zurich; (41) 1-2423000; fax (41) 1-2423131. In addition, it has 16 offices throughout Switzerland where you can get international plane and train tickets, book accommodations, and obtain travel information. SSR operates a student hotel in Lucerne and offers river rafting and canoeing trips. **SSR-Reisen** also distributes the *National Student Discount Directory*.

For Further Information

For general tourist information, contact the **Swiss National Tourist Office**, 608 Fifth Avenue, New York, NY 10020; (212) 757-5944.

Let's Go: Germany and Switzerland ($16.95) is a good guide tailored to the student budget. An excellent book to read in preparation for your trip is *Insight Guide: Switzerland* ($19.95). For more information on *Let's Go* and *Insight Guides*, see pages 56–57.

WORK

Anyone who wishes to work in Switzerland must obtain a work permit before entering the country; application for the permit is made by the prospective

Swiss employer. The possibilities for finding permanent employment in Switzerland are very limited.

Internships/Traineeships

Programs offered by members of the Council on International Educational Exchange are listed below.

Association for International Practical Training. *IAESTE Trainee Program.* On-the-job training for undergraduate and graduate students in technical fields such as engineering, computer science, agriculture, architecture, mathematics, and the natural and physical sciences. See page 19 for more information. *Hospitality/Tourism Exchange Program.* On-the-job training for young people beginning a career in the hotel and food-service industries. Participants must have graduated or be currently enrolled in a university or vocational school and possess at least six months of training or experience in the chosen field. Training usually runs from 6 to 18 months. Consult Appendix I for the address to write for more information.

Syracuse University. *Graduate Internship in International Studies.* Geneva. Summer. Internships with international organizations. Graduates in international relations or related fields. Apply by February 15.

Voluntary Service

For persons interested in voluntary-service work, the Year Abroad Program sponsored by the **International Christian Youth Exchange** offers persons ages 18 to 30 voluntary-service opportunities in the fields of health care, education, the environment, construction, and more. See page 25 for more information.

STUDY

The **Cultural Affairs Office** at the Embassy of Switzerland (see "Travel," above) distributes a fact sheet entitled *Educational Facilities in Switzerland with Instruction in English*, as well as a list of Swiss universities.

Following are the study programs offered by CIEE-member institutions. Unless otherwise noted, consult Appendix I for the addresses of the colleges and universities listed in this section.

Semester and Academic Year

Engineering

Iowa State University. *Lausanne Exchange*. Lausanne. Academic year. Civil, rural, mechanical, micro, electrical, and chemical engineering, as well as math, computer science, physics, and materials science. Study at École Polytechnique Fédérale de Lausanne. Juniors, seniors, and graduate students in special cases with three years of French and 3.0 GPA. Contact: Dr. Peter Reilly, Chemical Engineering, 242 Sweeney, Iowa State University, Ames, IA 50011; (515) 294-5968.

General Studies

Cornell University. *Cornell Abroad at University of Geneva.* Academic year. Wide range of studies available with instruction in French; internships available with international organizations. Excursions and dormitory housing. Juniors and seniors with 3.0 GPA and four semesters of college French. Apply by February 15 for fall and academic year; October 15 for spring.

International Student Exchange Program (ISEP). Academic year. Direct reciprocal exchange between U.S. universities and the Université de Fribourg and Université de Lausanne. Full curriculum options. Rolling admissions. Open only to students at ISEP-member institutions. Contact ISEP for list of members.

Iowa State University. *Lausanne Exchange.* Academic year. Courses available in wide range of disciplines at Université de Lausanne. Juniors, seniors, (and graduate students in special cases only) with three years of French and 3.0 GPA. Apply by November 15. Contact: Dr. Peter Reilly, Chemical Engineering, 242 Sweeney, Iowa State University, Ames, IA 50011; (515) 294-5698.

Kent State University. *KSU Semester in Geneva.* Fall and spring semesters. International relations and the UN, international business, and French language. Internships available. Sophomores to seniors with 2.5 GPA. Rolling admissions.

LaSalle University. *LaSalle-in-Europe.* Fribourg. Academic year. Liberal arts, science, and international studies; instruction in English, French, and German. First-year college students and sophomores with one year of college French or German and 2.5 GPA. Apply by April 1.

State University of New York College at Cortland. *University of Neuchâtel.* Semester and academic year. Humanities, and French language and literature. Excursions and dormitory housing. Sophomores to seniors with intermediate to advanced French and 2.5 GPA. Apply by March 7 for fall and academic year; October 15 for spring. Contact: Office of International Programs, SUNY College at Cortland, PO Box 2000, Cortland, NY 13045; (607) 753-2209.

Webster University. *Study Abroad in Geneva.* Quarter, semester, and academic year. High-school graduates to graduate students. Apply four months before projected start of study. Contact: (800) 753-6765.

Hospitality Administration

Iowa State University. *HOTELCONSULT.* Lausanne. Fall and spring semesters. Hotel and restaurant management at Institut Hôtelier César Ritz; internships possible. Sophomores to seniors. Apply one semester in advance. Contact: International Programs, College of Family and Consumer, Iowa State University, 122 MacKay, Ames, IA 50011; (515) 294-3527.

International Relations

World Learning/School for International Training. *College Semester Abroad.* Geneva. Fall and spring semesters. Intensive French-language study, academic seminar including U.N. contributors, international organizations and field-study methods seminars, independent-study project, educational travel, and homestay. Sophomores to seniors with 2.5 GPA. Apply by May 7 for fall; October 7 for spring. Contact: College Semester Abroad Admissions, (800) 336-1616.

Summer and Short-Term

French Language and Swiss Culture

State University of New York College at Cortland. *University of Neuchâtel.* Summer. Four-week program of French language and French-Swiss culture. Undergraduates and graduates. Apply by April 1. Contact: Office of International Programs, SUNY College at Cortland, PO Box 2000, Cortland, NY 13045; (607) 753-2209.

University of Utah. *Neuchâtel French Language Program.* University of Neuchâtel. Summer. French language study for four weeks preceded by two and a half weeks of travel study in Europe. Undergraduates, graduate students, and others with 2.0 GPA and (recommended) one or two quarters of college French. Apply by March 1.

General Studies

University of North Carolina at Chapel Hill. *UNC Program to Switzerland.* Thun. Sophomores to seniors. Apply by February 1.

Webster University. *Study Abroad in Geneva.* Summer. High-school graduates to graduate students. Apply four months in advance. Contact: (800) 753-6765.

Hospitality Administration

Iowa State University. *HOTELCONSULT.* Lausanne. Summer. Offered in cooperation with Boston University. Hotel and restaurant management at Institut Hôtelier César Ritz; internships possible. Sophomores to seniors. Apply two to three months in advance. Contact: International Programs, College of Family and Consumer, Iowa State University, 122 MacKay, Ames, IA 50011; (515) 294-3527.

University of Massachusetts at Amherst. *Summer Program in Hotel, Restaurant, and Travel Administration.* Sophomores to seniors. Some French required. Apply by January 15.

International Relations

Augsburg College. *Global Issues and World Churches.* Geneva. Introduction to international nongovernmental organizations (NGOs), especially ecumenical church agencies. Excursions to Italy and Germany. Sophomores to seniors. Apply by March 15.

UKRAINE

Of the new countries that have come into being and the old countries that have been reborn during the turbulent recent years in Eastern Europe, perhaps none is more of a welcome and baffling surprise to its own inhabitants than Ukraine, whose independence is a result of glasnost gone amok. The Chernobyl disaster pulled Ukrainians together, and the activism that rose from the tragedy evolved into the triumphant drive for statehood that culminated in the declaration of independence from the now-dissolved USSR in the summer of 1991.

A country that bears the marks of centuries of rule by a plethora of outsiders, Ukraine today is bounded on its western end by Galicia and the miraculously intact old city of Lvov, with its Polish squares, Viennese opera house, ghostly Jewish quarter, and Soviet monuments summing up centuries in the space of a few blocks. Moving eastward across the endless fields of wheat, the church roofs become round, and centuries of lopsided union with Russia become apparent long before one reaches Kiev—architectural, political, and cultural reminders of Russia's influence still mark the region. To the south are the Black Sea coast, the port of Odessa, and the beaches and resorts of the Crimea, long the favorite getaway of Russian nobles and Soviets of every stature, and the site of the spas frequented by Russia's chronically ill writers of the 19th century.

Ukraine means, literally, "on the border." Its people live on a seemingly eternal border between Europe's east and west. From the first millenium B.C., Ukraine was a crossroads, its Black Sea coast the home to Greek, Roman, and Byzantine settlements, its fertile interior the domain of a succession of nomadic groups. Ukrainians have lived for centuries under the rule of the Mongols, Russia, Poland, Lithuania, and Austria-Hungary, with only the briefest periods of self-rule in between. Whenever Europe's borders have been redrawn, those borders have cut through Ukraine.

This was not always the case. By the 9th century A.D., the Kievan Rus had come into being, the dominant Slavic state in Eastern Europe. At its peak in the 10th and 11th centuries, it stretched from the Crimea to the heart of present-day European Russia, bringing with it Orthodox Christianity. The Mongol invasions in the 1300s brought an end to the only long era of Ukrainian statehood. But nothing in the 700 years of partitions and cultural repressions that followed did much to diminish Ukrainians' national identity. Nearly every generation has revolted, whether in the Cossack revolution of the 1600s or the remarkably durable Ukrainian Insurgent Army, which continued to wage a guerrilla war for independence against the Soviets for 10 years after World War II ended.

To be sure, the Poles left their mark, bringing Catholicism to western Ukraine; but the conversion did not go as intended, instead resulting in the centuries-old Uniate church, a blend of Roman Catholic and Eastern Orthodox ritual and tradition. And the Russians, who ruled eastern Ukraine for most of the past 300 years, made what seemed to be inroads in their efforts to assimilate Ukrainians into Russia. By suppressing Ukrainian culture and at times the language itself, the tsars and later the Soviets managed to create a large population of Ukrainians who couldn't speak their own language. The effects of Russian and Soviet repressions of Ukrainian culture are being undone today at a pace that startles Ukrainians themselves. Even in Kiev, the Ukrainian capital where nearly everyone spoke Russian until recently, the lilt of Ukrainian fills the streets, and Ukrainian music, art, and literature are undergoing a stunning renaissance.

Centuries as an agrarian province for other powers and decades of Soviet industrialization and pillage in Russia's shadow have left this new country in an economic and political free-fall. Still mistaken for a southern swath of Russia, it is sometimes overlooked on the international stage as its neighbors to the north and west are pulled into the new Europe. But with its nuclear arsenal and most of the Black Sea fleet in its ports as a bargaining chip, Ukraine can command regional and international attention to its needs. Ukrainians have watched their salaries plummet under inflation much worse than Russia's, but to wonder how long Ukrainians will endure this time of crisis is to forget how small a crisis this really is when put in historical perspective. Rich in mineral resources, with a highly developed manufacturing industry and a high agricultural output, Ukrainians have reason to believe in a brighter future.

—Steve Koppelman, New York, New York

Official name: Ukraine. **Area:** 233,100 square miles. **Population:** 51,994,000. **Population density:** 223 inhabitants per square mile. **Capital and largest city:** Kiev (pop. 2,637,000). **Language:** Ukrainian. **Religion:** Orthodox, Ukrainian Catholic, Moslem. **Per capita income:** US $2,500. **Currency:** Hryvnia. **Literacy rate:** 99%. **Average daily high/low:** Kiev: January, 24°F/14°F; June, 75°F/56°F. **Average number of days with precipitation:** Kiev: January, 18; June, 11.

TRAVEL

U.S. citizens must have a passport and visa to enter Ukraine. They also must possess an invitation from within Ukraine or proof of advance hotel reservations. Visas valid for the specified length of the visitor's stay are available for $30. For more information, contact the **Embassy of Ukraine**, 3350 M Street NW, Washington, DC 20007; (202) 333-7507.

Getting Around

Ukraine's transportation system is not extensive or designed for tourists. As in Russia, to get the most out of travel in Ukraine, you have to use your wits. The best way to get around Ukraine is by **train**. The second alternative, of course, is **bus** travel. In Kiev, you can get around via the Metro. **Boat** service also runs along the Dnieper. At press time, **air** transportation was still provided by Aeroflot, although this may be changing.

For Further Information

Ukraine has no official tourist representative in the U.S. However, you can obtain information on travel and package tours in Ukraine from Russia's **Intourist** (see page 210).

At press time, there were no good guides to Ukraine. However, *On the Loose in Eastern Europe* ($15.50) has a good chapter on Ukraine. For a good introduction to Ukraine, read *Insight Guide: Eastern Europe* ($19.95). For more information on *On the Loose* and *Insight* guides, see pages 56–57.

WORK

In order to work in Ukraine, it is necessary to obtain a work visa. To be granted the visa, you must secure an invitation in writing from a Ukrainian company. Work visas are issued by the **Embassy of Ukraine** (see "Travel," above), as well as at Ukrainian consulates. For more information contact the embassy.

Internships/Traineeships

Association for International Practical Training. *IAESTE Trainee Program.* On-the-job training for undergraduate and graduate students in technical fields such as engineering, computer science, agriculture, architecture, mathematics, and the natural and physical sciences. See page 19 for more information.

STUDY

Below are educational programs offered by CIEE-member institutions. Unless otherwise noted, consult Appendix I for contact addresses.

Semester and Academic Year

General Studies

University of Wisconsin at Green Bay. Kharkov. Semester and academic year. Study at Kharkov State University. Russian, general studies. First-year college students to seniors. Apply by March 15 for fall and academic year; October 15 for spring.

Russian Language and Ukrainian Culture

Whitworth College. *Kiev University Exchange Program*. Kiev. Semester and academic year. Offered in conjunction with Kiev University. Russian-language study, Ukrainian-language study, history, literature, and contemporary Ukrainian life. Juniors and seniors with 2.5 GPA. Apply by February 1 for fall and academic year; October 1 for spring.

Summer and Short Term

General Studies

University of Pennsylvania. *Penn-in-Kiev*. Kiev. Summer. Ukrainian-language study, advanced Russian-language study, Ukrainian culture and civilization. First-year college students to seniors. Apply by March 1.

Political Science

Old Dominion University. *ODU Abroad: Odessa*. Summer. Russian language and political science. Preference given to students with at least elementary Russian. Apply by March 1. Contact: Study Abroad Office, BAL 304, Old Dominion University, Norfolk, VA 23529; (804) 683-5378.

Russian Language and Ukrainian Culture

University of Alabama. *Study Tour of the Former Soviet Union*. Russia, Ukraine, and Georgia. Three weeks in May. Undergraduates and graduate students. Apply by March 1. Contact: (205) 348-5256.

UNITED KINGDOM

Visitors to the United Kingdom will arrive complete with images ranging from stately manors and the royal family to black taxis and Page 3 pinups. What they will find is so much more. The United Kingdom is juggling to find its place in a changing environment. Just 50 years ago, the UK was at the forefront of the world's economy and politics. Now, as its role has diminished with the end of the empire, and after a period of increased political isolation, the UK seems to have retreated into its own corner of Europe.

The United Kingdom refers to four distinct states: England, Scotland, Wales, and Northern Ireland. England, with London as its capital is the economic lifeline and is divided between a relatively prosperous South and a poorer, more industrial North. Scotland, Wales, and Northern Ireland have their own native cultures and languages, and nationalistic fervor exists in all three states, most notably in Northern Ireland. The long-term effects of these on the Union, however, remain to be seen. This is why the UK is often considered to be several cultures coexisting instead of one coherent unit. London is undeniably the nation's economic capital, but the recession has hit hardest here. Recent growth has been restricted to cities such as Bristol, Manchester, and Glasgow, where decaying districts have been restored, companies have relocated, and a new optimism has arisen.

Although the UK joined the European Community in 1973, few Britons would call themselves true Europeans. They consider themselves to be very separate from continental Europe and divided by more than the English Channel—unique customs, languages, and certainly a different outlook on life. The idea of a European union has caused division both in Parliament and among the people. Being reduced to just a state within a single European country may prove too difficult for a country so proud of its uniqueness.

While the opening of the Channel Tunnel in 1994 will bring the UK closer to continental Europe physically, if not emotionally, the influence of foreign cultures is nothing new to Britain. Since WWII, immigration from Africa, the West Indies, and the Indian subcontinent has created a multiracial population that is challenging the traditionally homogeneous society.

The Conservative Party has led Parliament in the UK since 1979 and has made sweeping changes that have not always been appreciated by a working class used to a welfare state. Many complain that the less well-off are no longer cared for in the UK as the government moves away from a paternalistic model toward a more independent one. The changes it has made have tended to enforce the divisions between rich and poor, North and South.

The British have an uneasy relationship with the past, both defending its traditions and railing against them. Traditions that are still dearly revered include the Commonwealth of Nations (a grouping of many of the old colonies of the empire), the continued practice of bestowing knighthoods, and even the monarchy.

Many aspects of British culture are now world renowned. British journalism, television, radio, music, and theater have set standards of excellence for the English-speaking world. Sports invented by the British are played all over the world—soccer, rugby, tennis, cricket, and horse-racing—although recently, British teams seem to be being beaten at their own games.

The British people are inherently friendly but reserved, very independent yet stubborn, and their dy sense of humor is well-known. The place to meet them is in the pub, a social institution that is often the center of the village or suburb where friends go to talk and unwind.

A fact often overlooked by the visitor who doesn't venture past London is that the UK is so rich in natural beauty—the romantic Lake District, the rugged Highlands of Scotland, the Welsh valleys, the Antrim coast of Northern Ireland. The countryside is dotted with quaint villages complete with cricket greens and friendly inns. Picturesque cities include Bath, Edinburgh, York, and Oxford. It is the unexpected surprises, found by those who venture beyond the stereotyped images of the United Kingdom, that will captivate the visitor.

—Cronan Enright, Dublin, Ireland

Official name: United Kingdom of Great Britain and Northern Ireland. **Size:** 94,226 square miles (about the size of Wyoming). **Population:** 55,486,800. **Population density:** 588 inhabitants per square mile. **Capital:** London. **Largest city:** Greater London (pop. 6,735,000). **Language:** English, Welsh, Gaelic (Scots, Irish dialects). **Religion:** Anglican, Roman Catholic. **Per capita income:** US$15,000. **Currency:** British pound. **Literacy rate:** 99%. **Average daily temperature:** London: June, 60°F; December, 41°F. Manchester: June, 58°F; December, 41°F. **Average number of days with precipitation:** London: June, 11; December, 15. Edinburgh: June, 15; December, 18.

TRAVEL

U.S. citizens need a passport but not a visa for visits of up to six months. Visas also are not required of students enrolled full-time in a course of study at a recognized educational establishment. For specific requirements, contact the nearest **British Consulate General**, with locations in Atlanta, Chicago, Houston, Los Angeles, New York, and Washington, DC.

Getting Around

If you want to travel throughout Britain by air, British Airways' **U.K. Airpass** is good for 3 to 12 trips within the U.K. Each one-way segment costs $58, but segments arriving in or departing from London cost $73. The U.K. Airpass is valid for a minimum stay of seven days and a maximum of three months. It must be purchased in the U.S. in conjunction with an international flight to the U.K. For more information, contact British Airways at (800) 247-9297.

A comprehensive **railroad** network covers Britain, where InterRail is valid but Eurailpasses are not. The best value for youths ages 16 to 23, or full-time students at British schools, is the **Young Person's Railcard**, which provides a 33-percent discount off any train ticket. Good for one year, this card can only be purchased in Britain, where it is available at BritRail Travel Centres. It costs £16 (US $24), a good deal when you consider that one-third off the usual £64 fare from London to Edinburgh will more than pay for your card. You'll need two photos and proof of your age and student status. In Scotland, **Rail Rover** tickets, available locally at all ScotRail offices, offer 4 days of travel in 8 for £59 (US $88), 8 consecutive days for £85 ($126), or 12 days in 15 for £110 ($163). ScotRail's **Area Rovers**, valid in either the West Highlands or the North Highlands, allow four days of travel within an 8-day period for £35 ($52).

BritRail offers a number of passes for travel throughout England, Scotland, Wales, and Ireland. The **BritRail Pass** is valid for travel in England, Scotland, and Wales. The **Youth Pass**, for those between 16 and 25, entitles you to 8 days of unlimited standard-class travel for $179, 15 days for $269, 22 days for $339, and one month for $395. Persons over 25 pay $219, $339, $425, and $495, respectively, for standard class; first class is more expensive.

BritRail also offers the **Youth Flexipass**, which allows standard-class travel on any 4 of 8 days for $155, any 8 of 15 days for $219, or any 15 days in two months for $309. For those over 26 years of age, the adult Flexipass allows standard-class travel on any 4 of 8 days for $189, any 8 of 15 days for $269, or any 15 days in one month for $395. More expensive first-class Flexipasses are available as well.

Those who plan to visit only England and Wales should consider BritRail's **England/Wales Pass**, which gives you four days of travel over an eight-day period for $149 standard class or $219 first class. If you'll be spending most of your time in Scotland, look into the **Freedom of Scotland Travelpass**. This all-standard pass allows 8 continuous days of travel for $145, 15 days for $205, or 22 days for $259. It also lets you take advantage of ferry service to such islands as Lewis, Bute, Arran, Skye, Harris, and North Uist. If you want unlimited travel throughout England, Scotland, Wales, Northern Ireland, and Ireland, the new **BritIreland Pass** gives you 5 days of standard train travel in 15 days for $269 or 10 days of travel in one month for $419. The pass also includes sea passage.

For those traveling extensively in both France and the U.K., Rail Europe's **BritFrance Railpass** lets you take advantage of these two countries' rail networks in their entirety. The second-class youth pass (for those under 26) allows 5 days of travel over 15 days for $229 or 10 days of travel within one month for $349, and includes one round-trip Channel crossing via hovercraft. The BritFrance Railpass, as well as all the above-mentioned rail passes, can be purchased from Rail Europe (see page 62) or Council Travel (see pages xiii–xvi).

Travel by train is not your only option; long-distance express **buses**, called coaches, provide service that's generally cheaper and nearly as fast as the trains. The only intercity bus network covering all of Great Britain is National Express; connections can be made with Scottish Citylink for travel to areas in Scotland not served by National Express. Foreign visitors can receive a 30-percent discount off standard fares for National Express and Scottish Citylink coach service with the **BritExpress Card**, valid for 30 days. The Tourist Trail Pass gives you unlimited access to this network. The **Young Person's Tourist Trail Card** allows travelers up to 23 years old or students of any age 5 consecutive days of travel for £45 (US $67), 8 days for £63 ($94), 15 days for £95 ($140), 22 days for £112 ($166), or 30 days for £133 ($197). The BritExpress Card can only be purchased in England, from the National Express office at 13 Regent Street, London SW1.

Another option in the U.K. is **hitchhiking**. The fastest hitching is on the expressways or "M-roads," where you are allowed to hitch only on the entrances or exits to the gas station and restaurant service complexes located along the road at regular intervals.

Rural areas of Britain are ideally suited to **bicycling**. The secondary roads are smooth and well maintained, and British drivers are courteous. As in most European countries, rural people tend to be more hospitable than their city cousins. With pubs and lodgings readily available in the villages of the countryside, you'll be well taken care of. On most trains (except a few express trains with limited baggage space) you can take your bicycle at no extra charge. However, rules vary from route to route; be sure to ask the ticket collector which trains accept bikes and where they should be taken for loading. To acquaint yourself with England's cycle routes, get the *CTC Route Guide to Cycling in Britain and Ireland*, published by the Cyclists' Touring Club. This and other practical guides, as well as a complete selection of Ordinance Survey Landranger Maps, are available through the British Travel Bookshop (see "For Further Information," below).

Eating and Sleeping

There are more than 200 **youth hostels** in England and Wales alone. For more information, contact the **Youth Hostels Association (E&W)**, Trevelyan House, 8 St Stephen's Hill, St Albans, Herts AL1 2DY, England; (44) 727-55215; fax (44) 727-44126. In London, contact the London Information Office and YHA Adventure Shop, 14 Southampton Street, Covent Garden, London WC2E 7HY; (44) 71-8361036.

In Northern Ireland, contact the **Youth Hostel Association of Northern Ireland**, 56 Bradbury Place, Belfast, BT7 1RU; (44) 232-324733; fax (44) 232-439699.

Scotland has nearly 100 youth hostels. The **Scottish Youth Hostels Association** also offers the Scottish Wayfarer Pass, allowing unlimited travel by train and ferry, one-third off selected coach services, and accommodations vouchers for use at any Scottish Youth Hostel, plus a free SYHA handbook and a Scotpass discount card. The 8-day pass costs £156 (US $230); the 14-day pass costs £246 ($365). For more information, contact the SYHA at 7 Glebe Crescent, Stirling FK8 2JA; (44) 786-51181; fax (44) 786-50198.

Information on all the above organizations can also be obtained from Hostelling International/American Youth Hostels (see page 54). For a list of independent hostels in England and Scotland, contact **Independent Hostel Owners in Ireland, England, Malta, Scotland, Germany** (see page 161).

For information on **YMCAs** and other inexpensive accommodations in England, contact the Y's Way (see pages 53–54). Many British universities offer affordable **dormitory lodgings** to travelers. For more information, contact Council Travel (see "Especially for Students and Young People," below) or consult Campus Travel Service's *US and Worldwide Travel Accommodations Guide* (see page 54). You can also order a copy of the *Holiday Accommodations at British Universities* guide from the **British Universities Accommodation Consortium (BUAC)**, Box C92, University Park, Nottingham NG7 2RD, England; (44) 602-504571. Enclose an international postal reply coupon.

Especially for Students and Young People

For travel information, train, plane, and ferry tickets, and accommodations bookings, you can check with the **Council Travel** office at 28A Poland Street (Oxford Circus), London W1V 3DB. Budget airfare information for all of Europe is available by calling the European sales number: (44) 71-2873337. Information on worldwide budget airfares can be obtained by calling (44) 71-4377767. If you prefer to arrange your accommodation before you leave, Council Travel offices (see pages xiii–xvi) can reserve rooms at British university dormitories starting at about $20 per night.

Another student travel organization is **Campus Travel**, 52 Grosvenor Gardens, London SW1W 0AG; (44) 71-7308832; fax (44) 71-7305739. You'll find Campus Travel branches at many universities and Youth Hostels Association locations.

In Britain, persons with the International Student Identity Card can obtain discounts on ferry service to mainland Europe and on international train and plane fares. A **Theatre Standby Scheme** offers discounted standby tickets at West End theaters; to find out what plays are giving discounts, look for an "S" with a circle around it in the entertainment section of the newspapers or go to the kiosk in Leicester Square. For a substantial listing of benefits open to young travelers, ask for *First Stop Britain* from the British Tourist Authority (see "For Further Information," below).

For Further Information

For general information, contact the **British Tourist Authority**, 551 Fifth Avenue, New York, NY 10176; (212) 986-2200; fax (212) 986-1188. You can find guidebooks, maps, and other useful publications at the adjoining British Travel Bookstore; (212) 490-6688. Ask for a free catalog. The Northern Ireland Tourist Board is at the same address; its phone number is (212) 922-0101.

For current information on London attractions, three weekly magazines—*Time Out, City Limits*, and *What's On in London*—list just about everything that is happening in the city. This is also a good place to look for classified ads about sharing flats, overland travel from London (the world center for that kind of trek), and for traveling companions.

There's no lack of tourist guides to the United Kingdom. For students and other young travelers, the best all-around guide is *Let's Go: Britain and Ireland* ($16.95). More detailed information on the city of London can be found in *Let's Go: London* ($11.95). Those who plan to travel in Scotland should should check out *Cadogan Guides'* extremely thorough *Scotland* ($16.95). For more information on *Let's Go* and *Cadogan* guides, see pages 56–57.

WORK

Getting a Job

In order to obtain a work permit in Britain, you must have a specific job offer. First priority is always given to British and European Community nationals; for almost all types of employment, the prospective employer must obtain a permit from the Department of Employment on your behalf. The employer is responsible for sending the permit to you; you will be required to present it at the port of entry.

CIEE, in cooperation with BUNAC (British Universities North America Club), can obtain permission for U.S. students to work in Britain for a period up to six months anytime during the year. In addition to work authorization, CIEE gives participants information on living and working in Britain and details on the best way to find work. Jobs are relatively easy to find upon arrival; participants work as secretaries, waiters, and in other similar positions. You can expect to make enough money to cover your daily living expenses and usually save something toward the cost of travel once you finish your job. To be eligible, you must be a U.S. citizen at least 18 years of age, enrolled as a full-time student in an accredited U.S. college or university, and residing in the U.S. at the time of application. Upon arrival in Britain you are required to have proof of minimum funds of $500 for support until you receive your first paycheck. There is a $160 fee for the service; application forms are available from CIEE's Work-Exchanges Department.

If you are thinking about working in the U.K., get a copy of the annually published *Summer Jobs in Britain* (1994 edition, $15.95), which lists names of employers and describes jobs available. Copies are available from CIEE (add $1 for book-rate or $2.50 for first-class postage).

For those who want to teach in Britain, send for a copy of *Teaching in Britain*, a fact sheet put out by the **British Information Services**, 845 Third Avenue, New York, NY 10022.

Farm Work

Tiptree International Farm Camp recruits people from all over the world to pick fruit and berries during the summer. Workers are paid according to the amount of fruit they pick but must pay for their room and board. Positions, which are available from about the second week of June until mid-July, are open only to students 18 to 25 years old. For more information, write the Camp Organizer, International Farm Camp, Hall Road, Tiptree, Colchester, Essex CO5 0QS.

Internships/Traineeships

The programs offered by organizations and institutions that are members of the Council on International Educational Exchange are listed below. Consult Appendix I for the addresses where you can write for further information. In addition to those listed below, Moorhead State University and Southwest Texas State University have internship programs open only to their own students.

Association for International Practical Training. *IAESTE Trainee Program.* On-the-job training for undergraduate and graduate students in technical fields such as engineering, computer science, agriculture, architecture, mathematics, and the physical and natural sciences. See page 19 for more information.

Hospitality/Tourism Exchanges Program. On-the-job training for young people beginning a career in the hotel, food service, and tourism industries. Participants must have graduated from or be enrolled in a university or vocational school and possess at least six months of training or experience in the chosen field. Training usually runs from 6 to 18 months.

Beaver College. *London Internship Program in Arts Administration, Business, Communications, Government, Social Services.* In cooperation with London Guildhall University. Semester students take two courses plus internship. Fall, spring, and summer. Juniors and seniors with 3.0 GPA. Apply by April 20 for fall; October 15 for spring; March 31 for summer.

Boston University. *London Internship Program.* Fall, spring, and summer. Sophomores to graduates; post-baccalaureate students. Twelve credits of course work plus a four-credit internship in one of the following areas: business, the arts, advertising, public relations, media, comparative legal studies, economics, communications, politics, and psychology, among others. 3.0 GPA and adviser's approval. Apply by July 15 for fall; November 15 for spring; April 1 for summer. Contact: (617) 353-9888.

Marymount College. *London Internship Program.* Individual work-study positions arranged for students based on their area of study. Fall and spring semesters. Juniors with 2.8 GPA.

Ohio University. *Residency at the Young Vic Theater.* Residency with mentors in the British theater. 10 weeks during the academic year. Open to graduate students in the M.F.A. program at Ohio University only. Apply by January 1. Contact: William Condee, School of Theater, 307 Kantner Hall, Athens, OH 45701; (614) 593-4445; fax (614) 593-0569.

The Consortium for Overseas Student Teaching. Student teaching. Quarter. Sophomores to seniors attending Ohio University only. Contact: Wes Snyder, Center for Higher Education and International Programs, 129 McCracken Hall, Athens, OH 45701; (614) 593-4445; fax (614) 593-0569.

Syracuse University. *Management Internships in London.* Summer. Six-week program with commercial, financial, or marketing firms in the London area. Apply by February 15. Juniors to graduates.

Law in London. Summer. Internship in comparative clinical legal education. Six-week program with a firm of solicitors, a barrister's chambers, or one of

a variety of legal entities in the London area. Any student in good standing at an American Bar Association–approved law school who has completed one year of full- or part-time legal study. Apply by February 15.
State University of New York at Oneonta. *England Student-Teaching Program*. Fall quarter. Elementary and secondary education student-teaching program in Hertfordshire schools. Open to students who have completed first quarter of student-teaching; SUNY Oneonta students only. Rolling admissions.

Voluntary Service

CIEE places young people in voluntary-service **workcamps** in Wales, organized by the United Nations Association of International Youth Service in Cardiff. At these workcamps, small groups of volunteers from various countries work on a range of nature conservation projects and recreational programs for at-risk children. Volunteers receive room and board in return for their labor. Interested persons must be at least 18 years old. The applications of U.S. residents are processed by CIEE. For more information, contact the International Voluntary Service Department at the CIEE.

Another organization sponsoring workcamps in Britain is the **Fourth World Movement**. For more information, see page 22.

Short-term voluntary service opportunities are also available through the 46-year-old **Winant-Clayton Volunteer program**. British participants come to the U.S. to do social work (the Claytons) and American participants go to Britain to do the same (the Winants). Participants pay for transportation to and from the site; room, board, and a small stipend are provided during the placement. There is a $15 application fee; the deadline is January 31 for placement the following summer. For details, write to the Winant-Clayton Volunteers, St. Bartholomew's Church, 109 East 50th Street, New York, NY 10022; (212) 751-1616, ext. 271.

Community Service Volunteers (CSV) matches volunteers with projects in Great Britain and Northern Ireland. Participants work with those who are disabled, elderly, homeless, or in trouble. After being placed, CSV provides you with room, board, and pocket money. Terms of service range from four months to a full year. A placement fee of £465 (US $693) is required. For more information, contact Overseas Volunteer Administrator, Community Service Volunteers, 237 Pentonville Road, London, N1 9NJ.

The Royal Society for Mentally Handicapped Children and Adults (MENCAP) organizes holidays for people with mental handicaps all over England. Participants are required to work from 9 to 16 days. For more information, contact the Royal Society for Mentally Handicapped Children and Adults, 119 Drake Street, Rochdale, Lancashire OL16 1PZ.

Other types of short-term volunteer work are also available. For persons interested in volunteering for an archaeological dig, the **Council for British Archaeology** (112 Kennington Road, London SE11 6RE) publishes a newsletter called *British Archaeological News* (six issues a year; $18 surface mail, $28 airmail) that lists information about archaeological projects in Great Britain as well as indicating which ones will accept volunteers. For persons interested in working on a restored narrow-gauge railway, the **Ffestiniog Railway Company** (Harbour Station, Porthmadog, Gwynedd, North Wales) recruits volunteers from around the world for the summer season.

You'll find additional opportunities for all types of community service described in *Volunteer! The Comprehensive Guide to Voluntary Service in the U.S. and Abroad* ($8.95), published by CIEE. Another good source of information is the **Scottish Community Education Council** (Atholl House, 2 Canning

Street, Edinburgh EH3 8EG). This organization provides information on opportunities for voluntary community work in Scotland. Write for their brochure listing available opportunities (enclose an international postal reply coupon).

STUDY

A good source of information on studying in Britain is **British Information Services (BIS)**. They publish *Study in Britain*, which gives information on how to apply to a British university and lists addresses for universities in the U.K. It is updated annually and appears each June. BIS can be contacted at 845 Third Avenue, New York, NY 10022-6691; (212) 752-5747; fax (212) 758-5395. The **British Council**, on the other hand, advises students who plan to pursue graduate study in Britain and publishes a brochure entitled *Postgraduate Study and Research in the United Kingdom*. They also help and advise on programs and produce a leaflet on postgraduate scholarships and awards. To request information, contact the British Council's Education Office at the British Embassy, 3100 Massachusetts Avenue NW, Washington, DC 20008; (202) 898-4407.

The study programs offered by CIEE-member institutions are listed below. Unless otherwise noted, consult Appendix I for the addresses of the colleges and universities listed in this section. In addition to the programs below, California State University at Sacramento, North Carolina State University Pepperdine University, State University of New York schools, University of Massachusetts at Amherst, University of Nebraska at Lincoln, University of North Carolina at Chapel Hill, University of Notre Dame, University of Oregon, University of Pennsylvania, and University of Wisconsin at Madison offer programs open to their own students only.

Semester and Academic Year

Art and Architecture

Beaver College. *Architecture, Art, Craft, and Design at Glasgow School of Art*. Scotland. Semester and academic year. Juniors and seniors with 3.0 GPA. Apply by April 20 for fall and academic year; October 15 for spring.

Studio Art at Sir John Cass School of Art, London Guildhall University. England. Semester and academic year. Juniors and seniors with 3.0 GPA. Apply by April 20 for fall and academic year; October 15 for spring.

Studio Art and Art History at the Slade School of Fine Art, University College London, University of London. England. Juniors and seniors with 3.0 GPA. Apply by February 1.

State University of New York at Buffalo. *Wolverhampton Exchange*. Wolverhampton, England. Semester and academic year. Graphics arts and design. Juniors to graduate students with 2.5 GPA. Apply by April 1 for fall and academic year; October 15 for spring. Contact: Study-Abroad Coordinator, Office of International Education, SUNY at Buffalo, 212 Talbert Hall, Box 601604, Buffalo, NY 14260-1604; (716) 645-3912.

University of Illinois at Urbana-Champaign. *Art and Design in Britain*. Various sites in England. Semester and academic year. Students from institu-

tions with programs in art and design only. Juniors and seniors. Apply by April 1 for fall; October 1 for spring.
University of Kansas. *Art and Design at Brighton University, England*. Brighton. Academic year. Art, graphic design, textiles, visual and performing arts, history of design. Juniors and seniors. Apply by February 15.

Asian and African Studies

Beaver College. *School of Oriental and African Studies, University of London*. England. Semester and academic year. Juniors and seniors with 3.0 GPA. Apply by April 20 for fall and academic year; October 15 for spring.

British Studies

University of Evansville. *University of Evansville's Harlaxton College*. Grantham, England. Semester and academic year. Sophomores to seniors with 2.5 GPA. Adviser's permission required. Apply by June 1 for fall and academic year; October 1 for spring.

Business

Beaver College. *Business Studies at Middlesex Polytechnic at Hendon*. London, England. Fall semester and academic year. Juniors and seniors with 3.0 GPA. Apply by April 20.
Bentley College. *Bentley College's Business Program in Lancaster, England*. Term and academic year. Full academic curriculum at Lancaster University. Juniors and seniors with 3.0 GPA. Apply by April 15 for fall term and academic year; November 1 for spring.
Old Dominion University. *ODU Abroad: Buckinghamshire*. Fall and spring semesters. Full business curriculum. Sophomores and juniors. Apply by April 1 for fall; October 1 for spring. Contact: Study Abroad Office, BAL 304, Old Dominion University, Norfolk, VA 23529; (804) 683-5378.
Rochester Institute of Technology. *Study in Sheffield, England*. Fall quarter (September to mid-November). European economy, society, business, and environment; and international business and marketing. Excursions and dormitory housing. Juniors. Contact: Center for International Business, PO Box 9887, Rochester, NY 14623-0887; (716) 475-2371/4995.
State University of New York College at Oswego. *Business Administration in London*. England. Semester and academic year. Business curriculum including accounting, international marketing, human resources, and economics at Thames Valley University. Apartment housing. Juniors and seniors with 2.5 GPA. Apply by April 1 for fall and academic year; November 1 for spring. Contact: Office of International Education, SUNY at Oswego, 102 Rich Hall, Oswego, NY 13126; (315) 341-2118.

Communications

State University of New York College at Brockport. *Communications Program*. Queen Margaret College at Edinburgh, Scotland. Fall and spring semesters. Juniors and seniors with 2.5 GPA and 3.0 in communications. Apply by February 15 for fall; September 15 for spring. Contact: Office of International Education, SUNY College at Brockport, Brockport, NY 14420; (716) 395-2119.
State University of New York College at Oswego. *Huron University*. London, England. Spring semester. Broadcasting. Undergraduates. Apply by

November 1. Contact: International Education, 102 Rich Hall, SUNY College at Oswego, Oswego, NY 13126; (315) 341-2118.

Criminal Justice

State University of New York College at Brockport. *Criminal Justice Program*. Brunel University in London, England. Fall semester. Juniors and seniors with 2.5 GPA. Apply by February 15. Contact: Office of International Education, SUNY College at Brockport, Brockport, NY 14420; (716) 395-2119.

Economics

Beaver College. *Single-Term Program in the Department of Economics, University College, London*. England. Fall and spring terms. Juniors and seniors with 3.0 GPA. Apply by April 20 for fall; October 15 for spring.
London School of Economics and Political Science, University of London. England. Single term and academic year. Juniors and seniors with 3.3 GPA. Apply by March 10 for fall and academic year; October 15 for spring.
University of North Carolina at Chapel Hill. *UNC at LSE*. Academic year. Study at London School of Economics. Juniors and seniors with 3.5 GPA. Apply by February 12.

Education

Beaver College. *Christ Church College*. Canterbury, England. Semester and academic year. Courses and field experience in elementary education. Juniors and seniors with 3.0 GPA. Apply by April 20 for fall and academic year; October 15 for spring.
College of Ripon & York St. John. Ripon and York, England. Spring semester. Courses and field experience in elementary education. Juniors and seniors with 3.0 GPA. Apply by October 15.
Ohio University. *Undergraduate Student/Preservice Teacher Education Program*. Sheffield, England. Spring quarter. Education courses at Sheffield Hallam University, and primary and secondary teaching-aide experience in Sheffield classrooms. Undergraduates. Apply by January 31. Contact: Wes Snyder, Center for Higher Education and International Programs, 129 McCracken Hall, Athens, OH 45701; (614) 593-4445.
University of Wisconsin at River Falls. *Overseas Practice Teaching*. Various sites in England, Wales, and Scotland. Fall and spring semesters. Individualized student teaching experience. Seniors with preparatory education courses. Apply three months before desired teaching time. Contact: Carol LeBreck, Coordinator, Karges Center, UW at River Falls, River Falls, WI 54022; (715) 425-3778/3705.

European Studies

Beaver College. *School of Slavonic and East European Studies, University of London*. England. Academic year. Juniors and seniors with 3.0 GPA. Apply by April 20.
Council on International Educational Exchange. *Nottingham Internship and Study Program at Nottingham Trent University*. England. Spring semester. Full course in European studies with unpaid internship (for academic credit). Sophomores to seniors with 2.75 GPA. Apply by October 15. Contact University Programs Department.

Fashion

Marymount College, Tarrytown. *London College of Fashion*. England. Semester and academic year. Specialized program in fashion design, merchandising, promotion, and theater arts; internships available. Juniors and seniors with 2.8 GPA. Rolling admissions.

General Studies

American Heritage Association. *Northwest Interinstitutional Council of Study Abroad—London*. England. Fall, winter, and spring quarters. Sophomores to seniors with 2.5 GPA. Apply by June 15 for fall; November 1 for winter; January 15 for spring. Contact: (800) 654-2051.

American University. *London Semester*. Fall and spring semesters. Political science, European Community, theater, history; internships available. Second-semester sophomores to seniors with 2.75 GPA. Apply by March 15 for fall; October 15 for spring. Contact: World Capitals Programs, American University, Dunblane House—Tenley Campus, Washington, DC 20016-8083; (202) 895-4900/4937.

Auburn University. *Nottingham Trent University, England*. Semester and academic year. Juniors and seniors with 3.0 GPA. Apply by March 15 for fall and academic year; October 15 for spring.

Ball State University/American Institute for Foreign Study. London Centre. England. Spring semester. Excursions and optional homestays. Sophomores to seniors with 2.75 GPA. Apply by November 15. Contact: Coordinator, London Centre, Center for International Programs, 708 North Calvert Street, Muncie, IN 47306; (317) 285-5422.

Beaver College. *City University*. London, England. Semester and academic year. Juniors and seniors with 3.0 GPA. Apply by April 20 for fall and academic year; October 15 for spring.

Goldsmith's College, University of London. England. Academic year and spring semester. Juniors and seniors with 3.0 GPA. Apply by April 20 for academic year; October 15 for spring.

Imperial College, University of London. England. Semester and academic year. Juniors and seniors with 3.0 GPA. Apply by April 20 for fall and academic year; October 15 for spring.

King's College, University of London. England. Semester and academic year. Juniors and seniors with 3.0 GPA. Apply by April 20 for fall and academic year; October 15 for spring.

London Guildhall University. England. Semester and academic year. Juniors and seniors with 3.0 GPA. Apply by April 20 for fall and academic year; October 15 for spring.

Middlesex Polytechnic at Trent Park. London, England. Semester and academic year. Juniors and seniors with 3.0 GPA. Apply by April 20 for fall and academic year; October 15 for spring.

Oxford Program in Social Science and Humanities. Oxford, England. Semester and academic year. Local faculty base specially arranged courses on Oxford-style teaching. Juniors and seniors with 3.2 GPA. Apply by April 20 for fall and academic year; October 15 for spring.

Queen Mary and Westfield College, University of London. England. Semester and academic year. Juniors and seniors with 3.0 GPA. Apply by March 10 for fall and academic year; October 15 for spring.

Queen's University of Belfast. Northern Ireland. Semester and academic year. Juniors and seniors with 3.0 GPA. Apply by April 20 for fall and academic year; October 15 for spring.

Royal Holloway College, University of London. Egham Hill, England. Semester and academic year. Juniors and seniors with 3.0 GPA. Apply by March 20 for fall and academic year; October 15 for spring.

University of Aberdeen. Scotland. Semester and academic year. Juniors and seniors with 3.0 GPA. Apply by April 20 for fall and academic year; October 15 for spring.

University of Birmingham. England. Semester and academic year. Juniors and seniors with 3.0 GPA. Apply by April 20 for fall and academic year; October 15 for spring.

University of Bristol. England. Academic year. Juniors and seniors with 3.2 GPA. Apply by March 20.

University College of North Wales. Bangor, Wales. Spring term and academic year. Juniors and seniors with 3.0 GPA. Apply by April 20 for academic year; October 15 for spring.

University College, University of London. England. Semester and academic year. Juniors and seniors with 3.0 GPA. Apply by March 10 for academic year; April 20 for fall; October 15 for spring.

University of East Anglia. Norwich, England. Semester and academic year. Juniors and seniors with 3.0 GPA. Apply by April 20 for fall and academic year; October 15 for spring.

University of Edinburgh. Scotland. Semester and academic year. Juniors and seniors with 3.0 GPA. Apply by March 20 for fall and academic year; October 15 for spring.

University of Essex. Colchester, England. Semester and academic year. Juniors and seniors with 3.0 GPA. Apply by April 20 for fall and academic year; October 15 for spring.

University of Glasgow. Scotland. Semester and academic year. Juniors and seniors with 3.0 GPA. Apply by April 20 for fall and academic year; October 15 for spring.

University of Lancaster. England. Semester and academic year. Juniors and seniors with 3.0 GPA. Apply by April 20 for fall and academic year; October 15 for spring.

University of Liverpool. England. Semester and academic year. Juniors and seniors with 3.0 GPA. Apply by October 15 for fall and academic year; April 20 for spring.

University of Manchester. England. Academic year. Juniors and seniors with 3.2 GPA. Apply by April 20.

University of Nottingham. England. Semester and academic year. Juniors and seniors with 3.0 GPA. Apply by April 20 for fall and academic year; October 15 for spring.

University of Reading. England. Semester and academic year. Juniors and seniors with 3.0 GPA. Apply by April 20 for fall and academic year; October 15 for spring.

University of Southampton. England. Academic year. Juniors and seniors with 3.0 GPA. Apply by April 20.

University of Surrey. Guilford, England. Academic year. Social sciences and engineering courses. Juniors and seniors with 3.0 GPA. Apply by April 20.

University of Sussex. Brighton, England. Semester and academic year. Juniors and seniors with 3.0 GPA. Apply by April 20 for fall and academic year; October 15 for spring.

University of Ulster. Coleraine and Londonderry, Northern Ireland. Semester and academic year. Juniors and seniors with 3.0 GPA. Apply by April 20 for fall and academic year; October 15 for spring.

University of Wales. Swansea. Semester and academic year. Juniors and seniors with 3.0 GPA. Apply by April 20 for fall and academic year; October 15 for spring.
University of York. England. Semester and academic year. Juniors and seniors with 3.0 GPA. Apply by April 20 for fall and academic year; October 15 for spring.
Boston University. Oxford. Semester and academic year. Modern British studies program with emphasis in politics, history, or literature. Study at St. Anne's College, Oxford University, with instruction by Oxford professors. Apartment housing. Sophomores to seniors with 3.0 GPA. Apply by March 15 for fall and academic year; October 15 for spring.
Brethren Colleges Abroad. *Cheltenham and Gloucester College of Higher Education, England*. Semester and academic year. Liberal arts and social sciences. Excursions and study tours. Sophomores to seniors with 3.0 GPA. Apply by April 15 for fall and academic year; November 30 for spring.
Brigham Young University. *BYU Study Abroad*. London, England. Fall, winter, and spring quarters. Live in BYU London Centre. Apply by February 1 for fall; October 1 for winter and spring.
Butler University. *Birkbeck College, University of London*. England. Fall and spring semesters. Study possible in humanities and business; internships available. Juniors and seniors with 3.0 GPA. Apply by April 15 for fall; October 15 for spring.
City University. London, England. Semester and academic year. Fully integrated program specializing in social sciences, communications, journalism, actuarial science, and engineering. Juniors and seniors with 3.0 GPA and previous study in field of interest. Apply by April 15 for fall and academic year; October 15 for spring.
King's College, University of London. England. Semester and academic year. Fully integrated program with study possible in all disciplines including prelaw and premedicine. Juniors and seniors with 3.0 GPA and previous study in field of interest. Apply by April 15 for fall and academic year; October 15 for spring.
London School of Economics. England. Academic year. Fully integrated program with study in social sciences including anthropology, economics, and international relations. Juniors and seniors with 3.0 GPA and previous study in field of interest. Apply by April 15.
Middlesex University. England. Semester and academic year. Fully integrated program with study possible in American studies, engineering, and performing arts. Juniors and seniors with 3.0 GPA and previous study in field of interest. Apply by April 15 for fall and academic year; October 15 for spring.
Queen Mary and Westfield College, University of London. England. Semester and academic year. Fully integrated program with study available in all disciplines. Juniors and seniors with 3.0 GPA and previous study in field of interest. Apply by April 15 for fall and academic year; October 15 for spring.
School of Oriental and African Studies, University of London. England. Semester and academic year. Fully integrated program with study available in many areas including languages, economics, and political science. Juniors and seniors with 3.0 GPA and previous study in field of interest. Apply by April 15 for fall and academic year; October 15 for spring.
University College, University of London. England. Semester and academic year. Fully integrated program with study possible in all disciplines with particular strengths in the arts, archaeology, and anthropology. Juniors and seniors with 3.0 GPA and previous study in field of interest. Apply by April 15 for fall and academic year; October 15 for spring.

University of Bristol. England. Academic year. Fully integrated program with study possible in all major disciplines. Juniors and seniors with 3.0 GPA and previous study in field of interest. Apply by April 15.
University of East Anglia. Norwich, England. Academic year, fall term, and two spring terms. Fully integrated program with study possible in wide range of disciplines. Juniors and seniors with 3.0 GPA and previous study in field of interest. Apply by April 15 for fall and academic year; October 15 for spring.
University of Edinburgh. Scotland. Semester and academic year. Fully integrated program with study possible in all disciplines for full year and in arts and social sciences for individual terms. Juniors and seniors with 3.0 GPA and previous study in field of interest. Apply by April 15 for fall and academic year; October 15 for spring.
University of Essex. Colchester, England. Semester and academic year. Fully integrated program with study possible in all disciplines. Juniors and seniors with 3.0 GPA and previous study in field of interest. Apply by April 15 for fall and academic year; October 15 for spring.
University of Glasgow. England. Semester and academic year. Fully integrated program with study possible in all disciplines. Juniors and seniors with 3.0 GPA and previous study in field of interest. Apply by April 15 for fall and academic year; October 15 for spring.
University of Kent. Canterbury, England. Academic year. Fully integrated program with study possible in all disciplines. Juniors and seniors with 3.0 GPA and previous study in field of interest. Apply by April 15.
University of Lancaster. England. Semester and academic year. Fully integrated program with study possible in all disciplines. Juniors and seniors with 3.0 GPA and previous study in field of interest. Apply by April 15 for fall and academic year; October 15 for spring.
University of Leeds. England. Academic year. Fully integrated program with study possible in all disciplines. Juniors and seniors with 3.0 GPA and previous study in field of interest. Apply by April 15.
University of Nottingham. England. Semester and academic year. Fully integrated program with study possible in architecture, classical studies, and natural sciences. Juniors and seniors with 3.0 GPA and previous study in field of interest. Apply by April 15 for fall and academic year; October 15 for spring.
University of St. Andrews. St. Andrews, Scotland. Academic year. Fully integrated program with study possible in all arts and sciences disciplines. Juniors and seniors with 3.0 GPA and previous study in field of interest. Apply by April 15.
University of Stirling. Scotland. Semester and academic year. Fully integrated program with study possible in all disciplines including environmental studies, film studies, and public relations. Juniors and seniors with 3.0 GPA and previous study in field of interest. Apply by April 15 for fall and academic year; October 15 for spring.
University of Sussex. Brighton, England. Spring semester and academic year. Fully integrated program with study possible in most arts and sciences disciplines. Juniors and seniors with 3.0 GPA and previous study in field of interest. Apply by April 15 for academic year; October 15 for spring.
University of Ulster. Coleraine, Northern Ireland. Semester and academic year. Fully integrated program with study possible in all major disciplines. Juniors and seniors with 3.0 GPA. Apply by April 15 for fall and academic year; October 15 for spring.
University of Westminster. London, England. Semester and academic year. Fully integrated study program; internships available. Juniors and seniors with 3.0 GPA. Apply by April 15 for fall and academic year; October 15 for spring.

University of York. England. Semester and academic year. Fully integrated program with study possible in all arts and sciences disciplines with particular strengths in English literature, education, and archaeology. Juniors and seniors with 3.0 GPA and previous study in field of interest. Apply by April 15 for fall and academic year; October 15 for spring.

Contact: Institute for Study Abroad, Butler University, 4600 Sunset Avenue, Indianapolis, IN 46208; (800) 858-0229.

Eckerd College. *Eckerd in London*. England. Fall and spring semesters. Variety of courses in humanities and social sciences. Housing at London Study Centre and excursions. Sophomores to seniors with 2.75 GPA. Apply by April 15 for fall; November 15 for spring.

Great Lakes College Association/Wabash College. *GLCA Scotland Program*. Aberdeen. Semester and academic year. Humanities and social sciences; advanced science courses also available. Sophomores to seniors. Apply by February 1. Contact: GLCA Scotland Program, Wabash College, Crawfordsville, IN 47933; (317) 364-4410.

Grinnell College. *Grinnell in London*. England. Fall semester. Music, art, English, political science, and theater; last third portion of program is travel/study. Sophomores to seniors with 2.5 GPA. Apply by March 1.

Hiram College. *Cambridge Quarter*. Cambridge, England. Fall quarter. English, history, and other liberal arts disciplines. Homestays and excursions. Sophomores to seniors with 2.5 GPA. Apply by March 15.

Hollins College. *Hollins Abroad*. London, England. Fall and spring semesters. Theater, art, architecture, literature, economics, history, law, and politics at University of London. Homestays. Juniors and seniors with 2.0 GPA. Apply by April 1 for fall; October 1 for spring. Contact: Hollins Abroad Office, PO Box 9597, Hollins College, Roanoke, VA 24020; (703) 362-6307.

International Student Exchange Program (ISEP). Academic year. Direct reciprocal exchange between U.S. universities and institutions in England (Lancashire, Plymouth, Sunderland); Northern Ireland; Scotland (Edinburgh, Glasgow); and Wales (Cardiff). Full curriculum options. Rolling admissions. Open only to students at ISEP-member institutions. Contact ISEP for list of members.

Iowa State University. *Arizona/Iowa Regents' London Study Program*. University College, London, England. Spring semester. English, history, theater, business, and other humanities and social sciences. First-year college students to seniors. Apply by November 1. Contact: Tom Emerson, Foreign Languages and Literatures, 300 Pearson Hall, ISU, Ames, IA 50011; (515) 294-4340.

James Madison University. *JMU Semester in London*. England. Fall and spring semesters. British art, architecture, literature, history, culture, music, and theater. Hostel housing and excursions. Sophomores to seniors with 2.8 GPA. Apply by November 15 for fall; February 1 for spring.

Lancaster University. Lancaster, England. Fall term, two spring terms, and academic year. Liberal arts curriculum available, plus business, pre-med, and natural sciences. Dormitory housing with British students. Sophomores to graduate students in good academic standing. Contact: Ethel Sossman, 111 East 10th Street, New York, NY 10003; (212) 228-0321.

Marymount College, Tarrytown. *City University*. London, England. Semester and academic year. Courses offered in social sciences, mathematics, and philosophy. Juniors and seniors with 2.8 GPA. Rolling admissions.

King's College. London, England. Semester and academic year. Wide range of academic disciplines offered. Juniors and seniors with 2.8 GPA. Rolling admissions.

London School of Economics. England. Academic year. Business, management, history, political science, and social sciences. Juniors and seniors with 3.3 GPA. Rolling admissions.

Oxford Brookes University. Oxford, England. Semester and academic year. Courses available in all major disciplines. Juniors and seniors with 2.8 GPA. Rolling admissions.

Queen Mary and Westfield College. London, England. Semester and academic year. Arts and sciences as well as business management. Juniors and seniors with 2.8 GPA. Rolling admissions.

University College, London. England. Semester and academic year. Arts and sciences as well as business management. Juniors and seniors with 2.8 GPA. Rolling admissions.

University of Essex. England. Semester and academic year. Courses available in all major disciplines. Juniors and seniors with 2.8 GPA. Rolling admissions.

University of Kent. Canterbury, England. Semester and academic year. Courses available in all major disciplines. Juniors and seniors with 2.8 GPA. Rolling admissions.

University of Lancaster. England. Semester and academic year. Courses available in all major disciplines. Juniors and seniors with 2.8 GPA. Rolling admissions.

University of St. Andrews. St. Andrews, Scotland. Semester and academic year. Courses available in most major disciplines. Juniors and seniors with 2.8 GPA. Rolling admissions.

University of Stirling. Scotland. Semester and academic year. Courses available in most major disciplines. Juniors and seniors with 2.8 GPA. Rolling admissions.

University of Westminister. London, England. Semester and academic year. Arts and sciences as well as business management, urban planning, and communications. Juniors and seniors with 2.8 GPA. Rolling admissions.

University of York. York, England. Semester and academic year. Courses available in all major disciplines. Juniors and seniors with 2.8 GPA. Rolling admissions.

Michigan State University. *Humanities and Social Science in England and Scotland*. London, York, and Lake District (England); and Edinburgh (Scotland). Spring semester. First-year college students to seniors. Apply by November 30. Contact: Office of Overseas Study, 108 International Center, Michigan State University, East Lansing, MI 48824-1035; (517) 353-8920.

Millersville University. *Humberside Exchange Program*. Hull, England. Academic year. Sophomores to seniors with 2.5 GPA. Apply by April 1.

Northern Arizona University. *Nottingham Exchange*. England. Fall and spring semesters. Variety of academic and professional disciplines at University of Nottingham. Sophomores (with 2.5 GPA) to graduate students. Apply by April 1 for fall; November 1 for spring.

Wolverhampton Exchange. England. Fall and spring semesters. Variety of academic and professional disciplines at University of Wolverhampton. Sophomores (with 2.5 GPA) to graduate students. Apply by April 1 for fall; November 1 for spring.

Northern Illinois University. *Academic Internships in London*. England. Semester and academic year. Internship plus two courses. Sophomores to seniors with 3.0 GPA. Apply by April 4 for fall and academic year; November 1 for spring. Contact: Foreign Study Office, Semester/Academic Year Programs, Northern Illinois University, Williston Hall 100, DeKalb, IL 60115-2854; (815) 753-0420/0304.

Old Dominion University. *ODU Abroad: Edge Hill College*. Ormskirk. Se-

mester and academic year. Full academic curriculum. Sophomores to juniors. Apply by April 1 for fall and academic year; October 1 for spring.
ODU Abroad: University of the West of England. Bristol. Semester and academic year. Full academic curriculum. Undergraduate and graduate students. Apply by March 1 for fall and academic year; September 1 for spring.
Contact: Study Abroad Office, BAL 304, Old Dominion University, Norfolk, VA 23529; (804) 683-5378.
Portland State University. *Northwest Interinstitutional Council on Study Abroad—London*. See listing under American Heritage Association.
Rosary College. *Rosary in London*. England. Fall semester. British life and culture and independent-study course; study tours and emphasis on experiential learning. Sophomores to seniors. Apply by March 15. Contact: Ann Charney, Director of Study Abroad, Rosary College, River Forest, IL 60305; (708) 524-6948.
Rutgers University. *Study Abroad in Britain*. Exeter, Bristol, Reading, York, London, St. Andrews, and Brighton, England; Glasgow, Scotland. Spring semester and academic year. Juniors with 3.0 GPA. Apply by February 1.
St. Lawrence University. *London Semester Program*. England. Spring and fall semesters. Internships available. Sophomores to seniors with 2.8 GPA. Apply by February 20 for fall; October 10 for spring.
Shoreline Community College. *London Spring Quarter*. England. Offered in cooperation with American Institute for Foreign Study. Social, historical, and cultural approach to contemporary British society. Excursions. Freshmen and sophomores. Apply by February 1. Contact: Coordinator, Study Abroad Program, Shoreline Community College, 16101 Greenwood Avenue North, Seattle, WA 98133; (206) 546-4602.
State University of New York College at Brockport. *Brunel Social Science Program*. Brunel University near London, England. Fall and spring semesters. Juniors and seniors with 2.5 GPA (3.0 GPA in major). Apply by April 1 for fall; November 1 for spring.
Leeds University Study Abroad. Leeds, England. Semester and academic year. Full university curriculum. Juniors and seniors with 2.7 GPA overall and 3.0 in major. Apply by April 1 for fall and academic year; November 1 for spring.
Middlesex University Program. Middlesex, England. Fall and spring semesters. Full university curriculum. Juniors and seniors with 2.5 GPA overall and 3.0 in major. Apply by April 1 for fall; November 1 for spring.
Oxford University Program. Oxford, England. Fall, spring, and late spring quarters. Full university curriculum with required tutorials. Juniors and seniors with 2.9 GPA overall and 3.0 in major. Apply by April 1 for fall; November 1 for spring; March 1 for late spring.
Contact: Office of International Education, SUNY College at Brockport, Brockport, NY 14420; (716) 395-2119.
State University of New York College at Buffalo. *Manchester Metropolitan University*. Manchester, England. Fall semester. Sophomores to seniors with 2.5 GPA. Apply by March 1. Contact: Office of International Education, GC 416, SUNY College at Buffalo, 1300 Elmwood Avenue, Buffalo, NY 14222-1095; (716) 878-4620.
State University of New York College at Cortland. *University of North London*. England. Semester and academic year. Full university curriculum options. Excursions and apartment housing. Sophomores to seniors with 2.5 GPA. Apply by March 7 for fall and academic year; October 15 for spring. Contact: Office of International Programs, SUNY College at Cortland, PO Box 2000, Cortland, NY 13045; (607) 753-2209.

State University of New York College at New Paltz. *Study Abroad in England*. London. Semester and academic year. Wide range of courses available at Middlesex University. Juniors and seniors. Rolling admissions. Contact: Office of International Education, HAB 33, SUNY College at New Paltz, New Paltz, NY 12561; (914) 257-3125.

State University of New York College at Oswego. *Huron University*. London, England. Semester and academic year. Undergraduates. Apply by April for fall and academic year; November 1 for spring.

London Exchange: Thames Valley University. England. Semester and academic year. Full university curriculum options in humanities and professional disciplines. Apartment housing. Sophomores to seniors. Apply by April 1 for fall and academic year; November 1 for spring.

Contact: International Education, 102 Rich Hall, SUNY College at Oswego, Oswego, NY 13126; (315) 341-2118.

Stetson University. Nottingham, England. Semester and academic year. Sophomores to seniors with 2.5 GPA (3.0 GPA in major). Apply by March 1 for fall and academic year; October 15 for spring.

Syracuse University. *Syracuse in London*. England. Semester and academic year. Sophomores to seniors with 3.0 GPA. Apply by March 15 for fall and academic year; October 15 for spring. Contact: (800) 235-3472.

Texas Tech University. *London Semester*. England. Fall and spring semesters. Humanities and business. Sophomores to seniors with 2.5 GPA. Apply by November 1 for spring; May 15 for fall.

Tufts University. *Tufts in London*. England. Academic year. Full university curriculum. Juniors with 3.0 GPA. Apply by February 1.

University of Alabama. *Study Abroad in England*. University of Hull in Hull, England. Academic year. Sophomores to seniors with 3.0 GPA. Apply by March 1. Contact: (205) 348-5256.

University College London. *Junior Year Abroad*. London, England. Semester and academic year. Sophomores to seniors with 3.0 GPA. Rolling admissions. Contact: Sara Hibbert, International Office, UCL, Gower Street, London WCIE 6BT, U.K.; (44) 71-3807185.

University of Colorado at Boulder. *Academic Year in Lancaster*. England. Juniors and seniors with 2.75 GPA. Apply by March 1.

University of Denver. *Spring Quarter in London*. England. British studies and arts and sciences. Excursions. Undergraduates with 2.5 GPA. Apply by February 1.

University of Essex. *International Programme*. Colchester, England. Semester and academic year. Full university curriculum. Dormitory housing. Sophomores to seniors with 3.0 GPA. Apply by April for fall and academic year; September for spring. Apply directly or through Beaver College, Butler University, or Marymount College.

University of Kansas. *Academic Year Abroad in Great Britain*. East Anglia, Essex, Exeter, Hull, Leicester, Kent, Reading, St. Andrew's, Stirling, Strathclude, Wales at Swansea, Wales at Aberystwyth. Semester and academic year at Stirling, Scotland. Juniors with 3.0 GPA. Apply by March 1 for fall (UK students: February 15); October 15 for Stirling spring.

University of Maryland. *Study in London*. Semester and academic year. Sophomores to seniors with 2.5 GPA. Apply by May 1 for fall and academic year and October 15 for spring.

University of North Carolina at Chapel Hill. *UNC Program to Bristol*. Bristol, England. Academic year. Sophomores to seniors with 3.0 GPA. Apply by February 14.

Year in Edinburgh. Edinburgh, Scotland. Academic year. Sophomores to seniors with 3.0 GPA. Apply by February 14.
Year in Glasgow. Glasgow, Scotland. Fall semester and academic year. Sophomores to seniors with 3.0 GPA. Apply by February 14 for fall and academic year.
Year Abroad in Lancaster. Lancaster, England. Academic year. Sophomores to seniors with 3.0 GPA. Apply by February 14.
Year in Leeds. Leeds, England. Academic year. Sophomores to seniors with 3.0 GPA. Apply by February 14.
UNC Exchange Program to Manchester. Manchester, England. Academic year. Juniors and seniors with 3.0 GPA. Apply by February 14.
Year in Sheffield. Sheffield, England. Academic year. Sophomores to seniors with 3.0 GPA. Apply by February 14.
UNC to St. Andrews, Scotland. Academic year. Sophomores to seniors. Apply by February 14.
UNC Program to Sussex. Sussex, England. Academic year. Juniors and seniors with 3.0 GPA. Apply by February 14.
University of Oregon. *Northwest Interinstitutional Council on Study Abroad—London.* See listing under American Heritage Association.
University of Sussex. *Junior Year Abroad.* Brighton, England. Spring semester and academic year. Sophomores to seniors with 3.0 GPA. Apply by April 1 for academic year; November 1 for spring.
University of Washington. *Northwest Interinstitutional Council on Study Abroad—London.* See listing under American Heritage Association.
University of Wisconsin at Madison. *Academic Year at the University of Warwick.* Coventry, England. Academic year. Liberal arts and physical sciences. Juniors to graduate students in good academic standing. Special exchanges for history and philosophy students. Open only to students at higher education institutions in Wisconsin or Wisconsin residents studying in other states. Apply by second Friday in February.
University of Wisconsin at Milwaukee. *Study in London.* England. Semester and academic year. Offered in conjunction with the University of Wisconsin at Madison. Sophomores to seniors with 3.0 GPA. Apply by April 15 for fall and academic year; October 15 for spring.
University of Wisconsin at Platteville. *London Study Centre at Thames Valley University.* England. Semester and academic year. Liberal arts, business administration, and criminal justice. Sophomores to seniors with 2.5 GPA. Apply by April 30 for fall and academic year; October 20 for spring.
University of Wisconsin at River Falls. *Wisconsin in Scotland.* Edinburgh. Semester and academic year. Sophomores to seniors with 2.25 GPA. Apply by April 1 for fall and academic year; November 1 for spring.
Washington State University. *Northwest Interinstitutional Council on Study Abroad—London.* See listing under American Heritage Association.
Webster University. *Study Abroad in London.* England. Quarter, semester, and academic year. High-school graduates to graduate students. Apply four months before projected start of study. Contact: (800) 753-6765.
Western Washington University. *Northwest Interinstitutional Council on Study Abroad—London.* See listing under American Heritage Association.
Whitworth College. *British Isles Study Tour.* Fall semester every three years (next offered in Fall, 1996). British history, literature, art, and politics. Sophomores to seniors with 2.5 GPA. Apply by December 15, 1995.

Health and Medicine

Beaver College. *Pre-Med Program at King's College, University of London.* England. Spring semester. Juniors and seniors with 3.0 GPA. Apply by October 15.

Interior Design

Marymount College, Tarrytown. *London Guild Hall University.* England. Semester and academic year. Project-based core course for interior design majors. Juniors and seniors with 2.8 GPA. Rolling admissions.

Literature

Michigan State University. *English Literature.* Wimbledon, England. Fall semester. Sophomores to graduate students. Apply by June 3. Contact: Office of Overseas Study, 108 International Center, Michigan State University, East Lansing, MI 48824-1035; (517) 353-8920.

State University of New York at Binghamton. *Semester in London.* England. Spring semester. Literature and theater. Internships available. Sophomores to seniors. Apply by October 15. Contact: Department of English, SUNY at Binghamton, PO Box 6000, Binghamton, NY 13902-6000; (607) 777-2000.

Performing Arts

Beaver College. *University of Surrey Department of Dance.* Guildford, England. Academic year. Juniors and seniors with 3.0 GPA. Apply by April 20.

Butler University. *University of East Anglia, London Drama Term.* London and Norwich, England. Academic year. Full year study program; includes a term in London with theater internship. Juniors and seniors with 3.0 GPA. Apply by April 15. Contact: Institute for Study Abroad, Butler University, 4600 Sunset Avenue, Indianapolis, IN 46208-3485; (800) 858-0229.

Marymount College, Tarrytown. *London Drama Program.* England. Semester and academic year. Conservatory-style theater and acting training program for drama majors; instruction by British instructors from London drama academies. Juniors and seniors with 2.8 GPA. Rolling admissions.

State University of New York College at Oswego. *Theater Management Program in London.* England. Semester and academic year. Study theater management and literature or contemporary European studies while working in a fringe theater. Apartment housing. Juniors and seniors with 2.5 GPA and background in theater. Apply by April 1 for fall and academic year; November 1 for spring. Contact: Office of International Education, SUNY at Oswego, 102 Rich Hall, Oswego, NY 13126; (315) 341-2118.

University of Minnesota. *Literature and Theater in London.* Spring quarter. Theater internships available. First-year college students to graduate students and adults. Apply by January 15. Contact: The Global Campus, 106C Nicholson Hall, 216 Pillsbury Drive SE, University of Minnesota, Minneapolis, MN 55455-0138; (612) 625-3379.

University of Oregon. *Theater in Great Britain.* London and Stratford-upon-Avon. Spring quarter (late March to early June). Contemporary theater seminar, attendance of numerous performances, and optional acting class. Excursions and dormitory housing. Sophomores to graduate students. Apply by January 15.

Political Science

Butler University. *INSTEP: London Semester.* England. Fall and spring semesters. Law, politics, government, and political economy; internships avail-

able. Juniors and seniors with 3.0 GPA and previous study in field of interest. Apply by April 15 for fall; October 15 for spring.
INSTEP: Cambridge Semester. Fall and spring semesters. Emphasis on politics, economics, and history; internships available. Juniors and seniors with 3.0 GPA and previous study in field of interest. Apply by April 15 for fall; October 15 for spring.

Contact: Institute for Study Abroad, Butler University, 4600 Sunset Avenue, Indianapolis, IN 46208; (800) 858-0229.

State University of New York College at Brockport. *Brunel Political Science Exchange Program*. London, England. Academic year. Juniors and seniors with 3.0 GPA. Apply by February 15. Contact: Office of International Education, SUNY College at Brockport, Brockport, NY 14420; (716) 395-2119.

University of Iowa. *Ireland in Comparative Perspective*. Belfast, Northern Ireland. Fall semester. Political science: politics of ethnic and cultural conflict, comparative study of intercommunal relations. Sophomores to seniors with 3.0 GPA. Apply by March 15.

Summer and Short-Term

Archaeology

University of Louisville. *A Panorama of Archaeology in England, Scotland, Wales*. Three weeks in summer. High-school graduates to graduate students and adults. Apply by April 1.

Art and Architecture

Flagler College. *Art History Summer School*. Cambridge, England. Two-week program in August. Offered with Consortium of Florida Colleges and Universities. British art history at University of Cambridge. Dormitory housing. High school graduates. Apply by May 1.

Michigan State University. *Art in London*. England. Summer. Studio art and art criticism. Sophomores to graduate students. Apply by April 15.
History of Art. London, England. Summer. Instruction and museum visits. Sophomores to graduate students. Apply by April 15.

Contact: Office of Overseas Study, 108 International Center, Michigan State University, East Lansing, MI 48824-1035; (517) 353-8920.

Ohio University. *Art in England*. London, England; and Edinburgh, Scotland. Four weeks in summer. Art history, studio art, or independent study. Undergraduates. Apply by March 1. Contact: Pat Kroutel, School of Art, 241 Siegfried Hall, Ohio University, Athens, OH 45701; (614) 593-7697.

Syracuse University. *Art and Architecture in London*. England. Six weeks in May and June. Exploration of London's layout, historical development, buildings, and art treasures in its museums and galleries. Undergraduates and graduate students. Apply by March 1. Contact: (800) 235-3472.

Business

Bentley College. *Bentley College's Business Program in Lancaster*. England. Summer term. Full academic curriculum at Lancaster University. Juniors and seniors with 3.0 GPA. Apply by November 1.
Bentley College's Summer School in England. Cambridge. Offered in association with Selwyn College of Cambridge University. International business and economics. Excursions. Juniors and seniors with 3.0 GPA. Apply by April 1.

Michigan State University. *Business Law Program in Cambridge.* England. June and July. International law and impact on international business in European Economic Community in addition to study of English legal system. Dormitory housing and excursions. Juniors and seniors. Apply by April 15. Contact: Office of Overseas Study, 108 International Center, Michigan State University, East Lansing, MI 48824-1035; (517) 353-8920.

Ramapo College of New Jersey. *Intersession in London.* England. Two weeks in January. International business. Excursions and residence hall housing. Sophomores to graduate students. Apply by November 30. Contact: Study Abroad Office, Ramapo College of New Jersey, 505 Ramapo Valley Road, Room D-204, Mahwah, NJ 07430-9926; (201) 529-7463.

Syracuse University. *The European Single Market: A London and Brussels Perspective.* London, England, with trip to Brussels, Belgium. Summer. Seniors and graduate students. Apply by March 1.

Management Internships in London. England. Summer. Placement in English financial institutions. Research paper to be submitted after internship. Undergraduates and graduates with basic accounting and computing skills. Apply by February 15.

Contact: (800) 235-3472.

University of Colorado at Boulder. *London Seminar in International Finance and Business.* Summer. Economic integration of European Community and effects on nations of Community and world finance. Juniors to graduate students with previous international finance or international economics. Apply by March 1.

University of South Carolina. *Summer Program.* Middlesbrough and London, England; Edinburgh, Scotland. Summer. Business Administration. Sophomores to graduate students who have had an introductory marketing course. Apply by March 1.

Communications

Michigan State University. *Mass Media and Reporting in Britain.* London, England. Summer. Working seminars with British media professionals. Juniors, seniors, and graduate students. Apply by April 15. Contact: Office of Overseas Study, 108 International Center, Michigan State University, East Lansing, MI 48824-1035; (517) 353-8920.

Southern Illinois University at Carbondale. *British Television Programming, Policy, and Production.* London, Bristol, and Manchester, England. Summer. Seminar on differences in programming, production, and administration between British and American broadcasting systems. Sophomores to graduate students and qualified professionals. Apply by March 1.

Southern Methodist University. *SMU in London.* England. Summer. International communications, journalism, and advertising. Excursions and site visits. Sophomores to seniors. Apply by March 15. Contact: Office of International Programs, SMU, 100 McFarlin Auditorium, Dallas, TX 75275-0391; (214) 768-2338.

Criminal Justice

Michigan State University. *Forensic Anthropology and Human Identification.* London and Cambridge, England. Summer. Forensic anthropology and identification, and skeletal biology; instruction and field experiences. Juniors, seniors, and graduate students. Apply by April 15. Contact: Office of Overseas

Study, 108 International Center, Michigan State University, East Lansing, MI 48824-1035; (517) 353-8920.

Economics

University of Kansas. *International Summer School in Economics at the London School of Economics*. Juniors and seniors with 3.0 GPA. Apply by March 18.

University of Nebraska—Lincoln. *Nebraska at Oxford*. Oxford, England. Four weeks in summer. British political and international economic policy. Sophomores to graduate students. Apply by March 15.

Education

Old Dominion University. *ODU Abroad: Student Teaching in the U.K.* Various cities. Summer. Supervised student teaching in British schools. Undergraduate education majors. Apply by March 1. Contact: Study Abroad Office, BAL 304, Old Dominion University, Norfolk, VA 23529; (804) 683-5378.

State University of New York College at Brockport. *British Educational Methods Program*. London, England. Summer. Juniors to graduate students. Apply by March 15. Contact: Office of International Education, SUNY College at Brockport, Brockport, NY 14420; (716) 395-2119.

State University of New York College at Fredonia. *Teacher Education Program*. Swansea, Wales; and Exmouth, England. Two weeks in June and July. Participants visit schools in Wales, meet headmasters and teachers, visit classrooms, and interact with teachers and students. Seniors, graduate students, teachers, and administrators. Apply by January 15. Contact: Dean, Educational Studies, Room W113, Thompson Hall, SUNY College at Fredonia, Fredonia, NY 14063; (716) 673-3449.

University of Louisville. *Education in Edinburgh*. Edinburgh, Scotland. Summer. First-year college students to graduate students. Apply by April 1.

University of New Orleans. *UNO in Bath, England: Seminars for Educators*. Bath, England. Three weeks in summer. Special education/education. Graduate students, elementary- and secondary-school teachers. Apply by April 1.

University of North Carolina at Chapel Hill. *UNC Summer Program to London*. Sophomores to seniors. Apply by March 15.

Engineering

Iowa State University. *Chemical Engineering Study Abroad Program*. London, England. Summer. Juniors majoring in chemical engineering. Apply by February 15. Contact: Dr. Peter Reilly, Department of Chemical Engineering, 231 Sweeney, Iowa State University, Ames, IA 50011; (515) 294-5968.

Film

Michigan State University. *Film in Britain*. London, England; and Edinburgh, Scotland. Summer. Sophomores to graduate students. Apply by April 15. Contact: Office of Overseas Study, 108 International Center, Michigan State University, East Lansing, MI 48824-1035; (517) 353-8920.

General Studies

American Heritage Association. ISIS at Kingston-upon-Thames, England. Summer. Apply by May 1.

Beaver College. *Scottish Universities' International Summer School*. Edinburgh, Scotland. Summer and short-term (2- to 3-week sessions). Courses in literature, culture, and history of England and Scotland. Juniors, seniors, and graduate students (by special arrangement for undergraduate credit) with 3.0 GPA. Apply by March 31.

Boston University. *Summer Program in London*. England. Intensive six-week summer program offering courses from six different program tracks: advertising, marketing, and public relations; the arts; management, finance, and economics; the media; prelaw; psychology and social policy. Sophomores to seniors with 3.0 GPA in major. Apply by April 1.

Brigham Young University. *BYU Study Abroad*. London, England. Summer. Live in BYU London Centre. Sophomores to seniors. Apply by February 1. *British Literary Masterworks Study Abroad Program*. London, England. Summer. Sophomores to seniors. Apply by February 1.

Council on International Educational Exchange. *London Summer Business and Liberal Arts Program at the University of Westminster*. England. Three three-week summer sessions that may be combined. Program involves University of Westminster courses and professors arranged specially for participants. Sophomores to graduate students, continuing-education students with 2.75 GPA, and professionals. Apply by March 1. Contact: University Programs Department.

Flagler College. *International Summer School at Cambridge University*. England. Four-week program in July. English art, history, politics, and literature. Excursions and dormitory housing. High-school graduates. Apply by May 1.

Louisiana State University. *LSU in London*. England. July and August. Six-week program in theater, English, and political science. Excursions. Sophomores to seniors with 2.5 GPA and graduate students with 3.0 GPA. Apply by April 1.

Loyola Marymount University. Canterbury, England. Summer. Courses offered in business, liberal arts, fine and communication arts, and science and engineering. Sophomores to seniors and high-school graduates not enrolled in college with 2.8 GPA. Rolling admissions.

Michigan State University. *Cambridge University International Summer School*. England. Juniors and seniors with 3.0 GPA. Apply by April 15. *History/Arts and Humanities in Britain*. London, England; and Edinburgh, Scotland. July. One-month program in British history, European intellectual history, and creative arts and humanities of Europe. Excursions and dormitory housing. First-year college students to graduate students. Apply by April 15. *Social Sciences in London*. England. Summer. Political, economic, and social processes in the industrial world. Sophomores to seniors. Apply by April 15.

Contact: Office of Overseas Study, 108 International Center, Michigan State University, East Lansing, MI 48824-1035; (517) 353-8920.

Moorhead State University. *Western Art and Culture: The Scottish Perspective*. Arboath, Scotland. June and July. Four-week study tour in Western thought as expressed in art and architecture. History, literature, art, studio art (optional), archaeology, and culture. Sophomores to adults. Apply by April 9. Contact: Jill I. Holsen, International Programs, Moorhead State University, Moorhead, MN 56563; (218) 236-2956.

New York University. *NYU in London*. England. Five weeks in July and August. Art, drama, politics, and history. Excursions and dormitory housing. Undergraduates. Apply by April 1. Contact: NYU in London, English Department, Faculty of Arts and Sciences, 19 University Place, 2nd Floor, New York, NY 10003; (212) 998-8800.

North Carolina State University. *The London Experience*. England. Summer. Art, architecture, music, theater, and other humanities. Undergraduates with 2.25 GPA. Apply by March 1.

A Summer at Oxford. England. History, literature, European art, and contemporary Britain. Excursions and residence hall housing. Sophomores to seniors with 2.5 GPA. Apply by March 1.

Ramapo College of New Jersey. *Summer Study in England*. Oxford. Early July to mid-August. British literature, folktales, history, and culture. Excursions and residence hall housing. Sophomores to graduate students. Apply by April 15. Contact: Study Abroad Office, Ramapo College of New Jersey, 505 Ramapo Valley Road, Room D-204, Mahwah, NJ 07430-9926; (201) 529-7463.

Southern Methodist University. *SMU in Oxford*. England. Five weeks in summer. British literature, history, political science, business, and economics at University College, Oxford. Excursions. Sophomores to seniors. Apply by March 15. Contact: Office of International Programs, SMU, 100 McFarlin Auditorium, Dallas, TX 75275-0391; (214) 768-2338.

State University of New York College at Oswego. *Huron University*. London, England. Summer. Contemporary British culture. High-school graduates to graduate students. Apply by April 1. Contact: International Education, 102 Rich Hall, SUNY College at Oswego, Oswego, NY 13126; (315) 341-2118.

University of Alabama. *Alabama at Oxford*. Oxford, England. Five weeks in summer. Culture, literature, English, and history at Wadham College. Apply by March 1. Contact: (205) 348-5256.

University of Hartford. *Discovering Britain*. Oxford, England. Three weeks in summer. British history, art, literature, and culture. First-year college students to graduate students. Apply by April 1.

University of Kansas. *Humanities in Great Britain*. London, Edinburgh, York, Oxford, Stratford-upon-Avon, and Exeter. Summer. First-year college students to seniors with 2.5 GPA. Apply by February 1.

University of Kentucky. *Cooperative Center for Study in Britain*. London, England. Summer. First-year college students to graduate students and adults. Apply by March 22.

Cooperative Center for Study in Britain. Glasgow, Scotland. Summer. Freshmen to graduate students and adults. Apply by March 22.

University of Michigan. *Summer Study in London, England*. Six weeks in summer. First-year college students to seniors. Apply by March 1.

University of Utah. *University of Cambridge International Summer School*. England. Two-, four-, and six-week programs in July and August. Humanities and social sciences. Sophomores to seniors with 2.7 GPA, and others. Apply by March 1.

University of Wisconsin at Platteville. *Summer Session in London at Thames Valley University*. England. Theater, art, history, and culture. Sophomores to seniors with 2.0 GPA. Apply by April 1.

Webster University. *Study Abroad in London*. England. Summer. High-school graduates to graduate students. Apply four months ahead. Contact: (800) 753-6765.

Health and Medicine

Michigan State University. *Nursing Progam in London*. England. Summer. Role and responsibilities of nurses in different health-care organizations. Juniors to graduate students and professional nurses. Apply by April 15.

Medical Ethics and History of Health Care. London, England. Summer. Program designed for medical and nursing students, as well as students in philosophy, health policy, and international relations. Juniors to graduate students. Apply by April 15.

Contact: Office of Overseas Study, 108 International Center, Michigan State University, East Lansing, MI 48824-1035; (517) 353-8920.

Old Dominion University. *ODU Abroad: A Comparison of Nursing in the U.S. and U.K.* University of the West of England, Bristol. Summer. Apply by March 1. Contact: Study Abroad Office, BAL 304, Old Dominion University, Norfolk, VA 23529; (804) 683-5378.

University of Louisville. *Nursing in London.* London, England. Summer. Course designed to guide registered nurses and nursing students in making personal choices in daily dilemmas. Freshmen to graduate students and registered nurses. Apply by April 30. Offered in alternate years.

History

New York University. *Cambridge Study Program/Victorian Britain.* England. Summer. All students and nonstudents interested in Victorian Britain. Apply by April 28. Contact: NYU/SCE, International Programs, 331 Shimkin, Washington Square, New York, NY 10003.

Rutgers University. *Summer Institute in Sussex.* Falmer, England. English social history. Undergraduates. Apply by March 1.

State University of New York College at Oswego. *Historical Tour of the British Isles—Undergraduate and Adult Version.* Britain, Scotland, and Wales. Two to three weeks in summer. Accommodations in bed-and-breakfast hotels. Juniors and seniors with 2.5 GPA for undergraduate tour; non-traditional students and working adults for adult tour. Undergraduates apply by April 1; adults apply by May 1.

Contact: Office of International Education, SUNY at Oswego, 102 Rich Hall, Oswego, NY 13126; (315) 341-2118.

International Relations

Lehigh University. *Lehigh in London.* England. Summer (late May to early July). Course in economic relations of advanced industrial societies and internship in a business or political/social organization. Homestays. Sophomores to seniors with 2.7 GPA. Apply by March 15. Contact: Office of Summer Studies, 205 Johnson Hall, 36 University Drive, Lehigh University, Bethlehem, PA 18015; (215) 758-3966.

Law

Ohio State University. *Prelaw Summer Study Program.* Oxford, England. Four weeks in July and August. Anglo-American legal system and American law studies. Excursions and dormitory housing. Undergraduates and recent graduates with 3.0 GPA. Apply by February 15.

University of Notre Dame. *Live and Learn Law in London.* London. From late June to early August. Study at Notre Dame Law Centre. Law students who have successfully completed one year of law study. Apply by April 1.

Literature

Flagler College. *English Literature Summer School.* Cambridge, England. Two-week program in August. Offered with Consortium of Florida Colleges and Universities. English literature from 16th to 20th centuries at University of Cambridge. Dormitory housing. High-school graduates. Apply by May 1.

Illinois State University. *Thomas Hardy's England.* Dorset, England. Offered in summer of even-numbered years. Six-week program in life and works of Thomas Hardy. Sophomores to graduate students with 2.5 GPA. Apply by

March 12. Contact: Dr. Bill Morgan, Illinois State University, 4240 English Department, Normal, IL 61761-6901; (309) 438-7158.

Michigan State University. *English Literature in London*. England. Summer. Classes as well as theater productions and museum visits. Sophomores to graduate students. Apply by April 15. Contact: Office of Overseas Study, 108 International Center, Michigan State University, East Lansing, MI 48824-1035; (517) 353-8920.

Ohio State University. *Summer Program in English Literature*. Bath. Five weeks in July and August. Shakespeare in performance and contemporary British and Irish literature. Excursions. Undergraduates with 2.7 GPA. Apply by March 15.

State University of New York at Brockport. *British Writers Summer Program*. Various sites in England and Scotland. Sophomores to seniors with 2.5 GPA. Apply by May 1.

Oxford University Summer Program. England. British literature (also available for hearing-impaired). Juniors and seniors with 2.5 GPA. Apply by May 1. Contact: Office of International Education, SUNY at Brockport, Brockport, NY 14420; (716) 395-2119.

University of Alabama. *Alabama at Oxford*. England. July and August. English literature and history. Excursions and dormitory housing. First-year college students to graduate students. Apply by April 1.

University of Louisville. *Study in London: Shakespeare and His Times*. Summer. First-year college students to graduate students. Apply by April 1.

University of Massachusetts at Amherst. *Oxford Summer Seminar*. Juniors to graduate students with 3.0 GPA. Apply by March 31.

Marketing and Public Relations

Michigan State University. *Packaging in England*. London. Summer. Packaging and development of packages for European market. Juniors and seniors. Apply by April 15. Contact: Office of Overseas Study, 108 International Center, Michigan State University, East Lansing, MI 48824-1035; (517) 353-8920.

Syracuse University. *Marketing Strategies in a Changing Environment*. London, England. Summer. Juniors and seniors. Apply by March 1. Contact: (800) 235-3472.

University of Alabama at Birmingham. *UAB in London*. England. Two weeks in December. Marketing. Juniors to graduate students, professionals, and teachers with marketing or business background. Contact: Dr. Duleep Doesthale, Center for International Studies, 306 Hill University Center, 1400 University Boulevard, UAB, Birmingham, AL 35294-1150; (205) 934-3328.

Performing Arts

Brigham Young University. *Theater in England*. Various cities. Six-week program from April to June. First-year college students to seniors. Apply by February 1.

Eckerd College. *Eckerd in London*. England. January term. Theater course. First-year college students to seniors with 2.75 GPA. Rolling admissions.

Michigan State University. *Acting and Theater in Great Britain*. London and Stratford-upon-Avon, England. Summer. Seminars, plays, and courses in acting and theater history. Excursions. Sophomores to graduate students. Apply by April 15. Contact: Office of Overseas Study, 108 International Center, Michigan State University, East Lansing, MI 48824-1035; (517) 353-8920.

New York University. *Tisch School of the Arts in London.* England. Five weeks in July and August. British film directors, writing for stage and screen, and contemporary British theater. Undergraduates (and graduate students for independent study). Apply by April 15. Contact: TSOA Student Affairs Office, 721 Broadway, 7th Floor, New York, NY 10003; (212) 998-1900.

Ohio University. *History and Drama: The English Stage Past and Present.* London and Stratford-upon-Avon, England. June. Three-week interdisciplinary course in social, historical, political, and practical aspects of theater. Excursions. Undergraduates. Apply by April. Contact: Professor Loreen Giese, Department of English, 342 Ellis Hall, Ohio University, Athens, OH 45701; (614) 593-2838.

State University of New York College at Brockport. *Edinburgh Festival Summer Program.* Edinburgh, Scotland. August. Seminars on educational theater and critical thinking at University of Edinburgh; students attend international productions of Edinburgh Festival/Fringe. Sophomores to graduate students and continuing-education students. Apply by March 1. Contact: Office of International Education, SUNY College at Brockport, Brockport, NY 14420; (716) 395-2119.

State University of New York College at New Paltz. *London Piano Festival.* England. Summer. Individual and group piano instruction, as well as lectures, masters classes, and course in music literature. Excursions. High-school students to graduate students. Rolling admissions.

London Theatre Seminar. England. Winter break (late December to mid-January). Theater arts lectures, seminars, and attendance of plays. High-school students to graduate students. Rolling admissions.

Contact: Office of International Education, HAB 33, SUNY College at New Paltz, New Paltz, NY 12561; (914) 257-3125.

University of Pennsylvania. *Penn-in-London I and II.* British theater and literature. Apply by March 1.

Photography

Michigan State University. *Photo Communication in England and Scotland.* London, Bath, York, and Bradford (England); Edinburgh and Glasgow (Scotland). Summer. First-year college students to graduate students. Apply by April 15. Contact: Office of Overseas Study, 108 International Center, Michigan State University, East Lansing, MI 48824-1035; (517) 353-8920.

Ohio University. *Photographic Field School in Visual Communication.* Edinburgh, Scotland. Ten weeks in summer. Magazine photography and visual usage in print media. Undergraduates. Apply by March 31. Contact: Terry Eiler, School of Visual Communication, 300 Siegfried Hall, Ohio University, Athens, OH 45701; (614) 593-4898.

Political Science

Butler University. *INSTEP: London.* England. Summer program with emphasis on law, politics, government, and political economy; internships available. Juniors and seniors with 3.0 GPA and previous study in field of interest. Apply by April 15.

INSTEP: Cambridge. England. Summer program with emphasis on politics, economics, and history; internships available. Juniors and seniors with 3.0 GPA and previous study in field of interest. Apply by April 15.

Contact: Institute for Study Abroad, Butler University, 4600 Sunset Avenue, Indianapolis, IN 46208; (800) 858-0229.

Michigan State University. *Political Science in London*. England. Summer. Sophomores to graduate students. Apply by April 15.
Public Affairs in Cambridge. England. Summer. Juniors and seniors. Apply by April 15.

Contact: Office of Overseas Study, 108 International Center, Michigan State University, East Lansing, MI 48824-1035; (517) 353-8920.

Syracuse University. *Politics in England*. London. Summer. Sophomores to seniors. Apply by March 1. Contact: (800) 235-3472.

Social Work

University of Alabama at Birmingham. *UAB in London*. Two weeks in December. High-school graduates to graduate students, professionals, and teachers. Contact: Dr. Duleep Deosthale, Center for International Studies, 306 Hill University Center, 1400 University Boulevard, University of Alabama at Birmingham, Birmingham, AL 35294-1150; (205) 934-3328.

Speech Science

Michigan State University. *Speech-Language Pathology and Audiology in London*. England. Summer. Juniors to graduate students. Apply by April 15. Contact: Office of Overseas Study, 108 International Center, Michigan State University, East Lansing, MI 48824-1035; (517) 353-8920.

Writing

Michigan State University. *American Thought and Language—Writing*. London, England. Summer. First-year college students and sophomores. Apply by April 15. Contact: Office of Overseas Study, 108 International Center, Michigan State University, East Lansing, MI 48824-1035; (517) 353-8920.

EXPLORING BRITISH CULTURE

Readings

Social and political issues dominate British writing; if the French are preoccupied with philosophical issues, the British concern is with social manners and political morality. For example, in *Pride and Prejudice* (1813), Jane Austen explores social convention; in *Hard Times* (1854), Charles Dickens confronts the devastating impact of industrialization on Great Britain; and in *The Mill on the Floss* (1860), George Eliot traces a young woman's efforts to free herself from the restrictive pressures of family life. Alan Sillitoe confronts the mores and institutions of British society in the short story "The Loneliness of the Long-Distance Runner" (1959), a 20th-century example of this type of literature.

E. M. Forster's novels *Howard's End* (1910), *Passage to India* (1924), and *Room with a View* (1908) have had successful screen adaptations in recent years.

Some of Virginia Woolf's most famous works are *Mrs. Dalloway* (1925), a stream-of-consciousness novel that follows a woman for a day in London; *Orlando* (1928), which follows the development of self-consciousness of its male, then female, protagonist through three centuries; and *To the Lighthouse* (1927), another stream-of-consciousness novel about an upper-middle-class couple from various points of view.

The satiric pen of Evelyn Waugh has attacked many of England's most revered institutions. One of his most famous works is *Brideshead Revisited* (1945), about the decline of the English aristocracy and the rediscovery of the protagonist's Catholic faith.

Perhaps the most interesting development in British literature has been the emergence of a number of younger writers from immigrant backgrounds. Timothy Mo, an Anglo-Chinese novelist, examines the trauma and comedy of one family's cultural adjustment in *Sour Sweet* (1982). Salman Rushdie, of Anglo-Indian ancestry, is the author of *Midnight's Children* (1981) and *The Satanic Verses* (1988); both works draw their considerable energy from a sense of being caught between two worlds and feeling at home in neither. Kazuo Ishiguro is a contemporary writer who was born in Japan and moved to Britain as a small child. His novel *Remains of the Day* (1989) is written in the voice of a deceased English aristocrat's valet and provides insight into the British class system. Mo, Rushdie, and other writers of immigrant backgrounds have given voice to a new Britain characterized by cultural contrast, ethnic diversity, and—at times—unsettling discord.

Films

Since the early 1970s a great number of relatively low-budget independent films have been produced in Great Britain, many with the help of funding from the BBC. These films often have a curious relationship to current British social ills and the continuing decline of "British Eminence." Dennis Potter's fantasy transformation of the "hard-boiled detective" genre, *The Singing Detective*, is a particularly good example. Others also receiving attention in the U.S. are Mike Leigh's *High Hopes* and *Life Is Sweet*, Stephen Frears's *My Beautiful Laundrette* (1985), *Prick Up Your Ears* (1987), and *Sammy and Rosie Get Laid* (1987), Neil Jordan's *Mona Lisa* (1986), and Bill Forsyth's *Local Hero* (1983) and *Gregory's Girl* (1981).

Monty Python classics such as *Monty Python and the Holy Grail* (1975) are a good introduction to wacky British humor, as is Charles Crichton's hit *A Fish Called Wanda*, written by and starring former Python John Cleese. Kenneth Branagh's adaptations of Shakespeare's *Henry V* (1989) and *Much Ado about Nothing* (1993) have been much acclaimed.

The team of Ismail Merchant and James Ivory have collaborated on adaptations of author E. M. Forster's novels, including *Room with a View* (1985), and *Howard's End* (1992), both written by novelist and screenwriter Ruth Prawer Jhabvala. The Merchant-Ivory team also adapted Forster's *Maurice* (1987). These films look at the changing values of British society just before World War I.

CHAPTER SEVEN

THE MIDDLE EAST AND NORTH AFRICA

This chapter encompasses a broad range of countries lying between the Caucasus Mountains and the Sahara, between the Atlantic and the Indian Ocean. A number of powerful bonds unite this region: Most of these countries share a common religion (Islam) and many share a common language (Arabic). Nevertheless, cultural diversity is the dominant characteristic of the area.

Located at the juncture of Europe, Africa, and Asia, the Middle East and North Africa have been of vital importance in world history. A number of strategic waterways such as the Bosporus, the Strait of Gibraltar, the Strait of Hormuz, and the Suez Canal guarantee the area's continued importance as a crossroads of the world's commerce. The discovery of vast petroleum reservoirs in the region has enhanced its importance.

The Middle East also is crucial to world history because many of the world's peoples trace the roots of their religion and culture to the region. The fertile river valleys of the Tigris and Euphrates and the Nile were home to some of the world's earliest civilizations. The surrounding land is rich with the artifacts of the ancient cultures of Assyria, Babylon, Egypt, and Phoenicia and Persia. These civilizations formed the backbone of Western culture. Travelers to the Middle East and North Africa can expect to see the strata of history evident here as in no other region of the world.

The Middle East

While most of the countries of the Middle East share the religion of Islam, the region was also the birthplace of Judaism and Christianity. These three religions have a history of mutual antagonism, but regional violence has escalated since the creation of the state of Israel in 1948 and the ensuing displacement of the Palestinian population. While the Palestinian-Israeli dispute continues to dominate international politics in the Middle East, it is not the only cause of the continuing war and violence in the region. Many complex rivalries and animosities combined to produce the region's most recent war, the Persian Gulf War of 1991, which involved Arab, European, Canadian, Australian, and American forces.

Peace in this region has yet to be achieved, as demonstrated by the faltering negotiations between Israel, the Palestinians, and neighboring Arab states. Moreover, with the collapse of the Soviet Union, a number of newly independent countries in the region—such as Armenia, Azerbaijan, and Georgia—have experienced unprecedented violence amounting to civil war. For this reason, many Americans are hesitant to travel or study in the region; yet the need for Americans to gain an understanding of the people, cultures, and languages of the region has never been greater. While there are good reasons for avoiding countries like Georgia, Iraq, and Lebanon at present, it is important not to make broad generalizations about the different countries of the Middle East. Those who consider their options and travel wisely have an unequaled chance to witness some of today's most important world events unfold from an entirely different perspective.

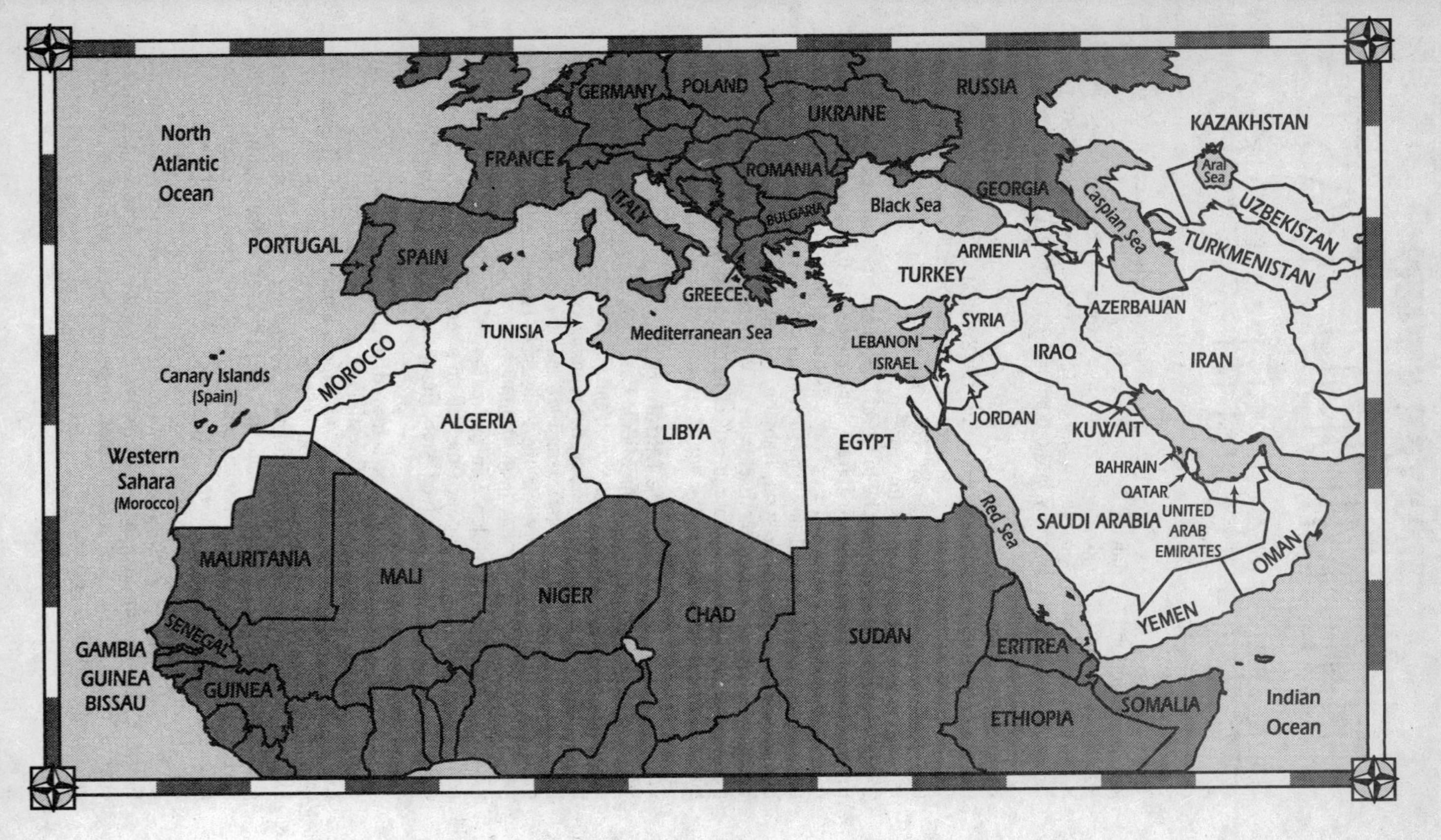
North Atlantic Ocean
GERMANY
POLAND
RUSSIA
UKRAINE
KAZAKHSTAN
FRANCE
ROMANIA
Aral Sea
ITALY
BULGARIA
Black Sea
GEORGIA
Caspian Sea
UZBEKISTAN
PORTUGAL
SPAIN
ARMENIA
TURKMENISTAN
TURKEY
GREECE
AZERBAIJAN
TUNISIA
Mediterranean Sea
SYRIA
LEBANON
ISRAEL
IRAQ
IRAN
MOROCCO
Canary Islands
(Spain)
ALGERIA
LIBYA
EGYPT
JORDAN
KUWAIT
Western Sahara
(Morocco)
BAHRAIN
QATAR
Red Sea
SAUDI ARABIA
UNITED ARAB EMIRATES
MAURITANIA
MALI
NIGER
OMAN
CHAD
SUDAN
YEMEN
SENEGAL
ERITREA
GAMBIA
GUINEA BISSAU
GUINEA
ETHIOPIA
SOMALIA
Indian Ocean

North Africa

For thousands of years civilization has flourished in the fertile strip between the Sahara and the Mediterranean. Egypt, Rome, and Carthage left their mark, but the longest-lasting influence is that of the Arabs whose language, religion, and culture still pervade the region. Other recent foreign influences have been those of Europe; the colonial powers of France, Italy, Spain, and Britain controlled the region during the first half of this century. Their former colonies, the modern nations of North Africa, did not gain their independence until the 1950s.

North Africa shares many characteristics with the Middle East, yet for years it has been more accessible to Western tourists, and more familiar with Western ways. Throngs of Europeans annually visit Tunisia and Morocco, attracted by sunny beaches, ancient ruins, vibrant cities, and exotic cultures. In the months leading up to publication of this book, many travelers have been frightened away from this region by civil strife involving Islamic militants and the secular governments of Algeria and Egypt. While U.S. citizens should exercise caution in traveling to these two countries, they should not be deterred from exploring this fascinating and important region.

Getting There

The cheapest fares available from the U.S. to the Middle East and North Africa are generally APEX fares (see Chapter Five for a general explanation of airfare types). There are also student fares to a limited number of destinations. Listed below are some examples of *one-way* summer fares that were in effect during 1993. More up-to-date information is available at Council Travel offices (see listing on pages xiii–xvi).

New York–Istanbul	$425
New York–Casablanca	$345
New York–Cairo	$499

In addition, student/youth flights are available from several European cities to the Middle East and North Africa. These can be booked at any Council Travel office or at a student travel bureau in Europe. Regulations vary depending on the airline, but generally holders of the International Student Identity Card or the GO 25 Card (see pages 9–11) are eligible. Listed below are sample *one-way* student fares for the 1993 peak summer season.

London–Tel Aviv	$239
Paris–Tel Aviv	$239
London–Istanbul	$255
Frankfurt–Tel Aviv	$239

The Mediterranean countries of North Africa are a short trip from Europe. From Algeciras, Spain, a variety of boats (including car ferries and hydrofoils) depart for the cities of Ceuta and Tangiers on the African continent, only a couple of hours away. From Palermo and Trapani in Sicily, you can find various types of passenger boat service to Tunisia. Several Greek islands, including Rhodes and Samos, are only a short boat trip from Turkey's Aegean coast. Ferry service is also available from Greece to Cyprus and from there to Lebanon and Israel. Student travel bureaus in Europe can provide you with more information.

Travel in the Middle East and North Africa

U.S. citizens may encounter travel restrictions in several countries. Currently, all travel to Lebanon, Libya, and Iraq by U.S. citizens is prohibited by the Department of State. Individuals seeking to travel to any of these countries must submit passport validation requests to the **U.S. Department of State**, Deputy Assistant Secretary for Passport Services, Attn: Office of Citizenship Appeals and Legal Assistance (Rm. 300), 1425 K Street NW, Washington, DC 20522-1705. Travel to Iran is not prohibited, but there are currency restrictions in place; for more information, contact the **Department of the Treasury**, Office of Foreign Assets Control, (202) 622-2480. In addition, at press time the U.S. Department of State has warned of violence within Afghanistan, Algeria, and Tajikstan. For up-to-date information on these and other countries in the Middle East and North Africa, obtain the latest Consular Information Sheets from the Department of State (see pages 8–9).

Historically, most Persian Gulf states have discouraged tourism. Saudi Arabia and Qatar do not issue tourist visas and require travelers to have a sponsor. Some Gulf states are gradually opening up to tourism, although tourist facilities are likely to be on the more expensive end. Jordan and Syria, however, both welcome tourists. Travelers who plan to include Israel in their itinerary should note that several Arab countries may refuse entry to travelers with **Israeli visas** stamped in their passports. These include Syria, United Arab Emirates, Yemen and others; check before you go. You will not encounter this problem entering Egypt. Jordan also recently began admitting travelers with Israeli visas, but officials are not always consistent. To avoid this problem, it's possible to have Israeli visa, entry, and exit stamps put on a separate sheet that can be stapled to the passport and removed on departure. However, evidence of entering Egypt from Israel can also be used as evidence to deny you access to certain other countries. It's possible to have a second short-term passport issued to ease travel to Israel and Arab states; to obtain a second passport, contact the Department of State's Office of Passport Services (see page 5). For more detailed information on entry requirements, contact the embassies of the countries you wish to visit (see addresses in the individual country sections that follow or "For Further Information," below).

In predominately Muslim countries, travelers of both sexes—but women in particular—will feel more comfortable if they are sensitive to local customs and act and dress accordingly. Remember, too, that there is a tremendous difference between urban and rural areas; what is acceptable in the city might not be acceptable in the country. In most Muslim countries, with some exceptions, single women will find it difficult to go out at night or to certain areas without attracting unwanted attention. One precaution is to travel with others; dressing in a conservative fashion is another. Light, ankle-length skirts and long-sleeved shirts or loose tunic/pants outfits suit local customs and are comfortable in the heat. It's also a good idea to bring a long scarf that can be used as a head covering. Local women are often protective of foreign women, and you can always hire a local male guide who can both show you the sights and discourage harassment. Women should not shirk from exploring the region; they should, however, be prepared for uncomfortable situations and unfamiliar restrictions.

Ramadan is the ninth month of the Islamic calendar, during which Muslims fast from dawn to sunset in commemoration of the revelation of the Koran to Mohammed. (In 1994, Ramadan begins on February 12; because the Islamic calendar is 11 days shorter than the Western calendar, Ramadan begins 11 days earlier in successive years.) If you try to get a meal in a restaurant during daylight hours in this month, you may be frowned upon or even refused service. Fasting means no eating, drinking, or smoking, and it is a simple matter of respect for a tourist to refrain from breaking the custom in public. If you want to eat during daylight hours, do so in private. The best solution is to adhere to local custom; at nightfall festive crowds fill the streets and the restaurants and cafés stay open late.

For Further Information

Basic advice on travel in the region can be found in the State Department's pamphlet, *Tips for Travelers to the Middle East and North Africa*, available from from the Superintendent of Documents, U.S. Government Printing Office, Washington, DC 20402.

A helpful book for understanding Middle East politics is *Political Tides in the Arab World*, which examines three types of government and how they have been affected by the Persian Gulf war. It's available for $4 from the Foreign Policy Association (see page 16). Among the better books concerning Arab-Israeli relations is *Arab and Jew*, a historical study of the conflict between the two peoples by former *New York Times* correspondent David Shipler. For a penetrating look at the lives of foreign workers in the Middle East, as well as the repercussions of the Iran-Iraq war, read *Expats* by former *Newsweek* Paris bureau chief Christopher Dickey. For an informed monthly update on Middle East affairs, try the magazine *Washington Report on Middle East Affairs*, $19 for a one-year subscription. For more information, contact Washington Report, PO Box 53062, Washington, DC 20009; (800) 368-5788.

There are many guidebooks for the countries most often visited by tourists, such as Egypt, Israel, Morocco, and Turkey (see the individual country sections that follow for some of these books). Among the few guides to less-visited countries, Lonely Planet Publications' *Arab Gulf States: A Travel Survival Kit* ($15.95), *Iran: A Travel Survival Kit* ($14.95), *Jordan and Syria: A Travel Survival Kit* ($8.95), and *Yemen: A Travel Survival Kit* ($11.95) are among the best. Although the 1990 edition is growing out of date, Lonely Planet's *West Asia on a Shoestring* ($14.95) is a good guide to consult if you're traveling further east. For more information on Lonely Planet Publications, see page 56.

Listed below are addresses where you can write for general information as well as details on visa requirements for the nations we do not cover later this chapter. **Note:** At press time, most of the newly independent states of the former Soviet Union continue to issue visas through the Russian Embassy (see page 210). These include Georgia, Kazakhstan, Kyrgyzstan, Tajikstan, Turkmenistan, and Uzbekistan.

- **Afghanistan:** Embassy of the Republic of Afghanistan, 2341 Wyoming Avenue NW, Washington, DC 20008; (202) 234-3770
- **Algeria:** Embassy of Algeria, 2137 Wyoming Avenue NW, Washington, DC 20008; (202) 265-2800
- **Armenia:** Embassy of Armenia, Consular Division, 122 C Street NW, Suite 360, Washington, DC 20001; (202) 628-5766
- **Bahrain:** Embassy of Bahrain, 3502 International Drive NW, Washington, DC 20008; (202) 342-0741
- **Iran:** Iranian Interests Section, Embassy of Pakistan, 2209 Wisconsin Avenue NW, Washington, DC 20007; (202) 965-4990

- **Jordan:** Embassy of the Hashemite Kingdom of Jordan, 3504 International Drive NW, Washington, DC 20008; (202) 966-2664
- **Kuwait:** Embassy of Kuwait, 2940 Tilden Street NW, Washington, DC 20008; (202) 966-0702
- **Oman:** Embassy of the Sultanate of Oman, 2342 Massachusetts Avenue NW, Washington, DC 20008; (202) 387-1980
- **Qatar:** Embassy of the State of Qatar, 600 New Hampshire Avenue NW, Suite 1180, Washington, DC 20037; (202) 338-0111
- **Saudi Arabia:** Royal Embassy of Saudi Arabia, 601 New Hampshire Avenue NW, Washington, DC 20037; (202) 333-4595
- **Syria:** Embassy of the Syrian Arab Republic, 2215 Wyoming Avenue NW, Washington, DC 20008; (202) 232-6313
- **United Arab Emirates:** Embassy of the United Arab Emirates, 600 New Hampshire Avenue NW, Suite 740, Washington, DC 20037; (202) 338-6500
- **Yemen:** Embassy of the Yemen Arab Republic, 600 New Hampshire Avenue NW, Suite 840, Washington, DC 20037; (202) 965-4760

WORK

For U.S. citizens, the chances of obtaining salaried employment in the Middle East and North Africa are slim unless they are fluent in the local language. **Teaching** is one area, however, where there are a few openings for Americans. Anyone interested in teaching in the region should write for a copy of *Teaching Opportunities in the Middle East and North Africa*, available for $14.95 from **AMIDEAST**, 1100 17th Street NW, Washington, DC 20036; (202) 785-0022.

You'll find internships and traineeships in Cyprus, Egypt, Israel, Morocco, Tunisia, and Turkey listed in the individual country sections later in this chapter. In addition, there are internship possibilities in the **IAESTE** programs in Jordan, Lebanon, Libya, and Syria; see page 19 for more information.

STUDY

You'll find study programs for individual countries in the Middle East and North Africa later in this chapter. In this section, we've listed only those study programs offered by CIEE members that take place in more than one country of the region. Unless otherwise noted, consult Appendix I for the addresses of the colleges and universities listed below.

Semester and Academic Year

General Studies

Eastern Michigan University. *Asian Cultural History Tour*. 45 cities in Egypt, Israel, Turkey, Greece, Ukraine, Russia, Thailand, India, Nepal, and China. Spring semester. History, art, comparative religion, and political science taught in an interdisciplinary context. Sophomores to seniors with 2.5 GPA. Apply by October 1. Contact: (800) 777-3541.

St. Olaf College. *Term in the Middle East.* Academic program in Istanbul, Turkey; Cairo, Egypt; Jerusalem, Israel; and Rabat, Morocco. Fall semester plus January. Social and political issues of contemporary Middle East. Sophomores to seniors. Apply by March 1.

Global Semester. Academic program in Cairo, Egypt; Bangalore, India; Hong Kong; and Kyoto, Japan, with stops in Switzerland, Israel, and Nepal. Fall semester plus January. Political, social, and cultural issues of countries visited. Sophomores to seniors. Apply by March 1.

Summer and Short-Term

History

University of Louisville. *Egypt and Greece.* Various cities. Ancient history. First-year college students to graduate students. Apply by April 1.

EGYPT

When most Americans envision Egypt, they think of the pyramids, the Sphinx, and King Tut. Indeed, the thousands of American tourists who visit Egypt each year come almost exclusively to visit Pharaonic Egypt. The monuments of ancient Egypt attract even larger numbers of European tourists, who also come for the Egyptian sun and Mediterranean and Red Sea beaches. However, to those who really want to get to know and understand the Arab world, Egypt offers the opportunity to study Arabic and gain insights into Islam, Arab history, and the politics, economics, and culture of the contemporary Middle East.

The roll call of civilizations and cultures in Egypt actually has been much more diverse than simply the Pharaonic and Arab. There are traces of ancient Persia in Egypt; the ancient Greek and Roman civilizations are visible in Egyptian monuments; and the Byzantine and Coptic Christian cultures are evident as well. Indeed, although today 85 percent of the population is Muslim, 15 percent remains Coptic Christian. In fact, the word *copt* comes from the same root word as Egypt, and the Copts regard themselves as the true Egyptians, undiluted by the intermingling of later Muslim conquerors. Throughout the 19th century and the early decades of the 20th century, France and Great Britain extended their influence over Egypt. Finally, in 1952, after a nonviolent revolution, Egyptians once again ruled themselves. Thus Egypt, although one of the world's oldest civilizations, is a relatively new independent nation-state.

Though a trite phrase, "Egypt, the gift of the Nile" is essential to understanding the nation. Ninety-six percent of Egyptian territory is uninhabited desert. In the remaining four percent live 50 million Egyptians, making the Nile valley and delta among the most intensely farmed and densely populated areas on earth. A quarter of all Egyptians live in metropolitan Cairo, one of the noisiest and most crowded cities on earth.

In general, Egyptians share a strong national pride, value family ties, and place importance on religion. Both Muslims and Christians believe that individual behavior must ultimately be judged by family and God. God is in every Egyptian's conversation: "See you tomorrow, *ensha'allah* [God willing]"; "I'm fine, *el hamduli'lah* [thanks be to God]." Both Muslims and Christians use the same phrases and acknowledge the same God's influence in their lives. But religion in Egypt is neither puritanical nor gloomy. Egyptians are optimistic, exuberant, posses a sense of humor, and have a great capacity to enjoy life.

—Molly Bartlett, Eugene, Oregon

Official name: Arab Republic of Egypt. **Area:** 386,650 square miles (three-quarters the size of Alaska). **Population:** 54,451,000. **Population density:** 140 inhabitants per square mile. **Capital and largest city:** Cairo (pop. 6,452,000). **Language:** Arabic, English. **Religion:** Sunni Muslim. **Per capita income:** US$700. **Currency:** Egyptian pound. **Literacy rate:** 44%. **Average daily temperature:** Cairo: June, 82°; December, 60°. **Average number of days with precipitation:** Cairo: June, 0; December, 1.

TRAVEL

U.S. citizens are required to have a passport and a visa to enter Egypt. Tourist visas valid for six months cost $15. Renewable 30-day visas are also available upon arrival in Egypt. For more information, contact the Consular Section of the **Embassy of the Arab Republic of Egypt**, 2310 Decatur Place NW, Washington, DC 20008; (202) 234-3903. There are also Egyptian consulates in Chicago, Houston, New York, and San Francisco.

Getting Around

One of the best ways to get around Egypt is by **train**. Trains connect Cairo with Alexandria and Port Said and will take you south up the Nile Valley to Luxor and Aswan. Good overnight service with sleeping cars is provided on the longer runs and discounts are available to students (see "Especially for Students and Young People," below).

Buses are another option, and are preferable to trains for shorter trips. They also provide service to areas not accessible by train, such as the Sinai and the Oases. **Shared taxis**, which drop off and pick up passengers along a fixed route, serve virtually every town and village in the Nile Valley. If you hitchhike, you will be expected to pay the equivalent of the shared taxi fare. As always, women should not hitchhike alone.

Probably the most relaxing as well as the most scenic way to get around the country is by traveling on the **Nile**, which has served as the country's major highway for thousands of years. Numerous passenger boats make the three- to four-day trip between Aswan and Luxor, which has become a standard part of most organized tours to Egypt. You can also choose to make this trip by felucca, the traditional sailboats that still provide local transportation up and down the river for many Egyptians, for much less money.

Eating and Sleeping

There are several youth hostels in Egypt. For more information, contact Hostelling International/American Youth Hostels (see page 54) or the **Egyptian**

Youth Hostels Association, 1 El-Ibrahimy Street, Garden City, Cairo (20) 2-3550329; fax (20) 2-3550329.

For Further Information

General tourist information is available from the **Egyptian Tourist Authority**, 630 Fifth Avenue, New York, NY 10111; (212) 332-2570; fax (212) 956-6439. The Egyptian Tourist Authority also has offices at 83-83 Wilshire Boulevard, Suite 215, Beverly Hills, CA 90211, and 645 North Michigan Avenue, Suite 829, Chicago, IL 60611. The Egyptian embassy (see "Travel," above) will provide copies of *Prism: Quarterly of Egyptian Culture* upon request.

Let's Go: Israel and Egypt ($16.95) is one of the best budget travel guidebooks to the region. For historical detail, however, *The Real Guide: Egypt* ($19) is an all-around better book. An excellent book to read in preparation for your trip is *Insight Guide: Egypt* ($19.95). For more information on *Let's Go, Real Guides*, and *Insight Guides*, see pages 56–57.

WORK

Finding regular salaried employment in Egypt is difficult for foreigners. A contract offer from an Egyptian company is required, and then you must apply for a work permit at a labor office in Egypt.

Internships/Traineeships

A program offered by a member of the Council on International Educational Exchange is listed below.

Association for International Practical Training. *IAESTE Trainee Program*. On-the-job training for undergraduate and graduate students in technical fields such as engineering, computer science, agriculture, architecture, mathematics, and the natural and physical sciences. See page 19 for more information.

STUDY

For information on Egyptian universities that offer courses for foreign students in Arabic language, Islamic history, Islamic religion, and Egyptology, contact the Cultural Counselor, **Egyptian Educational Bureau**, 1303 New Hampshire Avenue NW, Washington, DC 20036; (202) 296-3888.

The **American University in Cairo**, a private university founded in 1919, welcomes students from American colleges and universities for a semester or full year. The language of instruction is English, but an intensive Arabic language program is available.

Below are the study programs offered by CIEE-member institutions. Unless otherwise noted, consult Appendix I for the address where you can write for more information. In addition to the programs below, the State University of New York schools offer programs to their own students only.

Semester and Academic Year

Arabic Language and Egyptian Culture

American University in Cairo. *Intensive Arabic*. Cairo. Fall semester. First-year college students to graduate students and adults. Apply by May 31.

General Studies

American University in Cairo. *Study Abroad for a Semester or a Year*. Cairo. Semester and academic year. Sophomores to graduate students. Apply by May 31 for fall or academic year; October 31 for spring.
Antioch University. *Egyptian and Islamic Studies*. Cairo. Fall term. Courses plus independent field project. Sophomores to graduate students; some knowledge of Arabic recommended. Apply by March 15. Contact: (800) 874-7986.
University of Wisconsin at Madison. *Academic Year in Cairo*. Cairo. Semester and academic year. Humanities, social sciences, management, engineering, and computer science. Juniors and seniors at any accredited institution of higher education in Wisconsin or Wisconsin residents studying at universities in other states. Apply by second Friday in February.

Summer and Short-Term

Arabic Language and Egyptian Culture

American University in Cairo. *Intensive Arabic*. Cairo. Summer. First-year college students to graduate students and adults. Apply by March 31.

Archaeology and Classical Studies

Southern Illinois University at Carbondale. *Travel Study Program to Greece and Egypt*. Summer. Seminars on ancient Greek and Egyptian experience. High-school graduates to college graduates and adults with college background. Apply by April 1.

Education

State University of New York College at Oneonta. *Egypt Student Teach*. Cairo. First half of spring semester. Student teach at Cairo American College, an international elementary and secondary school. Excursions. Juniors and seniors who have completed first quarter of student teaching. Rolling admissions. Contact: International Education Office, Netzer Building 332C, SUNY College at Oneonta, Oneonta, NY 13820-4015; (607) 436-3369.

General Studies

American University in Cairo. Cairo. Summer. First-year college students to graduate students. Apply by March 31.
University of Louisville. *Egyptian Society and Culture*. Cairo. Three weeks in summer. Social sciences, political sociology. Excursions. First-year college students to graduate students and adults. Apply by April 1.

EXPLORING EGYPTIAN CULTURE

Readings

The most internationally recognized of Egypt's contemporary writers is Naguib Mahfouz, winner of the 1988 Nobel Prize for literature and known for his masterful ability to paint a vivid picture of Egyptian daily life. Mahfouz's famous *Cairo Trilogy*, first published in 1956, recently appeared in English as *Palace Walk* (1990), *Palace of Desire* (1991), and *Sugar Street* (1992). Banned in Egypt, *Children of Gebelawi* (1981) is an allegory that retells—in the setting of a Cairo alley—the stories of Mohammed, Moses, Jesus, and Adam and Eve. *Midaq Alley* (1975), also set in a poor neighborhood in Cairo, is the story of a working-class girl and the local barber. An insider's look at the city of Alexandria, *Miramar* (1975) offers the classic plot of interconnected characters living in a small hotel, while *Fountain and Tomb* (1975) is a series of tales woven into a novel—seen from a child's viewpoint—about the complex society of Cairo.

Although he lacks Mahfouz's international reputation, Yusuf Idris is Egypt's finest writer of short stories and is widely read and appreciated by Egyptians. A former physician in the Nile delta and a political prisoner under Farouk and Nasser, Idris has long made poverty and social injustice his themes. His books, including *Rings of Burnished Brass* and *The Cheapest Nights*, are collections of sharp, gritty stories that portray rural life in Egypt. *The Sinners* explores the repercussions experienced by a village after a peasant woman abandons her newborn baby in a ditch.

A writer of a more popular, commercial fiction, Fathy Ghanem portrays a young, ambitious Cairo journalist who is betrayed by both his colleagues and the women who love him in *The Man Who Lost His Shadow*. Lawyer and diplomat Yahya Haqqi writes in *Good Morning! and Other Stories* of the experiences that deeply influenced him as an official in an Upper Egyptian town, where he was asked to carry out orders that were in conflict with the interests of the common people.

One of the most prominent women authors in Egypt today is psychiatrist and feminist Nawal El Saadawi. Her book *The Hidden Face of Eve* (1982) provides a personal and often upsetting portrait of the lives of women in the Middle East. Saadawi has written powerful fiction as well, like *The Fall of the Imam, God Dies by the Nile* (1985) and, probably her best, *Women at Point Zero* (1983), which is about a woman who is condemned to death for killing a pimp. Editor Nayra Attiya conveys the strength and spirit of five contemporary women of the lower and lower-middle classes in *Khul-Khaal: Five Egyptian Women Tell Their Stories* (University Press).

Some of the better books on Egypt by nonnatives are the *The Other Nile* (1987) by Charlie Pye-Smith, a witty and insightful account of the author's journeys down the Nile into Sudan; Christopher Pick's compilations of famous foreigners' impressions, *Egypt: A Traveller's Anthology* (London: John Murray); and the informative travelogue *Egypt: The Eternal Smile* (1980), by Allen Drury.

Films

Since the late 1920s, Egypt has been the principal Arab filmmaking center. Most of the films coming out of the country are typically melodramas or farces with dreamy settings and outrageous plot lines of love, jealousy, wealth, and glamour, all embellished throughout with song and dance. This successful formula all but guarantees success at the box office, if not with the critics.

Alongside the commercial industry, however, is a relatively small number of independent filmmakers who make higher-quality pictures that can compete on an international scale. Chief among these independent filmmakers is Youssef Chahine. Both *Black Waters* and *Cairo Station* (1958) are portraits of working-class Egypt; *Cairo Station* is about a lame newspaper seller who goes insane from thwarted love. Two of his later films, *The Land* and *The Sparrow,* are insightful, political impressions of conflicting Egyptian social forces. The maturation of Chahine's style continues with two of his more recent films, *Alexandra . . . Why*? and *An Egyptian Story*, both heavily autobiographical films dealing with the struggle to find a satisfactory balance between one's own culture and the encroaching Western one.

A promising new director is Daoud Abdel Sayed; his first film *The Vagabonds* (1985) was well received. Since then he has made *The Search for Sayed Marzouk* (1991), which explores the frustrations and anxieties of the Egyptian people through the story of a naive man, and *Kit Kat* (1992), which skillfully displays the lively atmosphere of the Cairo streets as a blind man overcomes his obstacles. Female director Asma El Bakri enjoyed success at international film festivals for her adaptation of Egyptian author Albert Kosseri's novel *Proud and Beggars*, about Egyptian society in the 1940s.

ISRAEL

For centuries, Muslims, Christians, and Jews have fought to control this small piece of relatively arid land. Today, the continuing struggle pits Arab against Jew for control of the homeland the Arabs call Palestine and the Jews call Israel.

Late in the 19th century, the Zionist movement was founded in Europe. Its goal was to create a Jewish state on the land the Hebrews inhabited in biblical times. During the first half of this century, Jews from Europe began immigrating to Israel—an immigration that swelled after 1945 with survivors of the Holocaust. In 1948, the State of Israel was born. Ever since, the politics of the region have been dominated by the competing claims of Arabs and Jews to this piece of land situated between the Jordan River and the Mediterranean Sea.

Partly as a result of wars with its Arab neighbors in 1948, 1956, 1967, and 1973, Israel now controls the disputed territory. But Arab Palestinians comprise nearly half the population of the land under Israeli administration (Israel proper and the occupied territories of the West Bank, Gaza, and the Golan Heights). A Palestinian uprising that began in 1987 in the occupied territories continues to challenge the political and moral authority of the Israeli occupation. Unrest in the occupied territories and Iraqi missile attacks during the Persian Gulf War are reminders of the uncertain future of Israel, a nation that despite its impressive military victories still finds security an elusive goal.

Today, for an insider's look at Israel, push and shove your way onto a bus. Each ride presents a microcosm of Israeli society as varied as the landscape stretching before you. An ultra-Orthodox Hasid, dressed in the black garb of his 18th-century Polish ancestors, sits next to a soldier on his way home for a short leave. An Arab woman in white headdress sits next to an *oleh hadash* (new immigrant) from Argentina, eating falafel. Suddenly the multilingual cacophony dies down. Six piercing beeps signal the beginning of the hourly news broadcast. The bus driver raises the volume on the radio so that passengers can follow world events.

With the places along your route—names like Jericho, Jerusalem, Bethlehem, and Masada—constantly reminding you that this is an ancient land, it is easy to forget that the State of Israel is a relative newcomer to the family of nations. Many Israeli Jews are recent immigrants. The new nation absorbed first the Ashkenazi Jews, refugees from central and eastern Europe, then the Sephardic Jews of the Middle East and North Africa, and next the Falashas, or Ethiopian Jews. The latest wave of immigrants is from the Soviet Union; Israel's efforts to absorb the newest arrivals—half a million in 1990 alone—have strained its limited resources. Each group of immigrants has brought with it its own language, food, music, dress, and traditions, but the renaissance of the Hebrew language has done much to unify these disparate groups. In fact, the efforts of the lexicographer Eliezer Ben Yehuda, the "father of Modern Hebrew," to fashion a modern language out of a biblical tongue are celebrated in a popular song.

The Israeli Defense Forces have also played a significant role in the absorption effort. Men and women alike are drafted at the age of 18, women for two years, men for three. This is followed by reserve duty—until the women become mothers and the men reach the age of 55—for up to 45 days a year. As a result, the army is more than a formidable defense force; it is "the great equalizer."

It may surprise you to learn that the overwhelming majority of Israeli Jews are secular. Nevertheless, religion pervades every aspect of life. Part of the reason for this is rooted in Israel's parliamentary democracy. Since no one party ever wins the majority necessary to take control of Israel's 120-member Knesset (Parliament), small religious parties holding no more than three or four seats can force concessions that affect the whole country. Their influence has resulted in unusual situations and arrangements: There is no bus service on the Sabbath (except in the northern city of Haifa); and on the day before Passover, the State of Israel sells the contents of its granaries to a wealthy Israeli Arab so as to not to be in possession of any leavened substance during the eight-day festival.

A trip to Israel offers the chance to visit important religious sites, ancient archaeological digs, and modern cities. You can relax on Mediterranean beaches, explore the Negev Desert, scuba dive in the Gulf of Aqaba, or ski on Mount Hermon. It also provides a chance to better understand the contemporary struggles of the different peoples who inhabit this ancient land.

—Carina Klein, New York, New York

Official name: State of Israel. **Area:** 7,847 square miles (about the size of Massachusetts). **Population:** 4,477,000. **Population density:** 570 inhabitants per square mile. **Capital:** Jerusalem (the United States and most of the international community recognize Tel Aviv as the capital). **Largest city:** Jerusalem (pop. 493,000, including East Jerusalem). **Language:** Hebrew, Arabic. **Religion:** Judaism, Islam. **Per capita income:** US$10,500. **Currency:** Shekel. **Literacy rate:** 81%. **Average daily high/low:** Jerusalem: January, 55°F/41°F; July, 87°F/63°F. **Average number of days with precipitation:** Jerusalem: January, 9; July, 0.

TRAVEL

A passport valid for nine months from the date of your arrival is required for U.S. citizens. Onward or return tickets are also required. However, a visa is not needed for tourist stays of less than three months. For specific requirements, check with the **Embassy of Israel** (3514 International Drive NW, Washington, DC 20008; (202) 364-5557) or check with an Israeli consulate in New York, Chicago, Boston, Houston, Los Angeles, New Orleans, Philadelphia, San Francisco, Detroit, or Newark. **Note:** Many Arab countries will not let you enter if you have evidence of a visit to Israel in your passport. On request, Israeli passport officials can put your visa stamp on a removable piece of paper when you enter the country.

Traveling in Israel itself has been little affected by Palestinian unrest in the occupied territories. However, travel into the West Bank or Gaza Strip is not always advisable. Before you go, consult the U.S. Department of State's **Consular Information Sheet** (see pages 8–9) on Israel for any travel warnings that may be in effect. You might also want to become more informed about the *intifadeh* and the political situation in the Middle East. *Conflicts and Contradictions*, by Meron Beneviste (an Israeli geographer), is a good examination of the dilemma of Israel/Palestine and the legitimate and powerful claims of two ancient peoples for the same land.

Getting Around

It's easy to get around Israel; distances are short and there is good and inexpensive **bus** service. Be aware that there is no bus service, however, between Friday afternoon and Saturday night (*shabbat*) except in Haifa. Egged Bus Cooperative has a virtual monopoly on bus routes throughout Israel. Students with the **International Student Identity Card** receive a 10-percent discount on all Egged fares. Egged also offers a number of bus tours to areas of interest; for more information, call Egged's U.S. office, (800) 682-3333.

Trains offer another travel option, though service is limited and, like buses, trains don't run during *shabbat*. One rail line runs from Nahariya through Haifa and Tel Aviv and north along the coast. A second route runs between Tel Aviv and Israel. Students with the International Student Identity Card receive a substantial 50-percent discount on train fares.

Shared taxis (carrying up to seven passengers) operate between cities and towns, leaving when filled and dropping off and picking up passengers along the way. They are cheaper than regular taxis but more expensive than buses; they operate on Saturday and late at night, when buses don't. Try to agree on a price before setting out. Most people find that the extensive public transportation system makes renting a car unnecessary. Renting a **car** is fairly easy, however, although you'll need an International Driving Permit (see page 52).

Hiking is a popular pastime in Israel. For information on hiking routes, contact the **Society for the Protection of Nature (SPNI)**, 13 Helena HaMalka Street, Jerusalem; (972) 2-252357.

Eating and Sleeping

There are about 30 **youth hostels** in Israel. For more information, contact Hostelling International/American Youth Hostels (see page 54) or the **Israel Youth Hostels Association**, PO Box 1075, 3 Dorot Rishonim Street, Jerusalem 91009; (972) 2-252706; fax (972) 2-250676. For information on **YMCA** accommodations, contact The Y's Way (see pages 53–54).

Several Israeli universities offer affordable dormitory lodgings to travelers. For more information, contact ISSTA Lines (see "Especially for Students and Young People," below) or consult Campus Travel Service's *US and Worldwide Travel Accommodations Guide* (see page 54).

Throughout Israel, there are 40 **Christian hospices**, most of them old monasteries. Located near important religious sites, these hospices are officially intended as inexpensive lodgings for Christians on pilgrimage, but many welcome tourists. For safety, cleanliness, and low-cost bed and breakfast, they're hard to beat. For a list of hospices, contact the **Ministry of Tourism**, Pilgrimage Promotion, Youth and Student Division, PO Box 1018, Jerusalem 91009; (972) 2-240553.

Especially for Students and Young People

Israel's student travel bureau and issuer of the International Student Identity Card is **ISSTA Lines**, 109 Ben Yehuda Street, Tel Aviv 63401; (972) 3-5440111; fax (972) 3-5440312. ISSTA Lines' 11 other offices in Israel include Jerusalem, Haifa, and Beersheba. They provide travel services and book accommodations for Israel and other countries. They can also provide information on student and youth discounts available in Israel.

For Further Information

For general tourist information, contact the Israel Government Tourist Office (see "Meeting the People," above), which can provide you with information on camping and youth hostels, among many other topics.

One of the best guidebooks for the independent traveler on a budget is *Israel: A Travel Survival Kit* ($16.95), which combines practical travel facts with authoritative historical references and covers both the modern state and the ancient biblical country. Another helpful budget guide is *Let's Go: Israel and Egypt* ($16.95). An excellent book to read in preparation for your trip is *Insight Guide: Israel* ($19.95). For more information on Lonely Planet, *Let's Go*, and *Insight* guides, see pages 56–57.

WORK

Persons interested in working in Israel are required to obtain a special work permit. The prospective employer must apply to the Ministry of the Interior in Israel for approval. When in Israel students may secure employment and obtain the necessary work permit while in the country. According to the Consulate General of Israel, Israeli missions abroad are in no position to offer job placement services or information; employment possibilities should be investigated while in Israel.

Internships

A program offered by a member of the Council on International Educational Exchange is listed below.

Association for International Practical Training. *IAESTE Trainee Program.* On-the-job training for undergraduate and graduate students in technical fields such as engineering, computer science, agriculture, architecture, mathematics, and the natural and physical sciences. See page 19 for more information.

Working on a Kibbutz

Kibbutz Aliya (110 East 59th Street, New York, NY 10022) is the U.S. representative for kibbutzim in Israel, and offers young Americans (ages 18 to 35) the opportunity to live and work in one of these communities that accept volunteer workers from all over the world. Further information is available from Kibbutz Aliya upon request.

A variety of programs that bring young people to Israel for periods of a summer, a semester, six months, or a year are sponsored by the **American Zionist Youth Foundation**, 110 East 59th Street, New York, NY 10022; (212) 339-6002. Other options include summer programs, long-term programs, a semester at an Israeli University, and a work/study program on kibbutzim.

Working on an Archaeological Dig

Another work possibility in Israel is volunteering for an archaeological dig. A listing of archaeological excavations open to volunteers is put together each January by the **Ministry of Education and Culture**, Department of Antiquities, PO Box 586, Jerusalem 91004. You must be at least 17 years of age, however, and be prepared to work for at least a week or two. In addition, volunteers must be physically fit and capable of doing strenuous work in a hot climate. The listing of such digs is also available from the Israel Government Tourist Office (see "Meeting the People," above), or the American Zionist Youth Foundation (see "Working on a Kibbutz," above).

STUDY

If you are interested in enrolling at an Israeli university, you can contact the New York offices of the following organizations:

- **American Friends of Tel Aviv University**, 360 Lexington Avenue, New York, NY 10017; (212) 687-5651.
- **American Friends of Haifa University**, 488 Madison Avenue, New York, NY 10022; (212) 838-8069.
- **Hebrew University of Jerusalem, Office of Academic Affairs**, 11 East 69th Street, New York, NY 10021; (212) 472-2288
- **American Society for Technion—Israel Institute of Technology**, 810 Seventh Avenue, New York, NY 10019; (212) 262-6200; fax (212) 262-6155.
- **American Associates of Ben-Gurion University of the Negev**, 342 Madison Avenue, Room 1924, New York, NY 10173; (212) 687-7721.
- **American Committee for the Weizmann Institute of Science**, 51 Madison Avenue, New York, NY 10010; (212) 779-2500.

The **Hebrew University of Jerusalem** offers scholarships to U.S. students in a number of different fields. For applications and information, contact the Office of Academic Affairs at the Friends of Hebrew University (above).

The following academic programs are offered by CIEE-member institutions. Unless otherwise noted, consult Appendix I for the addresses of the colleges and universities listed in this section. In addition to the programs below, Pepperdine University, Syracuse University, and University of Wisconsin at Madison offer programs open to their own students only.

Semester and Academic Year

General Studies

Boston University. Haifa. Semester and academic year. Hebrew language and liberal arts studies at University of Haifa. Eight-week stay at a kibbutz prior to enrollment in university. Freshmen to seniors with 3.0 GPA; one semester of Hebrew language recommended. Apply by March 15 for fall and academic year; October 15 for spring.

Hebrew University of Jerusalem. *Freshman Program*. Jerusalem. Academic year. Humanities, social sciences, and Hebrew language. Dormitory housing. High-school graduates in good academic standing. Apply by April 15.

Graduate Studies Program. Jerusalem. Semester and academic year. Seminars and tutorials in Jewish studies, politics and society of Israel, comparative religion, modern Middle Eastern studies, etc. Dormitory housing. Students who hold a bachelor's degree at least. Apply by April 15 for fall and academic year; November 4 for spring.

Israeli Universities Option. Jerusalem. Four-year undergraduate degree program which begins with one-year *Freshman Program* (see above), followed by three-year regular academic program. Dormitory housing. High-school graduates in good academic standing.

Nativ Program. Jerusalem. Academic year. Offered in conjunction with Department of Youth Activities of United Synagogues of America (USY). University study in combination with leadership training, Jewish living, Israeli life, and kibbutz experience. Courses in Jewish, Israel, and Middle East studies, and Hebrew language. Excursions. High-school graduates in good academic standing. Apply by April 15. Contact: USY–Nativ, 155 Fifth Avenue, New York, NY 10010; (212) 533-7800 ext. 3231.

One Year Program. Jerusalem. Semester and academic year. Humanities, social sciences, and Hebrew language. Sophomores to seniors with 3.0 GPA. Apply by April 15 for fall and academic year; November 4 for spring.

Rutgers University. *Study Abroad in Israel*. Haifa. Academic year. Juniors with 3.0 GPA. Apply by March 1.

State University of New York—Empire State College. *Semester Program in Israel*. Jerusalem and other sites. Fall and spring semesters. Offered in cooperation with College Consortium for International Studies (CCIS). Geography, Hebrew language at all levels, history, Israeli studies, and Jewish studies; individualized tutorials and field studies. Internships and voluntary-service opportunities. Sophomores to graduate students and adults with 2.5 GPA. Apply by June 1 for fall; November 1 for spring.

Syracuse University. *Ben-Gurion University of the Negev*. Beersheba. Semester and academic year. Hebrew language, and Middle East and Jewish anthropology, biology, history, literature, political science, psychology, and sociology. Sophomores to seniors with 3.0 GPA. Apply by March 15 for fall and academic year; October 15 for spring.

Tel Aviv. Fall and spring semesters. Sophomores to seniors with 3.0 GPA. Apply by March 15 for fall; October 15 for spring. Contact: (800) 235-3472.

University of North Carolina at Chapel Hill. *UNC Program to Hebrew University of Jerusalem*. Jerusalem. Academic year. Business, Hebrew language, Jewish studies, math, Middle Eastern studies, and natural sciences. Sophomores to graduate students with 3.0 GPA. Apply by March 15.

UNC Program to Ben-Gurion University of the Negev. Beersheba. Sophomores to graduate students with 3.0 GPA. Apply by February 14.

University of Notre Dame. *International Study Program in Jerusalem.* Jerusalem. Spring. Arabic, theology, history, and government. Sophomores to graduate students with 2.5 GPA. Apply by October 15.

Political Science

Earlham College. *Great Lakes Jerusalem Program.* West Bank and Gaza Strip. Fall semester. Peace studies, sociology, politics, and history. Sophomores to seniors. Apply by January 31. Contact: International Programs Office, Earlham College, Richmond, IN 47374; (317) 983-1424.

Summer and Short-Term

Archaeology and Classical Studies

Michigan State University. *Archaeology, Modern Hebrew, and History of Religion.* Haifa University in Haifa. Summer. Sophomores to graduate students with elementary Hebrew. Apply by April 15. Contact: Office of Overseas Study, 108 International Center, Michigan State University, East Lansing, MI 48824-1035; (517) 353-8920.

Ramapo College of New Jersey. *Excavation at Tel Hadar.* Five weeks in June and July. Offered in cooperation with New Jersey Archaeological Consortium. Courses in field archaeology and Biblical archaeology plus excavation of Canaanite, Geshurite, and Aramaean strata at Tel Hadar. Excursions and kibbutz housing. Sophomores to graduate students and nonstudents. Apply by April 30. Contact: Study-Abroad Office, Ramapo College of New Jersey, 505 Ramapo Valley Road, Room D-204, Mahwah, NJ 07430-9926; (201) 529-7463.

University of Connecticut. *Archaeological Dig in Sepphoris, Israel.* Five weeks in summer. Offered in cooperation with Duke University. Archaeology of Roman Palestine, Israel in Talmudic times, and Hebrew language. First-year college students to graduate students. Apply by March 1.

University of Wisconsin at Madison. *Archaeological Summer Program at Caesarea Maritima.* Archaeological dig at a Roman/ Byzantine port city. Modern field techniques and Middle Eastern cultural history. Sophomores and above. Apply by third Friday in March.

Communications

New York University. *Journalism Program in Israel.* Four weeks in early summer. Israeli culture, history, politics, and journalism with specific emphasis on government relations, censorship, and border nation relations. Juniors to graduate students. Apply by April 1. Contact: Israel Program, Department of Journalism, College of Arts and Sciences, NYU, 10 Washington Place, 5th Floor, New York, NY 10003; (212) 998-7970.

General Studies

Hebrew University of Jerusalem. *Summer Courses.* Jerusalem. Archaeology, Israel studies, Jewish studies, comparative religion, Middle East studies, and international relations. Excursions and dormitory housing. Undergraduates, graduate students, and adults with one year of university study. Apply by May 1 for July session; June 1 for August session.

State University of New York at Oneonta. *Israel Program.* Tel Aviv and other sites. Summer. Economic, social, political, and religious institutions of

modern Israel. Excursions and optional kibbutz stay. High-school students to college seniors and continuing-education students. Rolling admissions. Contact: International Education Office, Netzer Building 332C, SUNY at Oneonta, Oneonta, NY 13820-4015; (607) 436-3369.
State University of New York—Empire State College. *Semester Program in Israel.* Jerusalem and other sites. Summer. Offered in cooperation with College Consortium for International Studies (CCIS). Geography, Hebrew language at all levels, history, Israeli studies, and Jewish studies; individualized tutorials and field studies. Internships and voluntary-service opportunities. Sophomores to graduate students and adults with 2.5 GPA. Apply by May 1.
Villanova University. *Jerusalem/Birzeit Summer Program.* Jerusalem and Birzeit. Early July to late August. First-year college students to seniors with 2.5 GPA. Apply by March 15.

Hebrew Language and Culture

Hebrew University of Jerusalem. *Hebrew Ulpan.* Jerusalem. Eight-week summer program from August through September and four-week winter program from late January to late February. Intensive Hebrew language program. Persons who have completed at least one year of university study. Apply by July 1 for summer; January 1 for winter.
Summer Courses. Jerusalem. Five-week Hebrew and Arabic-language program. Undergraduates, graduate students, and adults with one year of university study. Apply by May 1.

International Relations

State University of New York College at New Paltz. *Israel Study Mission.* Various locations. Summer. Study tour of Israeli society and Israeli-Palestinian conflict, including meetings with Israeli and Palestinian political figures, journalists, scholars, religious leaders, and students. First-year college students to graduate students. Rolling admissions. Contact: Office of International Education, HAB 33, SUNY College at New Paltz, New Paltz, NY 12561; (914) 257-3125.

EXPLORING THE CULTURE

Readings

The works of a number of Israeli writers are readily available in translation in the United States. One of the most popular and influential Israeli writers is Amos Oz, who writes in Hebrew about contemporary Israeli society. Oz's first book, *Elsewhere, Perhaps* (1966) depicts life on a kibbutz, and his novel *In the Land of Israel* (1983) chronicles his conversations with people from all walks of life about Israel and the Palestinian conflict. *Black Box* explores the breakdown of a marriage. Another major Israeli novelist is Abraham B. Yehoshua, whose most recent work, *Five Seasons*, deals with a widower coming to terms with his changed life. Nobel Prize–winner Shmuel Agnon's book *In the Heart of the Seas* is about a journey to Israel in 1947.

David Grossman, a leading Israeli author, writes in *The Smile of the Lamb* (1983) of a young Israeli soldier forced to grapple with living according to traditional values of morality and justice while enforcing the Israeli occupation of the West Bank. His latest book, *Sleeping on a Wire: Conversations with*

Palestinians in Israel (1993) focuses on the poignant situation of the Arabs (and their descendants) who remained in Israel after the 1948 war. In Grossman's *See Under: Love* (1989), set in Israel in the late 1950s, a child tries to make sense of the "Nazi Beast" he hears about all around him.

Arabesques, by Anton Shammas, is the story of an Israeli Arab family and was the first novel written in Hebrew by an Israeli Arab. It caused a sensation when it was first published in 1986. The first definitive collection in English of Palestinian writing has been recently published: *Anthology of Modern Palestinian Literature*, edited by Salma Khadra Jayyusi. This massive volume includes works of poetry, fiction, and personal accounts of the Palestinian experience from the turn of the century to the present. Kathryn Abdul-Baki offers an unusual point of view as an English-speaking Arab writer, born of an Arab father and an American mother, in her collection of stories of the Middle East, *Fields of Fig and Olive* (1991). *A Season of Stones* (1991), by Western author Helen Winternitz, is an insider's account of life in a Palestinian village in the Israeli-occupied territory.

MOROCCO

Although Morocco is closer to the United States than most of the nations of Europe, few Americans are familiar with this land of dramatic landscape, colorful history, and ancient traditions. Morocco lies in the northwest corner of Africa, little more than an hour's ferry ride from Spain across the Strait of Gibraltar. It is bordered by the Mediterranean and the Atlantic to the north and west, and the Sahara desert to the south and east. Great mountain peaks, hills, fertile valleys, and expansive plains provide the backdrop for the villages and farmland that make up rural Morocco. This exotic scenery has long attracted Hollywood directors, and many well-known films have been made there, including *Lawrence of Arabia*, and more recently, *The Last Temptation of Christ*.

In ancient times the Phoenicians, Carthaginians, and Romans all made use of these shores. But Morocco's national history began in the eighth century A.D. with the arrival of Arabs from across North Africa, making Morocco "Al Maghrib Al Aqsa," Islam's westernmost territory. The indigenous Berbers gradually converted to Islam, and a series of Arab dynasties ruled Morocco until the 20th century.

Part of Morocco was annexed by Spain in the 19th century, and the rest of Morocco became a protectorate of France in 1912; the country regained its independence in 1956. The current form of government is a constitutional monarchy, although King Hassan II has enjoyed almost absolute power since he inherited the throne in 1961. He leads a country of 26 million Moroccans who are predominantly Sunni Moslems with a mixture of Berber and Arab heritages. The national language is Arabic, although French is taught in schools and spoken by many Moroccans. Berber languages are still spoken in the more remote areas.

While Morocco remains a predominantly rural society, a major effort toward industrialization is well underway. A consistently high birthrate has created a population that is largely young, and unemployment has been a major concern in recent years, particularly in the major cities.

Elements of the old and the new often appear in striking juxtaposition. It is typical to see a mother wearing a long caftan and veil walking with a daughter dressed in blue jeans and high heels. Men wear Western suits under their djellabahs. In the valleys of the Atlas Mountains, the way of life for the Berbers in fortress towns has remained unchanged for centuries, while their counterparts in Casablanca make their homes in high-rise apartments.

The influence of the French is everywhere, but because they built modern facilities outside the old town walls, Morocco's imperial cities remain much as they were in previous centuries. Fez was a powerful center of art, intellectual life, and commerce in medieval times. To wander its narrow winding streets, accessible only on foot or by mule, is truly to take a trip back in time. To the south, the city of Marrakesh stands in a palm-covered plain at the foot of the snowcapped High Atlas. Rabat, Morocco's capital, boasts well-preserved monuments and an imposing fortress that faces the Atlantic.

The medina—the old Arab quarter, usually including a market—of any Moroccan city dazzles the visitor with fortune-tellers, hustlers, and merchants in their seemingly endless throng of activity. Traditional ceramics, textiles, and wood and metal work can be purchased by anyone willing to go through a lively bargaining process. Getting around Morocco takes energy, but a quiet moment in the evening can bring the smell of saffron in the air, friendly conversation over mint tea, and the call to prayer echoing from the minaret of a nearby mosque.

—Brooke Pickering, New York, New York

Official name: Kingdom of Morocco. **Size:** 172,413 square miles (larger than California). **Population:** 26,181,000. **Population density:** 151 inhabitants per square mile. **Capital:** Rabat (pop. 556,000). **Largest city:** Casablanca (pop. 2,600,000). **Language:** Arabic, Berber. **Religion:** Sunni Moslem. **Per capita income:** US $990. **Currency:** Dirham. **Literacy rate:** 35%. **Average daily high/low:** Rabat: January, 63°F/46°F; June, 78°F/60°F. **Average number of days with precipitation:** Rabat: January, 9; June, 2.

TRAVEL

A passport is required for U.S. citizens visiting Morocco, but a visa is not required for stays of up to 90 days. For further information, contact the **Embassy of Morocco**, 1601 21st Street NW, Washington, DC 20009; (202) 462-7979. You can also contact the **Moroccan Consulate General** in New York, (212) 758-2625.

Getting Around

Algeciras, Spain, is the starting point for many travelers going to Morocco from Europe. The **ferry** across the Strait of Gibraltar takes about 90 minutes to Ceuta or about 2½ hours to Tangier.

The quickest way to get around is by **train**. Interrail passes are no longer valid on trains in Morocco. The main north-south rail line connects Tangier, Rabat, Casablanca, and Marrakesh. Another line runs from Casablanca and Rabat to Fez and east to the Algerian border. Train travel in first- or second-class compartments is the most comfortable means of public transportation and only a little more expensive than bus fare. Third- and fourth-class cars, while cheap, are extremely cramped.

Morocco's **bus** network is much more extensive than its rail system. On the down side, buses are usually crowded, poorly ventilated, and slow-moving, making frequent roadside stops to pick up and discharge passengers. The fastest and most comfortable service is offered by the national bus company, Compagnie de Transports de Maroc (CTM).

Intercity service is also provided by ***grands taxis***, as opposed to *petits taxis*, which operate only within city limits. Also, collective taxis provide long-distance service for groups. **Collective taxis**, in the form of minivans, board at designated taxi stands bound for specific destinations. They are faster than buses and easier to negotiate than *grands taxis*, as passengers pay a common flat fare.

You may find a car best for exploring out-of-the-way places. Morocco's road system is generally good, though many roads are narrow. Road signs are in Arabic and French. Primary roads (indicated with a P) are in better condition than secondary (S) roads. **Car** rentals are available in major cities from both Moroccan and international companies.

Eating and Sleeping

Morocco is full of inexpensive hotels, the cheapest usually being in the *medina*, or old town. There are also several **youth hostels** throughout Morocco, including Casablanca, Fez, Marrakesh, Rabat, and Tangier, among other cities. For more information, contact Hostelling International/American Youth Hostels (see page 54) or **Fédération Royale Marocaine des Auberges de Jeunes**, Boulevard Okba Ben Nafii, Meknès; (212) 5-524698.

For Further Information

General tourist information can be obtained from the **Moroccan National Tourist Office**, 20 East 46th Street, New York, NY 10017; (212) 557-2520.

A good budget-travel guide to Morocco and neighboring countries is *Morocco, Algeria, and Tunisia: A Travel Survival Kit*, available for $16.95 from Lonely Planet Publications. *Let's Go: Spain and Portugal* ($16.95) has a chapter on Morocco sufficient for a brief visit. An excellent book to read in preparation for your trip is *Insight Guide: Morocco* ($19.95). For more information on Lonely Planet, *Let's Go*, and *Insight* guides, see pages 56–57.

WORK

It is necessary to obtain a work permit to work in Morocco. Application for the permit is made by the employer. First priority for employment is given to Moroccan citizens.

Voluntary Service

CIEE places young people in voluntary-service workcamps in Morocco organized by Chantiers Jeunnesse Maroc in Rabat. These workcamps bring together volunteers from various countries for a three-week period to do gardening and environmental work. Volunteers must be 18 years of age or older and speak French. Room and board are provided. The applications of U.S. residents are processed by CIEE. For more information contact CIEE's Voluntary Service Department.

STUDY

The following are academic programs offered by CIEE-member institutions. Unless otherwise noted, consult Appendix I for the addresses of the colleges and universities listed in this section. In addition to the programs below, the University of Wisconsin at Madison offers programs open to their students only.

Semester and Academic Year

General Studies

State University of New York at Binghamton. *Arabic Studies in Tangier.* Semester and academic year. Intensive language study. Sophomores to graduate students with elementary proficiency in modern standard Arabic. Apply by April 1 for fall and academic year; October 1 for spring. Contact: Department of Classical and Near Eastern Studies, SUNY at Binghamton, PO Box 6000, Binghamton, NY 13902-6000; (607) 777-2000.

World Learning/School for International Training. *College Semester Abroad.* Rabat. Fall and spring semesters. Arabic-language study, life and culture seminar, field-study methods seminar, and independent-study project, homestay, and educational travel to Fez, Meknes, High Atlas, and Marrakesh. Sophomores to seniors with 2.5 GPA. Apply by May 7 for fall; October 7 for spring. Contact: College Semester Abroad Admissions at (800) 336-1616.

International Relations

University of Minnesota. *Minnesota Studies in International Development (MSID).* Academic year. Predeparture coursework at the University of Minnesota fall quarter; internship in development-related research or action project in winter and spring quarters required. Juniors to graduates and adults with interest in development. 2.5 GPA and two years of French or one year of Arabic. Apply by May 1. Contact: The Global Campus. 106C Nicholson Hall, 216 Pillsburg Drive SE., Minneapolis, MN 55455-0138; (612) 625-3379.

Summer

General Studies

University of Wisconsin at Milwaukee. *Summer in Morocco.* Rabat. Summer. Offered in conjunction with the University of Wisconsin at Madison. Sophomores to seniors with 2.75 GPA. Apply by February 12.

EXPLORING MOROCCAN CULTURE

Readings and Films

English translations of works by native Moroccan writers have been slow to appear, but recently a few English-language publishers have taken an interest in the literature of this country. Contemporary storyteller Mohammed Mrabet is one of Morocco's leading writers. His tales, translated by American writer

Paul Bowles, are filled with intrigue and unexpected plot twists (often inspired by some creative pipe-smoking). *Love with a Few Hairs* (1968) depicts the contrasts between sophisticated Western culture and ancient Moroccan beliefs in the story of a young Moroccan man who marries an Arab girl. *The Boy Who Set the Fire and Other Stories, The Lemon*, and *M'Hashish* are other good collections of Mrabet's stories, all translated by Bowles.

Driss Chraibi is another modern-day Moroccan writer who, like many of his peers, shows a deep concern for the identity of postcolonial Morocco. *The Simple Past*, translated by Hugh A. Harter, is a semi-autobiographical account of a young man who travels from his native Morocco to Paris. Critically acclaimed author Tahar Ben Jalloun's *The Sand Child* is a light novel about a girl whose father brings her up as a boy. Also concerned with growing up in Morocco is *Messaouda* (1986), by Abdelhak Serhane, a semi-autobiographical account of the cruelty experienced by a boy in a poor village. The condition of women in Moroccan society is addressed by Morocco's leading sociologist Fatima Mernissi in *Beyond the Veil: Male-Female Dynamics in Modern Moslem Society* (1987) and *Doing Daily Battle: Interviews with Moroccan Women* (1989).

The most celebrated and prolific non-native writer on Morocco today is Paul Bowles, an American and longtime resident of the country. His books and stories, written in a readable, economic style, offer an insightful view into the culture. His novel *The Sheltering Sky* (1949) was made into a movie in 1990 by director Bernardo Bertolucci. Both the novel and the film are about the bizarre journey of an American couple through the Sahara desert. *The Spider's House* (1982) is an excellent political novel set in the city of Fez during the fight for independence, while *The Delicate Prey and Other Stories* (1980) and *Midnight Mass* (1983) are both story collections. Bowles has also written many travel journal–style accounts of the country: *Points in Time* (1982) and *Their Heads Are Green and Their Hands Are Blue*.

The city of Marrakesh is highlighted in Nobel Prize–winner Elias Canetti's *The Voices of Marrakesh* (1984), and in *A Year in Marrakesh* (1984), by Peter Mayne. *Smara: The Forbidden City* (1932), by Michel Vieuchange, is the journal of the then 26-year-old adventurer who traveled 900 miles alone through southern Morocco disguised as a Berber woman in order to visit the ruins of Smara, an abandoned city never seen before by a European.

TUNISIA

Even the name of Tunisia's main airport, Tunis-Carthage International, reminds arriving visitors that this nation, located at the crossroads of the Mediterranean, has a long and proud history. Phoenicians, Carthaginians, Romans, Arabs, Turks, French—all have left their mark on Tunisia.

Arab conquerors, arriving in the seventh century, called Tunisia "the green land." In fact, the relatively well-watered north, once the granary of Rome, still grows oranges, olives, and other produce for the tables of Europe. But today, agriculture has been supplanted by the tourist industry and petroleum, from the nearly uninhabited desert that comprises the southern two-thirds of the country, as the leading contributors to the economy.

Everywhere you go you'll find streets, schools, mosques, and other sites named after Habib Bourguiba, the national hero who led Tunisia in its drive for independence from France in 1956 and then served as president for 31 years. Although ousted from power in 1987, his political legacy lives on in the equal legal status of women and the country's ties with the West.

Today, Tunisia is a North African nation with cultural, racial, and linguistic ties to both Europe and the Middle East. This delicate balance is evident everywhere. The Avenue Habib-Bourguiba, hub of the cosmopolitan capital city of Tunis, is lined with cafés serving mint tea and French pastries, while just a few blocks from the city center is the entrance to the medina and the world of the souks, or traditional outdoor markets, that offer a dizzying array of colors, sights, and smells as well as a chance to test your bargaining skills (most Tunisians speak both Arabic and French).

But you won't want to spend all of your time in Tunis. The electric train known as the TGM is an easy and inexpensive way to get out of the city, and the ride offers a slice of Tunisian life most tourists never see. Your fellow passengers will probably strike up a conversation with you as the train whisks past the ruins of Carthage and the picturesque port city of Sidi Bou Said. The last stop will be the beaches of La Marsa. Don't be surprised to see women in bikinis, or even topless. While Islam is the religion of Tunisia, 75 years of mostly French rule and 1.3 million tourists annually, mostly from Western Europe, have had an impact.

—Carina Klein, New York, New York

Official name: Republic of Tunisia. **Area:** 63,170 square miles (about the size of Missouri). **Population:** 8,276,000. **Population density:** 131 inhabitants per square mile. **Capital and largest city:** Tunis (pop. 1,000,000). **Language:** Arabic, French. **Religion:** Islam. **Per capita income:** US$1,253. **Currency:** Tunisian dinar. **Literacy rate:** 62%. **Average daily temperature:** Tunis: June, 94°/66°F; December, 59°/40°F. **Average number of days with precipitation:** Tunis: June, 5; December, 14.

TRAVEL

U.S. citizens will need a valid passport to travel to Tunisia; however, visas are not required for stays of up to four months. For further information, check with the **Embassy of Tunisia**, 1515 Massachusetts Avenue NW, Washington, DC 20005; (202) 862-1850. There are also Tunisian Consulates General in New York and San Francisco.

Getting Around

Tunisia is easily reached by **ferry** from the Italian cities of Genoa, Palermo, or Trapani; or from Marseilles, France. The Tunisian **rail** network serves the major intercity routes and links the country to Algeria. Tunisian trains are comfortable and convenient, but service is less frequent than **buses**, the most common mode of transport. Buses, however, can be crowded and slow. Perhaps the fastest mode of transportation are **louages**, intercity taxis serving fixed routes. *Louages* display their destination on a sign and usually carry five people at a posted per person rate.

Tunisian roads, both surfaced and unpaved, remain in relatively good condition. With the exception of the Tunis-Hammamet superhighway, however, they tend to be narrow. Road signs everywhere are in Arabic and French. Renting a car is relatively easy and cheap, although advance reservations are advisable during the summer tourist season. **Rental cars** are practically the only way to see the southern Sahara region of Tunisia. Bicycles and motorcycles are also available to rent.

Eating and Sleeping

There are about 30 **youth hostels** in Tunisia. For more information, contact Hostelling International/American Youth Hostels (see page 54) or **Association Tunisienne des Auberges de Jeunesse**, 10 rue Ali Bach Hamba, BP 320-1015 Tunis RP; (216) 1-353277; fax (216) 1-352172.

Especially for Students and Young People

Tunisia's student travel bureau and issuer of the International Student Identity Card is **Sotutour**, 2 rue de Sparte, 1000 Tunis RP; (216) 1-348314; fax (216) 1-348284. The organization provides information on student travel and offers a variety of one-week tours, including one that involves four days of camel-trekking in the Sahara.

For Further Information

For general travel information, contact the **Cultural Section in Charge of Tourism** at the Tunisian Embassy (see "Travel," above).

Probably the best guide to the country is *Cadogan Guides' Tunisia* ($17.95). *The Real Guide: Tunisia* ($17) is also good. Budget travelers visiting nearby countries will want to read *Morocco, Algeria, and Tunisia: A Travel Survival Kit* ($16.95). Travelers making a brief trip from Italy will find the Tunisia chapter helpful in *Let's Go: Italy* ($16.95). An excellent book to read in preparation for your trip is *Insight Guide: Tunisia* ($19.95). For more information on *Cadogan Guides, Real Guide*s, Lonely Planet, *Let's Go*, and *Insight* guides, see pages 56–57.

WORK

To hold a regular job in Tunisia, you will need a work permit; a job contract is required before applying. Generally, permits are only granted to those with skills that are not readily obtainable in Tunisia itself. For more information, contact the **Ministère de la Formation et de l'Emplois**, 13 rue Khartoum, 1002 Tunis, Tunisia; (216) 1-682724.

Internships/Traineeships

A program offered by a member of the Council on International Educational Exchange is listed below.

Association for International Practical Training. *IAESTE Trainee Program*. On-the-job training for undergraduate and graduate students in technical fields such as engineering, computer science, agriculture, architecture, mathematics, and the natural and physical sciences. See page 19 for more information.

Voluntary Service

CIEE places young people in voluntary-service workcamps in Tunisia organized by the Association Tunisienne d'Action Volontaire in Tunis. These workcamps bring together volunteers from various countries for two weeks to accomplish a range of construction and restoration projects. Volunteers must be 18 years of age or older and speak French. Room and board are provided. The applications of U.S. residents are processed by CIEE. For more information, contact the International Voluntary Service Department at CIEE.

STUDY

Although there are no study programs offered by CIEE members in Tunisia, a short term of study in the country is easy to arrange, especially at language schools, where you can take courses in French or Arabic.

EXPLORING TUNISIAN CULTURE

Readings

Tunisia's most prominent novelist today, and about the only one who has been translated into English, is Albert Memmi. Although out of print now, his novel *The Pillar of Salt* deals with the author's problem of identity as a North African Jew. Translated by North African travel writer Paul Bowles, *Five Eyes* is a collection of stories by five contemporary Maghrebi writers.

Books about Tunisia by foreigners are much more accessible to the non-Arabic speaker. *About Tunisia* (1961) is J. Anthony's account as an American diplomat in the country before independence, and *Among the Faithful* (1937), by D. Martin, contains sensitive and nonjudgmental descriptions of Tunisian family life. For a good overall background and historical account, try *Tunisia* (1970), by Wilfrid Knapp.

TURKEY

Turkey is a country very much in transition. It is a Muslim country, but one receptive to Western influence. On the same beach, you might see a Turkish woman sunbathing in a bikini while another wades in the shallow water fully dressed in heavy layers of clothing including the traditional head scarf and long, full Turkish pants. Both will point to different interpretations of the Koran to explain their attire, or relative lack thereof. Although bars are still rare in Turkey (in most Muslim countries, drinking alcohol is frowned upon), beer and an anise-like liquor called raki are produced and consumed here. For the most part, however, teahouses, rather than bars, are where people gather socially. Traditional teahouses are almost exclusively male, but many have become used to and even cater to male and female tourists, especially in the larger cities.

Turkey, one of the largest countries in the Middle East, borders on Greece, Bulgaria, Georgia, Armenia, Azerbaijan, Iran, Iraq, and Syria. Culturally, it is as varied as the six different countries it adjoins. Istanbul, the former capital of the Ottoman Empire and a gateway connecting Europe and Asia, is a cosmopolitan city, at once an architectural mosaic of ancient mosques and palaces, working-class neighborhoods with traditional wooden houses, and modern areas complete with skyscrapers. In the western part of the country, tourism has become an important part of the economy. This is most noticeable on the Aegean coast, with its impressive beaches and historic ruins. As you head east, the country becomes poorer and more traditional, although Ankara, the capital city in the center of the country, is a notable exception. The villages along Turkey's northern coast, on the Black Sea, are farming and fishing communities, and the northeast is a rainy mountainous region that grows most of the tea that is drunk in Turkey. The deserts of the southeast, near Iran and Iraq, are the home of the Kurdish-speaking people.

Although attitudes toward Westerners vary in different regions of the country, in general Turks are friendly and interested in meeting people from other countries. One of the best ways to meet them is to go shopping. There are plenty of interesting goods to be bought in flea markets and shops, including the brightly colored, handwoven carpets for which the country is famous. Many areas in Turkey are known for their characteristic styles of carpets and kilims. If you express interest in one, the owner will most likely invite you to sit down and have tea with him as you discuss the carpet. Turks are great businessmen and love to haggle; you'll want to break out your best bargaining skills and match wits with the carpet merchant. Even if you don't buy it, chances are you'll wind up having a lively conversation. But watch out—you may end up the proud owner of a carpet you never realized you needed!

—Mary Leonard, New York, New York

Official name: Republic of Turkey. **Area:** 301,381 square miles (slightly larger than Texas). **Population:** 58,580,000. **Population density:** 194 inhabitants per square mile. **Capital:** Ankara (pop. 2,553,000). **Largest city:** Istanbul (pop. 6,700,000). **Language:** Turkish, Kurdish, Arabic. **Religion:** Islam. **Per capita income:** US$1,160. **Currency:** Turkish Lira. **Literacy rate:** 81%. **Average daily high/low:** Istanbul: January, 45°F/35°F; July, 81°F/65°F. **Average number of days with precipitation:** Istanbul: January, 12; July, 3.

TRAVEL

A passport is required for U.S. citizens traveling to Turkey; however, a visa is not needed for tourist stays of up to three months. For further information, check with the **Embassy of the Republic of Turkey**, 1714 Massachusetts Avenue NW, Washington, DC 20036; (202) 659-8200. There are also Turkish consulates in Chicago, Houston, Los Angeles, and New York.

Getting Around

Travel in Turkey is inexpensive, whatever way you go. **Bus** service is quick, comfortable, and cheap. **Trains** are even less expensive than buses, but they are generally slower and don't serve Turkey's popular western coast. Shared **taxis** (called *dolmus*) follow fixed routes between cities and allow you to get off and on wherever you like. *Dolmus* can be identified by their yellow bands (regular taxis have checkered bands). Hitchers, too, have an easy time in Turkey, where drivers stop for waving hands. Drivers may ask for payment, but will charge you less than the bus. Road signs in English make driving a breeze.

Those traveling to eastern Turkey from Istanbul or any other Western city should consider Turkish Airlines. Domestic fares on Turkish Airlines are reasonable, and flying will save you from a 36-hour ordeal by bus. You can also purchase a **Visit Turkey Pass** in conjunction with an international flight on Turkish Airlines. The Visit Turkey Pass allows two domestic flights for $189, three for $249, or five for $349. The pass is good for one month. As Turkish Airlines offers discount fares to youths under 25, however, you might find that regular one-way tickets are cheaper than the pass. For more information, contact Turkish Airlines at (800) 874-8875. Another option is Turkish Maritime Lines, which operates passenger ships along the Mediterranean, Aegean, and Black Sea coasts.

Eating and Sleeping

Budget travelers will want to check into a *pansiyon*; these small, inexpensive hotels usually include breakfast for under $10 a night, and cost even less in eastern Turkey. Turkey's only official youth hostel is the **Yücelt Interyouth Hostel**, at Caferiye Sok 6/1, Sultanahmet 34400, Istanbul; (90) 1-5136150. However, a number of student residences throughout Turkey double as hostels. For more information, contact either of Turkey's student and youth travel organizations (see "Especially for Students and Young People," below). For information on campgrounds, contact the Turkish Government Tourism Office (see "For Further Information," below).

Especially for Students and Young People

There are two student/youth travel organizations in Turkey, both issuers of the International Student Identity Card:

- **GENCTUR**, Yerebatan Caddesi 15/3, Sultanahmet 34410, Istanbul; (90) 1-5265409; fax (90) 1-5226223
- **7 TUR**, Inönü Caddesi 37/2, Gümüssuyu 80090, Istanbul; (90) 1-2525921; fax (90) 1-2525924

The International Student Identity Card is widely accepted throughout Turkey. Both organizations distribute guides to discounts available to cardholders.

For Further Information

General tourist information is available from the **Turkish Government Tourism Office**, 821 United Nations Plaza, New York, NY 10017; (212) 687-2194; fax (212) 599-7568.

The most complete guide to the country for budget travelers is *Turkey: A Travel Survival Kit* ($14.95) from Lonely Planet Publications. For the most historical detail, however, consult *Cadogan Guides' Turkey* ($16.95). Also good is *The Real Guide: Turkey* ($13.95). An excellent book to read in preparation for your trip is *Insight Guide: Turkey* ($19.95). For more information on Lonely Planet, *Cadogan Guides, Real Guide*s, and *Insight Guide*s, see pages 56–57. *Let's Go: Greece and Turkey* includes extensive information on traveling in all parts of the country. It's available for $16.99 in most bookstores and at Council Travel offices.

WORK

If you want to work in Turkey, you'll have to obtain a work visa prior to entering the country, and to get a work visa, you'll have to have a job already in Turkey. If you'll be staying less than six months (or working for the government), you must submit a copy of the employment contract and an official letter with a description of your position (including the duration of the job) when applying for the visa. If you're planning to stay more than six months in an advisory, technical, or managerial capacity in the private sector, you must obtain the approval of the State Planning Organization and submit this along with the contract and letter at the time of application. For more information contact the Turkish Embassy (see "Travel," above).

Internships/Traineeships

The following program is offered by a member of the Council on International Educational Exchange.

Association for International Practical Training. *IAESTE Trainee Program.* On-the-job training for undergraduate and graduate students in technical fields such as engineering, computer science, agriculture, architecture, mathematics and the natural and physical sciences. See page 19 for more information.

Voluntary Service

CIEE places young people in voluntary-service workcamps in Turkey organized by Genctur in Istanbul. At these workcamps, groups of up to 20 people from various countries work on projects involving construction, gardening, or archaeology. Most camps are two weeks in length. Volunteers must be at least 18 years old and willing to work an average of eight hours a day for two to three weeks. They receive room and board in return. The applications of U.S. residents are processed by CIEE. For more information, contact the International Voluntary Service Department at CIEE.

STUDY

Requests for specific information on studying in Turkey should be directed to the Educational Counselor's Office of the Turkish Embassy (see "Travel," above).

Following are the study programs offered by CIEE-member institutions. Unless otherwise noted, consult Appendix I for the addresses of the colleges and universities listed in this section.

Semester and Academic Year

General Studies

Beloit College. *Turkey Exchange Program.* Istanbul. Spring semester. International relations, economics, business, Turkish studies, Turkish language and other disciplines; study at Marmara University with Turkish students (instruction in English). Juniors and seniors with 2.75 GPA. Apply by November 1.

Summer and Short-Term

Business

Ball State University. *Summer Study Abroad in Turkey*. Istanbul. Six-week program at Istanbul University's Silivri campus. Excursions. Sophomores to graduate students with 2.5 GPA. Apply by April 1. Contact: Management Science Department, College of Business, WB 255, Ball State University, Muncie, IN 47306; (317) 285-5313.

EXPLORING TURKISH CULTURE

Readings and Films

Due more to neglect than lack of talent, the majority of Turkish authors have not been translated into English. One exception is Yasar Kemal, saved from obscurity by his wife who has translated almost all of his works. His latest novels, however, are likely to be more accessible: *The Sea-Crossed Fisherman*, a psychological drama, contrasts the struggles between an old man trying to save the dolphins and a desperate city fisherman, and *The Saga of the Seagull*, also situated in a fishing village in Istanbul. Another recent novel, *The Birds Have Also Gone*, is a tender story about bird catchers on the Çukurova plain.

A few other Turkish authors, including Mehmet Nusret Nesin and Edouard Roditi, have been translated and published recently in the U.S. A collection of 21 of Nesin's stories, ranging widely in style, is available under the title *Turkish Short Stories from Four Decades* (1991) from Three Continents Press in Washington, DC. New Directions puts out Roditi's *The Delights of Turkey*, his collection of 20 short stories—some gentle, some risqué—set in rural Turkey and in Istanbul. For a sampling of Turkish authors, try a short-story anthology like *A Dot on the Map*, published by Indiana University's Turkish Studies Department.

Yilmaz Güney was the first serious Turkish screenwriter and director to be recognized internationally. Rejecting the usual schmaltzy melodramas that draw the biggest crowds in Turkey, he was the first to address the social concerns of modern-day Turkey in his films, which include *Yol, The Herd*, and *The Enemy*. Erden Kiral's 1984 movie, *The Mirror*, is based on the novel *The White Ox*, by Osman Sahin, about a peasant who discovers that the local landowner is in love with the peasant's wife. A politically sensitive film, *Blackout Nights* (1990), by director Yusuf Kürçenli, is based on an autobiographical novel by prolific Turkish poet Rifat Ilgaz. It recreates his arrest as a suspected communist at the end of WWII while attacking larger issues of censorship and political oppression. Prominent director Ömer Kavur's *Secret Face* is another internationally recognized film.

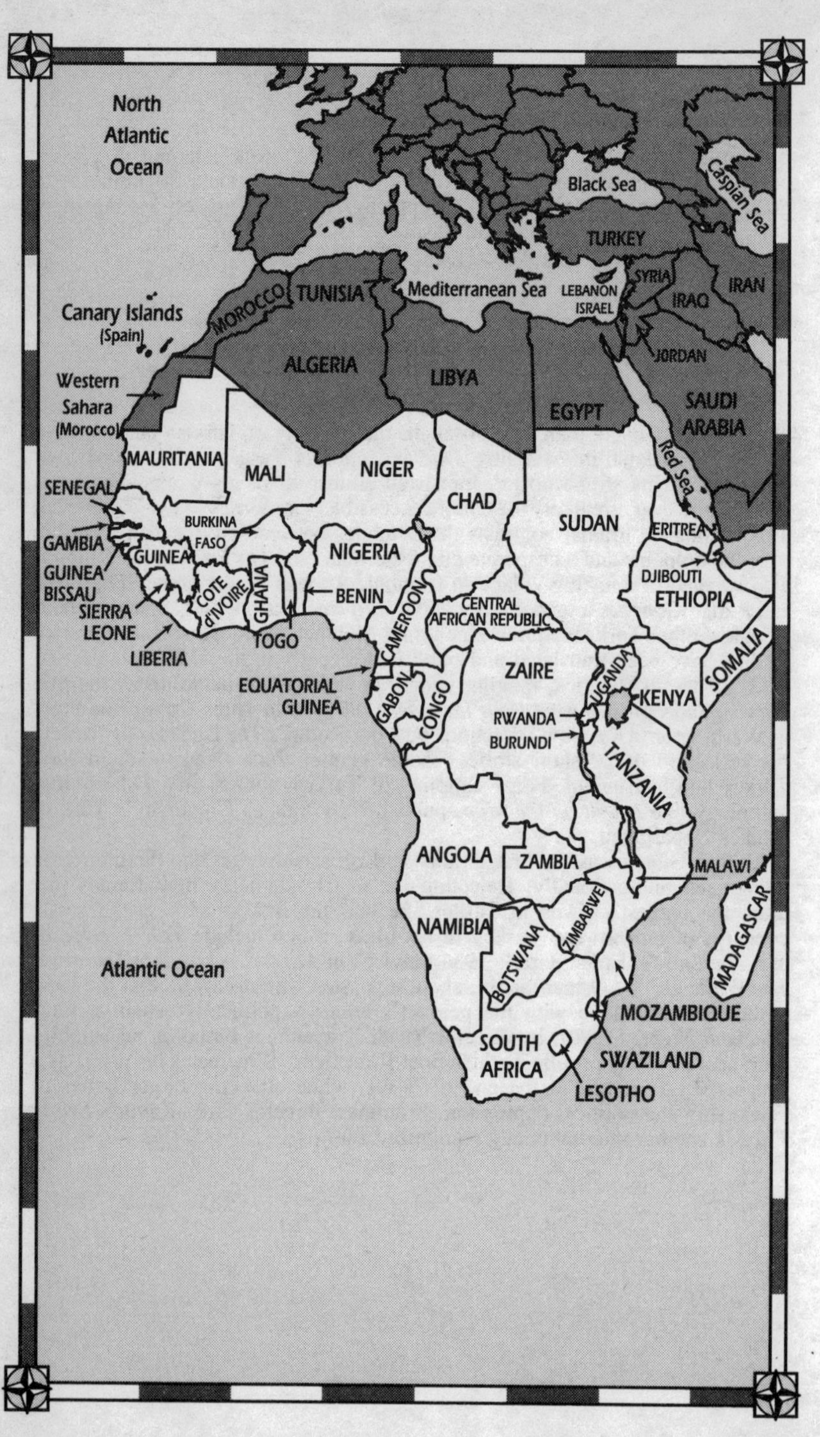
North Atlantic Ocean
Black Sea
Caspian Sea
TURKEY
SYRIA
IRAN
IRAQ
LEBANON
ISRAEL
JORDAN
Mediterranean Sea
MOROCCO
TUNISIA
Canary Islands (Spain)
ALGERIA
LIBYA
EGYPT
SAUDI ARABIA
Western Sahara (Morocco)
Red Sea
MAURITANIA
MALI
NIGER
CHAD
SUDAN
ERITREA
SENEGAL
GAMBIA
BURKINA FASO
GUINEA
GUINEA BISSAU
SIERRA LEONE
LIBERIA
COTE d'IVOIRE
GHANA
TOGO
NIGERIA
BENIN
CAMEROON
CENTRAL AFRICAN REPUBLIC
DJIBOUTI
ETHIOPIA
SOMALIA
EQUATORIAL GUINEA
GABON
CONGO
ZAIRE
UGANDA
KENYA
RWANDA
BURUNDI
TANZANIA
ANGOLA
ZAMBIA
MALAWI
MADAGASCAR
NAMIBIA
BOTSWANA
ZIMBABWE
MOZAMBIQUE
Atlantic Ocean
SOUTH AFRICA
SWAZILAND
LESOTHO

CHAPTER EIGHT

AFRICA SOUTH OF THE SAHARA

A vast continent, Africa offers the visitor an array of impressions and experiences not easily forgotten. A region of immense cultural and linguistic diversity—in fact, more than 800 languages are spoken here—Africa comprises a mass of countries within artificial boundaries arbitrarily drawn by the European colonial powers late in the last century. As a result, many African nations, most of which have come into existence as independent states only within the last 40 years, are still struggling to forge a sense of nationhood among disparate ethnic and linguistic groups.

Substantial economic growth continues to elude most African nations, a disproportionate number of which are classified by the United Nations in the lowest economic bracket. Some regions have been hit hard by a deadly mixture of recurring drought, poor land management, political conflict, and rapid population growth that has often resulted in famine. These problems are typified by conditions in Liberia and Somalia. Countries like Ghana and Zimbabwe, however, have a decidedly brighter future.

A visit to Africa can do much to broaden one's image of this complex and rapidly changing continent. Africa offers perceptive students, volunteer workers, and adventurous travelers the chance to experience a radically different way of life while gaining a new perspective on themselves and the world. Among those who have had the chance to experience Africa as more than just a casual tourist, few leave the continent unchanged.

TRAVEL

The Essentials

A trip to sub-Saharan Africa is a trip off the beaten tourist path and requires some initiative and preparation. One way to prepare is to talk to people who have traveled there. Another way is to read some of the books you'll find recommended in this chapter. These—especially the literary works by African authors—will help put you in touch with the worlds you are about to encounter.

Before traveling to any part of Africa, be sure you understand the political realities of the region or country you're planning to visit. Political instability (at press time, in countries as diverse as South Africa and Sudan) can present certain problems for the traveler. It is important to stay informed and to be flexible in your travel plans. Unfortunately, coverage of African political news in the U.S. press is notoriously poor. Instead, you might need to turn to *Jeune Afrique*, *Africa News*, *Africa Report*, *West Africa*, or *South*, periodicals that are available in most libraries. For daily newspaper coverage of events in Africa, read *Le Monde*, *The Guardian*, *The Nairobi Times*, and the *Christian Science Monitor*.

Other preparations you'll need to make involve **health**. For travel to many of the countries of sub-Saharan Africa, you must be vaccinated against yellow fever, cholera, typhoid, and polio. It is best to contact your local public health service office for details on the latest health requirements for individual countries; information is also available from the major international air carriers as well as from the consulates of each country. Be sure your doctor records your shots on an **International Vaccination Card**. Then carry it with you at all times; failure to present this card at some borders may lead to a second inoculation. Further information about health problems and precautions for travelers can be found in the "Health" section of Chapter Two.

Travelers to the region should also be aware of the prevalence of AIDS in Burundi, Rwanda, Uganda, Zaire, and to a lesser degree in Kenya and Tanzania. In sub-Saharan Arica, AIDS has spread almost entirely by heterosexual intercourse; men and women are equally infected. Transmission of AIDS through contaminated blood and blood products also is common, because some countries do not screen blood for HIV before transfusion. Travelers to the region should try to avoid blood transfusions unless they know HIV-antibody screening has been done. It is also possible to pick up the virus from an unsterilized needle, so if you need an injection in Africa, make sure the needle either is new or has been properly sterilized. More information on precautions against AIDS can also be found in Chapter Two of this book.

In addition to your passport, you'll need a **visa** to enter most countries of sub-Saharan Africa. Visas can be obtained in the United States at the embassy or a consulate of the country you are traveling to; in most cases, your passport must accompany the visa application. Since it can take up to three weeks for a visa to be processed, start collecting the necessary visas well before your departure date. If you don't have a well-planned itinerary, however, it might be best to obtain the necessary visas at the appropriate consulates as you travel through Africa. In this case, be sure to pack plenty of extra passport photos, and keep your ears open to find out which consulates are most hospitable.

You may also be required to show an onward ticket out of the country when crossing the border. To this end, booking an airline ticket with plenty of stopovers is a good idea. In lieu of an onward ticket, however, proof of sufficient funds should gain you passage. While "sufficient funds" can vary from country to country, major credit cards are widely recognized as proof.

Getting There

There are APEX fares from the U.S. to major African cities such as Lagos and Nairobi. Sample fares available during the summer of 1993 are listed below. For more up-to-date information, check with a Council Travel office (see pages xiii–xvi).

	Round-trip	**One-way**
New York–Nairobi	$1,689	$829
New York–Johannesburg	$1,989	$905
Los Angeles–Nairobi	$2,039	$889

If you are already in Europe, it is relatively inexpensive to fly to most major African cities. Students and young people are eligible for special discounted fares between Europe and Africa. These can be booked at any Council Travel office or a student travel bureau in Europe. Regulations vary depending on the airline, but generally holders of the International Student Identity Card (see pages 9–10) or the Go 25 Card (see page 11) are eligible. Sample *one-way* student fares available during the summer of 1991 are listed below.

Berlin–Nairobi	$614	Paris–Lagos	$475
Berlin–Johannesburg	$748	Paris–Douala	$495
Amsterdam–Johannesburg	$704	London–Lagos	$485
Paris–Abidjan	$475		

Traveling around Africa

If you're going to cover long distances within Africa and your time is short, **air travel** is your best bet. You'll save money if you make your initial reservations to the farthest point you are traveling to and arrange your intermediary travel via stopovers. If you wait until you're in Nairobi to decide you want to go to Johannesburg, your costs may be double what they would have been had you booked through to Johannesburg with a stopover in Nairobi.

Train travel in Africa is inexpensive but slow. The railroads were built for colonial purposes—to transport raw materials from the interior of Africa to the coast, where they could be shipped off to other parts of the world. As a result, you may not be able to travel along the coast by rail, but will find lines running from the coastal capital cities into the interior. Some of these lines will treat you to some spectacular scenery along the way.

Road conditions vary throughout Africa but generally follow predictable patterns. Roads around and between major cities are usually paved and in good repair. Outside of the main intercity routes, road conditions are dictated by the relative stability of each country and the economic state of affairs. Always place greater value on word of mouth than on maps. **Bus service** of some type covers all parts of the continent and many routes have frequent service. However, buses tend to be crowded and make many stops to pick up and discharge passengers, which means slow going.

Another, often speedier option is the **shared taxi**. Called by different names in different countries, the shared taxi can also take many forms: car, truck, or van. Basically, a shared taxi is any vehicle running between two points along a fixed route, waiting at designated spots to fill up with passengers before departing for its destination. Taxis are generally more expensive than buses, but in some countries, by very little.

Hitching, too, is a recognized form of travel in Africa. Trucks are most likely to pick up hitchers, which they carry in back, on top of the load. But although it is easy to get a ride, you will be expected to pay. Normally, the fare is less expensive than it would be on a bus traveling the same distance. **Note:** In Africa, it is impolite to stick out your thumb. Hitchers wave their hands. And as always, women should never hitch alone.

Eating and Sleeping

Africa has an abundance of cheap places to stay, many of which are listed in the guidebooks published by Lonely Planet Publications (see page 56). Another source of information on accommodations in most major cities is the local tourist office, which will be centrally located and easy to find. The only countries offering youth hostels are Kenya, Namibia, South Africa, and Zimbabwe; see these country sections for more information.

For Further Information

The best guidebooks on Africa are those published by Lonely Planet (see page 56). The recently updated *Africa on a Shoestring* ($27.95) contains over 1,000 pages of detailed information on 55 African countries. Those who don't want to carry around a big book, however, should check out Lonely Planet's more focused regional guides, including *West Africa: A Travel Survival Kit* ($19.95), *Central Africa: A Travel Survival Kit* ($10.95), and *East Africa: A Travel Survival Kit* ($15.95). Lonely Planet also publishes several country-specific Travel Survival Kits. The most accurate maps of Africa are those published by Michelin, including North East Africa, North West Africa, Southern Africa, and Côte d'Ivoire.

A useful reference guide to all aspects of political, economic, and cultural affairs in Africa is the annually updated *Africa South of the Sahara*, by Europa Publications. At $295, this encyclopedic tome is probably too expensive to buy yourself, but you can find it in a good library.

You'll find information about visas and other requirements in the individual country sections later in this chapter. Listed below are the addresses of embassies of countries not covered in the separate sections of this chapter.

- **Angola:** Angolan Permanent Representative to the U.N., 747 Third Avenue, 18th Floor, New York, NY 10017; (212) 861-5656.
- **Benin:** Embassy of the Republic of Benin, 2737 Cathedral Avenue NW, Washington, DC 20008; (202) 232-6656
- **Burkina Faso:** Embassy of Burkina Faso, 2340 Massachusetts Avenue NW, Washington, DC 20008; (202) 332-5577
- **Burundi:** Embassy of the Republic of Burundi, 2233 Wisconsin Avenue NW, Suite 212, Washington, DC 20007; (202) 342-2574
- **Cape Verde:** Embassy of the Republic of Cape Verde, 3415 Massachusetts Avenue NW, Washington, DC 20007; (202) 965-6820
- **Central African Republic:** Embassy of the Central African Republic, 1618 22nd Street NW, Washington, DC 20008; (202) 483-7800
- **Chad:** Embassy of the Republic of Chad, 2002 R Street NW, Washington, DC 20009; (202) 462-4009
- **Comoros:** Embassy of the Federal and Islamic Republic of the Comoros, 336 East 45th Street, Second Floor, New York, NY 10017; (212) 972-8010
- **Congo:** Embassy of the Republic of the Congo, 4891 Colorado Avenue NW, Washington, DC 20011; (202) 726-5500
- **Djibouti:** Embassy of the Republic of Djibouti, 1156 15th Street NW, Washington, DC 20005; (202) 331-0202
- **Guinea:** Ambassador of Equatorial Guinea, 57 Magnolia Avenue, Mount Vernon, NY; (914) 667-9664
- **Eritrea:** Office of the Provisional Government of Eritrea, 1418 15th Street, Suite 1, PO Box 65685, Washington, DC 20035; (202) 265-3070
- **Ethiopia:** Embassy of Ethiopia, 2134 Kalorama Road NW, Washington, DC 20008; (202) 234-2281
- **Gabon:** Embassy of the Gabonese Republic, 2035 20th Street NW, Washington, DC 20009; (202) 797-1000
- **Gambia:** Embassy of The Gambia, 1155 15th Street NW, Suite 1000, Washington, DC 20005; (202) 785-1399
- **Guinea:** Embassy of the Republic of Guinea, 2112 Leroy Street NW, Washington, DC 20008; (202) 483-9420
- **Guinea-Bissau:** Embassy of Guinea-Bissau, 918 16th Street NW, Mezzanine Suite, Washington, DC 20006; (202) 872-4222
- **Lesotho:** Embassy of the Kingdom of Lesotho, 2511 Massachusetts Avenue NW, Washington, DC 20008; (202) 797-5533
- **Mali:** Embassy of the Republic of Mali, 2130 R Street NW, Washington, DC 20008; (202) 332-2249

- **Mauritania:** Embassy of the Islamic Republic of Mauritania, 2129 Leroy Place NW, Washington, DC 20008; (202) 232-5700
- **Mauritius:** Embassy of Mauritius, 4301 Connecticut Avenue NW, Suite 441, Washington, DC 20008; (202) 244-1491
- **Mozambique:** Embassy of Mozambique, 1990 M Street NW, Suite 570, Washington, DC 20036; (202) 293-7146
- **Rwanda:** Embassy of the Republic of Rwanda, 1714 New Hampshire Avenue NW, Washington, DC 20009; (202) 232-2882
- **Sao Tome and Principe:** Permanent Mission of Sao Tome and Principe, 801 Second Avenue, Suite 1504, New York, NY 10017; (212) 697-4211
- **Seychelles:** Permanent Mission of Seychelles to the United Nations, 820 Second Avenue, Suite 203, New York, NY 10017; (212) 922-9177
- **Sudan:** Embassy of the Republic of the Sudan, 2210 Massachusetts Avenue NW, Washington, DC 20008; (202) 338-8565
- **Zaire:** Embassy of the Republic of Zaire, 1800 New Hampshire Avenue NW, Washington, DC 20009; (202) 234-7690

For up-to-date information on entry requirements as well as any important travel advisories, obtain a **Consular Information Sheet** for the countries you plan to visit from the Department of State (see pages 8–9). The Department of State also publishes a useful pamphlet, *Tips for Travelers to Sub-Saharan Africa*, available free from the Superintendent of Documents, U.S. Government Printing Office, Washington, DC 20402. At press time, Department of State travel warnings were in effect for Angola, Somalia, and Sudan.

WORK

The ministries of education of the various African countries often have information on **teaching** positions in their high schools and universities. A university degree is required, and teaching certification or experience is helpful; three-year contracts are common. For the address of the ministry of education in the country you are interested in, contact its embassy or a consulate.

Another option is **voluntary service**. To help fill the great need for technical and educational assistance in Africa, a number of organizations based in the United States operate programs there, and many place volunteers in these programs. Some of these are church-related, while others are privately run or government agencies. Most of the voluntary-service organizations listed in Chapter Three (including the Peace Corps) make placements in African countries. CIEE's publication *Volunteer! The Comprehensive Guide to Voluntary Service in the U.S. and Abroad* (see page 26) will also give you excellent leads on voluntary-service programs in Africa. While some service programs will require you to have technical skills and/or teaching experience, others will accept you without any previous experience.

There are also a number of internship/traineeship possibilities in Africa. In the individual country sections that follow, you'll find information on programs offered by member institutions and organizations of CIEE.

STUDY

There are a growing number of study programs in Africa sponsored by U.S. institutions and designed primarily for American students. You'll find the study programs of CIEE-member universities listed in the country sections that follow. It's also possible for a well-qualified American undergraduate to enroll directly in an African university. Graduate students planning to conduct research in an African country must notify its government of their plans and obtain the proper visa before going; in most African countries, research is not possible on a tourist visa.

EXPLORING THE CULTURES OF AFRICA

In many of the individual country sections that follow, you'll find recommendations of books to read and films to see. However, the notion of African national literatures is somewhat misleading since European colonizers created the present "nations" of Africa without regard for indigenous ethnic patterns. Many of today's African writers actually represent a region rather than a particular country. Thus, to get a listing of applicable readings or film suggestions, be sure to check not only the specific country you are going to but also that of neighboring countries with similar cultures.

A number of anthologies include works of African authors from different regions of the continent. *Stories from Central and Southern Africa* (1983), edited by Paula Scanlon, features short fiction from Zambia, Zimbabwe, Malawi, and South Africa. *African Short Stories* (1985), edited by Nigerian novelist and poet Chinua Achebe and C. L. Innes, is an excellent collection of stories from the last 25 years. *Unwinding Threads* (1983), edited by Charlotte H. Bruner, is a collection of fiction by African women. *Ten One-Act Plays* (1968), edited by Cosmo Pieterse, contains plays from East, South, and West Africa, and *Woza Afrika!* (1986), edited by Duma Ndlovu, is a collection of contemporary plays from southern Africa.

If you are having trouble finding works referred to in this chapter in your local bookstore or library, contact one of the following publishers:

- **Heinemann Publishers**, 361 Hanover Street, Portsmouth, NH 03801; (603) 431-7894
- **Three Continents Press**, 1901 Pennsylvania Avenue NW, Suite 407, Washington DC 20006; (202) 223-2554
- **Red Sea Press**, 15 Industry Court, Trenton, NJ 08638; (609) 771-1666

BOTSWANA

Situated at the center of the Southern African Plateau, Botswana is often described as an island of peace and prosperity surrounded by Zambia to the north, Zimbabwe to the east, Namibia to the west and northwest, and South Africa to the south. Located in the central and southern regions, the Kalahari Desert, where the nomadic !Kung San and other hunter-gatherers live, dominates 84 percent of the country's terrain. In some areas, the Kalahari sands can reach depths of 100 meters. With fewer than two million people and entirely landlocked, Botswana is the size of France or Texas and has become prosperous through the mining and sale of high-quality diamonds and the export of beef.

Independent since 1966, Botswana, formerly the Bechuanaland Protectorate, was one of Britain's three High Commission Territories. The other two were Swaziland and Basutoland (now Lesotho). Administratively, Botswana has 10 districts, eight of which follow the boundaries of eight "tribal" reserves established by the colonial authorities. The largest group is the BaNgwato of the Central District. This is the group and district from which Botswana's first president, Sir Seretse Khama, emerged. Khama, also a traditional Paramount Chief of the BaNgwato, is credited with founding the Botswana Democratic Party that has ruled Botswana since independence.

Botswana is proud of its heritage as a multiparty, multiracial democracy. At least six political parties exist and have entered candidates in recent elections. Though most current public servants are African, a few Europeans and Indians continue to hold influential, leading positions in government, commerce, and education. In addition to the government press, several independent newspapers keep Botswana informed on issues and events.

Botswana is a multilingual nation, but the official languages of Botswana are Setswana and English. In addition to these and other languages you will hear Zulu, Xhosa, and Afrikaans spoken around the capital city of Gaborone in southern Botswana. To the east, along the Zimbabwe border, and in and around Francistown, you will hear Shona, Ndebele, and Kalanga. In the north, on the Zambian border, the languages of the Subiya, Lozi and Yei peoples predominate; and, to the west and northwest along the Namibian–Caprivi Strip border, various San, Hambukushu, and Herero dialects are common.

Tourism is big business in Botswana. In addition to encountering domesticated goats, cattle, horses, and donkeys, you will come to know free-roaming wildlife as well as those animals protected by the numerous and expansive game reserves scattered throughout the country.

Maun is both the administrative and commercial center of the Ngamiland/Northwest District, and the traditional capital of the BaTawana Tribal Authority. The focal point of the nation's tourist industy, Maun has a population of approximately 20,000 people. It is from the Maun airport—reportedly the busiest in southern Africa between March and November—that photographers and big-game hunters enter into the best-kept safari secret in Africa: the Okavango Delta. This delta is the final resting place of the Okavango River, which flows southward from Angola's Highlands, fans out into flora-rich marsh and is swallowed by the thirsty Kalahari sands. In Maun, nestled on the Thamalakane River, indigenous African rondavel homesteads contrast intriguingly with the European banks, shops, restaurants, and hotels.

—Roland A. Foulkes, Gainesville, Florida

Official name: Republic of Botswana. **Area:** 231,804 square miles (slightly smaller than Texas). **Population:** 1,300,000. **Population density:** 5 inhabitants per square mile. **Capital and largest city:** Gaborone (population 138,000). **Language:** English (official), Tswana, Shona. **Religion:** Indigenous beliefs, Christianity. **Per capita income:** US$920. **Currency:** Pula. **Literacy rate:** 80%. **Average daily high/low:** Francistown: January, 88°F/65°F; June, 74°F/41°F. **Average precipitation:** Francistown: January, 4.2″; June, 0.1″.

TRAVEL

U.S. citizens need a passport but no visa for stays of up to 90 days. For more information, contact the **Embassy of the Republic of Botswana**, Suite 7M, 3400 International Drive NW, Washington, DC 20008; (202) 244-4990.

Getting Around

Botswana's main roads are paved, but most are gravel. **Buses** and minibuses serve major towns, but to get to more remote spots it's best to rent a four-wheel-drive vehicle. You can also try hitching.

In eastern Botswana, one **rail** line runs from South Africa north through Botswana and into Zimbabwe, stopping at Gaborone and Francistown and points in between. First- and second-class cars are shared sleepers; third class has soft seats, and fourth class has hard seats.

For Further Information

The best travel information on Botswana and neighboring countries is Lonely Planet's new *Zimbabwe, Botswana and Namibia: A Travel Survival Kit* ($16.95). For more information on Lonely Planet Publications, see page 56.

WORK

In order to work in Botswana, you must secure employment before traveling to the country. You must also obtain a work permit, which the employer is responsible for securing on your behalf. For further information, contact the **Commissioner of Labour**, Private Bag 0072, Gaborone, Botswana.

STUDY

Below you'll find an academic program offered by a CIEE-member institution. Consult Appendix I for the address to write for more information.

Semester and Academic Year

Natural Sciences

World Learning/School for International Training. *College Semester Abroad: Kalahari Conservation and Ecology*. Gaborone, Maun, Okavango. Fall and spring semesters. Intensive language study, field-study seminar, and independent-study project. Homestays and excursions. Sophomores to graduate students with 2.5 GPA. Apply by May 7 for fall; October 7 for spring. Contact: College Semester Abroad Admissions at (800) 336-1616.

CAMEROON

Cameroon has a long history of European involvement that reads like a sort of *Who's Who* of Western imperialism. European contact with Cameroon dates from the 15th century, when the Portuguese arrived. In fact, although the predominant European influence in Cameroon today is French, Cameroon's name comes from the Portuguese *camaroês*, or "giant shrimp," which live in abundance on the country's Atlantic coastline. Later, slave traders—chiefly Dutch and American—were active in the area. In the 19th century the Germans took control of the territory and created Cameroon's present boundaries. After Germany's defeat in the First World War, Britain and France divided the territory, with France controlling the largest portion. In 1960, Cameroon finally emerged as an independent nation.

Cameroon stretches from the central African coast to the banks of the largely evaporated Lake Chad in the Sahel, encompassing tropical rain forest, desert, and cool mountain highlands. More than 100 ethnic groups live within its borders. There are religious differences between the north and the south; the north is Muslim, and residents of the south ascribe to either indigenous religions or Christianity. The south is more commercial and Westernized than the north.

While not immune to political unrest, especially between north and south during the early '60s, Cameroon has had a relatively stable, albeit authoritarian government. Tension remains between the northern and southern regions of the country and there is sometimes violent intragovernmental jockeying for position. However, the social and economic life of Cameroon continues undisturbed.

Relative stability has prevailed in the economic arena as well. Cameroon is one of the few African nations to be a self-sufficient food producer, and it exports its flourishing cocoa and coffee crops. By avoiding the conspicuous "show" projects, such as large international centers and superhighways, that many newly independent African nations produced in quantity and concentrating instead on long-term-yield projects such as education and agriculture, Cameroon avoided the heavy borrowing that has come back to haunt much of Africa. Cameroon has a sufficient economic base and has recently embarked on a number of internationally and commercially oriented ventures.

—Mario Miraldi, New York, New York

Official name: Republic of Cameroon. **Area:** 179,714 square miles (somewhat larger than California). **Population:** 11,390,000. **Population density:** 63 inhabitants per square mile. **Capital:** Yaoundé (pop. 700,000). **Largest city:** Douala (pop. 852,000). **Language:** French and English (both official), Foulbé, Bamiléke, Ewondo, Donala, Mungaka, Bassa. **Religion:** Christianity, Islam, animism. **Per capita income:** US$1,010. **Currency:** CFA Franc. **Literacy rate:** 65%. **Average daily temperature:** Yaoundé: June, 74°F; December, 75°F. **Average number of days with precipitation:** Yaoundé: June, 17; December, 4.

TRAVEL

U.S. citizens visiting the country need a passport and a visa. In addition, proof of innoculation against cholera and yellow fever are required. For specific regulations, check with the **Embassy of the Republic of Cameroon**, 2349 Massachusetts Avenue NW, Washington, DC 20008; (202) 265-8790.

Getting Around

The road system in Cameroon is fair and improving. The major arteries in the north and the southwest are paved, but roads into the southeastern portion of the country are not as good and often are damaged by heavy storms. Car rentals can be arranged from Hertz, Avis, and Eurocar. **Cameroon Airlines** offers good service from Douala and Yaoundé to all major towns. Buses are few and far between; public transport consists mainly of **shared taxis**. A **rail** line links Douala and Yaoundé and goes on into the interior; service is slow and infrequent, but provides a cheap and interesting way to travel.

For Further Information

For general information, contact the **Cultural Service of the Embassy of the Republic of Cameroon** (see "Travel," above). You can find reliable travel information on Cameroon in the recently updated *Central Africa: A Travel Survival Kit*, available for $10.95 from Lonely Planet. Lonely Planet's *Africa on a Shoestring* ($27.95) also contains information on Cameroon. For more information on Lonely Planet, see page 56.

WORK

It is very difficult for foreigners to secure regular, salaried employment in Cameroon. Before leaving the U.S., a work visa must be issued (proof of employment is required). For more information, contact the Embassy of the Republic of Cameroon (see "Travel," above) or the **Ministry of Labor**, Yaoundé, Cameroon, Africa.

STUDY

A program offered by a CIEE-member institution is described below. Consult Appendix I for the contact address.

Semester and Academic Year

General Studies

World Learning/School for International Training. *College Semester Abroad*. Dschang and Yaoundé. Fall and spring semesters. Intensive French-language training, life and culture seminar, field-study methods seminar, and independent-study project. Homestays, villages stay, and excursions. Sophomores to seniors with 2.5 GPA and three semesters of college French. Apply by May 7 for fall; October 7 for spring. Contact: College Semester Abroad Admissions at (800) 336-1616.

EXPLORING THE CULTURE OF CAMEROON

Readings

Mongo Beti is probably the best known Cameroonian writer; *Mission to Kala* (1964) is a satiric tale about a man who must retrieve a fellow villager's wife after she has run off. Beti's other works include *Perpetua and the Habit of Unhappiness* (1978), which conveys his concerns about post-independence Africa, and *Remember Ruben* (1980), set just prior to Cameroonian independence.

Ferdinand Oyono used colonial Cameroon as his canvas in *Road to Europe* (1989) and *The Old Man and the Medal* (1969). Set in the Bula country of southern Cameroon, the former tells the story of a young man who seeks to "become somebody" by using the rules of the colonial system to his advantage. The latter is a satiric story of a villager who is awarded a medal by the French. His pride turns to doubt and finally contempt for the system, which the medal represents.

Also set in colonial Cameroon is Kenjo Jumbam's book *The White Man of God* (1980), which describes the confusion of a boy coming to terms with the Christian Western world presented to him through a local priest. Another novel, Mbella Sonne Dipoko's *Because of Women* (1969), is a delicate story of a man who quarrels with his pregnant wife over another woman.

CÔTE D'IVOIRE

Côte d'Ivoire, or the Ivory Coast, is probably the most cosmopolitan nation in West Africa. Centrally situated on the Gulf of Guinea and dominated by the French for more than three centuries, it was once a major export center for ivory, slaves, and other "commodities." Today its residents include about 30,000 French nationals, many Lebanese and Vietnamese, and even ambassadors from both the P.L.O. and Israel.

In Abidjan, the nation's capital, the shining clusters of skyscrapers, the luxurious hotels, the dozens of European banks, and the superhighways swooping over estuaries cannot quite obscure the city's slums. No other nation in West Africa so dramatically embodies the contrasts between rich and poor, new and old.

The contrast is particularly dramatic because of the enormous wealth of those who are rich. Imported luxury cars are surprisingly common in the streets of Abidjan. Cash crops such as cocoa, rubber, pineapples, and bananas are grown on giant plantations near the coast—many of them owned by President-for-Life Félix Houphouët-Boigny, who is believed to be a billionaire. The president recently has been busy overseeing the relocation of the capital from Abidjan to Yamoussoukro, the former village (now a city) where he was born, and the government is spending hundreds of millions of dollars to make the new capital a monument to his rule. Meanwhile, political groups and the press are struggling for freedom of expression, and no one knows what will happen when the president, who is in his late 80s, eventually dies.

Houphouët's rule has achieved some notable successes, however. Poverty in Côte d'Ivoire is less severe than in nearby countries such as Guinea and Liberia. Most years, villagers are able to grow ample supplies of staples such as corn and yams, cassavas, and tomatoes. In addition, most of the country has electricity, potable water supplies, and well-funded schools run by government-supplied teachers.

Ivorians are justifiably proud of their artisanship. They specialize in linen tapestries painted with folk-art animal designs, cotton textiles in bright colors, silver filigree jewelry, and striking wooden sculptures of animals. However, stores aren't limited to stocking traditional merchandise; Abidjan also has some of the largest cassette tape outlets in the world.

Any traveler to Côte d'Ivoire should try to get out of Abidjan to see the rest of the country. The intercity bus system is excellent, and many urban Ivorians jump at the chance to take a visitor to their ancestral village. Don't turn them down.

—Jason Zweig, New York, New York

Official name: Republic of Côte d'Ivoire. **Area:** 124,503 square miles (about the size of New Mexico). **Population:** 12,977,000. **Population density:** 104 inhabitants per square mile. **Capital and largest city:** Abidjan (pop. 2,700,000). **Language:** French, Akan, Kru, Voltaic, Malinke. **Religion:** Christianity, Islam, indigenous. **Per capita income:** US$820. **Currency:** CFA Franc. **Literacy rate:** 45%. **Average daily temperature:** Abidjan: June, 79°F; December, 81°F. **Average number of days with precipitation:** Abidjan: June, 18; December, 6.

TRAVEL

U.S. citizens visiting Côte d'Ivoire need a passport but no visa for stays of up to 90 days. For specific requirements, contact the **Embassy of the Republic of Côte d'Ivoire**, 2424 Massachusetts Avenue NW, Washington, DC 20008; (202) 797-0300.

Getting Around

Côte d'Ivoire has one of the best internal transportation systems in all of West Africa. **Air Ivoire** provides regular service from Abidjan to the country's other major cities. Luxury express **buses** also link the major cities, which are connected by a relatively well maintained system of roads. **Bush taxis** provide service throughout the country. In addition, a single **rail** line crosses the country north from Abidjan to Ouagadougou in Burkina Faso, and is a good way of getting to many towns in the interior.

For Further Information

You can find reliable travel information on Côte d'Ivoire in the recently updated *West Africa: A Travel Survival Kit*, available for $19.95 from Lonely Planet Publications. *Africa on a Shoestring* ($27.95) also contains information on Côte d'Ivoire. For more information on Lonely Planet, see page 56.

WORK

It is very difficult for foreigners to secure regular, salaried employment in the Côte d'Ivoire. For more information, contact the Embassy of the Republic of the Côte d'Ivoire (see "Travel," above).

Voluntary Service

Goshen College offers a study-service term in Côte d'Ivoire that is open primarily to Goshen students; sometimes a limited number of spaces are available to students at other colleges and universities.

STUDY

A study program offered by a CIEE-member institution is described below. Unless otherwise noted, consult Appendix I for the address where you can write for more information.

Semester and Academic Year

General Studies

International Student Exchange Program (ISEP). Academic year. Direct reciprocal exchange between U.S. universities and Université Nationale de Côte d'Ivoire. Full curriculum options. Rolling admissions. Open only to students at ISEP-member institutions. Contact ISEP for list of members.

GHANA

Ghana is a kaleidoscope of cultural traditions, tribes, languages, and increasingly, Western influences. Known as some of the friendliest people in Africa, Ghanaians show an extraordinary generosity toward visitors—both in the bustling cities where vendors offer their goods amidst the blur of taxis, and in the villages where locals work against a backdrop of maize or grazing cattle. The arts in Ghana have a long history, particularly in gold working and the weaving of the rich Kente cloth of the Ashanti region. Today, however, one can also sense the presence of Western capital in Ghana's capital of Accra, where businessmen walk among the shops and tall bank buildings. These paradoxes may be more evident to the visitor than to the Ghanaians themselves, who combine new ways with their enduring cultural traditions.

Modern-day Ghana takes its name from the ancient Sudanic Empire that dominated a wide area of West Africa (modern day Mali) from the 4th to the 11th centuries. This highly organized empire amassed wealth through trading minerals, spices, and other goods with North Africa. During the 12th century, Arab invasions caused groups of inhabitants to move south, settling by A.D. 1200 in what is now the northern half of Ghana. They soon established themselves as the ruling class, coming to be known as the *Akans* (leaders). Later, other distinct groups also migrated and the main tribes that established themselves continue to exist, the most powerful being the Ashanti.

Lured by rich gold deposits, the first Europeans arrived at what came to be known as the Gold Coast during the late 15th century. The Portuguese were first, followed by the Dutch and the British. In 1874 the British made the Gold Coast a crown colony, consolidating their rule in 1902 with the annexation of the Ashanti region. However, an independence movement arose in 1948 with anticolonial riots from which Kwame Nkrumah emerged as the leader. Under his leadership Ghana became the first country in Africa to win independence from its colonial rulers on March 6, 1957.

The intermingling of native and Western culture is manifest throughout Ghana, especially in the south. While Ghanaians speak any number of four major languages and numerous dialects, the country's official language is English. In schools modeled after Britain's educational system, teachers wear Western-style clothing and instruct their students in English. The mixture of cultures is felt most keenly in the larger southern cities such as Accra or Kumasi, in vast urban marketplaces and streetside stands that offer everything from richly dyed clothes and palm oil to British literature and imported tea. Religious practices are also varied. Muslims perform ablution outside mosques, while on another street singing pours forth from a Christian church. Many of those who live in the north are Muslim, while Christianity predominates in the south. Indigenous religious beliefs influence Ghanaian culture throughout the country.

The traveler who picks up a local newspaper will likely find Flight Lieutenant J. J. Rawlings' photograph on the front page. He came to power in 1981, following a succession of coups, an increase in corruption, and a severe economic decline during the 1970s. Since then Ghana has enjoyed a period of political stability; starting in 1983 the World Bank and the International Monetary Fund have helped cut the inflation rate from 100 percent to less than 15 percent. In November 1992 Ghanaians reelected Rawlings as their president, a move that should ensure continued political and economic stability.

—Sophie B. Wadsworth, Tacoma, Washington

Official name: Republic of Ghana. **Area:** 92,098 square miles (about the size of Wyoming). **Population:** 15,616,000. **Population density:** 169 persons per square mile. **Capital and largest city:** Accra (pop. 949,000). **Language:** English, Akan, Mossi, Ga-Adangme, Ewe. **Religion:** Christianity, animism, Islam. **Per capita income:** US$380. **Currency:** Cedi. **Literacy rate:** 60%. **Average daily temperature:** Accra: June, 78°F; December, 81°F. **Average number of days with precipitation:** Accra: June, 10; December, 2.

TRAVEL

For U.S. citizens, both a passport and a visa are required. You'll also need an onward or return ticket and a guarantee of financial support from a bank or employer to cover your stay in the country. Finally, a certificate of immunization against yellow fever is required. For specific regulations, check with the **Embassy of the Republic of Ghana**, 3512 International Drive, Washington, DC 20008; (202) 686-4520.

Getting Around

Ghana's **rail** system is limited to the southern portion of the country and is subject to frequent interruptions in service. The most prevalent form of transport are **tro-tros** (also called mammy-lorries), which are usually modified trucks or vans fitted with benches and packed with people. From the point of departure, these travel to nearby villages and neighboring districts. If you want to travel farther, you'll have to change at least once. For longer distances, the best mode of transportation are the larger **buses**, both government- and privately owned. Some private buses run on schedule and leave without waiting to fill up.

The traveler who wishes to avoid these obstacles can find inexpensive domestic **flights** between the cities of Accra, Tamale, and Kumasi. Another, more interesting alternative is to travel along Lake Volta. Passenger **boats**, freighters, and smaller vessels regularly depart Akosombo for northern ports.

For Further Information

You can find reliable travel information on Ghana in the recently updated *West Africa: A Travel Survival Kit*, available for $19.95 from Lonely Planet Publications. *Africa on a Shoestring* ($27.95) also contains information on Ghana. For more information on Lonely Planet, see page 56.

WORK

It is very difficult for foreigners to secure regular, salaried employment in Ghana. For more information, contact the Embassy of Ghana (see "Travel," above). For another type of work experience, see the internship and voluntary-service sections below.

Internships/Traineeships

A program offered by a member of the Council on International Educational Exchange is listed below.

Association for International Practical Training. *IAESTE Trainee Program*. On-the-job training for undergraduate and graduate students in technical fields such as engineering, computer science, agriculture, architecture, mathematics, and the natural and physical sciences. See page 19 for more information.

Voluntary Service

CIEE places young people in voluntary-service workcamps in Ghana organized by the Voluntary Workcamp Association of Ghana in Accra. These workcamps bring together international and Ghanaian youth for three-week periods during July, August, September, and December to build schools, health clinics, drains, and public latrines in rural areas. Volunteers must be 18 or older, and may choose to stay for a period of up to three months. The applications of U.S. residents and an orientation are handled by CIEE. For more information, contact the International Voluntary Service Department at CIEE.

The International Ecumenical Workcamp, a voluntary-service workcamp in Ghana, provides people at least 18 years of age from all over the world the opportunity to work on a rural development construction project. The term of service is four weeks. Apply by May 13 to **International Christian Youth Exchange** (see Appendix I for address). For persons interested in longer-term voluntary-service work, the same organization's **Year Abroad Program** offers persons ages 18 to 30 opportunities in the fields of health care, education, the environment, construction, and more. See page 25 for more information.

Adults can perform community-service work in Ghana through the Global-Service Program sponsored by **AFS Intercultural Programs**, 313 East 43rd Street, NY, NY 10017; (800) 237-4636. Service projects are arranged individually according to the participant's interests or expertise. Included are planned excursions and cultural activities. Projects run from three to seven weeks and are open to all interested persons at least 19 years old.

STUDY

The following are the educational programs offered by CIEE-member institutions. Unless otherwise noted, consult Appendix I for the addresses of the colleges and universities listed in this section.

Semester and Academic Year

General Studies

Council on International Educational Exchange. *Undergraduate Program at the University of Ghana at Accra, Legon.* Semester and academic year. Juniors with 3.0 GPA. Contact University Programs Department for application deadlines.

State University of New York College at Brockport. *Accra Program.* Fall semester and academic year. Study at Institute of African Studies at University of Ghana. Juniors and seniors with 2.5 GPA. Apply by February 15. Contact: Office of International Education, SUNY College at Brockport, Brockport, NY 14420; (716) 395-2119.

World Learning/School for International Training. *College Semester Abroad.* Accra area, Kumasi, Cape Coast, Elimina. Fall and spring semesters. African arts and culture; independent study project. Homestays and excursions. Sophomores to seniors with 2.5 GPA. Apply by March 7 for fall; October 7 for spring. Contact: College Semester Abroad Admissions at (800) 336-1616.

Summer and Short-Term

General Studies

University of Louisville. *Pan-African Studies in Ghana.* First-year college students to graduate students. Apply by April 30.

Performing Arts

State University of New York College at Brockport. *Ghana Summer Fine Arts Program.* Accra, Legon. Five weeks in July and August. African drumming and dance, and African culture. Excursions and dormitory housing. Sophomores to seniors with 2.5 GPA. Apply by April 1. Contact: Office of International Education, SUNY College at Brockport, Brockport, NY 14420; (716) 395-2119.

University of Maryland. *Performing Arts in Ghana.* Accra. Summer. Aspects of Ghanaian dance as related to the society at large. Dormitory housing at University of Ghana. Apply by March 15.

EXPLORING THE CULTURE OF GHANA

Readings

A number of novels by contemporary Ghanaian authors are available in English. Ayi Kwei Armah, one of Ghana's most prominent writers, is the author of *Two Thousand Seasons* (1979), in which he reconstructs one thousand years of African history, and *The Beautyful Ones Are Not Yet Born* (1969), which deals with political corruption in a newly independent African nation among other books. *This Earth, My Brother* (1972), by the poet and novelist Kofi Awoonor, is an allegorical novel in which a lawyer searches for meaning and identity in post-colonial Africa.

Those interested in poetry and theater should read J. C. DeGrafts's *Beneath the Jazz and Brass* (1975) and *Muntu: A Play* (1983). Kojo Laing's book of poetry, *Godhorse* (1989) is varied, evocative, and humorous. The play *The Blinkards* (1974), by Kobina Sekye, is a witty send-up of the pretensions of the Ghanaian nouveaux riches. For a look at contemporary Ghanaian theater, read the plays of Asiedu Yirenki, especially the collection *Kivalu and Other Plays* (1980).

KENYA

Kenya's surprising diversity will astound the visitor. Its people live in conditions ranging from the bustling modernity of Nairobi to the traditional rhythms of its rural villages—places where the pace of life hasn't changed appreciably in centuries. Its cultural spectrum includes over 40 distinct ethnic groups, the largest of which are the Kikuyu of central Kenya and the Luo of the country's western regions.

The country's startling geography encompasses the jagged snowcapped peaks and year-round glaciers of Mount Kenya—Africa's second highest mountain—and the plunging depths of the Great Rift Valley, which slices southward through the African continent. The arid Sahara desert in the north contrasts with the lush, verdant central highlands whose fertile soil and cool, crisp nights reminded British colonial settlers of their homeland. Kenya's wide diversity of plant life is matched only by the spectacular wildlife found in its celebrated game parks.

The country's innumerable contradictions challenge the visitor to take a closer look. Kenyans are, in general, incredibly friendly and welcome outsiders with much warmth and curiosity. Nairobi, Mombasa, and the regions surrounding them are readily accessible to outside visitors and are well traveled by tourists. Although venturing away from these beaten paths requires some added planning, the understanding of the country that such a trip provides makes the extra effort well worthwhile.

The seemingly random nature of Kenya's eclectic population and geography is just what it might seem—a coincidence. The country was arbitrarily drawn into being when the British colonized the area around the turn of this century to access its raw materials and harvest cash crops from its fertile soil. The coffee, tea, banana, pineapple, and sisal plantations established by the British still account for a large percentage of Kenya's gross national product. This was not the region's first contact with peoples from other parts of the world: The coastal regions around Mombasa had been cosmopolitan trading centers long before the arrival of the British. As far back as the 1500s, Arab and East Indian merchants would sail across the Indian Ocean to trade for ivory and other valuable local commodities.

Centuries of trading have left a lasting effect on the country. Kenya's national language, Kiswahili, developed from the Bantu languages originally spoken by the coastal ethnic groups and contains many words from Arabic, sprinkled with words of Indian, Portuguese, and English origin. A significant number of East Indians have made Kenya their home, comprising a large segment of the merchant population.

In 1963, following the lengthy Mau Mau rebellion, Kenya gained its independence from the crumbling British empire. However, colonial rule also left its imprint, ranging from the privileged status generally afforded to white visitors to the national obsession with drinking tea. English is the official language in the government and school systems, both of which operate on the British model. In Nairobi most people speak both Kiswahili and English, in addition to the language of their ethnic group. In more isolated parts of the country, however, it isn't uncommon to meet people who speak neither English nor Swahili. This shouldn't deter the traveler; there is generally someone who speaks English or is adept at hand signals.

Long considered by Western governments to be the most stable democracy in sub-Saharan Africa, Kenya has come under increasing criticism in recent years for political repression and human rights violations. Under pressure from Western aid donors, current president Daniel Arap Moi recently legalized opposition parties—although, according to observers, elections continue to suffer from widespread intimidation tactics on the part of the government. Stability can only be a relative term in a country whose president, one of the richest people in the world, lives within miles of one of the world's largest shantytowns.

Complicating the political environment, the divisive force of tribalism continues to play a powerful role in how Kenyans view themselves. In fact, most Kenyans—including those living in Nairobi—identify first and foremost with their ethnic group and traditional homeland, not with their country. The country is haunted by the struggle to incorporate its people's traditional customs and beliefs into a modern, secular state.

Western visitors will be struck by the vast differences between Kenyan culture and their own. As in most parts of sub-Saharan Africa, the pace of life and concept of time are far more relaxed than in the West. This outlook includes greeting the astounding rush-hour crushes on Nairobi city buses and *matatus* (private gypsy cabs) with smiles and laughter, and spontaneously welcoming guests into one's home and to one's table. It is considered rude to turn down offers of food and tea—which results in many very full, very wired visitors. Travelers who limit their experience of Kenya to a Western hotel in Nairobi and a guided safari (Swahili for "trip") get only the most superficial glimpse of what the country has to offer.

—Keith Yazmir, San Francisco, California

Official name: Republic of Kenya. **Area:** 224,960 square miles (slightly smaller than Texas). **Population:** 25,241,000. **Population density:** 112 inhabitants per square mile. **Capital and largest city:** Nairobi (pop. 959,000). **Language:** Swahili (official), Luhya, Luo, Meru, Kikuyu. **Religion:** Roman Catholic, Protestant, Islam. **Per capita income:** US$380. **Currency:** Kenyan shilling. **Literacy rate:** 50%. **Average daily temperature:** Nairobi: June, 61°F; December, 64°F. **Average number of days with precipitation:** June, 9; December, 8.

TRAVEL

U.S. citizens need a passport and a visa to enter Kenya. Yellow fever and cholera vaccinations may be requested. A copy of a return or onward ticket or a letter from a travel agent is also needed. For specific requirements, check with the **Embassy of the Republic of Kenya**, 2249 R Street NW, Washington, DC 20008; (202) 387-6101. There are also Kenyan consulates in Los Angeles and New York.

Getting Around

Bus service extends to all parts of the country, and is provided by vehicles ranging from comfortable air-conditioned buses on a few main routes to *matatus*, crowded minibuses which provide cheap transportation on local routes. Try to choose one that is already full of people; otherwise you'll have to wait around until more are rounded up. In cities like Nairobi, taxis are plentiful. **Train** service is also available, although most only travel at night. In addition, a number of small domestic **airlines** provide fairly inexpensive service to the various regions of the country—a timesaver but also an opportunity to see the breathtaking landscape from above.

The majority of people in rural areas travel by flagging down vehicles, whether *matatus*, trucks, or cars. Generally speaking, when offered a ride you are expected to pay a small amount to the driver. At the other extreme, you can rent your own **car** or jeep in Nairobi or Mombasa (the minimum age is usually 23). Be warned: Gas is expensive and accidents can be costly if your insurance is not comprehensive. Your U.S. driver's license is valid in Kenya, but remember to stay on the *left* side of the road. Kenya's famed game preserves and national parks are accessible to motorists driving their own cars, but most visitors choose to see them as part of an organized tour. Travelers should be aware that there have been incidents of petty crime in game preserves as well as in Nairobi.

Eating and Sleeping

Youth hostels are just catching on in Kenya. For more information, contact Hostelling International/American Youth Hostels (see page 54) or the **Kenya Youth Hostels Association**, PO Box 48661, Nairobi; (254) 2-723012. For a list of independent hostels, contact **Kenya Backpackers Hostels**, Mrs. Roche, Third Avenue Parklands, Nairobi.

For Further Information

General information is available from the **Kenya Tourist Office**, 424 Madison Avenue, New York, NY 10017; (212) 486-1300. One of the best guidebooks to the country is *Kenya: A Travel Survival Kit*, available for $13.95 from Lonely Planet Publications. Also good is *The Real Guide: Kenya* ($12.95). An excellent book to read in preparation for your trip is *Insight Guide: Kenya* ($19.95). For more information on Lonely Planet, *Real Guides*, and *Insight Guides*, see pages 56–57.

WORK

In order to work in Kenya, it is necessary to obtain a work permit; application for the permit must be made by the employer. Permits are issued only when there are no Kenyan applicants for the job. For further information contact the Embassy of Kenya (see "Travel," above).

Internships/Traineeships

Programs sponsored by CIEE members are described below. Consult Appendix I for the addresses of the institutions listed in this section.

Ramapo College of New Jersey. *Summer Internship Program and Study Travel Tour*. Program combines six weeks of student teaching with a three-week study tour. Students serve as interns in a rural high school or in an urban, pre-college institute. Permission of program directors and at least three weeks prior living experience in a non-Western environment are required. Apply by May 2.

STUDY

Following are educational programs offered by member institutions of the Council on International Educational Exchange. Unless otherwise noted, consult Appendix I for the addresses where you can write for more information.

Semester and Academic Year

General Studies

International Student Exchange Program (ISEP). Academic year. Direct reciprocal exchange between U.S. universities and Kenyatta University. Full curriculum options. Rolling admissions. Open only to students at ISEP-member institutions. Contact ISEP for list of members.

Kalamazoo College. *Kalamazoo in Kenya*. Nairobi. Fall semester and academic year. Study at University of Nairobi. Juniors and seniors with 2.75 GPA. Apply by February 15.

Ramapo College of New Jersey. *Kenya Study—Travel Tour*. Various locations. Three weeks in July. History, culture, and ethnic groups of Kenya. Sophomores to graduate students and adults. Apply by April 20. Contact: Study Abroad Office, Ramapo College of New Jersey, 505 Ramapo Valley Road, Room D-204, Mahwah, NJ 07430-9926; (201) 529-7463.

St. Lawrence University. *Kenya Semester Program*. Nairobi. Fall and spring semesters. Academic courses plus one-month internship with private or public agency. Apply by February 20 for fall; October 10 for spring.

World Learning/School for International Training. *College Semester Abroad*. Lamu, Nairobi, Zanzibar (Tanzania). Fall and spring semesters. Coastal studies. Intensive Swahili-language study, development-studies seminar, independent-study project, village stays, educational travel, and homestay. Sophomores to seniors with 2.5 GPA. Apply by May 7 for fall; October 7 for spring. Contact: College Semester Abroad Admissions at (800) 336-1616.

College Semester Abroad. Nairobi. Fall and spring semesters. Intensive language study, independent-study project, seminar in Kenyan life and culture, field-study methods seminar, and rural-development seminar. Excursions to Tanzania and rural Kenya; homestay. Sophomores to seniors with 2.5 GPA.

Apply by May 7 for fall; October 7 for spring. Contact: College Semester Abroad Admissions at (800) 336-1616.

International Relations

American University. *Kenya Study Tour*. Fall semester (12 weeks in Washington, DC, and three weeks in Kenya). International environment and development focusing on global policy issues. Second-semester sophomores to seniors with 2.75 GPA. Apply by March 15. Contact: World Capitals Programs, Dunblane House—Tenley Campus, American University, Washington, DC 20016-8083; (202) 895-4900/4937.

Summer and Short-Term

General Studies

University of Illinois at Urbana-Champaign. *Summer Program in Kenya*. Kiswahili language and Kenyan history and culture. Juniors to graduate students with 3.0 GPA. Apply by December 15.

University of Minnesota. *Minnesota Studies in International Development (MSID)*. Academic year. Predeparture coursework at the University of Minnesota fall quarter; internship in development-related research or action project in Kenya during winter and spring quarters required. Juniors to graduates and adults with interest in development. A 2.5 GPA is required; apply by May 1. Contact: The Global Campus, University of Minnesota, 106 Nicholson Hall, 216 Pillsbury Drive SE, Minneapolis, MN 55455-0138; (612) 625-3379.

EXPLORING THE CULTURE OF KENYA

Readings and Films

The works of Ngugi Wa Thiong'o, currently the best-known Kenyan writer, have been highly influential for the last 30 years. Many are considered so volatile by the Kenyan government that he was imprisoned and ultimately exiled. Among his most important works are *Ngaahika Ndeenda: I Will Marry When I Want* (1982), written with Ngugi Wa Mirii, and *Matigari* (1986), about a fictional freedom fighter who emerges from the forest after the rebellion to look for the "new" Kenya. Other novels by Thiong'o are *Weep Not, Child* (1964), set before and during the Mau Mau insurgency, and *Petals of Blood* (1978), which presents his view of contemporary Kenya. The novel *Devil on the Cross* (1982), which shows his increasing political commitment, was written on scraps of toilet paper during his imprisonment.

The Mau Mau rebellion, which helped end colonial rule in Kenya, is dealt with in *Mau Mau Detainee* (1975), by J. M. Kariuki, a Kikuyu tribesman and participant in the uprising. Meja Mwangi's *Carcass for Hounds* is also set during the rebellion, in the Laikipia district. Other books by Mwangi include *Kill Me Quick* (1973), about two unemployed youths in Nairobi, and *Going Down River Road* (1976), a vivid story of a construction worker whose life crumbles around him. Recently, both Thiong'o and Mwangi have turned to film in order to communicate more directly with their audiences. *Carcass of Hounds* was made into a film entitled *Cry Freedom* (1980, not to be confused with the Hollywood treatment of Stephen Biko's life of the same name) by Nigerian film director Ola Balogun. Thomas Akare's work is harder and less sentimental. In *The Slums* (1981), he presents a powerful look at the "other" Nairobi to which the rich bring their cars to be washed by the novel's protagonists.

A book that looks at the relationships of Africans and Europeans under colonialism is Mugu R. Gatheru's autobiography, *Child of Two Worlds* (1964). Gatheru, the son of a tribal ritualist, became a professor of African history after studying in Kenya, India, Britain, and America. In addition, a couple of nonfiction works provide insights into the lives of contemporary Kenyans. Tepit Ole Saitoti's *The Worlds of the Maasai* examines the complexities of that traditional society as it struggles to survive in the modern world. *Three Swahili Women: Life Histories* (1989), by Sarah Mirza and Margaret Strobel, presents a picture of life in the coastal region of the country.

MADAGASCAR

Situated off the eastern coast of Africa, this island has historically been a crossroads of cultures. Africans, Indonesians, Indians, Asians, and Arabs have come to Madagascar at different points in history. The result is a unique people, the Malagasy. Correspondingly, the country is a cultural treasure chest. Each corner of the island seems to afford a new find: the capital city and coasts bustle with rickshaws from India (called *pousse-pousses*); the south is the home of traditional Indonesian dances with delicate hand motions set to African rhythms; the hillsides of the high plateau sport a patchwork of rice paddies cultivated along a series of terraces.

Visitors to Madagascar land in Antananarivo, the capital city. Keep your eyes peeled during the flight: the landscape features lush green areas interspersed among rich red earth. Antananarivo itself is a city of point and counterpoint: its chic cafés, boulangeries, and coiffeurs are surrounded by barefoot street vendors selling newspapers, fresh fruit, and anything else that may be of value to a passerby. There are two official languages in Madagascar, French and Malagasy, the native tongue. Although most people in the capital speak some French, an effort to learn and speak Malagasy will be rewarded a hundred times over.

While rich in cultures, Madagascar is economically one of the poorest countries in the world. In the poorer sections the houses are pieced together with shards of tin, the clothes with scraps of fabric and mismatched thread; the cars, tables, and doorsteps redefine the meaning of the word *recycle*. The poverty take its toll on the roads of the island. Transportation can be slow and reliable by land, more convenient but more expensive by air.

Recent political turmoil has left the country in a state of flux, and tensions between the two major political factions occasionally erupt. Long-standing disputes with France over the sovereignty of several islands off Madagascar's northern tip remain, although internal strife has died down a great deal in the face of recent reforms. Traveling in Madagascar requires a great deal of persistence, but it is a wholly unique and rewarding experience.

—Will Wadman, Providence, Rhode Island

Official name: Democratic Republic of Madagascar. **Area:** 226,657 square miles (slightly smaller than Texas). **Population:** 12,185,000. **Population density:** 53 inhabitants per square mile. **Capital and largest city:** Antananarivo (pop. 802,000). **Language:** Malagasy (official), French. **Religion:** Animism, Christianity, Moslem. **Per capita income:** US$200. **Currency:** Franc. **Literacy rate:** 53%. **Average daily high/low:** Antananarivo: January, 79°F/61°F; July, 68°F/48°F. **Average number of days with precipitation:** Anatananarivo: January, 21; July, 10.

TRAVEL

U.S. citizens must have a passport and visa to enter Madagascar. Proof of yellow fever and cholera immunization is also required. For further information, contact the **Embassy of the Democratic Republic of Madagascar**, 2374 Massachusetts Avenue NW, Washington, DC 20008; (202) 265-5525. Madagascar also has consulates in New York, Philadelphia, and Palo Alto.

Getting Around

Air Madagascar maintains an extensive domestic network, serving 58 destinations. Road conditions are generally poor and transportation is slow. Train service, however, is even slower. The quickest way to get around the country is by private **taxi**. The most common way to get around is by shared taxi or bus. Regular **boat** service connects cities around the coast.

Following a period of political instability, at press time travel conditions have stabilized according to the U.S. Department of State's most recent **Consular Information Sheet** (see pages 8–9). Street crime in the city of Antananarivo is still a risk, however, and generally occurs near public transportation areas and at night.

For Further Information

You can find reliable travel information on Madagascar in the recently updated *Madagascar and Comoros: A Travel Survival Kit*, available for $10.95 from Lonely Planet Publications. *Africa on a Shoestring* ($27.95) also contains information on Madagascar. For more information on Lonely Planet, see page 56.

STUDY

Below you will find an academic program offered by a CIEE-member institution. Consult Appendix I for the contact address.

General Studies

World Learning/School for International Training. *College Semester Abroad*. Antananarivo, Fort Dauphin. Fall and spring semesters. Area/French language studies. Intensive language study, homestay, area-studies seminar, field-study seminar, independent-study project. Sophomores to graduate students with 2.5 GPA and one and a half years college-level French. Apply by May 7 for fall; October 7 for spring. Contact: College Semester Abroad Admissions at (800) 336-1616.

NAMIBIA

In 1946, South Africa annexed the southwest African territory now known as the Republic of Namibia. From 1946 to 1968 it was known as South-West Africa, and in 1968 it was renamed Namibia by the United Nations. Namibia achieved independence from South Africa on March 21, 1990. It is one of 10 countries that comprise Southern Africa. With 1,280 kilometers of desolate coastline along the Atlantic and the vast shifting dunes of the Namib Desert spreading into the interior some 80 to 130 kilometers, Namibia shares its remaining borders with Angola to the north, with the Caprivi Strip in the northeast (bordering Zambia), Botswana to the east, and South Africa to the south. More than half the size of Alaska, Namibia rests on a high, semiarid-to-desert plateau that slopes down to the Kalahari Desert on the Botswana border.

Though Namibia possesses some of the richest, most abundant and most valuable natural resources in Africa (including gem diamonds, copper, lead, zinc, cadmium, uranium, salt, silver, coal, natural gas, fish, cattle), the majority of Namibians live in extreme poverty. Namibia's only deep-water port, Walvis Bay, was annexed by South Africa in 1977. With 137 airports of various sizes throughout Namibia, the largest located in the capital city of Windhoek, movement around the country is not a problem.

Prior to Namibian independence in 1990, South Africa's racist apartheid laws kept blacks and whites separate and unequal in Namibia. All areas of public life are now officially integrated. In most towns, motels, hotels, cafés, and restaurants are open to all. However, individual Afrikaners (or other whites) continue to practice apartheid in some of the remote rural and central urban areas. The legacy of apartheid can be seen most clearly in the structure of Windhoek, which is really two cities: the ultramodern center and business district with its fashionable shops, cinemas, hotels, German cafés and restaurants linked to spacious white suburbs; and the nearby black township of Katutura characterized by oppressive compounds and small, flimsy houses.

Like its neighbor to the east, Namibia has an abundance of wildlife. Thanks to its expansive open spaces, Namibia has some of the few great migratory herds remaining in Africa. They include kudu, giraffe, springbok, wildebeest, elephant, gemstock, zebra, eland, warthog, impala, and leopard. More than 10 national parks provide safe areas for these animals. The two most popular game reserves are the Etosha Pan Game Reserve and the Kalahari Gemsbk Park.

The area north of Windhoek and surrounding the extinct Erongo volcano near Karibib is rich in San rock paintings, the rainbow-colored lava rocks of the Burnt Mountain, and a petrified forest. Dinosaur prints can be found farther east near Kalkfeld. Famous rock paintings and challenging mountaineering also can be found northwest of Usakos at Namibia's version of the Matterhorn, the 2,000-meter Spitzkoppe. The Ai-Ais hot springs and the Fish River Canyon have superb camping facilities.

The first people to inhabit the area were a late Stone Age hunting and gathering people known as the Khoisan-speaking San (Bushmen). Today they are found in the Kalahari along the Botswana border. Various Nama and Bantu peoples migrated later from north-central and west Africa around the 3rd century A.D. Namibia, once a German protectorate, has had permanent white settlements since the 1600s. Today whites in Namibia number fewer than 100,000, yet English, German, and Afrikaans are widely spoken by blacks and whites alike. Approximately 10,000 pastoral Ovahimba, Ovajimba, and Herero people make their home in the Kaokoveld Mountains of the northwest. East of these mountains and to the north is the home of the Ovambo, who comprise 50 percent of the population—roughly 600,000. The 75,000 Damara are the second-largest indigenous group. The Herero, who now number 60,000, live primarily in the Waterberg region south of Tsumeb.

Namibia's independence in 1990 set the stage for a host of changes in the country. While Namibia and South Africa hold discussions over Walvis Bay, the violence that accompanied struggle for independence is over, and the country is focusing on normalizing commerce, education, and agriculture. President Sam Nujoma, his South-West African People's Organization, other political parties, and their friends abroad are working to create a united and prosperous nation.

—Roland A. Foulkes, Gainesville, Florida

Official name: Republic of Namibia. **Area:** 317,818 square miles. **Population:** 1,520,000. **Population density:** 4 inhabitants per square mile. **Capital and largest city:** Windhoek (pop. 114,000). **Language:** Afrikaans, English (official), several indigenous languages. **Religion:** Lutheran. **Per capita income:** US $1,240. **Currency:** South African Rand. **Literacy rate:** 16%. **Average daily high/low:** Windhoek: January, 85°F/63°F. **Average number of days with rainfall:** Windhoek: January, 8; June, 0.3.

TRAVEL

U.S. citizens visiting Namibia are required to have a passport and visa, as well as an onward/return ticket and proof of sufficient funds. For further information, contact the **Embassy of Namibia**, 1605 New Hampshire Avenue NW, Washington, DC 20009; (202) 986-0540; fax (202) 986-0443.

Getting Around

Namibia is a dry country twice the size of France divided into four natural regions: the coastal Namib desert, the central plateau, the eastern grasslands, and the forested north. A natural wonderland, Namibia is home to a vast array of unique flora and fauna. To see the animals close-up, head north to Etosha National Park.

Main roads and railways radiate from the capital of Windhoek, in the country's center. Aside from the main line to South Africa, **train** service is fairly slow and infrequent. **Bus** service can take you to main towns, but no farther. Your best bet is probably to rent a **car** or four-wheel-drive vehicle. An International Driver's Permit is required in Namibia. Main roads are paved, and even the less-traveled gravel roads are in good condition. Hitching is also acceptable. Most drivers will stop for you; however, on minor routes, they may be few and far between. Namib Air flies from Windhoek to main towns throughout the country.

For Further Information

You can ask for general information from the **Embassy of Namibia** (see "Travel," above). In Namibia, a wide range of tourist information, including the *SWA Accommodations Guide*, is available from **Namibia Tourism**, Private Bag 13346, Windhoek 9000; (264) 61-220241. Also try the Windhoek Publicity Association, PO Box 1868, Windhoek 9000; (264) 61-228160.

The best information on travel in Namibia and neighboring countries can be found in Lonely Planet's new *Zimbabwe, Botswana and Namibia: A Travel Survival Kit* ($16.95). An excellent book to read in preparation for your trip is *Insight Guide: Namibia* ($19.95). For more information on Lonely Planet Publications and *Insight Guides*, see pages 56–57.

WORK

In order to work in Namibia, the embassy recommends that you secure a job before departure. It is also necessary to obtain a work permit once you get to Namibia. Permits are issued by the **Ministry of Home Affairs**, Permanent Secretary, Private Bag 13200, Windhoek 9000, Namibia. For more information contact the Embassy of Namibia (see "Travel," above).

STUDY

The following are educational programs offered by a CIEE-member institution. Consult Appendix I for the contact address and phone.

Semester and Academic Year

General Studies

Augsburg College. *Southern Africa Societies in Transition: The View from Namibia*. Windhoek. Fall term. Courses explore the complex political, social, and economic dynamics of building a new nation as well as issues facing all of Southern Africa. Excursions and brief homestays. Sophomores to seniors. Apply by April 1.

Women's Studies

Augsburg College. *Women and Development: A Southern Africa Perspective*. Windhoek. Spring term. Courses introduce central issues facing Southern Africa with emphasis on the position of women. Excursions and brief homestays. Sophomores to seniors. Apply by October 15.

NIGER

A country of extremes, Niger stands at a cultural and geographical crossroads in Africa. Landlocked on the southern edge of the Sahara, two-thirds of the country is desert. Bordered by Algeria, Libya, Chad, Nigeria, Benin, Burkina Faso, and Mali, Niger is today a mostly Muslim country that encompasses five major groups of people identified by language and livelihood. A land threatened by recurrent drought and encroaching desert, it also possesses important natural resources such as uranium and petroleum.

A nation of traders and merchants at the edge of trans-Saharan route, Niger has been in contact with outside cultures throughout history. The western part of present-day Niger belonged to the Songhai empire, established in the 7th century A.D. by Berbers who in the 11th century accepted Islam. Eastern Niger was part of the Kanen-Bornu states. The southern region saw the rise of Hausa city-states in the 14th century, which were conquered by Fulani in the 19th century. However, the French occupied and colonized Niger from 1897 until the country's independence in 1960.

The southern strip of land along the border with Nigeria, about 90 miles wide extending from the Niger River to Lake Chad, is considered the "lush" savanna of the country and is home to 90 percent of Niger's population. While it *is* lush in comparison to the extreme condition of the desert in the north, this area receives only about 20 inches of rain a year—an amount that permits farming but always threatens desertification. Niamey, the capital and largest city, is conveniently located in this region on the banks of the Niger River. Although this busy river port sports some European-influenced architecture, including an attempt at a skyscraper, its character has been shaped by the physical landscape of the country and aboriginal customs: Unpaved streets, mud houses, open-air markets, multiple local languages, and camels walking down the dusty main boulevards are a constant reminder of the climate, the region, and the traditions of the Hausa and Djerma peoples.

Extending north between the arable savanna of the southern border and the desert is the Sahel, land used as pasture. Agadez is one of the most impressive cities in the north, and the first city beyond the desert via the major trans-Saharan route. A city built of mud brick, Agadez has an impressive 16th-century mosque and ruins of the sultan's palace from the same era. It is also a perfect base for excursions to the Air Mountains in the northeast. Some of the attractions in this area include the thermal waters at Tafadek and the effervescent wells at Igouloulef. Several oases in the region delight travelers, including Timia and Iferouane, which has prehistoric sights. To the northwest of Agadez is Arlit, a dusty town whose uranium mines may have saved Niger from economic disaster; the reserves in the Arlit region are among the largest in the world.

Beyond the Air Mountains is the Tenere desert, which is famous for some of the most spectacular sand dunes in the Sahara; travel through this region is difficult and requires a fair amount of planning. The north of Niger is also home to Tuareg nomads who raise cattle, camels, and goats. (They are known as the "blue men of the Sahara" because their indigo-dyed clothes have turned their hands permanently blue.) The Tuareg are one of the most famous tribal groups of the Sahara desert. They speak a Berber language and have a highly stratified caste system that includes serfs and slaves. Although Muslim, they have a matrilineal succession of chiefs and the women have a considerable amount of freedom. The fascinating traditions of the Tuareg are but one piece of the ethnic puzzle that makes up Niger, compelling the visitor to get to know its people and their history.

—Dagny Galt, Boulder, Colorado

Official name: Republic of Niger. **Area:** 489,189 square miles. **Population:** 8,154,000. **Population density:** 16 inhabitants per square mile. **Capital and largest city:** Niamey (pop. 350,000). **Language:** French, Hausa, Fulani. **Religion:** Sunni Moslem. **Per capita income:** US $290. **Currency:** CFA Franc. **Literacy rate:** 28%. **Average daily high/low:** Niamey: January, 93°F/58°F; June, 101°F/77°F. **Average number of days with precipitation:** Niamey: January, 0; June, 6.

TRAVEL

U.S. citizens need a passport and visa to enter Niger. Proof of yellow fever and cholera vaccination is also required. For further information, contact the **Embassy of the Republic of Niger**, 2204 R Street NW, Washington, DC 20008; (202) 483-4224.

Getting Around

There are no rail lines in Niger, but there is a good system of paved roads and a **bus** network to go along with it. You can also travel in the back of **trucks** or in a **shared taxi**.

At press time, the latest Department of State **Consular Information Sheet** advised that travel north of the central city of Tahoa ''is especially dangerous, because of possible armed attack.'' It also warned that ''areas bordering Mali and Algeria are sites of banditry or violent attack.'' Overland travel between Niger and Algeria is prohibited.

For Further Information

You can find reliable travel information on Niger in the recently updated *West Africa: A Travel Survival Kit*, available for $19.95 from Lonely Planet Publications. Lonely Planet's *Africa on a Shoestring* ($27.95) also contains information on Niger. For more information on Lonely Planet, see page 56.

WORK

In order to obtain information on working in Niger, it is necessary to write to the **Ministry of Foreign Affairs**, Niamey, Republic of Niger, West Africa. The Embassy of Niger in the U.S. does not provide this information.

STUDY

Below is a study program offered by a CIEE-member institution. Consult Appendix I for the contact address.

Semester and Academic Year

Language and Culture of Niger

Boston University. Niamey. Fall semester. Language and cultural immersion in French and Hausa offering students individual field placements and community-service opportunities. Sophomores to college graduates and graduate students in good academic standing. Apply by March 15.

NIGERIA

Nigeria is not for the faint of heart. The incessant barrage of intense heat, colors, sounds, and tastes tests the culture-shock threshold of all but the most resilient. The country—Africa's most populous—shows the strains of a large population competing for scarce resources at almost every turn; however, in this somewhat hostile environment you'll also see an aggressive enjoyment of life.

The Niger and Benue rivers form a Y that divides the country into north and south, and the south into distinct southeastern and southwestern regions. The south is home to Lagos—the capital until recently, when it was moved to the more central city of Abuja—as well as most of the country's larger cities; it is also the focus of the government's efforts toward social and economic development. Each of the major regions is populated by different ethnic groups, the chief of which are the Yoruba in the southwest, the Ibo in the southeast, and the Hausa-Fulani in the north. Nigeria has struggled with these ethnic divisions since its amalgamation into one territory under British control, but especially since independence in 1960. In 1967 ethnic animosities culminated in a civil war that left an estimated one million Nigerians (mostly Ibos) dead. Today Nigeria maintains a fragile national unity, but the federal government remains shaky, with six military coups since independence—a record for Africa.

Although Nigeria is the second-largest African oil-producing nation (after Libya), massive migration from rural to urban areas, an unstable industrial base, rampant inflation, and governmental corruption and mismanagement have created immense poverty and one of the most precarious economies in Africa. Social reform has been frustratingly slow, and the cities to which rural migrants flock have become dangerous and overcrowded.

Despite these modern ills, Nigeria has succeeded in preserving its traditional cultures. Indigenous beliefs are much in evidence, although most contemporary Nigerians profess to be adherents of Islam or Christianity. Despite the influx of Western-style stores, the Nigerian love of bargaining is still on display in the open-air markets. You will also have the opportunity, especially in the south, to experience colorful traditional festivals on every occasion, be it a birth, a funeral, the time for planting, or the harvest. In fact, no matter how much you learn about Nigeria before your departure, prepare to be surprised by its contradictions and amazing diversity.

—Sarah Wood, New York, New York

Official name: Federal Republic of Nigeria. **Area:** 356,667 square miles (about three times the size of Nevada). **Population:** 88,500,000. **Population**

density: 248 inhabitants per square mile. **Capital:** Abuja. **Largest city:** Lagos (pop. 1,300,000). **Language:** English (official), Hausa, Yoruba, Ibo. **Religion:** Islam, Christianity. **Per capita income:** US$230. **Currency:** Naira. **Literacy rate:** 51%. **Average daily temperature:** Lagos: June, 78°; December, 80°. **Average number of days with precipitation:** Lagos: June, 8; December, 0.

TRAVEL

U.S. citizens need a passport and a visa to enter Nigeria. Proof of yellow fever and cholera vaccinations is also required. For further information, check with the **Embassy of the Republic of Nigeria**, 2201 M Street NW, Washington, DC 20037; (202) 822-1500. You can also check with the Nigerian consulate in New York.

Getting Around

At press time, the latest Department of State Consular Information Sheet advised that the international airport at Lagos does not meet minimum security standards of the International Civil Aviation Organization. Other Nigerian airports are reported to have nonfunctioning radar. Nigerian airports are also targets for a large amount of petty crime. Plane tickets are inexpensive but often overbooked; unless you pay a tip—or *dash*—to the proper airport personnel, you may find that your seat's not guaranteed.

Nigeria's road system, however, is one of the best in Africa and includes an expressway linking Ibadan and Lagos, the country's two largest cities. **Buses** connect the main cities, but are no less expensive than **taxis**—only safer. The fastest means of transport is provided by shared taxis (cars and minibuses), which speed along fixed routes, leaving when full and picking up and dropping off passengers along the way. **Hitchhiking** is relatively easy but the driver will expect some payment. A limited **rail** system provides a cheap but slower alternative for those with more time.

For Further Information

You can find reliable travel information on Nigeria in the recently updated *West Africa: A Travel Survival Kit*, available for $19.95 from Lonely Planet Publications. Lonely Planet's *Africa on a Shoestring* ($27.95) also contains information on Nigeria. For more information on Lonely Planet, see page 56.

WORK

To work in Nigeria, it is necessary to secure a job and obtain a work permit before arriving in the country. The employer must provide you with a written job offer, which you must present at the Embassy of Nigeria in order to be issued the permit. For more information, contact the Embassy of Nigeria (see "Travel," above).

Voluntary Service

For persons interested in voluntary service work the Year Abroad Program sponsored by the International Christian Youth Exchange offers persons ages 18 to 30 voluntary-service opportunities in the fields of health care, education, the environment, construction, and more. See page 25 for more information.

STUDY

The following educational programs offered by CIEE-member institutions. Unless otherwise noted, consult Appendix I for the addresses of the colleges and universities listed in this section.

Semester and Academic Year

General Studies

Brown University. *Brown in Nigeria*. Ibadan. Semester and academic year. Full enrollment at University of Ibadan in faculty of choice with Nigerian students. Dormitory accommodations. Juniors in good academic standing and with demonstrated academic interest in Africa. Apply by April 15 for fall and academic year; October 15 for spring.

University of Pennsylvania. *Penn-Ibadan Link Program*. Ibadan. Semester and academic year. Offered in conjunction with the University of Ibadan and the Institute of African Studies. Nigerian and West African studies. Juniors and seniors. Apply by March 15 for fall and academic year; October 15 for spring.

World Learning/School for International Training. *College Semester Abroad*. Lagos, Ibadan, and Ife. Fall and spring semesters. Intensive language study with excursions to sites in northern Nigeria, seminar on Nigerian life, field-study methods seminar, culture and development. Sophomores to seniors with 2.5 GPA. Apply by May 7 for fall; October 7 for spring. Contact: College Semester Abroad Admissions at (800) 336-1616.

Summer and Short-Term

General Studies

University of Pennsylvania. *Penn-in-Ibadan*. Summer. Examination of indigenous traditional culture and contemporary society. Apply by April 1.

EXPLORING NIGERIAN CULTURE

Readings

Nigeria has produced many of the more popular African writers writing in English today. Chinua Achebe, probably the most famous African novelist, is best known for *Things Fall Apart* (1962), which explores what happens to traditional African life as it falls under the influence of Western culture. *Arrow of God* and *No Longer at Ease* (1963) also explore this theme, while the novel *A Man of the People* is about politics and government corruption in 1960s Nigeria.

Wole Soyinka, winner of the 1985 Nobel Prize for literature, also addresses problems of contemporary life. *Ake* (1983) is the autobiography of his childhood. *A Play of Giants* (1984) portrays a group of dictatorial African leaders in an embassy in New York. Soyinka has turned to film in the last few years; his directorial debut was the film *Blues for a Prodigal* (1984).

A number of other Nigerian writers have also distinguished themselves. T. Obinkaram Echewa's novel *The Crippled Dancer* (1986) concerns feuding and intrigue within an Igbo village. Buchi Emecheta's *In the Ditch* (1987), about the problems of a Nigerian woman living in London, and *Second Class Citizen* (1983), which tells the story of the same woman's early years in Nigeria, have found a large international audience. Flora Nwapa writes about unconventional African women in such books as *Efuru* (1966).

SENEGAL

Senegal, the westernmost nation on the African mainland, was the point of embarkation for slaves being shipped to the New World. Today it is the point of arrival for most travelers to West Africa.

Until independence in 1958, Senegal was controlled by France for the better part of three centuries. The French colonial agenda, however, was only a partial success. Today, while many Senegalese speak French and are Catholic, most are Muslims who speak African languages such as Wolof, Malinke', or Pulaar. Unfortunately, the most visible legacies of French colonialism are also the most tragic: the slave warehouse on the island of Goree' and an environment ravaged by the French focus on the cultivation of peanuts.

The central district of Dakar, Senegal's capital, is clean and open to the sun and sea. It bears the imprint of Leopold Senghor, the nation's president for its first 20 years of independence. Senghor, who loved France, had many of the public buildings designed in French style and named the streets after French heroes. But the rest of Dakar—and the rest of Senegal—are marked by its African heritage. Herds of goats pass through city streets, urban dwellers cook over open charcoal stoves, and brightly dressed nomads drive their flocks through the sandy northern savannah.

The transformation of Senegal into a multiparty democracy in 1983 has encouraged political activity and a freer press. There are several independent newspapers, and European and American papers are often available in Dakar. The Senegalese love music, and a few of their stars—reggae performer Alpha Blondy and rock star Youssou N'Dour among them—are well known in the United States. In Senegal itself, cassette tapes play everywhere, and the periodic village festivals are full of music and dance. Much of the music is unforgettably beautiful.

Sadly, in the extreme north, along the Senegal River, the savannah is being transformed into desert. In the 19th century the French covered northern Senegal with peanut farms. This turned the Senegalese away from traditional farming methods and crops, and ultimately turned thousands of acres of rich land into desert.

If your French is weak, get a visa to enter The Gambia, a tiny English-speaking country entirely surrounded by Senegal. An express bus links Dakar and Banjul, the Gambian capital. The Gambia is a silver of a nation, 200 miles long and about 10 miles wide, that stretches along the banks of the River Gambia in central Senegal and boasts fine beaches, picturesque towns reminiscent of the Caribbean, markets buzzing with commerce, and villages with a lively traditional life.

—Jason Zweig, New York, New York

Official name: Republic of Senegal. **Area:** 75,750 square miles (about the size of Utah). **Population:** 7,952,000. **Population density:** 104 inhabitants per square mile. **Capital and largest city:** Dakar (pop. 1,400,000). **Language:** French (official); Wolof, Serer, Peul, Tukulor, and other regional languages. **Religion:** Islam. **Per capita income:** US$615. **Currency:** CFA Franc. **Literacy rate:** 10%. **Average daily temperature:** Dakar: June, 79°; December, 74°. **Average number of days with precipitation:** Dakar: June, 2; December, 0.1.

TRAVEL

U.S. citizens need a passport but not a visa for visits of less than 90 days. Onward/return tickets and proof of yellow fever vaccination are also required. For further information, check with the **Embassy of the Republic of Senegal**, 2112 Wyoming Avenue NW, Washington, DC 20008; (202) 230-0540.

Getting Around

Senegal's main roads run north to south from Mauritania to Guinea-Bissau, but they are mostly concentrated on the western side of the country, near the coast. The roads are well served by **buses** and **taxis**. For travel westward, the **train** from Dakar to Bamako, Mali, is most convenient. A shorter line runs between Dakar and St. Louis to the north.

Boat travel is a good alternative for travel south along the coast. Le Diola runs twice weekly between Dakar and Ziguinchor. Hourly ferries connect Dakar with Goree Island.

For Further Information

For general tourist information, contact the **Senegal Tourist Office**, 888 Seventh Avenue, New York, NY 10106; (212) 757-7115; fax (212) 757-7220. You can find reliable travel information on Senegal in the recently updated *West Africa: A Travel Survival Kit*, available for $19.95 from Lonely Planet Publications. Lonely Planet's *Africa on a Shoestring* ($27.95) also contains information on Senegal. An excellent book to read in preparation for your trip is *Insight Guide: Gambia and Senegal* ($19.95). For more information on Lonely Planet and *Insight Guides*, see pages 56–57.

WORK

It is very difficult for foreigners to obtain regular, salaried employment in Senegal. A job must be arranged before arriving in the country and a work permit is required. For more information contact the **Ministry of Labor**, Administrative Building, Dakar, Senegal.

STUDY

Programs sponsored by CIEE-member institutions are described below. Unless otherwise noted, consult Appendix I for the address where you can write for more information.

Semester and Academic Year

General Studies

Kalamazoo College. *Kalamazoo in Senegal.* Dakar. Academic year. Study at University of Dakar. Juniors and seniors with 20 quarter-hours of French and 2.75 GPA. Apply by February 15.

University of Wisconsin at Madison. *Academic Year in Senegal.* St. Louis. Academic year. Wolof-language study, West African history and culture, letters and humanities, law and political science, economics and business, law and computer science. Instruction in French. Juniors and seniors in good academic standing with four semesters of college French. Apply by second Friday in February.

International Relations

University of Minnesota. *Minnesota Studies in International Development (MSID).* Academic year. Predeparture coursework at the University of Minnesota fall quarter; internship in development-related research or action project in Senegal during winter and spring quarters required. Juniors to graduates and adults with interest in development; 2.5 GPA and two years of French. Apply by May 1. Contact: The Global Campus, University of Minnesota, 106C Nicholson Hall, 216 Pillsbury Drive SE, Minneapolis, MN 55455-0138; (612) 625-3379.

EXPLORING SENEGALESE CULTURE

Readings

Sembene Ousmane's novel *Xala* (1983) is an amusing story about a Senegalese businessman caught between the traditional way of life and the modern world—and particularly between monogamy and polygamy. His other books include *God's Bits of Wood* (1970), considered a classic, and his recently reissued book of short stories, *Tribal Scars and Other Stories* (1974). Ousmane works mostly with film at present, having found in it a more expressive medium for his work.

Nafissatou Diallo's novels also describe the traditional and modern aspects of Senegalese society. Her last novel, *Fary, Princess of Tiali*, is a West African Cinderella story about the marriage of a young girl who travels to the village of Mboupbene to become a princess by marriage. The novel describes the inner workings of the family, the mystic rituals of the region's holy men, the splendor of a traditional royal wedding, and the economic poverty of the lower classes.

SIERRA LEONE

Sierra Leone (which means "Lion Mountains") was named by Portuguese explorers. In the 18th century the British wanted to expand trade in West Africa and find a place for freedmen to settle after slavery was abolished in the British Empire. The first settlements in Sierra Leone of freed slaves from the Americas were made in 1787; however, most of the original settlers fell prey to either disease or hostile locals. While the freedmen settlers and their descendants, or "Krios" as they came to be called, enjoyed a privileged status under British rule, they never made up more than a small percententage of the population and do not currently have much political power, although they comprise a disproportionately large percentage of the country's intellectuals and professionals.

Today, some 18 different ethnic groups call Sierra Leone home. But since independence in 1961, its politics have been characterized by a struggle between the two largest groups, the Temnes and the Mendes, which are about equal in numbers. The result has been political instability, including a high incidence of civil violence and military coups.

Corruption and mismanagement have led to Sierra Leone's transformation from one of Africa's richest nations to one of its poorest. The diamond industry, from which Sierra Leone derives much of its export wealth, is crippled by the smuggling of up to one-third of the gems out of the country. Agriculture and tourism are being developed, especially because the diamond industry is proving so difficult to manage. Agricultural exports include palm kernels, cocoa, ginger, and coffee. Government officials are encouraging the planting of rice, a staple crop whose native consumption is so great that rice has to be imported from other countries.

Sierra Leone is noted for its lush tropical vegetation, beautiful mountains, and unspoiled beaches. Tourism has grown rapidly along the mountainous Freetown peninsula, where during the winter season the limited number of resort hotels fill to capacity with Europeans seeking warm weather, beaches, and cheap prices. Tourist enclaves have also cropped up at Bo, a city southeast of Freetown. However, you'll encounter few tourists in other areas of the country, including the mountainous interior, where roads are poor and tourist facilities are virtually nonexistent. Tourism is an important source of income, one that is being expanded with the hopes of turning around Sierra Leone's economic downslide.

—Raquel Hodgson, Berkeley, California

Official name: Republic of Sierra Leone. **Area:** 27,925 square miles (slightly larger than West Virginia). **Population:** 4,274,000. **Population density:** 153 inhabitants per square mile. **Capital and largest city:** Freetown (pop. 469,000). **Language:** English (official); Mende, Temne, Creole. **Religion:** animism, Islam, Christianity. **Per capita income:** US$325. **Currency:** Leone. **Literacy rate: 21%. Average daily high/low:** Freetown: January 85°F/75°F; June, 86°F/75°F. **Average number of days with precipitation:** Freetown: January, 0.8; June, 23.

TRAVEL

U.S. citizens need a passport and a visa to visit Sierra Leone. Proof of vaccinations against cholera and yellow fever are also required. For specific requirements, contact the **Embassy of Sierra Leone**, 1701 19th Street NW, Washington, DC 20009; (202) 939-9261.

Getting Around

Despite its small size, Sierra Leone is not always easy to get around, especially in the rainy season. The transport system is limited to government **buses** and ***poda podas*** (local trucks). Bus service is reasonably good between Freeport and the larger centers of population. Pickup trucks or vans tend to be slow, crowded, unreliable, and uncomfortable. Roads (not entirely paved and sometimes impassable) connect Sierra Leone to the neighboring countries of Liberia and Guinea.

At press time, the latest Department of State **Consular Information Sheet** advised that because of civil strife, a number of areas are closed to travelers. Check with the Department of State (see pages 8–9) for more up-to-date information.

For Further Information

You can find reliable travel information on Sierra Leone in the recently updated *West Africa: A Travel Survival Kit*, available for $19.95 from Lonely Planet Publications. Lonely Planet's *Africa on a Shoestring* ($27.95) also contains information on Sierra Leone. For more information on Lonely Planet, see page 56.

WORK

It is very difficult for foreigners to obtain regular, salaried employment in Sierra Leone. For more information contact the Embassy of Sierra Leone (see "Travel," above). For another type of work experience, see the internship and voluntary service sections below.

Internships/Traineeships

Programs offered by members of the Council on International Educational Exchange are listed below.

Association for International Practical Training. *IAESTE Trainee Program.* On-the-job training for undergraduate and graduate students in technical fields such as engineering, computer science, agriculture, architecture, mathematics, and the physical and natural sciences. See page 19 for more information.

Voluntary Service

For persons interested in voluntary service work, the Year Abroad Program sponsored by the **International Christian Youth Exchange** offers persons between 18 and 30 voluntary-service opportunities in the fields of health care, education, the environment, construction, and more. See page 25 for more information.

STUDY

The following is an educational program offered by a member of the Council on International Educational Exchange. Consult Appendix I for the address of the institution listed in this section.

Semester and Academic Year

General Studies

Kalamazoo College. *Kalamazoo in Sierra Leone*. Freetown. Fall and winter quarters (September 15 to February 15). Study at Fourah Bay College, University of Sierra Leone. Juniors and seniors with 2.75 GPA. Apply by February 15.

EXPLORING THE CULTURE OF SIERRA LEONE

Readings

William Conton's book *The African*, published in 1960, remains the best known Sierra Leonean work. It tells the story of a young man's education and his eventual rise to power as a nationalist leader. Recently, poet and novelist Syl Cheney-Coker has also risen to some prominence, drawing not only on Sierra Leone for his material, but also all of Africa as well as Europe and the United States. *The Graveyard Also Has Teeth* (1980) is a collection of some of his poems. For an example of his fiction, read *The Last Harmattan of Alusine Dunbar* (1991), which traces black pioneers returning from America just after the Revolution to the West African coast, and tells the story of their settlement up until today.

SOUTH AFRICA

South Africa has established itself as one of the chief economic powers of the continent by taking advantage of its mineral wealth, location, and fair climate. Because of the traditional governmental policy of apartheid, however, this wealth is concentrated almost exclusively in the hands of white South Africans.

Apartheid—formally implemented in South Africa in the late 1940s and now on the path to abolition—is a concept of government that segregates the population along four main racial categories: black, white, "coloured" (an ambiguous grouping comprising Indians and biracial persons, although interracial marriage was strictly outlawed until recently), and Asian.

The new constitution drafted in 1993 will do much to dismantle apartheid. The infamous homelands, in which black South Africans were internally exiled since apartheid's inception, are slated for abolishment. Citizens no longer need to carry a racially coded passbook. Yet although the official government line has changed dramatically in recent years, it will take some time for old attitudes to change and for old wounds to finally heal.

Cape Town, with one of the world's most beautiful settings, is probably South Africa's friendliest and most loved city. Cape Town lies on a peninsula nestled between the mountains and two great oceans, the Indian and the Atlantic. Known for its superb beaches, climate, food, and wine, Cape Town is also the home of two of South Africa's greatest schools, the Universities of Cape Town and Stellenbosch. In Cape Town one will also find the recently opened Victoria and Albert Waterfront, an extremely successful urban renewal project filled with trendy bars, shops, and restaurants.

On the opposite side of the country, easily accessible by frequent and inexpensive plane service, lies the city of Durban. While Cape Town is considered relaxed and slow-paced, Durban is wild and crazy. It is here that one finds some of the best nightlife in the country. The land surrounding Durban is often referred to as The Valley of a Thousand Hills. This is Zulu country, where one is just as likely to find a man driving a team of oxen as an ordinary automobile.

Inland, in the Afrikaner-dominated Transvaal, is Johannesburg, one of the largest cities in Africa and the industrial and financial center of Southern Africa. In 1886, one of the richest gold veins in the world was discovered there. Jo'burg, as it is commonly called, was strictly segregated until recently. Most black workers still have to commute back to the townships every night after working in and around Johannesburg.

On the border with Mozambique is Kruger National Park, where the nature enthusiast will find more than 122 species of mammals, ranging from elephants and rhinoceros to zebra and impala.

South Africa has a great many things to offer the tourist, but it is not a completely free country and it is impossible to ignore this fact. The only certain thing is that South Africa is in a difficult period of adjustment.

—Gregory F. Ferro, Tucson, Arizona

Official name: Republic of South Africa. **Area:** 472,359 square miles (about twice the size of Texas). **Population:** 40,600,000. **Population density:** 85 inhabitants per square mile. **Capitals:** Pretoria (administrative), Bloemfontein (judicial), and Capetown (legislative). **Largest city:** Johannesburg (pop. 2,100,000). **Language:** Afrikaans, English (both official), Nguni, Sotho languages. **Religion:** Protestant, Roman Catholic. **Per capita income:** US$2,600. **Currency:** Rand. **Literacy rate:** 99% (whites), 69% (Asians), 62% (Indians and biracial persons), 50% (Africans). **Average daily high/low:** Cape Town: January 78°F/60°F, July 65°F/45°F; Johannesburg: January 78°F/58°F, July 63°F/39°F. **Average number of days with precipitation:** Cape Town: January, 3; July, 10. Johannesburg: January, 12; July, 1.

TRAVEL

U.S. citizens need a passport to enter South Africa, but the visa requirement has been dropped. Proof of yellow fever vaccination is required if entering from an infected area. For specific regulations, check with the **Embassy of South Africa**, 3201 New Mexico Avenue NW, Washington, DC 20016; (202) 966-1650. South Africa also has consulates in Beverly Hills, Chicago, and New York.

Although no country other than South Africa recognizes the independent **homelands** of Bophuthatswana, Ciskei, Transkei, and Venda, you will have to observe visa regulations for entering or passing through those territories from South Africa. Visas are required for stays of more than 14 days in Bophuthatswana and Transkei and more than seven days in Ciskei. Visas are not required to enter Venda, although as with the other three, you do need your passport. You may also need a reentry visa to return to South Africa from the homelands. For more information, contact the Embassy of South Africa, or the embassies of Bophuthatswana, Ciskei, Transkei, and Venda in Pretoria.

Getting Around

South Africa has a good modern system of highways ranging from expressways to an extensive network of secondary roads, most of which are paved. The best way to get around is to rent a **car**, although some rental agencies will prohibit you from driving into townships or homelands. The next best way is by shared minibus taxis. South Africa is said to be one of the easiest countries to hitchhike in, though not near major cities. There are numerous regional **bus** companies; Autonet and Greyhound cover long-distance routes. Autonet, a partially privatised government network, offers three types of service: the higher-priced Translux, the economy-class Transcity, and Transtate. Translux and Transcity buses are faster and air-conditioned, but Transtate stops at many more places. South Africa has an extensive railway network, but after becoming privatized recently it scaled back passenger service to routes between main cities. Passenger trains are called ''name trains.'' The very expensive luxury express Blue Train runs between Pretoria and Cape Town. Except for the Blue Train, **name trains** give foreign travelers a 25-percent discount off the price of first-class tickets. Another option for getting around between major cities is South African Airways.

Owing to the existence of interfactional violence, care should be taken on visits to townships. Travel in the company of persons familiar with the area. Travelers should also be cautious if visiting the ''independent homelands.''

Eating and Sleeping

In general, lodgings in South Africa aren't cheap. South Africa has 16 **youth hostels**. For more information, contact Hostelling International/American Youth Hostels (see page 54) or the **South African Youth Hostels Association**, PO Box 4402, Cape Town 8000; (27) 21-4191853; fax (27) 21-216937. For a list of independent hostels, contact **South Africa Backpackers Hostels**, Back Pack, 73 Church Street, Cape Town 8000.

Especially for Students and Young People

South Africa's student and youth travel agency is **SASTS**, PO Box 1381, Cape Town 8000; (27) 21-216438; fax (27) 21-251169. SASTS is not affiliated with any government institutions and operates according to a nonracial policy.

SASTS offices are located on these campuses: the University of Cape Town, the University of Natal at Durban, the University of Natal at Pietermaritzburg, the University of the Witwatersrand in Johannesburg, and Rhodes University in Grahamstown. All of these offices provide a variety of services, including booking accommodations, providing travel information, and selling plane, train, and bus tickets.

For Further Information

General tourist information is available from the **South African Tourism Board**, 747 Third Avenue, New York, NY 10017; (800) 822-5368; fax (212) 826-6928. The best travel guide to South Africa and neighboring countries is Lonely Planet's new *South Africa, Lesotho and Swaziland: A Travel Survival Kit* ($16.95). An excellent book to read in preparation for your trip is *Insight Guide: South Africa* ($19.95). For more information on Lonely Planet and *Insight Guides*, see pages 56–57.

WORK

It is necessary to obtain a temporary employment visa in order to work in South Africa. Applicants must submit an offer of employment from the prospective employer to the South African Consulate three months before the date of departure. For more information, contact the **South African Consulate General**, 333 East 38th Street, New York, NY 10016.

Internships/Traineeships

The following program is sponsored by a member of the Council on International Educational Exchange.

Association for International Practical Training. *IAESTE Trainee Program*. On-the-job training for undergraduate and graduate students in technical fields such as engineering, computer science, agriculture, architecture, mathematics, and the natural and physical sciences. See page 19 for more information.

STUDY

Students who wish to enroll directly in a South African university should ask the South African Embassy (see "Travel") for their list of local universities.

Below are academic programs offered by a CIEE-member institution. Consult Appendix I for the contact address.

Semester and Academic Year

General Studies

World Learning/School for International Training. *College Semester Abroad*. Johannesburg, Cape Town, Natal, Transvaal, and Orange Free State. Fall and spring semesters. Area studies. Orientation, intensive language study, homestay, field-research seminar, independent-study project, field trip. Sophomores to graduate students with 2.5 GPA. Apply by May 7 for fall; October 7 for spring. Contact: College Semester Abroad Admissions at (800) 336-1616.

College Semester Abroad, Durban. Johannesburg, Durban, Transvaal, Cape Province. Fall and spring semesters. Area studies. Orientation, intensive language study, homestay, field-research seminar, independent-study project, field trip. Sophomores to graduate students with 2.5 GPA. Apply by May 7 for fall; October 7 for spring. Contact: College Semester Abroad Admissions at (800) 336-1616.

EXPLORING SOUTH AFRICAN CULTURE

Readings

Woza Albert!, by Percy Mtwa, Mbongeni Ngema, and Barney Simon (first performed in 1984, published in 1988), is a play that illustrates both the ridiculous and the tragic contradictions of apartheid. It is based on the idea that Christ's second coming takes place in South Africa, and is a brilliant example of the concept of ''laughing to keep from crying.'' Powerful and more strictly tragic are D. M. Zwelonke's *Robben Island* (1973) and Hugh Lewin's *Bandiet—Seven Years in a South African Prison* (1981). *Bandiet* is an account of the author's imprisonment, and *Robben Island* is a novel set in South Africa's harsh island prison where a leader of the Poko branch of the resistance refuses to crack under torture.

For books from the last couple of years, read *Coming Home and Other Stories*, by Farida Karodia (1988), and *Have You Seen Zandile?* (1990), a play by Gcina Mhlophe, Thembi Mtshali, and Maralin Vanrenen, about a child forced to move from Durban to the Transkei homeland. Though Karodia now lives in Canada, she was raised in South Africa and makes it the setting for her work, which also includes the novel *Daughters of the Twilight* (1986).

For a historical perspective on South Africa, read Thomas Mofolo's *Chaka*. Contemporary issues dominate most works by prominent African writers. Among these are Eskia Mphahlete's *Down Second Avenue* (1985) and Alex La Guma's novel *Time of the Butcherbird* (1979) and his short stories ''A Walk in the Night'' and ''The Stone Country.'' You might also want to read *Ushaba: The Hurtle to Blood River* (1974), by Jordan K. Ngubane, South Africa's leading Zulu-language novelist.

In white South African fiction, apartheid is also the dominant theme. The late Alan Paton's *Cry the Beloved Country* (1948) was one of the first internationally acclaimed books to deal with apartheid, and was followed by his *Ah! But Your Land Is Beautiful*. Other important white South African writers include Athol Fugard (*Master Harold and the Boys*), Peter Abrahams (*Tell Freedom* and *Mine Boy*), Nadine Gordimer (*A Soldier's Embrace* and *Crimes of Conscience*), and Andre Brink (*A Dry White Season*).

The most important white South African writer today is probably the Afrikaaner J. M. Coetzee. *The Life and Times of Michael K.* (1984) is a black man's odyssey from municipal gardening to an abandoned farm, war, labor camps, and finally back to Cape Town. *From the Heart of the Country* (1977) is a tale of madness set in the African veldt.

Films

A Dry White Season (1990), based on the novel by Andre Brink and directed by Euzhan Palcy, is a tragic and moving story about apartheid told by an

Afrikaaner narrator, although the main actors in the tragedy are black. *Come Back, Africa*, by Rogosin, dramatizes the squalor and desperation of the slums, as well as the concentrated oppression specifically aimed at breaking up black families and communities. Although the major historical figure in *Cry Freedom* (1987) is Stephen Biko, the movie actually focuses on Donald Woods, a white journalist who has contact with the South African martyr. *Mapantsula* (1989), directed by Oliver Schmitz, tells the story of a petty criminal in Soweto who stands firm against police oppression, providing a lively look at the underside of life in a black township. Both *Mapantsula* and *The Stick* (1989), directed by Darrell Roodt, were formerly banned by the South African government.

SWAZILAND

Swaziland is named for its principle people, the Swazis. Part of the Nguni linguistic group that moved south along Africa's east coast during the Bantu migration prior to the third century A.D., Swazis trace their roots to a single clan, called the Dlamini, that occupied the shores of present-day Mozambique. This clan stayed on the coast until the middle 18th century, when King Ngwane III led his people inland under pressure from competing clans. However, it wasn't until a century later that King Mswazi established a genuine nation. The Swazi people's name derives from the name of this legendary king.

Modern Swaziland is a small, landlocked country between South Africa and Mozambique, shaped by its past struggles with colonial powers. Annexed by the British, Swaziland was granted nominal independence in 1881 under an Anglo-Boer convention that took away large tracts of its territory. The British reestablished control of Swaziland as a protectorate after winning the South African War of 1899–1902. Swazis struggled with their loss of self-determination. Under Queen Labotsibeni and her son King Sobhuza II, Swazi resistance took the form of repurchasing land from the British, often with money earned in the coal mines of South Africa. Sobhuza II's deft diplomacy led to the creation of Swazi political parties and elections in 1964, and finally the granting of complete independence in 1968.

More than in most modern African nations, traditional culture is at the center of Swazi life. Even middle-class businessmen are known to wear the traditional robe to work. Traditional Swazi society revolves around the king, who owns most of the country's land and resources in theoretical trusteeship for his people. This is one reason why the repurchase of land from the British was such an important part of Swaziland's independence movement. This idea also allowed King Sobhuza II to suspend the country's original constitution and create a new one which placed all power in his person. Although there is a parliamentary system, final authority remains in the hands of Sobhuza's successor, King Mswati III.

Swazi tradition is best encapsulated in the sacred Incwala ceremony, during which the king gives his subjects permission to eat the first crops of the year. In preparation for the ceremony, the king goes into retreat and a group of men gather foam from the shores of Mozambique, where their ancestors lived. The culmination of the ceremony involves the king dancing before the people. The country's connection to the king is also demonstrated in the annual Umhlanga Dance, in which potential queen mothers participate. These ceremonies both take place in Lobamba, the royal city. The Dlamini remain dominant in Swaziland—you'll encounter that name wherever you go—although they're not necessarily royal. On the other hand, you can meet genuine princes, although they may be impoverished farmers.

In spite of its small size, Swaziland has a variety of ecological features ranging from rain forests to mountains to dry savannas. This geographic diversity can be enjoyed in the country's five nature preserves. While proudly independent, Swaziland nevertheless is much affected by its neighbors. A large number of refugees from Mozambique have added a touch of Portuguese culture and cuisine. Even more important is South Africa, on which Swaziland depends for much of its economic life. Not only do most goods entering or leaving Swaziland have to pass through South Africa, but a full five percent of the population makes its livelihood there. The result is a society under considerable strain as it struggles to retain its traditional values. You will find, however, that Swazis generally seek harmony in their lives. Even a brief visit to this country will convince you of their warmheartedness and sociability.

—Dan Fuchs, Nashville, Tennessee

Official name: Kingdom of Swaziland. **Area:** 6,704 square miles. **Population:** 859,000. **Population density:** 126 inhabitants per square mile. **Capital and largest city:** Mbabane (pop. 46,000). **Language:** Swazi, English. **Religion:** Christian, indigenous beliefs. **Per capita income:** $900. **Currency:** Lilangeni. **Literacy rate:** 65%. **Average daily high/low:** Mbabane: January, 77°F/59°F; June, 66°F/42°F. **Average number of days with precipitation:** Mbabane: January, 15; June, 3.

TRAVEL

U.S. citizens need a passport to visit Swaziland, but a visa is not necessary for tourist stays of up to 60 days. Temporary residence permits are issued in Mbabane for longer stays. For more information, contact the **Embassy of the Kingdom of Swaziland**, 3400 International Drive NW, Suite 3M, Washington, DC 20008; (202) 362-6683.

Getting Around

There is no passenger train service in Swaziland. A good system of **buses** covers the country, though the slightly more expensive minibus taxis are usually used for shorter distances. Roads in Swaziland are well maintained. Rental **cars** are available and you can cover much of the country in a few days. It's also common to hitchhike.

For Further Information

The best travel guide to Swaziland and neighboring countries is Lonely Planet's new *South Africa, Lesotho and Swaziland: A Travel Survival Kit* ($16.95). For more information on Lonely Planet Publications, see page 56.

WORK

In order to work in Swaziland, it is necessary to obtain a work permit. The Embassy of Swaziland recommends that you secure a job before going to the country. However, it is possible to go to Swaziland on a tourist visa, seek employment, and once a job is secured, apply for a work permit. Those interested in opening their own businesses need to obtain a resident permit. For more information, contact the Embassy of Swaziland (see "Travel," above).

Internships/Traineeships

The following program is sponsored by a member of the Council on International Educational Exchange.

Ohio University. *Undergraduate Student Exchange/Preservice Teacher Education Program.* Ngwane Teacher Training College, Ngwane. Summer. Open only to sophomores, juniors, and seniors attending Ohio University. Apply by March 1. Contact: Wes Snyder, Center for Higher Education and International Programs, 129 McCracken Hall, Athens, OH 45701; (614) 593-4445; fax (614) 593-0569.

TANZANIA

Tanzania is a land of rare beauty and unusual interest, boasting such world-famous sites as Mount Kilimanjaro, Lake Victoria, the Great Rift Valley, Olduvai Gorge, and the Serengeti Plain. It also has a variety of ethnic groups, the most widely known being the Masai, who have proudly retained their nomadic lifestyle. But the attraction for which Tanzania is most famous is neither its topography nor its people, but its wildlife. In fact, more than a quarter of the country's area is protected as national parks and game preserves. Yet in spite of these well-known attractions, little has been done to develop tourism and only a few adventurous travelers stray from the beaten path to visit Tanzania.

For most of the last five hundred years, Tanzania has been dominated by foreign powers—Arab, Persian, Portuguese, German, and British. After gaining its independence from Britain in 1961, Tanganyika annexed the island of Zanzibar off the East African coast and became Tanzania in 1964.

For most of its short history as an independent nation, Tanzania was led by Julius Nyerere, or Mwalimu (teacher) as he was often called. Under Nyerere's leadership, Tanzania experimented with an African style of socialism called *Ujamaa*. Major corporations were nationalized and private enterprise discouraged. Tanzanians, a diverse group of over 120 tribes, each with its own language and culture, were encouraged to further national unity by learning Swahili, a language that has long served as a lingua franca among traders on the East African coast. Ironically, a language that developed in conjunction with the Arab and Persian exploitation of Africans has become the language of an African nation trying to assert its freedom and identity.

The Tanzanian socialist experiment, however, has not been particularly successful. In spite of receiving the highest per capita foreign assistance in Africa, Tanzania is one of the 25 poorest countries in the world. Agriculture dominates the economy and over 90 percent of the population lives in rural areas. But under the leadership of Ali Hassan Mwinyi, who assumed the presidency after Nyerere stepped down in 1985, the country has gradually moved toward more open economic system, with positive results.

Tanzanians are a peaceful and friendly people who rarely criticize one another either publicly or privately. They treat each other, and especially the elderly, with respect. Women are regarded as subservient to men and do most of the work. The lives of most Tanzanians also are heavily influenced by witchcraft, spirits, and magic.

—Erna Loewen-Rudgers, Mbeya, Tanzania

Official name: United Republic of Tanzania. **Area:** 364,886 square miles (three times the size of New Mexico). **Population:** 26,869,000. **Population density:** 73 inhabitants per square mile. **Capital and largest city:** Dar es Salaam (pop. 1,300,000). **Language:** Swahili, English (both official). **Religion:** Christianity, Islam, Animism. **Per capita income:** US$240. **Currency:** Tanzanian shilling. **Literacy rate:** 85%. **Average daily temperature:** Dar es Salaam: June, 76°; December, 81°. **Average number of days with precipitation** (inches): Dar es Salaam: June, 6; December, 11.

TRAVEL

U.S. citizens need a passport and a visa to enter Tanzania. Proof of yellow fever and cholera vaccination is also required for visitors entering from infected areas, and sometimes from those arriving from noninfected areas as well. For specific requirements, check with the **Embassy of Tanzania**, 2139 R Street NW, Washington, DC 20008; (202) 939-6125.

Getting Around

Major urban centers within Tanzania are connected by roads; however, most are unpaved. **Bus** service along certain routes is liable to be canceled at any point for indefinite periods. The three main rail lines radiate out from Dar es Salaam north to Arusha (near Mount Kilimanjaro and the Kenyan border), west to Lake Tanganyika, and southwest into Zambia. Whatever way you go, be prepared for long delays.

Ferries are generally more reliable than ground transportation. They operate along the coast of Lake Tanganyika, providing service to Burundi and Zambia (cargo boats provide connections to Zaire) and along Lake Victoria, providing service to Uganda and Kenya. Boats also connect Dar es Salaam to the islands of Zanzibar, Mafia, and Pemba in the Indian Ocean.

For Further Information

General tourist information is available from the **Tanzania Tourist Corporation**, 201 East 42nd Street, New York, NY 10017. Reliable information on travel in Tanzania can be found in Lonely Planet's *East Africa: A Travel Survival Kit* ($15.95). Lonely Planet's newly updated *Africa on a Shoestring* ($27.95) also contains information on Tanzania. For more information on Lonely Planet Publications, see page 56.

WORK

In order to work in Tanzania, it is necessary to write to the embassy expressing your desire to obtain employment, the field you're interested in working in, and your qualifications. The embassy will then refer you to the appropriate ministry in Tanzania. Should you secure a job, a residency visa is required, which is issued in Tanzania. For more information, contact the Embassy of Tanzania (see "Travel," above).

Voluntary Service

Global Volunteers places participants in rural communities to work on economic and human-development projects in Tanzania. Projects include tutoring, construction work, and health care. Volunteers serve for three weeks; no special skills are required. For more information, contact Global Volunteers, 375 East Little Canada Road, St. Paul, MN 55117; (612) 482-1074.

STUDY

Study programs offered by CIEE-member institutions are listed below. Unless otherwise noted, consult Appendix I for the addresses where you can write for more information. In addition to the programs below, the University of Wisconsin at Madison offer programs open to their own students only.

Semester and Academic Year

General Studies

Brown University. *Brown in Tanzania*. Dar es Salaam. Academic year. Full enrollment in six yearlong liberal arts courses with Tanzanian students at University of Dar es Salaam. Dormitory accommodations with Tanzanian roommates. Juniors in good academic standing and with demonstrated academic interest in Africa. Apply by February 15.

International Student Exchange Program (ISEP). Academic year. Direct reciprocal exchange between U.S. universities and University of Dar es Salaam. Full curriculum options. Rolling admissions. Open only to students at ISEP-member institutions. Contact ISEP for list of members.

Natural Sciences

World Learning/School for International Training. *College Semester Abroad—Wildlife Ecology and Conservation*. Arusha, Moshi, Serengeti National Park, and other sites. Fall and spring semesters. Intensive Swahili, wildlife ecology and conservation seminar, field-study methods seminar, homestays, field visits, and independent-study project. Sophomores to seniors with 2.5 GPA and previous coursework in environmental studies or biology. Apply by May 7 for fall; October 7 for spring. Contact: College Semester Abroad Admissions at (800) 336-1616.

TOGO

Togo is a splinter-thin strip of land wedged between Ghana and Benin. It was part of Germany's only West African colony from 1894 to 1919, when France and Great Britain split the territory between them. Britain took the western area and added it to Ghana. The French granted Togo independence in 1960.

Togo's population of nearly four million people is divided among almost 40 ethnic groups. The climate ranges from the scorching savannah of the north to breezy inland lakes to a lush semitropical zone along the coast. From lagoons on the Atlantic, the land rises to a peak of more than three thousand feet in the central mountains. The port cities—including the capital, Lomé—are full of a profusion of fresh seafood, including some of the finest lobster you will ever taste. Game reserves in the north shelter herds of antelope and buffalo. If you are very lucky, you might even spot one of West Africa's last remaining elephants—all this in a country only 350 miles long and 32 miles wide at the seashore.

Unlike some of West Africa's larger, dirtier capitals that ring with constant clanging and honking, Lomé is a city built on a comfortably human scale. It is a thriving port and market center; goods pour ashore through its free-trade zone, then fan out through the region along traditional trading routes. Lomé's pristine, relatively uncrowded beaches attract tourists from Europe and elsewhere. Everything from luxury hotels to cheap corner cafés caters to the traveler, and all are welcome.

Togo is opening up further. The autocratic president, General Gnassingbé Eyadéma, who seized power in 1967, announced in 1991 that he would allow multiparty elections and a new, democratic constitution. The elections provided, at long last, a legal outlet for dissent and free political expression, and in August 1991 Kokou Koffgoh took office as president. If Africa can move peacefully toward greater democracy, Togo could become an even more interesting place to visit.

—Jason Zweig, New York, New York

Official name: Republic of Togo. **Area:** 21,622 square miles (about the size of West Virginia). **Population:** 3,810,000. **Population density:** 176 inhabitants per square mile. **Capital and largest city:** Lomé (pop. 600,000). **Language:** French (official), Gur, Kwa. **Religion:** Animism, Christianity, Islam. **Per capita income:** US$390. **Currency:** CFA Franc. **Literacy rate:** 45% (males). **Average daily temperature:** Lomé: June, 78°F; December, 80°F. **Average number of days with precipitation:** Lomé: June, 10; December, 2.

TRAVEL

U.S. citizens need a passport but not a visa for stays of up to three months. However, the government does require yellow fever and cholera vaccinations. For specific regulations, check with the **Embassy of the Republic of Togo**, 2208 Massachusetts Avenue NW, Washington, DC 20008; (202) 234-4212.

Getting Around

Roads in Togo are excellent except in the far north, where there isn't much traffic anyway. Paved roads link the different regions of the country, making it possible to drive from Lomé to the capital cities of neighboring Benin or Ghana in just a few hours. Traveling these roads is cheap and comfortable, with **minibuses** and **taxis** being the chief means of public transport. There are also two short **rail** lines from Lomé to K'palimé and Blitta. A third line runs east along the coast from Lomé through Aného and on into Benin. First-class cars are more comfortable and less crowded than second.

Eating and Sleeping

Hotel and boardinghouse accommodations in main cities are economical. Near Lomé, it's also possible to stay at one of several organized beach campsites.

For Further Information

You can find reliable travel information on Togo in the recently updated *West Africa: A Travel Survival Kit*, available for $19.95 from Lonely Planet Publications. Lonely Planet's *Africa on a Shoestring* ($27.95) also contains information on Togo. For more information on Lonely Planet Publications, see page 56.

WORK

It is very difficult for foreigners to obtain regular, salaried employment in Togo. For more information contact the Embassy of the Republic of Togo (see "Travel," above).

STUDY

Below is an educational program offered by a CIEE-member institution. Consult Appendix I for the address where you can write for more information.

Semester and Academic Year

General Studies

International Student Exchange Program (ISEP). Semester and academic year. Direct reciprocal exchange between U.S. universities and Université du Bénin in Lomé. Full curriculum options. Rolling admissions. Open only to students at ISEP-member institutions. Contact ISEP for list of members.

UGANDA

The civil strife that characterized Uganda's history after independence in 1962 is still remembered by many. But slowly visitors are returning to Uganda to witness a state and people hard at work to create political and economic order. The beauty of the land and its people is once again surfacing and replacing the images of past military coups and mass killings that brought international condemnation of the former dictatorial governments. While the present government still restricts certain political activities and government opposition, it has been praised for getting the country back on track toward development. A landlocked country that sits on the northern shores of Lake Victoria, Uganda's location on the line of the equator furnishes the country with a tropical climate, but the tropical heat is allayed by the altitude of the land. A profusion of lush forests is made possible by the abundance of water; lakes cover almost one-fifth of Uganda's area. In the south, rivers flow to Lake Victoria, the third largest lake in the world, from which the Nile flows into Lake Mobutu. Thus, it is not surprising that rivers and lakes mark many of the country's borders with neighboring countries: Sudan to the north, Zaire to the west, Rwanda and Tanzania to the south, and Kenya to the east. Uganda's international borders and the basis of its present economic system were created under the influence of British rule from about 1894 to 1926. The British replaced older and much smaller political entities and economies (which remained a focus for cultural, economic, and political competition) with a consolidated colonial rule. As a typical colony Uganda became a supplier of raw materials for Britain and a market for manufactured goods from Europe. But throughout the country's history many of the indigenous, and often rivalrous, groups and kingdoms sought cultural and political separation from their neighbors and Britain.

The coalition government put in place when Uganda gained independence in 1962 quickly disintegrated. As different groups struggled for control, the army stepped in and the era of military dictatorship began. It has been said that the country deteriorated with each post-independence government. The military coup led by Idin Amin Ada in 1971 is infamous for ushering in a time of excessive dictatorial powers and mass killings of some 300,000 Ugandans; the rule of Milton Obote was also fraught with slaughter. As of 1986 the National Resistance Movement has been in power and has tried to restore economic and social order under the leadership of President Yoweri Museveni. The country is undergoing a constitutional revision, with elections scheduled for 1995; the last elections were held in 1989.

A visit to Uganda may begin at Entebbe or Kampala, the co-capitals. In addition to its lively markets and Sikh temples, Kampala's attractions include the Kibuli Mosque and the Kasubi Tombs of the kings of the Baganda people. Kampala is the only large urban center in the nation and has about 10 times as many people as Jinja, the second-largest city. Jinja is known for the magnificent views over Lake Victoria, close to where the Nile leaves the lake. Western Uganda attracts visitors to the hot springs near Sempaya and the pygmy tribes near the village of Ntandi in the Semliki Valley's forests. Kasese, in southwestern Uganda, is a well-known base from which to organize a trip up the Ruwenzori Mountains. Other places of interest include the volcanoes along the Uganda-Rwanda border, the Mountains of the Moon, and the Ssese Islands. These islands are found south of Entebbe in Lake Victoria. They are worth a trip because they are unspoiled; they managed to escape the ravages of civil wars. Its inhabitants, the Basese, are a distinct tribal group with their own language and culture.

But it is when driving through the rain forests and savannahs of Uganda that the scenery engulfs the visitor in the richness of the land. The country's national parks and game reserves are teeming with wild fauna and flora, to the delight of nature enthusiasts. They are perfect places to appreciate the natural beauty of Uganda and to explore some of the world's most bountiful expanses.

—Ramid Shontu, Jackson, Mississippi

Official name: Republic of Uganda. **Area:** 93,354 square miles (slightly smaller than Oregon). **Population:** 18,690,000. **Population density:** 200 inhabitants per square mile. **Capital and largest city:** Kampala (pop. 773,000).

Language: English (official), Luganda, Swahili. **Religion:** Christian, Moslem, indigenous. **Per capita income:** $290. **Currency:** Shilling. **Literacy rate:** 52%. **Average daily high/low:** Entebbe: January, 80°F/64°F; June, 77°F/63°F. **Average number of days with precipitation:** Entebbe: January, 9; June, 14.

TRAVEL

U.S. citizens need a passport and visa to travel to Uganda. A tourist visa costs $20. For specific requirements, contact the **Embassy of the Republic of Uganda**, 5909 16th Street NW, Washington, DC 20011; (202) 726-7100; fax (202) 726-1727.

Getting Around

Uganda has a fairly good road system, although some sections are still being repaired from the country's civil war years. The most common form of public transportation is the **minibus**. Regular long-distance buses are less expensive, slower, but safer than minibuses, which are often crowded beyond capacity. Even cheaper and slower than the bus is the **train**. The two rail lines run from Tororo west to Kasese and northwest to Pakwach. There is also ferry service across Lake Victoria from Jinja to Tanzania.

At publication time, the U.S. Department of State's **Consular Information Sheet** on Uganda stated that "sporadic bandit and rebel activity" was a danger in certain parts of Uganda. It also warned against highway travel at night.

For Further Information

Reliable information on travel in Uganda can be found in Lonely Planet's *East Africa: A Travel Survival Kit* ($15.95). Lonely Planet's newly updated *Africa on a Shoestring* ($27.95) also contains information on Uganda. For more information on Lonely Planet Publications, see page 56.

WORK

It is necessary to arrange a job prior to entering Uganda. You must secure a work permit that the employer applies for on your behalf. For more information, contact the Embassy of the Republic of Uganda (see "Travel," above).

STUDY

Following is a study program sponsored by a CIEE-member institution. Consult Appendix I for the contact address.

Summer and Short-Term

General Studies

Lisle Fellowship. *Uganda: New Images for a New Age*. Three weeks in summer. History and culture of the "new" Uganda. Recent high-school graduates, college students, and adults. Apply by April 1.

ZAMBIA

Zambia was originally organized by the British South Africa Company as Northern Rhodesia during the late 19th century. As was so often the case with other African countries, its borders unified neither tribal nor linguistic groups. However, in this century a nationalistic movement was able to transcend internal differences and bring about the eventual bloodless revolution that resulted in the creation of an independent Zambia in 1964.

Thirty years after independence Zambia still sees itself as a "front-line" state battling the legacies of colonialism—most notably poverty—while at the same time risking its own security and economic stability to help neighboring countries: Zimbabwe in the 1970s and now, black South Africans. The man who led Zambia to independence, Kenneth Kaunda, was president under a "one-party participatory democracy" until 1991. During the food riots of June 1990, the nation suffered its worst violence since independence, caused by the government efforts to diversify the economy. These efforts included cutting off food subsidies, which led to price increases. However, the food subsidies were restored by Kaunda to contain the unrest and in 1991 multiparty elections brought Frederick Chiluba to the presidency.

Much of Zambia's economy is based on copper mining; a decline in world copper prices over the last 20 years has caused Zambia's economy to spiral downward. Recently, new cash crops have been introduced to supplement Zambia's traditional agricultural exports of maize, tobacco, and cotton. But Zambia, faced with a large international debt, remains in economic difficulty.

There is a great deal of political unrest in Zambia; however, Zambians are quick to point out that the soldiers and the government cause most of the trouble for tourists, while the people themselves are quite friendly. Do not wear khaki or military-style clothing, and do not take pictures of borders, post offices, or other government establishments. As long as you act with deference and do not challenge soldiers' authority, they will probably leave you in peace, requiring only a bribe or other "present."

—Kimberly Sherman, Baton Rouge, Louisiana

Official name: Republic of Zambia. **Area:** 290,586 square miles (about three times the size of Oregon). **Population:** 8,445,000. **Population density:** 29 inhabitants per square mile. **Capital and largest city:** Lusaka (pop. 982,000). **Language:** English (official), various Bantu dialects. **Religion:** Animism, Christianity, Hindu, and Islam. **Per capita GDP:** US$580. **Currency:** Kwacha. **Literacy rate:** 54%. **Average daily temperature:** Lusaka: June, 61°F; December, 75°F. **Average number of days with precipitation:** Lusaka: June, 0.4; December, 17.

TRAVEL

U.S. citizens need a passport and visa to enter Zambia. For specific requirements, check with the **Embassy of the Republic of Zambia**, 2419 Massachusetts Avenue NW, Washington, DC 20008; (202) 265-9717.

Getting Around

The main roads are quite good but many of the rural routes are often impassable in the rainy season. Hitching in Zambia is not as common as it is in other African countries due to crime caused by the poor economy. **Zambia Railways** runs passenger trains from Lusaka north to Zaire, and south to Victoria Falls and Zimbabwe. The **Tanzania Zambia Railway Authority** operates the line northeast to Tanzania. **Zambia Airways** serves all major cities and tourist centers. Ferry service across Lake Tanganyika connects Zambia with Tanzania.

For Further Information

General tourist information is available from the **Zambian National Tourist Board**, 237 East 52nd Street, New York, NY 10022; (212) 308-2155. Reliable information on travel in Zambia can be found in Lonely Planet's recently updated *Africa on a Shoestring* ($27.95). For more information on Lonely Planet Publications, see page 56.

WORK

To obtain employment in Zambia, you can either secure a job before traveling to the country or get a tourist visa and look for employment once you get there. A work permit is necessary and can be obtained before or after you arrive in Zambia. Interested persons should write to the **Ministry of Home Affairs**, PO Box 50997, Lusaka, Zambia, or to the **Ministry of Information and Broadcasting**, PO Box 51025, Lusaka, Zambia.

STUDY

A study program offered by a CIEE-member institution is described below. Consult Appendix I for the address where you can write for more information.

Semester and Academic Year

General Studies

International Student Exchange Program (ISEP). Academic year. Direct reciprocal exchange between U.S. universities and University of Zambia. Full curriculum options. Rolling admissions. Open only to students at ISEP-member institutions. Contact ISEP for list of members.

ZIMBABWE

Zimbabwe, a landlocked country in Southern Africa, combines great natural beauty with a society that has become peaceful after a bloody interracial war. Zimbabwe was the British colony of Southern Rhodesia until 1965, when white Rhodesians declared independence from Britain and formed a racially repressive government. Blacks, who comprise over 95 percent of the population, fought a guerrilla war against the white Rhodesian regime until a 1980 settlement renamed the nation Zimbabwe, ruled by a black majority government headed by Robert Mugabe. Today, blacks and whites work alongside each other. Although racial tensions persist, one is more likely to encounter a widespread feeling of reconciliation and determination to build a better country together. The excitement of independence is giving way to the challenges of economic growth. The last few years of drought and high inflation have made life more difficult for the average citizen.

Americans may be surprised by the lingering British influence on the country's customs, language, and school system. Many Zimbabweans still celebrate British holidays such as Boxing Day and take their tea with milk, and English is still the primary language taught in high schools and used in newspapers (in part because the two main ethnic groups, the Shona and the Ndebele, speak different languages). In addition, the capital, Harare, is quite cosmopolitan and boasts nightclubs, large hotels, department stores, and public gardens.

But in the countryside, where over three-quarters of the black population lives, Zimbabwe's traditional way of life remains strong. Most rural blacks are farmers or livestock herders. They continue to eat the traditional diet of cornmeal, known as *sadza*, with meat or vegetable stew. Zimbabweans are family-oriented; a visit to someone's home usually includes a hearty meal and plenty of conversation. While foreigners can get by without fluency in Shona or Ndebele, communication in the rural areas is easier if you can manage a simple conversation. Zimbabweans will appreciate your effort in learning their language. They will also share with you the struggles of their past and the hopes for the country's future.

Despite economic hardships, Zimbabweans are proud of their past and eager to show visitors the beauty of their country. The tropical savannah landscape encompasses some stunning highlights, including Victoria Falls, an abundance of ancient cave paintings, and game parks alive with elephants, lions, and giraffes. The ruins of Great Zimbabwe, capital of a 14th-century gold-trading empire, are also a spectacular sight. Traveling to these spots is made easy by a network of reliable buses.

—Elizabeth Grossi, New York, New York

Official name: Republic of Zimbabwe. **Area:** 150,803 square miles (about the size of Montana). **Population:** 10,720,000. **Population density:** 71 inhabitants per square mile. **Capital and largest city:** Harare (pop. 730,000). **Language:** English (official), Sinde bele, Shona. **Religion:** Traditional African religions, Christianity. **Per capita income:** US$540. **Currency:** Zimbabwean dollar. **Literacy Rate:** 67%. **Average daily temperature:** Harare: June, 57°F; December, 69°F. **Average number of days with precipitation:** Harare: June, 1; December, 16.

TRAVEL

U.S. citizens need a passport but not a visa for travel in Zimbabwe. An onward or return ticket is also required. Visitors must declare currency upon arrival. For specific requirements, check with the **Embassy of Zimbabwe**, 1608 New Hampshire Avenue NW, Washington, DC, 20009; (202) 332-7100.

Getting Around

A good **rail** network connects the major regions of the country and links Zimbabwe to South Africa. There is also an extensive road system, most of which is well maintained. Various types of **buses** serve the country, providing everything from intercity express service to local service in the cities and countryside. They are slow and usually crowded, but cheap and serve most of the country. In addition, **Air Zimbabwe** connects the country's major urban centers and tourist attractions, including Victoria Falls. Contact Air Zimbabwe at (800) 228-9485.

Eating and Sleeping

There are youth hostels in Bualwayo and Harare. For more information, contact Hostelling International/American Youth Hostels (see page 54), or contact the **Youth Hostel Association of Zimbabwe**, PO Box 8521, Causeway, Harare; (263) 4-796436. For a list of independent hostels, contact **Zimbabwe Backpackers Hostels**, Backpackers Con-O-Shon, 932 Delport Road, Airport, Box AP99, Harare; (263) 4-5074115.

For Further Information

General tourist information can be obtained from the **Zimbabwe Tourism Office**, 1270 Avenue of the Americas, New York, NY 10020; (212) 332-1090. The best guide to Zimbabwe and neighboring countries is Lonely Planet's new *Zimbabwe, Botswana and Namibia: A Travel Survival Kit* ($16.95). For more information on Lonely Planet Publications, see page 56.

WORK

For information on obtaining employment in Zimbabwe, call the **Embassy of Zimbabwe**, 1608 New Hampshire Avenue NW, Washington, DC, 20009; (202) 332-7100. The embassy will direct you to the appropriate Zimbabwean Ministry, depending upon the type of occupation you are seeking.

STUDY

Programs sponsored by CIEE-member institutions are described below. Unless otherwise noted, consult Appendix I for contact addresses and phone numbers.

Semester and Academic Year

General Studies

Associated Colleges of the Midwest. *Zimbabwe Program*. Harare. Spring semester. Language, culture, development issues, and independent-field project. Homestays and excursions. Sophomores to seniors. Apply by October 10.

Michigan State University. *Undergraduate Student Exchange Program*. University of Zimbabwe in Harare. African academic year (from March to December). Sophomores to seniors. Apply by November 30. Contact: Office of Overseas Study, 108 International Center, Michigan State University, East Lansing, MI 48824-1035; (517) 353-8920.

Pitzer College. *Scripps-Pitzer in Zimbabwe*. Various locations in Zimbabwe. Fall and spring semesters, and African academic year (beginning with spring semester). Five-month spring semester featuring rural and urban components, language study, special core seminar, independent study or internship, and opportunity to enroll in regular courses at University of Zimbabwe. Four-month fall semester with larger fieldwork component. Sophomores to seniors. Apply by May 15 for fall; October 15 for spring and academic year.

Syracuse University. *Syracuse University in Zimbabwe*. Harare. Semester and academic year. Economic development, environmental issues, gender questions, history, geography, literature, and culture, with focus on Southern Africa Development Community (SADC). Independent study, field coursework, or internship. Excursions and optional homestays. Juniors and seniors. Apply by March 15 for fall and academic year; October 15 for spring. Contact: (800) 235-3472.

World Learning/School for International Training. *College Semester Abroad*. Harare, Mashonaland, Zvishavane, Bulawayo, Victoria Falls. Fall and spring semesters. Shona-language study, life and culture seminar, independent-study project, homestay, and educational travel. Sophomores to seniors with 2.5 GPA. Apply by May 7 for fall; October 7 for spring. Contact: College Semester Abroad Admissions at (800) 336-1616.

Summer and Short-Term

Education

Michigan State University. *Education, Society, and Learning in an African Context*. Harare. July. Focus on issues of human diversity and the role of social institutions; visits to local schools. Excursions and dormitory housing. Juniors to graduate students. Apply by April 15. Contact: Office of Overseas Study, 108 International Center, Michigan State University, East Lansing, MI 48824-1035; (517) 353-8920.

EXPLORING THE CULTURE OF ZIMBABWE

Readings

Among the many books that explore the colonial period and its injustices is Wilson Katiyo's *A Son of the Soil* (1976), about a black boy growing up in colonial Rhodesia. The underside of colonial Rhodesia is starkly presented in Dambudzo Marechera's *The House of Hunger* (1978).

Bones (1990), by Chenjerai Hove, is a novel about the guerilla war for freedom in Zimbabwe, told through interior monologues by representative colonial "types" and by spirits. *Harvest of Thorns* (1991), by Shimmer Chinodye, is another take on conflict in the Zimbabwean consciousness; Benjamin Tichifa, the protagonist, is torn between the old colonial regime and the new African one.

Since independence, more of an interest has emerged in books that deal with modern Zimbabwean issues as well as those that reinforce Zimbabwean identity by celebrating its history, culture, and heroes. Solomon Mutswairo's *Chaminuka: Prophet of Zimbabwe* (1983) is a historical novel about Zimbabwe's legendary 19th-century man of peace. In a similar vein, Mutswairo's *Mapondera: Soldier of Zimbabwe* (1978) tells the story of this man's struggle against the British in the 19th century. *The Polygamist* (1972), by Ndabaningi Sithole, is an essentially autobiographical novel that tells the story of a man who returns to his people (the Ndebele) as a converted Christian.

CHAPTER NINE

SOUTH ASIA

Separated from the rest of the continent by the Himalayas, South Asia is dominated by India, which at its present rate of growth is projected to become the world's most populous nation early in the next century. India itself is a kaleidoscope of peoples, religions, languages, and cultures. The smaller nations on its northern fringes—Bangladesh, Bhutan, Nepal, and Pakistan—as well as the island-nation of Sri Lanka, each with its own distinct character, add to the richness of this region. A source of much that is honored and cherished, this immense diversity has also been at the root of the civil and political strifc that has produced bitter conflicts within and between the nations of the region. To a large degree, recent antagonism between India and Pakistan and violence in India itself is the product of political manipulation of the differences between Hindus and Muslims.

With the exception of the ancient kingdom of Nepal, the modern nations of South Asia have only emerged as independent states since the end of the Second World War. Once divided into a number of different kingdoms, even India as a nation is a recent invention. However, the Indus River valley was one of the earliest centers of civilization. Here, in the third millenium B.C., the Hindu religion emerged. Five hundred years before Christ, India was the birthplace of Buddhism. Islam spread to the region from the Middle East in the 11th century A.D. and remains a major religion in the area. Buddhism, which had its origins in India, is the dominant religion in Sri Lanka and Bhutan.

In 1947 Britain relinquished its colonial control of the Indian subcontinent, creating the Muslim-dominated states of Pakistan and Bangladesh in the process. The British presence thoroughly infiltrated all levels of society through its transformation of the education system and the bureaucracy in the 19th century. In most nations of South Asia, English remains the language by which people from different linguistic groups communicate with each other. Britain's worldwide empire also uprooted many, transporting South Asian workers to the Caribbean, Africa, and the South Pacific islands as well as to England itself. For these reasons, the nations of South Asia, which in antiquity bore the germ of a broader Asian culture, have in many ways developed a closer relation to the West than most other Asian countries.

Getting There

Food, lodging, and land transportation in South Asia are generally inexpensive. Getting there will be your main expense. From the U.S., the cheapest airfares to South Asia are APEX or other excursion fares. You'll find up-to-date information on such fares at Council Travel offices. To give you some idea of cost, here are sample *one-way* fares in effect during the summer of 1993.

Los Angeles–Bombay	$ 809
New York–Delhi	$1,258
San Francisco–Calcutta	$ 839

From Europe, special student/youth fares, which enable you to save up to 50 percent off regular commercial fares, are available from several European cities to destinations in South Asia. These can be booked at any Council Travel

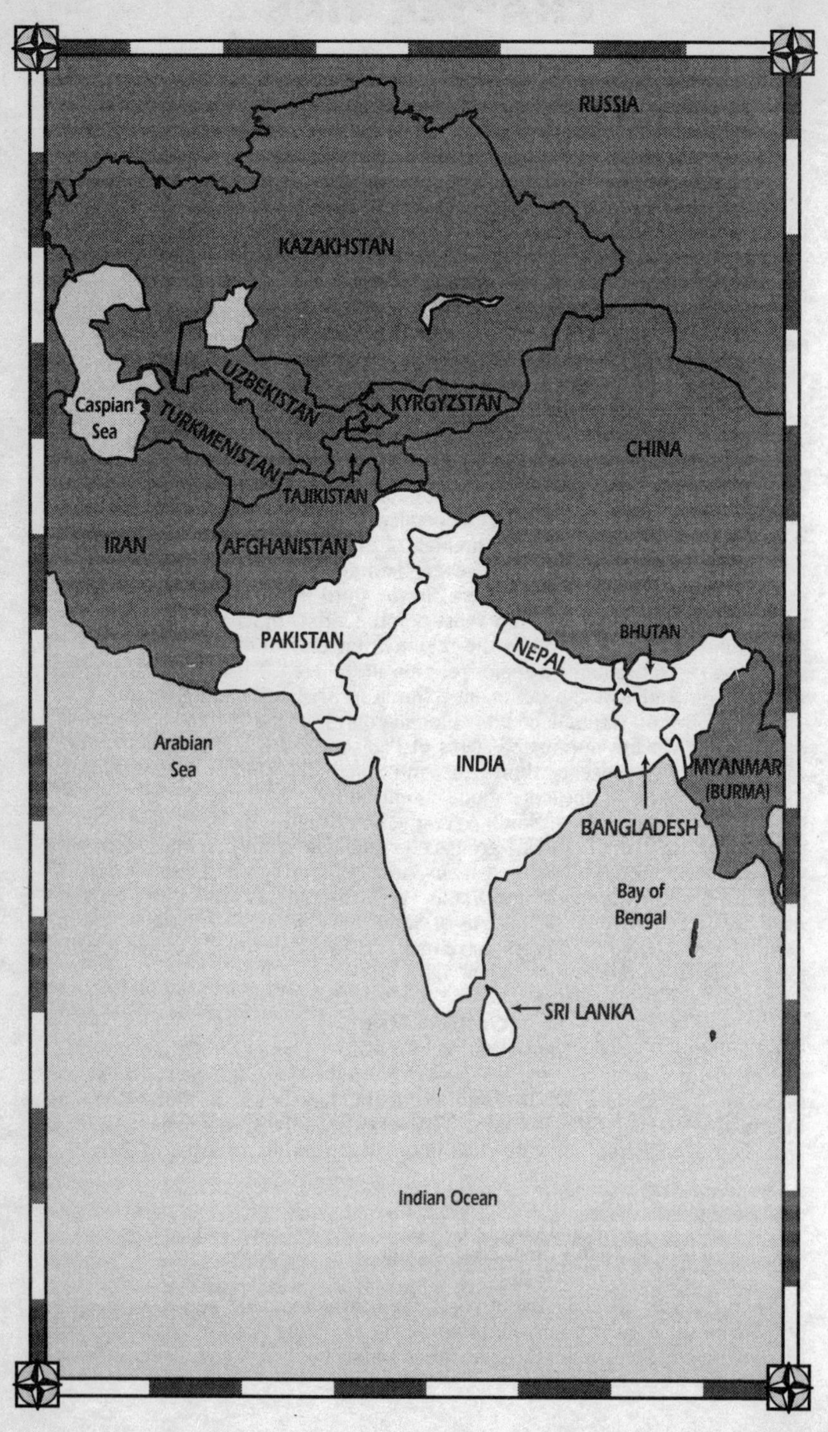
RUSSIA
KAZAKHSTAN
Caspian
Sea
UZBEKISTAN
TURKMENISTAN
KYRGYZSTAN
TAJIKISTAN
CHINA
IRAN
AFGHANISTAN
PAKISTAN
NEPAL
BHUTAN
Arabian
Sea
INDIA
MYANMAR
(BURMA)
BANGLADESH
Bay of
Bengal
SRI LANKA
Indian Ocean

office or a student travel bureau in Europe. Regulations vary depending on the airline, but generally holders of the International Student Identity Card or the Go 25 Card (see pages 9–11) are eligible. Sample *one-way* fares in effect during 1993 are listed below.

Frankfurt–Delhi	$635
Paris–Karachi	$535
Frankfurt–Bombay	$505
Paris–Delhi	$535

Special student/youth fares are also available from a number of other cities in Asia. For further information, contact a Council Travel office. Sample *one-way* fares in effect during 1993 are listed below.

Bangkok–Calcutta	$189
Hong Kong–Bombay	$469
Bangkok–Kathmandu	$245

Overland trips from Europe to India and Nepal and beyond were once quite popular among more adventurous travelers. Overlanding is still an option, although conditions in the Middle East have narrowed the options. Today the only sure route is through Turkey, Russia, and other republics of the former Soviet Union. U.S. citizens will be taking their chances passing through Iran or Afghanistan. It's much easier to travel in the other direction overland from Southeast Asia or China. One of the most famous routes into South Asia follows the path of the ancient silk traders along the Karakoram Highway between Pakistan and China. A number of tour operators specialize in overland adventure tours in which the group usually rides in back of a truck, stopping at leisure and camping in the open air. For information on overland tour operators, contact **Council Travel** (see pages xiii–xvi).

Getting around South Asia

Because India comprises more than half of South Asia, getting around in South Asia for the most part involves travel in India, which is discussed later on in this chapter. If you plan on visiting several distant points within the region and want to make the most of your time, consider travel by **air**. In addition to Indian Airlines, other local lines include Bangladesh Biman, Royal Nepal Airlines, and Pakistan International Airlines. Below are some sample *one-way* fares in effect during 1993 from Council Travel. Fares are likely to be even cheaper if purchased at points of departure.

Delhi–Kathmandu	$143
Calcutta–Karachi	$195
Delhi–Dhaka	$166

The suspension of ferry service between India and Sri Lanka makes flying the only option. If you choose **overland** travel between other countries, you'll have to mix and match your modes of transportation. Direct **trains** operate only between India and Pakistan. To get from India to Bangladesh, you'll have to take the train or bus to near the border and taxi the rest of the way, then cross on foot and board another bus. Likewise, to enter Nepal you must take a bus to the border, cross on foot, and pick up another bus. Travel to the tiny

Buddhist kingdom of Bhutan is purposefully made difficult by a prohibitive daily expenditure requirement of over $200 per day; Bhutan also limits the number of tourists to 4,000 annually.

Traveling conditions will also be affected by the **weather**. The Indian subcontinent experiences two monsoon seasons. Beginning in June, the monsoon comes from the southwest and blows northward during the summer. From October to December, the monsoon comes from the northeast. While the downpours frighten away most tourists, travel during the monsoon seasons can be a pleasant surprise. It seldom rains all day, and the rains break the humidity and heat.

Eating and Sleeping

You can find all sorts of inexpensive accommodations throughout South Asia, from Sri Lanka to Nepal. Hostelling information for India, Nepal, and Sri Lanka is given in the country sections that follow.

In Bangladesh, there are nearly 30 youth hostels. The local hosteling organization is the **Bangladesh Youth Hostel Association**, 42/2 Azimpur Road, Dhaka 1205; (880) 2-503445; fax (880) 2-833212.

There are also a number of youth hostels in Pakistan, as well as about 50 government-operated "rest houses" open to members of Hostelling International. For more information, contact the **Pakistan Youth Hostels Association**, Garden Road, Aabparà. Sector G-6/4, Islamabad; (92) 51-826899; fax (92) 51-826417. You can also contact Hostelling International/American Youth Hostels (see page 54) for information on hosteling in these countries.

For Further Information

General information on travel in this region is contained in the State Department's pamphlet, *Tips for Travelers to South Asia*, available free from the Superintendent of Documents, U.S. Government Printing Office, Washington, DC 20402.

Two excellent guides for overland travelers in the Middle East and South Asia are Lonely Planet's *Karakoram Highway: The High Road to China* ($14.95) and *West Asia on a Shoestring* ($14.95), although the latter, last published in 1990, is growing out of date. For countries not covered in this chapter, two of the best guides are *Pakistan: A Travel Survival Kit* (fourth edition, $15.95) and *Bangladesh: A Travel Survival Kit* (second edition, $10.95). Travelers heading further north should check out *Tibet: A Travel Survival Kit* (second edition, $13.95). For more information on Lonely Planet Publications, see page 56.

The majestic Himalayas attract climbers the world over to northern India, Nepal, Bhutan, and Tibet. Trekkers and climbers will find many interesting books published by The Mountaineers Books (see page 57). Among these are *Sivalaya: Explorations of the 8000-metre Peaks of the Himalaya* ($9.95), *Mount Everest National Park* ($18.95), and *Trekking in Tibet* ($16.95). One of The Mountaineers' most interesting titles is *Himalayan Passage: Seven Months in the High Country of Tibet, Nepal, China, India, and Pakistan* ($16.95), by Jeremy Schmidt.

A good source for books on current affairs of all Asian nations is **The Asia Society**, 725 Park Avenue, New York, NY 10021; (212) 288-6400. Ask for a current publications catalog.

Listed below are the embassies you can write for information on the visa requirements of the countries not covered in individual sections later in this chapter.

- **Bangladesh:** Embassy of the People's Republic of Bangladesh, 2201 Wisconsin Avenue NW, Washington, DC 20007; (202) 342-8373
- **Bhutan:** Consulate of the Kingdom of Bhutan, 2 United Nations Plaza, 27th Floor, New York, NY 10017; (212) 826-1919
- **Pakistan:** Embassy of Pakistan, 2315 Massachusetts Avenue NW, Washington, DC 20008; (202) 939-6200

WORK

It is generally quite difficult for Americans to get any type of regular employment in the region. However, voluntary-service opportunities and internship positions are available and are discussed in the individual country sections that follow. In addition, the **Association for International Practical Training's** *IAESTE Trainee Program* operates in Pakistan; see page 19 for more information.

STUDY

You'll find a number of study programs listed in the individual country sections later in this chapter. In the section below are study programs offered by CIEE-member institutions that take place in more than one country of the region. Unless otherwise noted, consult Appendix I for the addresses of the sponsoring institutions.

Semester and Academic Year

General Studies

Eastern Michigan University. *Asian Cultural History Tour*. 45 cities in India, Nepal, China, Thailand, Egypt, Israel, Turkey, Greece, Ukraine, and Russia. Spring semester. History, art, comparative religion, and political science taught in an interdisciplinary context. Sophomores to seniors with 2.5 GPA. Apply by October 1. Contact: (800) 777-3541.

St. Olaf College. *Global Semester*. Academic program in Cairo, Egypt; Bangalore, India; Hong Kong; and Kyoto, Japan, with stops in Switzerland, Israel, and Nepal. Fall semester plus January. Political, social, and cultural issues of countries visited. Sophomores to seniors. Apply by March 1.

World Learning/School for International Training. *College Semester Abroad*. New Delhi and Dharamsala, India; Kathmandu, Nepal; Dolpo, Bhutan; and Kham, Tibet (conditions permitting). Fall and spring semesters. Intensive language, seminar in Tibetan studies, field-study methods, village excursions, homestay, and independent-study project. Sophomores to seniors with 2.5 GPA. Apply by May 7 for fall; October 7 for spring. Contact: College Semester Abroad Admissions at (800) 336-1616.

INDIA

It has been said that anything one says about India is true. A place of striking extremes, India has the highest mountains in the world, the lushest jungles, and the driest deserts. It is where zealous materialism exists side by side with severe asceticism, and where millionaire maharajahs share quarters with the most destitute persons of the world. From loud and gritty Bombay to the silent majesty of the desert palaces of Rajasthan, India is bewildering urban chaos as well as untouched tranquility.

India is a very extroverted country. This is especially apparent in its delightful disregard of the strict Western distinction between public and private life. It is not uncommon to see gregarious groups of young boys cheerfully splashing and lathering up as they bathe on the sidewalk, women unpacking and setting up their cooking pots on the train-station platform, spindly bodies crouching along the railway tracks in the early morning to perform their daily duties, and barbers setting up shop along the busy roadway with only a hand mirror and an umbrella. At first overwhelming, any initial feelings of astonishment quickly fade into a sense of freedom as you witness life in its most natural and exuberant forms.

Indian society esteems the well-being of the group before the privacy of the individual. The rewards and responsibilities of life are shared among members of the same caste, and particularly of the extended family, which is organized under the joint family system. In this unit, one of the most fundamental structures of Indian society, the oldest male member is the head and under his roof live his younger brothers, his sons, and their respective families. The structure of the system engenders the basic and deeply rooted Indian ideals of collective solidarity and mutual dependence. Even with the long presence of the British—who brought their own cherished values of independence and personal freedom—the dedication, loyalty, and interdependence of family and friends have remained steadfast in India.

Although some customs remain the same, the influx of many other new ideas has changed India considerably since the Indus Valley civilization left its mark over 5,000 years ago. The religion of Hinduism, which was born in this valley, is based on tolerance of other races and creeds, and India is certainly used to assimilating them. Conquerors with new ways and religions have made their way into India from the Aryans of southern Russia, to the Persians, Greeks, Muslims, Turks, Moghuls (from Afghanistan), and finally the Europeans, creating a melting pot of civilizations. Even today Indians are very friendly to foreign tourists, especially English-speaking ones. English has become the language of opportunity for most Indians, promising social mobility, good jobs, and an escape from poverty. Although crucial to the unity of this country of over 200 languages and dialects, the introduction of English has also made an unfortunate contribution to the caste system, giving birth to an entirely new strata made up of a wealthy, British-educated ruling elite.

In the south, English is spoken quite frequently among the majority of the inhabitants, an act of resistance against the central government's enforcement of Hindi as the national language. Quite unlike the rest of the country, the southern states have been less exposed to Aryan invaders—and tourists—and have on the whole resisted the incursion of Islam. While the Moghul mosques, forts, and tombs of northern India show its strong Muslim influence, Hinduism is at its most pure and intense in the south. Still surviving are the ancient Indian customs of temple building, vegetarianism, classical dance forms, and traditional Hindu festivals.

Although 83 percent of Indians are Hindus, India is a land of many creeds, including Islam, Christianity, Sikhism, Jainism, Zoroastrianism, and Buddhism. Religion is a way of life in India; it rules the average person's every action and thought. Contrary to the impressions given by Kama Sutra legends and tourist photos of erotic temple sculptures, Indian society and religion are tightly bound to conservative tradition. In all but the most progressive circles, premarital sex is taboo, marriages are arranged, and gender roles are as strictly defined as they were thousands of years ago.

In contrast to this moral austerity, many of the traditions associated with religion are some of the most vibrant and colorful manifestations of Indian culture. With over two million gods in the Hindu pantheon, India is reputed to have the most festivals of any nation. These parties are elaborate and boisterous, usually celebrating a special day in the cycle of a god's life and involving vast pilgrimages of devotees bearing the god's image throughout the village, surrounded by a procession of caparisoned elephants, performing monkeys, noisy bands, and firecrackers.

Yet while religion is the very life of India in many ways, it is ironically the greatest threat to the coherence of the country today. As religious zeal intensifies in many parts of the world, India has also provided fertile ground for extremism and intolerance. Conflicts among Hindus, Muslims, and Sikhs have become especially bitter, as have conflicts related to the desire of several states, particularly Punjab, Darjeeling, and Kashmir, to separate from India. Another of India's toughest challenges is population control. With nearly 900 million people—a figure projected to reach one billion by the year 2000—India is three times as populous as the U.S., yet it is only one third the size! But as the most populous democratic nation in the world, India has the potential to be a major global force.

Despite the unpredictability of Indian politics, this country has consistently fascinated travelers from all over the world since the beginning of time. Impossible and unforgettable, India is a magical land of wonder, joy, and mystery.

—Amy Carden, Cincinnati, Ohio

Official Name: The Republic of India. **Area:** 1,266,595 square miles (about one third the size of the U.S.). **Population:** 866,000,000. **Population density:** 683 inhabitants per square mile. **Capital:** New Delhi (pop. 8,300,000). **Largest city:** Calcutta (pop. 10,800,000). **Language:** 16 languages, including Hindi (official) and English (associate official). **Religion:** Hindu, Islam, Christianity, Sikh. **Per capita income:** US$350. **Currency:** Rupee. **Literacy rate:** 48%. **Average daily temperature:** Bombay: June, 84°F; December, 79°F. New Delhi: June, 94°F; December, 60°F. **Average number of days with precipitation:** Bombay: June, 20.5; December, 0.1. New Delhi: June, 2.6; December, 2.

TRAVEL

U.S. citizens traveling to India will need a passport and visa, which must be obtained before arrival in India. Single-, double-, or triple-entry tourist visas are valid for one month; multiple-entry tourist visas are valid for six months or one year. For specific requirements, check with the **Embassy of India**, 2536

Massachusetts Avenue NW, Washington, DC 20008; (202) 939-9839. There are also Indian consulates in Chicago, New York, and San Francisco.

Keep all official bank receipts for money exchanged so that you'll be able to convert your rupees back into American dollars when you leave. When you pay in rupees for your transportation out of India, you'll be asked to show a receipt to prove that you have obtained your rupees officially.

Getting Around

India covers so vast a territory that you may well want to fly between certain major cities rather than make arduous journeys overland. Domestic **air** service is provided by Indian Airlines and the smaller Vayudoot. Airfares are not much more expensive than the price of comparable rail service, but airlines in India have been rated as some of the least safe in the world. Indian Airlines offers the **Discover India Pass**, which entitles you to 21 days of unlimited travel for $400. Indian Wonderfares passes allow you seven days of unlimited travel within north, south, east, or west India for $200. Indian Airlines also offers a 25-percent discount off U.S. dollar prices of regular fares all year for youth under 30. Indian Airlines passes are available only to foreign visitors and must be issued in the U.S. by the international carrier arranging your flight to India.

India's **rail** network connects even the most remote areas of the country, except Kashmir. Since rail travel is popular among Indians, it's a good way to meet the people and experience the diversity of India's different cultures. Indian trains have five confusing labeled classes: air-conditioned, first-class air-conditioned sleeper, air-conditioned chair car, second-class reserved, and second-class unreserved (only second-class cars are not air-conditioned). Although there are no student discounts on rail travel in India, trains are generally inexpensive. If you plan to take trains frequently, it might be worthwhile to invest in an **Indrail Pass**, which entitles the bearer to unlimited travel for a fixed period of time. Indrail passes can be purchased only by foreign tourists and must be paid for in U.S. dollars, although they may be purchased within India itself. For further information, contact **Hariworld Travels**, 30 Rockefeller Plaza, Shop 21, North Mezzanine, New York, NY 10012; (212) 957-3000.

With the Indrail pass, it's possible to stay overnight in the railroad stations, either for a fee in the "retiring rooms" (beds and private rooms) or for free on couches in the first-class or second-class waiting rooms.

Buses in India are used primarily for local transportation. In urban areas, buses are the primary component of the mass transit system. In rural areas, buses complement the rail system, fanning out to villages from train stations. An increasing number of air-conditioned, long-distance buses provide links between the country's major cities, creating a comfortable alternative for getting around India. Rental **cars** are not readily available in India; however, cars with drivers are quite inexpensive. The price, which may be negotiable, depends on the size of the car, the time spent, and the distance covered. In the major cities, taxis are readily available. An alternative to taxis are three-wheeled scooters, with metered fares running about half those of regular taxis. In addition, cycle rickshaws still operate in many cities and smaller towns. Perhaps the most efficient and interesting way to travel locally is by bicycle. You can find inexpensive rental shops anywhere.

Eating and Sleeping

Accommodations and meals in India are very inexpensive. Low-cost hotels can be found in most towns, and are listed in the various publications of the government tourist offices in addition to more expensive Western-style hotels. There are around 40 **youth hostels** throughout India. For more information, contact Hostelling International/American Youth Hostels (see page 54) or the **Youth Hostels Association of India**, 5 Nyaya Marg, Chanakyapuri, New Delhi 110 021; (91) 11-3011069.

Especially for Students

India's student travel agency and issuer of the International Student Identity Card is **STIC Travels**, Hotel Imperial, Room 6, Janpath, New Delhi 110001; (91) 11-3324789; fax (91) 11-3712710. STIC also has branch offices in Bombay, Calcutta, and Madras. STIC issues Indrail Passes, distributes lists of inexpensive hotels and guesthouses, and has information on low-cost flights within India and the region. In India, the International Student Identity Card entitles the holder to discounts on some accommodations and on STIC-operated tours.

For Further Information

For general tourist information, contact the **Government of India Tourist Office**, 30 Rockfeller Plaza, Suite 15, North Mezzanine, New York, NY 10112; (212) 586-4901. For an analysis of the past year's social, political, and economic events, read *India Briefing*, an annual survey of contemporary Indian affairs published by The Asia Society (see page 372).

The most comprehensive travel guide to India is *Cadogan Guides' India* ($14.95). However, budget travelers may find more information suited to their needs in Lonely Planet's newly revised *India: A Travel Survival Kit* ($19.95). Lonely Planet also publishes *Kashmir, Ladakh, and Zanskar: A Travel Survival Kit* ($10.95) and *Trekking in the Indian Himalaya* ($10.95), a hiker's guide.

WORK

It is necessary to secure a job in India before getting the required business visa to enter the country for working purposes. Business visas can be obtained by contacting the Indian embassy (see "Travel," above). For more information, contact the **Ministry of Labor and Employment**, Shral Shakti Bhavan Rafi Marg, New Delhi 110001, India; (91) 11-3710240.

Voluntary Service

Sisters of Charity of Nazareth sponsor a volunteer program in India for those interested in health care, social service, education, and ministry. Participants serve from two weeks to three months. Room and board are provided. For service periods of three months or more, at least nine months' prior notification is required. For more information, contact Sisters of Charity of Nazareth, SCNA Center, PO Box 172, Nazareth, KY 40048.

For persons interested in longer-term voluntary-service work, the **International Christian Youth Exchange's** Year Abroad Programs offers persons ages 18 to 30 voluntary service opportunities in health, education, environment, construction, and so on. See page 25 for more information.

In addition, the **Partnership for Service Learning** sponsors service opportunities in India; for more information see page 26.

STUDY

The **American Institute of Indian Studies (AIIS)** is a cooperative organization comprised of 47 U.S. colleges and universities with a special interest in Indian studies. The organization offers a variety of research fellowships for study in India to graduate students, researchers, and university faculty members, as well as a limited number of performing arts fellowships. AIIS also offers intensive language training programs in India for people with two years of formal training in Hindi. For further details, contact AIIS, 1130 East 59th Street, Chicago, IL 60637; (312) 702-8638; fax (312) 702-6636.

For an overview of Indian educational institutions and advice for the foreign student, ask for the booklet *Studying in India*, available from the Ministry of Education and Culture at the Embassy of India (see "Travel," above).

The following educational programs are offered by CIEE-member institutions. Unless otherwise noted, consult Appendix I for the addresses of the colleges and universities listed below.

Semester and Academic Year

General Studies

Associated Colleges of the Midwest. *India Studies*. Pune. Spring term at an ACM college and six months in India. Courses in Marathi language, literature, history, philosophy, art, and music. Sophomores to seniors. Apply by April 1 for early response; final deadline November 1.

Davidson College. *Davidson College Fall Semester in India*. Madras. Offered only in even-numbered years. Courses in India past and present, issues in contemporary India, art history, and independent study. Excursions. Juniors and seniors with 2.75 GPA and (preferably) Asian studies background. Apply by March 1.

State University of New York College at Oneonta. *Semester in India*. Delhi and other locations. Fall semester. Indian culture and society. Brief homestays. Sophomores to seniors. Rolling admissions. Contact: International Education Office, Netzer Building 332C, SUNY College at Oneonta, Oneonta, NY 13820-4015; (607) 436-3369.

University of Wisconsin at Madison. *College Year in India*. Madurai, Varanasi, Hyderabad, or Trivandrum. Academic Year. Intensive language instruction in Tamil, Hindi, Telugu, or Malayalam. Individualized program combining fieldwork, independent study, dance and music performance studies available. Juniors to recent graduates in good academic standing. Participants normally complete summer language course in Madison prior to departure. Apply by second Friday in February.

World Learning/School for International Training. *College Semester Abroad*. New Delhi, Udaipur, Ahmedabad, Sadra. Fall and spring semesters. Intensive Hindi language, life and culture, village stay, field-study seminar, and independent-study project. Homestays. Sophomores to seniors with 2.5 GPA. Apply by May 7 for fall; October 7 for spring. Contact: College Semester Abroad Admissions at (800) 336-1616.

International Relations

University of Minnesota. *Minnesota Studies in International Development (MSID)*. Academic Year. Predeparture coursework during the fall quarter at the University of Minnesota; internship in development-related research or action project in India during the winter and spring quarters required. Juniors to graduates and adults with interest in development; 2.5 GPA required. Apply by May 1. Contact: The Global Campus, University of Minnesota, 106C Nicholson Hall, 216 Pillsbury Drive SE, Minneapolis, MN 55455-0138; (612) 625-3379.

Religious Studies

Antioch University. *Buddhist Studies*. Bodh Gaya. Fall term. Courses in philosophy, contemporary culture, history, beginning Hindi or Tibetan, and meditation. Orientation held in London. Sophomores to graduate students in good academic standing. Apply by March 15. Contact: (800) 874-7986.

Summer and Short-Term

General Studies

Lisle Fellowship. *India: Peace and the Social and Environmental Dynamics of Change*. Three weeks in mid-summer. Cosponsored by Gandhi Peace Foundation. Recent high-school graduates, college students, and adults. Apply by April 1.

New York University. *Asian Studies in India*. Bombay. Offered in summer of even-numbered years. Seniors and graduate students. Apply by April 15. Contact: Graduate Admissions Office, 32 Washington Place, New York, NY 10003.

State University of New York College at Oneonta. *India: A Study in Contrasts*. Delhi and other locations. Winter session (three weeks in January). Indian society and culture. First-year college students to graduate students and continuing-education students. Rolling admissions. Contact: International Education Office, Netzer Building 332C, SUNY College at Oneonta, Oneonta, NY 13820-4015; (607) 436-3369.

Performing Arts

University of Wisconsin at Madison. *Summer Arts Program in Kerala*. Trivandrum, Kerala. Summer. Performing arts, theater and drama, language and culture study. Juniors to graduate students in good academic standing. Apply by third Friday in March.

EXPLORING INDIAN CULTURE

Readings

Ever since the British installment of English-language schools for Indians, writing in English has been well established in India. R. K. Narayan is commonly considered India's leading novelist in English. His novels are usually set in the imaginary southern town of Malgudi—said to be Mysore, where the author lives—and often present a delightful character involved in a strange predicament. Some of his finest works include *The Guide*, which won him India's highest literary honor in 1958, *A Tiger for Malgudi* (1983), and *Grateful to Life and Death* (1953), a story about the simple and moving life of an English teacher.

A new novel to come out of India that has generated a lot of hype is Vikram Seth's *A Suitable Boy* (1993). Its unusual length (1,336 pages) and its reactionary style have prompted comparisons with Tolstoy and Dickens.

Anita Desai's widely acclaimed novels generally deal with the position of women in an ever-changing India. *Clear Light of Day* (1980) is about a middle-class family forced to confront an increasingly difficult world; *Fire on the Mountain* (1977) is the tragic story of a girl's visit to her grandmother in the hill country that ends with rape and murder; and the humorous *In Custody* (1984) depicts a college teacher who is asked to interview a famous visiting poet. Her latest novel is *Baumgartner's Bombay* (1989). Kamala Markandaya's *Nectar in a Sieve* (1955) is an extremely powerful and sensitive novel about a poor, rural family on the margins of survival. *Two Virgins* (1973), by the same author, deals with the clash between tradition and modernity in India's painful evolution into the contemporary world. Also by Markandaya are *A Handful of Rice* (1966), *The Golden Honeycomb* (1977), and *Shalimar* (1983).

Although a Westerner (married to an Indian), Ruth Prawer Jhabvala is considered one of India's foremost contemporary writers. The praised *Out of India* (1986), a collection of exotic, langorous tales, expresses the essence of the author's often difficult Indian experience. *Heat and Dust*, winner of the Booker Prize for best novel in 1975, portrays the relationship between an English colonial wife and a mysterious Indian prince. Other books by Jhabvala about India include *Amrita* (1956), *A Backward Place* (1965), *Travelers* (1973), and *An Experience of India*, another collection of short stories.

Best-selling recent books on India include two by Dominique Lapierre. *City of Joy* (1986) was a big hit in Europe and India when it came out and was adapted to the screen in America in 1992. *Freedom at Midnight* (1976), written with Larry Collins, is a riveting account of India's progress to independence from Britain. On the same theme but from a different author, *Midnight's Children* (1981), by Salman Rushdie—the Pakistani author of the notorious *Satanic Verses*—is the story of 1,001 children born in the first hour of Indian independence.

Films

India's movie industry, supported by the world's largest film-going public, annually produces more films than any other country in the world. In the opinion of many Westerners, it also produces the world's worst films. Indian films, predominantly produced in the Hindi language, emphasize spectacular and emotional excess at the expense of strong story lines and narrative realism, and usually fall under the following genres: mythologicals, historicals, song-and-dance, and superhero films. Two particularly popular and typical examples of the latter examples are Manmohan Desai's superheroic *Naseeb* (1981) and Mehboob Khan's more folkorically tinged *Mother India* (1957). In addition, many of the song-and-dance spectacles can be found on U.S. cable television's arts and culture channels on Sunday mornings.

Since the early 1980s, more and more Indian films have been made in opposition to these commercially successful movies, with a number of film-makers following the example of Satyajit Ray, India's most internationally renowned filmmaker. Ray's first three films, making up the *Apu Trilogy*, are remarkable and probably his most well known. These films—*Pather Panchali* (1955), *The Unvanquished* (*Aparajito*) (1956), and *The World of Apu* (1959)—present a series of young, rural, poverty-stricken characters trapped between Indian traditions and Western ideas.

Other well-known figures in the "New Indian Cinema" are Ritwak Ghatak, who explores rural and urban social attitudes in *Ajantrik*, and Shyam Benegal, whose film *The Role*—ostensibly the biography of a popular female film star—is an important commentary on the position of women in Indian culture as well as an encapsulation of the history of Indian film genres. Mira Nair's big success was *Salaam Bombay!* (1988), a poignant and vivid view of street life as seen by a small boy. Her latest film, *Mississippi Masala* (1991), is about a young Indian woman living in Mississippi who falls in love with a black American there, to the distress of both of their families.

The critically acclaimed filmmaking team of Englishman James Ivory, Indian Ismail Merchant, and Ruth Prawer Jhabvala (see "Readings") have collaborated on several films about India. *Bombay Talkie* (1970) is a romantic drama about a sophisticated American woman who falls for two Bombay filmmakers, and *Shakespeare Wallah* (1965) is a slow-moving film about an English acting troupe whose tour of India is interrupted by romance.

Two excellent British films set in India are E. M. Forster's *A Passage to India* (1984) and *Gandhi* (1982). Written, directed, and edited by David Lean, *A Passage to India* is a powerful film about a young English woman who accuses an Indian doctor of rape.

NEPAL

A rapidly developing tourist industry has brought far-reaching changes to this once isolated kingdom, situated between India and China in the middle of the Himalayan Mountains. As a result, today you can find five-star hotels and Western restaurants serving pizza and linguine in Kathmandu, the country's capital. While these amenities bring the comforts of home to the Westerners who visit Nepal, they can also shelter the traveler from the rustic but far more interesting conditions typical of the country.

By Western standards, Nepal is an impoverished country; its average annual per capita income is approximately US $160 per year. However, this poverty is rarely oppressive, and few sick or starving people wander the streets. Kathmandu is bustling, muddy, and polluted, yet it remains a beautiful city filled with temples, open-air markets, and merchants peddling mangoes and oranges on their bicycles. Barefooted, bare-bottomed children run through the streets playing with discarded bicycle tires and asking unsuspecting tourists for "one rupee," "pen," or "balloon." Women in colorful saris, *lungis*, or Punjabi suits battle the flies for the perfect tomato or head of cauliflower. Many of the side streets reek of rotting meat, courtesy of the merchants who sell chunks of fresh goat and buffalo to loyal customers, and major thoroughfares are filled with dilapidated taxis, bicycles, rickshaws, cows, and city buses overflowing with gaudy decorations and passengers who sit on the dashboards, hang out of the windows, or stand on the bumpers.

Despite the crowds and often oppressive smells of the city, the most pervasive feeling in Kathmandu is one of warmth and friendliness. The Nepalese people exude goodwill and will do anything to help a confused visitor—perhaps an influence of the two dominant religions in Nepal, Hinduism and Mahayana Buddhism (most people practicing a unique combination of the two).

The countryside beyond Kathmandu is even more rustic, friendly, and beautiful. In the monsoon season, from July to mid-September, the white-capped

Himalayas are obscured by mist and clouds. Even then, however, breathtaking scenery is provided by the green-terraced hillsides that the locals plant with rice paddies and banana trees.

Much of the country is inaccessible by road. Instead, the footpaths that crisscross the mountains are literally the highways of Nepal. Not surprisingly, the Nepalese people are exceptionally strong and surefooted, and even small children scramble along the mountain paths with fifty-pound loads of firewood and fodder on their backs. People will think nothing of walking several days to visit a friend or relative. Tea shops dot the roadsides, and weary travelers are always welcome to sit down to the typical Nepalese meal of *dal bhaat*, which consists of rice, lentils, and vegetables such as potatoes or green beans.

The friendliness of the Nepalese people is as overwhelming as the mountains that attract most visitors to Nepal. The lack of electricity, running water, and toilet paper hardly seems to matter in this small country with an enormous heart.

—Victoria R. Clawson, Bernardsville, New Jersey

Official name: Kingdom of Nepal. **Area:** 56,136 square miles (about the size of Wisconsin). **Population:** 19,611,000. **Population density:** 349 inhabitants per square mile. **Capital and largest city:** Kathmandu (pop. 422,000). **Language:** Nepali (official). **Religion:** Hindu, Buddhist. **Per capita income:** US $160. **Currency:** Nepalese rupee. **Literacy Rate:** 29%. **Average daily high/low:** Kathmandu: 65°F/35°F; July, 84°F/68°F. **Average number of days with precipitation:** Kathmandu: January, 1; July, 21.

TRAVEL

U.S. citizens need a passport and a visa to visit Nepal. Visas valid for 30 days can be obtained before leaving the U.S. from the Nepalese embassy. Visas are also issued on arrival at the Kathmandu airport. For specific information, contact the **Royal Nepalese Embassy**, 2131 Leroy Place NW, Washington, DC 20008; (202) 657-4550. You can also contact the Nepalese Consulate General in New York.

Getting Around

Nepal has no railroads and a limited number of roads passable to motor vehicles. However, if there's a road leading where you want to go, you can be sure there's a **bus** that can take you there. **Bicycles** are an excellent way of seeing the towns and countryside in the area around Kathmandu and can be rented in Kathmandu itself. **Motorbikes** can also be rented by the hour. If you're in a hurry, Royal Nepal Airlines operates flights to all areas of the country. While in Kathmandu, you can get around by bus, taxi, or rickshaw; but because the city is quite compact, perhaps the best—and certainly the cheapest—alternative is simply to walk.

Trekking

Trekking in Nepal is an unforgettable experience; the scenery is beautiful, the paths are safe, and villagers are hospitable. It is hard work, especially at higher altitudes, so make sure you're in good health and try to travel with as little gear as possible. You'll need to get a trekking permit from the Central Immigration Office in Kathmandu; it will take a minimum of three working days. All your trekking equipment—down jacket, pack, boots, and bags—can be rented right in Kathmandu or Pokhara. There are many trekking agencies in Nepal that can arrange a trek for you. For safety reasons, you should not trek alone. There have been a number of robberies and even attacks on trekkers over the last couple of years, although these are rare.

The trekking season in Nepal is governed by the monsoon season of rains which begins in mid-June and lasts until mid-September. Therefore, the months between October and May are good months to trek. Blue skies and clear views make autumn the best season for trekking, but springtime (February and March) treks will yield breathtaking views of hillsides covered with wildflowers and rhododendrons. As the government's *Trekking in Nepal* brochure puts it, "The botanists and students of leeches will enjoy the summer season (July to September)." This brochure, which includes general tourist information, is available free from the Royal Nepalese Embassy (address above). They will also send you a copy of *Travellers' Information: Nepal*, which covers basic information like currency exchanges, airport taxes, and goverment-office hours. A valuable source of information is *A Guide to Trekking in Nepal*, recently updated by Stephen Bezrucha and available for $16.95 from The Mountaineers Books (see page 57). Bezrucha has also put together *Nepali for Trekkers: Language Tape and Phrasebook*, also available from The Mountaineers. The Mountaineers also publishes *Royal Chitwan National Park: Wildlife Heritage of Nepal* ($18.95). Also recommended is Stan Armington's *Trekking in the Nepal Himalayas*, available for $11.95 from Lonely Planet Publications (see page 56).

Eating and Sleeping

There are a few **youth hostels** in Nepal. For more information, contact Hostelling International/American Youth Hostels (see page 54) or the **Nepal Youth Hostels Association**, Mahendra Youth Hostel, Jawalkhel, Lalitpur, Nepal; (977) 21003.

For Further Information

General tourist information is available from the **Royal Nepalese Embassy** (see "Travel," above). Probably the best guide to the country is Lonely Planet's newly updated *Nepal: A Travel Survival Kit* ($12.95). Lonely Planet also publishes the *Nepali Phrasebook* ($4.95), which includes a special chapter for use while trekking. Two other good guides are *The Real Guide: Nepal* ($14) and Moon Publications' *Nepal Handbook* ($12.95). An excellent book to read in preparation for your trip is *Insight Guide: Nepal* ($19.95). For more information on Lonely Planet, *Real Guide*s, Moon Publications, and *Insight Guide*s, see pages 56–57.

WORK

Work permits are required for Nepal, and obtaining one is extremely difficult. Generally, they are only issued to embassy staff, to those working on government projects, or to foreigners working with the airlines.

Voluntary Service

Sisters of Charity of Nazareth sponsors a volunteer program in Nepal for those interested in health care, social services, education, or ministry. Participants serve from two weeks to three months; room and board are provided. For service periods of three months or more, at least nine months' prior notification is required. For more information, contact the Sisters of Charity of Nazareth, SCNA Center, PO Box 172, Nazareth, KY 40048.

STUDY

The following are the academic programs offered by CIEE-member institutions. Unless otherwise noted, consult Appendix I for the addresses of the colleges and universities listed in this section.

Semester and Academic Year

General Studies

Cornell University. *Cornell-Nepal Study.* Kirtipur, Kathmandu. Fall and spring semesters. Offered in conjunction with Tribhuvan University. Culture and peoples of Nepal, or environmental and ecological diversity. Excursions and residence hall housing with Nepalese students. Juniors to second-year graduate students in good academic standing.

Pitzer College. *Experience in Nepal.* Various locations. Fall and spring semesters. Offered in affiliation with Tribhuvan University. Nepali language, culture, independent study, and community-service projects. Homestays and trekking excursions. Apply by May 15 for fall; October 15 for spring.

University of Wisconsin at Madison. *College Year in Nepal.* Kathmandu. Intensive language study (Nepali or Tibetan), independent-study project, and cultural-immersion program. Fieldtrips, homestays. Participants complete a summer course in Nepali or Tibetan at Madison prior to departure. Juniors to recent graduates in good academic standing. Apply by second Friday in February.

World Learning/School for International Training. *College Semester Abroad.* Kathmandu. Fall and spring semester. Intensive language study, life and culture seminar, field-study methods seminar, village trek, homestay, and independent-study project. Sophomores to graduate students with 2.5 GPA. Apply by May 7 for fall; October 7 for spring. Contact: College Semester Abroad Admissions at (800) 336-1616.

EXPLORING NEPALESE CULTURE

Readings and Films

Fiction from Nepal is collected in *Nepalese Short Stories* (1976), edited by Karuna Kar Varilya, in which some of Nepal's best storytellers write on a variety of themes. *The Mountain is Young*, by Han Suyin, centers on the story of a sensual native (in this case a Nepalese man) who awakens a frigid English woman to the pleasures, and pains, of passionate love. Despite its perhaps trite theme and its length, Suyin's romance offers some clear insights into the life of the Nepalese aristocracy. *Blackout*, by once-censored author Tara Nath Sharma, is a novel about life in the hills, while *Wake of the White Tiger* is an acclaimed novel, by Diamond Shumshere Rana, that takes place during the early era of the authoritarian Rana warlords.

Excellent, informative books of general reading on Nepal include *The Heart of Nepal*, by Duncan Forbes, and *Nepal, Land of Mystery*, and *The Forgotten Valley*, by Karl Eskelund. Works about the condition of Nepalese women include two books by Lynn Bennett. *Dangerous Wives and Sacred Sisters* (1983) is an exploration of the lives of Hindu women in Nepal, while *The Status of Women in Nepal* is a more academic study.

SRI LANKA

The name Sri Lanka means "beautiful island," a fitting name for an isle known as the "Pearl of the Indian Ocean." Its beauty and strategic location at the crossroads of ancient trade routes have made Sri Lanka famous, and coveted, throughout the centuries. The island was known to the ancient world as Taprobane and later as Serendip, and until 1972 it was named Ceylon. Shaped like a teardrop right off the coast of India, it has been profoundly influenced by the history and the peoples of this powerful neighbor. However, it has also had its share of contact with peoples from much farther away throughout the centuries, and currently faces ethnic strife.

When Buddhism was brought from India during the 3rd century B.C., Sri Lanka already had two centuries of recorded history. The Veddas, Sri Lanka's indigenous population, were pushed into the interior when the Sinhalese, who migrated from northern India, conquered the island in the 6th century B.C. Other groups from Asia arrived later—the Tamils in the 11th century A.D. and Moors in the 12th and 13th centuries—but the island was seldom united under a single ruler. Seven indigenous kingdoms reigned over the island in the 16th century when European powers began a struggle for control of the island. Portugal ruled from 1505 to 1655, to be defeated and replaced by the Dutch. They in turn were ousted in 1796 by the British, who ruled until Sri Lanka achieved independence in 1948.

Although a very small number of aboriginal Vedda are found in Sri Lanka today, the allure of the country has remained constant. From tropical beaches to ancient hilltop cities, Sri Lanka offers a wide range of experiences for visitors. Coral reefs and sandy coves fringe the lowlands, where agriculture still employs more than half of Sri Lankans. The land rises inland toward the central region, where mountains rise to its highest point at Mount Pidurutalagala (8,281 feet). The highlands are covered in evergreen forests and the hill country is perfect for hiking, walking, and for visiting plantations and archaeological ruins, all in a cooler climate that provides a respite from the hot lowlands. From these heights numerous small rivers flow down to the coast. Colombo, Sri Lanka's capital, is a port city near the mouth of the Kelani River with a long history and fascinating architecture.

The hill country is dotted with wildlife sanctuaries and magnificent towns such as Kandy, Sri Lanka's religious and cultural center on the banks of the Mahaweli River. The former capital of the Kingdom of Kandy, this city dates back to the early centuries A.D. and has much to offer. One of its most revered sites is the Dalada Maligawa, or Temple of the Tooth, the island's main Buddhist shrine where a tooth of Buddha is kept. The temple and the city are the location for the famous Esala Perahera procession, which is held nightly for about two weeks in August in reverence to Buddha. Dry plains extend north of the hill country, where the deserted ruins of Sri Lanka's ancient capitals stand as powerful reminders of the strength of Buddhist culture. The most extensive and important of Sri Lanka's ancient cities is Anuradhapura, which was a major capital in 380 B.C.—here stands the Bo-tree, regarded as the oldest tree in the world. Other major sites in the region include Mihintali, Polonnaruwa, and the impressive rock fortress of Sigiriya.

It is unfortunate that the ongoing conflict between the Sinhalese and Tamil separatists has prevented Sri Lanka, a country where agriculture employs more than half of the people, from concentrating on national development. Travelers are often dissuaded from visiting the northern and eastern regions controlled by the Liberation Tigers of Tamil Eelam, a group waging a war of independence. In the past they have used violent tactics, including blowing up Sri Lanka's president in Colombo in 1993 during a political rally; riots in 1983 left more than 4,000 dead. This civil strife has disrupted the country's struggle for economic and industrial development, as well as having discouraged tourism. Nevertheless, a visit to Sri Lanka can yield a wealth of experiences worth the extra effort required to avoid getting caught in the middle of its civil conflict.

—Jandar Romishe, Honolulu, Hawaii

Official name: Democratic Socialist Republic of Sri Lanka. **Area:** 25,322 square miles (about the size of West Virginia). **Population:** 17,423,000. **Population Density:** 687 inhabitants per square mile. **Capital and largest city:** Colombo (pop. 1,200,000). **Language:** Sinhalese, Tamil (both official). **Religion:** Buddhism, Hinduism. **Per capita income:** US$380. **Currency:** Rupee. **Literacy Rate:** 90%. **Average daily high/low:** Colombo: January, 86°F/72°F; July, 85°F/77°F. **Average number of days with precipitation:** Colombo: January, 7; July, 12.

TRAVEL

U.S. citizens must have a passport, onward or return ticket, and proof of sufficient funds (US$30 per day) to visit Sri Lanka. Visas are not required for stays of up to three months. For further information, contact the **Embassy of the Democratic Socialist Republic of Sri Lanka**, 2148 Wyoming Avenue NW, Washington, DC 20008; (202) 483-4025. There are also Sri Lankan consulates in Honolulu, Los Angeles, Newark, New Orleans, and New York.

Getting Around

Paved roads link the major cities. However, most roads remain unpaved. In addition to Ceylon Transport Board (CTB) **buses**, there are a number of private minibus companies. You can also rent cars and motorcycles. **Trains** are less crowded than those in India, but rail lines are mostly confined to the southern part of the island.

Eating and Sleeping

There is a wide range of inexpensive accommodations in Sri Lanka, from guest houses and hotels to YMCAs. For information on **youth hostels** in Sri Lanka, contact Hostelling International/American Youth Hostels (see page 54) or the **National Youth Hostel Association of Sri Lanka**, 26 Charlemont Street, Colombo 6; (94) 1-587880.

For Further Information

A good general guide to the country is the recently updated fifth edition of *Sri Lanka: A Travel Survival Kit*, available for $13.95 from Lonely Planet Publications (see page 56).

WORK

In almost all cases, it is necessary to obtain an employment permit in order to work in Sri Lanka. However, foreign students studying in the country are permitted to hold jobs without obtaining a permit. Unless you are working for the U.S. government, it is very difficult to secure regular salaried employment. For more information, contact the Embassy of Sri Lanka, Information Section (see "Travel," above).

Internships/Traineeships

A program sponsored by a member of the Council on International Educational Exchange is listed below.

Florida A&M University. *NAFEO Sri Lanka Internship Program.* Sponsored in cooperation with NAFEO, the National Association for Equal Opportunity in Higher Education, this summer program enables students to work at the USAID Sri Lanka Mission. Positions are available in such areas as computer programming, finance, budgets, and operations. Open to students at Florida A&M University only. Apply by March 1. Contact: Program Coordinator, Office of International Programs, 302-304 Perry Paige South, 1730 South ML King Boulevard, Tallahassee, FL 32307.

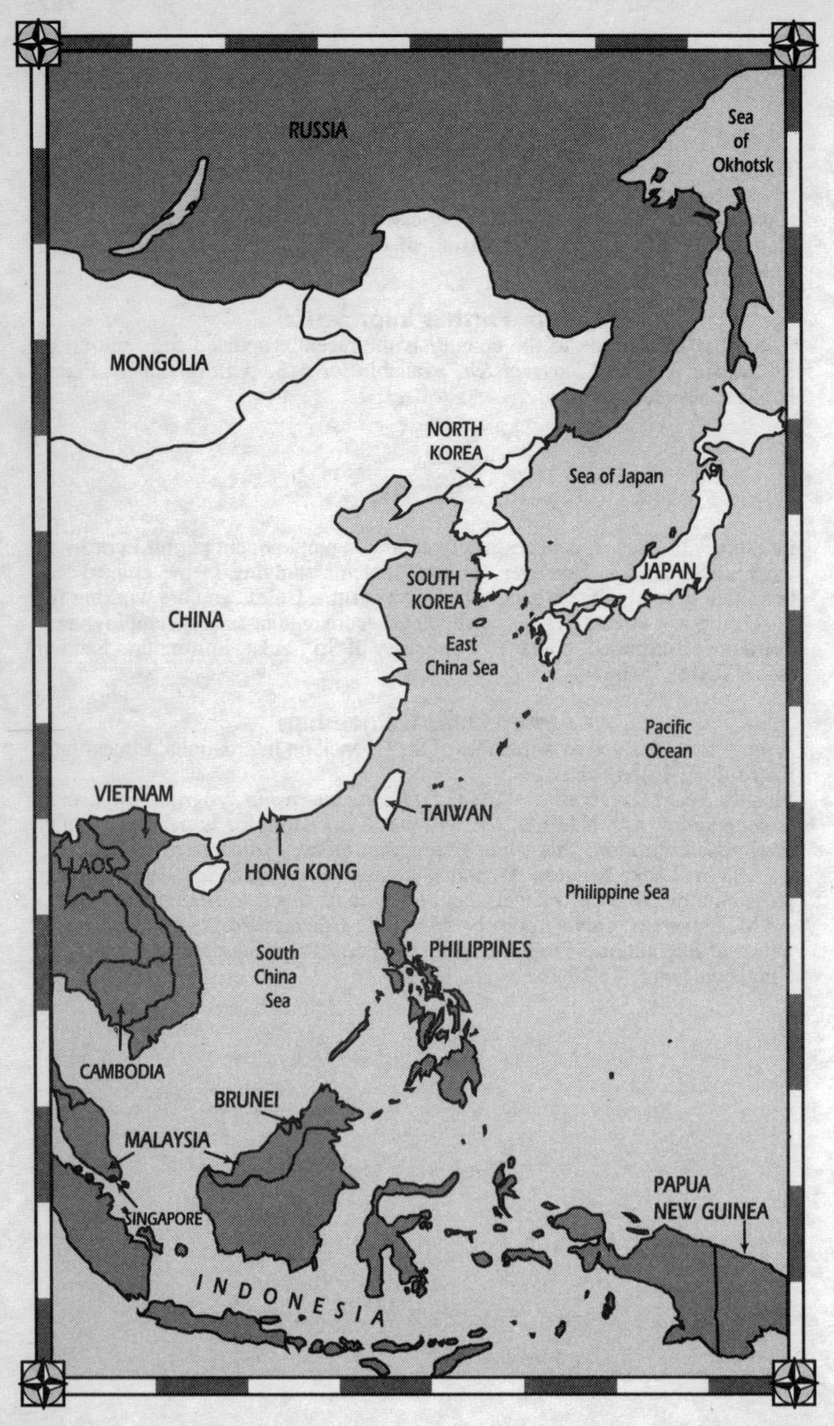
RUSSIA
Sea
of
Okhotsk
MONGOLIA
NORTH
KOREA
Sea of Japan
SOUTH
KOREA
JAPAN
CHINA
East
China Sea
Pacific
Ocean
VIETNAM
TAIWAN
LAOS
HONG KONG
Philippine Sea
South
China
Sea
PHILIPPINES
CAMBODIA
BRUNEI
MALAYSIA
SINGAPORE
PAPUA
NEW GUINEA
INDONESIA

CHAPTER TEN

EAST ASIA

East Asia encompasses a diversity of peoples that account for nearly a third of the world's population. In fact, almost a fourth of the earth's people live in China alone. A vast nation comprising numerous ethnic groups in its own right, China has historically been the dominant country within the region, greatly influencing the cultures, languages, religions, and social structures of surrounding East Asian countries. In this century, the smaller nations on China's periphery—Taiwan, South Korea, Japan, and the British colony of Hong Kong—began to surpass China economically. Many predict, however, that if market liberalization proceeds apace, China will once again become the undisputed power in the region.

Since the Second World War, regional politics have stressed the tensions between the communist nations of China and North Korea and the emerging capitalist democracies. These tensions persist in China's sometimes hostile, sometimes conciliatory attitude toward Taiwan and Hong Kong and in the growing concern over North Korea's nuclear potential. However, this paradigm has lost its usefulness in a region whose "democratic" nations have managed to temper free-market capitalism with state-centered economic planning and strict social control. In fact, many glimpse the future in China's combination of economic liberalization and political repression. It's worth noting, too, that many other factors enter into the region's geopolitics. One factor is a deep-seated distrust of Japan among other Asian nations (in spite of their emulation of Japan's economic success). Another is the strong desire for reunification felt by China, Hong Kong, and Taiwan, which may very well win out over their mutual antagonisms in the near future. Should the two Koreas also become one, East Asia could consist of three very powerful countries.

The countries of East Asia are fast becoming more prominent in the picture Americans have of the world. In large part, this interest arises from the astounding economic vitality of these countries whose products now flood Western markets. Today, U.S. trade with Asia surpasses its trade with Europe. The greater portion of the world's economy now circulates around the Pacific Rim, bringing together two cultural spheres that are only beginning to get to know each other.

Getting There

Today, a variety of excellent **airfares** have brought down the price of travel to Asia. Many carriers to Asia offer APEX and promotional fares, and student fares are available to a number of cities. Sample *one-way* fares from the U.S. to Asia in effect for the summer of 1993 are listed below. For more up-to-date information on fares to Asia, contact any Council Travel office (see pages xiii–xvi).

Seattle–Tokyo	$439	New York–Beijing	$749
San Francisco–Hong Kong	$649	New York–Seoul	$659

From Europe, persons with the International Student Identity Card or the Go 25 Card (see pages 9–11) can get special discounted fares on scheduled flights from a number of European capitals to Hong Kong, Osaka, Seoul,

Taipei, or Tokyo. Sample *one-way* student/youth fares in effect during 1993 are listed below.

London–Hong Kong	$659
Paris–Seoul	$790
London–Osaka	$719

Many of these student/youth fares allow stopovers in Bangkok, Thailand. Contact a Council Travel office or a student travel bureau in Europe or Asia for complete information.

Student/youth fares are also available on scheduled flights connecting East Asian cities with cities in South and Southeast Asia. On some of these flights you'll save up to 50 percent on the regular fares. Sample *one-way* student/youth fares in effect during the summer of 1993 are listed below.

Bangkok–Tokyo	$415
Bangkok–Hong Kong	$199
Hong Kong–Singapore	$269

If you want to travel **overland** between Europe and East Asia, you might consider traveling through the Soviet Union on the Trans-Siberian Railroad. The world's longest train route, the Trans-Siberian makes 91 stops, takes you one-quarter of the way around the globe, and passes through seven time zones and 100 degrees of longitude. Nonstop, from Moscow to Nakhodka, the trip takes eight days. From Nakhodka, ship passage can be arranged to Yokohama, Japan. Two other routes take you to Beijing, China, via Manchuria or Mongolia. Russian transit visas are considerably less expensive than tourist visas. For further information, see "Travel" in the Russia section of Chapter Six.

Another popular overland route used to be to cross China from India or Nepal through Tibet to Hong Kong or Beijing. However, it has become difficult to enter Tibet from India or Nepal without being part of an organized tour group. Thus, your best bet may be to fly over Tibet. Traveling across China is an experience in itself, and one for which you'll want to allow plenty of time.

Traveling around East Asia

Largely because of geography, but also because of politics, most travel between the countries of East Asia is by **air**. Of the five nations covered at length in this chapter, only China and Hong Kong share a common border. Thus, for the most part, overland transport—while viable within individual countries—is simply not an option for international travel in the region.

Air service between the nations of East Asia is convenient and fairly inexpensive for persons eligible for student/youth fares; eligibility for these fares is the same as for the student fares discussed above. Sample *one-way* fares available from Council Travel in 1993 are listed below.

Tokyo–Hong Kong	$369
Tokyo–Seoul	$359
Seoul–Hong Kong	$389

If travel by air doesn't appeal to you, you can travel more cheaply by **boat** between several countries. From Hong Kong, vessels depart for a number of Chinese cities, including Guangzhou (Canton) and Shanghai, as well as the island of Taiwan. From Taiwan, boats travel to Okinawa, where you can get connecting service to a number of cities in Japan; several of these boats make stops on some of the smaller islands that are part of the Japanese archipelago. There is also frequent ferry service between Shimonoseki, Japan and Pusan, South Korea. Combined, these various shipping lanes make a convenient circuitous route, and boat service can be surprisingly cheap.

The United States government discourages travel to **North Korea** by U.S. citizens. The North Korean government, however, has eased its own restrictions on foreign tourism and recognizes U.S. passports. However, visas are required. Since North Korea maintains no diplomatic or consular representative in the United States, U.S. citizens interested in traveling to North Korea must apply for a visa at a North Korean embassy in a third country such as China, Denmark, Egypt, Malaysia, Norway, Pakistan, or Singapore.

Of the other countries not covered in this section, the Portuguese colony of **Macau** is easily visited from Hong Kong. U.S. citizens need a passport but not a visa for stays of up to 60 days. For more information, contact the **Embassy of Portugal**, 2125 Kalorama Road NW, Washington, DC 20008; (202) 328-8610.

Mongolia, a seldom-visited but fascinating country, will attract the adventurous traveler. Tourist visas good for 90 days can be arranged with confirmed bookings through the Mongolian Travel Agency (Zhuulchin). For more information, contact the **Embassy of Mongolia**, 2833 M Street NW, Washington, DC 20007; (202) 333-7117. The first travel guide to this remote country is *Mongolia: A Travel Survival Kit*. Brand-new in 1993, it's available for $13.95 from Lonely Planet Publications (see page 56).

For Further Information

While there are many excellent guidebooks to the separate countries of East Asia (which will be noted later in this chapter), one of the few general guides to the entire region is Lonely Planet's *North-East Asia on a Shoestring*. While this book doesn't go into great depth in any one country, it's useful for getting around between countries. The third edition, updated in 1992, is available for $15.95 from Lonely Planet Publications (see page 56). *A Traveller's Guide to Asian Culture*, by Kevin Chambers, gives a broad overview of cultural trends from India to Japan, from antiquity to the present century. It's available for $13.95 from John Muir Publications, PO Box 613, Santa Fe, NM 87504; (800) 888-7504. Also published by John Muir are *Asia Through the Back Door* ($15.95), a budget traveler's guide by Rick Steves and John Gottberg, and *2 to 22 Days in Asia* ($9.95), a travel itinerary planner.

The Asia Society, a nonprofit organization dedicated to increasing Americans' understanding of Asian cultures, publishes and distributes a variety of books and is generally an excellent source of information on social and political trends in the region. For a publications catalog and information about the society's other services, write to The Asia Society, 725 Park Avenue, New York, NY 10021. A good source for general-interest books on East Asia, especially Japan and Korea, is the **Charles E. Tuttle Company**, 28 South Main Street, Rutland, VT 05701; (800) 526-2778. For Asian literature and films on video, try **Cheng and Tsui Company**, 25-31 West Street, Boston, MA 02111; (617) 426-6074.

Studying in East Asia

You'll find a number of study programs listed in the individual country sections later in this chapter. In the section below, we've listed only the study programs of CIEE-member institutions that take place in more than one country. Unless otherwise noted, consult Appendix I for the addresses of the colleges and universities listed in this section.

Semester and Academic Year

Education

Southern Illinois University at Carbondale. *Special Education in Japan and Hong Kong*. Site visits to facilities for mentally and physically handicapped. Juniors to graduate students and special education teachers. Apply by April 1.

General Studies

St. Olaf College. *Global Semester*. Academic program in Cairo, Egypt; Bangalore, India; Hong Kong; and Kyoto, Japan, with stops in Switzerland, Israel, and Nepal. Fall semester plus January. Political, social, and cultural issues of countries visited. Sophomores to seniors. Apply by March 1.

Summer and Short-Term

Business

Old Dominion University. *ODU Abroad: Management Seminar in Korea and Hong Kong*. Summer. College seniors and graduate students. Apply by March 1. Contact: Study Abroad Office, BAL 304, Old Dominion University, Norfolk, VA 23529; (804) 683-5378.

CHINA

China, the world's oldest living civilization, has an indomitable heritage, culture, and tradition. Foreigners visiting China today will find themselves witnesses to a turning point in the nation's long history, as the government continues to support far-reaching social and economic changes while repressing demands for democracy and political change. We have yet to see if, after a century of cultural and economic isolation, China will embrace the capitalist ideals of internationalism and modernity. We should note, however, that in the past couple of years China has encouraged limited capitalist enterprises and has stressed market-oriented socialism as it tries to compete in the world market.

Much of the turmoil of Chinese history is written on the faces of the Chinese people. The older generation remains fearful and cautious of politics. In 1949, the communist government under Mao Tse-tung declared a Chinese nation at last independent of foreign domination and internal chaos. But domestic politics soon turned to repression, particularly during the Cultural Revolution of the late 1960s and '70s. As a result, older Chinese have witnessed family and friends being subjected to accusations, jailed, shipped off to labor camps and in many cases killed. Now, young people, too—as a result of the government's bloody repression of the student prodemocracy movement in 1989—have become victims of a party leadership intent on enforcing its claim to authority. The Chinese people have been numbed by innumerable swings of the political pendulum and masterful manipulation of "truth" for political ends. If fear and apathy seem to be dominating the nation's political life, at the moment it is because the Chinese are tired of sacrificing in the name of China for the political elite.

Over the last decade, greater economic freedom has resulted in an improved standard of living and more contact with the outside world. The young have been at the forefront of this trend. Free markets, black markets, "strange" clothes, "decadent" ways, and foreign ideas, music, and language have been heartily embraced. The world's largest Kentucky Fried Chicken outlet was built 100 meters from Mao's memorial. Material rewards have also been adopted to provide incentive for higher economic productivity. Although Chinese government officials still oppose "bourgeois philosophies and social doctrines," they have embraced reform policies to encourage decentralization of industry and agriculture and to attract foreign investment. Slowly and expensively, the Chinese are being introduced to the luxuries of TVs, refrigerators, and washing machines. The age of electronic communications has hit China and is expected to effect changes in the society from the bottom up. Satellites for TV reception are bringing the world, and the long-dreaded "foreign ideas," to the living rooms of a country that has long sought to control the flow of information. Even the local TV broadcasts have become more daring in challenging the restrictions imposed by the government; an anchorwoman explained that it is almost impossible for the government to keep up with the proliferation of TV broadcasts.

Social changes are also evident. Lovers, previously invisible in public areas, crowd parks, benches, boating houses, and any space they can find—something that would not have been possible a few years ago. More fundamental social change is resulting from the government's strict enforcement of the controversial one-child-per-family policy implemented to control population growth—a policy that challenges the age-old Chinese tradition of the extended family.

However dramatic China's economic and social reforms have been, political reform has lagged behind. This fact fueled much of the popular frustration that led to the student prodemocracy movement in the spring of 1989. TV images of Chinese citizens in open defiance of the regime granted the world an opportunity to transform its stereotypical preconceptions of China. No longer are the Chinese seen as a vast, passive population, a people undistinguished in all but their reliance on the glories of their past.

The foreigner drawn to China should try to understand China's attraction to the West as well as the history behind its urgency to "catch up" to its Western counterparts. China was once the world's leading civilization. When it reopened its doors to the world in the late 19th century, however, it was stunned to discover that the industrial civilizations of the West had long surpassed it in almost every dimension. Nor was this discovery without its irony. It was, after all, the Chinese who invented the compass, which enabled the European powers to extend their empires and cultural influence all over the globe. It was the Chinese who invented gunpowder as well, which armed the West to conquer and colonize. And it was also the Chinese who invented paper currency, which facilitated international trade and the growth of capitalism. Today, the awakened sleeping giant that is China is reaching another vital juncture. The course it will take, both in pace and direction, is yet unpredictable but of critical importance to the rest of the world.

—Ching-Ching Ni, Oberlin, Ohio

Official name: People's Republic of China. **Area:** 3,696,100 square miles (slightly larger than the U.S.). **Population:** 1,151,486,000. **Population density:** 409 inhabitants per square mile. **Capital:** Beijing (pop. 6,800,000). **Largest city:** Shanghai (pop. 7,300,000). **Language:** Chinese (Mandarin, Wu Hakka, Yue, Xiang, Gan, Min, Zhuang, Hui, Yi). **Religion:** Atheism (official), Confucianism, Buddhism, Taoism (traditional). **Per capita income:** US$360. **Currency:** Yuan. **Literacy rate:** 70%. **Average daily temperature:** Beijing: June, 75°; December, 25°. **Average number of days with precipitation:** Beijing: June, 13; December, 2.

TRAVEL

U.S. citizens will need both a passport and a visa for travel to China. Transit visas are also required for any stop in China. Travelers to Tibet must apply for approval from the Tourist Administration of the Tibetan Autonomous Region. For specific information, contact the **Embassy of the People's Republic of China**, 2300 Connecticut Avenue NW, Washington, DC 20008; (202) 328-2517. There are also Chinese Consulates General in Chicago, Houston, Los Angeles, New York, or San Francisco.

Getting Around

The Chinese government continues to encourage tourism from the West. Though some locations are off-limits to foreigners, you can generally travel around the country with a minimum of restrictions. From a practical point of view, however, those unable to speak Chinese will find independent travel difficult. Learning a little Chinese—even a limited number of phrases—will make things easier, and more enjoyable. Contact with Chinese people is limited not only by linguistic and cultural barriers, but also by government policies. Tourists—as well as foreign students, businessmen, and diplomats—are generally placed in accommodations exclusively for foreigners rather than being allowed to mingle freely with the local population. However, these policies are more strictly followed in the north around Beijing; travelers will find more freedom in other parts of the country.

A special **currency** is designated for foreigners in China. *Renminbi* (people's money) is the currency of China, but foreigners are supposed to use foreign-exchange certificates (FECs) for all expenses. In practice, FECs must be used for all accommodations, train and plane tickets, hotel restaurants, and Friendship (hard-currency) stores. They are not supposed to be accepted in normal stores, or exchanged for *renminbi*. However, these rules are not strictly adhered to. Since only FECs can be used in the hard-currency stores, they are in high demand. Most people will accept them as payment; only in very small stores or seldom-visited areas will you have a problem with FECs. Often, you will be given change in *renminbi* after paying in FECs. It's also easy to exchange FECs for *renminbi* on the street.

China's transportation system is extensive. **Buses** are common. Intercity **trains** have two classes of service: hard seat and soft seat. Hard seats are wood or vinyl-covered benches seating three across; soft seats are linen-covered seats in a private car or compartment. Soft-seat prices are double that of hard seats. Overnight trains have hard sleepers and soft sleepers in addition to seats. Foreigners are charged somewhat more for tickets than Chinese locals and are usually directed into special lines at train stations. Students studying in China may be allowed to pay the local price. It should also be noted that a person can only buy tickets for trains originating in that city (that is, you can't buy a ticket from Shanghai to Nanjin in Beijing).

Intercity **air** service often runs late and service onboard is minimal, but it will get you where you want to go. China's regional domestic carriers are China Eastern Airlines, China Southern Airlines, and China Northwest Airlines. Service to Hong Kong and other Asian cities is provided by Dragon Air. Regular tickets are fairly inexpensive, but foreigners must pay twice the regular fare on domestic flights.

The **bicycle** is probably the most popular form of transportation in China. Chinese bicycles are basic and can be rented everywhere by the hour, day, or week. They can also be loaded on the luggage racks on top of buses with no questions asked. Taking them on a train, however, will involve more red tape.

Eating and Sleeping

There are inexpensive hotels and guest houses throughout China and one official youth hostel in Beijing. For more information, contact the **CYTS Tours Corporation**, 23B Dong Ziao Min Xiang, Beijing 100006; (86) 1-512770; fax (86) 1-5138691.

For Further Information

For general travel information, contact the **China National Tourist Office**, 60 East 42nd Street, Suite 3126, New York, NY 10165; (212) 867-0271.

Another good source of information is the **National Committee on U.S.-China Relations**, 777 United Nations Plaza, New York, NY 10017; (212) 922-1385. For $20, it will supply you with a custom-made *Briefing Kit on the People's Republic of China*. Because these kits are individualized, allow four weeks for their preparation in advance. Orders should include the dates of your trip, your itinerary, and any special interests in China that you may have.

Budget travelers will find *China: A Travel Survival Kit* a helpful guidebook to take along; however, because it was last updated in 1991, it may be slightly out of date. It's available for $19.95 from Lonely Planet Publications (see page 56). Travelers to Tibet should read *Tibet: A Travel Survival Kit* ($13.95), also published by Lonely Planet. Overlanders will also enjoy Lonely Planet's *Karakoram Highway: The High Road to China* ($14.95). Other good guides include *Fielding's China* ($17), published by Pelton & Associates.

A number of guidebooks to various regions of China is available from **China Books and Periodicals**, 2929 24th Street, San Francisco, CA 94110; (415) 282-2994. China Books publishes and distributes many other books of interest, including many of the works of fiction and film listed in the "Exploring Chinese Culture" section, below.

For an excellent summation of recent Chinese affairs, read *China Briefing*, prepared annually by The Asia Society. It can be ordered for $15.85 plus $4.50 postage from The Asia Society, 725 Park Avenue, New York, NY 10021.

WORK

Westerners are not permitted to work in China unless they have permission from the Chinese government. Chinese institutions of higher learning offer yearlong **teaching** posts to foreign applicants. Applicants should have a master's degree or higher and at least two years' teaching experience. Applicants are encouraged to contact individual colleges and universities in China directly. For further information, contact the Consulate General of the People's Republic of China, 520 12th Avenue, New York, NY 10036.

Western Washington University sponsors a China Teaching Program for people who want to teach English as a second language in the PRC. Participants are required to attend two short-term training sessions offered in the summer. Chinese language, geography, history, culture, and TESOL methodology, as well as preparation for living in China are covered. Teaching positions are negotiated with institutions of higher learning in China, and participants are placed twice a year (spring and fall). An undergraduate degree is required; applicants from a variety of fields are accepted. In addition, a placement-only option, which enables qualified individuals to forego the training session, is available to people who have teaching experience and extensive knowledge of China. Participants are typically placed in one-year assignments. For more information, contact China Teaching Program/Western Washington University, Old Main 530, Bellingham, WA 98225-9047; (206) 650-3753

Voluntary Service

WorldTeach sponsors a volunteer teaching program in China; for more information, see page 27.

STUDY

An excellent book for anyone planning to study, live, or work in China is *Living in China: A Guide to Teaching & Studying in China Including Taiwan*, by authors Weiner, Murphy, and Li. Extremely thorough, the book includes chapters on the Chinese educational system, planning your trip, adjusting to the culture, working, and traveling, and even includes a detailed directory of all colleges and universities in China and Taiwan that accept foreigners. Available from China Books & Periodicals (see "For Further Information," above) for $16.95 plus $2.50 postage.

If you are thinking of enrolling in a Chinese university, contact the Embassy of the People's Republic of China (see "Travel," above) for its fact sheet on the enrollment of foreign students in China.

The following educational programs are offered by CIEE-member institutions. Unless otherwise noted, consult Appendix I for the addresses where you can write for more information. In addition to the programs below, Pepperdine University and State University of New York schools offer study programs open only to their own students.

Semester and Academic Year

Chinese Language and Culture

Beloit College. *Fudan Exchange Program.* Fudan University, Shanghai. Fall semester and academic year. Sophomores to graduate students with intermediate Chinese and 2.75 GPA. Apply by April 1.

Brethren Colleges Abroad. Dalian Foreign Languages University. Semester and academic year. Chinese language from beginning to advanced levels, literature, history, arts; three weeks of study tours. Sophomores to seniors with 2.7 GPA. Apply by May 1 for fall and academic year; December 1 for spring.

Council on International Educational Exchange. *Advanced Graduate Students Program.* Peking University in Beijing. Supplementary studies or research after the completion of a master's degree and for students currently enrolled in a doctoral program who would like to further their primary research. Students attend university classes and are assigned a supervisor/mentor to aid them. Students may request assignment to a specific professor. Contact: University Programs Department.

China Cooperative Language & Study Program at Peking University. Beijing. Fall and spring semesters. Sophomores to graduate students with two years of Mandarin, one Chinese area studies course, and 2.75 GPA. Apply by April 15 for fall; October 15 for spring. Contact: University Programs Department.

China Cooperative Language & Study Program at Nanjing University. Semester and academic year. Sophomores to graduate students with one year of college Mandarin, one Chinese area studies course, and 2.75 GPA. Apply by April 15 for fall and academic year; October 15 for spring. Contact: University Programs Department.

Research Program for Scholars. Peking University in Beijing. For post-doctoral students to further research their fields of specialty. Program participants work in close contact with university faculty members. Contact: University Programs Department.

Moorhead State University. *China Program.* Nankai University in Tianjin. Semester and academic year. Juniors and seniors with some Chinese-language study. Apply by February 1 for fall and academic year; June 15 for spring.

Portland State University. *Study in China.* Zhengzhou. Semester and academic year. Juniors to graduate students with two years of college Chinese. Rolling admissions.

State University of New York College at Oswego. *Chinese Language, Culture, Civilization Program in China.* Beijing. Semester and academic year. Chinese language, literature, history, and civilization; instruction in Chinese. Study at Capital Normal University. Excursions and dormitory housing. Sophomores to seniors with 2.5 GPA and interest in China. Apply by April 1 for fall and academic year; November 1 for spring. Contact: Office of International Education, SUNY at Oswego, 102 Rich Hall, Oswego, NY 13126; (315) 341-2118.

University of Massachusetts at Amherst. *University of Massachusetts in China.* Beijing. Juniors to graduate students with two years of college Mandarin Chinese. Apply by March 1.

University of Oregon. *OSSHE Beijing Program.* Fall semester. Sophomores and above with 2.75 GPA. Apply by March 1.

Whitworth College. *Jilin Teachers College Exchange Program.* Jilin. Semester and academic year. Chinese language (Mandarin), civilization and culture, and Teaching English as a Foreign Language training. Juniors and seniors with

2.5 GPA and two years of college Mandarin Chinese. Apply by February 1 for fall and academic year; October 1 for spring.
Nanjing University Exchange Program. Nanjing. Semester and academic year. Offered in conjunction with Nanjing University. Chinese language (Mandarin), civilization, and culture. Juniors and seniors with 2.5 GPA and one year of college Mandarin Chinese. Apply by February 1 for fall and academic year; October 1 for spring.

Education

State University of New York College at Cortland. *Beijing Institute of Physical Education*. Semester and academic year. Teacher training, coach training, anatomy of sport, biomechanics, exercise physiology, history of physical education, and humanities offerings. Excursions and dormitory housing. Juniors and seniors with one year of Mandarin and 2.5 GPA. Apply by March 7 for fall and academic year; October 15 for spring. Contact: Office of International Programs, SUNY College at Cortland, PO Box 2000, Cortland, NY 13045; (607) 753-2209.

General Studies

American University. *Beijing Semester*. Fall semester. Courses in intensive Mandarin, Chinese politics, business, culture, and civilization. Juniors and seniors with 2.75 GPA. Apply by March 15. Contact: World Capitals Program, American University, Dunblane House–Tenley Campus, Washington, DC 20016-8083; (202) 895-4935/4937.
State University of New York College at Cortland. *Capital Normal University*. Beijing. Semester and academic year. Liberal arts, education, and sciences. Excursions and dormitory housing. Juniors and seniors with one year of Mandarin and 2.5 GPA. Apply by March 7 for fall and academic year; October 15 for spring. Contact: Office of International Programs, SUNY College at Cortland, PO Box 2000, Cortland, NY 13045; (607) 753-2209.
World Learning/School for International Training. *College Semester Abroad*. Kunming, Dali, Lijiang, Shanghai, Xian, and Beijing. Fall and spring semesters. Orientation, intensive language study, homestay, independent-study project, study tour. Sophomores to graduate students with 2.5 GPA. Apply by May 7 for fall; October 7 for spring. Contact: College Semester Abroad Admissions at (800) 336-1616.
College Semester Abroad—Yunnan Province: Language and Cultures. Kunming, Lijang, Dali. Fall and spring semesters. Intensive language, life and culture, field-study methods seminar, homestay, independent study, educational travel. Sophomores to seniors with 2.5 GPA. Apply by May 7 for fall; October 7 for spring. Contact: College Semester Abroad Admissions at (800) 336-1616.

Summer and Short-Term

Chinese Language and Culture

Boston University. *Intensive Chinese Language and Culture*. Beijing. Nine-week summer program offering Chinese language study at all levels and courses in Chinese civilization, history, politics, and economics. Sophomores to college graduates in good academic standing. Apply by March 1.

Council on International Educational Exchange. *China Cooperative Language and Study Program at Peking University*. Beijing. Summer. Sophomores to graduate students with one year of college Mandarin, one Chinese area studies course, and 2.75 GPA. Apply by April 1. Contact: University Programs Department.

Shanghai Summer Language & Culture Program at Fudan University. Co-sponsored with University of Colorado at Boulder. Sophomores to graduate students with 2.75 GPA. Apply by April 1. Contact: University Programs Department.

Miami University. *Chinese Language and Culture Program*. Shanghai. Summer. First-year college students to graduate students and teachers. Apply by February 28.

Michigan State University. *Intensive Chinese Language and Culture Studies Program*. Shanghai. Summer. Juniors to graduate students with one year of college Chinese. Apply by April 15. Contact: Office of Overseas Study, 108 International Center, Michigan State University, East Lansing, MI 48824-1035; (517) 353-8920.

Portland State University. *Summer Session in Zhengzhou, China*. Four-week program in intensive language and culture. High-school graduates to graduate students and nonstudents. Rolling admissions.

University of Alabama. *Study Tour of the People's Republic of China*. Huaxi, Shanghai, Xian, Beijing. Eight weeks in June and July. Offered in cooperation with Giuzhou University. First-year college students to graduate students. Apply by April 1.

University of Minnesota. *Chinese in Tianjin*. Tianjin. Summer. Language and culture studies. High-school students to graduate students and adults with one year of college level Chinese. Apply by March 1. Contact: The Global Campus, 106C Nicholson Hall, 216 Pillsbury Drive SE, University of Minnesota, Minneapolis, MN 55455-0138; (612) 625-3379.

Washington State University. *Intensive Chinese Language Summer Program*. Chengdu, Xian, and Beijing. Six weeks in summer from late June to early August. Intensive language study, Chinese history and culture. Sophomores to graduate students and adults with 3.0 GPA with some Asian studies coursework. Apply by April 15.

Education

University of Louisville. *A Study of Education and Culture in China*. Xiamen. Two weeks in summer. Study at Xiamen University. Culture as a basis of foreign-language teaching, Chinese culture, and education. Undergraduates to graduate students and adults. Apply by April 1.

International Relations

Ramapo College of New Jersey. *Summer Study in China*. Shanghai. Chinese history, politics, culture, economics, business, and language (Mandarin). Dormitory housing. Sophomores to graduate students. Apply by April 2. Contact: Study Abroad Office, Ramapo College of New Jersey, 505 Ramapo Valley Road, Room D-204, Mahwah, NJ 07430-9926; (201) 529-7463.

EXPLORING CHINESE CULTURE

Readings

After the death of Mao Tse-tung in 1976, Chinese writers began to reflect on the Cultural Revolution. The first post–Cultural Revolution novel to be translated into English, Gu Hua's *A Small Town Called Hibiscus* (1982) shows the effect of political events on ordinary country people, starting in the early 1960s and ending with the fall of the Gang of Four in the late 1970s. The stories of Wang Meng, China's Minister of Culture during the liberalizing early 1980s, take a satirical view of Chinese society. In the title piece of *The Butterfly and Other Stories* (1983), a high official reviews his fall from power and subsequent rehabilitation. Zhang Xianliang depicts sexual relations inside a labor camp in the controversial *Half of Man Is Woman* (1988).

China's foremost woman writer is Zhang Jie, whose novella *Love Must Not Be Forgotten* (1986) contemplates loveless marriage. Another important woman writer, Wang Anyi, in *Lapse of Time* addresses the problems of young people returning to the cities after years of reeducation in the countryside during the Cultural Revolution. Also by Wang Anyi is the *Three Loves* trilogy, of which two, *Love in a Small Town* (1988) and *Love on a Barren Mountain* (1991), have been translated into English. One of China's youngest women writers, Ai Bei, currently resides in the United States, having fled her homeland after the Tiananmen Square massacre of 1989. Several of her stories and a novella are collected in *Red Ivy, Green Earth Mother* (1990).

Mo Yan became internationally known when his novel *Red Sorghum* was made into a film by Zhang Yimou. His stories have been collected in *Explosions and Other Stories*. Liu Heng is another rising star, both in China and abroad; his novella *The Obsessed* was the basis for another film by Zhang Yimou, *Judou*. Liu's first full-length novel, *Black Snow* (1992) deals with a young man's return to Beijing after three years in a labor camp and his subsequent involvement in the city's underworld.

Films

Contemporary Chinese film is exemplified by China's so-called Fifth Generation directors, the fifth class (1982) to graduate from the Beijing Film Academy (founded in 1956, but suspended by the Cultural Revolution). Breaking with the tradition of Maoist didacticism—yet always with an eye on the censors—the best young directors of this class rely on rich images and a relative scarcity of narrative, creating movies that are at once engrossing and ambiguous.

The most successful of this generation is Zhang Yimou, who became widely known in the U.S. through his movie *Red Sorghum* (1987), based on a story of rural China by the writer Mo Yan. *Judou* (1990), based on the story "The Obsessed" by Liu Heng, was originally banned in China for its depiction of adultery and is the first Chinese film to have been nominated for an Academy Award. Also nominated was *Raise the Red Lantern* (1991), which depicts a young woman's life as one of a Shanghai merchant's four wives in 1920s China. Zhang's most recent release is *The Story of Qiu Ju* (1992), an unusually funny movie (for Zhang) in which a pregnant woman goes to court to force an apology from the village chief for beating her husband.

Xie Fei directed *Black Snow* (1990), based on Liu Heng's novel, recording the underside of urban China. *A Girl from Hunan* (1986) recreates a turn-of-the-century Chinese village.

The Fifth Generation also includes the directors Chen Kaige and Tian

Zhuangzhuang. Tian Zhuangzhaung's *Horse Thief* (1986) depicts a Tibetan peasant's struggles to feed his family, and his expulsion from society. In Chen's *Yellow Earth* (1984), set in 1930s China, a communist soldier with a penchant for collecting folk songs encounters peasant life. *The Big Parade* (1985) documents the training of soldiers for the Red Army's annual parade in Tiananmen Square. In *Life on a String* (1991), a blind musician wanders the countryside waiting for the magical restoration of his sight. Chen's most recent film, *Farewell to My Concubine* (1992), encapsulates the last 50 years of Chinese history and was co-winner of the Palme d'Or at Cannes.

The first American film to be made in China was Peter Wang's *A Great Wall* (1987), which humorously chronicles the return of native Chinese Leo Fang and his American-born wife to China.

HONG KONG

Arguably the most densely populated city in the world, Hong Kong is a vibrant center of trade and services riding the current explosive economic growth in Southern China. This British colony of six million is no longer a major manufacturing center, but has instead become the world's bridge to China by serving as a critical link for transportation, finance, and investment. And while business, finance, and the thriving economy are clearly the most important issues to most Hong Kong residents, social and political awareness is growing—largely a result of the upcoming return to Chinese sovereignty in July 1997.

Hong Kong has a well-deserved reputation for sophistication and internationalism but the visitor should not be fooled by the Western gloss, for the population is 98 percent Chinese and, underneath Hong Kong's cosmopolitan face, Chinese tradition thrives. Perhaps the most interesting aspect of Hong Kong today is the unique blend of East and West, the combination of internationalism, capitalism, and Chinese culture. Hong Kong is a place where hundreds of foreign financial institutions coexist with ivory and jade carvers and local vendors of snake wine and Chinese herbal medicines, where early morning joggers mingle with elderly locals entranced in their daily *tai qi* exercises, where Taoist and Buddhist temples sit alongside shopping malls, mah-jongg parlors alongside movie theaters, and Rolls-Royces mix with crowded trams. A typical Hong Kong street scene includes a businessman chatting on his cellular phone while waiting for his driver, and an old lady burning incense and paper money outside her shop in honor of a dead relative or the local god of the day, and a man out for a walk, swinging his bird cage in one hand and clutching a McDonald's bag in the other. Chinese tradition is the anchor in this fast-paced, materialist, rapidly changing city.

While Hong Kong offers the visitor a true taste of Chinese culture, the international community also plays a large role in society. Obvious beyond their numbers, Hong Kong is home to large groups of British, Americans, Europeans, Indians, and Japanese—all who have left their marks upon the colony. Since food plays a significant role in Chinese life, Hong Kong boasts some of the best Chinese restaurant food in Asia including dim sum, Szechuan, and Shanghai specialties. The foreign communities have also made their culinary presence felt in a wide range of restaurants and bars frequented by locals and expatriates alike.

Most visitors to Hong Kong only get to know the business and tourist centers of Kowloon and Central. But the territory offers numerous less well-known attractions that provide relaxing escapes from the city crowds, in addition to spectacular views of Hong Kong's tropical and lush landscape. Among the offerings are peaceful, and sometimes rugged, hiking trails that snake through the center of hilly Hong Kong island and the New Territories; several undeveloped mountain areas that have been transformed into country parks; remote beaches; and small traditional fishing villages that dot the many outlying islands and are easily accessible by ferry.

In addition to its own attractions, Hong Kong has value as a regional center for travelers. Hong Kong today maintains its traditional role as a jumping-off point for trips into China and is an excellent place to plan and arrange trips throughout the region. A wide range of travel services are available including consular services for most countries. Hong Kong is no longer the bargain paradise it was in the '70s, but local transportation is both simple and cheap and various types of accommodations are available, including modestly priced hotels.

—Robert and Mary Ann Williams, Hong Kong

Hong Kong is a dependency of the United Kingdom. Area: 409 square miles (about one-fourth the size of Rhode Island). **Population:** 5,700,000. **Population density:** 14,035 inhabitants per square mile. **Capital and largest city:** Victoria (pop. 767,000). **Language:** English (official), Chinese (Cantonese). **Religion:** Buddhism, Taoism, Christianity. **Per capita income:** US$14,341. **Currency:** Hong Kong dollar. **Literacy rate:** 90%. **Average daily temperature:** Victoria: June, 82°F.; December, 63°F. **Average number of days with precipitation:** June, 18; December, 3.

TRAVEL

U.S. citizens are required to have a passport; however, a visa is not required for stays of up to 30 days with proof of onward transportation by sea or air. For specific requirements, check with the **British Embassy**, 3100 Massachusetts Avenue NW, Washington, DC 20008; (202) 462-1340. There are also British consulates in Atlanta, Boston, Chicago, Cleveland, Los Angeles, and New York.

Getting Around

The city center is located on Hong Kong Island, which is connected to the surrounding islands by **ferry** service. The mainland peninsula known as Kowloon is also a busy commercial district. Beyond Kowloon, the New Territories include a number of new cities and smaller villages punctuating rural land. You can travel between Hong Kong Island and Kowloon by boat and subway, as well as by car or bus via the Cross-Harbour Tunnel.

Train service in Hong Kong is fast, extensive, and easy to use. And all station signs are printed in Chinese and English. The three-line MTR (Mass Transit Railway), which serves Hong Kong Island and Kowloon, operates from 6 A.M. to 1 A.M. Hong Kong's second main railway, the KCR (Kowloon-

Canton Railway) runs through the New Territories to the Chinese border at Lo Wu. A third line, the LRT (Light Rail Transit) connects the New Territories cities of Tuen Mun and Yuen Long.

Hong Kong doesn't offer much in the way of rail passes. Don't waste your money on the Tourist Ticket, which actually costs more than it's worth, giving you HK$20 worth of travel on the MTR and KCR for HK$25. (The extra price is justified by touting it as a "souvenir.") For long stays, however, you might want to invest in a **Common Stored Value Ticket**, available in denominations of HK$50 (US$7), HK$100 (US$14), and HK$200 (US$28). For help in getting around, pick up a free copy of the *MTR Guidebook*, which explains the proper buses and trams to use when the trains don't go directly to your destination.

Buses in Hong Kong fall into three types: double-deckers, minibuses, and maxicabs. Minibuses and maxicabs are smaller and faster and most commonly used by local residents. On Hong Kong Island, the cheapest mode of transportation is the tram system, still operable after 89 years.

Boat service between the outlying islands and along the mainland coast is widespread and inexpensive. In fact, crossing the harbor via the Star Ferry is cheaper than taking the train across, and much more interesting. If you get tired of the pace of the city and want a change, take a ferry ride to some of Hong Kong's outer islands, where you can spend some time in a sedate farming village or on a beautiful beach. Another trip popular with tourists is the ferry to Macao, a tiny Portuguese colony on the coast of China scheduled to revert to Chinese control in 1999. Ferries also take passengers to the Chinese city of Guangzhou.

Bicycle rental is another attractive way to get around outside of the busy streets of Hong Kong Island and Kowloon. The country roads of the New Territories are worth exploring by bike but the less-populated islands are probably the best places for cycling. For information on bicycle rentals, contact the Hong Kong Tourist Association (see "For Further Information," below) or the **Hong Kong Cycling Association**, Room 1013, Queen Elizabeth Stadium, 18 Oi Kwan Road, Wan Chai.

For persons interested in seeing Hong Kong as part of a **group tour**, the Hong Kong Student Travel Bureau (see address in "Especially for Students and Young People," below) offers a selection of tours available throughout the year. Options include half-day and one-day tours by bus, ferry, or junk. The organization also offers an array of tours into the People's Republic of China geared to students and young people; details are available at **Council Travel** offices (see pages xiii–xvi).

Eating and Sleeping

There are several **youth hostels** outside of Hong Kong Island and Kowloon. For further information, contact Hostelling International/American Youth Hostels (see page 54) or contact the **Hong Kong Youth Hostels Association**, Room 225-226, Block 19, Shek Kip Mei Estate, Sham Shui Po, Kowloon; (852) 7881638.

In Kowloon, especially along Nathan Road, there are a number of hostels not associated with the above organizations, although most are in extremely poor repair. **YMCAs** are considered a better option. Contact the Y's Way (see pages 53–54). Hong Kong Student Travel Ltd. (see "Especially for Students and Young People," below) has a list of other inexpensive accommodations in the city.

Especially for Students and Young People

Hong Kong Student Travel Ltd. has 10 offices scattered around the territory. Its main office is at Room 501-9, Trade Square, 681 Cheung Sha Wan Road, Kowloon; (852) 7253983; fax (825) 7253847. This organization offers a variety of services for students and youths: providing information, arranging tours, booking accommodations, and selling air, rail, and bus tickets.

Holders of the International Student Identity Card get reduced fares on international flights from Hong Kong and discount rates on a selection of accommodations including the YMCA International House, the STB hostel, and a number of hotels. In addition, many retail stores and restaurants offer discounts to cardholders; a list of these discounts is available at Hong Kong Student Travel Ltd. offices.

For Further Information

For general information, contact the **Hong Kong Tourist Association**, 590 Fifth Avenue, New York, NY 10036-4706; (212) 869-5008. Information on the nearby Portuguese colony of Macau can be obtained from the Macau Tourist Information Bureau, PO Box 1860, Los Angeles, CA 90078; (800) 331-7150.

One of the best guides to Hong Kong and nearby points of interest is Lonely Planet's *Hong Kong, Macau, and Canton: A Travel Survival Kit*. It's available for $14.95 from Lonely Planet Publications. Also good is *The Real Guide: Hong Kong and Macau* ($11.95). An excellent book to read in preparation for your trip is *Insight Guide: Hong Kong* ($19.95). *Insight Pocket Guide: Hong Kong* ($9.95) is a useful itinerary planner. For more information on Lonely Planet, *Real Guide*s, and *Insight Guide*s, see pages 56–57. Those relocating to Hong Kong for a longer term will find all sorts of helpful tips on everyday living in *Update Hong Kong*, available for $19.95 from Intercultural Press (see page 3).

A comprehensive look at Hong Kong's history and analysis of the last years of colonial rule can be found in *City on the Rocks: Hong Kong's Uncertain Future*, by Kevin Rafferty.

WORK

U.S. citizens interested in regular employment in Hong Kong will need a work permit. You must apply for the permit before departing for Hong Kong at the nearest British Consulate; allow 8 to 12 weeks for processing.

Internships/Traineeships

A program offered by a member of the Council on International Educational Exchange is listed below. For further information, consult Appendix I for the appropriate address.

Syracuse University. *Retailing and Fashion Internships in Hong Kong*. Summer. Undergraduate students are placed in American retailing or fashion companies. Housing and tuition for six credits are included in program fee. Apply by March 1.

STUDY

The following academic programs are offered by CIEE-member institutions. Consult Appendix I for the address where you can write for more information.

Semester and Academic Year

Business

Bentley College. *Bentley College's Business Program in Hong Kong*. Semester and academic year. Offered in association with Chinese University of Hong Kong. Full university curriculum plus Chinese language and culture. Juniors and seniors with 2.7 GPA. Apply by April 15 for fall and academic year; November 1 for spring.

General Studies

International Student Exchange Program (ISEP). Academic year. Direct reciprocal exchange between U.S. universities and Chinese University of Hong Kong. Full curriculum options. Rolling admissions. Open only to students at ISEP-member institutions. Contact ISEP for list of members.

Summer and Short-Term

Business

Bentley College. *Bentley College's Study Tour to Hong Kong and China*. Hong Kong and Kunming, China. Winter and summer sessions. Financing business in Hong Kong and China. Juniors to graduate students with 2.7 GPA. Contact Bentley College for application deadlines.

EXPLORING HONG KONG CULTURE

Film

Although dominated by low-budget productions, Hong Kong is the center of the Chinese-language film world. In fact, many mainland Chinese and Taiwanese films are co-produced by Hong Kong companies.

Since the 1950s, Hong Kong has been known for martial arts movies. Perhaps the greatest master of the kung fu film was director King Hu, who combined martial arts and historical epic. His films include *The Fate of Lee Khan* (1973), *Raining in the Mountain* (1978), and the three-hour spectacular *A Touch of Zen* (1975).

Of course, the man who made kung fu an international craze was the actor Bruce Lee, who died at the age of 32. Although he had appeared in earlier films, director Lo Wei's *Fists of Fury* (1972) made Lee an international star. Lee's other kung fu films include Lo Wei's *The Chinese Connection* (1973), set in turn-of-the-century Shanghai; *Enter the Dragon* (1973), a Hollywood production in which Lee fights opium smugglers for the British intelligence;

and *Return of the Dragon* (1973), in which Lee visits relatives in Italy and fights off gangsters trying to take over their Chinese restaurant.

Although the martial-arts genre is no longer confined to Hong Kong, Lee's direct heir is Peking Opera–trained actor/director Jackie Chan. In *Project A* (1983) and *Project A II* Chan plays a sailor who quits China's Coast Guard in 1903 to hunt pirates his corrupt superiors refuse to arrest. Chan's films also include *Police Story* (1985), *Police Story II* (1988), and *Police Story III* (1991), as well as *Armor of God* (1987) and *Armor of God II* (1991).

Few directors can equal John Woo for his mastery of the cinematic gunfight. In *A Better Tomorrow* (1986), gangsters fight it out between Hong Kong, Saigon, and New York (continuing the battle in the sequels, *A Better Tomorrow II* and *III*). *The Killer* (1989) features a professional assassin who makes his last hit to pay for an eye transplant for a woman he inadvertently blinded in a shootout. *Bullet in the Head* (1990) shows Chinese gangsters at work in Saigon during the Vietnam War.

Ann Hui is particularly sensitive to the communist threat in *Boat People* (1982), which depicts a refugee family escaping Vietnam; yet she also displays a typical Hong Kong nostalgia for China's past in *The Romance of Book and Sword* (1987), in which a dynastic struggle takes place between Han Chinese and Manchu warlords. Hui's most recent film, *Zodiac Killers* (1991), follows two Chinese youths through Tokyo's underworld.

JAPAN

One of the first things many Americans notice when visiting Japan is the proliferation of vending machines along most city streets. Even more surprising than their sheer number is the fact that many of them dispense beer and whiskey. Unlike what one might expect to see in America, however, Japanese youths do not line up illicitly at these beer machines after school.

This phenomenon reveals the strength of the "shame" concept in Japanese society. Japanese students will generally refrain from buying vending-machine beers for fear of the shame this would bring upon them should they be caught. Such a view also accounts for the strength of the group as a social unit, which sometimes overrides even familial obligations. An emphasis on groups, some say, can be found in all levels of Japanese society, from the obligatory high-school activities clubs to the process of consensus decision-making that prevails in the Japanese corporation. In its worst form, it can lead to such phenomena as *ijime*, the collective bullying of school children who don't fit in, sometimes resulting in death.

Such theories contain much truth, but visitors should keep in mind that few countries are the object of as much theorizing—among outsiders and among themselves—as Japan. Visitors will detect a very strong national and racial identity among the Japanese. This sometimes can lead to the feeling that Japan is pitted against the world, giving rise to such verbal coinages as *gaiatsu* (foreign pressure). On the other hand, Japan has a long history of adopting foreign influences and ideas, and the liberal number of foreign words in most Japanese people's active vocabulary lulls many Western visitors into a false sense of cultural familiarity.

One major factor in Japan's development was its isolation during a period of European expansion. Although Japan's first contact with the West came with the landing of a Portuguese vessel in the 16th century, the reigning shoguns made it their policy over the next 300 years to protect their archipelago from outside influences. Some say this policy was the result of reports made by an early Japanese mission to South America about Spain's harsh treatment of the indigenous peoples.

The great change began in 1854, when Commodore Perry anchored American gunships in Tokyo Bay and persuaded the Japanese to open their ports to foreign trade. Internal conflict aroused by this event came to a head in 1868 with the Meiji Restoration, in which the shogunate was overthrown by an intelligentsia that perceived the advantages of assimilating western technology and the corresponding political forms. Yet this was also the period in which the cult of the emperor was invented. Thus were the Japanese people thrown, in a very short time, from a culturally insular state to one in which they were systematically inundated with selected western ideas.

Imperialism was the logical extension of Westernization, and Japan proved it could be a match for the Western powers after trouncing Russia in 1905. For Japan, the first half of this century was characterized by a drive to control East Asia and the Pacific which ended with the detonation of atomic bombs in Hiroshima and Nagasaki and the American occupation. Today, most of those who lived through the war remember the privation their families suffered and say that they were captive to a military government. To a younger generation, the history of Japanese aggression in Korea, China, and Burma remains distant and ill-understood, owing in part to the careful scrutiny to which history textbooks are subjected by the Ministry of Education. The moral fallout of the war is exemplified by the ambiguous status of hundreds of thousands of resident Koreans—descendants of forcibly expatriated laborers—who are refused the rights of citizenship to this day.

The explosive economic expansion Japan experienced throughout the 1970s and '80s is now over, but despite a profusion of luxury items, the real living conditions of most Japanese have always been quite modest. Few people own real estate; most live in what by U.S. standards are extremely cramped rented quarters. Major Japanese corporations recently reported losses for the first time in many years, and the Japanese people are beginning to feel the effects of a worldwide economic slump. Such unquestioned staples of Japanese society as lifetime employment are now under siege as ailing companies begin laying off workers or encouraging them to retire early.

As if economic woes weren't enough, the dominant Liberal Democratic Party has lately seen its reputation tarnished by political corruption scandals rivaling those of Italy. These center around the indictment and arrest of Shin Kanemaru—the party's leading figure—for dealings with organized crime groups known as *yakuza*. The massive public demonstrations that preceded Kanemaru's ouster from the LDP were a surprising sign of the extent of this discontent among a populace that once seemed to implicitly trust its leadership. But even more surprising were the actions of several prominent members of the LDP who killed the prime-ministership of Kiichi Miyazawa in a no-confidence vote and then formed new spin-off parties aimed at "reform."

The overall impression many visitors have of Japan is one of security. Even in the hectic urban sprawl of Tokyo, you can walk through a crush of bodies without losing your wallet. Only in those neighborhoods that gather together enterprises on the borderline of legality—like hostess bars, massage parlors, and love hotels—or in the flophouse communities where day-laborers live hand-to-mouth does one sense the underside of life in Japan. To be sure, crime exists, but it is so highly organized that it seldom finds expression in random acts.

Indeed, Japan can be quite peaceful, and it's the mundane things—like a relaxing soak in the public bath after a day at work, or the common sight of small vegetable-garden patches between suburban homes—that contribute most to the aura of tranquility. Away from the cities, you'll discover why the Japanese have been entranced by the beauty of nature since the beginning of their civilization, and you'll experience the warmth of their hospitality and curiosity about foreigners. You'll also find that the character of the people differs greatly among the various distinct regions of this mountainous archipelago. By all means travel, if you can, away from the cities and the most popular temples. Taste the local specialities, enjoy the local festivals, and you'll come away with a knowledge of the hidden diversity of this fascinating country.

—Max Terry, New York, New York

Official name: Japan. **Area:** 145,856 square miles (about the size of Montana). **Population:** 124,017,000. **Population density:** 850 inhabitants per square mile. **Capital and largest city:** Tokyo (pop. 8,100,000). **Language:** Japanese. **Religion:** Shintoism, Buddhism. **Per capita income:** US$17,100. **Currency:** Yen. **Literacy rate:** 99%. **Average daily temperature:** Tokyo: June, 70°; December, 43°. **Average number of days with precipitation:** Tokyo: June, 12; December, 5.

TRAVEL

A passport is required to enter Japan, but U.S. citizens don't need a visa for stays of up to 90 days. For further information, check with the **Embassy of Japan**, 2520 Massachusetts Avenue NW, Washington, DC 20008; (202) 939-6800.

Getting Around

The Japanese **rail** system is probably the world's most efficient. Japan Railways (JR) operates 26,000 trains each day through nearly 5,000 stations across the country. Several non-JR lines offer competitive service. The cheapest are the local trains, which stop at every station along the line; then come the express trains, the limited express trains, and the *shinkansen*, or "bullet trains," which travel at speeds of up to 130 miles per hour. Most JR trains (except locals) offer more comfortable "Green Car" service at extra cost.

JR's **Japan Rail Pass** offers unlimited travel on JR trains and buses for periods of 7, 14, or 21 days. Passes can be purchased for either of two classes: Ordinary or Green. Though passes are available only to foreign visitors and must be purchased outside of Japan, prices are set in yen. In 1993, Ordinary-class passes cost ¥27,800 ($226) for 7 days, ¥44,200 ($359) for 14 days, and ¥56,600 ($460) for 21 days. The seven-day pass almost pays for itself on a single round-trip *shinkansen* excursion to Kyoto from Tokyo. Persons traveling to Japan on a student visa are not eligible for the Japan Rail Pass. Contact a Council Travel office (see pages xiii–xvi) for further information.

Train and subway networks in Japan's major cities can be somewhat confusing. Once you board the right train, it's easy to tell where to get off, as station names are marked clearly in English on most platforms. Since you have to buy local tickets from machines with destination names in Japanese only, you might not be sure how much to pay. The answer is to purchase the cheapest ticket; when you arrive at your destination, the ticket collector will tell you how much you owe. Those spending time in Tokyo will find *Tokyo: A Bilingual Atlas* a good guide to rail and subway lines. Both it and *Japan: A Bilingual Atlas* can be purchased in the U.S. from the publisher, **Kodansha International**, 114 Fifth Avenue, New York, NY 10011; (800) 631-8571.

Buses make up an integral part of urban transportation networks, but because their routes are not marked in English, they can be somewhat difficult to use. Buses usually depart from the same area near major train stations. Just keep repeating the name of your destination and someone will point out the right bus. Or, if you know the right characters, write it down. You're likely to use buses in the countryside and the mountains. On major intercity routes, however, take the train instead of the bus, as the highways are often crowded and driving is slow.

Domestic **airlines** are almost prohibitively expensive, but if you're pressed for time, you'll find extensive air service between Japanese cities. Japan Airlines (JAL) flies only between the major cities, while two other carriers, All Nippon Airways (ANA) and Japan Air System (JAS) provide more comprehensive service to both major cities and the smaller provincial centers.

Japan also offers extensive **ferry** service between the islands. Many lines give discounts to student travelers. You should always ask, as this information is not always publicized.

Touring the countryside by **bike** is perhaps the best way to enjoy the lush, natural beauty of Japan. If you plan to tour, bring your own bicycle with you on the plane. Buying and even renting bicycles in Japan can be quite expensive. For information on cycling organizations, routes, and cylists' accommodations, contact the **Japan Bicycle Promotion Institute**, Nihon Jitensha Kaikon Biru, 9-3 Akasaka 1-chome, Minato-ku, Tokyo 107; (81) 3-3583-5444; fax (81) 3-3582-1099. There's also an English-language cycling newsletter published in Japan, *Oikaze*. For information or to subscribe (overseas price: $15), write *Oikaze*, c/o Harrell, 2-29-6 Uehara 7B, Shibuya-ku, Tokyo 151.

Sleeping

If you find yourself without reservations and need a place to stay, you'll find an information booth in nearly every major train station. The people staffing these booths are usually very helpful, and in many cases will call to arrange a room for you; however, not all will speak English. If you can't communicate, use the **Japan Travel-Phone System** (see "For Further Information," below).

Affordable travel in Japan is easier with an International Youth Hostel Card. There are more than 450 **youth hostels** in Japan. The complete "Youth Hostels Map of Japan," is available on request from the Japan National Tourist Organization (see "For Further Information," below). For more information, contact Hostelling International/American Youth Hostels (see page 54) or **Japan Youth Hostels Inc.**, Hoken Kaikan, 1-2 Sadohara-cho, Ichigaya, Shinjuku-ku, Tokyo 162; (81) 3-3269-5831. The northern island of Hokkaido has the greatest concentration of hostels, as well as an alternative accommodations network called **Toho**, which caters to cyclists and other outdoor enthusiasts. Cyclists can also stay at **Cycling Terminals**; for more information on these, contact the Japan Bicycle Promotion Institute (see "Getting Around," above).

Camping is popular among the Japanese, who enjoy over 2,500 organized campgrounds in Japan. A partial list is available from the JNTO (see above).

Although youth hostels are by and large the cheapest alternative, try to spend a few nights in some other types of lodgings, such as smaller, more traditional Japanese inns called *ryokan*. While some *ryokan* are astronomically priced, many cost under ¥5000 ($50) per night without meals. Somewhat more comfortable are ***minshuku***, guest houses run by families, similar to American bed-and-breakfasts. The cost usually remains in the range of ¥5000, with two meals included. It is advisable to make reservations ahead of time. For information and free reservations, contact the **Welcome Inn Reservation Center**, Second Floor, Kotani Building, 1-6-6 Yurakucho, Chiyoda-ku, Tokyo 100; (81) 3-3580-8353; fax (81) 3-3580-8256. The JNTO can also provide you with the *Directory of Welcome Inns*. Another helpful organization is the **Japanese Inn Group**, c/o Sawanoya Ryokan, 2-3-11 Yanaka, Taito-ku, Tokyo 110; fax (81) 3-3822-2252. Other types of affordable lodgings include ***kokuminshukusha*** (people's lodges), which are government-operated accommodations in scenic areas, and ***kokumin kyukamura*** (people's vacation villages), which offer camping and sports facilities.

Those planning to live in Japan for some time but who haven't arranged permanent accommodations will probably want to check into a ***gaijin* house**. Usually found in larger cities, *gaijin* houses are boardinghouses that cater to foreigners. You should be able to find a single room for $300 to $400 per month. As a rule, prices are higher in city centers, lower in the suburbs. *Gaijin* houses are generally well kept, some with western-style and some with Japanese-style rooms. While living in a community of foreigners can sometimes isolate you from Japanese life, gaijin houses are good places to meet people and get your bearings.

Especially for Students and Young People

A good source of student and youth travel information is **CIEE**, Sanno Grand Building, Room 102, 14-2 Nagata-cho, 2-chome, Chiyoda-ku, Tokyo 100. The office also issues the International Student Identity Card and can book airline tickets for you.

Japan's national student travel organization is the **National Federation of University Cooperative Associations (NFUCA)**, Shinjuku TR Building, 2F, 2-2-13 Yoyogi, Shibuya-ku, Tokyo 151; (81) 3-3379-6311; fax (81) 3-3320-0220. Branch offices are in Kyoto and Fukuoka. NFUCA sells plane and ferry tickets, books accommodations, and provides information on student discounts.

For Further Information

The best source for general travel information is the **Japan National Tourist Organization**, 630 Fifth Avenue, New York, NY 10011; (212) 757-5640; fax (212) 307-6754. (**Note:** At press time, the Japanese government was debating whether to close the JNTO to save money, but even if such action is authorized, it will probably take a few years to go into effect.) The JNTO also operates a toll-free English-language telephone service, the **Japan Travel-Phone System**, designed to help English speakers who need travel information or emergency aid. In Tokyo, the number is 3503-4400; in Kyoto, it's 371-5649; outside these two cities, dial 0120-222-800 for information on eastern Japan or 0120-444-800 for information about western Japan. *Write these numbers down;* they can be of great assistance in a number of cases, whether it's helping you find your way to a shrine or easing communications with non-English-speaking desk clerks.

With detailed information on accommodations and plenty of clear maps, a good guide for budget travelers is *Japan: A Travel Survival Kit*, available for $21.95 from Lonely Planet Publications (see page 56). *Gateway to Japan*, by June Kinoshita and Nicholas Palevsky, gives a very thorough summary of Japanese history and culture, as well as a detailed province-by-province guide to restaurants, hotels, and sights. Published by Kodansha International (see "Getting Around," above), the book costs $19. Those interested in traditional Japanese architecture will find Peter Popham's *Wooden Temples of Japan* an interesting guide. It's one of the *Travel to Landmarks* series distributed by St. Martin's Press. A good source for all types of hard-to-find books on Japan is the Charles E. Tuttle Company (see page 391).

The **Japan Information Center** is located in the Consulate General of Japan, 299 Park Avenue, 18th Floor, New York, NY 10171; (212) 371-8222. The center has an auditorium for film showings and lectures, a reading room, a photo and film library, and a number of free publications. Another organization devoted to promoting an understanding of Japan in the United States is the **Japan Society**, 333 East 47th Street, New York, NY 10017; (212) 832-1155; fax (212) 755-6752.

WORK

Getting a Job

Foreigners need an employment visa in order to be authorized to work in Japan. Obtaining a work visa involves finding an employer willing to offer you a job and sponsor your application for a visa. Most Americans in Japan are employed by the U.S. government, Christian missions, schools, or U.S. companies with branch offices in Japan. Positions of English-speaking persons are often listed in the help-wanted sections of English-language newspapers such as the *Japan Times* and the *Asahi Evening News*. If you secure employment prior to leaving for Japan, the employer may file for a "Certificate of Eligibility" in advance on your behalf. Upon receipt of this certificate, you may contact the Japanese Embassy or Consulate nearest you to have your visa affixed in your passport before leaving. Persons unable to secure a job before departure can enter as tourists for up to 90 days, look for work, and if a position is found, apply for an employment visa. You will, however, have to leave Japan in order to get the visa stamped in your passport. You can apply for the visa in any country outside Japan (such as Korea), which can take time as well as money. English teachers usually have little trouble getting the necessary visa; for others, it may be more difficult.

If you're seriously considering working in Japan, get a copy of *Jobs in Japan*, a 268-page guide for English-speaking foreigners seeking work in Japan. Written by John Wharton, it's available for $14.95 (plus $4 first-class postage) from The Global Press, 697 College Parkway, Rockville, MD 20850; (202) 466-1663.

Teaching English

There are a number of possibilities for people interested in teaching English in Japan, including both regular salaried employment and informal tutoring. For those interested in either possibility, *Teaching English in Asia*, also written by John Wharton and available from Global Press (address above), is a useful primer filled with basic information on English-teaching methodologies as well as tips on popular classroom activities and dealing with Japanese students. The book costs $12.95 (plus $4 first-class postage).

Persons considering teaching in Japan should be aware of the **Japan Exchange and Teaching Program (JET)**, which offers 12-month positions as assistant English teachers assigned to public or private schools or local boards of education; participants are assigned duties related to English education at the secondary-school level. Applicants must be under 35 years of age, have a bachelor's degree, and possess excellent English-speaking skills. A functional command of the Japanese language is also required; study of or living experience in Japan is preferred, in addition to some background in the teaching of English as a Second Language. The program is co-sponsored by the Ministry of Foreign Affairs, the Ministry of Education, the Ministry of Home Affairs, and the local governments of Japan. For further information, contact the Embassy of Japan, Office of JET Program, 2520 Massachusetts Avenue NW, Washington, DC 20008.

English teaching positions offered by CIEE-member organizations are described below. Consult Appendix I for the addresses where you can write for further information.

- **Earlham College's Teaching English in Japan** program involves two-year English teaching assistant positions in rural schools. Applicants should be college graduates with Japanese language preparation and some knowledge of TESOL principles. Contact: The Institute for Education on Japan, Earlham College, Drawer 202, Richmond, IN 47374; (317) 983-1324.
- **The Overseas Service Corps YMCA** program sends people to teach conversational English as a Second Language in community-based YMCAs in Japan for two years. A salary and housing are provided, along with round-trip airfare. Applicants must have a B.A. degree; teaching experience and training are desirable. For more information, write to the International Office for Asia, YMCA of the USA, 909 4th Avenue, Seattle, WA 98104; (206) 382-5008.

Internships/Traineeships

Programs offered by a member of the Council on International Educational Exchange are listed below.

Association for International Practical Training. *IAESTE Trainee Program*. On-the-job training for undergraduate and graduate students in technical fields such as engineering, computer science, agriculture, architecture, mathematics, and the natural and physical sciences. See page 19 for more information. *Hospitality/Tourism Exchanges Program*. On-the-job training for young people beginning a career in the hotel, food service, and tourism industries. Participants must have graduated, or be currently enrolled in a university or vocational school and possess at least six months of training or experience in the chosen field. Training usually runs from 6 to 18 months. Consult Appendix I for the address where you can write for further information.

Voluntary Service

CIEE places young people in voluntary-service workcamps in Japan organized by NICE, a newly founded voluntary service organization in Tokyo. On these workcamps, a group of 10 to 15 volunteers from different countries works together on a variety of environmental and cultural projects. Room and board are provided. Volunteers must be between the ages of 18 and 35. The applications of U.S. residents are processed by CIEE. For more information, contact CIEE's Voluntary Service Department.

For persons interested in long-term voluntary-service work, the Year Abroad Program sponsored by the **International Christian Youth Exchange** offers persons ages 18 to 30 voluntary-service opportunities in the fields of health care, education, the environment, construction, and more. See page 25 for more information.

STUDY

Admission to Japanese universities is based almost entirely on entrance examinations given by the respective institutions. It should come as no surprise that it's very difficult for foreign students to compete with Japanese students in these entrance examinations. National and private universities will admit foreigners as long as they can prove that their command of the Japanese language is good enough to enable them to take courses conducted exclusively in Japanese. In most cases, selection is based on the Japanese Language Proficiency Test and the General Examination for Foreign Students. Information about these exams can be obtained from the **Testing Division of the Association of International Education, Japan (AIEJ)**, 4-5-29 Komaba, Meguro-ku, Tokyo 153; (81) 3-34673521; fax (81) 3-34673834.

Several private universities in Japan—including International Christian University, Obirin University, Sophia University, Waseda University, Nanzan University, Kansai Gaidai University, Keio University, Nagoya Gakium University, and Seinan Gakiun University—offer special language programs and courses in Japanese and English for foreigners. (For more information about the programs of International Christian University, see the program listings at the end of this section.)

Other possibilities for study in Japan include enrollment in one of the many institutions that offer intensive language instruction for foreigners who want to learn Japanese. To find out which ones are accredited, contact the Association for the Promotion of Japanese Language Education. One can also study full or part time at one of the many cultural arts schools in Japan, which offer many different courses—either in English or Japanese—in such subjects as martial arts, flower arrangement, tea ceremony, calligraphy, Zen, and shiatsu. Tourist information centers around Japan can provide information on the courses available and how to apply.

Monbusho, the Ministry of Education, Science, and Culture of the Government of Japan, offers scholarships to those who want to pursue Japanese studies or study at a Japanese university as a research student. For further information, contact the Embassy of Japan (see "Travel") or the Consulate General of Japan near you. Embassies and consulates can also provide you with the booklet *ABC's of Study in Japan*.

Following are the academic programs offered by CIEE-member institutions. Unless otherwise noted, consult Appendix I for the addresses where you can write for more information. In addition to the programs listed below, Pepperdine University, State University of New York schools, University of Nebraska at Lincoln, University of Notre Dame, University of Oregon, and University of Wisonsin at Madison offer study programs open only to their own students.

Semester and Academic Year

Business

Brethren Colleges Abroad. Sapporo. Semester and academic year. Japanese language, literature, culture, bilingual case-study business courses, and independent-study project at Hokusei Gakuen University. Study tours. Sophomores to seniors with 2.7 GPA. Apply by May 1 for fall and academic year; December 15 for spring.

Council on International Educational Exchange. *Cooperative Japanese Business & Society Program at the Center for Japanese Studies*. Tokyo. Semester and academic year. Sophomores to graduate students with previous study of basic business courses and 2.75 GPA. Apply by April 1 for fall and academic year; October 15 for spring. Contact: University Programs Department.

General Studies

Associated Colleges of the Midwest/Great Lakes College Association. *Japan Studies*. Tokyo. Academic year. Eleven-month program of study at International Division of Waseda University. Homestays. Freshman to seniors with 3.0 GPA; Japanese not a prerequisite for application but required prior to departure. Apply by February 4. Contact: ACM/GLCA Japan Studies Program, Earlham College, Drawer 13, Richmond, IN 47374; (317) 983-1224.

Council on International Educational Exchange. *Cooperative Japanese Studies Program at the Center for Japanese Studies*. Tokyo. Semester and academic year. Courses in social sciences and Japanese language. Juniors to graduate students with 2.75 GPA. Apply by April 1 for fall and academic year; October 15 for spring. Contact: University Programs Department.

Michigan State University. *Year in Japan*. Kobe. Academic year at Konan University. Juniors and seniors. Apply by March 1. Contact: Office of Overseas Study, 108 International Center, Michigan State University, East Lansing, MI 48824-1035; (517) 353-8920.

Obirin University. *Reconnaissance Japan Program*. Tokyo. Semester and academic year. Japanese studies and language. Juniors with 3.0 GPA; some Japanese language preferred. Apply by April 1.

State University of New York College at Buffalo. *Kansai Gadai*. Osaka. Academic year. Juniors and seniors with 3.0 GPA. Apply by February 1. Contact: Office of International Education, GC 416, SUNY College at Buffalo, 1300 Elmwood Avenue, Buffalo, NY 14222-1095; (716) 878-4620.

State University of New York College at Oneonta. *Seinan Program*. Seinan Gakuin University at Fukoka. Academic year. Japanese language, history, arts, culture, trade, sports, philosophy, society, government, and economics. Apartment housing. Sophomores to seniors. Rolling admissions. Contact: International Education Office, Netzer Building 332C, SUNY College at Oneonta, Oneonta, NY 13820-4015; (607) 436-3369.

University of Hartford. *Study in Japan*. Kanuma. Semester and academic year. Offered in conjunction with Asian Study Consortium. Liberal arts and sciences. First-year college students to seniors. Rolling admissions.

University of Nebraska—Lincoln. *Senshu University Exchange*. Tokyo. Fall semester. Japanese language, business, and civilization. Excursions and brief homestays. Sophomores to seniors in good standing at member institutions of the Association of Big Eight Universities. Apply by March 15.

Whitworth College. *Shikoku Christian College Exchange Program*. Zentsuji. Semester and academic year. Offered in conjunction with Shikoku Christian College. Japanese language and society, cross-cultural communication issues. Juniors and seniors with 2.5 GPA and one year of college Japanese. Apply by February 1 for fall; October 1 for spring.

World Learning/School for International Training. *College Semester Abroad*. Tokyo, Yokohama, Kyoto, and Hiroshima. Fall and spring semesters. Intensive language, life and culture seminar, field-study methods seminar, independent-study project. Homestays and excursions. Sophomores to seniors with 2.5 GPA. Apply by May 7 for fall; October 7 for spring. Contact: College Semester Abroad Admissions at (800) 336-1616.

Japanese Language and Culture

Gustavus Adolphus College. *Kansai Gaidai*. Hirakata. Semester and academic year. Homestays. Juniors and seniors with 3.0 GPA and one year of Japanese. Apply by March 1 for fall and academic year; October 1 for spring.

Ohio University. *Japanese Culture and Language Abroad*. Nagoya. Fall quarter (early September to late November). Intermediate and advanced Japanese language study. Excursions and housing with Japanese students. Students and non-students with one year of college Japanese. Apply by June 1. Contact: Dr. Koda, Department of Linguistics, 103 Gordy Hall, Ohio University, Athens, OH 45701; (614) 593-4564.

Southern Illinois University at Carbondale. *International Studies in Japan*. Nakajo. Semester and academic year. Housing with Japanese students. Undergraduates to graduate students with 2.75 GPA. Apply by March 1.

Southern Methodist University. *SMU in Japan*. Nishinomiya, near Osaka. Fall semester and academic year. Japanese language and culture, history, religion, and business courses at Kwansei Gakuin University. Sophomores to seniors with one year of college Japanese for fall; two years for year program. Apply by March 15. Contact: Office of International Programs, SMU, 100 McFarlin Auditorium, Dallas, TX 75275-0391; (214) 768-2338.

Stanford University: *Kyoto Center for Japanese Studies*. Academic year. Sophomores to seniors with two years of college Japanese. Apply by January 31.

State University of New York College at Brockport. *Kansai Gaidai Japanese Language and Asian Studies Program*. Osaka. Academic year. Juniors and seniors with 2.5 GPA. Apply by February 15. Contact: Office of International Education, SUNY College at Brockport, Brockport, NY 14420; (716) 395-2119.

State University of New York College at Oswego. *Japanese Language, Culture, Civilization Program at Tsukuba University*. Academic year. Japanese language, literature, history, and civilization. Apartment or dormitory housing. Sophomores to seniors with 2.5 GPA and one year of Japanese. (Students with fluent Japanese may take regular university courses at University of Tsukuba; special scholarships available.) Apply by April 1. Contact: Office of International Education, SUNY at Oswego, 102 Rich Hall, Oswego, NY 13126; (315) 341-2118.

University of Alabama. *Kansai Gaidai*. Hirakata. Semester and academic year. Homestays available. Sophomores to seniors with 3.0 GPA. Apply by March 1 for fall and academic year; May 15 for spring. Contact: (205) 348-5256.

Whitworth College. *Seiwa College Exchange Program*. Nishinomiya-shi. Semester and academic year. Offered in conjunction with Seiwa College. Language study, cross-cultural studies, comparative linguistics, Asian studies, Japanese religions, Christianity in Japan, family life in Japan, business management in Japan, Japanese literature. Juniors and seniors with 2.5 GPA and one year of college Japanese. Apply by February 1 for fall; October 1 for spring.

Summer and Short-Term

Business

Bentley College. *Bentley's Study Tour to Japan*. Three-week summer program including courses on Japanese economy and business practices. Excursions. Juniors to graduate students with 2.7 GPA. Apply by March 1.

Council on International Educational Exchange. *Cooperative Japanese Business & Society Program at the Center for Japanese Studies*. Tokyo. Summer. Sophomores to young professionals with previous business courses and 2.75 GPA. Apply by March 1. Contact: University Programs Department.

Economics

University of Alabama. *Bama in Chiba*. Chiba University in Chiba City. Late May to mid-June. Introduction to Japanese economy, history, corporate culture, business, monetary policy, manufacturing, agriculture, foreign policy, and culture. Excursions. Undergraduates and graduate students with basic economics. Apply by March 1. Contact: College of Commerce and Business Administration, Study Abroad, University of Alabama, Box 870221, Tuscaloosa, AL 35487-0221; (205) 348-7842.

Education

Earlham College. *Studies in Cross-Cultural Education*. Morioka. Twenty-week program in summer and fall. Culture, education, and Japanese language; internship in local junior or senior high school. Homestays. Undergraduates with one year of Japanese. Contact: Carmelita Nussbaum, Drawer 13, Earlham College, Richmond, IN 47374; (317) 983-1224.

Japanese Language and Culture

Council on International Educational Exchange. *Cooperative Japanese Language Program at the Center for Japanese Studies at Waseda Hoshien*. Tokyo. Three or six weeks in summer. Sophomores to young professionals with 2.75 GPA. Apply by March 1. Contact University Programs Department.

Earlham College. *Hokkaido Intensive Program*. Hokkaido Tokai University in Sapporo. Twenty-week program in spring and summer. Intensive language and culture study plus internship. Homestays. Students with beginning Japanese only. Apply by November 14. Contact: Carmelita Nussbaum, Drawer 13, Earlham College, Richmond, IN 47374; (317) 983-1224.

International Christian University. *Summer Intensive Course in Japanese Language*. Tokyo. Sophomores to graduate students with one year of college Japanese. Apply by April 1.

Michigan State University. *Intensive Japanese Language Study*. Hikone and Otsu. Juniors and seniors with two years of college Japanese. Apply by April 15. Contact: Office of Overseas Study, 108 International Center, Michigan State University, East Lansing, MI 48824-1035; (517) 353-8920.

Portland State University. *Summer Session in Sapporo.* High-school graduates to graduate students and nonstudents. Offered even-numbered years only.
State University of New York at Buffalo. *Summer Program of Japanese Language and Culture at Tokyo University of Agriculture and Technology.* Intensive Japanese language. Optional homestays. First-year college students to graduate students with one year of Japanese and 2.5 GPA (3.0 in Japanese). Apply by April 15. Contact: Study-Abroad Coordinator, Office of International Education, SUNY at Buffalo, 212 Talbert Hall, Box 601604, Buffalo, NY 14260-1604; (716) 645-3912.
University of Utah. *Kobe, Japan Language Program.* Kobe YMCA College. Six or seven weeks in summer. Homestays. Undergraduates, students, and others with 2.0 GPA and (recommended) one or two quarters of college Japanese. Apply by March 1.

EXPLORING JAPANESE CULTURE

Readings

Japan's rapid industrialization, often perceived as Westernization, produced conflicting ideals in the Japanese psyche. In Jun'ichiro Tanizaki's *Some Prefer Nettles* (1928), a man is simultaneously attracted to two women who embody the opposite poles of East and West, ideas characterized as old or new. Similarly, the protagonist of *Naomi* becomes enchanted, and finally defeated, by his lover's Western mystique. Tanizaki's most famous novel, *The Makioka Sisters* (1942–48), chronicles the disappearance of old ways of life in the years preceding World War II.

Yasunari Kawabata, Japan's first Nobel Laureate, is known for his depictions of ill-fated love affairs set in hot spring resorts, such as *Snow Country* (1947) and *Thousand Cranes*. Kawabata's protégé, Yukio Mishima, perhaps more than any of his contemporaries, personally internalized the conflicting ideals of Japan and the West as he understood them. *Confessions of a Mask* (1949) is a somewhat autobiographical novel of a boy's coming of age. *The Temple of the Golden Pavilion* (1956) is based on the true story of a young Buddhist priest who burns down his temple. More accessible are Mishima's short stories, of which there are many collections; "Patriotism" (1960), a tale of lovers' suicide, is among the best.

Japan's youngest generation of writers—much like their American counterparts—seem to be having an increasingly difficult time extracting meaning from their materialistic society. Haruki Murakami's first two novels seem to embody a vague desire to escape from the world: *A Wild Sheep Chase* (1990) and *Hard-Boiled Wonderland and the End of the World*. In a new collection of Murakami's stories, *The Elephant Vanishes* (1993), various characters are confronted by mysteries which they (or the author) refuse to deeply explore. The work of Banana Yoshimoto, Japan's most recent young best-selling author, is now available in English. The novel *Kitchen* (1991) features a young woman who moves in with a friend and loses herself in household chores after her grandmother dies.

Films

Perhaps the most memorable creations of Japanese cinema are Tomoyuki Tanaka's mutant monster heroes: Godzilla, Rodan, and Mothra. Godzilla, at least, is still going strong, appearing in a new feature just about every year.

The preoccupation with nuclear fallout and other man-made environmental catastrophes evident in such science-fiction/horror movies is also the theme of Katsuhiro Otomo's animated film *Akira* (1987), which takes place in Neo Tokyo after World War III.

Next to Godzilla, the most famous fixture of Japanese film is probably the director Akira Kurosawa. One of the directors responsible for the popularity of samurai movies, Kurosawa's work in this genre includes *Yojimbo* and *Sanjuro*, as well as the legendary *Seven Samurai* (1954), which was the model for John Sturges's famous western *The Magnificent Seven*. The samurai film is taken to new depths in *Ran* ("Chaos," 1985), which mixes elements of *King Lear* and the history of feudal Japan. In *Rhapsody in August* (1990), a Japanese-American (played by Richard Gere) visits his Japanese grandmother and listens to her recollections of the atomic bombing of Nagasaki.

Nagisa Oshima represents a generation of filmmakers influenced by the French director Jean-Luc Godard. *Cruel Story of Youth* chronicles the love affair of two high-school dropouts set against a bleak urban backdrop. His most recent films are renowned for their eroticism: *In the Realm of the Senses* (1976) concerns a sexually insatiable wife; in *In the Realm of Passion* (1980) the spirit of a betrayed husband haunts his wife and her lover.

SOUTH KOREA

The Korean Peninsula extends from Northeast China toward Japan dividing the Yellow Sea from the Sea of Japan. This location has seemingly guaranteed its history of internal conflict and foreign domination. Following a long period of dependency on China beginning in the 7th century A.D., Korea was colonized in 1874 when Japan imposed on it the Treaty of Kwanghwa, which secured Japanese commercial access and related interests. After Japan's victory in the Sino-Japanese War of 1894–1895, Korea became a Japanese protectorate and was annexed as a Japanese colony in 1910.

Between 1910 and 1945, Japan's harsh colonial regime attempted to eradicate Korean culture and incorporate Korea totally into the Japanese empire. In 1945, Japan relinquished control of Korea. However, soon after gaining independence from the Japanese, Korea was the theater of a power struggle between the Chinese/Soviet–supported communists in the north and the U.S.-backed forces in the south. As a result of this continuing struggle, Korea was divided at the 38th parallel into the People's Democratic Republic of Korea (North Korea) and the Republic of Korea (South Korea). In 1953, a truce meant to create a demilitarized zone and to provide for a framework for ending the war was signed by both sides. This was, and remains, a geographic, economic, and political division. A series of elected and nonelected governments in the south, and the softening of positions in the north, eventually led to high-level talks between the two Koreas beginning in 1990.

The majority of South Korea's 44 million citizens are culturally homogeneous Koreans. They share this quality with their northern brothers and sisters. A small Chinese minority numbers about 20,000. Korean is the official language and English is widely taught in the high schools. Energized by hosting the 1988 summer Olympics in Seoul, the tourist industry has grown tremendously in the intervening years. This rapid growth contributed to increased activity in the related sectors of tour operations, facilities, and sites development. All require more trained, multilingual personnel. By the end of the 1980s, 51 of Korea's 107 universities and colleges were offering majors in hotel administration and associated tourist fields.

With a population of 10 million, Seoul is the hub for the entire nation. It has been the center of educational opportunities, culture, art, professional training, leadership, and social and economic development. Established 100 years before Columbus's arrival in the Americas, the city of Seoul is characterized by the harmonious blend of ultra-modern buildings, ancient palaces, shrines, and monuments. It is a busy metropolis with many first-class Euro-American–style hotels, shops, bars, and restaurants. Also, there is a strong U.S. military presence, which is seemingly all-pervasive.

Beyond Seoul you will find Korea's pastoral beauty on Kanghwado Island, north of Seoul's port city of Inch'on. The island's largest temple, Chondungsa, is about one and a half hours' drive from Seoul. Near Suwon, some 41 kilometers south of Seoul, Korea's 20-year-old Folk Village provides a romantic view of rural life in Korea as it was in centuries past. Known as the Citrus Island, Chejudo is Korea's largest and most famous island. It is a popular honeymoon resort and tourist shop. In Cheju City you can visit Samsonghyol (the Cave of the Three Family Spirits) where it is believed that three gods—that is, the island's forefathers, Ko, Po, and Yang—appeared. You will find Korea's highest mountain on Chejudo as well. This volcanic cone named Hallasan was last active in A.D. 1007. Beaches, waterfalls, and unusual villages are part of the spectacular scenery of this island.

Back on the peninsula, in the Diamond Mountains, the impressive Soraksan Range is located along the eastern coast north of Kangnung City. Considered Korea's "culture city" with its royal Onung (Five Tombs) and Tomb of Kim Yu-Shin, the Pulguksa and other Buddhist temples, the Punhwangsa Pagoda, and fortress ruins, Kyongju is an ancient Shilla capital nested in a secluded basin between Taegu and the Pusan Expressway. About 15 minutes from the city you can enjoy all the amenities, including boating and swimming, of the Pomun Lake Resort.

—Roland A. Foulkes, Gainesville, Florida

Official name: Republic of Korea. **Area:** 38,025 square miles (about the size of Virginia). **Population:** 43,134,000. **Population density:** 1,134 inhabitants per square mile. **Capital and largest city:** Seoul (pop. 10,700,000). **Language:** Korean. **Religion:** Buddhism, Christianity. **Per capita income:** US$5,600. **Currency:** Won. **Literacy rate:** 96%. **Average daily high/low:** Seoul: January, 35°F/15°F; July, 87°F/71°F. **Average number of days with precipitation:** Seoul: January, 8; July, 16.

TRAVEL

U.S. citizens need a passport but not a visa for stays of up to 15 days. Multiple-entry tourist visas are valid for 60 months, with each period of stay not to exceed 90 days. For further information, check with the **Embassy of the Republic of Korea**, Consular Office, 2600 Virginia Avenue NW, Washington,

DC 20037; (202) 939-5660. For information on travel to North Korea, see page 391.

Getting Around

Seoul is South Korea's transportation hub, with highways, rail lines, and flight lanes fanning out from there to the rest of the country. From Seoul, Korean Air and Asiana Airlines provide direct domestic service to 10 cities.

Travel by **rail** has been facilitated by a new super-express train, the Saemaul-ho, which runs along three principal routes: Seoul-Pusan, Seoul-Yosu, and Seoul-Kwangju. There are special ticketing counters for English-speaking visitors in the stations of Seoul, Taejon, Kimchon, Chonan, Tongdaegu, Pusan, Iri, Mokpo, and Kyongju. Since weekend and holiday trains fill up, advance booking is recommended.

Buses connect more destinations than do trains (particularly on the east coast). While buses are not quite as comfortable, they are generally just as fast as the super-express trains, and less expensive. Each city also has its own local bus system. In Seoul and Pusan, however, the subway is easier to use.

Ferries are a pleasant way to travel among coastal areas and outlying islands. The most heavily traveled routes are those from Pusan to Cheju, P'ohang to Ullungdo, and Mokp'o to Hongdo. Also, a coastal hydrofoil operates along the southern coast between Pusan and Yosu via the Hallyosudo Waterway. Many travelers take the ferry between Korea and Japan. The most commonly travelled route is between Shimonoseki and Pusan, on the Pukwan ferry.

Eating and Sleeping

In Seoul there are plenty of cheap **boardinghouses**, none especially luxurious but great places to meet fellow travelers. Another less expensive option to the western-style hotel is the traditional Korean inn or ***yogwan***, which gives you comfortable but basic lodgings, supplying you with a mattress, quilt, and pillow.

There are nine **youth hostels** in South Korea. Since Korean youth hostels often book large groups, it's often difficult to find a room; book ahead of time. For more information, contact the **Korea Youth Hostels Association**, #604 Seoul Youth Center, 27 Soopyo-Dong, Joong-ku; (82) 2-266-2896; fax (82) 2-279-8002.

Especially for Students and Young People

South Korea's student travel bureau and issuer of the International Student Identity Card is the **Korea International Student Exchange Society (KISES)**, Room 505, YMCA Building, 9 ChongNo 2-ka, ChongNo-Ku, Seoul; (82) 2-733-9494; fax (82) 2-732-9568. KISES has branch offices in Kangnam, Pusan, Daegu, and Daejon. It provides a variety of services to students, including selling plane and ferry tickets, booking accommodations, distributing tourist information, and arranging special tours. KISES can also arrange homestays with Korean families.

For Further Information

General tourist information, including a list of hotels, hostels, and Ys, is available from the **Korean National Tourism Corporation**, Two Executive Drive, Seventh Floor, Fort Lee, NJ 07024; (201) 585-0909; fax (201) 585-9041.

The best guide for the budget traveler is *Korea: A Travel Survival Kit*, with a chapter on visiting North Korea, available for $11.95 from Lonely Planet Publications. *South Korea Handbook* is another good guide to the country. You can order it for $14.95 from Moon Publications. An excellent book to read in preparation for your trip is *Insight Guides: Korea* ($19.95). For more information on Lonely Planet, Moon Publications, and *Insight Guide*s, see pages 56–57.

For a review of social, political, and economic events of the last decade, read *Korea Briefing*, updated annually by the Asia Society. To order, send $14.85 (plus $4.50 postage and handling) to the Asia Society, 725 Park Avenue, New York, NY 10021.

WORK

U.S. citizens need a work permit in order to hold regular employment in South Korea. To apply, it is necessary to secure a job offer before residing in the country. A letter of support from the prospective employer is necessary. The application process takes about two months. For further information, contact the Korean Embassy (see "Travel," above).

Internships/Traineeships

A program offered by a member of the Council on International Educational Exchange is listed below.

Association for International Practical Training. *IAESTE Trainee Program*. On-the-job training for undergraduate and graduate students in technical fields such as engineering, computer science, agriculture, architecture, mathematics, and the natural and physical sciences. See page 19 for more information.

Voluntary Service

For persons interested in voluntary-service work, the Year Abroad Program sponsored by the **International Christian Youth Exchange** offers persons ages 18 to 30 voluntary-service opportunities in health care, education, the environment, construction, and more. See page 25 for more information.

STUDY

The following educational programs are offered by CIEE-member institutions. Unless otherwise noted, consult Appendix I for the addresses of the colleges and universities listed below.

Semester and Academic Year

General Studies

Council on International Educational Exchange. *Cooperative Studies Program at Sogang University*. Seoul. Fall and spring semesters. Korean language at all levels, economics, business, international relations, history, and Korean studies. Homestays available. Sophomores to graduate students with 2.75

GPA. Apply by April 15 for fall; October 15 for spring. Contact University Programs Department.

International Student Exchange Program (ISEP). Semester and academic year. Direct reciprocal exchange between U.S. universities and Korea and Yonsei universities. Full curriculum options. Rolling admissions. Open only to students at ISEP-member institutions. Contact ISEP for list of members.

Old Dominion University. *ODU Abroad: Yonsei University*. Seoul. Semester and academic year. Full university curriculum. Undergraduate and graduate students. Apply by March 1 for fall and academic year; October 1 for spring. Contact: Study Abroad Office, BAL 304, Old Dominion University, Norfolk, VA 23529; (804) 683-5378.

Whitworth College. *Keimyung University Exchange Program*. Taegu. Semester and academic year. Business/management, economics, education, teaching, history, Korean-language study, mathematics, political science, psychology, statistics. Juniors and seniors with 2.5 GPA. Apply by February 1 for fall and academic year; October 1 for spring.

Soong Sil University Exchange Program. Seoul. Semester and academic year. Offered in conjunction with Soong Sil University. Business/management, computer sciences, history, independent study, Korean-language study, political science/politics. Juniors and seniors with 2.5 GPA. Apply by February 1 for fall and academic year; October 1 for spring.

Summer and Short-Term

General Studies

International Student Exchange Program (ISEP). Summer. Direct reciprocal exchange between U.S. universities and Korea University. Full curriculum options. Rolling admissions. Open only to students at ISEP-member institutions. Contact ISEP for list of members.

State University of New York at Stony Brook. *Chonnam*. Fall semester and academic year. Juniors to graduate students with one year of Korean and 3.0 GPA. Apply by April 1.

Yonsei University in Seoul. Semester and academic year. Korean studies. Juniors proficient in Korean. Apply by April 1 for fall; November 1 for spring. Contact: Dean for International Programs, SUNY at Stony Brook, Stony Brook, NY 11794-2700; (516) 632-7030.

International Relations

University of Pennsylvania. *Penn-in-Seoul*. Seoul. Summer. Offered in conjunction with Seoul National University. International relations, political science, economics. Internship with Korean multinational corporation. Sophomores to seniors. Apply by March 1.

EXPLORING KOREAN CULTURE

Readings

During the period of the Japanese occupation, the Korean language was formally outlawed and Koreans were forced to speak Japanese. For this reason, Korean writers continue to attach enormous importance to their native tongue.

The writer Hwang Sun-won's personal story is fairly typical of many Korean intellectuals of his generation who grew up under occupation rule and spent their university years studying in Tokyo. An astute social critic, Hwang perceptively describes the ways Koreans of all walks of life communicate in words and signs. Selected works are translated in *Masks and Other Stories*.

The best new collection of modern Korean writers, both in poetry and prose, is *Modern Korean Literature: An Anthology*, edited by Peter H. Lee. Zong Insob's collection, *Folk Tales from Korea*, offers more traditional fare, as does Suzanne Crowder Han's *Korean Folk and Fairy Tales*.

TAIWAN

A part of China since 1684, the island of Taiwan became a separate nation in 1949, when Chiang Kai-shek's Kuomintang (Nationalist Party) was driven off the mainland by Mao Tse-tung's communist forces. For many years after, though the communists controlled the People's Republic of China, the most populous nation on earth, the government-in-exile on Taiwan was recognized as the official government of China by the Western world. This period came to an end in 1971, when the Nationalists lost China's U.N. seat. Today, few nations continue to support the Taiwanese government's claim to be the legitimate ruler of mainland China.

Taiwan's relationship to China is complicated, to say the least. In general, the Taiwanese see themselves as Chinese, and continue to see the mainland as their homeland, as is evident in such mundane affairs as nightly news weather reports covering both countries and Hong Kong. Today, Taiwanese businessmen are spending an increasing amount of time on the mainland opening enterprises in Shanghai and other nearby cities. In recent years, these Nationalists have gradually relinquished their ambition of regaining control of the mainland and have begun to adapt to present realities. In 1991, Taiwan officially declared an end to all counter-revolutionary actions, in effect recognizing the legitimacy of the communist government. In spite of China's furor over the U.S. sale of F-15 fighters to Taiwan in 1992, official representatives of the China and Taiwan met for their first peaceful talks in Singapore in 1993. Although the talks mostly concerned minor matters of commerce, they represented a giant step forward in cooperation between the two. Many believe that China and Taiwan (as well as Hong Kong) will one day reunite. The question remains: On whose terms?

Despite what may seem a lack of international political recognition, Taiwan has enjoyed booming economic growth and now has the highest standard of living in Asia after Japan. Taiwan represents a model of development in which economic success is achieved through a rigid, authoritarian system. In this light, one must distinguish between the majority native Taiwanese and the mainland Nationalists who occupied the island during the Revolution and remain the dominant political force to this day. Chiang Kai-shek and his son, Chiang Chingkuo, ruled this island with military discipline and incurred no small amount of local resentment. Their successor, President Lee Teng-hui, has begun to liberalize the country, permitting the existence of opposition parties, the chief of which is the Democratic Progressive Party. In a 1993 victory for Lee over conservative Nationalist leaders, the party elected the country's first native Taiwanese prime minister, Lien Chan.

Taiwan is one of the last living repositories of traditional Chinese culture.

Buddhism, Taoism, and Confucianism, banished from the mainland, are still practiced here as an intermingling set of beliefs and social customs.

But while Taiwanese youths receive a traditional Confucian education, many are strongly attracted to what they perceive as more liberal Western lifestyles. English teachers are in high demand throughout this country that seeks to consolidate its relationships with Western nations such as the United States. Such relationships seem especially important now, as Hong Kong prepares to be reabsorbed by China and U.S. military forces plan to scale down their own activities in the region. Taiwan has plenty of reasons to feel concern for its future, but as it embarks on a course of skillful diplomacy with China, the country feels an increasing optimism.

—Howard Beans, Albany, New York

Official name: Republic of China. **Area:** 13,885 square miles (about twice the size of Hawaii). **Population:** 20,658,000. **Population density:** 1,478 inhabitants per square mile. **Capital and largest city:** Taipei (pop. 2,724,000). **Language:** Mandarin Chinese (official), Taiwan, Hakka dialects. **Religions:** Buddhism, Taoism, Confucianism. **Per capita income:** US$7,380. **Currency:** New Taiwan dollar. **Literacy rate:** 90%. **Average daily temperature:** Taipei: June, 80° F; December, 63° F. **Average number of days with precipitation:** Taipei: June, 14; December, 3.

TRAVEL

U.S. citizens need a passport and visa for travel to Taiwan. Visas for stays of up to two months are issued free of charge. The U.S. does not have official diplomatic relations with Taiwan, but does have friendly semi-official ties. Instead of an embassy or consulate, Taiwan's interests in the United States are represented by the **Coordination Council for North American Affairs**, 4201 Wisconsin Avenue NW, Washington, DC 20016-2137; (202) 895-1800. Additional offices are located in Atlanta, Boston, Chicago, Honolulu, Houston, Kansas City, Los Angeles, Miami, New York, San Francisco, and Seattle.

Getting Around

Travel in Taiwan is both cheap and efficient. The main rail line runs from Taipei along the western coastal plain to Kaohsiung in the south. A second line runs down the east coast to Taitung. **Trains** vary from locals to high-speed luxury expresses that travel the length of the island in four hours.

Buses serve all parts of the island, and those that drive along the new Taipei-Kaohsiung freeway are faster than the trains when there's no holiday traffic. While it's possible to rent a car and drive it yourself (you'll need an International Driving Permit), few foreigners do so. Unless you can read the Chinese road signs and are willing to battle heavy traffic, you'll be better off taking a **taxi**, which is quite inexpensive by American standards.

The principle domestic airlines are China Air Lines (CAL) and Far Eastern Air Transport (FAT). However, with good ground transportation available, you probably won't need to use either of them.

Eating and Sleeping

Taiwan has only a few **youth hostels**. For more information, contact Hostelling International/American Youth Hostels (see page 54) or **Chinese Taipei Youth Hostel Association**, 12F-14, 50 Chung Hsiao W. Road, Section 1, Taipei; (886) 2-3318366; fax (886) 2-3316427. Also contact the Kan Wen Culture and Education Foundation (see "Especially for Students and Young People," below).

Especially for Students and Young People

Taiwan's student travel organization is the **Kan Wen Culture and Education Foundation**, 9F-B, 148 Fu Hsing S. Road, Sec 2, Taipei. A list of establishments offering discounts to holders of the International Student Identity Card is available from the Kan Wen Culture and Education Foundation.

For Further Information

General travel information can be obtained from the Travel Section of the **Coordination Council for North American Affairs**, One World Trade Center, Suite 7953, New York, NY 10048; (212) 466-0691; fax (212) 432-6436. The Coordination Council also has Travel Sections in Chicago and San Francisco.

The best budget guidebook to Taiwan is Lonely Planet's *Taiwan: A Travel Survival Kit* ($11.95). An excellent guide to read in preparation for your trip is *Insight Guide: Taiwan* ($19.95). For more information on Lonely Planet Publications and *Insight Guides*, see pages 56–57.

WORK

Foreigners need a work permit for regular paid employment in Taiwan. For further information on working in Taiwan, contact the Coordination Council for North American Affairs (address above).

Teaching English

English teachers are especially in demand in Taiwan, where to a large extent the economy depends on international trade and commerce.

The **YMCA's Overseas Service Corps** sponsors a volunteer teaching program in Taiwan; participants teach conversational English as a Second Language in community-based YMCAs for one year. A bachelor's degree is required; teaching experience and training are desirable. In addition to a monthly stipend, housing is arranged through the YMCA in the form of an apartment or homestay. Transportation from Taiwan back to the U.S. is provided by the YMCA but note that volunteers are responsible for airfare from the U.S. to Taiwan. For more information, contact the International Office of Asia, YMCA of the USA, 909 4th Avenue, Seattle, WA 98104; (206) 382-5008.

Internships/Traineeships

AIESEC-US sponsors a reciprocal internship program for students in economics, business, finance, marketing, accounting, and computer science. See page 19 for more information.

Voluntary Service

For persons interested in voluntary-service work, the Year Abroad Program sponsored by the **International Christian Youth Exchange** offers persons ages 18 to 30 voluntary-service opportunities in the fields of health care, education, the environment, construction, and more. See page 25 for more information.

STUDY

An excellent book for anyone planning to study, live, or work in Taiwan is *Living in China: A Guide to Teaching & Studying in China Including Taiwan*, by Weiner, Murphy, and Li. Extremely thorough, the book includes chapters on the Chinese educational system, planning your trip, adjusting to the culture, working, and traveling, and even includes a detailed directory of all colleges and universities in China and Taiwan that accept foreigners. Available from China Books & Periodicals—2929 24th Street, San Francisco, CA 94110; (415) 282-2994—it costs $16.95 plus $2.50 postage.

For additional information on study in Taiwan, contact the Cultural Division of the Coordination Council for North American Affairs (see "Travel," above), indicating your level of study.

The following educational programs are offered by CIEE-member institutions. Unless otherwise noted, consult Appendix I for the addresses of the colleges and universities listed in this section.

Semester and Academic Year

Chinese Language and Taiwanese Culture

University of Massachusetts at Amherst. *University of Massachusetts in Taiwan*. Taichung. Semester and academic year. Intensive Chinese-language study. Field trips. Sophomores to graduate students with 3.0 GPA and two years of college Mandarin Chinese. Apply by March 1.

General Studies

Council on International Educational Exchange. *China Cooperative Language & Study Program at National Chengchi University*. Taipei. Semester and academic year. Economics, Chinese civilization and culture, and Mandarin language. Homestays and apartment housing. Sophomores to graduate students with at least one year of college Mandarin. Apply by April 15 for fall and academic year; October 15 for spring. Contact: University Programs Department.

Summer and Short-Term

Chinese Language and Taiwanese Culture

University of Massachusetts at Amherst. *Summer at Tunghai*. Tunghai. Sophomores to graduate students and recent graduates (for undergraduate credit only) with 3.0 GPA and one year of college Mandarin Chinese. Apply by March 1.

CHAPTER ELEVEN

SOUTHEAST ASIA

A region whose premier cities rank among the world's most vibrant capitals yet stand but a stone's throw from some of the world's most traditional communities, Southeast Asia will challenge your mind and indulge your senses. From super-clean, super-modern, non-smoking Singapore with its mélange of Chinese, Indian, Arab, and Malaysian peoples to the chaotic din of traffic-clogged Bangkok, you'll witness the power of human enterprise and the different forms its future might take. From Buddhist Thailand to Muslim Indonesia and Malaysia to the Catholic Philippines, you'll marvel at the array of cultures scattered across these archipelagic and peninsular lands. Be it a tour of Cambodia's ancient Angkor Wat or visions of the frenetic art of Balinese dance, you're sure to be amazed.

Despite the generally tolerant character of the different peoples who inhabit this region, many have suffered through years of political strife in their emergence from the period of European colonialism and World War II. Some, like the Thais, have managed to peacefully negotiate their differences. Other countries have not been so fortunate. Witness the military coup in which Burma became Myanmar, as well as the continuing troubles with Cambodia's Khmer Rouge. From the conquest of the Philippines in 1898, the United States has had a history of direct involvement in Southeast Asia, although this lapsed somewhat after the failed intervention in Vietnam. Recently, even the U.S. military presence in the Philippines has been phased out. At the same time, heavy investment in these countries has made Japan the dominant economic power. Add to these factors a dispute between China and the Association of Southeast Asian Nations (ASEAN) over large tracts of the South China Sea and you'll see that these nations' mutual security is far from stable.

For many Americans, Southeast Asia remains one of the most mysterious regions of the world. Indonesia, Malaysia, and Thailand are known for their lush forests and picture-perfect beaches. Deep in the heart of these countries you'll find such peoples as Thailand's Hill Tribes and the Dani of Indonesia's Irian Jaya. Venture further—into Cambodia, Laos, or Vietnam—and you'll touch a world long off-limits to U.S. citizens but now eager to make contact. Whether you're interested in remote antiquity or the near future, exotic cultures or enchanting natural beauty, idyllic days or outdoor adventure, Southeast Asia is sure to be much more than you expect.

Getting There

At press time, many international carriers were offering APEX and/or budget fares from several U.S. cities to Bangkok, Manila, and Singapore. Sample *one-way* fares available through Council Travel for the summer of 1993 are listed below.

Seattle–Bangkok	$689	Dallas–Singapore	$709
Los Angeles–Bangkok	$689	New York–Manila	$649

From the East Coast, one of the cheapest ways to get to destinations in Southeast Asia is via Europe. Holders of the **International Student Identity Card** or the **GO 25 Card** (see pages 9–11) may take advantage of special

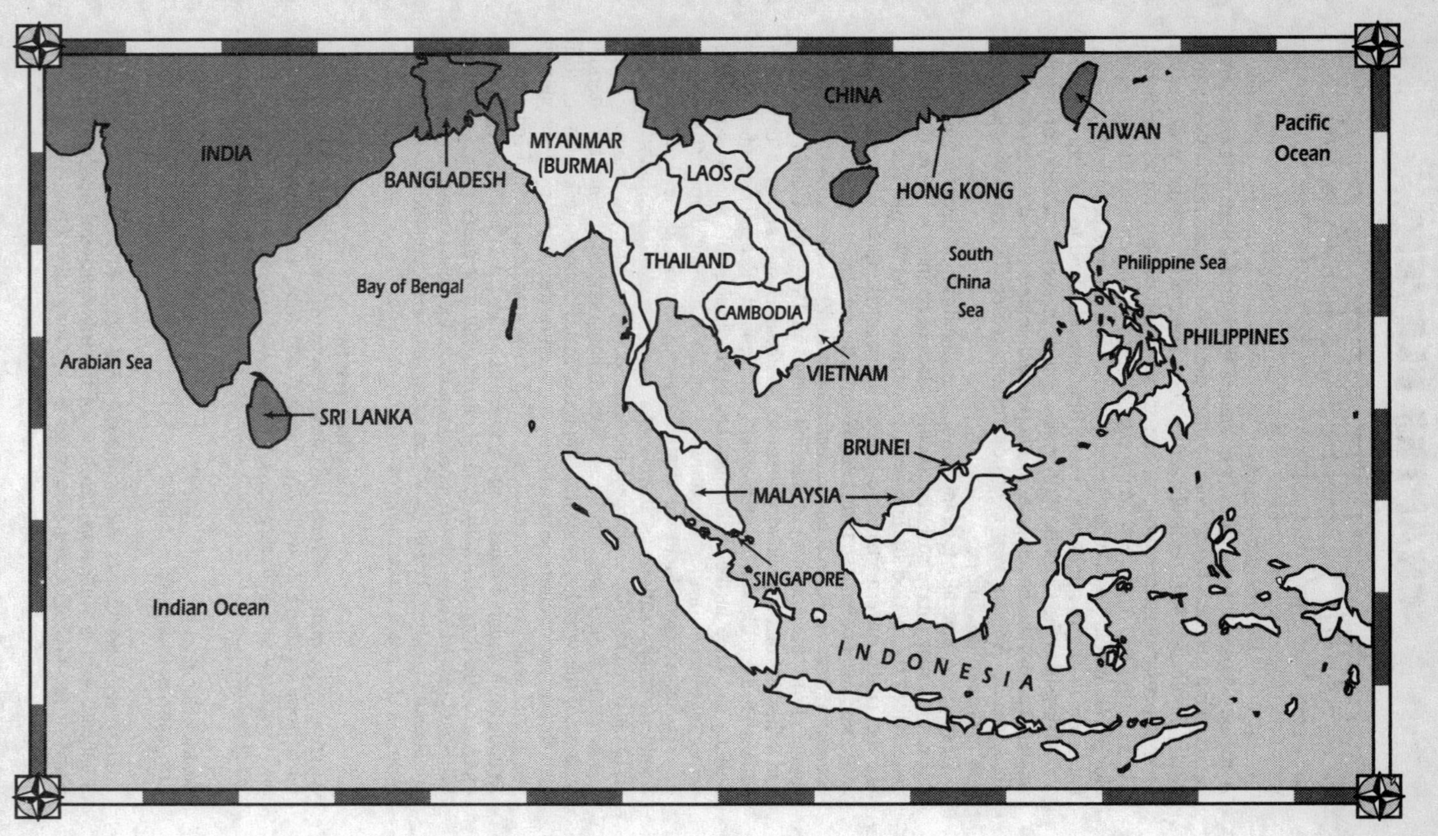

INDIA
BANGLADESH
MYANMAR (BURMA)
LAOS
CHINA
TAIWAN
Pacific Ocean
HONG KONG
THAILAND
CAMBODIA
VIETNAM
South China Sea
Philippine Sea
PHILIPPINES
Bay of Bengal
Arabian Sea
SRI LANKA
BRUNEI
MALAYSIA
SINGAPORE
Indian Ocean
INDONESIA

youth/student fares on scheduled flights connecting various European cities with Bangkok, Kuala Lumpur, Singapore, Jakarta, Manila, and Penang. These fares are excellent bargains. Sample *one-way* student fares available through Council Travel for the summer of 1993 are listed below.

London–Bangkok	$525	Frankfurt–Bangkok	$645
London–Singapore	$545	Paris–Jakarta	$759

In the East Asia and South Asia chapters, we've listed sample fares from cities in these regions to destinations in Southeast Asia. For fares between Southeast Asia and Australia, check the chapter on Australia that follows.

Traveling around Southeast Asia

Bus and **train** service extends along the length of the Malay peninsula linking Singapore, Malaysia, and Thailand. To get to the islands of the Philippines or Indonesia, the most convenient means of travel is by **plane**. Airfares in Southeast Asia are generally low. In Bangkok particularly, it's possible to get especially good bargains on flights to other cities in the region, as well as round-the-world tickets. Sample *one-way* student/youth fares that were in effect for the summer of 1993 are listed below; eligibility requirements are the same as for the student/youth fares from Europe described above. Check with Council Travel for more information (see pages xiii–xvi).

Bangkok–Singapore	$169
Bangkok–Jakarta	$259
Bangkok–Manila	$279

If you're looking for a truly memorable experience, try traveling by **ship**. In Thailand, Malaysia, Singapore, Indonesia, and the Philippines, you'll find a variety of old steamers, freighters, and modern cruise ships setting sail for points throughout the region. Local ships are a bargain, even for first-class travel. And as very few travelers take advantage of ocean travel, it's a great way to see a different side of Asia.

Most travelers use **Bangkok** as a central base from which to arrange trips to other less accessible countries, such as Vietnam, Laos, Cambodia, and Myanmar (Burma). For travel to such countries as Cambodia and Vietnam, which have no official diplomatic representatives in the U.S., the easiest way to get a visa is through a travel agent in Bangkok that specializes in this service. The largest such tour operator in Thailand is **Diethelm Travel**, Kian Gwan Building 11, 140/1 Wireless Road, Bangkok, 10500. For information on travel to Myanmar, contact the **Myanmar National Tourist Office**, 106 Tweed Place, Chapel Hill, NC 27514; (919) 493-7500; fax (919) 493-7500.

For Further Information

At press time the most up-to-date guidebook to the region was Lonely Planet's *Southeast Asia on a Shoestring*. The seventh edition of this longtime budget-travel favorite is available for $19.95 from Lonely Planet Publications. Another excellent guide is the *Southeast Asia Handbook*, by Carl Parkes. Full of useful information, detailed maps, and thorough historical background, the first edition (1990) costs $16.95 and is available from Moon Publications.

Lonely Planet also publishes a number of other guides to the region. Budget travelers to Myanmar can't do without the newly updated *Myanmar (Burma):*

A Travel Survival Kit ($8.95). The countries of Indochina are well researched in the yet more recent *Vietnam, Cambodia, and Laos: A Travel Survival Kit* ($15.95). Cambodia is dealt with in greater detail in *Cambodia: A Travel Survival Kit* ($12.95).

Insight Guide: Southeast Asia ($19.95)—covering Brunei, Indonesia, Malaysia, the Philippines, Singapore, and Thailand—is a great book to read in preparation for your trip. A good introduction to the many different cultures throughout the region is *A Traveler's Guide to Asian Culture*, by Kevin Chambers, available for $13.95 from John Muir Publications. Also available from John Muir is the budget guide *Asia Through the Back Door* ($15.95). For information on all the above publishers, see pages 56–57.

A good source for books on Southeast Asia—including fiction and history—is the Asia Society, 725 Park Avenue, New York, NY 10021. Write for their catalog. For a look at modern Southeast Asia through other travelers' eyes, try *Video Night in Kathmandu*, by Pico Iyer, and *Music in Every Room*, by John Krich.

Information on entry requirements for countries not included in this chapter can be obtained from the following addresses:

- **Brunei:** Embassy of Brunei Darussalam, Watergate, Suite 300, 2600 Virginia Avenue NW, Washington, DC 20037; (202) 342-0159; fax (202) 342-0158.
- **Laos:** Embassy of Laos, 2222 S Street NW, Washington, DC 20008; (202) 332-8416.
- **Myanmar (Burma):** For visa information, contact the Embassy of Myanmar, 2300 S Street NW, Washington, DC 20008; (202) 535-1311.

STUDY

A number of study programs take place in individual countries of Southeast Asia. Below you will find a programs that visit several regional destinations. Consult Appendix I for the contact addresses and phone numbers.

Semester and Academic Year

General Studies

Eastern Michigan University. *Asian Cultural History Tour*. 45 cities in Thailand, China, India, Nepal, Egypt, Israel, Greece, Turkey, Ukraine, and Russia. Spring semester. History, art, comparative religion, and political science taught in interdisciplinary context. Sophomores to seniors with 2.5 GPA. Apply by October 1. Contact: (800) 777-3541.

St. Olaf College. *Term in Asia*. Japan, Hong Kong, China, and Thailand. Fall semester plus January. Three-month homestay in Chiang Mai, Thailand. Sophomores to seniors. Apply by March 1.

INDONESIA

Tourists in Indonesia frequently remark upon the apparent timelessness of the cultural traditions they encounter. Yet a discerning traveler is likely to be equally taken by the country's dynamism and the rapid changes transforming Indonesian society. In the 40-odd years since it declared its independence from colonial rule, Indonesia has emerged as a major Southeast Asian political force, experienced tremendous economic growth, and managed to foster a palpable, albeit arguably fragile, atmosphere of social unity.

These achievements are particularly striking in a land where hundreds of ethnic groups, speaking more than 250 distinct languages, are scattered over an archipelago comprising nearly 14,000 islands. Subjected to 350 years of colonial rule, Indonesians have only recently come to envision themselves as a unified nation. Five major faiths are recognized within the country and various animist religions and mystical, spiritual sects have their adherents as well. Though approximately 90 percent of the population claims to be Muslim, that figure includes a broad spectrum ranging from the devoutly orthodox to those who are merely Muslims on paper. "Unity in Diversity," the slogan emblazoned on the national seal of the Republic of Indonesia, is more than a motto. It is a challenge that is continually negotiated by the modern state and its citizenry.

Due partly to increased exports of natural commodities, Indonesia has recently become the focus of much world attention. As in the past, when the islands of Indonesia were known to Europeans as the Spice Islands, foreign commercial interests play an important role in the country's fortunes. Ancient maritime empires based in Java and Sumatra carried on trade with Chinese, Indian, and later Arab merchants. In time, the Portuguese established a niche in the archipelago. Among the most important foreign influences was that of the Dutch, who created an expansive colonial empire known as the Netherlands East Indies. Indonesia's revolution and the eventual capitulation and expulsion of the Dutch remains a major theme in official rhetoric and the "Spirit of '45" still figures importantly in the popular imagination.

Today executive power in Indonesia is in the hands of the president. The incumbent, Suharto, has run largely unopposed since being elected acting president in 1967. Prior to assuming office, Suharto commanded the armed forces, which continue to play a major role in local and national politics. Opposition to state policies is strongly suppressed.

Although it is the world's fourth most populous country, Indonesia is rarely on the itineraries of American travelers. Those who do visit generally go only to the most populated island, Java, or the neighboring island of Bali. But visitors with more time and the inclination to experience the less familiar might also want to venture to such islands as Sumatra, Kalimantan (Indonesian Borneo), or Irian Jaya (New Guinea). Obviously, a longer stay will enable the traveler to make a deeper exploration into the richness of the complex cultures that make up Indonesia.

—Anne Schiller, Ithaca College, New York

Official name: Republic of Indonesia. **Area:** 735,268 square miles (about three times larger than Texas). **Population:** 193,000,000. **Population density:** 262 inhabitants per square mile. **Capital and largest city:** Jakarta (pop. 8,800,000). **Language:** Bahasa Indonesian (official), Javanese, and other regional languages. **Religion:** Islam. **Per capita income:** US$490. **Currency:** Rupiah. **Literacy rate:** 85%. **Average daily temperature:** Jakarta: June, 81° F; December, 80° F. **Average number of days with precipitation:** Jakarta: June, 7; December, 14.

TRAVEL

U.S. citizens need a passport valid six months beyond the length of stay for travel to Indonesia, but a visa is not required for stays of less than two months. You must also have an onward or return ticket. Also, be sure that you plan to enter Indonesia through an approved gateway city. Most popular gateway cities are approved, but you should check just in case. If you plan to enter through an unapproved city, you must obtain a visa in advance. For more information, check with the **Embassy of the Republic of Indonesia**, 2020 Massachusetts Avenue NW, Washington, DC 20036; (202) 775-5200; fax (202) 775-5365. Indonesian Consulates General are located in New York, Los Angeles, Houston, Chicago, and San Francisco.

Getting Around

Probably the most convenient means of getting around this vast archipelago is by **air**. Domestic flights are moderately priced, but be sure to book well in advance. Garuda Indonesia Airways offers a **Visit Indonesia Pass**. The basic pass, valid on Garuda Indonesia and Merpati Airlines, lets you visit three cities for $300. Up to 10 additional cities may be added for $100 each, though you may not depart from the same city twice. The pass is valid for up to 60 days and must be purchased in the U.S. For more information, contact Council Travel (see pages xiii–xvi) or Garuda Indonesia Airlines, (800) 342-7832.

A slower but more interesting way to get around the islands is by **boat**. The national shipping line, PELNI, operates large, air-conditioned passenger ships with regular sailings between all major seaports. Ferries also operate between Java and Sumatra, Java and Bali, and Bali and Lombok, as well as between Sumatra and Malaysia. Including cargo ships, the possibilities for sea transport are endless, though you should count on some delays and stay flexible.

A **rail** system connects the main cities of Java and there are three unconnected local rail lines on the island of Sumatra; however, in most other parts of this vast nation, rail transport is not possible. More common are **buses**, both express intercity coaches and local buses serving the countryside. You can also rent a **car** or hire one with a driver. You'll also find motorcycles for rent in a number of locations (an International Driver's Permit is required). **Note:** To reduce the number of traffic fatalities, the police have recently imposed very high fines for traffic violations. Drive carefully.

In the cities, transportation is provided by taxis, buses, and minibuses. In some cities you'll find *becaks*, bicycle rickshaws that can be hired by the hour or according to the distance traveled; you should settle on a price before you get in, however.

Eating and Sleeping

There are a number of **youth hostels** throughout Indonesia. For more information, contact Hostelling International/American Youth Hostels (see page 54) or the **Indonesian Youth Hostels Association**, Graha Permuda Lantai 8, Jalan Gerbang Permuda 3, Senayan, Jakarta 10270; (62) 21-588156; fax (62) 21-588313. It's also easy to find inexpensive boardinghouses or to rent rooms with families.

For Further Information

For general travel information, contact the **Indonesia Tourist Promotion Office**, 3457 Wilshire Boulevard, Los Angeles, CA 90010; (213) 387-2078.

At press time, the most recently published guide to Indonesia was *Indonesia: A Travel Survival Kit*, available for $23.95 from Lonely Planet Publications. Lonely Planet also publishes *Bali and Lombok: A Travel Survival Kit* ($13.95). Another excellent guide to the country is *Indonesia Handbook*, by Bill Dalton, available for $19.95 from Moon Publications. Moon also publishes Dalton's *Bali Handbook* ($12.95). Insight Guides make excellent pre-trip reading. Insight Guides publishes *Insight Guide: Indonesia, Insight Guide: Bali*, and *Insight Guide: Java* ($19.95 each). All three contain a wealth of information and beautiful photos to get you excited for your trip. More information on *Insight Guides*, Lonely Planet, and Moon Publications can be found on pages 56–57.

WORK

Foreigners need an employment visa to work in Indonesia which can be obtained at the Embassy of Indonesia or any U.S. consulate. It is necessary to secure a job before going to the country and applying for the visa. Upon approval from the Office of Immigration under the Ministry of Justice in Jakarta, a visa will be issued. Getting a permit for casual work is impossible; for long-term employment, the applicant must have a skill that is not available locally. For more information, contact the **Embassy of the Republic of Indonesia**, Consular Office, 2020 Massachusetts Avenue NW, Washington, DC 20036; (202) 775-5317.

Voluntary Service

Global Volunteers, 375 East Little Canada Road, St. Paul, MN 55117; (612) 482-1074, sponsors a three-week service program in Indonesia. Volunteers teach English, math, basic sciences, and computer literacy, as well as help with construction and landscaping.

In addition, **Goshen College** offers a study-service term in Indonesia that is primarily open to Goshen students; sometimes a limited number of spaces are available to students at other colleges and universities.

STUDY

Students who would like to enroll directly in a university in Indonesia should request a fact sheet from the Indonesian Embassy (see "Travel," above) entitled *Information for Foreign Nationals Who Want to Study at Indonesian Universities*.

The following educational programs are offered by CIEE-member institutions.

Unless otherwise noted, consult Appendix I for addresses of the colleges and universities listed in this section.

Semester and Academic Year

General Studies

World Learning/School for International Training. *College Semester Abroad*. Sumatra. Fall and spring semesters. Environmental studies. Orientation, intensive language study, homestay, field-study seminar, independent-study project, field trip. Sophomores to graduate students with 2.5 GPA. Apply by May 7 for fall; October 7 for spring. Contact: College Semester Abroad Admissions at (800) 336-1616.

College Semester Abroad. Bali, Ubud, Peliatan. Fall and spring semesters. Intensive language study, seminar on Indonesian and Balinese culture, field-study methods seminar, village homestay, and independent-study project. Sophomores to seniors with 2.5 GPA. Apply by May 7 for fall; October 7 for spring. Contact: College Semester Abroad Admissions at (800) 336-1616.

Indonesian Language and Culture

Beloit College. *Indonesian Exchange Program*. Salatiga (Central Java). Fall semester. Intensive Indonesian language and area studies courses; study at Satya Wacana University with Indonesian students. Juniors and seniors with 2.75 GPA. Apply by April 1.

Council on International Educational Exchange. *Cooperative Southeast Asian Studies Program at the Institut Keguruan Dan Ilmu Pendidikan (IKIP) Malang*. Java. Fall and spring semesters. Sophomores to seniors with 2.75 GPA and one Asian studies course. Apply by April 1 for fall; October 1 for spring. Contact University Programs Department.

Summer and Short-Term

General Studies

Lisle Fellowship. *Modernization in Paradise: Encounters of the Human Kind*. Bali. Balinese culture and education with special focus on interaction between tradition and modernization. Recent high-school graduates, college students, and adults. Apply by April 1.

EXPLORING INDONESIAN CULTURE

Readings

In *The Fugitive*, set in 1945, Pramoedya Ananta Toer portrays the revolution against Dutch colonial rule from an Indonesian point of view. T. B. Simatupang deals with this period in *Report from Banaran: The Story of the Experiences of a Soldier during the War of Independence*.

Twilight in Djakarta (1957), by Lubis Mochtar, is a disturbing novel about political corruption in post-independence Indonesia. Finished in jail, Mochtar's book paints a vivid portrait of the seamier side of daily life in the Indonesian capital. *The Outlaw and Other Stories* collects Mochtar's work spanning the period from the 1950s through the '70s.

Ismail Marahimin is another contemporary Indonesian author who has received international recognition. In *And the War Is Over* (1977), set at the end of the Second World War, Marahimin brilliantly portrays three cultures—each alien to the others—in an ironic story of Javanese and Dutch prisoners plotting an escape from their Japanese captors.

The Year of Living Dangerously (1978), by C. J. Koch, involves a foreign reporter involved in the political turmoil of the last years of Sukarno's dictatorship in the mid-1960s. The book was later made into a film.

Bali, A Paradise Created (1989), by Adrian Vickers, analyzes the way Bali has been promoted as paradise for tourists. A classic look at Balinese culture is *Island of Bali* (1932), by Miguel Covarrubias. More recently, Ana Daniel documents her experience of learning traditional Balinese dance and puts the art into a cultural context in *Bali: Behind the Mask* (1981).

MALAYSIA

Malaysia, with an estimated population of approximately 18 million, is a mélange of cultures and peoples: Malays make up 48 percent of the population, Chinese comprise 35 percent, Indians 10 percent, and various indigenous ethnic groups make up the rest. The tension between these groups as they vie for political and economic power in this relatively prosperous nation is a constant source of problems—and, at times, factional violence—but also creates a cultural vibrancy not found in more racially uniform countries.

Malaysia's large Chinese population arrived in large numbers in the late 19th century to work on the country's rubber plantations and in its tin mines, many fleeing from the war and famine in China. Today, the Chinese in Malaysia dominate the economy, a position obtained by hard work and perseverance. However, the Malays, who consider themselves to be the indigenous population of Malaysia, hold most of the political power.

Malaysia is divided into two regions. Peninsular Malaysia extends from the southern tip of Thailand to the island nation of Singapore; East, or Insular, Malaysia includes Sabah and Sarawak, the two states that share the tropical island of Borneo with the Indonesian state of Kalimantan. Malaysia's strategic location—smack in the heart of Southeast Asia and alongside the Straits of Molucca—has made it an attractive addition to any imperial power's portfolio. Over the years the country has been dominated by the Portuguese, the Dutch, and, most recently, the British, who granted independence to Malaya in 1957. In 1963, Malaya changed its name to Malaysia after the British colonies of Sabah and Sarawak agreed to join the republic. Today the country is booming economically, thanks to a lucrative combination of plentiful natural resources, a solid infrastructure, and a relatively well-educated labor force.

The state religion is Islam and everywhere there is evidence of a nationwide surge of Islamic consciousness. On the East Coast women wear black robes and remain veiled in purdah; laws have been passed that forbid conversion attempts to any religion except Islam; and punishments meted out by Islamic courts seem harsh by Western standards (such as the stoning to death of adulterers).

Peninsular Malaysia's East and West Coasts show the traveler two completely different sides of Asian culture. The East Coast has remained rather isolated against the tide of industrialization and remains a bastion of sleepy fishing villages, deserted beaches, and colorful markets filled with exotic fruits and batik sarongs. This is home for many easygoing Malays, who work as farmers or fishermen. The West Coast is populated primarily by Chinese and is more business-oriented as a whole. Filled with excitement and energy, the West Coast boasts historic sights and a vibrant nightlife. The island of Borneo offers yet another experience for the traveler: rain forests, incredible national parks, and perhaps a visit to a jungle-surrounded longhouse to peer at a collection of dusty skulls. Sarawak has recently come into international attention, as press coverage has focused on the struggle of the Penan tribespeople to save their ancestral homelands from indiscriminate logging, a policy that threatens to destroy Malaysia's rain forests forever.

—Edythe Antal, Baltimore, Maryland

Official name: Malaysia. **Area:** 127,316 square miles. **Population:** 17,981,000. **Population density:** 141 inhabitants per square mile. **Capital and largest city:** Kuala Lumpur (pop. 1,000,000). **Language:** Malay, Chinese, Tamil, English. **Religion:** Islam, Buddhism, Hinduism, Confucianism, Taoism. **Per capita income:** US$2,460. **Currency:** Ringgit. **Literacy rate:** 80%. **Average daily temperature:** Kuala Lumpur: June, 81°; December, 80°. **Average number of days with precipitation:** Kuala Lumpur: June, 13; December, 18.

TRAVEL

U.S. citizens need a passport but not a visa for stays of up to three months. For specific requirements, check with the **Embassy of Malaysia**, 2401 Massachusetts Avenue NW, Washington, DC 20008; (202) 328-2700. **Warning:** While in Malaysia, remember that the Malaysian government has strong laws against drugs. The penalties for trafficking and possession of illegal drugs—even of minuscule amounts—are severe and can include death.

Getting Around

In addition to roads, both ferry and air lines connect Malaysia to the countries of Indonesia, Singapore, and Thailand. Malaysia and Thailand are also connected by rail.

Malayan Railways or Keratapi Tanah Melayu (KTM) offers **train** service on two lines through Peninsular Malaysia. The west coast line runs from Singapore through Kuala Lumpur to Thailand. The second line branches off from the west coast at Gemas and travels northeast to Thailand. The six-hour trip from Singapore to Kuala Lumpur costs approximately US$30. Malayan Railways also offers the **Explorer Pass** for travel throughout Peninsular Malaysia and Singapore. The second-class pass for students and youth under 30 costs approximately $32 for 7 days, $43 for 14 days, and $54 for 21 days. The first-class pass costs approximately $55 for 10 days and $120 for 30 days.

The roads in Peninsular Malaysia are among the best in Southeast Asia. **Buses** run on all the main roads. This highway network, which provides access to the beautiful beaches and tropical rain forest of the peninsula's east coast, also makes the country good for those who wish to rent a car. **Shared taxis** are a great budget-travel option, costing about as much as an air-conditioned bus or second-class train. The roads are not as good in Malaysian Borneo and public transportation is often provided by trucks or four-wheel-drive vehicles.

The national **airline**, Malaysia Airlines, has good connections between Malaysian Borneo and Peninsular Malaysia. Malaysia Airlines also offers a **Discover Malaysia Pass**, which costs $138 for five flights within Peninsular Malaysia or Sabah or Sarawak (not the whole country). The Discover Malaysia Pass gives a 40-percent discount off flights outside of the main region. It's valid for 21 days and may be purchased in the U.S. or in Malaysia within 14 days of arrival in conjunction with an international flight on Malaysia Airlines. For more information, contact Council Travel or call Malaysia Airlines at (212) 697-8994.

Eating and Sleeping

Throughout Malaysia, **Chinese hotels** are the least expensive places to stay. However, you should be selective; many of the cheapest double as brothels. MSL Travel has a complete list of budget accommodations (see "Especially for Students and Young People," below).

There are several **youth hostels** on Peninsular Malaysia, including two in Kuala Lumpur. For more information, contact Hostelling International/American Youth Hostels (see page 54) or the **Malaysian Youth Hostels Association**, 21 Jalan Kampung Attap, 50460 Kuala Lumpur; (60) 3-2306870; fax (60) 3-2741115. For a list of independent hostels, contact **Backpackers Hostels** in Malaysia, Box 11417, 50744 Kuala Lumpur; (60) 3-2321428; fax (60) 3-2934792.

Especially for Students and Young People

Malaysia's student travel organization is **MSL Travel**, First Floor, Asia Hotel, 69 Jalan Haji Hussin, 50300 Kuala Lumpur; (60) 3-2989722; fax (60) 3-2933707. MSL also has offices on the island of Penang and in Petaling Jaya. You'll find that these offices provide a full range of services, including booking accommodations, and selling bus, rail, and plane tickets. MSL can also provide information on student discounts in Malaysia. You can also contact the branch office of Australia's **STA Travel**, Letter Box 32, 10 Jalan P Ramlee, 50250 Kuala Lumpur; (60) 3-2305720; fax (60) 3-2305718.

For Further Information

General tourist information is available from the **Malaysian Tourist Information Center**, 818 West Seventh Street, Los Angeles, CA 90017; (213) 689-9702.

The best guidebook for the budget traveler is *Malaysia, Singapore and Brunei: A Travel Survival Kit*, available for $14.95 from Lonely Planet Publications. *Insight Guide: Malaysia* makes great preparatory reading. Information on Lonely Planet and *Insight Guides* can be found on pages 56–57.

WORK

Foreigners are required to secure a work permit in order to work in Malaysia. Permits are issued by the **Director General of Immigration**, Department of

Immigration Malaysia, Block 1, Level 2-7, Jalan Damansutra, Damansara Town Center, Damansara Height, 50550 Kuala Lumpur, Malaysia. You'll need to find a Malaysian who agrees to assure your maintenance and repatriation. For more information, contact the Embassy of Malaysia (see "Travel," above).

Internships/Traineeships

A program offered by a member of the Council on International Educational Exchange is listed below. For further information, consult Appendix I for the appropriate addresses.

Association for International Practical Training. *Hospitality/Tourism Exchanges Program.* On-the-job training for young people beginning a career in the hotel, food service, and tourism industries. Participants must have graduated, or be currently enrolled in a university or vocational school, and possess at least six months of training or experience in the chosen field. Training usually runs from 6 to 18 months.

STUDY

Below is an educational program offered by a CIEE-member institution. Consult Appendix I for the contact address and phone number.

Semester and Academic Year

General Studies

Western Michigan University. *Malaysia: Study Abroad in Southeast Asia.* Kuala Lumpur. Semester or academic year, summer. Offered in conjunction with Sunway College. Business, communications, computer science, and pre-engineering/pre-science. Sophomores. Apply by June 15 for fall; October 15 for spring; February 15 for summer.

THE PHILIPPINES

About 500 miles off mainland Southeast Asia is an archipelago comprised of 7,100 islands and islets known as the Philippines. Because of the physical characteristics of Philippine geography, there are noticeable changes in dialect, language, and even styles of clothing as one moves through the different regions of the archipelago. Despite these differences, however, there has been a concerted effort to develop a national identity and move the country out from under the shadows of its Spanish- and American-influenced past.

The Spanish ruled the Philippines from 1521 to 1898; the islands are named after King Philip II of Spain. They were so successful in introducing Catholicism to the islands of the archipelago that the Philippines today is the only predominantly Roman Catholic country in Asia. (The Muslim south resisted Spanish attempts at Christianization and has maintained an Islamic identity.) Aside from religion, the Spanish introduced Western technology, Western economic and political institutions, and a public education system, all of which aided the spread of nationalism among the Filipinos.

When the archipelago was ceded to the United States in 1898, Filipinos were more than happy to be relieved of their Spanish masters and welcomed the professed commitment of the United States to Philippine independence. However, it took the U.S. government 48 years to make good on its promise. In the interim, the Philippines became acquainted with political democracy and equal economic opportunity. English became the medium of instruction, and remains the language of education, business, and government transactions. The Philippines became the first Southeast Asian country to have an elective legislative body, and when the Philippine constitution was drawn up in 1935, it closely resembled its American model.

Today, the country is recovering from a period of economic instability and political turmoil that reached its peak with the 1986 coup against Ferdinand Marcos. The Philippine government under Corazon Aquino, however, was not able to fulfill many of its promises of improvement; Aquino was succeeded by Fidel V. Ramos. The country is beset by a weak economy, widespread poverty, communist insurgents, and a powerful military. Nevertheless, Filipinos are filled with hope about their future.

It is the Filipino's basic nature not to dwell on the negative but rather to adapt to new situations. In the past years, there has been a proliferation of restaurants, boutiques, discos, and resorts all over the country. This is characteristic of the Filipino's innate desire to enjoy, to entertain, and to be entertained. It is not uncommon to find a Filipino, whether living in a modest nipa hut in the remote province of Vigan or in a grand home in the bustling city of Manila, celebrating the arrival of a guest. The numerous foreigners who come to the Philippines are always moved by the enthusiastic welcome they receive. The immense pride of the Filipinos in their culture and country compels them to receive guests with open arms, exclaiming "Mabuhay! (Welcome)"

—Moyen F. Lagdameo, Franklin Lakes, New Jersey

Official name: Republic of the Philippines. **Area:** 115,831 square miles (about the size of Arizona). **Population:** 65,758,000. **Population density:** 567 inhabitants per square mile. **Capital:** Quezon City. **Largest city:** Manila (pop. 1,800,000). **Language:** English, Tagalog (and its official form, Pilipino). **Religion:** Roman Catholic, Protestant, Islam. **Per capita income:** US$700. **Currency:** Philippine peso. **Literacy rate:** 88%. **Average daily temperature:** Manila: June, 83°; December, 78°. **Average number of days with precipitation: Manila:** June, 17; December, 11.

TRAVEL

U.S. citizens need a passport but not a visa for stays of up to 21 days. Onward or return tickets are required for entry through international airports in Manila and Cebu. For further information, check the **Embassy of the Philippines**, 1671 Massachusetts Avenue NW, Washington, DC 20036; (202) 483-1533. The Philippines also has consulates general in Chicago, Houston, Honolulu, Los Angeles, New York, San Francisco, and Seattle.

Getting Around

The most common form of land transportation is the **bus**, with dozens of companies providing low-cost service. Rail service is virtually nonexistent except on Luzon, the largest island in the Philippines, where there is one line. An expensive alternative is to rent a **car** in Manila, Cebu City, or Davao City. In cities throughout the Philippines, however, cars with drivers can be hired at rates that may be cheaper than renting a car. The **jeepney** (usually a U.S. Army-surplus vehicle with added benches) is another popular form of transportation, crowded but cheap.

Within Manila, the elevated Light Rail Transit (LRT) train makes 15 stops from north to south of the metropolitan area. The other local railway is the Metro Tren. The Metroferry transports commuters along the Pasig River.

There are several options for getting around the islands. Philippine Airlines provides good domestic service to 45 points outside of Manila. There are also many smaller **airlines**. Regularly scheduled ferries provide convenient transportation among the main islands.

Eating and Sleeping

There are a number of **youth hostels** throughout the Philippines. For more information, contact Hostelling International/American Youth Hostels (see page 54) or **Youth and Student Hostel Foundation of the Philippines** (YSHFP), 4227 Tomas Claudio Street, 1700 Parañaque, Metro Manila; (63) 4-832-0680; fax (63) 4-818-7948.

Especially for Students and Young People

The Philippines' student travel agency is **YSTAPHIL**, which is also the secretariat of YSHFP. The organization provides information and a range of student/youth travel services, including a number of organized tours. The organization also provides a list of travel services, shops, restaurants, bars, and clubs that offer discounts to holders of the International Student Identity Card and International Youth Card.

For Further Information

General travel information is available from the **Philippine Center**, 556 Fifth Avenue, New York, NY 10036; (212) 575-7915; fax (212) 302-6759. The Philippine Center's west coast office is at 3460 Wilshire Boulevard, Suite 216, Los Angeles, CA 90010; (213) 487-4527; fax (213) 386-4063.

One of the better guides for the budget traveler is *Philippines: A Travel Survival Kit*, available for $14.95 from Lonely Planet Publications. Also good is Moon Publications' *Philippines Handbook* ($12.95). *Insight Guide: Philippines* is an excellent book to read in preparation for your trip. Information on *Insight Guide*s, Lonely Planet, and Moon Publications can be found on pages 56–57.

WORK

Foreigners are required to have a work permit for regular employment in the Philippines. Application is made by the employer after a job has been offered. Generally speaking, work permits are only granted when the foreigner has a needed skill that is not available locally. For more information, contact the

Consulate of the Philippines, Visa Section, 556 Fifth Avenue, New York, NY 10036; (212) 764-1330.

Internships/Traineeships

A program offered by a member of the Council on International Educational Exchange is listed below. For further information, consult Appendix I for the appropriate addresses.

Association for International Practical Training. *IAESTE Trainee Program.* On-the-job training for undergraduate and graduate students in technical fields such as engineering, computer science, agriculture, architecture, mathematics, and the natural and physical sciences. See page 19 for more information.

Voluntary Service

The **Partnership for Service Learning** sponsors a study/service program in the Philippines which includes study at an accredited college in the host country and service work in the local community. Generally participants are involved in human-services work, teaching, health care, recreation, and community development. For more information see page 25.

STUDY

A program offered by a CIEE-member institution is listed below. Consult Appendix I for the address of this institution.

Semester and Academic Year

General Studies

International Student Exchange Program (ISEP). Semester and academic year. Direct reciprocal exchange between U.S. universities and institutions in Manila, Iloio City, Miag-gao, and Quezon City. Full curriculum options. Rolling admissions. Open only to students at ISEP-member institutions. Contact ISEP for list of members.

SINGAPORE

Singapore is a geographic afterthought edging the Malay Peninsula, rich in strategic position and trading history. Its very name evokes a sense of the East of Conrad and Kipling and Sydney Greenstreet—you will find ample atmospheric touches such as rickshaws, Hindu temples, colonial buildings, and banyan trees. This city-state is a cultural carnival, with a panoply of religious and ethnic influences permeating everything from cuisine to architecture.

The visitor will delight in the clean, fast, prompt, reliable public transportation; in the courtesy and diversity of the population; in shopping malls that surpass those of the U.S. in comfort, convenience, and variety. Of course, it's not all modernized—historic districts capture the Malay, Chinese, and colonial pasts; the Zoo is the centerpiece of a natural preserve that is rain forest in the raw; and the famous Raffles Hotel has been restored to its prewar elegance. Take a tour into adjoining Malaysia or ride the aerial tram to the museums and parks of Sentosa Island, or visit the sites that testify to the city's two millennia as a crossroads of commerce and cultures.

But even more compelling than Singapore's past or its attractions are its present and future. Singapore is involved in constructing a "strategically planned" society that seeks to blend the "good life" for the individual with social controls that are reminiscent of the norms of a small American Midwestern town.

Singapore is diverse, fascinating, prosperous, safe—and a bit dull by the standards of cities such as Berkeley, Los Angeles, or New York. You can't buy *Playboy* or *Cosmopolitan*, but you can feel secure when you stroll about the city. You can't chew gum in the subway, but you can walk or sit without worrying that someone else's discarded gum will cling to you. Singapore is largely smoke-free, litter-free, and crime-free; strict penalties exist for antisocial behavior, from drug use to sexual harassment to urinating in stairwells, and high-tech surveillance devices help ensure that they are carried out. But the prime "enforcement" measure is the public itself, and values which stress civility, propriety, and mutual responsibility.

Singapore represents a national attempt to develop what we would call a "collective vision" of the best of all possible futures, to become "a tropical city of excellence." In doing so, it is challenging the Western paradigm of how to achieve such a world. Rather than relying on individual civil liberties and the free market as most modern societies have done, Singapore asks, "How can we balance freedom, safety, social responsibility, and planning to produce the highest quality of life for all citizens?" Think of your visit to Singapore as a visit to this new paradigm for the future.

—Derek M. Mills, Westminster, Colorado

Official name: Republic of Singapore. **Area:** 224 square miles (smaller than New York City). **Population:** 2,756,000. **Population density:** 12,303 inhabitants per square mile. **Capital and largest city:** Singapore (pop. 2,703,000). **Language:** Malay, Chinese (Mandarin), Tamil, English (all official). **Religion:** Buddhism, Christianity, Islam, Taoism. **Per capita income:** US$12,700. **Currency:** Singapore dollar. **Literacy rate:** 87%. **Average daily temperature:** June, 82°; December, 79°. **Average number of days with precipitation:** June, 13; December, 19.

TRAVEL

U.S. citizens need a passport but not a visa for stays of up to 14 days. Applications for extension of stay may be submitted for consideration to the Singapore Immigration Department. You'll also need a return or onward ticket. For further information, check with the **Embassy of Singapore**, 1824 R Street NW, Washington, DC 20009-1691; (202) 667-7555; fax (202) 265-7915.

Getting Around

There are a number of ways to get around this small, mostly urban island-nation. For those who want to travel north, a causeway connects the island with the Malaysian mainland, and there is both **bus** and **train** service from Singapore to Kuala Lumpur. Malayan Railways' **Explorer Pass** is good for train travel throughout Peninsular Malaysia and Singapore. The second-class pass for students and youth under 30 costs approximately $32 for seven days, $43 for 14 days, and $54 for 21 days. The first-class pass costs approximately $55 for 10 days and $120 for 30 days.

Singapore's Mass Rapid Transit (MRT) train system has two main lines: the north-south line runs from Yishun to Marina Bay and the east-west line connects Pasir Ris near the airport to Boon Lay. The two main bus lines, Singapore Bus Service (SBS) and Trans Island Bus Service (TIBS), travel to all parts of the city and environs. **Explorer** tickets allow you unlimited access to either line for one or three days. Perhaps the best option is the **TransitLink Farecard**, a stored-value pass good for travel on SBS, TIBS, and the MRT.

Most road signs are in English and you'll be able to rent a **car** without any problem (an International Driving Permit is required); driving is on the left-hand side of the road. Taxis in Singapore are metered, honest, and decently priced. Trishaws (pedicabs) can also be rented. Travelers with disabilities will want to pick up a copy of *Access Singapore*, a guide to facilities for the disabled published by the Singapore Council of Social Services, 11 Penang Lane, Singapore 1024.

Eating and Sleeping

Singapore is a food-lover's paradise. The predominant cuisines are Chinese, Indian, and Malaysian, and you'll find you can eat well and cheaply. Accommodations in Singapore, however, are generally more expensive than in any other city in Southeast Asia. There are no official youth hostels, but there are several **Ys** in Singapore where relatively inexpensive accommodations can be found. The cheapest lodgings are **guest houses**, which are usually apartments with as many beds crammed into them as possible. Some include breakfast.

In addition, the University of Singapore offers affordable **dormitory lodgings** to travelers. For more information, contact one of Singapore's student travel organizations (see "Especially for Students and Young People," below).

Especially for Students and Young People

CIEE/Council Travel's newest international office is **CIEE Travel**, 110-D Killiney Road, Tai Wah Building, Singapore 0932; (65) 738-7066; fax (65) 733-7421. CIEE Travel offers discount airfares and can arrange sightseeing tours, as well as direct you to budget accommodations.

Australia's **STA Travel** has six Singapore branches in addition to its main office at 1 Tanglin Road, 02-17 Orchard Parade Hotel, Singapore 1024; (65) 734-5681; fax (65) 737-2591. It can also arrange budget airfares and accommodations.

For Further Information

General information on tourism can be obtained from the **Singapore Tourist Promotion Board (STPB)**, 590 Fifth Avenue, 12th Floor, New York, NY 10036; (212) 302-4861. The STPB also has offices in Chicago and Los Angeles.

The best guidebook for the budget traveler is *Malaysia, Singapore and Brunei: A Travel Survival Kit*, available for $14.95 from Lonely Planet Publications. *Insight Guide: Singapore* makes great preparatory reading while *Insight Pocket Guide: Singapore* is a concise but comprehensive itinerary planner.

Information on both Lonely Planet and *Insight Guides* can be found on pages 56–57.

WORK

To work in Singapore, it is necessary to get a work permit which is obtained by the employer, who must prove that the skills necessary for the position are not available among the country's work force. Due to economic expansion in Singapore, the country is facing a labor shortage of qualified personnel, thus opening up employment opportunities for foreigners. For more information contact the Embassy of the Republic of Singapore (see "Travel," above).

Internships/Traineeships

A program sponsored by a CIEE-member institution is listed below.

Syracuse University. *International Business Interships in Singapore*. See "Study."

STUDY

Programs offered by CIEE-member institutions are listed below. Unless otherwise noted, consult Appendix I for the addresses where you can write for more information.

Summer and Short-Term

Business

Adventist Colleges Abroad. Singapore. Quarter program in conversational Chinese (Mandarin), Asian culture, and international finance. Excursions to Malaysia, Indonesia, and Thailand. Sophomores, juniors, and seniors with 2.5 GPA. Only open to students of Adventist Colleges Abroad consortium institutions. Apply by March 25.

Syracuse University. *International Business Internships in Singapore*. Seven-week program includes six-week internship with American companies based in Singapore. Juniors to graduate students. Apply by February 15.

THAILAND

In the streets of Bangkok, Thailand's capital and center of business and politics, visitors can observe the many images of modern Thailand. Buddhist monks in saffron robes walk in single-file during the early morning hours collecting food and alms. Students sporting identical uniforms and haircuts crowd the buses on their way to school. Motorcycles, trucks, and the ubiquitous *tuk-tuks* roar through the overcrowded streets that have made Bangkok traffic legendary for its slowness. Well-heeled professionals carrying attachés and cellular phones scramble to strike deals in one of the world's fastest growing economies. Young men and women from rural areas come and go, attracted to the promise of better economic opportunities and repelled by the high cost and impersonal lifestyles found in Bangkok.

Social scientists routinely contrast the struggle between "tradition" and "change," and this is clearly seen in contemporary Thailand. Despite its designation as a "NIC" or Newly Industrialized Country, Thailand is still predominately an agricultural society with traditional village values and structures. In the political sphere, the 1992 pro-democracy protests that led to the downfall of the military-backed government is being called a watershed event in the development of a more representative political system.

Roughly the size of France, Thailand is divided into four major regions. The city of Chiang Mai in the north attracts visitors for its cooler climate and fascinating hill tribe cultures. The Northeast, or "Issan," is the largest region and reflects Khmer and Lao influences. Central Thailand is the richest agricultural area and the area from which the major Thai dynasties were founded. Southern Thailand is famous for its tropical beaches and islands as well as a strong independent streak that has produced communist and Muslim national movements.

Visitors to Thailand should be especially respectful of the twin pillars of Thai society: Buddhism and the royal family. Buddhist temples can be found in every city and village, and appropriate dress should be worn when visiting; women should also be careful to avoid any accidental contact with monks. The exportation of Buddhist images or antiques is also restricted. Thais show great reverence for the members of the royal family. King Bhumibol Adulyadej, the ninth king in the current Chakri dynasty and the world's longest reigning monarch, has worked diligently to promote rural development, the preservation of local arts and handicrafts, and other worthy causes. King Bhumibol's stature is such that during times of national crisis, his calls for peace and restraint are heeded by all sides.

—Andrew Shaw, New York, New York

Official name: Kingdom of Thailand. **Area:** 198,456 square miles (about twice the size of Wyoming). **Population:** 56,814,000. **Population density:** 286 inhabitants per square mile. **Capital and largest city:** Bangkok (pop. 6,000,000). **Language:** Thai, Chinese, Malay. **Religion:** Buddhist. **Per capita income:** US$1,170. **Currency:** Baht. **Literacy rate:** 89%. **Average daily temperature:** Bangkok: June, 84°; December, 78°. **Average number of days with precipitation:** Bangkok: June, 10; December, 1.

TRAVEL

U.S. citizens need a passport to enter Thailand; however, a visa is not required for visitors staying 15 days or less, and possessing an onward/return ticket, and entering through airports at Bangkok, Chiang Mai, or Phuket. Tourist visas good for stays of up to 60 days are available for $15. For further information, check with the **Royal Thai Embassy**, 2300 Kalorama Road NW, Washington, DC 20008; (202) 234-5052.

Getting Around

An efficient **rail** system connects all major points in the north and northeast with Bangkok. A southern line leads to Malaysia and Singapore. State Railways of Thailand offers an **Explorer Pass** to students and youths under 30. The Explorer Pass allows 7 days of unlimited rail travel for approximately US$32, 14 days for approximately US$40, or 21 days for approximately US$48.

Bus service is crowded but inexpensive and available throughout the country. Buses are fairly comfortable; air conditioning is available and some buses even show video movies. Thailand is a good country for renting a **car**; traffic is manageable outside of Bangkok, where traffic jams are the rule. Highways are in good condition, and most directional signs are also in English. Avis and Hertz are represented, but you might get a better deal with local companies. You can also rent motorcycles and scooters. An International Driving Permit is required.

An enjoyable alternative to land transport is passenger **boat** service from Bangkok north along the Chao Phya River to Ban Pan and Ayutthaya, the ancient capital of the Kingdom of Siam. Thai Airways provides frequent **air** service from Bangkok to the other major cities as well as to the island of Phuket. Thai Airways's **Discover Thailand's Natural Heritage Pass** allows four domestic flights for $239. Additional flights may be added on for $50 each. Valid for 90 days, the pass must be purchased in the U.S. in conjunction with an air ticket to Thailand. For more information, consult Council Travel (see pages xiii–xvii).

Council Travel offers a variety of tour options in Thailand, including trekking in the mountains of the north and visits to important historical, archaeological, and scenic sites. Some tour itineraries also include Burma and other parts of Southeast Asia. Contact a Council Travel office for more information.

Eating and Sleeping

There are several **youth hostels** in Thailand, including four in Bangkok and two in Chiang Mai. For more information, contact Hostelling International/American Youth Hostels (see page 54) or the **Thai Youth Hostels Association**, 25/2 Phitsanilok Road, Sisao Theves, Dusit, Bangkok 10300; (66) 2-282-0950; fax (66) 2-281-6834. For less money than you'd pay for a hotel room, you can find a nice room in a **guest house**. Ask at tourist information centers in Bangkok. It's also possible to find lodgings in a number of **Buddhist monasteries**, or *wats*; however, you will be expected to participate in the religious life of the community to varying extents, depending upon the institution. For information on **YMCA** accommodations, contact The Y's Way (see pages 53–54).

Especially for Students and Young People

Thailand's student travel organization is the **Educational Travel Centre (ETC)**, Room 318, Royal Hotel, 2 Rajdamnoen Avenue, Bangkok 10200 (66) 2-2240043; fax (66) 2-2246930. Their office provides travel information, books accommodations, and sells plane, bus, and train tickets. Australia's **STA Travel** also has three offices in Bangkok; the main office is STA Travel, Wall Street Tower Building, 14th Floor, Room 1405, 33 Surawong Road, Bangrak, Bangkok 10500; (66) 2-2332582; fax (66) 2-2801388.

For Further Information

For general tourist information, contact the **Tourism Authority of Thailand**, Five World Trade Center, Suite 3443, New York, NY 10048; (212) 432-0433;

fax (212) 912-0920. The Tourism Authority of Thailand also has offices in Chicago and Los Angeles.

There is no shortage of guides to Thailand. The all-time favorite guidebook for budget travelers is Joe Cummings' *Thailand: A Travel Survival Kit*, now in its fifth edition. It's available for $13.95 from Lonely Planet Publications. Also good is Carl Parkes's *Thailand Handbook*, a new guide available for $16.95 from Moon Handbooks. Other competitors include *Cadogan Guides' Thailand* ($14.95) and *The Real Guide: Thailand* ($17). An excellent book to read in preparation for your trip is *Insight Guide: Thailand*. Publisher information for all these books can be found on pages 56–57.

An interesting book for anyone expecting extensive interaction with the people and culture of Thailand is *A Common Core: Thais and North Americans*, by John Paul Fieg, available for $11.95 from Intercultural Press (see page 3).

WORK

In order to work in Thailand, a nonimmigrant visa (rather than a tourist visa) is necessary. Then, to get a work permit, you will need to apply at the **Department of Labor** (Phanon Fuang Nakhon, Bangkok 10200, Thailand) and have an employment contract in which your prospective employer specifically states the terms and length of employment. Foreigners seeking casual employment should not expect to be able to find work or obtain the necessary work permit.

Internships/Traineeships

Programs offered by a member of the Council on International Educational Exchange are listed below.

Association for International Practical Training. *IAESTE Trainee Program*. On-the-job training for undergraduate and graduate students in technical fields such as engineering, computer science, agriculture, architecture, mathematics, the physical and natural sciences. See page 19 for more information.

Hospitality/Tourism Exchanges Program. On-the-job training for young people beginning a career in the hotel, food service, and tourism industries. Participants must have graduated from, or be enrolled in, a university or vocational school and possess at least six months of training or experience in the chosen field. Training usually runs from 6 to 12 months. Consult Appendix I for the appropriate address.

Voluntary Service

AFS Intercultural Programs sponsors a Global-Service Program that enables adults to do community-service work in Thailand. Service projects are arranged individually according to the participant's interests or expertise. The program runs from three to seven weeks and is open to all interested persons at least 19 years of age. For more information, contact AFS Intercultural Programs, 220 East 42nd Street, 3rd Floor, New York, NY 10017; (800) 237-4636.

In addition, **WorldTeach** sponsors a volunteer teaching program in Thailand; for more information, see page 27.

STUDY

The following programs are offered by CIEE-member institutions. Unless otherwise noted, consult Appendix I for the addresses of the colleges and universities listed in this section.

Semester and Academic Year

General Studies

International Student Exchange Program (ISEP). Bangkok. Semester and academic year. Direct reciprocal exchange between U.S. universities and Thammasat University. Full curriculum options. Rolling admissions. Open only to students at ISEP-member institutions. Contact ISEP for list of members.

University of Wisconsin at Madison. *College Year in Thailand*. Chiang Mai. Individualized program of independent study and fieldwork. Intensive language study. Participants complete summer course in Thai language and culture at Madison prior to departure. Juniors and seniors in good academic standing. Apply by second Friday in February.

World Learning/School for International Training. *College Semester Abroad*. Chiang Mai, Bangkok, and Sukhothai. Fall and spring semesters. Intensive language, seminar in Thai life and culture, field-study methods seminar, and independent-study project. Excursions to homestays. Sophomores to seniors with 2.5 GPA. Apply by May 7 for fall; October 7 for spring. Contact: College Semester Abroad Admissions at (800) 336-1616.

Thai Language and Culture

Council on International Educational Exchange. *Cooperative Southeast Asian Studies Program at Khon Kaen University*. Fall semester. Sophomores to seniors with 2.75 GPA and one Asian studies course. Apply by April 15. Contact: University Programs Department.

Summer and Short-Term

General Studies

International Student Exchange Program (ISEP). Bangkok. Summer. Direct reciprocal exchange between U.S. universities and Thammasat University. Full curriculum options. Rolling admissions. Open only to students at ISEP-member institutions. Contact ISEP for list of members.

State University of New York College at Oneonta. *Thailand Program*. Bangkok and other sites. Summer. Asian studies at Suan-Dusit Teacher's College. Sophomores to seniors. Rolling admissions. Contact: International Education Office, Netzer Building 332C, SUNY College at Oneonta, Oneonta, NY 13820-4015; (607) 436-3369.

Whitworth College. *Payap University Exchange Program*. Chiang Mai. Offered in conjunction with Payap University. Computer science, international marketing, theology, music, and Thai language and culture. Juniors and seniors with 2.5 GPA. Apply by February 1 for fall and academic year; October 1 for spring.

EXPLORING THAI CULTURE

Readings

Thailand is unique in the region for never having been under colonial rule, and its society and culture make for an interesting comparative study alongside the rest of Southeast Asia. For an excellent account of turn-of-the-century Thai society in contrast with China, read *Letters from Thailand*. Translated by Susan Fulop Morrell, these letters from Bangkok were written by a Chinese visitor to his family.

An important writer as well as a leading personality in contemporary Thailand, Kukrit Pramoj has been a movie actor, journalist, and Prime Minister. His historical novel *Si Phaendin* (''Four Reigns'') follows the life of a woman as she comes of age in the Royal Thai court during the turn of the century. This book covers the crucial period of 1892–1946, when ''Siam'' evolved into the modern state of Thailand.

Pira Sudham is one of the most important chroniclers of rural Thai society. *Monsoon Country* (1987)—written in English while the author was living in England—is a semi-autobiographical account of a poor farmer boy who by the strength of his intellect gains an education in Bangkok and London. *People of Easarn* (1988) describes life in Thailand's poorest region.

A new release, *Behind the Painting and Other Stories*, introduces English readers to Siburapha (Kulap Saipradit). Siburapha began as a writer of popular romances but took a political turn after World War II. Imprisoned from 1952 to 1957, he later found asylum in China. *Behind the Painting and Other Stories* contains one love story and three political tales.

VIETNAM

For Americans, at least, Vietnam is a name freighted with near mythic significance. Now increasingly accessible, travel to Vietnam is perhaps the best way to begin to dispel wartime images and appreciate the country and culture within a broader historical context. More important, visiting Vietnam enables the traveler to view the Vietnamese people on their own terms, instead of through the distorting lenses of the various foreign powers against whom they have struggled.

By any economic measure, Vietnam is currently among the world's poorest nations, having been ravaged by decades of war, socialist experimentation, and isolation from international commerce. The average citizen's annual per capita income hovers around US$200, and severe shortages in the country's basic infrastructure are readily apparent. The collapse of its communist benefactors in Central and Eastern Europe and the former Soviet Union has added to Vietnam's hardships, as has the ongoing U.S. trade embargo. Nevertheless, enormous strides have been taken with market reforms introduced by the socialist government in the last couple of years, and given the nation's large petroleum and mineral resources as well as the dynamism of its educated workforce, there is reason to be hopeful about the future, especially as relations with the U.S. improve. With signs that the 19-year-old American embargo may soon end, a host of U.S. companies are seeking to establish footholds in Vietnam.

Against the images of poverty and a war-scarred land that Americans remember, Vietnam's physical beauty is unexpectedly alluring. Lush tropical scenery abounds; the terrain is washed by rivers that flow down from verdant inland mountains through dense jungle forests to the pristine coastlines of the South China Sea.

The Vietnamese people tend to be warm and friendly, eager to renew contacts with the Western world. Despite successive periods of domination by foreign powers—China, France, the U.S.—the Vietnamese are a proud people, with rich artistic, literary, and religious traditions that remain strong today.

Evidence of former north-south divisions linger on in the stark contrast between Hanoi and Ho Chi Minh City. Every inch the stately capital, Hanoi is a city of elegant tree-lined avenues, lakes, and parks. Soviet-inspired edifices dot the city (Workers' Cultural Palace, Ho Chi Minh's Mausoleum). Vestiges of nearly 100 years of colonial rule, graceful French-style villas now in dusty disrepair, line the boulevards of the central city. One of Hanoi's most striking sights is an imposing replica of the Paris Opera House, which sits at the end of a narrow downtown street.

By contrast, Ho Chi Minh City is a bustling commercial hub, which plays the role of New York City to Hanoi's Washington, DC. Ho Chi Minh City functions at both a geographical and an ideological distance from the capital city, experimenting more openly with free-market principles and foreign cultural influences. One of the best ways to see this busy metropolis is to venture out into the crowded streets on the back of a motorscooter or in a hired pedicab.

Exploring Vietnam invokes a barrage of intense sensory impressions. Despite the scarcity of automobiles in the cities, you will be struck by the din and the dust raised by the continuous traffic of passing motorscooters and bicycles, with the occasional ox-drawn cart or diesel exhaust–spouting truck or bus. Given the tropical climate, much of life is lived out of doors, and sidewalks are lined with vendors selling everything from quick meals to haircuts, French *baguettes* to farm produce, dental work to bicycle repairs. Western visitors attract considerable curiosity and attention from local citizens, whose recent international contacts were largely limited to former Eastern-bloc tourists.

Vietnam is poised to enter a period of rapid social and economic change, during which it could emerge once again as a significant force within Southeast Asia. Visitors today are in a unique position—able to appreciate Vietnam's recent past, and to catch a glimpse of its future.

—Margaret Shiba, New York, New York

Official name: Socialist Republic of Vietnam. **Area:** 127,330 square miles (the size of New Mexico). **Population:** 67,568,000. **Population density:** 530 inhabitants per square mile. **Capital:** Hanoi (pop. 3,100,000). **Largest city:** Ho Chi Minh City (pop. 3,900,000). **Language:** Vietnamese (official), Chinese. **Religion:** Buddhism, Confucianism, Taoism. **Per capita income:** US$230. **Currency:** Dong. **Literacy rate:** 88%. **Average daily temperature:** Ho Chi Minh City: June, 81°; December, 78°. **Average number of days with precipitation:** Ho Chi Minh City: June, 21; December 7.

TRAVEL

Since Vietnam has no official diplomatic representative in the U.S., visas must be issued outside the country. Most travelers obtain tourist visas from the

Vietnamese Embassy in Bangkok, Thailand. However, you can also obtain a visa from the **Vietnamese Mission to the United Nations**, which sends applications to be processed in Canada. Contact the mission at 20 Waterside Plaza, New York, NY 10010; (212) 679-3779.

Still, it may be easier and less expensive to arrange a visa and onward ticket to Vietnam through one of Bangkok's many travel agents. One of the largest agencies is **Diethelm Travel**, Kian Gwan Building II, 140/1 Wireless Road, Bangkok 10330; (66) 2-255-9150; fax (66) 2-256-0248. Diethelm Travel also has offices in Phnom Penh, Cambodia, and Vientiane, Laos. At press time a new office in Ho Chi Minh City was in the planning stages.

The U.S. government continues to keep its some restrictions in place, limiting the amount of money U.S. citizens can spend in Vietnam ($200 per day, not including transportation), a well as the value of articles they can bring back into the U.S. (up to $100). The use of credit cards is prohibited. In addition, direct flights between the U.S. and Vietnam are not allowed. While these restrictions shouldn't deter budget travelers, for current regulations, contact the **Licensing Section**, Office of Foreign Assets Control, Department of the Treasury, Washington, DC 20220.

Getting Around

Air Vietnam makes daily flights between Ho Chi Minh City and Hanoi. It's possible to make stopovers in several cities along the way. Tickets must be bought with American dollars, but the flights are reasonably priced. However, tickets are hard to reserve or purchase outside of Vietnam.

The national **rail** line winds up along the coast from Ho Chi Minh City to Hanoi and points north. Trains come in two classes, hard-seat and hard-sleeper, and are very slow, taking two days to travel the 1,000 miles from Hanoi to Ho Chi Minh City. Reservations can only be made for trains originating from the city you're in. Tickets must be paid for in U.S. dollars and prices are artificially inflated above what locals have to pay, making long trips almost as expensive as flying. However, you may be able to insist on paying in Vietnamese dong, in which case you will still pay more than the locals, but less than you would in dollars.

Buses go everywhere. Most cities have several stations which serve as points of departure to different parts of the country; make sure you're in the right terminal. Most Vietnamese buses are very old and suffer frequent breakdowns, though some express buses, which make few stops, run smoothly. Most buses, however, are faster than trains, though somewhat less comfortable.

Vietnam's highway system is generally good. **Cars** with drivers can be rented from government and private concerns, but you can't drive yourself without a Vietnamese license. In the cities, pedicabs are an inexpensive way to get around. Probably the best way to get around between cities and villages is by **bicycle**, as many Vietnamese do themselves. The terrain is flat and you can stow your bike on both trains and buses. And while it's difficult to rent one, you can buy a cheap bike or bring your own. Hitchers generally have no problem finding rides, but, as always, should exercise caution.

Another option for seeing the country is on the numerous passenger **boats** and ferries that operate out of the Red River and Mekong River deltas.

For Further Information

One of the best guidebooks to Vietnam is Lonely Planet's *Vietnam, Cambodia, and Laos: A Travel Survival Kit*. Newly updated in 1993, this carefully researched book is full of detailed advice for the budget traveler to this seldom-visited country. It's available for $15.95 from Lonely Planet Publications. *Insight Guide: Vietnam* will get you excited to start your trip. You can find information on Lonely Planet and *Insight Guides* on pages 56–57.

WORK

Voluntary Service

Volunteers in Asia sponsors a volunteer teaching program in Vietnam for graduates with a B.A. degree and teaching experience. Volunteers serve for two years. Preference is given to students from the San Francisco Bay area, as four months of training there is required before departure. For more information, contact Volunteers in Asia Vietnam Program, PO Box 4543, Stanford, CA 94309; (415) 723-3228.

STUDY

The following educational programs are offered by CIEE-member institutions. Unless otherwise noted, consult Appendix I for the addresses of the institutions listed below.

Semester and Academic Year

General Studies

World Learning/School for International Training. *College Semester Abroad.* Hanoi, Hue, Da Nang, Nha Trang, and Ho Chi Minh City. Fall and spring semesters. Intensive language, seminar on Vietnamese life and culture, field-study methods seminar, homestays, independent-study project, and excursions. Sophomores to seniors with 2.5 GPA. Apply by May 7 for fall; October 7 for spring. Contact: College Semester Abroad Admissions at (800) 336-1616. *College Semester Abroad.* Ho Chi Minh City, Nha Trang, Da Nang, Hue, and Hanoi. Fall and spring semesters. Intensive language seminar on Vietnamese life and culture, field-study methods seminar, homestays, independent-study project, and excursions. Sophomores to seniors with 2.5 GPA. Apply by May 7 for fall; October 7 for spring. Contact: College Semester Abroad Admissions at (800) 336-1616.

Vietnamese Language and Culture

Council on International Educational Exchange. *Cooperative Southeast Asian Studies Program at the University of Hanoi.* Fall and spring semesters. Vietnamese language, history, and society. Sophomores to seniors with 2.75 GPA and one Asian studies course. Apply by April 15 for fall; October 15 for spring. Contact: University Programs Department.

CHAPTER TWELVE

AUSTRALIA AND THE SOUTH PACIFIC

Scattered across the vast South Pacific is an array of small islands that can be loosely grouped into Polynesia, which stretches from New Zealand to Hawaii, and Melanesia, which extends from Fiji to New Guinea. Most Americans know little about these islands, thinking only of white beaches, turquoise lagoons, and lush palm forests. These images are not unfounded, but the region also has a varied cultural and political life well worth exploring. Formerly colonies of Britain or France, a number of independent nations—with, to many, unfamiliar names like Kiribati, Vanuatu, Tuvalu—have emerged in the South Pacific in the last two decades.

Australia, on the other hand, occupies a larger portion of the American psyche. A number of popular films, ranging from *Gallipoli* to *Crocodile Dundee* to *Strictly Ballroom*, have provided a fresh perspective on this rugged, vast land and the uniquely wry character of its people. As airfares to the region decrease, Australia and its surrounding islands are seeing a sharp rise in visitors from the U.S.—succumbing, perhaps, to promises of "another shrimp on the barbie." Many see Australia and its kiwi-growing neighbor, New Zealand, as one of the few remaining frontiers. Both Australia and New Zealand are virtual havens for nature enthusiasts, with unparalleled opportunities for all types of outdoor activities including bushwalking, scuba diving, mountain climbing, and surfing. This is not to mention the unique collection of indigenous flora and fauna—the kangaroo, the platypus, the Tasmanian Devil, and the kookaburra are only part of the exotic menagerie. There are also clean, modern cities, such as Auckland, Sydney, and Melbourne, that provide the artistic and cultural enticements associated with metropolises—museums, nightclubs, opera, and a great pub music scene.

Romantic images of the South Pacific, such as the paintings of Gauguin, persist. Indeed, many of the less inhabited islands may seem to be paradise on earth. Equally enticing are images of Australia's Outback as one of the planet's last great open areas where humans have not yet had much impact on nature. Part of the interest in this portion of the world is that it is one of the last to be industrially developed. In the South Pacific islands, and even in the modern nations of Australia and New Zealand, the feeling of an unspoiled vastness remains.

Getting There

APEX and promotional fares are offered by most carriers flying between the U.S. and Australia. Some fares even include stopovers in Honolulu, Tahiti, Fiji, or other South Pacific islands. Sample *one-way* fares from the U.S. to the South Pacific region in effect during the summer of 1993 are listed below. For more up-to-date information, contact any Council Travel office (see pages xiii–xvi).

San Francisco–Sydney	$824
Los Angeles–Auckland	$730

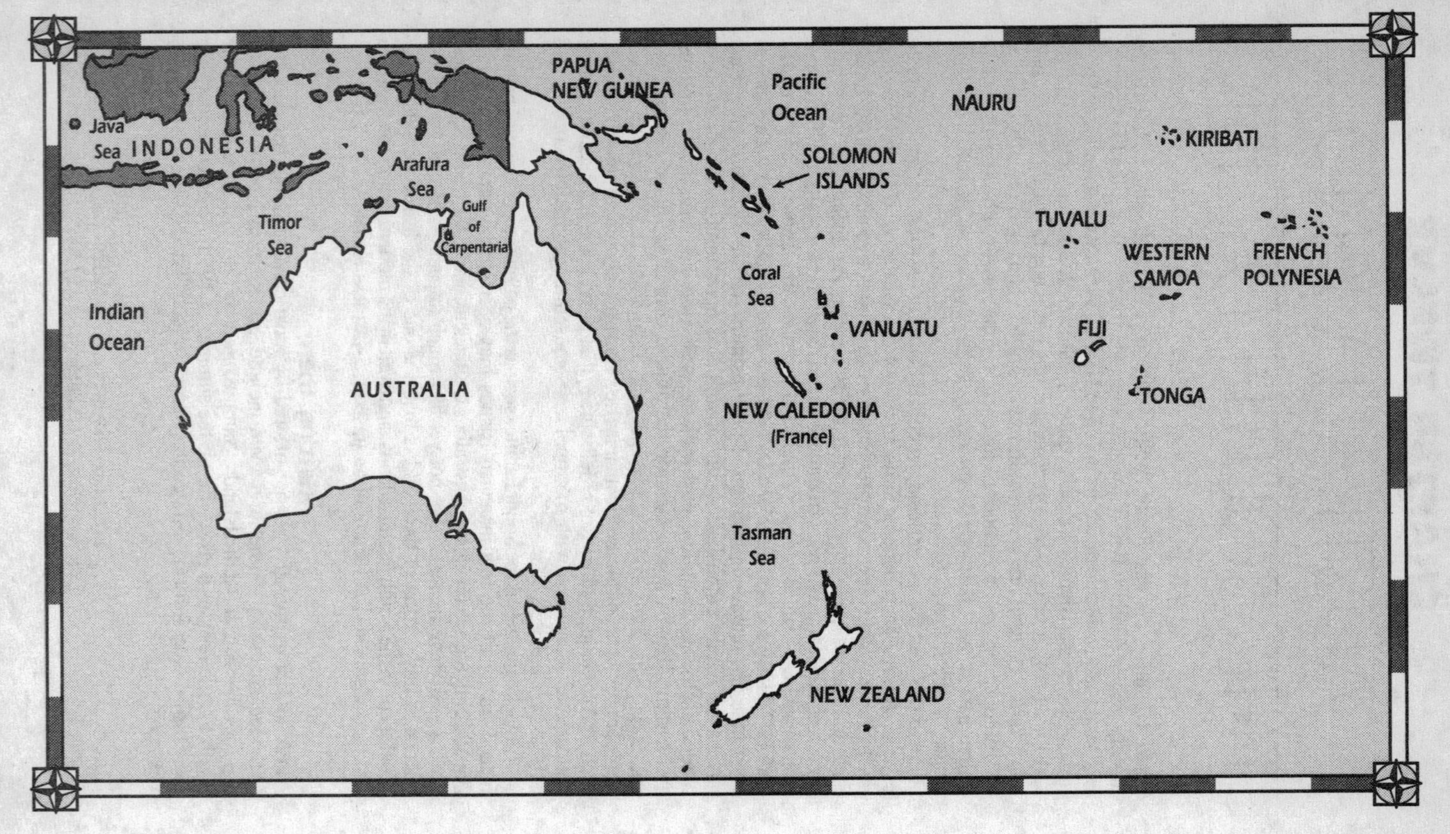
Java Sea
INDONESIA
PAPUA NEW GUINEA
Pacific Ocean
NAURU
KIRIBATI
SOLOMON ISLANDS
Arafura Sea
Gulf of Carpentaria
Timor Sea
TUVALU
WESTERN SAMOA
FRENCH POLYNESIA
Coral Sea
Indian Ocean
VANUATU
FIJI
AUSTRALIA
TONGA
NEW CALEDONIA (France)
Tasman Sea
NEW ZEALAND

Los Angeles–Nandi	$694
Honolulu–Sydney	$696

Holders of the International Student Identity Card or the Go 25 Card (see pages 9–11) are eligible for reduced airfares from several major European cities to points in Australia and the South Pacific. With some student/youth fares, stopovers in Asian cities along the route are permitted. Council Travel offices have up-to-date information.

If you're departing from an Asian city, you can also take advantage of student/youth fares to Sydney. To be eligible, you must meet the same requirements as those described above for youth/student fares from Europe. These fares can be booked through any Council Travel office. Sample fares in effect during the summer of 1993 are listed below:

Bangkok–Sydney	$489
Singapore–Sydney	$409
Hong Kong–Sydney	$729

Getting Around

The island-nations of the South Pacific are connected by regular **air** service, provided mostly by Air Pacific and Polynesian Airlines. Routes from Australia or New Zealand to the smaller islands are also served by larger carriers. Because the archipelagos of the South Pacific are so far-flung, travel between these island countries can be an expensive matter. Within each country's island chain, however, domestic air service is generally quite cheap. Some sample *round-trip* regional airfares in effect during the summer of 1993 are listed below.

Sydney–Auckland	$ 356
Auckland–Nandi	$ 538
Sydney–Papeete	$1,386

A number of regional air passes or special multi-flight fares make Pacific travel a little more affordable. For those planning to do a lot of traveling by air within both Australia and New Zealand, the Ansett group of airlines has arranged a discount fare structure called **Down Under Discount Deals**, which can save you up to 60 percent off regular fares when you purchase at least two sectors in conjunction with your international flight to Australia and New Zealand. For more information, contact Ansett at (800) 366-1300.

Air New Zealand has devised a new **Coral Route** fare structure, which includes a round-trip flight from Los Angeles to Australia or New Zealand with a variable number of South Pacific island stopovers en route in one direction. One Coral Route fare lets you visit four countries in three months for $1,169. Choose from Tahiti, Cook Islands, Hawaii, Fiji, Western Samoa, Tonga, New Zealand, and, for $100 extra, Australia. A one-year Coral Route fare costs $1,469, allowing you to visit seven destinations among those listed above plus Vanuatu, Solomon Islands, and New Caledonia. Various other shorter-term Coral Route fares are also available. For more information, contact Air New Zealand, (800) 262-1234.

Polynesian Airways' **Polypass** ($999) is valid for 30 days of unlimited travel over the airline's South Pacific routes. In addition, it includes one round-trip to Polynesia from the U.S. The Polypass cannot be used for travel beginning in the months of December or January. It can be purchased in the U.S. through Polynesian Airways, (800) 592-7100. The best deal in Pacific air travel, at $383, is Polynesian Airlines' **Pacific Triangle Fare**. Good for a full year, this fare allows one trip each, in a continuous direction, between Western Samoa, Fiji, and Tonga.

Air Pacific offers several **Pacific Air Passes**, which include either New Zealand or Australia. From Fiji for $449 you can travel between Apia, Western Samoa, Tonga, and Vanuatu; $499 adds Honiara to this itinerary. The Pacific Air Pass is good for 30 days. It can be purchased in the U.S. through Qantas Airlines, (800) 227-4500.

Solomon Airlines and Air Caledonie offer the **Discover Pacific Pass**, which costs from $399 for two flights to $899 for six flights. Solomon Airlines also has the **Discover Solomons Pass**, which gives four flights for $199, with additional flights for $50 each for travel among 24 island destinations including Guadalcanal. Air Vanuatu's **Discover Vanuatu Pass** costs $199 for any four flights within 30 days to destinations within Vanuatu. For more information on all these passes, call Air Promotion Systems, 5777 West Century Boulevard, Suite 875, Los Angeles, CA 90045; (800) 677-4277.

Air Niugini offers a **Visit Papua New Guinea Pass** good for four flights within the country for $299, with additional flights costing $50 each. Contact Air Niugini at (714) 752-5440.

While travel by plane is certainly the most effortless and direct way to get around the islands, it isn't the only way. Once you're in the South Pacific, it isn't too difficult to find a **boat** going where you want, assuming you're headed for one of the larger ports. Unique to this part of the world and the Caribbean, however, is a large number of private yachts in need of extra crew and willing to take on island-hopping travelers. Crew members usually work for free and share the cost of food and other necessities. You can try your luck at marinas and boating clubs, or look for notices in newspapers and boating magazines. If you accept a ride on a boat, you can't get off until you've reached your destination. Women should be especially careful, or travel in pairs with men.

For Further Information

The comprehensive *South Pacific Handbook*, by David Stanley, is the best general guide to this little-known but vast expanse of islands. It's available for $15.95 from Moon Publications. David Stanley has spent many years wandering the Pacific and knows the region well. His books show you how to get around (especially helpful if you want to crew on yachts) and give a good account of South Pacific history and culture. Among his other guides (also available from Moon Publications) are *Tahiti-Polynesia Handbook* and *Micronesia Handbook*, both $11.95.

Lonely Planet publishes a plethora of detailed travel guides to the South Pacific's many island groups. There are *Travel Survival Kit*s for Micronesia, New Caledonia, Papua New Guinea, Rarotonga and the Cook Islands, Samoa, Solomon Islands, Tahiti and French Polynesia, Tonga, and Vanuatu. You can find information on Moon Publications and Lonely Planet Publications on pages 56–57.

Listed below are addresses where you can write for general information as well as details on visa requirements on some of the smaller nations not covered in separate country sections later in this chapter.

- **French Polynesia:** Embassy of France, 4101 Reservoir Road NW, Washington, DC 20007; (202) 944-6000

- **Marshall Islands:** Office of the Representative of the Marshall Islands, Suite 1004, 1901 Pennsylvania Avenue NW, Washington, DC 20006; (202) 234-5414
- **Micronesia:** Embassy of the Federated States of Micronesia, 1725 N Street NW, Washington, DC 20036; (202) 223-4383
- **Nauru:** Consulate of the Republic of Nauru, PO Box A.M., Agana, Guam, 96910; (671) 649-8300
- **Palau:** Office of the Palau Representative, 444 North Capitol Street, Suite 308, Washington, DC 20008; (202) 624-7793
- **Papua New Guinea:** Embassy of Papua New Guinea, Suite 300, 1615 New Hampshire Avenue NW, Washington, DC 20009; (202) 745-3680
- **Solomon Islands:** British Embassy, 3100 Massachusetts Avenue NW, Washington, DC 20008; (202) 462-1340
- **Tahiti:** Embassy of France, 4101 Reservoir Road NW, Washington, DC 20007; (202) 944-6000
- **Tonga:** Consulate General of Tonga, 360 Post Street, Suite 604, San Francisco, CA 94108; (415) 781-0365
- **Vanuatu:** British Embassy, 3100 Massachusetts NW, Washington, DC 20008; (202) 462-1340

STUDY

Listed below are study programs offered by CIEE-member institutions which take place in more than one country. Consult Appendix I for the contact addresses and phone numbers.

Summer and Short-Term

Agriculture

Iowa State University. *ISU/Ag Travel Course*. Various sites in Australia and New Zealand. Winter break. Agriculture, agronomy, farm management, and international agriculture. Undergraduates and graduate students. Apply by October 15. Contact: Ken Larson, 1126 Agronomy Hall, ISU, Ames, IA 50011; (515) 294-3281.

Michigan State University. *Food and Agricultural Systems—Down Under*. Australia and New Zealand. Mid-May to mid-June. Four-week program on Australian and New Zealand agro-ecosystems with special emphasis on selected food and environmental issues. Juniors to graduate students. Apply by April 15. Contact: Office of Overseas Study, 108 International Center, Michigan State University, East Lansing, MI 48824-1035; (517) 353-8920.

AUSTRALIA

Australia, the only continent occupied by a single country, is a young nation in which egalitarianism runs deep amid increasing ethnic diversity. Its indigenous people are the Aborigines who migrated to Australia at least 30,000 years ago and invented, among other things, the boomerang and an amazingly sophisticated sign language. Great Britain claimed the continent in 1770, but did little with it until the American Revolution, when it decided to use the region to house its convicts. The prisoners were followed by thousands of European (mostly British) settlers, who were soon joined by American miners in search of gold discovered in 1853. Today, 4 in 10 Australians are either immigrants or the children of immigrants—active people looking to build a new life. Originally from European nations, but now increasingly from elsewhere, immigrants have helped push the nation towards the adoption of multiculturalism as national policy.

A member of the British Commonwealth, Australia recognizes Queen Elizabeth II as its official head of state, but is governed by a prime minister and parliament seated in Canberra, a planned city created to serve as the nation's capital.

Sixty percent of Australia's 17 million people live in the five largest cities, all with populations exceeding one million and all located on the coast. This leaves much of Australia's 7.6 million square kilometers very sparsely populated. And with good reason: 50 percent of Australia has less than 12 inches of rainfall a year. This aridity has not limited the development of Australia's flora and fauna. Indeed, it may have even favored the marsupials, animals like kangaroos with pouches for their young. Australia is the only continent where this fauna grouping has become so prevalent, evolving for millions of years in almost complete isolation. Australia boasts intriguing indigenous animals like the koala, the Tasmanian devil, the platypus, and the kookaburra, as well as imported (now wild) buffalos, rabbits, and camels.

While an Asian or African visitor would probably see Australia as a Western nation, Australia is taking advantage of its Pacific Rim location, and enthusiasm for expanding Asian trade and communications is rising. Americans or Europeans might see many cultural similarities between their nations and Australia but the differences are substantial. Australian society is neither European nor North American—nor is it merely a mixture of the two. A unique history, cultural makeup, and topography have all had a hand in the construction of the sardonic, egalitarian Australian character.

Australians have a heritage of anti-authoritarianism, directness, and a self-mocking brand of humor. For example, in restaurants, service is usually friendly but never servile. The implicit assumption is that of equality, and tipping is usually not expected. Today, there is an increased confidence in being Australian and an increasing examination of just what that means.

—Simon Avenell, Perth, Australia

Official name: Commonwealth of Australia. **Area:** 2,966,200 square miles (about three-fourths the size of the U.S.). **Population:** 16,849,496. **Population density:** 5.8 inhabitants per square mile. **Capital:** Canberra, Australian Capital Territory (ACT). **Largest city:** Sydney (pop. 3,600,000). **Language:** English. **Religions:** Protestant, Roman Catholic. **Per capita income:** US$18,054. **Currency:** Australian dollar. **Literacy rate:** 89%. **Average daily temperature:** Melbourne: June, 50°; December, 65°. Sydney: June, 56°; December, 70°. **Average number of days with precipitation:** Melbourne: June, 16; December, 11. Sydney: June, 12; December, 13.

TRAVEL

U.S. citizens will need a passport and visa to enter Australia. The standard tourist visa is valid for one year and allows for a stay of up to three months during that year. There is a $25 charge for visitor visas allowing stays of up to six months and multiple-entry visas valid for a period of four years. Proof of onward or return transportation is required for each entry, however. For specific details, check with the **Australian Embassy**, 1601 Massachusetts Avenue NW, Washington, DC 20036-2237; (202) 797-3000; fax (202) 797-3362. There are Australian consulates in Chicago, Honolulu, Houston, Los Angeles, New York, and San Francisco.

Getting Around

Keep in mind that Australia is a very large country, with much of it sparsely populated. Most of the nation's population is concentrated in the five state capitals: Sydney, Melbourne, Brisbane, Adelaide, and Perth. The traveler will have to cross long distances between these population centers.

Due to the great distances involved, Aussies often travel by **air**. There are numerous airpass options offered by various domestic airlines in Australia, as well as special discount plans for overseas visitors. All must be purchased outside Australia. Ansett Airlines' **Visit Australia Pass** gives you four one-way flights for US $444. If you include Perth or the Hayman Island resort, the price is $514. Other options include Ansett's **Explore Australia Air Pass**, which gives you a 35-percent discount off full economy fares when you combine three to seven segments, or a 40-percent discount for eight or more segments. Those planning on a lot of air time within both Australia and New Zealand will want to check out Ansett's **Down-Under Discount Deals** (see page 455). You can reach Ansett Airlines at (800) 366-1300. Australian Airlines' **Explorer Pass** also gives you four flights for $444. Its **Blue Roo Pass** gives discounts of 40 to 60 percent off individual fares. Australian Airlines passes can be obtained through Qantas Airways, (800) 227-4500. Eastwest Airlines has two regional airpasses priced in Australian dollars. The **Sun Air Pass**, for A$749 (US$500) lets you fly in one direction for 21 days along a circular route between Cairns and Sydney, stopping at such points as Hamilton Island, Brisbane, Ayers Rock, and Alice Springs. The **System Air Pass**, for A$849 (US$569) gives you 21 days of flight in one direction along Australia's east coast from Cairns to Hobart, over to Melbourne and down to Tasmania. Both passes let you make as many stops as you like. Contact Eastwest at (800) 354-7471. Council Travel (see pages xiii–xvi) can also provide information on all the above passes.

Australia's **rail** system is a more leisurely and cheaper alternative for getting around the country. The rail network links the five state capitals and serves Alice Springs in the Northern Territory as well. The famous trans-Australian run from Adelaide to Perth covers some 1,316 miles and takes two days and two nights. You might consider the following rail passes:

- The **Austrailpass** entitles you to unlimited rail travel for 14 days for $348 economy or $580 first class, 21 days for $452 economy or $716 first class, and 30 days for $548 economy or $880 first class. There are also passes for 60 and 90 days.
- The **Austrail Flexipass** allows 8 days of travel within a 60-day period for

$256 economy class and $424 first class, or 15 days of travel in a 90-day period for $380 economy class and $600 first class.

- The **Kangaroo Road 'n' Rail Pass** combines unlimited train passage with travel on Australian Coachlines (see below). Valid for 14, 21, or 28 days. Prices range from $524 to $920 for economy class and $832 to $1,024 for first class.

The above passes don't include meals and sleeper berths on long-distance trains, which will cost extra. Passes must be purchased before entering Australia. For more information, contact Council Travel (see pages 00–00) or call ATS Tours at (800) 423-2880.

Bus travel is generally faster and almost as cheap as the train. The three major bus companies—Pioneer, Bus Australia, and Greyhound—combine service to comprise Australian Coachlines. Australian Coachlines' **Aussie Pass** entitles you to unlimited travel on the networks of Pioneer and Greyhound. This flexible pass is available in a variety of combinations ranging from 7 days in one month for A$343 (US$230) to 90 days in six months for A$2,100 (US$1400). Those who want to combine rail and bus travel will want to look into the Kangaroo Road 'n' Rail Pass (described above). Tasmanian Redline Coaches' **Tassie Pass** gives you unlimited access to all of Tasmania by bus. Costs vary from A$111 (US$73) for the 7-day "Budget" pass to A$177 (US$120) for the 21-day "Bushwalker." Travelers wanting to see New Zealand as well as Australia should consider the **Down Under Pass**, which allows travel on Australian Coachlines and New Zealand's Mt. Cook Line. The pass costs from A$450 (US$300) for 9 days to A$1,419 (US$950) for 45 days. Students and members of Hostelling International receive discounts on most bus lines.

Renting a **car** in Australia costs about the same as renting one in the United States. Aussies drive on the left-hand side of the road—which, in the outback, might be poorly paved or full of wild buffalo. The biggest car rental companies in Australia are Hertz, Avis, Budget, and Thrifty, and you can get rates and make reservations by calling their toll-free numbers in the U.S. Campervans and mobile homes can also be rented for longer journeys. American Automobile Association (AAA) members can take advantage of motorist services offered by the **Australian Automobile Association (AAA)**, GPO Box 1555, Canberra City, ACT 2601; (61) 62-247-7311; fax (61) 62-257-5320. **Ferries** operate between the mainland and Tasmania. Hitchhiking is common. As long as the hitchhiker stands off the road, it is legal in all states of Australia except Queensland.

Eating and Sleeping

There are more than 100 **youth hostels** throughout Australia. Many discounts on travel, events, food, and more are available to Hostelling International members. For more information, contact Hostelling International/American Youth Hostels (see page 54) or the **Australian Youth Hostels Association**, Level 3, 10 Mallett Street, Camperdown, New South Wales 2050; (61) 2-565-1699; fax (61) 2-565-1325.

Backpackers Resorts of Australia is a network of independent hostels providing low-cost accommodations catering to the outdoors crowd. Write them at PO Box 1000, Byron Bay, New South Wales 2481; (61) 18-666888.

Many Australian universities offer affordable **dormitory lodgings** to travelers during the vacation months of December through February, and August through September. The Australian Tourist Commission (see "For Further Information," below) can provide you with a list of university accommodations; however, at press time, it was somewhat out of date. Another source is Campus Travel Service's *U.S. and Worldwide Travel Accommodations Guide* (see page 54).

There are many commercial **campgrounds** around the country—one of the cheapest accommodation alternatives. Most cater to "caravaners" (persons with RVs) rather than tent campers, but you can still pitch a tent and take advantage of the hot showers and laundry facilities. Most tourist offices in Australia have a list of campgrounds.

Especially for Students and Young People

Australia's student travel agency and issuer of the International Student Identity Card is **STA Travel**, 224 Faraday Street, Calton, Melbourne VIC 3053; (61) 3-3476911; fax (61) 3-3470608. STA has numerous offices in cities throughout Australia, including Adelaide, Brisbane, Cairns, Canberra, Darwin, Perth, Sydney, and Townsville. STA provides a wide range of services for student travelers, including plane or bus tickets, accommodation bookings, tours, and travel information.

For Further Information

For general tourist information, contact the **Australian Tourist Commission**, 489 Fifth Avenue, 31st Floor, New York, NY 10017; (212) 687-6300. The ATC also has offices in Chicago and Los Angeles. To order a copy of their free 130-page *Destination Australia* guide, call (800) 333-0199.

There are several guides designed especially for the budget traveler in Australia. *Australia: A Travel Survival Kit* is one of the best; you can order it for $21.95 from Lonely Planet Publications (see page 54). Lonely Planet also publishes *Bushwalking in Australia* ($12.95). Those planning only a short stay might want to read *2 to 22 Days in Australia*, an itinerary planner available for $9.95 from John Muir Publications, PO Box 613, Santa Fe, NM 87504; (800) 888-7504.

WORK

To obtain employment in Australia it is necessary to find an employer who is prepared to file temporary residence sponsorship papers with the Department of Immigration, Local Government, and Ethnic Affairs. The employer sponsors a particular position for a specified period of time and the Immigration Department will decide whether or not to approve the sponsorship, taking into account such factors as the need for the skills the applicant has to offer, and whether or not the position being offered is one that can be filled through local labor sources.

If you are a **teacher** of Japanese or Chinese language, mathematics or science, your skills are in demand in the public schools. Australia is currently experiencing a shortage of teachers in these disciplines. To find out about openings in these areas, write to the Education Department of the state you are interested in working in; for specific addresses contact the Embassy of Australia (see "Travel," above).

Internships/Traineeships

Listed below are the programs offered by institutions and organizations that are members of the Council on International Educational Exchange. Consult

Appendix I for the addresses where you can write for more information. In addition to the programs below, Moorhead State University offers a program open only to its own students.

Association for International Practical Training. *IAESTE Trainee Program.* On-the-job training for undergraduate and graduate students in technical fields such as engineering, computer science, agriculture, architecture, mathematics, and the natural and physical sciences. See page 19 for more information. *Hospitality/Tourism Exchanges Program.* On-the-job training for young people beginning a career in the hotel and food-service industries. Participants must have graduated, or be currently enrolled in a university or vocational school and possess at least six months of training or experience in the chosen field. Training usually runs from 6 to 18 months.

Boston University. *Sydney Internship Program.* A semester of coursework is combined with an internship in one of the following areas: advertising, marketing, public relations, management, finance, economics, the arts, media, politics and international relations, pre-law, psychology, and social policy. Fall and spring semesters; summer. Sophomores to post-baccalaureate students with a 3.0 GPA. Apply by March 15 for summer and fall; October 15 for the spring. Contact: (617) 353-9888.

Ohio University. *The Consortium for Overseas Student Teaching.* Student teaching in local and independent schools. Quarter. Sophomores to seniors attending Ohio University only. Contact: Wes Snyder, Center for Higher Education and International Programs, 129 McCracken Hall, Athens, OH 45701; (614) 593-4445; fax (614) 593-0569.

Voluntary Service

The **Australian Trust for Conservation Volunteers** sponsors service opportunities for six-week terms that involve tree planting, erosion control work, and fence construction. Participants stay in trailers, tents, farm houses, or shearers' quarters; no special skills are required. For more information, contact the Australian Trust for Conservation Volunteers, PO Box 423, Ballarat, Victoria, Australia 3350. Be sure to enclose an international postal reply coupon to cover the cost of postage for shipping the informational materials.

STUDY

Persons considering applying to an Australian institution of higher education should write to the **Australian Education Office (AEO)** to obtain information on study-abroad, summer and graduate opportunities, as well as general information pertaining to fees, application procedures, and exchange programs. The Education Office can advise you on study at all of Australia's higher education institutions and assist you with your enrollment process. The address for the AEO is 1601 Massachusetts Avenue NW, Washington, DC 20036; (202) 332-8285; fax (202) 332-8304.

Students considering direct enrollment should be aware that Australian students entering a university are generally at a higher educational level than their American counterparts. As a result, the sophomore year of an American university is typically considered the equivalent of the first year at an Australian university.

The school year in Australia extends from late February to late November.

In general, student life in Australia is lived with zest. While you are certain to be challenged academically, students can still find time to enjoy extracurricular activities that are unique to Australia. Visa regulations allow full-time students to work up to 20 hours a week on a casual basis during their course of study and full-time during vacations.

Following are educational programs offered by CIEE-member institutions. Unless otherwise noted, consult Appendix I for the addresses of the colleges and universities listed below. In addition, Pepperdine University, State University of New York schools, University of Nebraska at Lincoln, and University of Notre Dame offer programs open to their own students only.

Semester and Academic Year

Business

Bentley College. *Bentley's Business Program in Australia*. Melbourne. Semester and academic year. Offered in association with faculties of business at Royal Melbourne Institute of Technology and Monash University. Australian economy and business, industry and environment, and culture. Excursions. Juniors and seniors with 2.7 GPA. Apply by April 15 for fall and academic year; November 1 for spring.

Education

University of Wisconsin at River Falls. *Overseas Practice Teaching*. Various sites. Fall and spring semesters. Individualized student-teaching experience. Seniors with preparatory education courses. Apply three months before desired teaching time. Contact: Carol LeBreck, Coordinator, Karges Center, UW at River Falls, River Falls, WI 54022; (715) 425-3778/3705.

Engineering

University of Illinois at Urbana-Champaign. *International Programs in Engineering*. Sydney. Semester and academic year. Priority given to engineering students. Undergraduates to graduate students. Apply by February 15 for fall and academic year; October 1 for spring.

General Studies

Butler University. *Australian National University*. Canberra, ACT. Academic year, calendar year (February to November), fall and spring semesters. Fully integrated program with study available in all arts and sciences disciplines. Juniors and seniors with 3.0 GPA and previous study in field of interest. Apply by March 15 for fall and academic year; November 15 for spring and calendar year.

Flinders University. Adelaide. Academic year, calendar year (February to November), fall and spring semesters. Fully integrated program with study possible in all arts and sciences disciplines. Juniors and seniors with 3.0 GPA and previous study in field of interest. Apply by March 15 for fall and academic year; November 15 for spring and calendar year.

Macquarie University. Sydney. Academic year, calendar year (February to November), fall and spring semesters. Fully integrated program with study possible in all arts and sciences disciplines including Aboriginal, Australian, and Pacific Area studies. Juniors and seniors with 3.0 GPA and previous study in field of interest. Apply by March 15 for fall and academic year; November 15 for spring and calendar year.

Monash University. Melbourne. Academic year, calendar year (February to November), fall and spring semesters. Fully integrated program with study possible in all arts and sciences disciplines. Juniors and seniors with 3.0 GPA and previous study in field of interest. Apply by March 15 for fall and academic year; October 15 for spring and calendar year.

Murdoch University. Perth. Academic year, calendar year (February to November), fall and spring semesters. Fully integrated program with study possible in all arts and sciences disciplines plus communications and environmental studies. Juniors and seniors with 3.0 GPA and previous study in field of interest. Apply by March 15 for fall and academic year; November 15 for spring and calendar year.

University of Adelaide. Academic year, calendar year (February to November), fall and spring semesters. Fully integrated program with study possible in all arts and sciences disciplines. Juniors and seniors with 3.0 GPA and previous study in field of interest. Apply by March 15 for fall and academic year; November 15 for spring and calendar year.

University of Canberra. Academic year, calendar year (February to November), fall and spring semesters. Fully integrated program with study possible in all arts and sciences disciplines plus sports studies and communications. Juniors and seniors with 3.0 GPA and previous study in field of interest. Apply by March 15 for fall and academic year; November 15 for spring and calendar year.

University of New South Wales. Sydney. Academic year, calendar year (February to November), fall and spring semesters. Fully integrated program with study possible in all arts and sciences disciplines including Australian studies, marine sciences, and engineering. Juniors and seniors with 3.0 GPA and previous study in field of interest. Apply by March 15 for fall and academic year; November 15 for spring and calendar year.

University of Queensland. Brisbane, Queensland. Academic year, calendar year (February to November), fall and spring semesters. Fully integrated program with study possible in all arts and sciences disciplines plus Australian studies, marine sciences, and journalism. Juniors and seniors with 3.0 GPA and previous study in field of interest. Apply by March 15 for fall and academic year; November 15 for spring and calendar year.

University of Sydney. Academic year, calendar year (February to November), fall and spring semesters. Fully integrated program with study possible in all arts and sciences disciplines including Australian and Asian studies. Juniors and seniors with 3.0 GPA and previous study in field of interest. Apply by March 15 for fall and academic year; November 15 for spring and calendar year.

University of Technology, Sydney. Academic year, calendar year (February to November), fall and spring semesters. Fully integrated program with study possible in communications, computer science, engineering, and business. Juniors and seniors with 3.0 GPA and previous study in field of interest. Apply by March 15 for fall and academic year; November 15 for spring and calendar year.

University of Western Australia. Perth. Academic year, calendar year (February to November), fall and spring semesters. Fully integrated program with study possible in all arts and sciences disciplines. Juniors and seniors with 3.0 GPA and previous study in field of interest. Apply by March 15 for fall and academic year; November 15 for spring and calendar year.

Contact: Institute for Study Abroad, Butler University, 4600 Sunset Avenue, Indianapolis, IN 46208-3485; (800) 858-0229.

Council on International Educational Exchange. *Cooperative Studies Program at Murdoch University*. Perth. Semester and academic year. Sophomores to seniors with 2.75 GPA. Apply by April 15 for fall; November 15 for spring. Contact: University Programs Department.

International Student Exchange Program (ISEP). Semester. Direct reciprocal exchange between U.S. universities and institutions in Perth, Geelong and Melbourne (Victoria), and Toowoomba (Queensland). Full curriculum options. Rolling admissions. Open only to students at ISEP-member institutions. Contact ISEP for list of members.

Marymount College, Tarrytown. *Macquarie University*. Sydney. Semester and academic year. Courses available in major disciplines. Juniors and seniors with 2.8 GPA. Rolling admissions.

Monash University. Melbourne. Semester and academic year. Courses available in all major disciplines. Juniors and seniors with 2.8 GPA. Rolling admissions.

University of Melbourne. Semester and academic year. Courses available in all major disciplines. Juniors and seniors with 2.8 GPA. Rolling admissions.

Michigan State University. *Australia: Its People, Government, Justice System, and Public Policies*. Sydney and Canberra. Spring semester. Sophomores to seniors. Apply by November 30. Contact: Office of Overseas Study, 108 International Center, Michigan State University, East Lansing, MI 48824-1035; (517) 353-8920.

Northern Arizona University. *Australia Exchange—Adelaide*. Australian academic year (February to November). Variety of academic and professional disciplines. Sophomores (with 2.5 GPA) to graduate students. Apply by November 1.

Australia Exchange—Newcastle. Australian academic year (February to November). Variety of academic and professional disciplines. Sophomores (with 2.5 GPA) to graduate students. Apply by November 1.

Old Dominion University. *ODU Abroad: Ballarat University College*. Ballarat. Semester and academic year. Full university curriculum. Sophomores to juniors. Apply by March 1 for fall and academic year; October 1 for spring. Contact: Study Abroad Office, BAL 304, Old Dominion University, Norfolk, VA 23529; (804) 683-5378.

Rollins College. *Rollins in Melbourne*. Semester and academic year. Australian studies at Monash University. Excursions. Sophomores to seniors with 2.8 GPA. Apply by March 15.

Rollins in Sydney. Fall term. Australian studies. Sophomores to seniors with 2.8 GPA. Apply by March 15.

State University of New York College at Buffalo. *University of Newcastle*. Fall semester (late July to late November), spring semester (late February to late June), and academic year (late November to late June). Full university curriculum options. Dormitory housing. Sophomores to seniors with 3.0 GPA. Apply by February 15 for fall and academic year; October 1 for spring.

University of South Australia, Adelaide. Fall semester. Liberal arts. Sophomores to seniors with 2.75 GPA. Apply by February 15.

Contact: Office of International Education, GC 416, SUNY College at Buffalo, 1300 Elmwood Avenue, Buffalo, NY 14222-1095; (716) 878-4620.

State University of New York College at Oswego. *General Studies in Australia*. Griffith University in Brisbane. Fall and spring semesters. Wide range of studies offered including environmental studies, education, Australian studies, and business. Dormitory or apartment housing. Juniors and seniors with 2.5

GPA. Apply by April 1 for fall; November 1 for spring. Contact: Office of International Education, SUNY at Oswego, 102 Rich Hall, Oswego, NY 13126; (315) 341-2118.

University of New South Wales. *Study Abroad Program.* Sydney. Semester and academic year. Fully integrated program in liberal arts, sciences, engineering, marine studies, and fine arts. Juniors and seniors with 3.0 GPA. Rolling admissions.

University of North Carolina at Chapel Hill. *Australia, Wollongong.* Semester and academic year. Sophomores to graduate students with 2.7 GPA. Apply by February 14 for fall and academic year; October 1 for spring.

World Learning/School for International Training. *College Semester Abroad.* Melbourne. Fall and spring semesters. Interdisciplinary seminar, field-study methods seminar, and independent-study project. Homestays and excursions. Sophomores to seniors with 2.5 GPA. Apply by May 7 for fall; October 7 for spring. Contact: College Semester Abroad Admissions at (800) 336-1616.

State University of New York at Buffalo. *University of Central Queensland.* Rockhampton. Fall semester (mid-July to late November), spring semester (mid-February to late June), and academic year (mid-July to late June). Full university curriculum options. Sophomores to seniors. Apply by February 15 for fall and academic year; October 1 for spring. Contact: Office of International Education, GC 416, SUNY at Buffalo, 1300 Elmwood Avenue, Buffalo, NY 14222-1095; (716) 878-4620.

State University of New York at Plattsburgh. Bond University at Gold Coast. Fall and spring semesters. Sophomores to seniors with 3.0 GPA. Apply by June 1 for fall; October 1 for spring. Contact: Director, Overseas Academic Programs, Hawkins Hall 102, SUNY at Plattsburgh, Plattsburgh, NY 12901; (518) 564-5827/2398.

University of North Carolina at Chapel Hill. *UNC at Chapel Hill Program to University of Melbourne, Australia.* Semester and academic year. Sophomores to graduate students with 3.0 GPA. Apply by February 14 for fall and academic year; October 1 for spring.

UNC at Chapel Hill Program to Murdoch University, Perth, Australia. Semester and academic year. Sophomores to graduate students with 3.0 GPA. Apply by February 14 for fall and academic year; October 1 for spring.

University of Wollongong. *Study Abroad.* Wollongong. Semester and academic year. Sophomores to graduate students with 3.0 GPA. Apply by May 1 for fall; November 1 for spring.

Natural Sciences

World Learning/School for International Training. *College Semester Abroad—Natural and Human Environment.* Cairns, Townsville, Brisbane, and North Queensland. Fall and spring semesters. Ecology and field-study seminar, independent-study project. Homestays and excursions. Sophomores to graduate students with 2.5 GPA. Apply by May 7 for fall; October 7 for spring. Contact: College Semester Abroad Admissions at (800) 336-1616.

Summer and Short-Term

Natural Sciences

North Carolina State University. *Summer Courses in Tropical Field Ecology.* Swain Reefs of Great Barrier Reef, off Queensland coast. June and

July. Three-week program in ecological theory combined with practical research experience in the field. Housing on chartered ship. Undergraduates and continuing-education students. Apply by March 1.

EXPLORING AUSTRALIAN CULTURE

Readings

Contemporary Australian literature is marked by a strong interest in the past. Peter Carey's *Oscar and Lucinda* (1988), a novel set in the mid-19th century, illustrates the strange turns that love, religion, commerce, and colonialism took in the Victorian Age. Patrick White's *Voss* (1957), an account of a German explorer leading an expedition deep into the hostile continent, also looks backward into Australian history.

A number of Australian books deal with the current and historical situation of the Aborigines. Randolph Stowe's *To the Islands*, for example, is the surreal saga of a disillusioned missionary on a voyage through the desert to the Aboriginal islands of the dead. Thomas Keneally, a Catholic writer, deals with the problems that arise when a half-caste Aborigine tries to enter mainstream Australian society in *The Chant of Jimmy Blacksmith* (1972). (This book is also a film, produced by Fred Schepisi in 1978.) For an historically accurate novel of the Aborigines, read Colin Johnson's *Dr. Wooreddy* (1989). Set in the 19th century, this book deals with the relationships the Aborigines had with the convicts, the pioneers, and other groups they encountered.

A woman's view of life in Australia is provided by several contemporary Australian writers. Jessica Anderson's romantic novel, *Tirra Lirra by the River* (1978), focuses on an old woman's reflections on her life in Australia during the 1920s, 1930s, and 1940s. Jill Ker Conway's *The Road from Coorain* (1989) is an autobiographical account of her youth, and *My Place* (1988), by Sally Morgan, presents the story of the author's Aboriginal family history. The struggle of growing up in Australia from a male point of view is the focus of *Johnno* (1975), by David Malouf.

Films

Beginning in the 1970s, a flurry of Australian filmmaking activity has produced a variety of films. Perhaps dominant among these, at least in terms of popularity and visibility outside Australia, are the "ocker" movies. An "ocker" is slang for the archetypal uncultivated Australian working man, boorish, uncouth, and chauvinistic, but always a good mate with a wonderful sense of humor. Bruce Beresford's *The Adventures of Barry McKensie* (1972) is a classic example of this type of film; more recent examples are the *Crocodile Dundee* films (1986, 1988) and Yahoo Serious's *Young Einstein* (1988).

Nationalism is a prime topic of Australian film and can often be found hand-in-hand with the concept of Australian "mateship." Peter Weir's *Gallipoli* (1981) is a historical drama about the World War I massacre of Australian soldiers by the Turks (and the British). Bruce Beresford's *Breaker Morant* (1979) is an anti-imperialist film about the British using three Australian soldiers as scapegoats during the Boer War. Both of these films frame an attitude toward the British colonial period through its effects on Australia's young men.

Australia's "Aboriginal question" is detailed in a number of films, including *The Last Wave* (1977), by Peter Weir, which depicts the distance between the Aborigine and white worlds. Nicholas Roeg's *Walkabout* (1971) compares and contrasts the two cultures through the interaction of a young Aboriginal male and two suburban white children.

Praised for its aesthetics, *Picnic at Hanging Rock* (1986; also a book) presents the Australian landscape brilliantly. This film, set in 1900, concerns a group of girls from an elite private school who go on a picnic at Hanging Rock, and disappear.

FIJI

Simply mention the word "Fiji" to most Americans, and it conjures up images of bright, sunny skies brushed with orange, yellow, and blue hues, isolated warm white sandy beaches, tall green palms swaying to and fro to the gentle rhythm of a tropical breeze, shimmering blue-green ocean waves caressing the cowries and tanning bodies resting on the beach. Majestic mountains matted with luscious banana plants, fragrant gardenias, and brilliant birds of paradise are also part of the mental pictures associated with Fiji. But there is more to Fiji than the "Endless Love" image Brooke Shields and her playmate gave to us years ago in *The Blue Lagoon*.

Comprising more than 500 islands with only 100 of these inhabited, and with a comparative area slightly smaller than New Jersey, the Fiji archipelago is located at the crossroads of the highly romanticized South Pacific. Its closest neighbor, Vanuatu, is approximately 1,000 kilometers away. New Zealand lies to the south, New Guinea and Australia to the west, Samoa and Tahiti to the east, the Solomon, Marshall, and Hawaiian Islands to the north and northeast.

Fiji's modern history began in the early 1800s with the opening of the phenomenally profitable sandalwood trade, prior to the imposition of British colonial rule in 1874. Although English is the official language, Fijian and Hindustani are spoken and written as well. Outside of New Zealand and Australia, Suva, situated on the southeastern end of Viti Levu Island, is the largest and most cosmopolitan city in the South Seas. The other major Fijian island is Vanua Levu, which lies to the northeast of Viti Levu.

The cosmopolitan nature of Suva, and Fiji as a whole, is shaped by the three key cultural influences of indigenous Fijians, Europeans, and Indians. The physical characteristics, the artwork, and other cultural features of indigenous Fijians suggest an African origin. Indeed, many Fijians will say that they originated in what is now the lakes region of East Africa some 40,000 to 50,000 years ago. Through successive waves of land and overseas migrations, what is now Fiji became their home. Today they make up 46 percent of the population.

Fortune-seeking Europeans began to settle Fiji in increasing numbers from 1840 onwards. The descendants of these Europeans comprise 5 percent of the population.

The import of indentured laborers from India began in 1879, and by 1916 they numbered 64,000. The Indians were considered better suited and more willing to work on the European-owned sugar plantations than were the indigenous Fijians. Today, 250,000 Muslim, Hindu, and Sikh Indians make up 49 percent of the total population of Fiji. As the Fijians have historically owned 83 percent of the land, many Indians turned to business as a source of livelihood. Thus, they are the middlemen—the wholesalers, distributors, trucking contractors, electricians, plumbers, carpenters, taxi drivers, office clerks, and shipping agents. They also are highly represented in the legal, accounting, and medical fields.

Fiji gained independence from Britain in 1970. Between 1970 and 1987, most landownership and political power were vested in the indigenous Fijian minority. In 1987, the Indian party rose to power in a parliamentary election. Its government was overthrown during that same year in a military coup by then Lieutenant Colonel (now Major General) Sitiveni Rabuka. Through him, the indigenous Fijians have reasserted their control of Fiji's political life.

Fiji's location, and its rich multicultural and cosmopolitan nature make it a highly valued tourist destination. Viti Levu is the major communications and transportation hub of the South Pacific and Suva is home to the University of the South Pacific, jointly operated by 11 island-nations, with two campuses and university centers as far apart as Tuvalu, Niue Island, Cook Island, Vanuatu, Western Samoa, Tonga, Kiribati, Solomon Islands, Nauru, and Tokelan. Despite past political unrest, most Fijians and Indians are at peace with one another and are extraordinarily hospitable to visitors. It's more than likely that you will be invited on several occasions to stay in local homes or asked to participate in village activities. Travelers are accepted with greater respect in Fiji than perhaps in any other country, as long as they respect the local culture in turn.

—Roland A. Foulkes, Gainesville, Florida

Official name: Republic of Fiji. **Area:** 7,056 square miles (about the size of New Jersey). **Population:** 744,000. **Population density:** 105 inhabitants per square mile. **Capital and largest city:** Suva (pop. 69,000). **Language:** English (official), Fijian, Hindustani. **Religion:** Christian, Hindu, Islam. **Per capita income:** US$1,840. **Currency:** Fijian dollar. **Literacy rate:** 85%. **Average daily high/low:** Suva: January, 86°F/74°F; July, 79°F/68°F. **Average number of days with precipitation:** Suva: January, 18; July, 14.

TRAVEL

A passport, proof of sufficient funds, and onward or return ticket are required for U.S. citizens traveling to Fiji. For holders of U.S. passports, a tourist permit is issued upon arrival and is good for a stay up to four months; tourist permits can be extended up to a maximum of six months. For further information, check with the **Embassy of Fiji**, 2233 Wisconsin Avenue NW, #240, Washington, DC 20007; (202) 337-8320.

Getting Around

While the international airport at Nandi is the hub of South Pacific **air** lanes, Suva, the nation's capital on the other side of the island of Viti Levu, is Fiji's domestic transportation center. The main domestic carrier is Fiji Air, with flights departing Suva several times a week to many surrounding islands. In general, airfares within the Fiji islands are extraordinarily low.

A variety of small shipping companies provides freight and passenger service between the inhabited islands. While traveling by **boat** takes longer than going by plane, the price is less and the trip more interesting.

Ground transportation on the two major islands—Viti Levu and Vanua Levu—is by bus, truck, or taxi. **Bus** service, fast and reliable, is the best way to go. **Car** rental is easy with all the familiar U.S. companies but costs much more than it does in the U.S. You can also hitch, but chances are you will end up having to pay.

Eating and Sleeping

You'll have no problem finding inexpensive accommodations in Fiji. One of the real delights of traveling in Fiji, however, is staying in Fijian **villages**. Villages are communal property, so it is polite to ask permission of a resident before passing through. If you would like to stay overnight, you must personally ask the village chief (turanga-ni-koro). It is customary to pay your hosts a small fee for their trouble and to present a small gift.

Yanggona, or **kava**, is a mild drink made from the dried root (*waka*) of the pepper plant which plays a central role in indigenous social ceremonies. You can't associate with Fijians and not drink kava at some time. With this in mind, it's a good idea to carry around a bag of *waka* wherever you go. A bundle of *waka* is a customary gift as thanks in exchange for hospitality. You can buy it in many places and it isn't expensive.

For Further Information

A comprehensive guidebook for the traveler who really wants to get to know the islands is David Stanley's *Fiji Handbook*, available for $8.95 from Moon Publications. The recently updated *Fiji: A Travel Survival Kit* is also very good. It's available for $11.95 from Lonely Planet Publications. For more information on Moon Publications and Lonely Planet, see pages 56–57.

WORK

It is necessary to obtain a work permit to work in Fiji. The prospective employer and employee apply jointly for the permit to the Director of Immigration. Foreigners are only hired when there are no Fiji nationals available possessing the required skills for the position. For more information, contact the Embassy of Fiji, 2233 Wisconsin Avenue NW, Washington, DC 20007.

STUDY

A study program offered by a CIEE-member institution is listed below. Unless otherwise noted, consult Appendix I for the address where you can write for more information.

Semester and Academic Year

General Studies

International Student Exchange Program (ISEP). Fall and spring semester. Direct reciprocal exchange between U.S. universities and University of the

South Pacific. Full curriculum options. Rolling admissions. Open only to students at ISEP-member institutions. Contact ISEP for list of members.

NEW ZEALAND

New Zealand is famous for its natural features and diverse topography, which include golden beaches, lakes, rivers, rolling hills, mountains, glaciers and sparse areas of volcanic activity. New Zealand's "green and clean" image has been preserved by its geographic isolation and the environmentally conscious attitude of most policy makers and local organizations such as Greenpeace. During the 1980s New Zealand declared itself a nuclear-free zone. This bold stand by the New Zealand government won praise around the world, despite strong political pressure from the United States to allow American war ships in New Zealand waters.

New Zealand is comprised of two main islands: the North Island and the South Island. The North Island houses approximately 75 percent of New Zealand's population. The largest city is Auckland, with a population of close to a million people. Auckland is known as the "City of Sails," because it is believed the number of sailboats per capita is higher than in any other city in the world. Wellington, known as the "Windy City," is the capital and the political heartbeat of New Zealand. Gisborne, also on North Island, is the first city in the world to see the new day, as it is located due west of the international dateline. Gisborne is located in Eastland, a beautiful area isolated from other regions in New Zealand and off the main tourist track.

Cook Strait separates the North and South islands. Once across "the ditch," the Southern Alps provide magnificent scenery. This mountain range forms the backbone of South Island and is highlighted by New Zealand's tallest mountain, Mount Cook. Christchurch and Dunedin are the largest cities on the South Island. Christchurch, appropriately nicknamed the "Garden City," is filled with elegant parks and grand architecture. Dunedin is a city with a distinctly Scottish background. It is home to the oldest university in New Zealand, the University of Otago. Close to the city, Otago Peninsula is known for its rugged coastline and world-famous albatross colonies. Also on South Island, Queenstown and Wanaka have become popular tourist centers because of the area's picturesque scenery and recreational sports offerings.

New Zealanders are colloquially known as Kiwis, named after the national emblem of New Zealand. The Kiwi is a flightless, nocturnal, native bird identified by its long slender beak.

Influenced by their beautiful natural surroundings, New Zealanders are generally relaxed, friendly and physically active people. Extraordinarily sports-oriented, they participate in a variety of outdoor activities, such as tramping (hiking), skiing, bungee jumping, white water rafting, and fishing (both fresh-water and deep-sea). Rugby is New Zealand's national sport and over the years the country has been proudly represented by the All Blacks (the national rugby team).

Life down under has become a lot more exciting in recent years. Gone are the days when New Zealand closed down for the weekend, and gone are the days of 11 P.M.–closing. Bars and nightclubs in the main cities can now apply for late licenses to accommodate the need for more nighttime entertainment. These changes can be attributed to American culture which has filtered through the New Zealand society to create a unique blend of British and American influences.

New Zealand was originally inhabited by the Maori people in the 13th century, although some believe this "great migration" from the Polynesian Islands could have begun as early as the 9th century. European influences followed, first with the sighting of New Zealand by Abel Tasman and then the circumnavigation and landing by James Cook, approximately 500 years later. Today New Zealand's society and culture reflects this early British influence. English is the main language spoken in New Zealand, but there is a demand by Maori people to preserve their language and culture, which has become Anglicized since the arrival of the early British settlers. Maori people refer to white people in New Zealand as *Pakeha* and to New Zealand as *Aotearoa*, which means "land of the long white cloud." Today Maori-Pakeha relations are relatively harmonious and there are fewer racial problems in New Zealand than in many other countries with colonial pasts.

New Zealand has a close relationship with Australia and other countries in the South Pacific. Despite this good relationship with Australia there is an intense rivalry on the sports field, and national patriotism does spill over from time to time. Kiwis and Aussies love to have a "dig" at each other; this is similar to the American-Canadian rivalry.

—David Hair, Gisborne, New Zealand

Area: 103,736 square miles (about the size of Colorado). **Population:** 3,308,000. **Population density:** 31 inhabitants per square mile. **Capital:** Wellington (population 148,000). **Largest city:** Auckland (population 850,000). **Language:** English, Maori (both official). **Religion:** Protestant, Roman Catholic. **Per capita income:** US$12,200. **Currency:** New Zealand dollar. **Literacy rate:** 99%. **Average daily temperature:** Wellington: June, 48°; December, 58°. **Average number of days with precipitation:** Wellington: June, 17; December, 12.

TRAVEL

U.S. citizens will need a passport and an onward or return ticket; for stays of less than three months, a visa is not required. Proof of sufficient funds may also be required. For specific requirements, check with the **Embassy of New Zealand**, 37 Observatory Circle NW, Washington, DC 20008; (202) 328-4800. There is also a Consulate General of New Zealand in Los Angeles.

Getting Around

The main air carriers in New Zealand are Air New Zealand and Ansett New Zealand. Ansett's **New Zealand Airpass** coupons permit a number of flights at discount prices. For example, a coupon good for three flights costs NZ$399 (US$220); eight flights cost NZ$897 (US$500). The pass must be purchased in the U.S. before departure. Those planning on a lot of air time within both Australia and New Zealand will want to check out Ansett's **Down Under Discount Deals** (see page 455). Contact Ansett at (800) 366-1300.

Mount Cook Airline flies mainly to tourist destinations such as Mount Cook and Rotorua. The **Kiwi Air Pass**, good for 30 days, allows one trip in each direction on each route Mount Cook flies for US$525.

Unless you're in a hurry, it's best to use ground transportation. Going by **train** and **bus** is inexpensive and gives you a chance to take in New Zealand's beauty. InterCity operates New Zealand's rail network, as well as the Wellington-Picton **ferry** across the Cook Strait. Express trains link Auckland and Wellington on North Island, and Christchurch, Dunedin, and Invercargill on South Island. The trains are fast and reliable, but buses travel to far more destinations. Most budget travelers take advantage of both. A good way to do this is to purchase **InterCity's Travelpass**, which provides transportation on InterCity trains, buses, and ferries on a set number of days. You can have 8 days of travel in 14 for NZ$396 (US$220), or 15 days in 22 for NZ$492 (US$275). The Travelpass can be purchased in New Zealand, or in the U.S. at a 10-percent discount through **Downunder Direct**, 6 West Lancaster Avenue, Ardmore, PA 19003; (800) 642-6224. Downunder Direct also offers a unique car rental plan which includes complete camping equipment, including gas stove and all cooking utensils.

The **Kiwi Coach Pass** provides bus service on Mount Cook Landline buses for varying numbers of days, ranging from 7 days within an 11-day period for US$176 to 33 days within a 45-day period for US$396. Travelers wanting to see New Zealand as well as Australia should consider the Down Under Pass, which allows travel on Australian Coachlines and New Zealand's Mt. Cook Line. The pass costs from A$450 (US$301) for 9 days to A$1,419 (US$950) for 45 days.

New Zealand's road system is exceptionally well maintained, except in a few very mountainous areas. Traffic is generally light and roads are well marked, but remember to drive on the *left* side of the road. Gasoline prices are high but controlled by the government so that the price is the same at every station in the country. While all the major **car** rental firms are represented in New Zealand, you'll probably be better off with less-expensive local agencies. Most rental contracts include unlimited mileage.

Bicycling is becoming an increasingly popular way to see New Zealand. The terrain is hilly but the country is compact and the climate is mild. Bicycles may be rented by the hour or the day in most cities, or you can bring yours with you (contact the airlines for more information). An informative guide for the cyclist is *Cycle Touring in New Zealand*, available for $14.95 from The Mountaineers Books (see page 57).

Hitchhiking is popular with students in New Zealand (helpful New Zealanders often give young people rides). Another way to see parts of New Zealand, and one that's popular among young people, is walking, or "tramping" as New Zealanders call it. The most famous trails are the Milford Track (November–March only), which has to be booked through the chief ranger at Fiordland National Park; the Routeburn Track, summer only unless you're experienced; and the Heaphy Track near Waikaremoana.

Eating and Sleeping

There are around 50 **youth hostels** scattered about New Zealand. Youth hostels in New Zealand have no curfew. Hostelling International members are eligible for discounts of up to 50 percent off air and land transportation. For more information, contact Hostelling International/American Youth Hostels (see page 54) or the **Youth Hostels Association of New Zealand** (YHA), PO Box 436, Christchurch 1; (64) 3-379-9970; fax (64) 3-365-4476.

There are also a number of independent hostels catering to backpackers. For information, contact **Budget Backpackers Hostels**, Rainbow Lodge, 99 Titiraupenga Street, Taupo; (64) 7-378-5754. Another independent group is **Backpackers Resorts New Zealand**, Box 452, Nelson; (64) 3-546-7598; fax (64) 3-546-7886.

Students visiting New Zealand during summer vacations (December to March) can usually take advantage of available space at **university dormitories**. This kind of accommodation is inexpensive and often near the center of town. Travel information offices can direct you to local dormitory accommodations. You can also contact Student Travel Services (see "Especially for Students and Young People," below) or consult Campus Travel Service's *US and Worldwide Travel Accommodations Guide* (see page 54). For information on **YMCA** accommodations, contact the Y's Way (see pages 53–54).

Especially for Students and Young People

New Zealand's student travel organization and issuing agency for the International Student Identity Card is **Student Travel Services (STS)**, 10 High Street, PO Box 4156, Auckland; (64) 9-309-9723; fax (64) 9-309-9829.

In addition to the main office, STS has offices in Christchurch, Dunedin, Hamilton, Palmerston North, and Wellington, as well as two others in Auckland. These offices can provide general information, book local tours, arrange accommodations, and sell plane and bus tickets. They can also inform you of discounts available to students throughout the country.

For Further Information

For general tourist information, contact the **New Zealand Tourist Office**, 501 Santa Monica Boulevard, Suite 300, Santa Monica, CA 90401; (800) 388-5494. Probably the most comprehensive guidebook for the budget traveler is the recently updated *New Zealand Handbook*, by Jane King. It can be ordered for $14.95 from Moon Publications. Also good is *New Zealand: A Travel Survival Kit*, available for $15.95 from Lonely Planet Publications. *Insight Guide: New Zealand* is an excellent book to read in preparation for your trip. You can find information on Moon Publications, Lonely Planet, and *Insight Guides* on pages 56–57.

WORK

Getting a Job

In order to get a full-time job in New Zealand, it is necessary to obtain a written offer of employment from the prospective employer. After securing a job offer, a work visa is necessary. For more information, contact the **Embassy of New Zealand** (see "Travel," above) or the **New Zealand Consulate General**, Suite 1350, Tishman Building, 15th Floor, 10960 Wilshire Boulevard, Los Angeles, CA 90024, whichever one is closer to you.

For American students seeking temporary work in New Zealand, the process is much simpler. **CIEE's Work in New Zealand program** gives college and university students the opportunity to seek temporary employment for up to six months between April 1 and October 31. The program is conducted through an agreement with the Immigration Division of the Department of Labour of New Zealand and the Student Travel Services (NZ). To qualify, an individual must be at least 18 years of age, a college or university student, and a U.S. citizen or permanent resident. The cost of the program is $160. Since the work-exchange program began in 1979, more than 1,600 U.S. students have participated, with most doing unskilled outdoor work such as shearing sheep, picking fruit, or working at ski resorts. For more information, contact CIEE's Work Exchanges Department.

Internships/Traineeships

The following program is offered by a member of the Council on International Educational Exchange.

Ohio University. *The Consortium for Overseas Student Teaching.* Student-teaching. Quarter. Sophomores to seniors attending Ohio University only. Contact: Wes Synder, Center for Higher Education and International Programs, 129 McCracken Hall, Athens, OH 45701.

Voluntary Service

For persons interested in voluntary service work, the Year Abroad Program sponsored by the **International Christian Youth Exchange** offers persons ages 18 to 30 voluntary-service opportunities in the fields of health care, education, the environment, construction, and more. See page 25 for more information.

STUDY

The school year in New Zealand extends from early March to late November. According to the New Zealand consulate in New York, the admission of overseas students to New Zealand educational institutions is limited due to the heavy domestic demand for available spots. The Embassy of New Zealand can provide you with a helpful information letter on studying in New Zealand called *New Zealand–United States Educational Contacts*. Below are the study programs offered by institutions that are CIEE members. Unless otherwise noted, consult Appendix I for the addresses where you can write for more information.

Semester and Academic Year

General Studies

Butler University. *University of Auckland.* Calendar year (February to November). Fully integrated program with study possible in all arts and sciences disciplines. Sophomores and juniors with 3.0 GPA and previous study in field of interest. Apply by November 15.

University of Otago. Dunedin, South Island. Calendar year (February to November). Fully integrated program with study possible in all arts and sciences disciplines. Sophomores and juniors with 3.0 GPA and previous study in field of interest. Apply by November 15. Contact: Institute for Study Abroad, Butler University, 4600 Sunset Avenue, Indianapolis, IN 46208-3485; (800) 858-0229.

Education

University of Wisconsin at River Falls. *Overseas Practice Teaching*. Various sites. Fall and spring semesters. Individualized student-teaching experience. Seniors with preparatory education courses. Apply three months before desired teaching time. Contact: Carol LeBreck, Coordinator, Karges Center, UW at River Falls, River Falls, WI 54022; (715) 425-3778/3705.

Summer

General Studies

University of Alabama. *Study Tour of New Zealand*. South Island and Christchurch. Sociology and resource development. First-year college students to graduate students. Apply by April 1.

EXPLORING THE CULTURE OF NEW ZEALAND

Readings

Maurice Shadbolt's *The New Zealanders* (1972) is a collection of enjoyable short stories. Prose and poetry are collected in *An Anthology of New Zealand Writing Since 1945*, edited by MacDonald Jackson and Vincent O'Sullivan. Janet Frame, arguably New Zealand's finest writer, shares her life growing up in a poverty-stricken New Zealand family in *An Angel at My Table* (1984) and *Owls Do Cry* (1982). (Both of these books have been made into excellent films.) As New Zealand's most famous Maori writer, Patricia Grace gives voice to a culture living amidst an alien society. Her short stories have been collected in *Waiariki* (1975) and *The Dream Sleepers and Other Stories* (1980).

Films

The last ten years or so have seen a burgeoning production of full-length fiction and documentary films in New Zealand. These films focus on many of the same themes which currently garner attention in films throughout the world; however, many also deal with questions of race, national identity, and cultural colonialism that are specific to New Zealand.

Two films, *Skin Deep*, by Geoff Steven, and *Came a Hot Friday*, by Ian Mune, provide perspectives on small-town New Zealand. *Skin Deep* exposes the inner workings of a local community through a satire on civic pride. *Came a Hot Friday* steps back to 1949 to give a stylized impression of the "small town" which combines two con men with guns, fast cars, fast women, liquor, and a dash of cultural colonialism.

As with Native Americans and Australian Aborigines, the societal status of New Zealand's Maori is an important and sometimes volatile topic. *Utu*, by Geoff Murphy, is an historical fiction about a Maori warrior rebellion in connection with the Anglo-Maori wars of the 1870s. The documentary *Patu*, by Merata Mita, on the other hand, takes a more contemporary stance by documenting the South African rugby team Springbok's 1981 tour of New Zealand and the opposition, attitudes, and violence it provoked.

WESTERN SAMOA

The lush vegetation of the islands of Western Samoa and their dramatic natural settings are some of the attributes that have always attracted visitors. Some come to admire the beauty of the land and the friendly inhabitants; others come to study its unique Polynesian culture, as did anthropologist Margaret Mead. Still, many others historically have visited the islands hoping to add them to the roster of possessions of specific countries. Although present-day Samoans are descended from Polynesians who arrived more than 2,000 years ago, the West is more familiar with the island's history after the arrival of Europeans in the 18th century. Since then, international powers have fought for control of the islands and the native Samoans have resisted the onslaught of cultural and political domination. The *fa'a Samoa*, or Samoan way, is part of the country's legacy that has withstood the pressure to change and conform to foreign standards. Western Samoa today is a stronghold of Polynesian culture, but also a country shaken by economic crises and trying to balance its traditions with the international trend toward market-oriented economies.

Western Samoa, with an area roughly equivalent to that of Rhode Island, encompasses two larger islands, two smaller ones, and several islets. Along with nearby American Samoa, it is part of the Polynesian Samoa Archipelago, and these two countries share a common history that diverged due to foreign interference. In 1771 the Dutch explorer Jacob Roggeveen was the first European to visit the islands, and the United States and Germany partitioned them in 1899; the U.S. took what became known as American Samoa. Western Samoa was a German colony until 1914, when New Zealand landed troops and seized it until an independent monarchy was established in 1962. Western Samoa's freedom from foreign domination marked the first Polynesian nation to gain its independence in the 20th century. The political and governmental arena of the country today revolves around traditional chiefs who assume most of the responsibilities and power.

Halfway between Hawaii and New Zealand, Western Samoa has close ties to other South Pacific islands such as Tahiti and Tonga. The largest islands of Western Samoa are Savai'i and Upolu, where the capital Apia is situated. Manono and Apolima are smaller and also inhabited. The rest of the smaller islands and islets are inhabited. All of them share a tropical climate with high humidity and little seasonal change. Of volcanic origin, these verdant and luxuriant islands are surrounded by coral reefs that protect the calm shores. Often described by visitors as paradise, the islands' mountains, rain forests, waterfalls, secluded coves, and turquoise beaches support that mystique. The mountainous areas are covered by forests of gigantic tree ferns, hardwoods, and banyan trees. Most of the people live in small coastal villages where they engage in subsistence fishing and agriculture.

With a largely agricultural economy, little if any industry, and a huge foreign debt, Western Samoa is considered a Third World country. But the daily reality of life is more complex than that. The Samoan way of life stresses the communal rather than the individual needs and priorities. While this lifestyle may be considered by some as outdated and backwards, it is also praised for the sense of community of the Samoans. Anthropologists such as Margaret Mead have pointed to a culture attuned with nature, lacking certain of the pressures exhibited by industrialized societies.

—Jonathan Galton, Stockton, Colorado

Official name: Independent State of Western Samoa. **Area:** 1,133 square miles. **Population:** 190,000. **Population density:** 167 inhabitants per square mile. **Capital and largest city:** Apia (pop. 35,000). **Language:** Samoan, English (both official). **Religion:** Protestant, Roman Catholic. **Per capita income:** US$115. **Currency:** Tala. **Literacy rate:** 90%. **Average daily high/low:** Apia: January, 86°F/75°F; June, 85°F/74°F. **Average number of days with precipitation:** Apia: January, 22; June, 7.

TRAVEL

U.S. citizens need a passport, but visas are not required for stays of up to 30 days. For more information, contact the **Western Samoa Mission to the U.N.**, 820 Second Avenue, Suite 800, New York, NY; (212) 599-6196.

Getting Around

Polynesian Airlines operates domestic flights between the islands of Upolu and Savai'i, as well as to nearby American Samoa. **Ferries** also operate regularly among the islands of Western and American Samoa. **Buses** comprise the main form of public transportation, but they often run late. **Car** rentals are easily available on Upolu, but International Driving Permits are not recognized in Western Samoa, so you may be required to obtain a local license. Probably the best way to get around on land is by taxi.

For Further Information

For general tourist information, contact the **Western Samoa Visitors Bureau**, PO Box 882, Apia, Western Samoa. You can also contact the **Western Samoa Trade and Tourism Office**, 465 Kapahula Avenue, Honolulu, HI 96815. A good guide for budget travelers is *Samoa: A Travel Survival Kit*, available for $10.95 from Lonely Planet Publications (see page 56).

STUDY

Below are two study programs offered by a CIEE-member institution. Consult Appendix I for the contact address.

Semester and Academic Year

General Studies

World Learning/School for International Training. *College Semester Abroad.* Apia, Savaii, Manono, and Apolima. Fall and spring semesters. Area studies. Orientation, homestay, field-research seminar, independent-study seminar, field trips. Sophomores to graduate students with 2.5 GPA. Apply by May 7 for fall; October 7 for spring. Contact: College Semester Abroad Admissions at (800) 336-1616.

Summer and Short-Term

General Studies

World Learning/School for International Training. *College Semester Abroad*. Apia, Upolu, and Savaii. Six weeks in summer from late June to early August. Orientation, language study, homestay, and field trip. Sophomores to graduate students with 2.5 GPA. Apply by March 7. Contact: College Semester Abroad Admissions at (800) 336-1616.

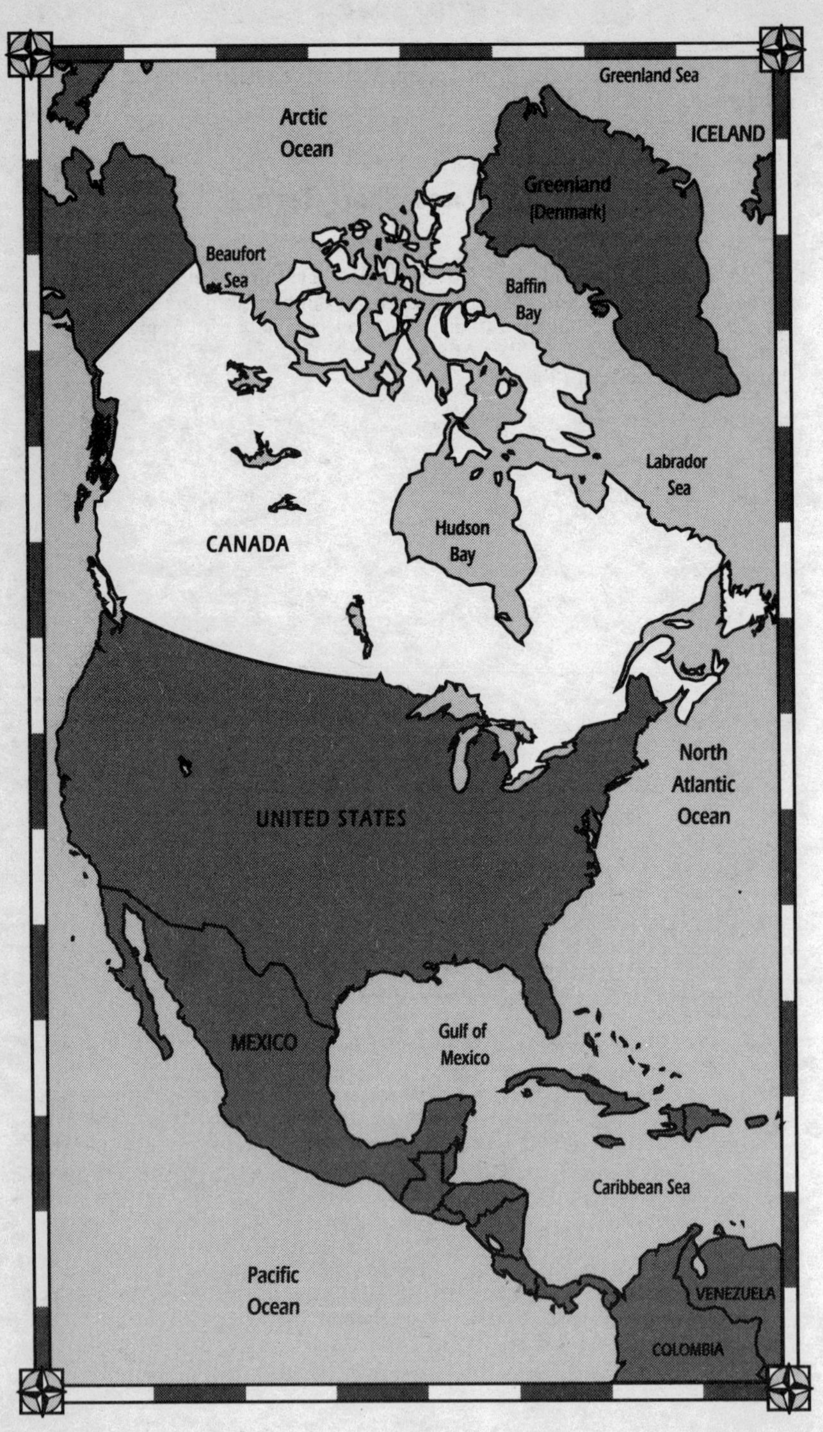

Greenland Sea
Arctic
Ocean
ICELAND
Greenland
(Denmark)
Beaufort
Sea
Baffin
Bay
Labrador
Sea
Hudson
Bay
CANADA
North
Atlantic
Ocean
UNITED STATES
MEXICO
Gulf of
Mexico
Caribbean Sea
Pacific
Ocean
VENEZUELA
COLOMBIA

CHAPTER THIRTEEN

CANADA

Although Canada is sometimes regarded as little more than the United States' 51st state, visitors soon become aware of the unique, refreshing qualities of this beautiful and diverse country. True, the United States and Canada have a lot in common, including many of the same natural features: the fjords of the Pacific coast, Rocky Mountain peaks, craggy Atlantic Ocean inlets, as well as the wheat fields, forests, and lakes in between. But when asked to define their national identity, most Canadians will launch into an explanation of how they differ from Americans. Whether this is symptomatic of an ingrained sense of inferiority or superiority is debatable, but it usually reflects Canadians' sheer practicality more than it does any overt anti-Americanism; while Canada shares much with the U.S., an awareness of the differences between the two countries will help us to understand Canada's uniqueness.

Larger than the U.S. in total area but only a tenth its size in population, Canada is one of the world's largest but least populated nations. This fact, combined with a European sense of social responsibility, is reflected its a high standard of living and clean, uncrowded, well-organized cities. The latter boast heavily subsidized cultural offerings, excellent public transportation, and little of the homelessness and poverty that plague many large American cities.

Someone once quipped that while Canada could have benefited from French culture, British government, and American know-how, it unfortunately was shaped by American culture, French government, and British know-how. Although this is an obvious oversimplification, it is true that Canada's close ties with all three countries are still very much apparent.

In fact, one of the most striking aspects of Canadian society is its diversity. While the American "melting pot" tends to blur cultural differences, Canadian society and governmental legislation have encouraged the country's many immigrant groups to nurture their customs and languages. Established by colonists loyal to the British Empire, Canada has long since dispensed with its political accountability to England, even as English-speaking Canadians maintain great respect for this heritage. At the same time, Canada's official bilingual French-English status has helped keep the French *joie de vivre* alive and well in the French province of Quebec, the Acadian communities of the Maritime Provinces, and other smaller pockets across the country. But the country is more than just a mix of French, British, and U.S. influences; different communities across the continent have become cultural centers for peoples from the Caribbean, Central and Eastern Europe, and the Pacific Rim.

Geography has also shaped Canada's diversity. The remote Yukon and Northwest Territories have a frontier atmosphere to this day. French Canada's geographic and political center, Quebec City, has the pulse and personality of a European capital. Toronto, Canada's fast-paced financial center, is often compared to New York City.

This diversity means that whether your objective is to experience another culture, enjoy stunning scenery, or join in the excitement of a dynamic city, Canada has much to offer. And it's all just across the border.

—Sarah Wood, Brooklyn, New York

Area: 3,849,000 square miles (slightly larger than the U.S.). **Population:** 26,835,500. **Population density:** 7 inhabitants per square mile. **Capital:** Ottawa (pop. 863,000). **Largest city:** Toronto (pop. 3,751,000). **Language:** English, French. **Religion:** Roman Catholic, Protestant. **Per capita income:** US$19,500. **Currency:** Canadian dollar. **Literacy rate:** 99%. **Average daily temperature:** Montreal: June, 66°; December, 21°. **Average number of days with precipitation:** Montreal: June, 11; December, 13.

TRAVEL

If entering Canada from the United States, U.S. citizens don't need a visa for stays of up to six months. However, you must show proof of citizenship, which may be in the form of a passport, driver's license, birth certificate, naturalization papers, or voter's registration. U.S. citizens entering Canada from a third country are required to have a valid passport. For more information, check with the **Canadian Embassy**, 501 Pennsylvania Avenue NW, Washington, DC 20001; (202) 682-1740. Canadian consulates are located in Atlanta, Boston, Buffalo, Chicago, Cleveland, Dallas, Detroit, Los Angeles, Minneapolis, New York, San Francisco, and Seattle.

Getting There

As with domestic travel within both Canada and the U.S., airfares between the two countries are constantly changing. You'll have to shop around a little to get the best deal. Council Travel offices can provide more information and make arrangements for you. Sample fares in effect during the summer of 1993 are listed below.

	One-way	Round-trip
San Francisco–Vancouver	$231	$263
New York–Montreal	$138	$154
Chicago–Toronto	$144	$177

Most visitors from the U.S. arrive by **car**. Crossing the border usually involves few formalities and is done in minutes. However, it's a good idea to pick up a **Nonresident Interprovincial Motor Vehicle Liability Insurance Card** from your insurance agent before you go. Although it is not required by law, it's a help if you run into any problems while you're in the country.

For persons wishing to travel by **train**, Amtrak provides service from the Eastern seaboard to Montreal and Toronto, where connections can be made to Via Rail, Canada's national railroad system. International **bus** service is also provided by Greyhound. Call Amtrak or Greyhound for schedules and fares, or check with a travel agent.

Getting Around

The domestic fare structure of Canadian **airlines** is similar to that in the United States. While none of the major airlines offer domestic air passes, you can arrange low-cost excursion fares with a number of stopovers across the country.

Book in advance to obtain the cheapest fares. Canada's main domestic carriers are **Air Canada**, (800) 776-3000, and **Canadian Airlines**, (800) 426-7000.

One of the most exciting ways to see Canada is by **train**. The 3,000-mile trip from Montreal to Vancouver takes four days and three nights. Other interesting rail trips can be made across the vast wilderness areas of Canada's northern frontier; one such trip is from Winnipeg to Churchill on the icy shores of Hudson Bay. Service is also available to New Brunswick and Nova Scotia. If you plan to travel extensively in Canada by train, you should look into Via Rail's **Canrail Pass**. Valid for 12 days of coach-class travel in a 30-day period, it costs Can$439 (US$334) for young people under 24 traveling during the high season (June 7 to September 30) and Can$299 (US$227) for the remainder of the year (excluding the weeks between December 14 and January 6). Those over 24 pay Can$489 (US$372) and Can$329 (US$250) respectively. Berths for overnight trips will cost extra. For further information, contact Council Travel (see page 00).

Road travel in Canada is another pleasant experience. Because Canada's population remains small in proportion to its land mass, roads and highways are less crowded than they are in the U.S. And the roadsides are not so developed, making for more scenic drives. Bus routes are plentiful and prices are comparable to those in the U.S. Driving your own car will allow you the most freedom. The largest car rental firm in Canada is Tilden Rent-A-Car; for information, call its U.S. affiliate, National Car Rental. Avis, Budget, and Hertz are other major car rental companies in Canada. In Canada most cars rent for a per-day (sometimes a per-week) fixed fee that includes a limited number of free kilometers. However, because unlimited mileage rates are generally not available in Canada, renting a car can be an expensive proposition if you plan to cover a lot of miles. A cheaper alternative might be to rent one in the U.S., where a number of companies still offer unlimited mileage options, and then cross into Canada (make sure the rental contract allows you to take the car across the border).

Ferries ply the waters off Canada's eastern and western coasts, connecting islands to the mainland. One of the newest is the high-speed Royal Sealink Express which runs from Vancouver to Victoria in about two and a half hours.

Canada is a cyclist's dream, though just as in the U.S., you should try to avoid major roads and use secondary routes. The best source of information is the **Canadian Cycling Association**, 1600 James Naismith Drive, Gloucester, Ontario K1B 5N4; (613) 748-5629; fax (613) 748-5692. In addition to numerous free brochures, the Association's available publications include *The Canadian Cycling Association Guide to Bicycling in Canada*, *The Canadian Rockies Bicycling Guide*, *The Great Canadian Bicycle Trail*, and *Newfoundland by Bicycle*. Call for current prices.

For those who like the great outdoors, another option is **hiking** or backpacking in Canada's spectacular national parks and vast wilderness areas. The **Sierra Club**'s several regional offices organize backpacking and camping expeditions. Contact the national office at 420-1 Nicholas Street, Ottawa, Ontario K1N 7B7. Another organization that organizes outdoor activities is the **Alpine Club of Canada**, PO Box 2040, Canmore, Alberta T0L 0M0; (403) 678-3200.

Eating and Sleeping

There are many **youth hostels** throughout Canada. For more information, contact Hostelling International/American Youth Hostels (see page 54) or

Hostelling International—Canada, 1600 James Naismith Drive, Suite 608, Gloucester, Ontario K1B 5N4; (613) 748-5638; fax (613) 748-5750. For a list of independent hostels in Canada, contact **Backpackers Hostels Canada**, c/o Thunder Bay International Hostel, Longhouse Village, RR 13, Thunder Bay, Ontario P7B 5E4; (807) 983-2042; (807) 982-2914.

Inexpensive lodging can also be found at most **YMCAs** and **YWCAs** across Canada. A listing of residences can be obtained from the National Council of YMCAs of Canada, 2160 Yonge Street, Toronto, M4S 2A9 Ontario; (416) 485-9447. The YWCA of Canada can be reached at 80 Gerrard Street East, Toronto, Ontario M5B 1G6; (416) 593-9886; fax (416) 971-8084. **Note:** Most YWCAs accommodate only women. In addition, most Canadian universities offer affordable **dormitory lodgings** from mid-May to mid-August; you can get information on these from Travel CUTS (see "Especially for Students and Young People," below) or from provincial government tourist offices.

There are virtually unlimited opportunities for **camping** in Canada. You can get specific information on sites and facilities from the various provincial government tourist offices (see "For Further Information," below). These offices can also give you information on affordable bed-and-breakfasts.

Especially for Students and Young People

Canada's major student travel organization and issuer of the International Identity Student Card is **Travel CUTS (Canadian Universities Travel Service)**, 187 College Street, Toronto, M5T 1P7 Ontario; (416) 977-5228; fax (416) 977-7112. Travel CUTS has 35 offices throughout Canada, including Burnaby, Calgary, Edmonton, Guelph, Halifax, Montreal, Ottawa, Quebec City, Saskatoon, Sudbury, Vancouver, Victoria, Waterloo, and Winnipeg. They can give you information about student/youth discounts, cheap accommodations, and budget airfares.

For Further Information

You can obtain general tourist information from Canadian consulates (see "Travel" for city locations) but the best sources of information are the various provincial tourist authorities listed below.

- **Alberta Tourism**, (800) 661-8888
- **Tourism British Columbia**, (800) 663-6000
- **Travel Manitoba**, (800) 665-0040
- **Newfoundland and Labrador Tourism**, (800) 563-6353
- **New Brunswick Department of Tourism**, (800) 561-0123
- **Northwest Territories Tourism**, (800) 661-0788
- **Nova Scotia Tourism and Culture**, (800) 341-7540
- **Ontario Travel**, (800) 668-2746
- **Prince Edward Island Department of Tourism**, (800) 565-0267
- **Tourisme Quebec**, (800) 363-7777
- **Tourism Saskatchewan**, (800) 667-7191
- **Tourism Yukon**, (800) 661-0788

The best general guide to the country is *Canada: A Travel Survival Kit*, newly revised and available for $19.95 from Lonely Planet Publications. *The Real Guide: Canada* ($15) is also good, but lacks the information on nature and history that Lonely Planet's book offers. Those planning to explore Canada west of the Rockies will find lots of useful information in *British Columbia*

Handbook and *Alaska-Yukon Handbook*, both available for $13.95 from Moon Publications. For information on the publishers of all these books, see pages 56–57.

WORK

Getting a Job

A work permit is required for regular full-time employment in Canada; application for the permit must be made from outside the country. In most cases, the permit will not be granted unless it is determined that no permanent resident of Canada is qualified for the job. For the specific requirements and procedures, contact the Canadian embassy or any Canadian consulate.

For college and university students, however, seeking summer employment in Canada, the process is much easier. CIEE, in cooperation with the Canadian Federation of Students, can obtain permission for you to work in Canada for a period of up to six months (May 1 to October 31). In addition to work authorization, CIEE gives participants information on living and working in Canada and details on the best way to find work. Past participants have worked in hotels, done hospitality work, housekeeping, conservation work, and reforestation, among other things. You can expect to make enough money to cover your daily living expenses and usually save something toward the cost of travel once you finish your job. To be eligible, you must be a U.S. citizen of at least 18 years of age, enrolled as a full-time student in an accredited U.S. college or university, and residing in the U.S. at the time of application. There is a $160 fee for the service; applications are available from **CIEE's Work Exchanges Department** (see page 17).

Internships/Traineeships

A programs offered by a member of the Council on International Educational Exchange is listed below.

Association for International Practical Training. *IAESTE Trainee Program.* On-the-job training for undergraduate and graduate students in technical fields such as engineering, computer science, agriculture, architecture, mathematics, and the physical and natural sciences. See page 19 for more information.

Voluntary Service

CIEE places young people in voluntary-service **workcamps** in Canada organized by the Canadian Bureau for International Education (CBIE). At these workcamps, volunteers from various countries work together on projects such as helping disabled children, providing social services, or helping with the maintenance and construction of recreational facilities. Volunteers receive room and board in return for their labor and must be 18 years of age or older. The applications of U.S. residents are processed by CIEE. For more information, contact the International Voluntary Service Department at CIEE.

Frontiers Foundation/Operation Beaver, 2615 Danforth Avenue, Suite 203, Toronto, Ontario M4C 1L6, sponsors voluntary-service projects throughout the year. The projects, which last from 3 to 18 months, usually involve renovation/construction (low-cost housing, community centers, schools) or recreation programs. Participants from all countries are eligible, but you must be at least

18 years old. Room, board, and transportation (within Canada) to and from the project site are provided.

STUDY

Many U.S. students enroll in Canadian universities and colleges each year. If you're planning to become one of them, you'll need special student authorization. You can get this from the Immigration Division of any Canadian embassy or consulate near you, but first you must present a letter of acceptance from the Canadian school that you will be attending, in addition to proof of funds. If you are going to study in the province of Quebec, a certificate of acceptance from the Quebec Immigration Service is also required. The **Canadian Bureau for International Education (CBIE)** also provides information for foreign students in Canada. Issued biennially, its *International Students Handbook* includes information on everything from Canadian political history to how to obtain housing in Canada. It can be ordered for Can$9 (about US$7) from CBIE, 85 Albert Street, Suite 1400, Ottawa, Ontario K1P 6A4; (613) 237-4820; fax (613) 237-1300. CBIE also offers free of charge the following leaflets: *Study in Canada: Information for International Students* (secondary and post-secondary levels); *Awards for Study in Canada* (graduate level and internships); and *Learning English or French in Canada*, published by the Council of Second Language Programs.

The Canadian Embassy has established a **Canadian Studies Graduate Student Fellowship** that enables doctoral candidates to complete their dissertations in Canada. Details are available from the Academic Relations Section, Canadian Embassy, 501 Pennsylvania Avenue NW, Washington, DC 20001; (202) 682-1740; fax (202) 682-7791.

The following are the educational programs offered by CIEE-member institutions. Unless otherwise noted, consult Appendix I for the addresses where you can write for further information.

Semester and Academic Year

General Studies

International Student Exchange Program (ISEP). Semester and academic year. Direct reciprocal exchange between U.S. universities and institutions in Calgary (Alberta); St. Catherines and Sudbury (Ontario); and Regina (Saskatchewan). Full curriculum options. Rolling admissions. Open only to students at ISEP-member institutions. Contact ISEP for list of members.

State University of New York at Plattsburgh. *Study in Toronto*. University of Toronto. Semester and academic year. Sophomores to seniors with 3.0 GPA. Apply by April 1 for fall and academic year; October 20 for spring.

Study in Quebec City. Université Laval. Semester and academic year. Sophomores to seniors with 2.5 GPA. Apply by April 1 for fall and academic year; October 15 for spring.

Study in Montreal. McGill University. Semester and academic year. Sophomores to seniors with 3.0 GPA. Apply by April 1 for fall and academic year; October 15 for spring.

Study in Ottawa. Carleton University. Semester and academic year. Sophomores to seniors with 3.0 GPA. Apply by April 1 for fall and academic year; October 15 for spring.

Contact: Study in Canada Programs, Center for the Study of Canada, SUNY at Plattsburgh, Plattsburgh, NY 12901; (518) 565-2086.

French Language and Canadian Culture

University of Iowa. *CIC Summer Study Program in Quebec*. Quebec City. Six weeks in summer. Study at the Université Laval. Offered in conjunction with the Committee on Institutional Cooperation. French-language study. Sophomores to seniors with 3.0 GPA and one year of college French. Apply by March 1.

Summer and Short-Term

Business

Michigan State University. *The Global Economy: Doing Business in Quebec*. July and August. Six-week program in business environment and practices, labor and industrial relations, political and economic climate in Quebec, and French language. Sophomores to seniors. Apply by April 15. Contact: Office of Overseas Study, 108 International Center, Michigan State University, East Lansing, MI 48824-1035; (517) 353-8920.

Education

State University of New York College at Brockport. *Dalhousie University Physical Education Exchange*. Halifax, Nova Scotia. Fall and spring semesters. Juniors and seniors with physical education major with 2.5 GPA. Apply by February 15 for fall; November 1 for spring. Contact: Office of International Education, SUNY College at Brockport, Brockport, NY 14420; (716) 395-2119.

French Language and Canadian Culture

Eastern Michigan University. *Intensive French in Québec*. Chicoutimi. Summer. Five-week language immersion program at University of Québec for beginning- to advanced-level students; additional courses in Québecoise culture. Homestays and excursions. First-year college students to graduate students. Apply by April 1. Contact: (800) 777-3541.

State University of New York at Plattsburgh. *French Immersion in the Summer*. Montreal, Quebec City, or Chicoutimi. Six-week sessions. High-school graduates entering college to graduate students in good academic standing. Apply by April 1. Contact: Study in Canada Programs, Center for the Study of Canada, SUNY at Plattsburgh, Plattsburgh, NY 12901; (518) 565-2086.

General Studies

University of New Orleans. *UNO Quebec Program*. Quebec. Five weeks in summer. First-year college students to graduate students. Apply by April 1.

Health and Medicine

State University of New York College at Brockport. *Comparative Health Systems Overseas Study Program*. Toronto. Summer. Graduate students in health administration with 2.5 GPA. Apply by May 1. Contact: Office of International Education, SUNY College at Brockport, Brockport, NY 14420; (716) 395-2119.

Natural Sciences

Michigan State University. Banff, Jasper, Kootenay, and Yoho national parks. Summer. Day trips and backpacking excursions from base camps to observe geology and ecology of region. Undergraduates. Apply by April 15. Contact: Office of Overseas Study, 108 International Center, Michigan State University, East Lansing, MI 48824-1035; (517) 353-8920.

EXPLORING CANADIAN CULTURE

Readings

Margaret Atwood is probably Canada's best-known contemporary writer. Her novel *Cat's Eye* (1989) focuses on an artist as she relives her Toronto childhood. In *The Handmaid's Tale* (1986), Atwood projects a futuristic North America dominated by patriarchial religious fundamentalists. Alice Munro, by contrast, writes about life in small rural Ontario towns in books such as *Lives of Girls and Women* (1971) and *Who Do You Think You Are?* (1978). Her short stories in *The Moons of Jupiter* are set in rural and urban Canada. Another contemporary Canadian writer, Robertson Davies, uses Canada and the character of its people in such novels as *Fifth Business* (1970), *The Rebel Angels* (1982), and *What's Bred in the Bone* (1985), as metaphors for the modern world and its more bizarre and disturbing aspects. Pierre Berton's novel *Why We Act Like Canadians* (1982), scrutinizes Canadian-American relations through a collection of letters written by a Canadian to an American friend.

Canada's multiculturalism is echoed in the mosiac of its literature. *Diamond Jubilee*, by John Chalmers and others, is a set of three anthologies of Alberta writers that includes works from many of the fifty identifiable ethnic groups in Alberta. Mordecai Richler, a popular Jewish Montreal writer, is another important Canadian literary figure. His latest novel, *Solomon Gursky Was Here* (1990) is a hilarious parody of an established Jewish Montreal family; *Home Sweet Home: My Canadian Album* (1984) is a lighthearted collection of his personal reminiscences.

French Canadian writers include Marie-Claire Blais (*A Season in the Life of Emmanuel*, 1966) and Roche Carrier (*The Boxing Match*, 1990). Anne Hebert is generally regarded as Canada's most important French poet of the 20th century (*Selected Poems*, 1987).

For a view of Canada from the eyes of an outsider, read *Maple Leaf Rag* (1988), by Stephen Brook. Brook is an Englishman who travels across Canada noting his perceptions humorously in this tongue-in-cheek travelogue.

Films

The bright lights of Hollywood have long drawn Canadian directors and actors southward, integrating them into the U.S. film industry. However, Canada's film community has recently been given a shot in the arm by a new crop of young filmmakers working north of the border. Toronto and Vancouver are new production centers for North American film. *Jesus of Montreal* (1989) is the most recent film by Canada's premier director, Denys Arcand. Combining weighty religious imagery, striking cinematography, and a complex play-within-a-play format, the story surrounds a group of Canadian actors and actresses who decide to perform a passion play and meet with resistance from various Canadian religious and social groups. Arcand's earlier film, *The Decline of the American Empire* (1986) is a lighter sexual comedy.

Another top Canadian director is Patricia Rozema. Her film *I've Heard the Mermaids Singing* (1987) is a whimsical comedy about an awkward "temp" worker in Montreal with a penchant for photography. Jacques Benoit's *How to Make Love to a Negro Without Getting Tired*, also set in Montreal, is a satire about interracial relationships. The top avant-garde director in Canada is Atom Egoyan; *Speaking Parts* is a bizarre, well-made film. Yves Simoneau's *Perfectly Normal* (1990) is another recent Canadian release. For a glimpse into life in rural Alberta in the 1940s, see *Bye Bye Blues* (1990), directed by Anne Wheeler. The film revolves around a middle-aged woman and the survival tactics she embraces when her husband becomes a POW in the Second World War.

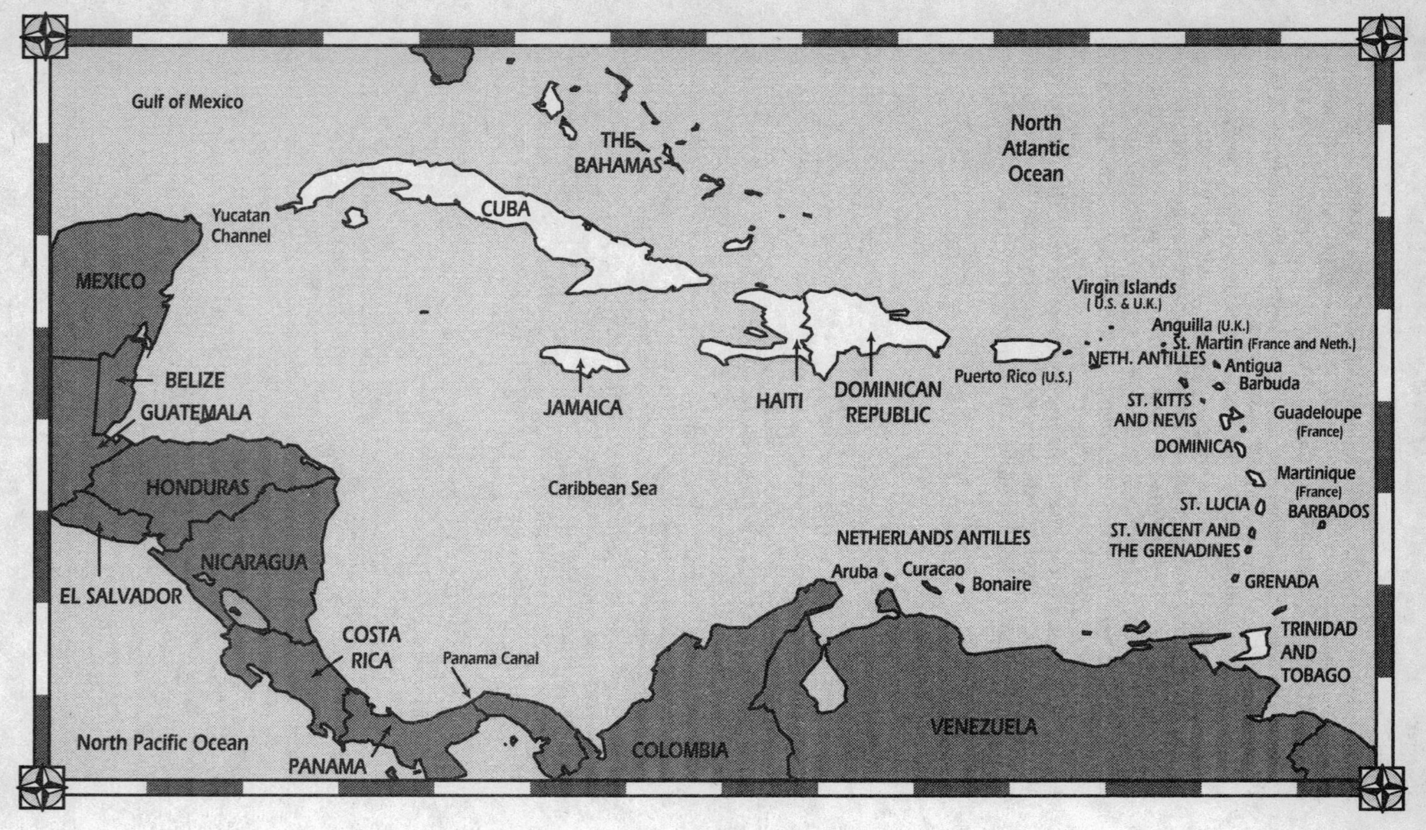
Gulf of Mexico
THE BAHAMAS
North Atlantic Ocean
Yucatan Channel
CUBA
MEXICO
Virgin Islands (U.S. & U.K.)
Anguilla (U.K.)
St. Martin (France and Neth.)
NETH. ANTILLES
Antigua
Barbuda
BELIZE
Puerto Rico (U.S.)
GUATEMALA
JAMAICA
HAITI
DOMINICAN REPUBLIC
ST. KITTS AND NEVIS
Guadeloupe (France)
DOMINICA
HONDURAS
Caribbean Sea
Martinique (France)
ST. LUCIA
BARBADOS
NETHERLANDS ANTILLES
ST. VINCENT AND THE GRENADINES
NICARAGUA
Aruba
Curacao
Bonaire
EL SALVADOR
GRENADA
COSTA RICA
Panama Canal
TRINIDAD AND TOBAGO
North Pacific Ocean
VENEZUELA
COLOMBIA
PANAMA

CHAPTER FOURTEEN

THE CARIBBEAN

Pristine beaches and crystal waters whose shimmering surface conceals a world of coral reefs teeming with aquatic life; tropical forests alive with the sounds of parrots; fresh-grilled fish and the rhythmic lilt of reggae music—these are a few of the images that come to mind when we think of the Caribbean. Indeed, for watersports enthusiasts and plain old beach bums alike, the Caribbean seems like paradise on earth. But as tourism thrives in this area of the world, many forget the underlying complexities of the region.

From the arrival of Columbus, such native peoples as the Arawaks and Caribs fared badly. Those that were not exterminated intermarried with African slaves and European colonizers. In fact, the entire population of the Caribbean islands has essentially been imported from another place at one time or another. But it is the varying mixture of these different races that has created such unique cultures among these many islands. With English-, French-, Spanish-, and Dutch-speaking populations, it would be misleading to point to a unified Caribbean identity; yet while the islands each have their own personalities, common threads in their histories have begun to weave a single Caribbean consciousness.

Although Haiti was the first country to gain its independence in the early 19th century, many islands in the region remain under U.S., British, French, and Dutch control. However, in recent years more of the islands of the Caribbean have become independent states; there are now thirteen independent island nations in the region. The newest Caribbean nations include Antigua and Barbuda, St. Kitts and Nevis, St. Lucia, and St. Vincent and the Grenadines.

Once, this part of the world brought great wealth to the colonial powers whose slave labor produced agricultural products like sugar for consumption in Europe. Today agriculture has been supplanted by tourism as the primary source of income on most islands. One exception is Cuba, which fights an uphill battle against a U.S. trade embargo. In general, Caribbean islanders have welcomed the influx of tourists; but in some areas where the contrast between wealthy visitors and less well-off locals is glaringly apparent, there is some latent hostility.

Not surprisingly, given its proximity to the area, the U.S. has a long history of involvement in the Caribbean, most brutally exemplified by its ill-explained 1983 invasion of Grenada. Today, the U.S. finds itself embroiled in faltering negotiations with the military government of Haiti over the restoration of that country's democratically elected president, Jean-Bertrand Aristide. Yet only a handful of Americans fully understand their nation's historic role in the region.

Few regions offer so much to discover. In addition to the stunning beauty of these islands and the seas that surround them, there is a world of history and intriguing cultures to explore. Yet although relatively few Americans head to the Caribbean to study or work, a variety of study and work opportunities do exist. Choosing to take advantage of these will be rewarded by a greater understanding of the nations of this fascinating and easily accessible region—one you'll want to return to again and again.

Getting There

It's easy to get a flight to the Caribbean from the United States; a variety of U.S. and Caribbean airlines provide nonstop service to the larger islands.

Miami and New York are the main gateways but nonstop flights are also available from a number of other U.S. cities. However, to get to some of the smaller, less-visited islands you may have to fly to a major international hub such as San Juan, Puerto Rico, and change planes. APEX fares are one of the cheapest ways to go, but be sure to check the ads in the travel section of a large Sunday paper for special promotional fares (see Chapter Five for a general explanation of airfares). Sample *one-way* fares in effect during the summer of 1993 are listed below. More information is available at Council Travel offices (see listing on pages xiii–xvi).

Miami–San Juan	$159	New York–Santo Domingo	$165
Miami–Nassau	$ 65	New Orleans–Kingston	$259

For persons planning a short-term stay (one week or less) at a tourist destination in the Caribbean, the cheapest way of traveling is to buy a **package** that includes airfare and accommodations. Many airlines serving the Caribbean offer a wide variety of packages; some even include low-cost car rentals. Most package deals give you the choice of a range of accommodations from budget to luxury categories. Since tour operators can make discount volume purchases, packages are generally cheaper than making your own arrangements. In fact, Council Travel arranges special low-cost spring-break packages geared toward students and teachers interested in making their vacation getaway an international experience. Check with a Council Travel office or look in the Sunday travel section of any major newspaper for more information on a wide range of Caribbean packages. Also, keep in mind the fact that airfares and room rates fluctuate widely with the changing of the seasons; July, August and the pre-Christmas season have the lowest rates.

Another way of getting to the Caribbean is by ship. A number of cruise ships depart for Caribbean destinations from Miami, Fort Lauderdale (Port Everglades), and other U.S. ports. Although cruise ships no longer cater just to the retired and wealthy, they are definitely not for those who want maximum contact with local cultures.

Getting Around

Island-hopping in the Caribbean can be done by either airplane or boat. A number of **airlines** serve the larger islands and the major tourist destinations, and smaller airlines provide scheduled service to even the smaller and more remote islands. Among the major regional airlines that serve the region are Liat and BWIA, both of which offer passes that can be bought in the West Indies.

Hundreds of cruise ships ply the Caribbean, but most of these are total vacations in themselves, not simply means of transportation. However, most groups of islands are connected by regular local **boat** service. For example, from Tortola, British Virgin Islands you can find frequent boat service to many other of the Virgin Islands (both British and U.S.) and from St. Maarten, Netherlands Antilles, you can catch boats to nearby French, Dutch, and British islands. Another option is to ask around the port area for information about crewing on a yacht. Unique to this part of the world and the South Pacific, a wide array of private yachts are often in need of extra crew and willing to take on island-hopping travelers. Crew members usually work for free and share the cost of food and other necessities. It helps to have some knowledge of sailing, but the most necessary factor is an outgoing personality.

From the U.S., arrangements can easily be made to visit any country of the region except **Cuba**. Americans are not barred from traveling to Cuba, but Treasury Department restrictions on U.S. travel agents, airlines, and individual citizens have made travel to Cuba difficult, unless one enters through a third country, such as Mexico or Jamaica. U.S. journalists, some researchers, and graduate degree candidates, as well as people with family on the island are exempt from these restrictions and can make arrangements through one authorized agency, Marazul Tours, 250 West 57th Street, Suite 1311, New York, NY 10107; (800) 223-5334. Others will need to make their travel arrangements through a travel agency or airline in a third country such as Canada or Mexico. To obtain a visa to visit Cuba, U.S. citizens need to apply to the Cuban Interests Section at the Embassy of Switzerland, 2630 16th Street NW, Washington, DC 20009; (202) 797-8518. A good travel guide is *Getting to Know Cuba* ($14.95), by Jane McManus, published by St. Martin's Press.

For Further Information

The U.S. Department of State publishes *Tips for Travelers to the Caribbean*, available free from the Superintendent of Documents, U.S. Government Printing Office, Washington, DC 20402. The most comprehensive guidebook to the region is the *Caribbean Islands Handbook* ($22), published in Britain and distributed in the United States by Prentice Hall. *Fielding's Caribbean* ($15), by Margaret Zellers, is also excellent, although not targeted to the budget traveler. Another good guide is *Frommer's Caribbean* ($18), also published by Prentice Hall. Those seeking to really get away from it all will enjoy Burl Willes's *Undiscovered Islands of the Caribbean*, available for $14.95 from John Muir Publications (see page 57).

Anguilla, the British Virgin Islands, Cayman Islands, Montserrat, and the Turks and Caicos comprise the British West Indies. U.S. citizens need proof of citizenship, photo identification, an onward/return ticket, and proof of sufficient funds for stays of up to three months. For further information, contact the **Embassy of the United Kingdom**, 3100 Massachusetts Avenue NW, Washington, DC 20008; (202) 462-1340.

Information on entry requirements of other countries not listed in this section can be obtained from the following addresses. They can also tell you where to find tourist information.

- **Antigua and Barbuda:** Embassy of Antigua and Barbuda, 3400 International Drive NW, Suite 4M, Washington, DC 20008; (202) 362-5122
- **Barbados:** Embassy of Barbados, 2144 Wyoming Avenue NW, Washington, DC 20008; (202) 939-9200
- **Dominica:** Consulate of the Commonwealth of Dominica, 820 Second Avenue, Suite 900, New York, NY 10017; (212) 599-8478
- **Grenada:** Embassy of Grenada, 1701 New Hampshire Avenue NW, Washington, DC 20009; (202) 265-2561.
- **Haiti:** Embassy of Haiti, 2311 Massachusetts Avenue NW, Washington, DC 20008; (202) 332-4090
- **St. Kitts and Nevis:** Embassy of St. Kitts and Nevis, 2100 M Street NW, Suite 608, Washington, DC 20037; (202) 833-3550
- **St. Lucia:** Embassy of St. Lucia, 2100 M Street NW, Suite 309, Washington, DC 20037; (202) 463-7378
- **St. Vincent and the Grenadines:** Embassy of St. Vincent and the Grenadines,

1717 Massachusetts Avenue NW, Suite 102, Washington, DC 20036; (202) 462-7806
- **Trinidad and Tobago:** Embassy of Trinidad and Tobago, 1708 Massachusetts Avenue NW, Washington, DC 20036; (202) 467-6490

Study in the Caribbean Region

In the individual country sections that follow, you'll find additional study programs listed. In this section we've listed only the study programs of CIEE-members institutions that take place in more than one country of the region. Unless otherwise noted, consult Appendix I for the addresses where you can write for further information.

Summer and Short-Term

International Relations

Michigan State University. *Summer School in the Caribbean.* Barbados, Trinidad, Tobago, and Guyana. Political science, sociology, and international relations. Sophomores to seniors. Apply by April 15. Contact: Office of Overseas Study, Room 108 International Center, Michigan State University, East Lansing, MI 48824-1035; (517) 353-8920.

Natural Sciences

Michigan State University. *Natural Science in the Caribbean.* British and U.S. Virgin Islands. Winter break (mid-December to early January). Environmental field studies by direct observation and from texts and lectures. Undergraduates. Apply by November 30. Contact: Office of Overseas Study, Michigan State University, Room 108 International Center, East Lansing, MI 48824-1035; (517) 353-8920.

Portland State University. *Natural History of the Virgin Islands.* British and U.S. Virgin Islands. Summer. Reef and shore biology and dynamics. High-school seniors to college graduates with four quarters of biology or geography. Apply by May 9.

BAHAMAS

Beginning just 50 miles off the coast of Florida, the 700 islands of the Commonwealth of the Bahamas are the vacation destination of three million tourists a year. Tourists are so important to the economy of the Bahamas that they provide nearly 70 percent of the country's gross national product. This has produced a standard of living well above most Third World countries. Unfortunately, tourism is not a stable industry, and the Bahamas' reliance on it makes its economy extremely vulnerable to volatile market conditions; a warm winter or a recession in North America can keep tourists away and instantly affect every Bahamian pocketbook. The government has attempted to diversify the economy, but a scarcity of natural resources—the sun, sea, and beautiful beaches excepted—makes it unlikely that other industries will soon replace tourism as the economic engine of the Bahamas.

Bahamian coral sand beaches may be the best known part of the islands, but they are certainly not the most interesting part. Foreign visitors with a keen eye for cultural nuances will detect in Bahamian culture a rich mosaic concocted from the historical blending of elements from Africa, England, the United States, and the rest of the Caribbean. Junkanoo music from the slave era and colorful parades mix with British-derived government and legal systems—complete with judges in traditional wigs—which in turn blend with American-style business practices. West Indian calypso and reggae music share the airwaves with Miami television and radio stations.

Politics in the Bahamas is worthy of special attention. The Bahamas has one of the oldest parliaments in the Western Hemisphere; its House of Assembly has governed the islands for over 300 years. Visitors are welcome to listen to the parliamentary debates in the historic House of Assembly building in downtown Nassau. Former Prime Minister Lynden O. Pindling brought political independence to the Bahamas in 1973, though the Bahamas remains a member of the British Commonwealth of Nations.

Although the congested city of Nassau with its mixture of British colonial and American modern architecture is the center of Bahamian society and home to 65 percent of the 250,000 Bahamian citizens, foreign visitors can learn much about the cultural roots of the Bahamas by visiting some of the small settlements on Abaco, Andros, Eleuthera, and other islands. Inexpensive mail boats (passengers welcomed) regularly ply the aquamarine sea between the 20 or so inhabited islands. It was on one of these islands—probably Samana Cay—that Columbus first stepped ashore in the Western Hemisphere, and it is in such places that the subsequent history of colonization, slavery, and emancipation can best be appreciated. A visit to a small settlement church or a boat-building shop will introduce visitors to two more important features of Bahamian life: religion and the sea. Down-home religion and the isolation imposed by the surrounding ocean have produced a society which, though modern, retains many of the close-knit qualities of human relationships that people usually ascribe only to the good old days. In the Bahamas, however, the old and the new live side by side.

—Dean W. Collinwood, Bountiful, Utah

Official name: Commonwealth of the Bahamas. **Area:** 5,380 square miles (about the size of Connecticut). **Population:** 251,000. **Population density:** 48 inhabitants per square mile. **Capital:** Nassau. **Largest city:** New Providence (population 171,000). **Language:** English. **Religion:** Protestant, Roman Catholic. **Per capita income:** US$7,178. **Currency:** Bahamian dollar. **Literacy rate:** 95%. **Average daily temperature:** Nassau: June, 80°F; December, 71°F. **Average number of days with precipitation:** Nassau: June, 12; December, 6.

TRAVEL

U.S. citizens do not need a visa for stays of up to eight months. However, proof of citizenship such as a birth certificate or passport is required, as is an onward or return ticket. With birth certificates, two additional forms of ID are necessary, one with a photo. For specific details, contact the **Embassy of the**

Bahamas, 2220 Massachusetts Avenue NW, Washington, DC 20008; (202) 319-2660. There are also Bahamian consulates in New York and Miami.

Getting Around

The Bahamas is probably the most accessible country to travelers from the United States after Canada and Mexico. Grand Bahama, for example, is only 60 miles from the east coast of Florida. In fact, from some islands it's easier to get to Florida than to Nassau, the nation's capital and largest city.

Getting around the Bahamas, on the other hand, is not easy except by **air**. Even by air, however, service to some of the less-visited islands is infrequent and often means going through either Nassau or Miami. Bahamas Air and Helda Air operate scheduled flights between various islands. In addition, inexpensive ferry service (which takes up to 16 hours) connects Nassau (New Providence Island) and Freeport (Grand Bahama), the nation's two main cities and tourist centers. A slow but interesting way of getting to other islands is via the **mail boats**, which carry passengers, mail, and merchandise. Another travel option is chartering a yacht and mapping your own course around the islands.

Cars can be rented in the main tourist resorts, as can bicycles, mopeds, and motorcycles. Bicycles are especially well-suited for the islands, since most are small and the terrain is flat. Driving is on the left-hand side of the road.

For Further Information

General tourist information is available from the **Bahamas Tourist Office**, 150 East 52nd Street, New York, NY 10022; (212) 758-2777; fax (212) 753-6531. There are also Bahamas Tourist Offices in Boston, Charlotte, Chicago, Dallas, Detroit, Houston, Los Angeles, Miami, Philadelphia, San Francisco, and Washington, DC.

One of the better ones is Fodor's *The Bahamas*, which comes in both a pocket-size and regular edition ($10.95). Birnbaum's *Caribbean, Bermuda & Bahamas 1991* ($14.95) includes a comprehensive guide to the region and maps. *The Caribbean Islands Handbook* ($22), published by Prentice Hall, also has a lengthy section on the Bahamas.

WORK

Getting a Job

It is necessary to obtain a work permit in order to work in the Bahamas. The prospective employer applies for the permit prior to the applicant entering the country. Positions are only granted to foreigners if there are no qualified Bahamians available. For more information, contact the **Ministry of Public Safety and Immigration**, PO Box N-3002, Nassau, Bahamas.

STUDY

If you wish to apply directly to a Bahamian university, the Embassy of the Bahamas (see "Travel," above) can help you with obtaining addresses for these institutions.

Programs offered by CIEE-member institutions are listed below. Unless otherwise noted, consult Appendix I for the addresses of the colleges and universities in this section.

Summer and Short-Term

Natural Sciences

Miami University. *Tropical Flora of the Bahamas*. Andros Islands. May. Two-week program in ecology and botany. Sophomores to graduate students with six hours of biology coursework. Apply by March 1.

State University of New York at Brockport. San Salvador Island. January. Oceanography program designed for biology, earth science, and geology majors. Juniors to graduate students. Apply by September 15. Contact: Office of International Education, SUNY at Brockport, Brockport, NY 14420; (716) 395-2119.

University of Alabama at Birmingham. *UAB in the Bahamas*. San Salvador Island. One week in June. Tropical ecology and marine biology. Sophomores to graduate students with coursework in biology. Contact: Dr. Ken Marion or Dr. Jim McClintock, Department of Biology, University of Alabama at Birmingham, Birmingham, AL 35294-1150; (205) 934-8308.

DOMINICAN REPUBLIC

According to its tourism bureau, the Dominican Republic, which occupies the eastern two-thirds of the island of Hispaniola, is "the best-kept secret in the Caribbean." In fact, in comparison to other Caribbean islands, the Dominican Republic is a relative latecomer to the tourist industry. As a result, it retains much of its intrinsic character and charm. But things are changing: Sugar, once its principle export, has been surpassed by tourism as the country's primary income generator, and a growing number of assembly plants, built by multinational companies attracted by low labor costs, are transforming the nation's economic base. There are now nine duty-free industrial parks in the Dominican Republic, many housed in former sugar refineries.

A relatively stable democratic system has been in place since the U.S. Marines ended their occupation of the country in 1966. Despite a long history of U.S. intervention, however, anti-American sentiment is not pronounced. Dominicans have a comfortable, Puerto Rico–like relationship with the U.S.; in fact, after Santo Domingo, New York City could be considered the country's second-largest city, thanks to its large Dominican population.

Discovered by Columbus in 1492, the Dominican Republic boasts the first Spanish settlement in the New World, the first cathedral, and the oldest university. For three hundred years the island was controlled by Spain, and for briefer periods after that was controlled by France and Haiti, which occupies the western part of the island. It nearly came under U.S. control in 1904 when a shaky Dominican government requested American statehood, a motion that was narrowly defeated in the U.S. Senate. Still, the U.S. has not hesitated to exert its political influence and the marines have occupied the country twice in this century. In 1966, after the most recent U.S. intervention, Joaquin Balaguer was elected president. Power has since alternated between his rule (re-elected four times) and parties of the center-left.

The Dominican people are primarily of African and Spanish descent (the native population was virtually exterminated in the 16th century), and baseball (not soccer) and merengue dancing are their passions. The population is fairly evenly divided between urban and rural areas, with Santo Domingo the political capital and Santiago, the second-largest city, the center of the nation's agricultural production.

In spite of a recent economic downturn, the last decade has been one of healthy economic growth. The booming tourist industry and foreign investment in new clothing and textile industries are signs that the Dominican Republic is a nation in transition.

—Nancy Robinson, Santiago, Dominican Republic

Official name: Dominican Republic **Area:** 18,704 square miles (about twice the size of Vermont). **Population:** 7,384,000. **Population density:** 394 inhabitants per square mile. **Capital and largest city:** Santo Domingo (pop. 2,400,000). **Language:** Spanish. **Religion:** Roman Catholic. **Per capita income:** US$998. **Currency:** Peso. **Literacy rate:** 83%. **Average daily temperature:** Santo Domingo: June, 80°F; December, 76°F. **Average number of days with precipitation:** Santo Domingo: June, 12; December, 8.

TRAVEL

U.S. citizens need a passport or proof of U.S. citizenship and a tourist card or visa to enter the Dominican Republic. The tourist card costs $10 (available from a consulate or the airlines serving the Dominican Republic) and is valid for 60 days. Multiple entry visas are valid for five years. For more information, check with the **Embassy of the Dominican Republic**, 1715 22nd Street NW, Washington, DC 20008; (202) 332-6280. There are Dominican Consulates General in Boston, Chicago, Los Angeles, Miami, New Orleans, New York, Philadelphia, and San Juan.

Getting Around

Domestic **air** service is offered by Agencia Portillo, Servicio Aéreo Dominicano, and Aeronaves Dominicanas. Several companies offer long-distance bus service between the country's cities and resorts, including Autobuses Metro, Terrabús, and Caribe Tours. Local **buses**, called *guaguas*, provide slow and crowded but very inexpensive service to virtually every village in the country. Additional long-distance transportation is provided by **shared taxis** called *carros públicos*, which travel on major highways picking people up and dropping them off along a specified route. Rail transport is virtually nonexistent.

Renting a **car** is another option for getting around the country. Main roads are generally well maintained, driving is on the right-hand side of the road, and a U.S. driver's license is valid. Both international and local companies operate in Santo Domingo and resort areas such as Puerto Plata. It's also possible to rent motorcycles and mopeds.

Especially for Students and Young People

The main student travel organization in the Dominican Republic is **ODTE**, PO Box 25135, Santo Domingo; (809) 686-3333; fax (809) 687-7401. ODTE also has offices in Santiago and La Vega. The organization arranges city and beach tours in Santo Domingo, and offers one-week packages (including accommodations and meals) at various beach resorts. Contact ODTE for information on discounts available to travelers with the International Student Identity Card in the Dominican Republic.

For Further Information

General tourist information is available from the **Tourist Information Center** at the Embassy of the Dominican Republic (see above) or by calling (800) 752-1151. The *Insiders' Guide to the Dominican Republic* is a good general guide. It's available for $14.95 from Hippocrene Books, Attn: Order Department, 171 Madison Avenue, New York, NY 10016; (718) 454-2366.

WORK

It is very difficult for foreigners to obtain work in the Dominican Republic. For more information, contact the Embassy of the Dominican Republic (see "Travel," above). For another type of work experience see the internship and voluntary-service sections below.

Voluntary Service

Amigos de las Americas sponsors a volunteer program in the Dominican Republic; see page 22 for more information. In addition, **Goshen College** offers a study-service term in the Dominican Republic that is open primarily to Goshen students; sometimes a limited number of spaces are available to students at other colleges and universities.

STUDY

The following programs are offered by CIEE-member institutions. Unless otherwise noted, consult Appendix I for the addresses of the colleges and universities listed in this section.

Semester and Academic Year

General Studies

International Student Exchange Program (ISEP). Semester and academic year. Direct reciprocal exchange between U.S. universities and Pontifícia Universidad Católica Madre y Maestra. Full curriculum options. Rolling admissions. Open only to students at ISEP-member institutions. Contact ISEP for list of members.

International Relations

Ohio State University. *Dominican Republic Program in International Development*. Santiago de los Cabelleros. Winter quarter. Intensive six-week program in agricultural economics, integrated rural development, and Dominican history and culture. Excursions and dormitory housing. Undergraduates with 2.7 GPA. Apply by November 16.

Spanish Language and Caribbean Culture

Council on International Educational Exchange. *Spanish Language & Caribbean Area Studies Program at the Pontifícia Universidad Católica Madre y Maestra*. Santiago. Semester and academic year. Sophomores to seniors with 2.75 GPA and four semesters of college Spanish for fall semester and academic year; five semesters for spring semester. Apply by May 1 for fall and academic year; October 15 for spring. Contact University Programs Department.

GUADELOUPE

Butterfly-shaped Guadeloupe is actually two islands, with the "wings" known as Grande-Terre and Basse-Terre—the two are connected only by a single bridge. As a *département* of France, Guadeloupe is represented in the French legislature by two senators and three deputies. Discovered by Spaniards, colonized by the French, and coveted by England, Guadeloupe has been home to many cultures. Slaves were brought from Africa and, later, East Indians were recruited to work in the sugarcane fields. These cultures have blended with a unique Caribbean flair.

The setting of these islands is idyllic, offering a wide array of natural features—all under a bright sun and a tropical climate. Travelers are enticed by the beaches that ring the islands; the color of the sand changes from dark volcanic hue to powdery-white tones according to the terrain of each island. Many of these beaches are secluded and protected by coral reefs. The color of the sea fluctuates from green to blue, and the water is warm year-round. Fishing villages hug the coastline, and marinas offer mooring to boats from all over the world. Fishing, deep-sea diving, windsurfing, and a host of other water sports are extremely popular with visitors—but basking in the sun seems to be the most prevalent activity.

While lush tropical vegetation encroaches on some of the beaches, the coastline can also plunge sharply down rocky cliffs and deep ravines—the promontories and precipices are especially dramatic in the northern shore of the island of Désirade, right off the coast of Grande-Terre. Basse-Terre's landscape is mountainous, dominated by the volcano Soufrière, which rises to almost 5,000 feet. Most of this island is a dense tropical rain forest—74,000 acres of it protected as a national park blessed with waterfalls, natural springs, green peaks, valleys, towering trees, and beautiful flowers. These natural treasures are easily reached by good roads. To reach the highest elevations, there is a good network of trails for serious hikers; civilization can seem very distant from here. Also called Basse-Terre, the department's political capital is a sleepy town that sits at the foot of Mount Soufrière's green slopes. A narrow, but marvelously scenic road circles the volcano and ends about 1,000 feet from the top—a climb that is permitted only if the semi-active volcano is not blowing too hard. The same road also leads to the Carbet Falls on the other side of the volcano, a breathtaking sight amid the dense forest.

Grande-Terre's terrain is characterized by rolling hills and sugarcane fields. A number of stately and still-functioning plantations and abandoned windmills dot the hills. The city of Pointe-à-Pitre is the island's commercial and cultural center while Gosier is located on Guadeloupe's "riviera." It's hard to imagine these popular beaches as landing site for invaders, but Guadeloupe was the battleground in a fierce war for possession of the island between the French and the British, who occupied it from 1759 to 1763. During the 18th century, the island was also a popular base for pirates feared throughout the Caribbean, who left marks in the history and culture of the island.

A visit should include excursions to the nearby islands that are part of the French *départment* of Guadeloupe; they were baptized by Christopher Columbus with Spanish names that were later translated to French by its settlers. They include: Marie Galante, Les Saintes (a cluster of little islands), Désirade, Saint Martin (the northern half), and Saint Barthélemy (St. Barts). Easily accessible to each other by boat or a short plane ride, each island has a distinct flavor and unique attractions. The islands' blend of French, Caribbean, and East Indian traditions erupt into a flurry of song, dance, and colorful parades for carnival, one of the archipelago's biggest celebrations; a perfect time to get to know the usually reserved but friendly people of these islands.

—Grace Jarret, Key West, Florida

Official name: Guadeloupe. **Area:** 530 square miles. **Population:** 335,260. **Population density:** 633 inhabitants per square mile. **Capital:** Basse-Terre. **Largest city:** Point-à-Pitre (pop. 25,312). **Language:** French, Creole. **Religion:** Roman Catholic. **Per capita income:** US$3,300. **Currency:** Franc. **Literacy rate:** 70%. **Average daily high/low:** Camp Jacob: January, 77°/64°; June, 80°/69°. **Average number of days with precipitation:** Camp Jacob: January, 23; June, 25.

TRAVEL

U.S. citizens need a passport and onward/return ticket; however, a visa is not required for stays of up to three months. For further information, contact the **Embassy of France**, 4101 Reservoir Road, Washington, DC 20008; (202) 944-6000.

Getting Around

Over 200 miles of **trails** make Guadeloupe ideal for hikers. From Pointe-à-Pitre, regular and frequent **bus** service departs for destinations all over the island. You can also flag down buses on the side of the road. Bus trips are generally short; it's possible to cover the entire island in one day. **Taxis** are available but more expensive. International and local **car** rental agencies operate on Guadeloupe. It's also common to hitch, although you're just as likely to have a bus stop for you. Numerous **air** and **boat** services operate between Guadeloupe and other nearby islands.

For Further Information

For general tourist information, contact the **French Government Tourist Office**, 628 Fifth Avenue, New York, NY 10020; (212) 757-1125. While there is no single guide to Guadeloupe, you can find reliable information in *Caribbean Islands Handbook* ($22), published in England and distributed in the U.S. through Prentice Hall Travel.

WORK

In order to work in Guadeloupe, it is necessary to arrange a job before arriving at the islands. A work permit, which is obtained by the employer, is necessary. Permits are issued by the French Ministry of Labor in France and usually take about two months to process.

STUDY

Below is a study program offered by a CIEE-member institution. Consult Appendix I for the contact address.

Summer and Short-Term

French Language and Caribbean Culture

North Carolina State University. *Summer in the Caribbean on Guadaloupe.* Late May to late June. French language, and Caribbean history and society at Université Antilles-Guyane. Excursions. Sophomores to seniors with two semesters of college French. Apply by March 1.

JAMAICA

Jamaica is 90 miles away from Cuba, and 340 miles from the U.S. mainland, yet it has closer links to Africa and England. At the time of Christopher Columbus's arrival on the island during his second trip to the New World in 1494, the inhabitants were the now-extinct Arawak Indians, who gave the island its name. Briefly a Spanish colony, the island retains a few traces of Spanish culture in the names of some of the island's more exotic destinations such as the tourist center of Ocho Rios and the well-known rafting spot of the Rio Grande, as well as in the architecture of its oldest towns. Jamaica's period as a British colony, and the introduction of an African population however, has most clearly defined its population, politics, and culture.

The descendants of African slaves brought from West Africa as labor for the sugar plantations now form 96 percent of the island's population. Indentured labor from India, China, and Europe, and the descendants of former British colonial rulers compose the remainder of the population. Jamaicans have mixed freely over the centuries, resulting in an interesting melting pot of facial features and skin tones.

The period of British rule has strongly influenced Jamaica's political institutions. By 1962, when the island attained its political independence, a two-party parliamentary democracy had been installed. Headed by a Prime Minister, the island is ruled by a bicameral Parliament with legislative and executive powers. The nominal head of state remains the Queen of England, represented locally by a Jamaican-born Governor General. Official business and conversation on the island is conducted in English, the official language. The educational system is also patterned after that of the United Kingdom.

However, the traditions carried over and retained by the African slaves and their descendants have the strongest influence on Jamaican culture. The local dialect most closely resembles broken English, but its African syntax plays tricks on the ear of the new arrival on the island. Reggae, made popular and internationalized by its most famous star, Bob Marley, is a hypnotic combination of bass rhythm, reminiscent of African drums, combined with lyrics of social significance. This music is heard everywhere on the streets of the island. Reggae Sunsplash, the festival held each summer, attracts participants and audiences from all over the world. Other, less well-known African traditions live on among the population in its dances, religious practices, and superstitions.

Kingston, the political and economic capital, is the center of Jamaica's modern development. The island, however, suffers from an unemployment rate of 22 to 30 percent. Traditionally a colonial, agricultural economy heavily dependent on sugar production, the island has since introduced light industry, crop diversification, tourism, and bauxite mining. The United States is the island's major trading partner. This, along with its proximity, has introduced a high level of knowledge about and interest in the United States.

The island has a tropical, maritime climate, which makes it a popular tourist destination for North Americans. At the same time, its mountainous interior provides alternatives for those seeking cooler, less crowded destinations. Jamaicans are hospitable, and enjoy sharing their island with visitors.

—Andrea Ewart Simon, Brattleboro, Vermont

Official name: Jamaica. **Area:** 4,232 square miles (about the size of Connecticut). **Population:** 2,489,000. **Population density:** 556 inhabitants per square mile. **Capital:** Kingston (pop. 100,000). **Largest city:** St. Andrew (pop. 393,000). **Language:** English. **Religion:** Protestant. **Per capita income:** US$150. **Currency:** Jamaican dollar. **Literacy rate:** 98%. **Average daily temperature:** Kingston: June, 82°; December, 79°. **Average number of days with precipitation:** Kingston: June, 5; December, 4.

TRAVEL

For visits of up to six months, U.S. tourists do not need a passport or a visa if they are arriving directly from the United States, Puerto Rico, or the U.S. Virgin Islands. However, tourists must have a return or onward ticket, proof of citizenship, photo ID, and sufficient funds. For specific requirements, check with the **Embassy of Jamaica**, 1850 K Street NW, Suite 355, Washington, DC 20006; (202) 452-0660. There are also Jamaican consulates in Atlanta, Chicago, Los Angeles, Miami, and New York.

Getting Around

One of the most interesting and least expensive ways of seeing more of Jamaica than its beaches is to take the **train** between Kingston and Montego Bay. The six-hour trip across the heart of the island provides beautiful scenery as well as a glimpse into the everyday life of Jamaicans. Another cheap way of getting around are the local **buses** that serve most areas of the island. Travel after dark by bus, however, is not recommended. In addition, there are minibuses that serve the most popular routes between the island's cities and resorts, leaving only when full and picking up and discharging passengers anywhere along the route. Although inexpensive, these are often overcrowded and chaotic.

You can easily rent a **car** in most resort areas as well as Kingston. Your U.S. driver's license is valid, but remember that driving is on the left-hand side of the road. Bicycle, moped, and motorcycle rentals are also available in tourist areas.

Eating and Sleeping

The University of the West Indies in Kingston offers affordable **dormitory lodgings** to travelers. For more information, contact JOYST (see "Especially for Students and Young People," below) or consult Campus Travel Service's *US and Worldwide Travel Accommodations Guide* (see page 54).

Especially for Students and Young People

Jamaica's student travel organization and issuer of the International Student Identity Card is **JOYST Caribbean Student Services**, 9 Eureka Crescent, Kingston 5; (809) 929-0411; fax (809) 929-7928. In addition to making travel arrangements, JOYST can provide information on discounts available to holders of the International Student Identity Card. JOYST also arranges homestays.

For Further Information

General tourist information is available from the **Jamaican Tourist Board**, 801 Second Avenue, New York, NY 10017; (800) 847-4279; fax (212) 758-9306. Other Jamaica Tourist Board offices are located in Chicago, Coral Gables, Dallas, Detroit, Los Angeles, and Philadelphia.

Probably the best guide to this country is *Jamaica Handbook*, available for $12.95 from Moon Publications (see page 57).

WORK

Getting a Job

In order to work in Jamaica it is necessary to obtain a work permit; the prospective employer applies for it on behalf of the applicant. For more information, contact the Embassy of Jamaica (see "Travel," above).

Internships/Traineeships

Two programs offered by members of the Council on International Educational Exchange are described below.

Association for International Practical Training. *IAESTE Trainee Program.* On-the-job training for undergraduate and graduate students in technical fields such as engineering, computer science, agriculture, architecture, mathematics, and the natural and physical sciences. See page 19 for more information.

Voluntary Service

Global Volunteers, 375 East Little Canada Road, St. Paul, MN 55117; (612) 482-1074, sponsors a two-week service program in Jamaica in which participants work with villagers in three agricultural communities. Volunteers tutor preschool and primary-school children, paint and repair buildings, help construct new community facilities, assist rural health-care workers, and provide technical training.

In addition, the **Partnership for Service-Learning** sponsors a study/service program in Jamaica; for more information, see page 26.

STUDY

Programs offered by CIEE-member institutions are listed below. Unless otherwise noted, consult Appendix I for the addresses of the colleges and universities in this section.

Semester and Academic Year

International Relations

University of Minnesota. *Minnesota Studies in International Development (MSID).* Academic year. Predeparture coursework at the University of Minnesota in the fall quarter; an internship in development-related research or an action project in Jamaica during the winter and spring quarters required. Juniors to graduates and adults with an interest in development. A 2.5 GPA is required; apply by May 1. Contact: The Global Campus, University of Minnesota, 106C Nicholson Hall, 216 Pillsbury Drive SE, Minneapolis, MN 55455-0138. (612) 625-3379.

World Learning/School for International Training. *College Semester Abroad.* Kingston. Fall and spring semesters. Women and Development. Field-study seminar, six-week homestay, rural village stay. Sophomores to graduate students with 2.5 GPA. Apply by May 7 for fall; October 7 for spring. Contact: College Semester Abroad Admissions at (800) 336-1616.

Performing Arts

State University of New York College at Brockport. *Jamaica Performing Arts Exchange Program.* Kingston. Fall and spring semesters. Jamaican art, dance, and culture at Cultural Training Centre. Homestays. Juniors and seniors with 2.5 GPA. Apply by March 15 for fall; November 1 for spring. Contact: Office of International Education, SUNY College at Brockport, Brockport, NY 14420; (716) 395-2119.

Summer and Short-Term

General Studies

State University of New York College at Brockport. *Summer Program in Jamaica*. Kingston. Cultural studies at University of the West Indies. Dormitory housing. Juniors and seniors with 2.5 GPA. Apply by May 1. Contact: Office of International Education, SUNY College at Brockport, Brockport, NY 14420; (716) 395-2119.

EXPLORING JAMAICAN CULTURE

Readings and Films

The novels of Roger Mais, especially *Brother Man* (1974) and *The Hills Were Joyful Together* (1981) are concerned with the victims of the oppressive cultural and economic legacy of colonialism. He brings the Jamaican slums alive, particularly the huge Kingston shantytowns, and through his portrayal indicts the ruling upper class. His book *Black Lightning* (1983) is a more heavily symbolic work employing a pastoral setting. The protagonist, Jake, is a blacksmith trying to confront human imperfection by creating a statue of Samson, whose tragic story mirrors Jake's own.

Another portrait of the Jamaican lower class is Michael Thelwell's sociological work, *The Harder They Come* (1980). See also Perry Henzell's 1973 film from which the book took its name. The film, something of a cult classic in U.S., is about a country boy who wants to be a reggae singer in Kingston but can't get his record played until he becomes an outlaw. The more infamous he becomes, the more records he sells. *A Habit of the Blood* (1989), by Lois Battle, provides a glimpse into the tawdry politics and the drug subculture of Jamaica. For an in-depth look at the life of Rastafarians, Leonard Barrett's *The Rastafarians: Sounds of Cultural Dissonance* (1988) examines the belief system, rituals, art, and music of this group.

Edgar White's plays, *The Nine Night* and *Ritual by Water* (1984), concern the conflict in consciousness among modern Jamaicans and West Indian expatriates. In *The Nine Night*, the protagonist returns to Jamaica from England to try to undo England's effect upon his family. *Ritual by Water* is about a worker at a youth center wrestling with ideals and despair.

For a historical perspective on Jamaica, read V. S. Reid's *New Day* (1949), which chronicles Jamaica from the 1865 rebellion to 1944, or Claude McKay's *Banana Bottom* (1933), about a young girl adopted by English missionaries and sent to England for her education. This book should be compared to Michelle Cliff's *Abeng* (1984), a young girl's rite of passage that explores Jamaican society's sensitive racial issues. *The Book of Jamaica* (1980), by Russell Banks, is a novel that explores the history, landscape, religion, and politics of this island. Another novel that provides a historical perspective is Alec Waugh's *Island in the Sun* (1955), in which the regime of a British governor confronts questions of colonialism, racial equality, and self-government.

MARTINIQUE

Often called "the island of flowers," Martinique is covered with hibiscus, bougainvillea, magnolia, oleander, anthurium, poinsettia, and many other flowering trees. Washed by the Caribbean Sea to the west and the Atlantic Ocean to the east, its varied terrain encompasses beaches, valleys, waterfalls, mountains, and rain forests. The rugged and elevated volcanic north beaches are black, and the rain forest that covers this region teems with hanging creepers, colossal trees, philodendrons, giant bamboos, and arborescent ferns. The landscape of the northern tip of the island rises inland to the towering Mount Pelée, a dormant volcanic cone. In contrast, the south has rounded hills used for cattle-raising. The alluvial flatlands of the south are blanketed with sugarcane fields that often extend as far as the long golden beaches.

One-third of Martinique's inhabitants live in Fort-de-France, the administrative capital and the commercial and cultural center of the island. It is situated on a good harbor with green mountains as a backdrop. The city was originally built around a French fort in the 17th century and abounds with citadels and parks. Park La Savane, next to Fort St. Louis, is adorned with a statue of Empress Josephine, first wife of Napoleon Bonaparte, who is a revered Martinique native. The Spanish abandoned Martinique in search of gold in Mexico and Peru and because of the fierce Caribs (who were later exterminated by the French). Twice occupied by Britain, the island became a French possession in 1635 and a French overseas *département* in 1946.

In Martinique, French and African traditions blend to create a French-Creole atmosphere encompassing the culture, cuisine, music, way of life, and people. The mixture of races in Martinique's society is a result of its history: French colonizers imported large numbers of Africans, after whom came East Indians and Chinese to replace the freed slaves. Later other immigrants made Martinique their home, including Syrians, Italians, and Lebanese. The traditions observed in Martinique today reflect its amalgam of cultures and are an integral part of West Indian life. Although French is the official language, Creole is the everyday language of the Martiniquais; it has West African grammatical structures and a vocabulary derived mostly from French, but is also influenced by the languages of other immigrants. Martinique's cuisine also reflects the rich traditions of the island, using subtle combinations of fresh seafood, local vegetables, and exotic spices.

A road trip around the island will take the visitor to secluded beaches, fishing villages, and modern resort towns. Route de la Trace is particularly spectacular as it traverses the rain forest and provides gorgeous views down into ravines and up at the deep green Carbet peaks. Several former plantation houses have been restored and now operate as hotels or restaurants. History is also alive in Saint Pierre, a lovely seaside town that was the first French settlement in Martinique; in 1902, Mount Pelée erupted and in three minutes the bustling cultural and economic center was wiped out by lava and a cloud of molten volcanic ash—all but one person perished. Today Saint Pierre is a small town with ruins from its fiery past, and with little worry about the mountain.

Festivals still take place during the year in many villages, each with its traditional events like *gommier* and *yole* races (Carib boat races), cockfights, horse races, and more. Carnival is a time-revered institution of the island, and is increasingly geared to the tourist industry. The Monday before Mardi Gras is characterized by burlesque weddings—guests wear masks, costumes, glitter, and feathers—and on Fat Tuesday itself everyone wears red. On Ash

Wednesday everyone dresses in black and white to bid farewell to Vaval, the king of the Carnival, and go with him to his resting place: the bonfire on the seafront. A feverish party atmosphere envelopes Carnival days, which are filled with music, an essential part of life in Martinique—biguine, mazurka, waltz, and zouk.

—Christiane Szeps, Harrisonburg, Virginia

Official name: Martinique. **Area:** 417 square miles. **Population:** 359,572. **Population density:** 801 inhabitants per square mile. **Capital and largest city:** Fort de France (pop. 101,540). **Language:** French (official) and Creole. **Religion:** Roman Catholic. **Currency:** Franc. **Per capita income:** US$3,650. **Average daily high/low:** Fort de France: January, 83°F/69°F; June, 86°F/74°F. **Average number of days with precipitation:** Fort de France: January, 19; June, 21.

TRAVEL

U.S. citizens need a passport and onward/return ticket; however, a visa is not required for stays of up to three months. For further information, contact the **Embassy of France**, 4101 Reservoir Road, Washington, DC 20008; (202) 944-6000.

Getting Around

Private **buses** operate in Fort-de-France and the suburbs, keeping no set schedule but leaving when full. **Shared taxis** or *taxis collectif* cover longer distances. **Cars** can be rented from local and international companies. Coastal **ferries** save driving time.

For Further Information

For general tourist information, contact the **French Government Tourist Office**, 628 Fifth Avenue, New York, NY 10020; (212) 757-1125. While there is no single guide to Martinique, you can find reliable information in *Caribbean Islands Handbook* ($22), published in England and distributed in the U.S. through Prentice Hall Travel.

WORK

In order to work in Martinique, it is necessary to arrange a job prior to going to the island. You are required to have a work permit, which is obtained by the employer from the French Ministry of Labor in France. According to the French Embassy, permits usually take about two months to process.

STUDY

Following are educational programs offered by CIEE-member institutions. Unless otherwise noted, consult Appendix I for the addresses of colleges and universities listed in this section.

Semester and Academic Year

Literature

James Madison University. *Martinique Spring Semester*. Schoelcher (FWI). French language and literature at Université des Antilles et de le Guyane. Homestays. Sophomores to seniors with 3.0 GPA and courses in French composition, conversation, and advanced grammar. Apply by February 15.

Summer and Short-Term

French Language and Creole Culture

Longwood College. *Summer Study Abroad Program in Fort-de-France, Martinique*. May and June. Four-week program in intensive French language and Creole culture. Homestays. Sophomores to graduate students and adults with two semesters of college French and 2.5 GPA. Apply by March 1. Contact: International Studies Office, Longwood College, Farmville, VA 23901; (804) 395-2172.

PUERTO RICO

Puerto Rico's tropical climate and strategic location at the crossroads of the Americas have historically made this Caribbean island a coveted possession. The Spanish, who colonized the island and exterminated its indigenous population, the Tainos, used Puerto Rico as a base for exploring and colonizing Latin America. The Spanish presence since the island's discovery by Columbus in 1493 has left an indelible mark in the history and character of Puerto Rico. But it was their progeny—who fostered a stronger allegiance for their country of birth rather than for the motherland—along with the influence of African slaves, that gave birth to a nation marked by the struggle for independence. Spain eventually surrendered Puerto Rico in 1898, not to the country's autonomy movement, but to the U.S. as a result of the Spanish-American War, marking a new era of foreign influence.

The visitor to today's Puerto Rico will find traces of the many cultures that have made their home on this Caribbean island over the centuries, blending to create the essence of today's Puerto Ricans. The old-world charm of Puerto Rico's colonial towns and plantation estates, together with a concept of time that is more relaxed than in industrialized countries, make Puerto Rico a popular destination—closely related to the U.S. and yet uniquely different.

The Puerto Rican Constitution was approved in 1952, when the island was granted its present U.S. commonwealth status. However, Puerto Rico's political status is still controversial, and debate goes on among commonwealth, statehood, and independence supporters. Its affiliation with the U.S. has been praised and attacked, both at home and abroad. Whatever the outcome of this debate over the long term, Puerto Rico will always have close ties to the U.S. while valuing and fostering its independence and uniquely Spanish-Caribbean character. Over the years a large proportion of Puerto Ricans have moved to the U.S., with the highest concentration in New York City. While Spanish has been the traditional language spoken in Puerto Rico, most Puerto Ricans speak some English, which is taught as a required second language.

Because of tourism's importance to the local economy, the development of this industry has been a high priority. The major international airport is in San Juan, and smaller airports are located in Ponce, Mayaguez, Aguadilla, and Arecibo. The network of paved roads is among the best-developed in Latin America, making this relatively small island very accessible to the visitor. Old San Juan, a colonial Spanish jewel, contains six sights designated as World Heritage Monuments and is a perfect starting point for a visit to the island.

Many visitors are discovering the beauty of the Caribbean National Forest, also known as El Yunque, a tropical rain forest preserve in the Sierra de Luquillo. This lush and mountainous region is accessible by road, although in the interior, roads narrow and wind through the mountains. Spending time in the interior is made more attractive by the *paradores puertorriqueños*, simple inns with bucolic appeal; some of them are secluded plantation estates. These pastoral attractions are never too far from coastal cities and quaint Spanish towns such as San German. For the visitor looking for a secluded beach getaway, the western shore of the island and the island of Vieques are less frequented by tourists.

Puerto Rico's historical and natural assets offer visitors a wide array of options for relaxation, learning, and simply having a good time. But to overlook the appeal of its people would be a mistake, for Puerto Ricans are friendly and outgoing. Their hospitality and warmth are as notorious as their zest for life.

—Lázaro Hernández, New York, New York

Official name: Puerto Rico. **Area:** 3,459 square miles. **Population:** 3,522,037. **Population density:** 958 inhabitants per square mile. **Capital and largest city:** San Juan (pop. 437,745). **Language:** Spanish (official) and English. **Religion:** Roman Catholic. **Literacy rate:** 89%. **Per capita income:** US $5,574. **Currency:** U.S. dollar. **Average daily high/low:** San Juan: January, 80°F/70°F; June, 85°F/75°F. **Average number of days with precipitation:** San Juan: January, 20; June, 17.

TRAVEL

U.S. citizens can travel freely to and from Puerto Rico without documentation, just as they would to any of the 50 states.

Getting Around

A good **bus** network connects cities and towns throughout Puerto Rico, although traveling in the eastern part of the island is easier than in the west. **Shared taxis**, usually minivans, also run to all parts of the island. Rental **car** agencies are plentiful and relatively cheap.

For Further Information

For general travel information, contact **Puerto Rico Tourism**, 575 Fifth Avenue, New York, NY 10017; (212) 599-6262. A good guide to the island is *Frommer's Puerto Rico*, available for $15 from Prentice Hall.

WORK

U.S. citizens interested in working in Puerto Rico can seek employment just as they would in any of the 50 states. No special work permits or visas are necessary.

STUDY

Below is an educational program offered by a CIEE-member institution.

Semester and Academic Year

Business

State University of New York College at Oswego. *Business Administration in Puerto Rico*. University of Puerto Rico, Mayagüez. Semester and academic year. Business curriculum including accounting, international marketing, and human resources. Instruction in Spanish (textbooks in English). Apartment housing. Juniors and seniors with three years of college Spanish and 2.5 GPA. Apply by April 1 for fall and academic year; November 1 for spring. Contact: Office of International Education, SUNY at Oswego, 102 Rich Hall, Oswego, NY 13126; (315) 341-2118.

General Studies

State University of New York College at Oswego. *Humanities and Social Sciences in Puerto Rico*. University of Puerto Rico, San Juan. Semester and academic year. Humanities and social sciences plus Caribbean literature, history, and civilization; instruction in Spanish. Dormitory housing. Juniors and seniors with three years of college Spanish and 2.5 GPA. Apply by April 1 for fall and academic year; November 1 for spring. Contact: Office of International Education, SUNY at Oswego, 102 Rich Hall, Oswego, NY 13126; (315) 341-2118.

Summer and Short-Term

General Studies

State University of New York College at Oswego. *Mayaguez Winter Study*. Mayaguez. Late December to mid-January. Arts and sciences, and business at University of Puerto Rico. Dormitory housing. High-school graduates to seniors. Apply by April 1. Contact: International Education, 102 Rich Hall, SUNY College at Oswego, Oswego, NY 13126; (315) 341-2118.

EXPLORING PUERTO RICAN CULTURE

Readings

Nationalist and racial concerns have characterized Puerto Rican literature in recent decades. Puerto Rican politics are the background to Enrique A.

Laguerre's *Benevolent Masters*, which traces a dignitary's ascent to power. *The Look*, by René Marquez, examines the life of a Puerto Rican youth involved with politics, drugs, the island's independence, and Chile during the Allende years. In *Macho Camacho's Beat* (1981), by Luis Rafael Sánchez, the realities of daily life in San Juan unfold as the radio persistently plays a popular song.

The Puerto Rican experience of emigration to the U.S. is also a common subject for contemporary Puerto Rican writers. Pedro J. Soto's *Spiks* vividly details the struggle over assimilation versus acculturation among Nuyoricans (Puerto Ricans born or raised in New York City). The same themes are explored by Piri Thomas in three autobiographical novels, *Down These Mean Streets* (1967), *Savior, Savior, Hold My Hand* (1973), and *Seven Long Times* (1975). Life in exile is humorously examined by Emilio Diaz Valcarel in *Schemes in the Month of March*. James Baldwin wrote about this subject in *If Beale Street Could Talk* (1974), in which New York and Puerto Rico are the settings for a novel of a love between two young people that helps them to deal with racial oppression.

Writers from other countries have also chronicled Puerto Rican life. Barry Levine spins a comic tale in *Benjy Lopez: A Picaresque Tale of Emigration and Return* (1980). Oscar Lewis's *La Vida* (1966) is a comprehensive chronicle of Puerto Rican life, a study of one thousand families from San Juan and their New York relatives. Written by Puerto Rican scholars but addressed to the general reader on the U.S. mainland, *Puerto Rico: A Political and Cultural Odyssey* (1983) is a collection of essays that function as a social, cultural, and political history.

CHAPTER FIFTEEN

MEXICO AND CENTRAL AMERICA

For nearly 300 years Mexico and the republics of Central America were all part of the Spanish empire. Because of this, these nations share a common heritage and many common characteristics. But making sweeping generalizations would be a serious error. For example, while the official language of most of these nations is Spanish, in Belize it is English. The largest population group in the region is the *mestizo*—a mixture of Spanish and Indian ancestry—but Guatemala remains predominantly Mayan. Most of these countries maintain a fairly low standard of living, but Costa Rica is surprisingly affluent. And while you can expect tropical weather in coastal areas, most cities of the region—including Mexico City, Guatemala City, and San José—lie inland far above sea level and enjoy surprisingly temperate climates.

Tapering south of the United States, this isthmus narrowly separates the Atlantic and Pacific oceans. As home of the strategically important Panama Canal, market for U.S. products, supplier of food and raw materials, and a major source of immigration, the region has long played a major role in the economy and society of the U.S. As the North American Free Trade Agreement nears completion, the integration of Mexico's economy with that of the U.S. will create enormous changes on both sides of the border. But in spite of their proximity and importance to the U.S., these nations remain little understood by most Americans.

Too often, relations with the United States have been reflected in local politics by power struggles between right and left, escalating to civil war. The most conspicuous examples are Nicaragua and El Salvador. Yet although political, social, and economic problems plague the region, the image of political instability and violence is not entirely accurate. Mexico, Costa Rica, and Belize have enjoyed decades of political stability and social peace. Nicaragua and El Salvador have each emerged from years of civil war and, though their problems are not over, chances for their peaceful resolution look good. Even 1993's abortive coup by Guatemalan President Serrano seems to promise that people will no longer tolerate authoritarian rule.

Still, inequities exist in these predominantly agricultural countries where the poor vastly outnumber the very rich. Related to the problem of economic disparity is the predicament of indigenous peoples, many of whom can't speak Spanish and whose traditional world is being encroached upon by the developing economies that surround them. Other problems in such highly industrialized urban areas as Mexico City include extremely dangerous levels of pollution and overcrowding. Yet in spite of such social and environmental ills, everyday life in Central America goes on with a kind of placid grace not seen in the U.S. Each town's central plaza becomes a place of midday rest and refuge from the afternoon heat and an outdoor social hall in the evenings. The people are friendly and courteous and almost always curious about travelers, especially in areas that don't see too many of them.

Many people travel to Mexico and Central America for no other reason than

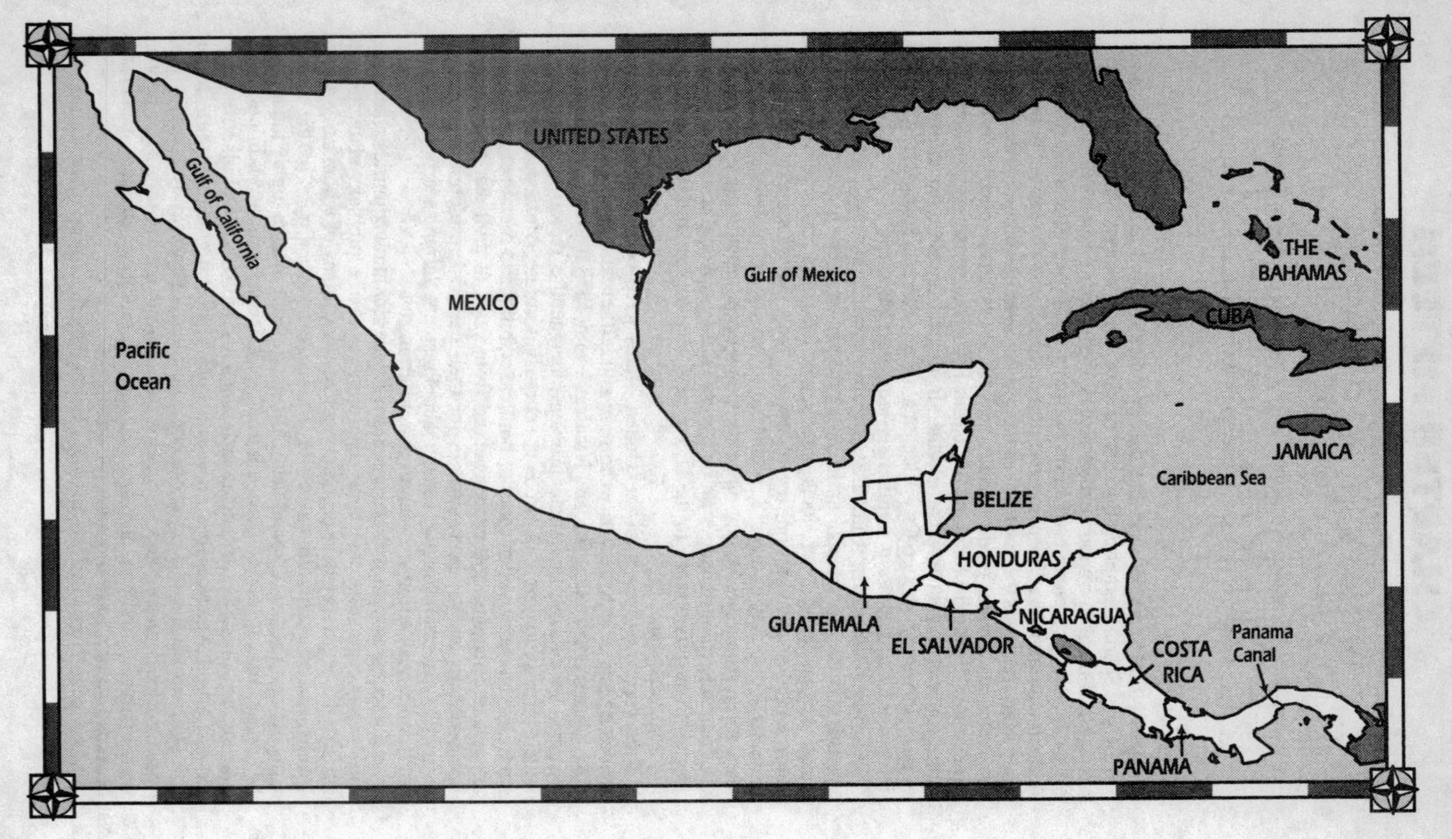
UNITED STATES
Gulf of California
MEXICO
Pacific
Ocean
Gulf of Mexico
THE
BAHAMAS
CUBA
JAMAICA
Caribbean Sea
BELIZE
HONDURAS
GUATEMALA
EL SALVADOR
NICARAGUA
COSTA
RICA
Panama
Canal
PANAMA

its warm weather and beautiful beach resorts like Acapulco and Cancún. Others go on pilgrimages to such ancient sacred sites as Tikal and Chichen Itza. For budget travelers, especially, Central America is an attractive destination. But North Americans are traveling to the region not only as tourists, but also as volunteers to help fight poverty, as scientists to explore the rain forest, as students to understand the region's language and culture, as businessmen to participate in the expanding economy, and as archaeologists to explore the mysteries of ancient cities that still rise as testimony to the great empires that flourished long before Columbus's arrival in the Americas. Whatever the reason, few travelers are disappointed.

The Essentials

Proof of U.S. citizenship is sufficient for travelers from the U.S. to enter Mexico and Panama, but passports are required for all countries in between. Many Central American countries also require proof of onward transportation and proof of sufficient funds, although requirements may be enforced somewhat arbitrarily. Especially when confronted with young travelers, officials may ask to see such proof. Check with the embassy or consulate for further information.

Getting There by Air

The cheapest fares from the U.S. to Mexico and Central America are generally APEX fares (see Chapter Five for a general explanation of airfares). Below are some sample *one-way* fares in effect during the summer of 1993. More information is available at Council Travel offices (see pages xiii–xvi).

New York–Mexico City	$219	New York–Guatemala City	$215
Los Angeles–Mexico City	$219	Miami–San José	$175
Houston–Mexico City	$129		

For persons planning a short-term stay (anywhere from four days to a couple of weeks), the cheapest way of traveling may be to buy a vacation **package** that includes airfare and accommodations. Generally speaking, packages are available to Mexico City, Guadalajara, and Mérida, as well as to beach resorts such as Cancún, Acapulco, Puerto Vallarta, Mazatlán, and Ixtapa. Packages range from budget to luxury, and can be booked through travel agents in the U.S. or through airlines flying to Mexico from the U.S. (including the Mexican carriers Mexicana and Aeroméxico). Packages are generally cheaper than making your own arrangements, since tour operators can mass-book hotels and make volume purchases. Council Travel arranges special low-cost spring vacation packages geared toward students and teachers interested in making their spring-break getaway an international experience. Options generally include Cancún among other destinations. Contact a Council Travel office for more information.

Other Means of Travel

Millions of Americans cross the border by **car** into Mexico each year. Until recently, however, civil war in El Salvador and Nicaragua discouraged most people from venturing beyond Mexico into Central America by car. Now that the region has become more stable, Americans are increasingly taking to the Pan-American Highway, which extends as far as eastern Panama, where it is interrupted by an expanse of marshland, resuming again in Colombia. While generally good, road conditions are inconsistent. Lack of maintenance and shortages of gasoline make passage through some parts of the road a real adventure. **Note:** Mexico has recently adopted a number of regulations governing entry of automobiles from the U.S.; see the Mexico section for more information.

If traveling by **train** or bus to Mexico, you will have to stop at a U.S. border town—such as El Paso or Brownsville, Texas, or San Diego, California—and walk across the border, where you can arrange connecting service to your destination. While the Mexican railway network is well developed and expanding, most other Central American countries have fairly minimal systems, usually connecting capital cities to ports and little else. Though they can be fun, trains generally travel less frequently, more slowly, and to fewer places than buses. As a result, the bus is the favorite mode of overland transportation in Central America. You'll find more specific information about traveling around Belize, Costa Rica, Guatemala, Honduras, and Mexico in the country sections that follow.

For Further Information

Probably the most comprehensive guidebook to Central America is the annually updated *Mexico & Central America Handbook* ($22), published in Britain and distributed in the United States by Prentice Hall. Also good is *Central America on a Shoestring*, available for $16.95 from Lonely Planet Publications (see page 56). As there are very few guidebooks for Central American countries other than Mexico and Guatemala, these books are helpful to those with a broader itinerary.

You'll find entry requirements and embassy addresses given in the individual country sections that follow. Addresses for the embassies of countries not covered in a separate section of this chapter are listed below.

- **El Salvador:** Embassy of El Salvador, 1010 16th Street NW, Third Floor, Washington, DC 20036; (202) 331-4032
- **Nicaragua:** Embassy of Nicaragua, 1627 New Hampshire Avenue NW, Washington, DC 20009; (202) 387-4371
- **Panama:** Embassy of Panama, 2862 McGill Terrace NW, Washington, DC 20008; (202) 483-1407

WORK

Except for Costa Rica, where **CIEE's Work Abroad Program** (see page 17) makes summer employment a possibility for U.S. students, stringent labor regulations and high unemployment rates make it almost impossible for foreigners to obtain employment in Mexico or Central America. Nevertheless, resourceful persons fluent in Spanish can find informal employment (mostly as English tutors) once they've arrived in the region. Persons with a degree in **TESOL** should check Chapter Three for teaching opportunities in Latin America.

You'll find internship possibilities for Mexico, Guatemala, and Costa Rica listed in the individual country sections later in this chapter. In addition, **AIESEC** offers internship possibilities in Panama; see page 19 for additional information about this program.

Voluntary Service

Whitworth College sponsors a *Central America Study Program*, which combines Spanish language study and community service. This program takes place in the spring and is open to sophomores, juniors, and seniors; 2.5 GPA and intermediate-level Spanish facility are required. For more information, contact: Coordinator, Off-Campus Programs, Station #2702, Whitworth College, Spokane, WA 99251.

STUDY

Persons considering study in Latin America might want to take a look at *Funding for Research, Study, and Travel: Latin America and the Caribbean*, edited by Karen Cantrell and Denise Wallen, even though most of the grants and scholarships listed in this 300-page reference work are for graduate study. The book is expensive ($32.50), so look for it in your college library or contact Oryx Press, 4041 North Central, Phoenix, AZ 85012; (602) 265-2651.

BELIZE

Ancient Maya heartland, pirate settlement, logger outpost, crown colony, and in 1981, independent nation—Belize (formerly British Honduras) has a remarkable heritage. It remains virtually unspoiled, untarnished by time and has become somewhat of a last frontier for the unassuming and adventurous traveler.

With a landmass no larger than the state of Massachusetts, Belize is a country of immense cultural and geographic diversity. Lush tropical rain forests, barren savannas, pine-forested mountains, tangled mangrove swamps, impressive limestone caves, and the world's second longest coral reef, all contribute to a bountiful legacy of ecological heterogeneity. Furthermore, its wide variety of fascinating flora and fauna, and its more than three hundred picturesque offshore islands make Belize a naturalist's paradise of breathtaking beauty and a haven for the outdoor enthusiast.

While the country is nestled between Mexico and Guatemala, it displays a distinctly Caribbean island atmosphere. This is immediately evident in its music, food, and way of life. With schools in every tiny village and compulsory education until grade eight, the country boasts a 90 percent literacy rate. Indeed, along with its democratically elected bipartisan government, its less apparent social class divisions and sociopolitical stability, Belize can truly be considered the anomaly of Central America.

The population (228,000) is composed of a colorful medley of cultures. The Afro-European Creoles, who live in Belize City and along the coast, contribute the largest ethnic group. The *mestizos* (*ladinos*) of Spanish colonist and Amerindian ancestry migrated to the region from the Yucatan in the 19th century. The Garifuna, descendants of African slaves and Carib Indians, live along the southern coast and practice a maritime way of life. Inland, the native Maya, with a cultural heritage spanning two millennia, still live in thatched wattle-and-daub houses within the vicinity of the hundreds of archaeological sites scattered across the countryside. During the 20th century, Lebanese, Chinese,

East Indians, German-speaking Mennonites, and more recently, Salvadorean and Guatemalan refugees have migrated to Belize.

Each of the six major towns—Corozal, Orange Walk, Dangriga, Punta Gorda, San Ignacio, and Belmopan, the new "planned" capital carved out of the jungle—has its own distinct ambience. In every community there is a high level of cultural integration readily expressed by the sharing of the Creole language. This linguistically interesting version of "broken English" has evolved as the lingua franca of its people. Although English is the national language, most people also speak Spanish.

Approximately one third of the country's population resides in Belize City, the old colonial capital built at sea level. It is the commercial and, to a large extent, cultural center of Belize. The city is renowned for its "swing bridge" and especially for its vibrant local market set alongside the wharf. Fishermen can be seen most any time unloading their daily catches of lobster, fish, and conch. Huge rainwater vats and a mixture of shabby, unpainted structures and colonial houses line the narrow, crowded streets. Vendors on bicycles hawk everything from pumpkin seeds to mahogany carvings, while rastafarians "hang out" in their favorite alleyways.

The economy is based on agriculture rather than industrial production; in fact, the entire country can be considered rural by North American standards. Each community retains a rustic flavor and the people thrive in a way of life that is rich in its own simplicity. Whitewashed wooden houses built on stilts display rusty red tin roofs that glisten in the brilliant sun. In the neighborhood, the graceful fronds of the coconut palms rustle as the morning wash flaps in the gentle breeze. This "laid back" atmosphere is occasionally shattered by the roar of the supersonic jets above, a frequent reminder of the British commitment to protect this fledgling nation.

Travelers expecting an exquisite holiday in the sun complete with fancy nightclubs, casinos, posh five-star hotels and international cuisine will be lost in the "jungles" and rural setting of Belize. There are no high-rise buildings, few luxury accommodations and a four-wheel-drive vehicle is essential for accessing the more remote spots. And yet, the intoxicating sound of punta music, the gracious gentility of the Belizean people, and the unspoiled beauty of the land are so contagious that once you've visited this tranquil nation, it's sure to lure you back.

—Cynthia Bennett Awe, Peterborough, Ontario

Official name: Belize. **Size:** 8,867 square miles (about the size of New Hampshire). **Population:** 228,000. **Population density:** 25 inhabitants per square mile. **Capital:** Belmopan (pop. 5,000). **Largest city:** Belize City (pop. 60,000.) **Language**: English and Spanish. **Religion:** Roman Catholic, Protestant. **Per capita income:** US$1,312. **Currency:** Belize dollar. **Literacy rate:** 93%. **Average daily temperature:** Belize City: June, 83°; December, 77°. **Average number of days with precipitation:** Belize City: June 13; December, 14.

TRAVEL

A passport is required for U.S. citizens but visas are not required for tourist stays of up to one month. Visitors wishing to stay longer than one month must receive permission at the local immigration office. A return or onward ticket is also required. For further information, contact the **Embassy of Belize**, 2535 Massachusetts Avenue NW, Washington, DC 20008; (202) 332-9636.

Getting Around

For many years, rivers were the only means of inland travel. Likewise, coastal towns were connected by boat. Today, small **boats** continue to navigate the waterways, especially in the sugar-producing north, but are no longer the primary mode of transport. One of the nicest trips is to travel by ferry from Punta Gorda to Guatemala. You can also explore the offshore cays by boat.

Buses run hourly between Belize City and major towns to the north and west. Service to the south is less frequent. The highway network between the major towns is good, but the many smaller unpaved roads are not as dependable, especially during rainy times, making four-wheel-drive vehicles a necessity in many parts.

The country's main airport is ten miles outside of Belize City. Most towns, however, are equipped with some form of landing strip, making regular **air** travel possible within the country. Maya Airways has daily flights to several towns and a number of other companies offer charter service to more out-of-the-way destinations.

For Further Information

General information can be obtained from the **Belize Tourist Board**, 15 Penn Plaza, 415 Seventh Avenue, New York, NY 10001; (800) 624-0686; fax (212) 695-3018. The best guide to Belize is Harry S. Pariser's *Adventure Guide to Belize*, available for $14.95 from Hunter Publishing, 300 Raritan Center Parkway, Edison, NJ 08818; (908) 225-1900. Also good is *The Real Guide: Guatemala and Belize* ($13.95). A good guide to the region's Mayan sites is *La Ruta Maya: Yucutan, Guatemala, and Belize*, available for $15.95 from Lonely Planet Publications. Nature lovers should check out *Belize: A Natural Destination* ($16.95), published by John Muir Publications. For more information on the *Real Guide*s, Lonely Planet, and John Muir Publications, see pages 56–57.

WORK

To work in Belize, it is necessary to obtain a temporary Employment Permit issued by the Director of Immigration and Nationality Services. Permits are granted only after securing a job offer. For further information, contact the **Immigration and Nationality Service** or the **Ministry of Labour and Local Government**, Belmopan, Belize.

Internships/Traineeships

A program sponsored by a member of the Council on International Educational Exchange is described below.

State University of New York College at Cortland. Internships in agencies involved in various aspects of development. Opportunities in communications, health, ecology, public administration, and other areas. Juniors and seniors in good academic standing. Apply by March 15 for fall; September 1 for spring. Contact: Office of International Programs, SUNY College at Cortland, PO Box 2000, Cortland, NY 13045; (607) 753-2209.

Voluntary Service

The Sisters of the Charity of Nazareth sponsors a volunteer program for those interested in health care, social service, education, or ministry. Participants serve from two weeks to three months; room and board are provided. For service periods of three months or more, at least nine months prior notification is required. For more information, contact the Sisters of Charity of Nazareth, SCNA Center, PO Box 172, Nazareth, KY 40048.

STUDY

Following is an educational program sponsored by a CIEE-member institution. Consult Appendix I for the contact address.

Natural Sciences

World Learning/School for International Training. *College Semester Abroad: Natural and Cultural Ecology*. Belize City, Monkey Bay, Belmopan, Cayo, Stann Creek District. Spring and fall semesters. Environmental studies. Orientation, 6-week homestay, field trips, field-research seminar, independent-study project. Sophomores to graduate students with 2.5 GPA and previous coursework in environmental studies, ecology, or anthropology. Apply by May 7 for fall; October 7 for spring. Contact: College Semester Abroad Admissions at (800) 336-1616.

COSTA RICA

Costa Ricans see their Central American nation as a rose among thorns. The country offers democracy, social stability, and relative economic prosperity in a region where all three are generally lacking.

The people of Costa Rica value their two-party democracy, tradition of nonviolence, and educational system. They also prize the traditional family structure that remains the central focus of their lives. A strong sense of history has helped keep these attitudes alive in the "Ticos" (the name by which the Costa Ricans are often called), and they will point with pride to the establishment of free and mandatory education for all citizens in 1869, the abolition of the death penalty in 1882, and the disbanding of a standing army in 1949.

But Costa Rica is not entirely immune to the maladies that plague the region. Rapid population growth, deforestation, and external debt (the highest per capita debt of any Third World nation) are among the problems confronting the country. And some question whether Costa Rica can continue to avoid the political strife and economic ills experienced by many of its Central American neighbors.

Although the country is officially neutral, Costa Ricans are strongly pro-American and view the United States as a friend and ally. Much economic support is gained by this relationship, both through the public and private sectors, and an increasing number of U.S. firms are locating their Latin American headquarters or branch offices in Costa Rica because of the nation's political and economic stability as well as the availability of an educated and hard-working labor force. Also visible are a growing number of retired Americans who have settled here to enjoy the good quality of life and pleasant climate at an economical price. Americans—whether businesspeople, retirees, students, or travelers—generally find Costa Rica safer, more comfortable, and less "foreign" than other Latin American nations.

—G. Bernard Yevin, Rockford, Illinois

Official name: Republic of Costa Rica. **Area:** 19,575 square miles (about twice the size of Maryland). **Population:** 3,111,000. **Population density:** 158 inhabitants per square mile. **Capital and largest city:** San José (pop. 890,000). **Language:** Spanish. **Religion:** Roman Catholic. **Per capita income:** US$1,810. **Currency:** Colone. **Literacy rate:** 93%. **Average daily temperature:** San José: June, 70°; December, 67°. **Average number of days with precipitation:** San José: June, 22; December, 6.

TRAVEL

U.S. citizens need only a passport to enter Costa Rica for stays of up to 30 days. Tourist cards are issued either on the plane or upon arrival at border crossings. An onward or return ticket is also necessary. For specific details, check with one of the **Costa Rican consulates** in Chicago, Houston, Los Angeles, Miami, New Orleans, or New York. The New York consulate is located at 80 Wall Street, Suite 718-19, New York, NY 10005; (212) 425-2620.

Getting Around

Traveling around Costa Rica is fairly easy, both because the country is compact and because it has one of the region's best transportation systems. **Roads** and **rail** lines link the capital with Puerto Limón on the Caribbean and Puntarenas and Puerto Caldera on the Gulf of Nicoya. In addition, the Pan-American Highway extends the length of the country, and express highways radiate from San José, connecting the capital to the other major cities of the central plateau as well as to Pacific ports and beaches. There are numerous companies in San José offering **car** and jeep rentals, including major U.S. companies such as Hertz, Avis, Budget, National, and Dollar, as well as local firms. Costa Rica is also great for **biking,** with relatively light traffic and good asphalt roads.

Eating and Sleeping

There are several **youth hostels** in various parts of Costa Rica. For more information, contact Hostelling International/American Youth Hostels (see page 54) or Costa Rica's national youth hostel association, **Red Costarricense de Albergues Juveniles (RECAJ)**, PO Box 1355-1002, Paseo de los Estudiantes, Avenida Central, calles 29 y 31, San José; (506) 244085.

Especially for Students and Young People

The student travel organization and issuer of the International Student Identity Card in Costa Rica is **OTEC Joven**, Calle 3, Avenida 1 y 3, Edificio Ferencz, 275 norte del Teatro Nacional, San José; (506) 220866; fax (506) 332321. At OTEC offices, you can get information on International Student Identity Card discounts, buy international air tickets, book accommodations, and sign up for tours. Tours offered by OTEC include a one-day Pacific island cruise, a one-day white-water rafting trip on the Reventazon River, and a three-day tour of Tortuguero National Park.

For Further Information

General information is available from the **Costa Rica Tourist Board**, PO Box 672712, Marietta, GA 30067-0046; (800) 327-7033. There are numerous guidebooks to Costa Rica. Two of the best are Harry S. Pariser's *Adventure Guide to Costa Rica* ($16.95, Hunter Publishing; see page 519) and *The New Key to Costa Rica* ($13.95, Ulysses Press), by Beatrice Blake and Anne Becher. A good one for budget travelers is *Costa Rica: A Travel Survival Kit*, available for $11.95 from Lonely Planet Publications (see page 56). The best coverage of parks and nature reserves can be found in *Costa Rica: A Natural Destination*, available for $16.95 from John Muir Publications (see page 57).

WORK

Getting a Job

It is very difficult for foreigners to obtain regular, salaried employment in Costa Rica. For more information, contact the **Direccion General de Migracion Extranjera**, San José, Costa Rica. If you are a student, or you're interested in voluntary-service work, see the programs below.

CIEE's Work in Costa Rica program allows U.S. college students to receive authorization to accept temporary employment in Costa Rica for up to four months during their summer vacation (June 1 to October 1). Participants are responsible for finding their own jobs; the most likely categories of employment include unskilled work in the service industries (especially tourism) as well as language institutes. The program is conducted with the cooperation of OTEC which provides an orientation and assists with problems that may arise. Participants should realize that the summer job market in a Third World country like Costa Rica will be quite different from that of the United States. Salaries may be low compared to the U.S. but should cover the cost of daily expenses. To qualify, an individual must be at least 18 years of age, a college or university student, and a U.S. citizen or permanent resident. The cost of the program is $160. For more information, contact the Work Exchanges Department at CIEE.

Internships/Traineeships

A program sponsored by a CIEE-member is listed below.

State University of New York College at Brockport. *Spanish-Speaking Internship Program*. San José. Fall and spring semesters and summer. Business. Juniors and seniors with intermediate Spanish. Apply by April 15 for fall and summer; November 1 for spring. Contact: Office of International Education, 101P Rakov Center, SUNY College at Brockport, Brockport, NY 14420; (716) 395-2119.

Voluntary Service

The Year Abroad Program sponsored by the **International Christian Youth Exchange** offers persons ages 18 to 30 voluntary-service opportunities in the fields of health care, education, the environment, construction, and more. See page 25 for more information.

In addition, **Global Volunteers** sponsors a two-week service program in Costa Rica where volunteers assist with two grassroots education programs. Participants tutor children and teach English as well as help in building schools. For more information, contact Global Volunteers, 375 East Little Canada Road, St. Paul, MN 55117; (612) 482-1074.

Goshen College also offers a study-service term in Costa Rica that is open primarily to Goshen students; sometimes a limited number of spaces are available to students at other colleges and universities.

STUDY

The following academic programs are offered by CIEE-member institutions. Unless otherwise noted, consult Appendix I for the addresses of the colleges and universities listed in this section.

Semester and Academic Year

General Studies

Associated Colleges of the Midwest. *Latin American Culture and Society*. San José. Fall semester; may be combined with *Tropical Field Research* for full academic year. Sophomores to seniors with at least one year of college Spanish. Apply by November 1 for early response; final deadline March 15. *Tropical Field Research: Natural and Social Sciences*. San José. Spring semester; may be combined with *Latin American Culture and Society* for full academic year. Sophomores to seniors with social science and natural science courses and one year of college Spanish. Apply by March 15 for early response; final deadline November 1.

International Student Exchange Program (ISEP). Academic year. Direct reciprocal exchange between U.S. universities and Universidad Nacional de Heredia. Full curriculum options. Rolling admissions. Open only to students at ISEP-member institutions. Contact ISEP for list of members.

University of Kansas. *Academic Year Abroad at the University of Costa Rica*. San José, Golfito. Sophomores with 3.0 GPA and five semesters of college Spanish. Apply by March 15 for fall; October 1 for spring and academic year (August 1 for early decision).

Summer and Short-Term

General Studies

American University. *Costa Rica Study Tour*. Spring semester (12 weeks in Washington, DC and three weeks in Costa Rica). International environment and development seminar focusing on global policy issues. Second-semester sophomores to seniors with 2.75 GPA. Apply by October 15. Contact: World

Capitals Programs, Dunblane House—Tenley Campus, American University, Washington, DC 20016-8083; (202) 895-4900/4937.
University of Alabama. *Alabama in Costa Rica*. San José. Four weeks in summer. Offered in cooperation with Centro Costarricense—Norteamericano. Latin American studies, history, and sociology. Homestays and excursions. Undergraduates and graduate students. Apply by March 1. Contact: (205) 348-5256.
University of New Orleans. *UNO Costa Rica International Summer School*. San Ramón. Summer. Study at the University of Costa Rica. First-year college students to graduate students. Apply by April 1.

Natural Sciences

Council on International Educational Exchange. *Ecology of the Rain Forest: Tropical Biology and Conservation at the Monteverde Institute*. Summer. Brief homestay. Sophomores to seniors with two semesters of college biology, environmental studies, or equivalent, and 2.75 GPA. Apply by March 15. Contact University Programs Department.
Ramapo College of New Jersey. *Study of Tropical Ecosystems*. Various locations. Two weeks in May. Tropical ecosystems (especially tropical forests), deforestation, and land use; field study at each site. Sophomores to graduate students. Apply by April 12. Contact: Study Abroad Office, Ramapo College of New Jersey, 505 Ramapo Valley Road, Room D-204, Mahwah, NJ 07430-9926; (201) 529-7463.

Spanish Language and Costa Rican Culture

Memphis State University. *MSU Summer Program in Costa Rica*. San José. One-month intensive Spanish-language program. Homestays and excursions. Undergraduates and graduate students with one year of college Spanish and in good academic standing. Apply by March 15. Contact: Dr. Nicholas W. Rokas, Department of Foreign Languages and Literatures, Memphis State University, Memphis, TN 38152; (901) 678-2501/2506.

GUATEMALA

Guatemala, like its Central American neighbors, has an intriguing past, a troubled present, and an uncertain future. Its Mayan roots are still strongly felt throughout the country—in its ancient ruins, its textiles and customs, and its languages. Eighty percent of Guatemala's population consists of indigenous people who are descended from the Maya and in many ways spend their days much as their ancestors did: tilling small plots of land and weaving, forming almost self-supporting communities in the western highlands and Alta Verapaz. Over 40 indigenous languages are spoken in Guatemala, as well as Spanish. The beautiful mountainous land and the low cost of Guatemalan transport add to the appeal for travelers exploring the region. The lowland area, the Petén, is covered with a dense rain forest which guards the Mayan ruins of Tikal, Ceibal, Nakum, and many other sites.

The Spanish language is only one of a number of legacies left by the Spaniards during their many years of rule, which began in 1523 when they arrived from Mexico City looking for precious metals. Many of the Spaniards who stayed in Guatemala intermarried with the indigenous people, forming the basis for the mestizo population, which now accounts for about 20 percent of the total. However, those of primarily European descent, the *ladinos*, wield much of the country's economic and political power, making their money from coffee, sugarcane, and banana plantations in the countryside.

Since it gained independence from Spain in 1821, Guatemala endured numerous military and civilian dictators, as well as extreme labor unrest and U.S. involvement. Most recently, the country experienced a period of extreme political violence and terror in the mid-1980s. This period has shaped much of the American impression of the country but, while the traveler should still use caution, Guatemala has recently undergone a period of relative political stability while the country deals with domestic unrest and the specter of human rights violations. This period was ushered in by the election in 1985 of Guatemala's first civilian president in thirty years. A new president, Jorge Serrano Elias, was sworn in in 1991, marking the first transfer of political power from one elected civilian to another. Serrano's move in May 1993 (with the aid of the army) to abolish Congress, the courts, and the Constitution put in jeopardy the country's recent political gains. However, partly because of international pressure, and partly due to the clamor raised by the Guatemalans themselves, Serrano's attempt to seize power was thwarted. In a surprise move, Ramiro de Leon de Carpio, former Attorney General of Human Rights and a frequent critic of the military, was sworn in as president to finish the remaining half of Serrano's five-year term. Although politicians had initially discounted him as unacceptable to the army high command, his election was applauded by Guatemalan civilians, and Guatemala continues perilously along the road toward democracy.

—Pearl Douglas, Charleston, West Virginia

Official name: Republic of Guatemala. **Area:** 42,042 (the size of Tennessee). **Population:** 9,266,000. **Population density:** 220 inhabitants per square mile. **Capital and largest city:** Guatemala City (pop. 1,095,000). **Language:** Spanish. **Religion:** Roman Catholic. **Per capita income:** US$1,810. **Currency:** Quetzal. **Literacy rate:** 55%. **Average daily temperature:** Guatemala City: June, 66°; December, 61°. **Average number of days with precipitation:** Guatemala City: June, 23; December, 4.

TRAVEL

U.S. citizens need a passport and tourist card or visa to enter Guatemala. Visas good for multiple stays of up to 30 days during a one-year period are issued free of charge with presentation of a U.S. passport and 2″ × 2″ photo at Guatemalan consulates in the U.S. Tourist cards valid for 30 days from the date of issue are available for US$5 on your airline flying into Guatemala or at the border with presentation of a passport. The initial 30-day period for holders of visas or tourist cards may be extended once in the country by reporting to the Immigration Office in Guatemala City. For further information, contact the **Embassy of Guatemala**, 2220 R Street NW, Washington, DC 20008; (202) 745-4952. There are Guatemalan consulates in Chicago, Los Angeles, Miami, New Orleans, and New York.

Getting Around

In Guatemala, the **bus** is king. Express buses traverse the Pan-American highway and slower ones cover the countryside, serving even the tiniest of villages. Only the wealthy own cars; the rest of the population relies entirely on the bus for transportation. For the most part, buses are very cheap and are easy to use, usually operating out of bus terminals located on the edge of town. Between towns you can hail buses and they'll usually stop for you. Most buses look like secondhand U.S. school buses, brightly painted and overcrowded. However, there are more comfortable first-class coaches going longer distances. Buses are a great way to meet people, and traveling on them is always an interesting experience. Because of the mountainous terrain, however, you may be in for a few rough rides.

Several domestic **airlines** depart from Guatemala City. Flying drastically cuts your travel time. Compare 45 minutes from Guatemala to Flores by plane with 18 hours by bus. Renting a **car** is sometimes risky unless you plan to stick to major roads. Even so, gas stations are few and far between (as are spare parts). Car theft and vandalism continue to be major problems. **Taxis** are available for intercity travel, but most don't have meters so be sure to set a price before getting in. **Biking** is very popular in Guatemala; in well-visited cities like Antigua, mountain bikes can be rented. Motorbikes can also be rented. Hitching is common, but it's polite to offer a small fee.

For Further Information

General information can be obtained from Guatemalan consulates (see "Travel," above) or from the **Guatemala Tourist Commission**, 299 Alhambra Circle, Suite 510, Coral Gables, FL 33134; (305) 442-0651; fax (305) 442-1013.

The best general guide to Guatemala is *The Real Guide: Guatemala and Belize* ($13.95). A good guide to the region's Mayan sites is *La Ruta Maya: Yucutan, Guatemala, and Belize*, available for $15.95 from Lonely Planet Publications. For more information on the *Real Guide*s and Lonely Planet Publications, see pages 56–57.

WORK

It is necessary to obtain a labor permit in order to be employed in Guatemala. You must secure a job before the permit will be issued. For further information, contact the **Ministerio de Trabajo y Prebision Social**, Palacio Nacional, 1er Nivel Zone 1, Guatemala City, Guatemala.

Voluntary Service

Global Volunteers sponsors a service program in Guatemala in which participants help construct health clinics, assist with reforestation, lay pipe for potable water systems, create community preschools, and assist with other infrastructure projects. The program runs for two weeks. For more information, contact Global Volunteers, 375 East Little Canada Road, St. Paul, MN 55117; (612) 482-1074.

STUDY

Listed below are the study programs sponsored by CIEE-member institutions. Unless otherwise noted, consult Appendix I for the addresses of these colleges and universities.

Summer and Short-Term

Economics

Lehigh University. *Lehigh in Guatemala*. Guatemala City. June. Economic development of the Third World, and political and cultural changes in Guatemala. Study at Universidad de Francisco Marroquin. Hotel accommodations and excursions. Sophomores to seniors with basic economics background and in good academic standing. Apply by March 15. Contact: Office of Summer Studies, 205 Johnson Hall, 36 University Drive, Lehigh University, Bethlehem, PA 18015; (215) 758-3966.

Health and Medicine

University of Utah. *Health Care in Guatemala*. Antigua. Four weeks in summer from late July to late August. Spanish-language study, health, and nursing. Volunteer work in health-care facilities. First-year college students to graduate students and adults; minimum age 18. Apply by March 1.

EXPLORING GUATEMALAN CULTURE

Readings

Guatemala's most famous author is Miguel Angel Asturias. The history and culture of Guatemala are recurrent themes in his work. *Men of Maize* (1949), considered his masterpiece, deals with the complexity of Indian culture in magic-realist style. *El Señor Presidente* (1946) offers a glimpse into social chaos and dictatorial rule, based on the dictatorship of Guatemalan president Cabrera. In *Weekend en Guatemala* (1956), he describes the downfall of the Arbenz government and *El Papa Verde* (1954) delves into the shady world of the United Fruit Company. Rigoberta Menchu provides an insider's look into life in the highlands in *Rigoberta Menchu: An Indian Woman in Guatemala* (1985), an account of the abuse of the Indian population and of the complexity of Indian culture.

Authors from other countries have also written about Guatemala. Henry J. Frundt's *Refreshing Pauses: Coca-Cola and Human Rights in Guatemala* (1987) is a tale of foreign greed and the Guatemalan effort to organize a union. *The Volcano Above Us*, by Norman Lewis, is a depressing but gripping novel about banana companies, trigger-happy troops, political instability, and racism. Paul Bowles recounts his experiences in Guatemala in *Up Above the World* (1982). Bowles also translated *The Beggar's Knife*, a short-story collection by Guatemalan writer Rodrigo Rey-Rosa. In *Guatemala: A Cry from the Heart* (1990), by David V. Schwantes, a Minnesota businessman joins an ecumenical group visiting Guatemala; his experiences and observations make him confront American policy on Central America. Francisco Goldman's novel *The Long*

Night of White Chickens (1992), set in the 1980s, is about a young man raised in Boston and his relationship with a Guatemalan orphan who is later murdered in Guatemala. Peter Daniel's *Tikal: A Novel about the Maya* (1983) is a novel that provides a hypothesis of reasons for the evacuation of Tikal more than 1,000 years ago, and has been praised for its detailing of Mayan customs.

HONDURAS

Flat land is at a premium in Honduras, especially in the nation's capital, Tegucigalpa, which is built on the slopes of the mountain El Picacho. Tegucigalpa was the site of some early Spanish gold mines; however, the Spanish soon realized there was little easily convertible wealth (gold, silver, copper) to be found in Honduras and moved on. Honduras was subsequently largely ignored by Spain as a colony and later as a trading partner, and remained fairly isolated until the United Fruit Company, with the support of the U.S. government, started to cultivate large cash-crop (chiefly banana) plantations in the arable Northwest. A succession of military and civilian rulers, internal rebellions, civil wars, and changes of government since independence in 1821 indicate a political instability that has scared away most foreign investment. The banana companies, which have used the lack of a stable Honduran government to their advantage, are the exception; Honduras was the original "banana republic."

Economically, Honduras shot itself in the foot by withdrawing from the Central American Common Market during the aftermath of the 1969 "Soccer War" with El Salvador. Only considerable U.S. aid has kept the Honduran economy from complete collapse. Honduras has traditionally been the poorest nation in Central America; at present, however, Nicaragua's drawn-out civil war has given Nicaragua that distinction. The result of Honduras's dependence on U.S. aid and U.S. companies for investment is the country's military alliance with the U.S., which has made it a base for U.S. military operations in Central America. The American influence is strong, from the *supermercados* and shopping malls that exist in defiance of the poverty of most Hondurans to the U.S. pop music that can be heard all over Tegucigalpa.

Most of Honduras is mountainous except the low swamplands (Paul Theroux's "Mosquito Coast") in the Northeast. Partly because of its inhospitable topography, Honduras is the least populous Central American republic although it is the largest in area. In contrast to the Spanish-speaking South, in many areas of the North coast both Spanish and English are commonly spoken, a result of West Indian laborers migrating to Honduras for work on coastal railways and banana and coffee plantations in the late 19th and early 20th centuries. There are no well-known tourist resorts, only the Bay Islands off the Caribbean Coast, which attract a mix of people seeking cheap beach life off the beaten path.

—Fraser Brown, New York, New York

Official name: Republic of Honduras. **Area:** 43,277 square miles (about the size of Tennessee). **Population:** 4,949,000 **Population density:** 114 inhabitants per square mile. **Capital and largest city:** Tegucigalpa (pop. 550,000). **Language:** Spanish. **Religion:** Roman Catholic. **Per capita income:** US$960. **Currency:** Lempira. **Literacy rate:** 73%. **Average daily temperature:** Tegucigalpa: June, 74°; December, 68°. **Average number of days with precipitation:** June, 13; December, 7.

TRAVEL

U.S. citizens need a passport to enter Honduras, but visas are not required for visits of up to three months. For specific regulations, check with the **Embassy of Honduras**, 3007 Tilden Street NW, Washington, DC 20008; (202) 223-0185.

Getting Around

Getting around by car is easy, but most Hondurans take the **bus**. There is frequent bus service along the country's main route, connecting the commercial center of San Pedro Sula with Tegucigalpa, the capital. Buses serve most of the rest of the country as well, except for parts of the Mosquito Coast which are still not accessible by road. **Cars** can be rented in San Pedro Sula or Tegucigalpa. The country's limited railroad network is confined to the banana-producing areas of the coast and transports a lot of bananas but not many people. Several small **airlines** offer daily flights between Tegucigalpa, San Pedro Sula, La Ceiba, and some Caribbean costal towns and islands. In the most isolated areas, travel is still by mule and on foot.

For Further Information

General tourist information is available from the **Information Department of the Embassy of Honduras**, 3007 Tilden Street NW, Washington, DC 20008; (202) 966-7702.

Good travel information about Honduras can be found in the *Mexico and Central American Handbook* ($22), published in England and distributed in the U.S. by Prentice Hall, or in *Central America on a Shoestring*, available for $16.95 from Lonely Planet Publications (see page 56).

WORK

It is very difficult for foreigners to obtain employment in Honduras. For more information contact the Embassy of Honduras (see "Travel," above).

Voluntary Service

For persons interested in voluntary-service work, the Year Abroad Program sponsored by the **International Christian Youth Exchange** offers persons ages 18 to 30 voluntary-service opportunities in the fields of health care, education, the environment, construction, and more. See page 25 for more information.

STUDY

Below is an academic program offered by a CIEE-member institution. Consult Appendix I for the contact address and phone number.

Semester and Academic Year

General Studies

International Student Exchange Program (ISEP). Fall and spring semesters. Direct reciprocal exchange between U.S. universities and Universidad José Cecilio del Valle. Full curriculum options. Rolling admissions. Open only to students at ISEP-member institutions. Contact ISEP for list of members.

Summer and Short-Term

Agriculture

Louisiana State University. *LSU in Honduras.* Spring. Educational and agricultural study. Sophomores to seniors with 2.5 GPA and graduate students with 3.0 GPA. Apply by February 1.

MEXICO

A 2,000-mile border—sometimes a shallow river but more often just an imaginary line in the desert—separates Mexico and the United States. While the border itself is crossed legally and illegally by thousands of people every day, the real division is a linguistic, economic, historic, and cultural one that is not so easily crossed. Nowhere else does the Third World rub shoulders so closely with one of the world's wealthiest nations. And while the two nations coexist peacefully but uncomfortably, each of them tries as much as possible to ignore the other. Yet as much as Americans and Mexicans each might like to be rid of their backyard neighbor, the futures of the two countries are inextricably linked.

In the 16th century, the Spanish defeated the Aztecs, took their land and silver, and enslaved or killed much of the native population. In the 19th century, Mexico gained its independence from Spain, but little changed for the average Mexican. Early in this century the Mexican Revolution brought far-reaching changes, including land redistribution and an end to the power of the traditional elite—the landed aristocracy, the church, and the military. But its promise of power to Mexican workers and campesinos was never realized; Mexico remains split by stark class differences.

Only recently does it appear that Mexico may be emerging from a decade-long financial crisis that has left the country demoralized and with a standard of living lower than that of 10 years ago. This crisis was brought about by a drop in the price of petroleum on world markets and Mexico's resultant inability to make the required payments on its foreign debt. One result of the crisis has been increased emigration—legal and illegal—across the U.S. border. Another has been challenges from both the left and right to the PRI, the political party that has controlled Mexico since the end of the Revolution. President Carlos Salinas de Gortari has taken important steps to give a greater role to the opposition and enforce fair elections. But the political stability of Mexico—like its economic future—is uncertain.

Nowhere is this uncertain future more evident than in Mexico City, the economic, political, and cultural heart of the country. With nearly 20 million people, the metropolitan area is by most counts the world's largest city. Not surprisingly, rapid population growth has strained the infrastructure of the city, producing overcrowding, pollution, and sprawling slums. But in spite of its problems, Mexico City—once the capital of New Spain and before that, of the Aztec empire—remains one of the world's most lively and interesting cities. Rising on the northern edge of the city are the ruins of Teotihuacan, once the center of a great empire that reached its zenith a millenium before the arrival of the Aztecs. Even now, Teotihuacan's Pyramids of the Sun and Moon are among the world's most impressive sights.

Although power radiates from Mexico City, it is in the villages of Mexico where the spiritual heart of the country beats. Here the pace of life is slower and traditional ties to the land, the church, and family are strong. Visitors to the highlands of central Mexico will encounter picturesque villages and a way of life that is attractive because it seems unaffected by the ills of modernity. But a closer examination will also reveal that these villages are not lost in time; like all of Mexican society today, they are products of the dynamic interplay between ancient Indian ways, the legacy of Spanish colonialism, and the contemporary cultural, political, and economic influence of Mexico's powerful northern neighbor.

Whether you come for unsurpassed beach resorts such as Acapulco or Cancún, the ruins of ancient Indian civilizations, or the natural beauty of its mountains, jungles, and deserts, strike out on your own to explore Mexico's cities, villages, and countryside. Your efforts will be richly rewarded as you develop a new perspective on the U.S.–Mexican relationship and encounter a very different way of life that's just across the border.

—Del Franz, New York, New York

Official name: United Mexican States. **Area:** 761,604 square miles (almost three times the size of Texas). **Population:** 90,007,000. **Population density:** 118 inhabitants per square mile. **Capital and largest city:** Mexico City (pop. 20,000,000). **Language:** Spanish. **Religion:** Roman Catholic. **Per capita income:** US$2,680. **Currency:** Mexican peso. **Literacy rate:** 88%. **Average daily temperature:** Mexico City: June, 63°; December, 54°. **Average number of days with precipitation:** Mexico City: June, 21; December, 4.

TRAVEL

U.S. citizens do not need a passport or a visa to enter Mexico for tourist or transit stays of up to 180 days. Tourist cards are issued free of charge upon presentation of proof of citizenship (a birth certificate, passport, or naturalization papers). They can be obtained at immigration offices at points of entry along the border, at Mexican consulates and tourist offices, or from airlines serving Mexico. Minors traveling alone must have notarized consent from one or both parents. For further information, check with the **Embassy of Mexico**, 1911 Pennsylvania Avenue NW, Washington DC 20006; (202) 728-1600. There are also **Mexican consulates** in most major U.S. cities.

Getting Around

Mexico's hundreds of **bus** companies lend credence to the saying that "In Mexico, where there's a road, there's a bus." Buses range from comfortable air-conditioned intercity buses to trucks with wooden benches, and half of the excitement of visiting a remote village may be the bus trip there. Traveling by bus is cheap and immerses you in Mexican culture in a way that is not possible if you drive or fly.

Mexico has a well-developed road system. While most major roads are two-laners, a network of brand-new four-lane highways is under construction, and many are already completed. However, these are toll roads, and many are quite expensive. For the most part, Mexican roads are characterized by unpredictable hazards that most U.S drivers are not accustomed to, including animals, slow-moving carts, people, and potholes. Mexican driving habits are also quite different; for example, passing is done with less margin of safety and little attention is paid to traffic lanes (which are seldom marked on the wider roads). Unleaded gasoline, used only by tourists with U.S. vehicles, can be found only in large towns and resorts. In spite of these obstacles, thousands of Americans drive in Mexico. A car provides comfort and independence and can be an enjoyable means of getting around, especially in northern Mexico, where traffic is light. In addition, hitchhiking is socially acceptable and done by both Mexicans and foreigners.

U.S. driver's licenses are acceptable in Mexico. If you're driving your own car, however, you'll have to provide other documents, buy Mexican insurance, and present a major credit card. If you exceed the time allotted to you on your tourist card, your car may be confiscated. For more information on bringing your car across the border, contact the Mexican Government Tourism Office (see "For Further Information," below). Those renting **cars** in Mexico should also be aware that driving restrictions apply in Mexico City. To reduce congestion and pollution, cars with certain numbers on their license plates cannot be driven on designated days. Make sure your rental car has the right numbers.

The Mexico rail network is widespread, although it's not nearly as comprehensive or frequent as bus service. Generally speaking, **trains** are also slower and subject to more delays than buses. On the other hand, they are usually more comfortable, more interesting, and even cheaper than the buses. Trains with sleeping cars provide overnight service between Mexico City and many other major cities of central Mexico, as well as cities along the U.S. border.

Air service is provided by several domestic airlines, the best known of which are Aeroméxico and Mexicana. In Mexico, travel by plane is convenient and a popular alternative for travelers covering long distances.

In this mountainous country of few navigable rivers, travel by boat is generally not an alternative. An exception are the car ferries that cross between the Baja Peninsula and various cities on the Mexican mainland.

Eating and Sleeping

If you avoid the most touristy places, Mexico can be one of the world's most inexpensive countries. There's an abundance of budget hotels in every Mexican city, but be aware that new establishments that resemble places you might see in the U.S. are generally on the more expensive side. Older-looking hotels are usually more economical, spacious, and comfortable. There is also a host of inexpensive youth hostels. For more information on **hostels**, contact Hostelling International/American Youth Hostels (see page 54) or the **Comisión Nacional del Deporte (CONADE)**, Dirección de Villas Deportivas Juveniles, Glorieta del Metro Insurgentes, Local C-11, Colonia Juarez, CP 06600, México DF; (52) 5-5252974. For a list of independent hostels, contact **Backpackers Mexico,** San Miguel International Backpackers Hostel, Organos 34, San Miguel de Allende, G.T.D. Mexico 37700 (52) 465-20674.

Dining in Mexico can also be quite cheap, and those who are used to American versions of Mexican food are in for a tasty surprise. Real Mexican cuisine is much more varied than the tacos and burritos familar to Americans. The staples of any Mexican meal are rice, beans, and tortillas, which are commonly served with a main dish of meat, chicken, or fish. The major meal of the day is eaten in the afternoon, usually between 2 and 5 P.M. Most restaurants serve a fixed-price *comida corrida*, or meal of the day.

Especially for Students and Young People

Mexico's student travel organization and issuer of the International Student Identity Card is **SETEJ Mexico**, Hamburgo No. 301, Colonia Juarez, 06600 Mexico DF; (52) 5-2110743. SETEJ has branch offices in four other cities: Cuernavaca, Guadalajara, Guanajuato, and Monterrey. At most SETEJ Mexico offices you can get travel information, book accommodations, and buy international train and plane tickets. You can also obtain a list of establishments offering discounts to holders of the International Student Identity Card at SETEJ offices.

For Further Information

General tourist information is available from the **Mexican Government Tourism Office**, 405 Park Avenue, Suite 1401, New York, NY 10022; (212) 421-6655; fax (212) 753-2874. Their toll-free number is (800) 446-3942. For information on roads in Mexico, call (800) 232-4639. Information on automobile regulations and taking your car into Mexico can be obtained by calling (800) 446-8277. You can get further information in Mexico by calling this 24-hour English-language hot line: 91-800-90392 (in Mexico City: 250-0123 or 251-0151).

There are a good number of guidebooks to Mexico. One of the favorites for students traveling on a budget is *Let's Go: Mexico* ($16.95), which also includes information on Guatemala and Belize. For good, detailed descriptions of Mexican culture and history in relation to the sights, try *The Real Guide: Mexico* ($11.95). Those who want to get off the beaten path might turn to *Mexico: A Travel Survival Kit* ($17.95) or *La Ruta Maya: Yucatan, Guatemala, and Belize* ($15.95), both published by Lonely Planet Publications. The best guide to the Yucatan Peninsula is *Yucatan Peninsula Handbook,* available for $14.95 from Moon Publications. For more information on *The Real Guides*, Lonely Planet, and Moon Publications see pages 56–57.

An extremely useful resource, Carl Franz's *The People's Guide to Mexico* ($18.95) is not a guidebook in the traditional sense; it does not describe hotels or the most interesting towns to visit. What it does do is provide, through a series of anecdotes, one of the best pictures of what travel in Mexico is all about. While most informative for the first-time visitor, the book also makes for interesting and enjoyable reading for the seasoned traveler. If you can't find it in bookstores, you can order it from John Muir Publications (see page 57). Franz also publishes a newsletter on Mexico. For a free copy, write or call Wide World Books and Maps, 1911 North 45th Street, Seattle, WA 98103; (206) 634-3453.

The uneasy relationship between Mexico and the United States is sure to enter into discussions you have with Mexicans. A recent book, *Limits to Friendship: The United States and Mexico* ($10.95, Random House), by Jorge G. Castaneda, provides a Mexican perspective on the political, economic, and cultural issues that divide the two countries. A good, concise analysis of foreign policy options from a U.S. point of view is provided by Peter H. Smith in

Mexico: Neighbor in Transition, available for $4 from the Foreign Policy Association (see page 16). Another look at the relationship from a U.S. perspective can be found in *Distant Neighbors* ($8.95, Viking), by *New York Times* correspondent Alan Riding. Finally, *Good Neighbors: Communicating with the Mexicans*, by John C. Condon, takes a look at Mexicans' and Americans' misconceptions about each other and suggests ways of overcoming these prejudices. It's available for $10.95 from Intercultural Press (see page 3).

WORK

Obtaining regular salaried employment in Mexico is nearly impossible for foreigners; it's not permitted unless specifically requested by a Mexican company. The employer then must apply for the requisite work permit, on the applicant's behalf, to the Mexican immigration authorities. For more information contact the **Embassy of Mexico**, Consular Section, 2827 16th Street NW, Washington, DC 20009; (202) 736-1000.

Internships/Traineeships

Internship programs offered by member institutions and organizations of the Council on International Educational Exchange are described below.

Association for International Practical Training. *IAESTE Trainee Program*. On-the-job training for undergraduate and graduate students in technical fields such as engineering, computer science, agriculture, architecture, mathematics, and the natural and physical sciences. See page 19 for more information.

Brigham Young University. *Spring Term Internship in Mexico*. Internships in pre-med and health-related fields. Six weeks in May and June; fluency in Spanish required. Students live with Mexican families and work in hospitals and other health-related facilities. Apply by December 1. Consult Appendix I for the address you can write to for more information.

State University of New York College at Brockport. *Spanish-Speaking Internship Program*. Cuernavaca. Fall and spring semesters and summer. Business. Juniors and seniors with intermediate Spanish. Apply by April 15 for fall and summer; November 1 for spring. Contact: Office of International Education, 101P Rakov Center, SUNY College at Brockport, Brockport, NY 14420; (716) 395-2119.

Voluntary Service

The Year Abroad Program sponsored by the **International Christian Youth Exchange** offers persons ages 18 to 30 voluntary-service opportunities in the fields of health care, education, the environment, and construction. See page 25 for more information.

The **Lisle Fellowship** sponsors a short-term study/service program, "Facing Changes: Challenges for Community Development and Artisans." This program is open to recent high-school graduates, college students, and adults. Apply by October 15. See Appendix I for the address where you can write for more information.

In addition, **Los Ninos–Helping Children at the Border** works with and helps support orphanages in the Mexican border cities of Mexicali, Tecate, and Tijuana. Short and long-term voluntary-service opportunities are available in the orphanages. No special skills are required, but participants must be at least 18 years old. For more information, contact Los Ninos, 1330 Continental Street, San Ysidro, CA 92073.

AFS Intercultural Programs sponsors a Global-Service Program which enables adults to do community-service work in Mexico. Service projects are arranged individually according to the interests or expertise of the participant. Projects run from three to seven weeks and are open to all interested persons 19 and older. For more information, contact AFS Intercultural Programs, 313 East 43rd Street, New York, NY 10017; (800) 237-4636.

Global Volunteers sponsors a two-week service program in Mexico where participants work with rural villagers on agricultural education, health care, and business development projects. Volunteer activities include tutoring children, painting, and digging latrines. For more information, contact Global Volunteers, 375 East Little Canada Road, St. Paul, MN 55117; (612) 482-1074.

Other voluntary-service opportunities are available through **The Partnership for Service-Learning** and **Amigos de las Americas**. For more information on these programs, see Chapter Three.

STUDY

The **Embassy of Mexico** (see "Travel") can provide information on language schools for foreign students as well as on independent postgraduate study.

The Universidad Autonoma de Guadalajara (UAG), a CIEE-member institution in Mexico, hosts a number of exchange students in programs sponsored by certain U.S. colleges and universities, as well as accepting students enrolling independently from the U.S. Contact the study-abroad office at your school for further information or write the UAG Exchange Department directly at Depto. de Intercambio Universitario, Av. Patria 1201, Lomas del Valle, Guadalajara, Jal. 44100; (3) 6417051, ext. 32204/32319.

The following study programs are offered by CIEE-member institutions. Unless otherwise noted, consult Appendix I for the addresses of colleges and universities listed in this section. In addition to these programs, California State University at Sacramento and University of Nebraska at Lincoln offer study programs open to their own students only.

Semester and Academic Year

Business

Bentley College. *Bentley's Business Abroad Program in Mexico*. Puebla. Semester and academic year. Offered in association with Universidad de las Américas. Full university curriculum plus visits to multinational companies. Excursions and optional homestays. Juniors and seniors with 2.7 GPA and one year of college Spanish. Apply by April 15 for fall and academic year; November 1 for spring.

General Studies

Alma College. *Program of Studies in Mexico*. Mexico City. Semester and academic year. Study at Universidad Iberoamericana. Homestays and excursions.

Sophomores to seniors with three semesters of Spanish and 2.5 GPA. Apply by March 15.

American Heritage Association. *Study in Querétaro.* Offered in conjunction with Portland State University and Western Washington University. Fall, winter, and spring quarters. History, economics, geography, literature, political science, and Spanish language (at all levels) at Universidad Autónoma de Mexico. Homestays available and excursions. Sophomores to seniors in good academic standing; no language requirement. Apply by July 1 for fall; November 15 for winter; February 1 for spring. Contact: (800) 654-2051.

Augsburg College. *Contemporary Issues in Mexico and Central America.* Cuernavaca. Spring term. Introduction to Latin American culture, politics, theology, and social change. Sophomores to seniors, preferably with one year of Spanish. Apply by October 15.

International Student Exchange Program (ISEP). Semester and academic year. Direct reciprocal exchange between U.S. universities and institutions in Guadalajara, Mexico City, and Monterrey. Full curriculum options. Rolling admissions. Open only to students at ISEP-member institutions. Contact ISEP for list of members.

Northern Illinois University. *Mexican and Latin American Studies.* Mexico City. Semester and academic year. Study at Universidad Autónoma de México; instruction in Spanish by Mexican faculty. Apply by June 1 for fall and academic year; November 1 for spring. Contact: Foreign Study Office, Semester/Academic Year Programs, Northern Illinois University, Williston Hall 100, DeKalb, IL 60115-2854; (815) 753-0420/0304.

Rollins College. *Latin American and Caribbean Affairs.* Mérida. Spring term. Offered in cooperation with University of the Yucatan; instruction in English and Spanish. Sophomores to seniors with 2.8 GPA. Apply by October 15.

Rutgers University. *Study Abroad in Mexico.* University of the Yucatán, Mérida. Academic year. Juniors with two years of college Spanish, 3.0 GPA, and Spanish literature courses. Apply by March 1. Contact: Department of Spanish and Portugese, 105 George Street, Rutgers University, New Brunswick, NJ 08903; (908) 932-9323.

State University of New York College at Cortland. *Mexican Studies.* Center for Bilingual Multicultural Studies, Cuernavaca. Spring semester. Sophomores to seniors in good academic standing with two years of college Spanish. Apply by March 1 for fall; October 15 for spring. Contact: Office of International Programs, SUNY College at Cortland, PO Box 2000, Cortland, NY 13045; (607) 753-2209.

University of North Carolina at Chapel Hill. *UNC Program to Mexico City.* Semester and academic year. Study at Universidad Autónoma de México. Juniors and seniors. Apply by February 14 for fall and academic year; October 1 for spring.

University of Notre Dame. *International Study Program in Mexico City.* Mexico City. Semester and academic year. Spanish-language study, Spanish and Latin American literature, and Latin American civilization. Sophomores and juniors with 2.5 GPA and two years of college Spanish with 3.0 GPA in Spanish. Apply by December 1 for fall and academic year; October 15 for spring.

University of Toledo. *Study Abroad in Mexico.* Guadalajara. Fall semester (from late August to late November). Spanish language and Mexican culture study at the Autonomous University of Guadalajara. Sophomores to graduate students with three semesters of college Spanish. Apply by February 28.

University of Wisconsin at Platteville. *Mexico Study Center*. Puebla. Semester and academic year at Universidad de las Americas. Sophomores to seniors with 3.0 GPA and two years of college Spanish. Apply by April 30 for fall and adademic year; October 20 for spring.

World Learning/School for International Training. *College Semester Abroad*. Oaxaca and Guanajuato. Fall and spring semesters. Intensive language study, Mexican culture and development seminar, field-study seminar, independent-study project. Homestays and excursions. Sophomores to seniors with 2.5 GPA. Apply by May 7 for fall; October 7 for spring. Contact: College Semester Abroad Admissions at (800) 336-1616.

International Relations

Augsburg College. *International Development and Human Rights in Latin America*. Cuernavaca. Spring term. Spanish language, political science, and economics; all taught in Spanish. Excursions and brief homestays. Sophomores to seniors with two years college Spanish. Apply by October 15.

Women and Development: Latin American Perspectives. Cuernavaca. Fall term. Spanish language, development, religion, and political science. Excursions and brief homestays. Sophomores to seniors, preferably with one year of Spanish. Apply by April 1.

Social Work

Augsburg College. *Social Policy and Human Services in Latin America*. Cuernavaca. Fall term. Spanish language, social work, sociology, education, and political science. Excursions and brief homestays. Sophomores to seniors, preferably with one year of Spanish. Apply by April 1.

Spanish Language and Mexican Culture

Beaver College. *Study in Mexico: Autonomous University of Guadalajara*. Semester and academic year. Intensive Spanish language. Students with sufficient language skills may enroll in integrated university courses. Homestays. Juniors and seniors with 3.0 GPA. Apply by April 20 for fall and academic year; October 15 for spring.

Central Washington University. Morelia, Michoacan. Fall, winter, and spring quarters. Accelerated Spanish with elective courses in Spanish or English; intensive study also available. Homestays. Undergraduates and graduates with 2.5 GPA and one term of Spanish; teachers welcome. Apply one month in advance.

Iowa State University. *ISU Cuernavaca Program*. Fall and spring semesters. Offered in conjunction with Northern Arizona University. Intensive Spanish-language study, culture and history of Mexico and Latin America. Sophomores to graduate students with 2.5 GPA. Apply by April 20 for fall; November 16 for spring. Contact: Department of Foreign Languages and Literature, 300 Pearson, Iowa State University, Ames, IA 50011.

Northern Illinois University. *Intensive Spanish Language*. Taxco. Semester and academic year. Intensive Spanish language, art history, literature, and history. Sophomores to seniors with 2.5 GPA. Apply by June 1 for fall and academic year; November 1 for spring. Contact: Foreign Study Office, Semester/Academic Year Programs, Northern Illinois University, Williston Hall 100, DeKalb, IL 60115-2854; (815) 753-0420/0304.

Ohio University. *Intensive Spanish Abroad*. Mérida. Winter quarter (early January to mid-March). Spanish conversation and composition, and Latin

American literature. Excursions. Undergraduates with two quarters of college Spanish. Apply by September. Contact: Professor David Burton, Department of Modern Languages, 220 Ellis Hall, Ohio University, Athens, OH 45701; (614) 593-2765.

State University of New York College at Brockport. *Multi-level Spanish Language Immersion Program*. El Centro Bilingue at Cuernavaca. Fall, winter, and spring quarters. Criminal justice emphasis; internships available. Homestays. Juniors and seniors with 2.5 GPA. Apply by April 15 for fall; November 1 for winter; November 15 for spring. Contact: Office of International Education, SUNY College at Brockport, Brockport, NY 14420; (716) 395-2119.

University of Colorado at Boulder. *Semester in Guadalajara*. Fall and spring semesters. Offered in cooperation with Centro de Estudios para Extranjeros at University of Guadalajara. Undergraduates with 2.75 GPA. Apply by March 1 for fall; October 15 for spring.

University of Maryland. *Maryland in Mexico City*. Mexico City. Semester and academic year. Spanish language and culture study. Sophomores with 2.5 GPA and two semesters of college Spanish with 3.0 GPA in Spanish. Apply by April 15 for fall and academic year; October 15 for spring.

University of Minnesota. *Spanish in Cuernavaca*. Cuernavaca. Fall, winter, and spring quarters. Spanish-language study at Cemanahuac Educational Community. Apply by June 15 for fall; October 15 for winter; December 31 for spring. Contact: The Global Campus, 106C Nicholson Hall, 216 Pillsbury Drive SE, University of Minnesota, Minneapolis, MN 55455-0138; (612) 625-3379.

University of Pennsylvania. *Semester in Oaxaca*. Oaxaca. Spring. Spanish language and Latin American studies. Sophomores to seniors with 3.0 GPA and two semesters of college Spanish for lower level and four semesters for advanced level. Apply by October 15.

University of Utah. *Cuernavaca Spanish Language and Mexican Culture Program*. Center for Bilingual Multicultural Studies. Spring quarter. Language, culture, civilization, and literature. Homestays. Apply by December 15.

University of Wisconsin at Green Bay. Mérida. Semester and academic year. Study at the University of Yucatán. Spanish-language study, Mexican and Mayan culture. First-year college students to seniors with Spanish proficiency. Apply by March 15 for fall and academic year; October 15 for spring.

Western Washington University. *Study in Mexico*. Morelia. Quarter and semester. Intensive Spanish study, English as a Second Language teaching methods. First-year college students to seniors with 2.5 GPA. Apply one month prior to beginning of program.

Whitworth College. *Iberoamericana Exchange Program*. Mexico City. Semester and academic year. Offered in conjunction with Iberoamericana University. Latin American studies, Spanish-language study, international relations, finance. Homestay. Juniors and seniors with 2.5 GPA and two years college Spanish. Apply by February 1 for fall and academic year; October 1 for spring.

Summer and Short-Term

Business

Bentley College. *Bentley College's Summer Program in Mexico*. Puebla. Offered in association with Universidad de las Americas—Puebla. Mexican business environment and Spanish language. Excursions. Sophomores to seniors with 2.7 GPA. Apply by April 1.

Fashion and Textiles

Iowa State University. *Mexico Study Tour*. Oaxaca, San Cristobal, Las Casas. Winter break (even-numbered years only). Mexican textile and apparel production and marketing. Juniors with three credit textiles course. Apply by October. Contact: Mary Littrell, Textiles and Clothing, 152 LeBaron Hall, ISU, Ames, IA 50011; (515) 294-5284.

Film

Michigan State University. *Filmmaking in Mexico*. Mexico City. Two weeks in late December and early January. Principles of making video ethnographic documentaries on location. Excursions. Juniors, seniors, and professionals. Apply by November 30. Contact: Office of Overseas Study, Michigan State University, 108 International Center, East Lansing, MI 48824-1035; (517) 353-8920.

General Studies

Alma College. *Program of Studies in Mexico*. Mexico City. Four to six weeks in summer. Latin American studies and intensive Spanish. Study at Universidad Iberoamericana. Homestays and excursions. Sophomores to seniors with 2.5 GPA. Apply by March 15.

Austin Community College. *ACC Study in Mexico Program*. Querétaro. Offered in conjunction with Texas Lutheran College. Five-week summer program with courses in anthropology, sociology, history, geography, and Spanish. Excursion and homestays. Freshmen to graduate students. Apply by April 1. Contact: Clint E. Davis, 1212 Rio Grande, Austin, TX 78701; (512) 459-2207 or (512) 495-7204.

International Student Exchange Program (ISEP). Summer. Direct reciprocal exchange between U.S. universities and institutions in Guadalajara, Mexico City, and Monterrey. Full curriculum options. Rolling admissions. Open only to students at ISEP-member institutions. Contact ISEP for list of members.

Loyola Marymount University. Cuernavaca. Summer. Courses offered in business, liberal arts, fine and communication arts, and science and engineering. Sophomores to seniors and high-school graduates not enrolled in college with 2.8 GPA. Rolling admissions.

Michigan State University. *Social Science in Mexico*. Querétaro, Mexico City, Guanajuanto, Morelia, and Pátzcuaro. Summer. Impact of social change on Mexico. First-year college students to graduate students. Apply by April 15. Contact: Office of Overseas Study, 108 International Center, Michigan State University, East Lansing, MI 48824-1035; (517) 353-8920.

University of Alabama. *Alabama in Yucatán*. Mérida. Three weeks in May. Latin American and Mexican studies. Undergraduates and graduate students. Apply by March 1. Contact: (205) 348-5256.

University of North Carolina at Chapel Hill. *UNC Program to Mexico City or Taxco*. Summer. Study at Universidad Autónoma de México. Juniors and seniors. Apply by March 15.

University of Toledo. *Study Abroad in Mexico*. Guadalajara. Three and six weeks in summer. Spanish language and Mexican culture study at the Autonomous University of Guadalajara. Sophomores to graduate students with three semesters of college Spanish. Apply by February 28.

Marketing and Public Relations

University of Arkansas at Little Rock. *Summer in Mexico*. Guadalajara. June. Offered in cooperation with Universidad Autonoma de Guadalajara. International marketing and Spanish language. Homestays. Undergraduates in good academic standing. Apply by March 1. Contact: Office for International Programs, UALR, 2801 South University Avenue, Little Rock, AR 72204; (501) 569-3374.

Spanish Language and Mexican Culture

Central Washington University. Morelia, Michoacan. Four to eight week summer program. Accelerated Spanish with elective courses in Spanish or English; intensive study also available. Homestays. Undergraduates and graduates with 2.5 GPA and one term of Spanish; teachers welcome. Apply one month in advance.

Davidson College. *Summer in Mexico*. Guadalajara. Offered in even-numbered years only. Sophomores and juniors with 2.75 GPA and intermediate Spanish. Apply by February 1.

Eastern Michigan University. *Intensive Spanish Language Program*. Queretaro. Summer. Courses at beginning to advanced levels. First-year college students to graduate students. Apply by April 15. Contact: (800) 777-3541.

Illinois State University. *Summer Program in Mexico*. Taxco. Seven-week program in June and July with courses in Spanish language, Spanish-American culture, and literature. Instruction in Spanish at Universidad Nacional Autónoma de México. Excursions and homestays. Sophomores to graduate students with one year of college Spanish and 2.5 GPA. Apply by March 12. Contact: 6120 Office of International Studies and Programs, Illinois State University, Normal, IL 61761; (309) 438-5112/3362.

Indiana University. *Overseas Study in Mexico*. Mexico City. Summer. Freshmen to seniors with one year of college Spanish and 2.8 GPA. Apply by early March.

Miami University. Puebla. Summer. Language workshops at Universidad de las Americas. Students with four semesters of Spanish. Apply by February 15.

New York University. *NYU in Mexico*. Mexico City. Summer. One-week graduate seminar on culture and society in contemporary Mexico; instruction in Spanish. Contact: Department of Spanish and Portuguese, Faculty of Arts and Sciences, 19 University Place, Room 400, New York, NY 10003; (212) 998-8770.

North Carolina State University. *Mexico Summer Program*. Cuernavaca. First-year college students to graduate students with two semesters of college Spanish and 3.0 GPA in Spanish, and elementary- and secondary-school teachers. Apply by March 1.

Southern Methodist University. *Xalapa Intensive Summer Language Program*. Xalapa. Six weeks from late May to early June. Intensive Spanish and culture of Mexico. Homestays and excursions. Sophomores to seniors with 2.75 GPA and one year of college Spanish. Apply by March 1. Contact: Office of International Programs, SMU, 100 McFarlin Auditorium, Dallas, TX 75275-0391; (214) 768-2338.

State University of New York College at Buffalo. *Summer Graduate Program in Culture and Spanish Language*. Mexico City. Homestays. Graduate students and elementary- and high-school teachers with graduate Spanish. Apply by April 1. Contact: Study Abroad Coordinator, Office of International Education, SUNY College at Buffalo, 212 Talbert Hall, Box 601604, Buffalo, NY 14260-1604; (716) 645-3912.

State University of New York College at Cortland. *Center for Bilingual Multicultural Studies*. Cuernavaca. Winter break (late December to mid-January). Intensive Spanish language, and Latin American history and culture. Sophomores to seniors with three semesters of college Spanish and 2.5 GPA. Apply by October 1. Contact: Office of International Programs, SUNY College at Cortland, PO Box 2000, Cortland, NY 13045; (607) 753-2209.

State University of New York College at Oswego. *Spanish Language, Mexican Culture, Civilization, History Program in Mexico City*. Six weeks in summer. Instruction in Spanish. Excursions and homestays. Undergraduates with one year of college Spanish and 2.5 GPA. Contact: Office of International Education, SUNY at Oswego, 102 Rich Hall, Oswego, NY 13126; (315) 341-2118.

Texas Tech University. *Mexico Field Course*. San Luis Potosi. Summer. Undergraduates and graduate students with two years of college Spanish. Apply by February 1.

University of Alabama at Birmingham. *UAB in Mexico*. Guadalajara. Mid-July to mid-August. Spanish language and Hispanic and pre-Columbian culture. High-school graduates to graduate students with one semester or two quarters of Spanish. Contact: Dr. Duleep Deosthale, Center for International Programs, 306 University Center, 1400 University Boulevard, University of Alabama at Birmingham, Birmingham, AL 35294-1150; (205) 934-3328.

University of Arkansas at Little Rock. *Summer in Mexico*. Guadalajara. Mid-June to mid-July. Offered in cooperation with Universidad Autonoma de Guadalajara. Spanish language and Mexican history. Undergraduates in good academic standing. Apply by March 1. Contact: Office for International Programs, UALR, 2801 South University Avenue, Little Rock, AR 72204; (501) 569-3374.

University of Colorado at Boulder. *Summer in Guadalajara*. Offered in cooperation with Centro de Estudios para Extranjeros at University of Guadalajara. Undergraduates with 2.75 GPA. Apply by March 1.

University of Iowa. *CIC Summer Study Program in Mexico*. Guanajuato. From mid-June to early August in summer. Offered in conjunction with the Committee for International Cooperation. Sophomores to seniors with two years of college Spanish with 3.0 GPA in Spanish; good overall academic standing. Apply by April 1.

University of Kentucky. *Kentucky Institute for International Studies in Morelia, Mexico*. Morelia. Summer. Language study. Excursions. Undergraduates to graduate students and adults. Apply by March 1.

University of St. Thomas. *UST Summer Program in Mérida*. Summer. Civilization, literature, Mexican studies, Spanish-language study. High-school students to graduate students, teachers, and professionals with two years of college Spanish. Apply by April 15.

University of Wisconsin at Madison. *Summer Program in Oaxaca*. Oaxaca. Spanish-language study, Spanish-American literature, and Mexican culture. Fieldtrips, homestays. Sophomores to seniors in good academic standing and with three semesters of college Spanish. Open only to students at higher education institutions in Wisconsin and Wisconsin residents studying outside the state. Apply by third Friday in March.

Western Washington University. *Study in Mexico*. Morelia. Four- and nine-week sessions in summer. Intensive Spanish study, cultural activities. Freshmen to graduate students with a 2.5 GPA and high-school teachers. Apply one month prior to beginning of the program.

Wichita State University. *Summer Program in Puebla*. First-year college students to graduate students with two years of high school Spanish and two semesters of college Spanish. Apply by April 1.

EXPLORING MEXICAN CULTURE

Readings

It has been said of Octavio Paz that his literary roles as a poet and as a cultural critic are just two sides of a single soulful outlook on Mexico, a subject he never tires of writing about. *The Labyrinth of Solitude* (1950), an analysis of the Mexican psyche from the Spanish Conquest to the 20th century, is perhaps his best-known book and a wonderful example of his prose style.

Carlos Fuentes, the son of a Mexican diplomat, spent his early years in the United States. As a result, when he returned to Mexico, he had to rediscover his homeland and his cultural identity. *The Death of Artemio Cruz* (1962), Fuentes's first and perhaps most popular novel, is the story of a man's life remembered as he is about to die. In his most recent work, *Christopher Unborn*, Fuentes presents an insightful yet humorous picture of his country in a story narrated by an unborn fetus and set in 1992, the 500th anniversary of Christopher Columbus's famous voyage. Some of his other works include *The Old Gringo, Terra Nostra, Distant Relations, Aura*, and *Where the Air Is Clear*.

The late Juan Rulfo wrote about Jalisco, the state in western Mexico from which he hailed. *The Burning Plains and Other Stories* (1953) explores the poverty and forlorn lives led by many of the people of his home state in lean, vivid prose. *Pedro Páramo* (1955), probably Rulfo's most popular work internationally, is a surrealistic view of life and death in rural Mexico.

Mariano Azuela explores Mexican culture and society at the time of the Mexican Revolution. Novels by Mariano Azuela include *The Trials of a Respectable Family* (1918), *The Firefly* (1932), and his classic work, *The Underdogs* (1915), which presents the revolution from the viewpoint of peasants. Two other novels by Azuela, *The Flies* and *The Bosses* (1918), are satiric and somber writings about the Mexican Revolution.

From an anthropological point of view Oscar Lewis provides oral histories of a working-class family in Mexico City in *The Children of Sanchez* (1979). His works also include *A Death in the Sanchez Family* (1969), *Pedro Martinez* (1966), and *Five Families* (1959). In *The Alamo Tree* (1984), Ernest Brawley writes about the effects of political, economic, and social changes on two Mexican families—one in Manzanillo, the other in Acapulco. Oster Patrick's *The Mexicans: A Personal Portrait of a People* (1989) presents biographies of a cross section of Mexicans—men, women, gays, intellectuals, farm workers, and so on—that reflects Mexican society and its problems. The fact that most Mexicans have some relative living and working in the United States has inspired many books. *Coyotes* by Ted Conover explores the secret world of illegal aliens in the U.S. Another poignant book that touches on this subject is *Across the Wire* (1993) by David Unger, which deals primarily with the Mexican underclass that lives in shantytowns just south of the border. Robert Moss's *Mexico Way* (1991) details an attempt by a U.S. government official to create a new state in northern Mexico.

The experiences of foreigners in Mexico are the subject of a number of books, including Harry LaTourette Foster's *A Gringo in Mañana Land* (1976),

Kenneth Gangemi's *The Volcanoes from Puebla* (1979), and John Lincoln's *One Man's Mexico* (1966). Mary Morris, an American writer, recounts her experiences in *Nothing to Declare: Memoirs of a Woman Traveling Alone*. Jim Conrad's *On the Road to Tetlama: Mexican Adventures of a Wandering Naturalist* (1991) is a travelogue of his adventures in the back country.

Films

Although the typical image of Mexico to emerge from American films is of a world of poverty plagued by corruption and violence, the long Mexican film tradition is characterized by infinitely more insightful explorations of the intricate mix of Mexican community and family relations.

Originally known for popular melodramas such as *Maria Candelaria* (1943), by Emilio Fernandez, that dominated the Latin American market, the Mexican film industry also harbored Luis Buñuel for much of the second half of his career. During his years in Mexico, Buñuel made several classics, including *The Young and the Damned (Los Olvidados)* (1950), an extremely brutal look at life in the slums of Mexico City. Some of his other movies include *El Bruto*, and *Exterminating Angel*.

In recent years Paul Leduc has made several innovative films based on historical and cultural themes. *Reed: Insurgent Mexico* provides a twist on the leftist journalist's account of the Mexican Revolution and also serves as a larger metaphor for Mexican-American relations. *Frida*, another Leduc film, is a beautiful biography of the life and work of Mexican painter Frida Kahlo. Presentations of her paintings are interspersed with fictionalized accounts of her relationships with her husband Diego Rivera, Leon Trotsky, Mexican communism, and her own vibrant approach to life.

Jaime Humberto Hermosillo presents some of the contradictions of modern Mexican society in *Doña Herlinda and Her Son* (1986). Doña Herlinda's son marries a feminist woman and his homosexual lover moves in with the family. Another charming film that deals with the intersexual relations between man and woman is *Danzón* (1991), by Maria Novaro. In this film an unmarried mother travels in search of her dancing partner, who has disappeared, and has the adventure of her life. Based on the book by the same title, *Like Water for Chocolate* (1992), written by Laura Esquivel and directed by Alfonso Arau, is a captivating movie that follows three generations of women of a Mexican family in a style that can only be described as magic-realist.

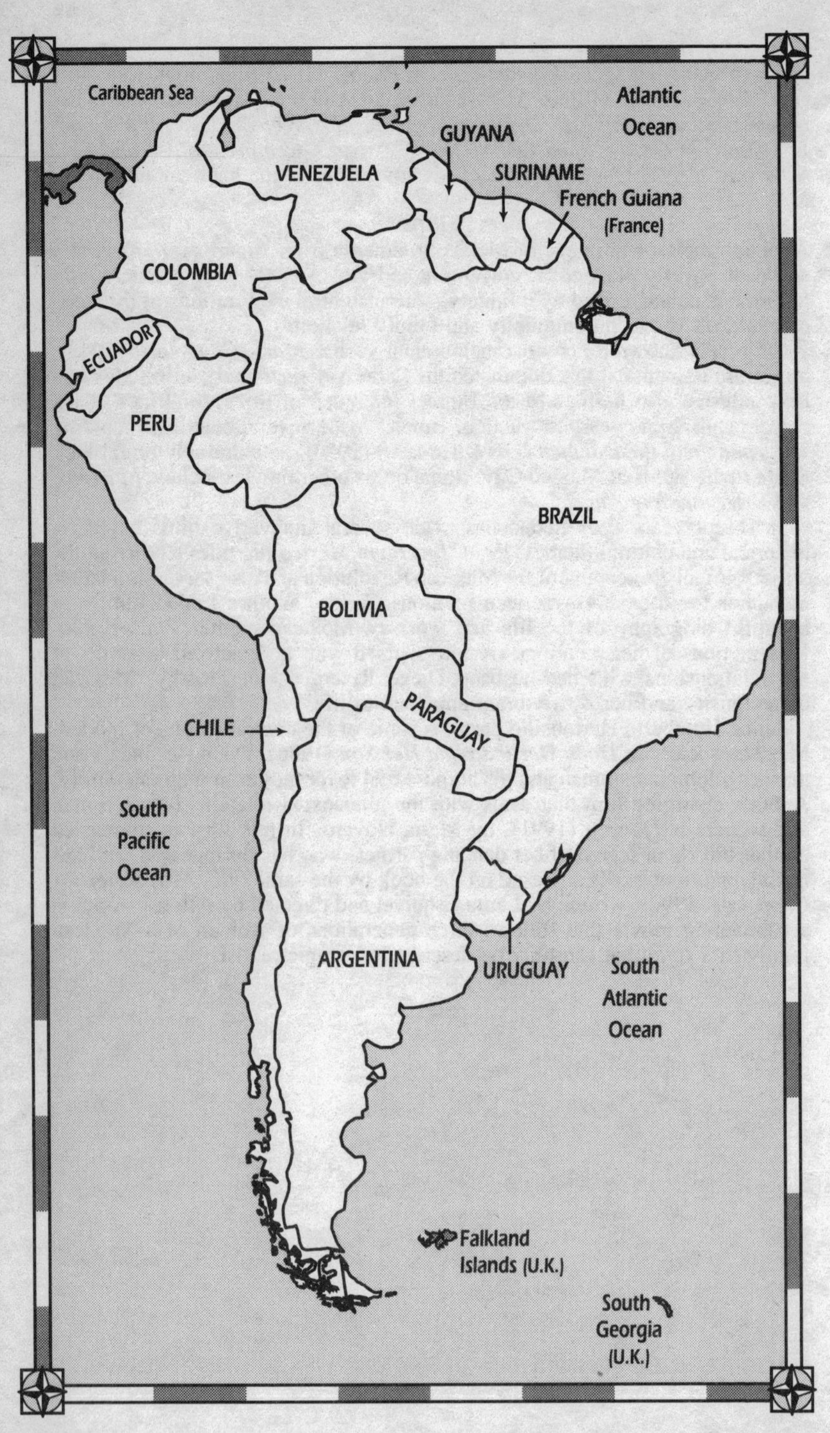
Caribbean Sea
Atlantic Ocean
GUYANA
VENEZUELA
SURINAME
French Guiana (France)
COLOMBIA
ECUADOR
PERU
BRAZIL
BOLIVIA
PARAGUAY
CHILE
South Pacific Ocean
ARGENTINA
URUGUAY
South Atlantic Ocean
Falkland Islands (U.K.)
South Georgia (U.K.)

CHAPTER SIXTEEN

SOUTH AMERICA

A wildly varied geography, indigenous tribes with roots in mysterious antiquity, and a Portuguese and Spanish colonial legacy combined with further European settlement make this continent an exciting destination for North American travelers, most of whom don't know enough about their southern cousins. If nature's your bag, there are the majestic Andes, the endangered Amazon rain forest, and the rocky shoreline of Patagonia. Ancient monuments like Machu Picchu and the indecipherable Nazca Lines abound, yet so do contemporary Indian peoples whose traditions remain at odds with industrial society. But it's the wider array of people that gives South America its multifaceted personality, a personality created by Indians, Africans, Asians, Spaniards, Portuguese, Germans, Italians, and others who have brought to this continent's capitals a decidedly more cosmopolitan flavor than Anglicized Canada and the United States.

Most U.S. citizens think only of skyrocketing inflation, military juntas, and cocaine barons when they consider South American politics—without remembering how their own country contributed to such problems in this century. But in spite of numerous obstacles, democracy is on the rise in South America. In countries like Argentina and Chile—infamous for the brutal rightist repression of the 1970s—the resignation of military leaders and popular election of new governments in the late 1980s signaled a new era. In Brazil, democracy was strengthened by the impeachment proceedings against former president Collor and the subsequent peaceful transition to a new administration. At press time, Venezuela's President Andrés Peréz had also recently agreed to step down to face corruption charges. While problems remain in countries like Colombia and Peru, the perceptive and careful traveler should encounter few difficulties.

Enjoy the beaches of Brazil and Uruguay, the alpine plain of Bolivia, and Argentina's vast pampas. Encounter practitioners of Afro-Caribbean religions such as voodoo and santeria or shake hands with a gaucho. Explore remote mountain villages or experience the continental European atmosphere of Buenos Aires. Follow the route Simón Bolívar took to liberate this continent from Spanish rule or study the works of Borges and García-Márquez in their own countries. Whatever your interests happen to be, you'll find in each of South America's 13 countries something much more than you imagined.

Getting There

The cheapest **airfares** from the United States to South America are generally APEX fares (see Chapter Five for a general explanation of airfares). Sample *one-way* fares in effect during the summer of 1993 are listed below. More information is available from Council Travel (see pages xiii–xvi).

New York–Rio de Janeiro	$415	New York–Buenos Aires	$545
Los Angeles–Santiago	$575	Miami–Caracas	$135
Miami–Montevideo	$429		

It's possible to travel **overland** from the United States through Central America, but you can only make it as far as Panama before hitting the impassable Darién

Gap, a swampy expanse that blocks the way to Colombia. However, you can skirt the gap by air or sea without much trouble and continue on your way. If you plan to drive your own car, however, you'll have a more difficult time; contact AAA (see page 52) for more information.

Getting Around South America

The ease or difficulty of getting around South America varies according to geography. In general, **overland** transportation is fairly easy in all countries, except in very mountainous regions, which includes most of Peru. Amazonian Brazil, of course, requires transport by air or water. The difficulty of travel in mountainous terrain, however, has its own rewards in the form of spectacular scenery and contact with native cultures, generally making the effort well worthwhile.

Traveling by **train** is one of the most interesting ways to see South America. However, with the exception of Argentina, you won't find much in the way of integrated national railway systems; most countries have only one or two lines with passenger service and Venezuela and Uruguay have none. Throughout the continent equipment is antiquated and travel is slow. Although not known for speed and efficiency, South American trains allow you to slow down, enjoy the scenery, and come into contact with workers and *campesinos*.

Buses are the most popular form of transportation in South America, and they range from luxury air-conditioned intercity express buses to trucks with wooden benches. No matter where you might want to go, if there's a road there's a bus that travels it. For anyone interested in traveling around the continent by bus, Autobuses Sudamericanos' **Amerbuspass** is a single ticket good for up to 10,000 kilometers of travel on the routes of 17 cooperating Latin American bus companies. Costs are $400 for 7 days, $700 for 15 days, and $1,300 for 30 days. For more information, contact the U.S. office of Autobuses Sudamericanos, 626 North Norton Avenue, Tucson, AZ 85719; (602) 795-6556.

Hitchhiking is fairly easy and safe in most parts of Latin America, although it's best not to take chances in areas with obvious political instability such as Peru. Of course, females should not hitchhike alone, and everyone will find it easier to get rides if they look neat and clean. Don't be surprised if the driver who gives you a ride asks for a fee. As in other areas of the world, it's best to get your information on hitchhiking from someone who has done or is doing it.

In most countries, it's also quite easy to rent a **car**; while there are certain advantages to this mode of transportation, it's an expensive alternative in South America. If you do plan to drive in South America, you'll need to get an international driving permit. All South American countries recognize the Inter-American Driving Permit; some also recognize the International Driving Permit. For more information on these permits, see page 52.

Air travel is certainly the fastest and most convenient way of covering long distances in South America. Nearly all the countries of the continent have air passes of some sort that allow foreign visitors unlimited travel in that country over a specified period of time. Generally speaking, these passes are good bargains for anyone planning to visit several regions of a country. You'll find more information on these passes in the individual country sections that follow.

There are also two passes that allow international air travel throughout the continent:

- AeroPeru offers the **Visit South America** pass, which allows six international flights including one flight from the U.S. to South America. The pass is good for 45 days of travel. Departing from Miami, it costs $999 in the low season or $1,184 in the high season. Departure from other U.S. cities can be arranged at extra cost. South American cities serviced by AeroPeru include Quito, Ecuador; Lima, Peru; Santiago, Chile; Buenos Aires, Argentina; La Paz, Bolivia; and Rio de Janeiro and São Paulo, Brazil. Flights to cities within Peru can be added on at $40 per flight segment; additional international destinations can also be added on at $100 each. The only problem with the Visit South America pass is that you'll have to do a lot of backtracking. For example, flying between Rio and Buenos Aires requires a connection through Lima. For more information, contact AeroPeru, (800) 777-7717.

- Air Paraguay offers a similar **Visit South America Airpass**. Like AeroPeru's pass, it consists of six coupons, each good for one international flight. However, it is valid for only 30 days. With departure from New York, for example, this pass costs $990 in the low season or $1,050 in the high season. Air Paraguay serves Asunción, Paraguay; Buenos Aires, Argentina; Montevideo, Uruguay; Rio de Janeiro and São Paulo, Brazil; Santa Cruz, Bolivia; and Santiago, Chile. Although you must use Asunción as a travel hub, you'll do less backtracking, since the city is more centrally located than Lima. Air Paraguay also offers a more flexible Optimum Fare pass which allows up to eight coupons to be used in up to three months. Costs vary according to destinations and number of coupons. For more information, contact Air Paraguay, (212) 268-9527.

Eating and Sleeping

You'll find an abundance of inexpensive **guest houses** and **hotels** in South American cities. The student travel offices listed under the individual country sections later in this chapter can often help you find inexpensive places to stay. You will also find information on national youth hostel organizations in the following sections.

For Further Information

Information on entry requirements are given in the country sections that follow. You can obtain information on countries not included in this chapter from the following embassies.

- **French Guiana:** Embassy of France, 4101 Reservoir Road NW, Washington, DC 20007; (202) 944-6000
- **Guyana:** Embassy of Guyana, 2490 Tracy Place NW, Washington, DC 20008; (202) 265-6900
- **Paraguay:** Embassy of Paraguay, 2400 Massachusetts Avenue NW, Washington, DC 20008; (202) 483-6960
- **Suriname:** Embassy of the Republic of Suriname, 4301 Connecticut Avenue NW, Suite 108, Washington, DC 20008; (202) 244-7488

Travelers to South America may be interested in joining the **South American Explorers Club**, headquartered in Ithaca, New York, with clubhouses in Quito, Ecuador, and Lima, Peru. For a $30 annual fee ($40 for couples), you receive a subscription to the quarterly *South American Explorer*, use of information and trip-planning services, as well as access to clubhouses in Quito and Lima, where you can store luggage and meet fellow travelers. For more information, contact the South American Explorers Club at the following addresses.

- **U.S.:** 126 Indian Creek Road, Ithaca, NY 14850; (607) 277-0488
- **Ecuador:** Toledo 1254, La Floresta, Apartado 21-431, Quito; (593) 2-566076.
- **Peru:** Av. Portugal 146 Breña, Casilla 3714, Lima 100; (51) 14-314480

The most consistently up-to-date guide to South America is the annually revised *South American Handbook*, produced in England and distributed in the U.S. by Prentice Hall. Designed especially for travelers who want to get off the beaten tourist path and explore South America on their own, this 1,344-page manual isn't cheap at $40 but it's worth the price, especially if you're planning to visit several countries in the region. Another excellent guide, especially for budget travelers, is *South America on a Shoestring*, available for $19.95 from Lonely Planet Publications. Outdoor enthusiasts will enjoy William C. Leitch's *South America's National Parks*, available for $15.95 from The Mountaineers Books. For more information on Lonely Planet and The Mountaineers, see pages 56–57.

WORK

Stringent labor regulations and high unemployment rates make it difficult for foreigners to obtain employment in South America. Nevertheless, resourceful persons with some knowledge of Spanish or Portuguese often find informal employment, mostly as English tutors or translators.

The internship and voluntary-service opportunities offered by members of the Council on International Educational Exchange are listed in the individual country sections later in this chapter. In addition, the **Association for International Practical Training** offers the IAESTE Trainee Program in Paraguay; see page 19 for more information about this program.

STUDY

Persons seeking scholarships or grants for study in South America might want to take a look at *Funding for Research, Study, and Travel: Latin America and the Caribbean* (see page 517).

You'll find study programs offered by CIEE-member institutions listed in the country sections that follow. Here we've included programs that take place in more than one country of the region.

Semester and Academic Year

General Studies

University of Wisconsin at Madison. *Comparative Year in Latin America.* Fall semester in Quito, Ecuador and spring semester in Santiago, Chile. Humanities and social sciences (and Spanish language study in Quito). Intensive language and culture orientation. Homestays and excursions. Juniors and seniors with 3.0 recommended GPA and five semesters of Spanish. Wisconsin residents or individuals attending any college or university in Wisconsin. Apply by February 11.

Social Work

Whitworth College. *Whitworth College/Central America Study Program.* Guatemala, Honduras, and other Central American countries. January and spring semester. Offered every three years (repeats in 1996). Study Spanish in Guatemala for four weeks, then to Honduras to work in rural service projects. Sophomores to graduate students with 2.5 GPA, Latin American studies coursework, and some Spanish language. Apply by April 1. Contact: Coordinator, Off-Campus Programs, Station #2702, Whitworth College, Spokane, WA 99251; (509) 466-3232.

ARGENTINA

The history of Argentina has been as hot and cold, as thrilling and melancholy as the strains of its national music, the tango. Once the envy of the developing world, and only 50 years ago as wealthy as France or Austria, this proud nation has suffered more than its share of political and economic reversals. Argentines have battled debilitating rates of inflation and brutal military dictatorships, but stubbornly, their morale remains high. They have now enjoyed a decade of relatively unimpeded democracy, and they live alongside some of the greatest natural resources and boldest natural beauty to be found in the hemisphere.

This sprawling nation—eighth largest in the world—has long drawn floods of immigrants, and in the early part of this century, Argentina served, like the U.S., as a "land of opportunity," attracting newcomers from all over Europe, and, in smaller numbers, from the Middle East and Asia. Expecting the usual Spanish-Indian and Afro-Caribbean blends that characterize most of Latin America, visitors are often surprised at the "European" features and Italian, English, or Slavic surnames of many Argentines. While some ethnic groups formed isolated communities in rural areas—Welsh farmers and Jewish cowboys set up shop in Patagonia—the great majority laid roots in the capital of Buenos Aires, which was transformed from a muddy pirate port into today's cosmopolitan metropolis of more than 11 million people. *Porteños,* as the people of Buenos Aires call themselves, are intensely proud of their city and rarely venture outside it. The wide boulevards, busy pedestrian malls, outdoor cafés, and wonderfully detailed churches and public buildings of Buenos Aires are indeed, as *porteños* proudly assert, reminiscent of Europe. But one need only take a ramshackle, colorfully painted bus into the neighborhoods of San Telmo or La Boca and watch an elderly couple dance a sensual, romantic tango on the street to be reminded that this is, in fact, a land apart.

As one ventures away from the capital, the wonders and contradictions of the country become clearer. To the west of the city, stretching out from the shore of the Rio Plata, lie Argentina's famous pampas, a land of incredibly rich topsoil. The vast herds of cattle grazing here, descended from the few hundred left behind by the first explorers, are the backbone of the Argentine economy and supplier of the innumerable *parrilladas*, or meat grills, found throughout the country. The pampas are also the ancestral home of the most famed of Argentine figures, the gaucho. Star of song and literature, this flamboyant cousin to the American cowboy can still be found, in greatly reduced numbers, on many Argentine cattle ranches.

Nestled amongst the Andes near the Chilean border, Argentina's surprisingly large wine industry flourishes, and many tours are available to friendly local *bodegas*, or vineyards. As the Andes stretch down into Patagonia, the stark southern cone of the country, they become the site of a spectacular lake district, dotted with vivid blue glacial pools. Local ski resorts like Bariloche are favorite vacation spots for Argentines and foreigners alike. With the exception of the lake district, Patagonia is almost entirely flat and dry, and its limitless horizons and unique culture and wildlife have enchanted poets and explorers since Darwin. In striking contrast, the northeastern part of the country is largely lush, sub-equatorial jungle, broken up here and there by tremendous waterfalls, the most spectacular of which is the famed Iguazú Falls.

Argentines are justifiably proud of their magnificent land, and eager to share it with outsiders. And while much is made of the way in which the national character is split between its Germanic and Latin elements, even a short time here reveals the inadequacy of such categories. Argentina has distinguished itself from both its neighbors and its ancestors, and despite past and present political and economic hardships, the land and its people remain rich in possibility.

—Michael Kovnat, Brooklyn, New York

Official name: Argentine Republic. **Area:** 1,663,000 square miles (about one-third the size of the U.S.). **Population:** 32,291,000. **Population density:** 30 inhabitants per square mile. **Capital and largest city:** Buenos Aires (pop. 10,500,000). **Language:** Spanish. **Religion:** Roman Catholic. **Per capita income:** US$2,134. **Currency:** Argentine peso. **Literacy rate:** 92%. **Average daily temperature:** Buenos Aires: June, 52°; December, 72°. **Average number of days with precipitation:** Buenos Aires: June, 7; December, 8.

TRAVEL

U.S. citizens will need a passport to enter Argentina; however a visa is not required for stays of up to three months. For specific regulations, check with the **Argentine Embassy**, 1600 New Hampshire Avenue NW, Washington, DC 20009; (202) 939-6400. There are also Argentine consulates in Chicago, Houston, Los Angeles, Miami, New Orleans, New York, and San Juan.

Getting Around

Because of the great distances involved, most tourists interested in seeing different parts of the country end up doing some flying. Foreign visitors can purchase **Visit Argentina** air passes that entitle them to a number of discounted coupons for flights within the country. Coupons are valid for 30 days and are honored by Aerolineas Argentinas and Austral Airlines. Four coupons cost $450; additional coupons cost $120 each. Visit Argentina passes must be purchased in conjunction with an international ticket to Argentina. For more information, contact Council Travel (see pages xiii–xvi) or Aerolineas Argentinas, (800) 333-0276.

Argentina has an extensive highway network. A variety of **bus lines** serve all parts of the country, providing comfortable and reliable service. But remember that distances are great: Express buses from Buenos Aires to Iguazú Falls take 24 hours; Buenos Aires to Bariloche is a 22-hour trip. **Hitchhiking** is popular and fairly easy throughout the entire country, except in the south, where traffic is light. All Argentine cities have **rental car** agencies. U.S. motorists should obtain either the **Inter-American Driving Permit** or the **International Driving Permit** (see page 52), both of which are recognized in Argentina.

Argentina has the best and most comprehensive **rail network** of any country of South America; however, it does not extend to the Brazilian frontier and Iguazú Falls in the northeast or cover much of the sparsely populated southern region of the country. The system fans out across the pampas to Bariloche and Mendoza in the west and into Bolivia and Paraguay in the north. Travel by train is inexpensive and comfortable. However, trains are slower than buses; the trip from Buenos Aires to Bariloche, for example, takes 30 hours. Argentinian Railroads offer the **Argempass**, providing unlimited first-class rail travel within the country. December 1992 prices were $149 for 30 days, $250 for 60 days, and $349 for 90 days. The Argempass can be purchased only in Argentina at train stations or travel agents.

Eating and Sleeping

There is a good number of **youth hostels** in Argentina. For more information, contact Hostelling International/American Youth Hostels (see page 54) or the **Asociación Argentina de Albergues de la Juventud (AAAJ)**, Talcahuano 214, 2 Piso, Oficina 6, Capital Federal, Buenos Aires; (54) 1-476-1001.

Especially for Students and Young People

Argentina has two student/youth travel organizations, both issuers of the International Student Identity Card.

- **ATESA** has offices at Tucumán 1584, 2° A y B, 1050 Buenos Aires; (54) 1-403630; fax (54) 1-311-6720. ATESA also has offices in Córdoba, Rosario, Salta, Mar del Plata, Tucumán, Mendoza, and Ushuaia.
- **ASATEJ** has offices at Florida 833, 3° piso, Oficina 319, 1005 Buenos Aires; (54) 1-311-6953; fax (54) 1-311-6840. Its mailing address is CC 307, 1000 Buenos Aires.

Both issue air, rail, and bus tickets, provide accommodations booking services, and arrange tours. Both can provide holders of the International Student Identity Card with information on discounts available to them in Argentina.

For Further Information

General tourist information is available from the **Argentine National Tourist Information Office**, PO Box 1758, Madison Square Station, New York, NY 10159-1758; (212) 765-8833.

One of the few guidebooks to focus on Argentina and nearby countries is *Argentina, Uruguay, and Paraguay: A Travel Survival Kit*, available for $16.95 from Lonely Planet Publications. An excellent book to read in preparation for your trip is *Insight Guide: Argentina* ($19.95). For more information on Lonely Planet and *Insight Guides*, see pages 56–57.

WORK

To work in Argentina, a foreigner must obtain a work visa. A work visa for U.S. visitors can only be obtained in the U.S. and proof of employment must be provided. For more information, contact an Argentinian Consulate (see "Travel," above) or the **Ministerio de Trabajo**, Av Julio a Roca 609, Buenos Aires 1067, Argentina.

Internships/Traineeships

Two programs sponsored by members of the Council on International Educational Exchange are described below.

Association for International Practical Training. *IAESTE Trainee Program.* On-the-job training for undergraduate and graduate students in technical fields such as engineering, computer science, agriculture, architecture, mathematics, and the natural and physical sciences. See page 19 for more information.

University of Illinois at Urbana-Champaign. *Semester or Year Program.* Buenos Aires. Juniors to graduate students with four semesters of college-level Spanish and 3.0 GPA. Apply by April 1. Contact: Study Abroad Office, 115 International Studies Building, 910 South Fifth Street, Champaign, IL 61820.

STUDY

The following academic programs are offered by CIEE-member institutions. Unless otherwise noted, consult Appendix I for the addresses of the colleges and universities listed in this section. In addition to the programs below, California State University offers a program open only to its own students.

Semester and Academic Year

General Studies

American University. *Buenos Aires Semester.* Fall semester. Argentine politics, economics, and culture. Internships with multinational organizations. Juniors and seniors with 2.75 GPA and two years of college Spanish. Apply by March 15. Contact: World Capitals Program, American University, Dunblane House—Tenley Campus, Washington, DC 20016-8083; (202) 895-4900 or 4937.

Council on International Educational Exchange. *Advanced Social Sciences Program at the Facultad Latinoamericana de Ciencias Sociales (FLACSO) and the Universidad de Buenos Aires.* Buenos Aires. Fall semester, spring semester, U.S. academic year, and Argentinean academic year. Advanced undergraduates and graduate students with three years of college Spanish, 3.0 GPA, and previous coursework in social sciences. Apply by April 1 for fall

semester and U.S. academic year; November 1 for spring semester and Argentinean academic year. Contact University Programs Department.
International Student Exchange Program (ISEP). Semester and academic year. Direct reciprocal exchange between U.S. universities and institutions in Buenos Aires. Full curriculum options. Rolling admissions. Open only to students at ISEP-member institutions. Contact ISEP for list of members.
State University of New York at Plattsburgh. *Study Program in Argentina.* Universidad del Salvador at Buenos Aires. Fall and spring semesters. Regular university courses with instruction in Spanish. Undergraduates with strong Spanish skills and 2.5 GPA. Apply by March 15 for fall; October 31 for spring. Contact: Director, Southern Cone Programs, Hawkins Hall 102, SUNY at Plattsburgh, Plattsburgh, NY 12901; (518) 564-5827/2398.
Universidad del Salvador. *Advanced Social Sciences Program.* See listing under Council on International Educational Exchange.
University of North Carolina at Chapel Hill. *UNC Program to Buenos Aires.* Semester and academic year. Sophomores to seniors with 2.8 GPA and fluent in Spanish. Apply by February 14 for fall and academic year; October 1 for spring.

Summer and Short-Term

General Studies

University of Illinois at Urbana-Champaign. *Summer Program in Argentina.* Buenos Aires. Juniors to graduate students with 3.0 GPA and four semesters of college Spanish. Engineering and other field experiences available. Apply by March 15.

EXPLORING ARGENTINE CULTURE

Readings and Films

Argentina's best-known literary figure in this century is the late Jorge Luis Borges. In books such as *Labyrinths* (1941) and *Fictions* (1949), Borges created unusual existential situations characterized by their erudite verbal pyrotechnics. His *Six Problems for Don Isidro Parodi* (1942) is a collection of six detective stories written "as a challenge to the frenetic action of American detective stories" and the "cold intellectualism of the British school."

Julio Cortazar also plays with the reader's perception of reality. His novel *Hopscotch* (1963), for instance, is divided into chapters that can be read in different orders, each arrangement suggesting a different meaning.

Manuel Puig, the author of *Heartbreak Tango* (1969) and *Betrayed by Rita Hayworth* (1968), was a younger writer whose surreal visions of modern life reveal the influence of Hollywood and American cartoons. *Kiss of the Spiderwoman* (1985), his most famous work thanks to the success of the movie version, is the story of two prisoners, one a political dissident and the other a homosexual window dresser. It provides a vividly realistic portrait of the political repression employed by the military government during its "Dirty War" against the Argentine Left in the 1970s. *Diary of the War of the Pig*, Adolfo Bioy Casares's 1969 novel, was eerily prophetic of the "Dirty War."

It details a war of extermination between the young—the killers—and the old—the willing victims.

In nonfiction, Jacobo Timerman's *Prisoner without a Name, Cell without a Number* (1985) is based on the well-known newspaper editor's imprisonment during the 1970s when the military dictatorship used imprisonment and torture as a routine political tool. Compare it with Lawrence Thornton's *Imagining Argentina* (1987), a novel about the redemptive imagination of a man whose wife has become one of the *desaparecidos* in the 1970s. The disappeared and the question of what became of their children is a subject poignantly explored in Luis Puenzo's *The Official Story* (1985). In this movie, the wife of an Argentine businessman wonders if her adopted daughter might have come to her by less-than-honorable means.

Another novel of Argentine life during the mid-1970s is Humberto Constantini's *The Gods, the Little Guys, and the Police* (1979), at once a whimsical fantasy and a frightening picture of political terror. The plot deals with Greek gods who concern themselves with the members of an apolitical group of poets suspected by the police of subversive activities. Ernesto Sabato's *On Heroes and Tombs* (1961) is a novel that presents a history of Argentina as represented by the obsessions of a well-to-do family.

While few tourists visit the remote region of Argentina known as Patagonia, as one of the world's last frontier regions it has captured the interest of a number of writers from around the world. The late Bruce Chatwin's *In Patagonia* (1977) is a classic account of the author's travels through that harsh landscape. In the same vein, be sure to check out Paul Theroux's *Patagonia Revisited* (1985) and Sara Mansfield Taber's *Dusk on the Campo: A Journey in Patagonia* (1991).

BOLIVIA

Few nations have the geographical diversity found in Bolivia, a country that encompasses both dry barren plains and verdant mountain valleys, snowcapped mountain peaks and tropical rain forests. Although it's landlocked, Bolivia campaigns quixotically through diplomatic channels to reclaim the corridor to the sea, which it lost to Chile in a military campaign more than a century ago.

On a dry, windswept plain 12,000 feet above sea level, La Paz, the nation's modern capital, coexists with indigenous villages where ancient Indian languages and customs still prevail. Although bleak, cold, and treeless, the altiplano (''high plateau''), which comprises about 30 percent of the nation's land area, contains about 62 percent of the nation's people. Studded with snowcapped peaks rising above 20,000 feet, the altiplano is a hostile environment of rare beauty. The altiplano is also one of the most mineral-rich regions on earth; large quantities of silver, gold, tin, copper, tungsten, lead, and zinc have been dug up and exported to satisfy the needs of the world's more industrial nations. The colonial splendor of San Luis Potosí (altitude 13,340), which sent more than two billion dollars worth of gold and silver to Spain, is still very much in evidence.

Ironically, the nation that produced so much of the world's gold and silver now has South America's lowest standard of living. First the deposits of gold, then silver, and now its tin have been largely depleted, forcing the nation to look elsewhere for economic viability. As a result, agriculture (chiefly cotton, sugar, and cattle) is becoming increasingly important as a contributor to GNP and producer of exports.

The tropical lowlands that sweep from the foothills of the Andes toward Brazil, Paraguay, and Argentina are said to be Bolivia's future. Here are few people but about half of the nation's land area. The area around Santa Cruz, center of the nation's agricultural and petroleum exports, has developed rapidly over the last 20 years. Santa Cruz, now Bolivia's second-largest city, is challenging La Paz as the nation's economic center.

Historically, Bolivia, perhaps more than any other Latin American nation, has been plagued by political and economic instability. Recently, however, the country has enjoyed unusual stability. For the first time in memory, power has been transferred peacefully from one elected leader to another. And the inflation rate, which hit an astronomical 24,000 percent a few years ago, has declined to manageable levels.

—Chad Isaaks, Jacksonville, Florida

Official name: Republic of Bolivia. **Area:** 424,165 square miles (the size of Texas and California combined). **Population:** 7,156,000. **Population density:** 16 inhabitants per square mile. **Capitals:** Sucre (legal) and La Paz (de facto). **Largest city:** La Paz (pop. 1,669,000). **Language:** Spanish, Quechua, Aymara. **Religion:** Roman Catholic. **Per capita income:** US $690. **Currency:** Bolivianos. **Literacy rate:** 78%. **Average daily high/low:** La Paz: January, 63°F/43°F; July, 64°F/33°F. **Average number of days with precipitation:** La Paz: January, 21; July, 2.

TRAVEL

U.S. citizens need a passport to enter Bolivia, but a visa is not required for stays of up to 30 days. For specific requirements, check with the **Embassy of Bolivia**, 3014 Massachusetts Avenue NW, Washington, DC 20008; (202) 483-4410.

Getting Around

Mountainous terrain and poorly developed road and railway systems make **air** travel an attractive alternative in Bolivia. Lloyd Aereo Boliviano, the national airline, serves most Bolivian cities. Its **Visit Bolivia Pass** is good for visiting six cities within the country for a period of 28 days and costs $150. It is sold only in the U.S. to travelers flying to Bolivia on Lloyd Aereo Boliviano (from Miami) and should be purchased in conjunction with your international ticket to Bolivia. For more information, contact Lloyd Aereo Boliviano, (305) 374-4600.

A surprising number of **rail** lines cross Bolivia. Trains come in two types, "slow" and the faster ferrobuses. Ferrobuses have first- and second-class cars, called *Pullman* and *Especiál*, respectively. Trains are less expensive than the bus and offer views of interesting scenery as well as contact with the rural population of the country. Rail lines connect most highland cities and link Bolivia to Chile, Peru, Argentina, and Brazil, but fail to connect Bolivia's two main cities, Santa Cruz and La Paz.

Buses are the most frequently used form of transportation in Bolivia, and service between the major cities is generally good. Only a few main roads are paved, however, and during the rainy season, buses providing service on unpaved roads are subject to frequent delays. **Rental cars** and four-wheel-drive vehicles are available. You should have both an International Driving Permit (see page 52) and your state driver's license.

Eating and Sleeping

For information on **youth hostels** in Bolivia, contact Hostelling International/American Youth Hostels (see page 54) or the **Asociación Boliviana de Albergues Juveniles**, PO Box 4294, Edificio Alborada, Piso 1, Of. 105, Juan de la Riva No. 1406, La Paz; (591) 2-361076.

For Further Information

Bolivia: A Travel Survival Kit is the best guidebook for the independent traveler on a budget who truly wants to get to know the country. It's available for $10.95 from Lonely Planet Publications (see page 56).

WORK

It is difficult for foreigners to obtain work in Bolivia. Employment and the necessary work visa (issued only when employment in Bolivia already is secured) must be obtained before traveling to Bolivia. For information contact the Embassy of Bolivia (see "Travel," above).

Voluntary Service

The Year Abroad Program, sponsored by the **International Christian Youth Exchange**, offers persons ages 18 to 30 voluntary-service opportunities in the fields of health care, education, the environment, construction, and more. See page 25 for more information.

STUDY

The following programs are offered by CIEE-member institutions. Unless otherwise noted, consult Appendix I for the addresses of the colleges and universities listed below.

Semester and Academic Year

General Studies

State University of New York at Stony Brook. *Stony Brook in Bolivia*. Fall and spring semesters. Social sciences and humanities. Juniors with two years of college Spanish. Apply by April 1 for fall; November 1 for spring. Contact: Dean for International Programs, SUNY at Stony Brook, Stony Brook, NY 11794-2700; (516) 632-7030.

World Learning/School for International Training. *College Semester Abroad*. Cochabamba, La Paz, Sucre, and Chapare. Fall and spring semesters. Intensive language study, interdisciplinary seminars on Bolivian life and culture and development issues, field-study methods seminar, and independent-study project. Homestays and excursions. Sophomores to graduate students with 2.5 GPA and three semesters of college Spanish. Apply by May 7 for fall; October 7 for spring. Contact: College Semester Abroad Admissions at (800) 336-1616.

EXPLORING BOLIVIAN CULTURE

Readings

Few Bolivian authors have been translated into English. Arturo Von Vacano's *Biting Silence* (1987) is dedicated "to liberty, although it may last 15 minutes," a reference to the political turmoil of a country where there have been more than 250 governments in the last century or so. It delves into the corruption of the political machinery and into the daily lives of the Bolivian populace.

Writers from other countries have also contributed to the available reading list on Bolivia. *Bolivia: Gate of the Sun* (1970) is a travelogue, by Margaret J. Anstee, that conveys the geographical diversity and the atmosphere of everyday life in Bolivia. Eric Lawlor's *In Bolivia* (1989) is another travelogue which searches out the essence of the country. His travels take him from La Paz through the forbidding countryside. Gudrun Pausewang's *Bolivian Wedding* (1972) chronicles the events of a single All Souls' Day in a Bolivian mountain town. *Gracias! A Latin American Journal* (1983) is an account of a six-month stay in Bolivia and Peru by a Dutch theologian, Henri Nouwen, who lived among the people.

BRAZIL

A few images of this enormous country shape most people's impressions of it. Prospectors and ranchers slash and burn their way through the ecologically delicate Amazon forest. Gold miners clamber over one another in an open pit mine. The Girl from Ipanema strolls seductively along a Rio beach. Clusters of futuristic buildings form a brave new capital in Brasilia. These images are accurate but incomplete, for Brazil is much more.

Brazil was the premier colony of Portugal. It was part of the Latin American independence movement, securing its freedom not with battles but with a single word from its new emperor, Pedro I. It was a hotbed of logical positivist philosophy, an influence still noted today in Brazilians named for Socrates, Newton, and Edison. In World War II, it harbored Nazi sympathizers but its soldiers fought alongside U.S. forces in Italy. Beginning in the 1960s, it endured a quarter-century of military dictatorship during which thousands of Brazilians were tortured, and many detainees "disappeared" or were killed. During this time, Brazil amassed the highest national debt in the Third World to build factories, power plants, and transportation networks—a debt which still plagues its economy today.

Except for the United States and Russia, Brazil is the largest country in the world to have essentially one language. In its forests, just 100,000 or so indigenous inhabitants remain. In spite of Brazil's European, African, and native heritage, there is no clear notion of racial difference. However, to be black or Indian is to be socially inferior, official proclamations to the contrary, though there is little agreement as to exactly who fits into each category.

Scholars have long felt that there are "two Brazils." One is modern, urban, and cosmopolitan, a Brazil of large and growing cities where all the material comforts are available to those who can afford to acquire them. The other is rural and backward, a land of primitive agriculture, illiteracy, and disease. Little connects these two worlds except the buses that bring people full of hope to the cities and that take many of them back again when their dreams die.

Brazilians are often intensely interested in Europe and the United States, and many middle- and upper-class Brazilians have traveled more extensively in Europe and the U.S. than they have within their own country or elsewhere in Latin America. Brazilians tend to be informal and hospitable. Visitors invariably find a warm welcome, particularly when they try to speak Portuguese, no matter how well.

—James Buschman, Alma, Michigan

Official name: Federative Republic of Brazil. **Area:** 3,286,470 square miles (about the same size as the U.S.). **Population:** 148,000,000. **Population density:** 45 inhabitants per square mile. **Capital:** Brasilia. **Largest city:** São Paulo (pop. 16,800,000). **Language:** Portuguese. **Religion:** Roman Catholic. **Per capita income:** US$2,540. **Currency:** Cruzeiro. **Literacy rate:** 81%. **Average daily temperature:** Rio de Janeiro: June, 70°F; December, 76°F. Manaus: June, 80°F; December, 80°F. **Average precipitation:** Rio de Janeiro: June, 2″; December, 5″. Manaus: June, 3.9″; December, 9″.

TRAVEL

Both a passport and a visa are required for U.S. citizens traveling to Brazil. To obtain a visa, tourists must have an onward or return ticket. For specific regulations, check with the **Embassy of Brazil**, 3006 Massachusetts Avenue NW, Washington, DC 20008; (202) 745-2700. There are Brazilian consulates in Chicago, Dallas, Houston, Los Angeles, Miami, New Orleans, New York, San Francisco, and San Juan.

Getting Around

Since Brazil is larger than the continental United States or the whole of Europe, and long-distance travel via road and rail is slow, most travelers intent on visiting different regions of the country generally resort to **air** transport for at least part of their journey. Fortunately, Brazil's domestic air transport network is among the world's best, providing comfortable and reliable service to even the most remote areas of the country. The **Brazil Air Pass**, valid on Varig Brazilian Airlines, gives you five flights in 21 days for $440. Additional flights cost $100 each. As airfares in Brazil have recently become quite expensive—it costs around US$200 for a flight from Rio to São Paulo—the Brazil Air Pass is a pretty good deal. The pass must be purchased in the U.S. in conjunction with an international ticket to Brazil. For more information, contact Council Travel (see pages xiii–xvi) or Varig Brazilian Airlines, (212) 682-3100.

The relatively few passenger trains in operation are used mainly for local transportation around urban areas. However, there is good intercity **rail** service between Rio and São Paulo, Belo Horizonte, and Brasilia. But remember: Distances are great; the relatively short trip between Rio and São Paulo will take about 10 hours, and traveling from São Paulo to Brasilia takes about 24 hours.

Most overland travel is by **bus**. Brazil has a rapidly expanding highway network which is especially well developed in the south. In other regions of the country, roads are not as good and travel is slower, but even in the Amazon region travel by road is now a realistic option, with paved roads extending as far as Manaus in the heart of the Amazon basin. Numerous bus companies provide comfortable and frequent service between the major cities of Brazil. Special luxury buses (called *leitos*) with fully reclining seats, curtained partitions, and attendants, make overnight trips. Less comfortable buses service even the most remote towns, although bus service on the unpaved roads of the Amazon basin is subject to frequent delays in the best of conditions, and is especially unreliable in the rainy season.

It is also possible to rent a **car** in most Brazilian cities. U.S. driver's licenses are valid in Brazil but many local rental companies require the International Driving Permit (see page 52). Hitching is possible for short local trips, but is generally discouraged for long-distance travel.

The best way to see the Amazon region is by **boat**. Riverboats still provide most of the transportation in this vast area, allowing you to travel the 2,000 miles up the Amazon to Iquitos, Peru, or to simply make a short hop between neighboring towns. The trip between Manaus and Belem, the two metropolises of the Amazon basin, takes five or six days, with stops at cities and towns along the way. There are also a number of ferry services on other rivers and along the coast.

Eating and Sleeping

Brazil has a large network of **youth hostels**. For more information, contact Hostelling International/American Youth Hostels (see page 54) or the national youth hostel organization, **Federaçao Brasiliera dos Albergues de Juventude**, Rua da Assembléia 10, S/1211, Centro, CEP 20119, Rio de Janeiro; (55) 21-2524829; fax (55) 21-2218753.

Especially for Students and Young People

Brazil's student travel organization and issuer of the International Student Identity Card is **STB**, Rua Estados Unidos 153, São Paulo, SP, CEP 01427-000; (55) 11-8874242; fax (55) 11-8872211. STB also has offices in Rio de Janeiro, Belo Horizonte, and Manaus. STB can book accommodations and transportation as well as provide information on discounts available to holders of the International Student Identity Card.

For Further Information

One of the most up-to-date guidebooks to Brazil is *Brazil: A Travel Survival Kit*, available for $17.95 from Lonely Planet Publications. *The Real Guide: Brazil* ($13.95) is also good, full of budget travel information as well as essays on history and culture. An excellent book to read in preparation for your trip is *Insight Guide: Brazil* ($19.95). For more information on Lonely Planet, *Real Guides*, and *Insight Guides*, see pages 56–57.

WORK

Getting regular salaried employment in Brazil is difficult for foreigners; work visas are only issued upon presentation of a work contract certified by the Brazilian Ministry of Labor. For more information, contact the Consular Section of the Brazilian Embassy (see "Travel," above). For those interested in **teaching** in Brazil, request a copy of their information sheet "Teaching Positions Abroad."

Internships/Traineeships

Two programs sponsored by members of the Council on International Educational Exchange are described below.

Association for International Practical Training. *IAESTE Trainee Program*. On-the-job training for undergraduate and graduate students in technical fields such as engineering, computer science, agriculture, architecture, mathematics, and the natural and physical sciences. See page 19 for more information.

Brigham Young University. *Internship in Brazil*. Spring term. (May 1 to June 22). Eight credit-hours of Portuguese language, with internships in business, education, and health services. Sophomores to seniors with two semesters of college Portuguese. Apply by February 1.

Voluntary Service

For persons interested in voluntary-service work, the Year Abroad Program sponsored by the **International Christian Youth Exchange** offers persons ages 18 to 30 opportunities in the fields of health care, education, the environment, construction, and more. See page 25 for more information. In addition, **Amigos de las Americas** sponsors voluntary-service opportunities in Brazil; see page 22 for more information.

STUDY

The following educational programs are offered by CIEE-member institutions. Unless otherwise noted, consult Appendix I for the addresses of the colleges and universities listed below.

Semester and Academic Year

Business

World Learning/School for International Training. *College Semester Abroad: International Business*. Fortaleza. Fall and spring semesters. Intensive language, life, and culture seminar; field-study methods seminar; and independent study project. Homestays. Sophomores to seniors with 2.5 GPA. Apply by March 7 for fall; October 7 for spring. Contact: College Semester Abroad Admissions at (800) 336-1616.

Natural Sciences

Antioch University. *Brazilian Ecosystems: The Protection and Management of Diversity.* Paraná State. Fall term. Courses in environmental research and conservation, Portuguese language, and independent field project in context of four-week internship. Juniors to graduate students majoring in science or environmental studies; some Spanish required, Portuguese preferred. Apply by March 15. Contact: (800) 874-7986.

General Studies

Brown University. *Brown in Brazil.* Rio de Janeiro. Fall semester. Enrollment in maximum of four courses at Pontifícia Universidade Católica. Excursions and homestays. Sophomores in good academic standing with three years of college Portuguese. Apply by February 15.

Council on International Educational Exchange. *Interuniversity Study Program at the University of São Paulo.* Fall semester, spring semester, U.S. academic year, and Brazilian academic year. Undergraduates with 3.0 GPA and two years of college Portuguese or Spanish (or one year of each language). Apply by March 15 for fall and U.S. academic year; November 1 for spring and Brazilian academic year. Contact University Programs Department.

International Student Exchange Program (ISEP). Semester and academic year. Direct reciprocal exchange between U.S. universities and Pontifícia Universidade Católica de Minas Gerais and Pontifícia Universidade Católica de Rio de Janeiro. Full curriculum options. Rolling admissions. Open only to students at ISEP-member institutions. Contact ISEP for list of members.

University of Maryland. *Study in Brazil.* Rio de Janeiro. Fall semester. Sophomores to seniors with two semesters of Portuguese. Apply by May 1.

University of North Carolina at Chapel Hill. *UNC Program to Rio de Janeiro.* Rio de Janeiro. Sophomores to seniors with 2.7 GPA and previous Spanish or Portuguese. Apply by February 14.

University of Wisconsin at Madison. *Academic Year at Universidade de São Paulo.* Portuguese language study, contemporary Brazil, anthropology, art, biology, communications, economics, film, geography, history, linguistics, political science, psychology, and sociology. Six-week homestay. Juniors to graduate students with 3.0 GPA and four semesters of either college Portuguese or Spanish or two semesters of each. Apply by February 15.

World Learning/School for International Training. *College Semester Abroad.* Belém, Santarém, and Manaus. Fall and spring semesters. Language study, seminar on Amazon studies and ecology, field-study methods seminar, homestay, independent-study project, field trips. Sophomores to seniors with 2.5 GPA. Apply by May 7 for fall; October 7 for spring. Contact: College Semester Abroad Admissions at (800) 336-1616.

Summer and Short-Term

Communications

University of Alabama at Birmingham. *UAB in Brazil.* Rio de Janeiro. Two weeks in June. International mass media and comparison of all forms of media in U.S. and Brazil. First-year college students to graduate students and professionals. Contact: Dr. Mark Hickson, Department of Communications Studies, University of Alabama at Birmingham, Birmingham, AL 35294-1150; (205) 934-3877.

General Studies

University of Illinois at Urbana-Champaign. *Summer Program in Recife.* Engineering students welcome. Field experiences available. First-year college students to graduate students with 3.0 GPA. Apply by March 15.

University of North Carolina at Chapel Hill. *Summer in Rio de Janeiro.* Four weeks in summer. Intensive Portuguese language study. First-year college students to graduate students with one semester of Portuguese or two semesters of Spanish. Apply by March 15.

World Learning/School for International Training. *College Semester Abroad.* Fortaleza, with excursions to Recife, Ceará, Bahia, and Amazonia. Fall and spring semesters. Language study, interdisciplinary seminars, development issues, field-study methods, homestay, and independent-study project. Sophomores to seniors with 2.5 GPA. Apply by May 7 for fall; October 7 for spring. Contact: College Semester Abroad Admissions at (800) 336-1616.

Natural Sciences

Michigan State University. *Social Issues, Environment, and Business.* São Paulo. Summer. Sophomores to seniors. Apply by April 15. Contact: Office of Overseas Study, 108 International Center, Michigan State University, East Lansing, MI 48824-1035; (517) 353-8920.

Portuguese Language and Brazilian Culture

University of Illinois at Urbana-Champaign. *Portuguese Language.* Basic through advanced Portuguese. Internships available. First-year college students to graduate students with 3.0 GPA. Apply by March 15.

EXPLORING BRAZILIAN CULTURE

Readings

Most Brazilian authors are closely identified with a particular region of the country, a fact that reflects the strong regional identities found in this vast and diverse country. Jorge Amado, the country's best-known contemporary novelist, writes about the Northeast. His books include *Gabriela, Clove and Cinnamon* (1958), the entertaining story of a young migrant worker whose beauty and cooking skill make her the most sought-after woman in town; *Dona Flor and Her Two Husbands* (1966), a farce about a woman whose dead ex-husband comes back to visit her after she has remarried; *Showdown*, a multigenerational saga set in the cacao-producing heartland of Amado's home state of Bahia; and *Jubiaba*, an interracial love story set in Bahia. *Dona Flor* and *Jubiaba* have been made into popular movies.

Marcio Souzas writes about the Amazon region in novels such as *The Emperor of the Amazon* (1980) and *Mad Maria* (1985). Inácio de Loyola Brandão offers a dark vision of 21st-century São Paulo in *And Still the Earth* (1985). Graciliano Ramos's *Barren Lives* (1938) is considered one of the best modern Brazilian novels. It reveals much about life in the Brazilian *sertão*. In

Of Men and Crabs (1967), Josue de Castro exposes the miseries, poverty, disease, and hunger of rural Brazil.

Less focused on a particular region, *Celebration* (1976), by Ivan Angelo, deals with Brazil's recent political past, specifically with the censorship imposed by the military government during the 1970s. Gilberto Freyre's writings are credited for the creation of a national identity in Brazil. *The Masters and the Slaves* (1943) is a monumental study of Brazilian civilization in which a first-person account reveals history. Nelida Piñon's *The Republic of Dreams* (1989) is a pointed chronicle of Brazilian history told through a family saga that begins in a Spanish village. A reading of this book should be compared to Errol Lincoln Uys's *Brazil* (1986), which follows two families over five centuries.

Clarice Lispector, one of the best-known contemporary female authors of Brazil, writes about a woman from the northeast who finds herself in the big city in *Hour of the Star* (1977). Rachel de Querioz's *The Three Marias* (1985), deals with the problems faced by women and men in a country where machismo is very much a part of everyday life. In *Dora, Doralina* (1984), a woman gradually achieves independence and dignity in modern Brazil. Daphne Patai's *Brazilian Women Speak: Contemporary Life Stories* (1988) allows ordinary women from the Northeast and Rio to speak about the struggles, constraints, and hopes of their lives.

For an understanding of the social and spiritual forces behind Rio's *carnaval*, Alma Guillermoprieto's *Samba* (1990) follows the carnival preparations from the beginning until the actual parade. João Trevisan's *Perverts in Paradise* (1986) is a fascinating survey of Brazilian gay life ranging from the papal inquisition to pop idols, transvestite macumba priests, and guerrilla idols. This contemporary account should be compared to Adolpho Caminha's *Bom Crioulo: The Black Man and the Cabin Boy*, Latin America's first novel of homosexual relations.

Films

Closely linked to the country's music, dance, and carnival traditions, Brazilian film is often vibrant, witty, and entertaining, while simultaneously satirical and politically aggressive.

In the 1960s, a group of young filmmakers began producing a series of low-budget independent films that initiated Cinema Nôvo (literally, "New Cinema"), Brazil's best-known film movement. In its initial stage, film topics revolved around the trials and tribulations of rural people and their communities. Glauber Rocha's *Barravento* (1961), for example, is a rhythmic but jolting presentation of the hardships, religion, and myths of a rural fishing village. Rocha's *Black God—White Devil* (1964) also looks at the mythic traditions of rural regions. Other films in this vein include *Vidas Secas* (1962), by Nelson Pereira dos Santos, and *Ganga Zumba*, by Carlos Diegues.

Among more recent Brazilian films is *Pixote* (1981), by Hector Babenco (who also directed the film adaption of Manuel Puig's *Kiss of the Spider Woman*), the story of an orphan growing up in the streets of Rio. *Dona Flor and Her Two Husbands* (1978), by Bruno Barreto, is the movie version of Jorge Amado's novel about a woman torn between her dead irresponsible husband who keeps returning to earth and her considerate but dull second husband. Carlos Diegues's *Bye Bye Brazil* (1980), is a comedy-drama about a group of traveling entertainers touring Brazil's small towns. Diegues's *Subway to the Stars* (1988) is set in contemporary Rio de Janeiro, where a young musician searches for his missing girlfriend and encounters the colorful citizens of the underworld. Also noteworthy are two films by Pereira dos Santos: *Tent of Miracles*, an interesting look at Brazilian racial problems and religions in the state of Bahia, and *How Tasty Was My Little Frenchman*, a critique of the Brazilian government.

Perhaps the best-known film about Brazil, however, is *Black Orpheus* (1959), by the French director Marcel Camus, a hauntingly beautiful and witty combination of Brazilian carnival and Greek mythology. Another film that delves into the psyche of the Brazilian character is *At Play in the Fields of the Lord* (1992), which is based on the 1965 novel by Peter Matthiessen. In this movie four fundamentalist missionaries try to convert Indians in Oriente province.

CHILE

The only country in South America that can boast of having two Nobel laureates in literature (Pablo Neruda and Gabriela Mistral), Chile has long considered itself one of the most sophisticated countries in the region. Its population is diverse, but the majority of Chileans are descendants of Spaniards who, in the mid-16th century, began to settle in this long narrow nation, nestled between the Andes and the Pacific Ocean. Unlike in Peru, they found little gold in this territory; consequently, few Spaniards ventured as far as the country's shores. The small number of colonialists that settled in Chile formed a close-knit society, becoming even closer as they battled the indigenous Araucanians.

Chile declared independence in 1810, and became the second country in the Western world to abolish slavery. Independence was not secured until 1818 when Bernardo O'Higgins—Chile's equivalent to George Washington—assumed leadership in the capital city, Santiago. Chile did not become the most popular place for European immigrants in Latin America, but thousands came because of its generally open society; to exploit the nitrate industry, and later the copper mines; and to exploit the south—an oasis of forests and lakes. The current Chilean north was once Peruvian and Bolivian territory, and mostly desert. Two bloody 19th-century wars, in which Chile was victorious, radically changed the country's geographic landscape, and the balance of power in South America.

Historically one of the few democracies in Latin America, Chile sustained representative government from the early 1830s to 1973, when it fell victim to the inability of its national leaders to resolve lingering economic problems. In 1973 the military toppled the only constitutionally elected Marxist president in the Western Hemisphere, Salvador Allende. Democracy was replaced by a 15-year military dictatorship, presided by Augusto Pinochet. In 1989, Patricio Aylwin was elected president, as were members of a national Congress. These were the initial steps in the complete transition to democracy, a process that may continue for another decade. Chileans take the changes in stride. Generally a peaceful, stoic, and sensitive people, they are pleased the transition is taking place—allowing them to concentrate on other issues and other facets of their lives. The country is looking for ways to deal with the $20 billion external debt left by Pinochet's government and the depletion of copper, the country's most important export.

Santiago, the capital, has one of the worst pollution problems in the world.

Conversely, Chileans are proud of one of the most efficient, cleanest, safest and cheapest subway systems in the world. The beaches of Chile, stretched beautifully along the Pacific Ocean, are among the best in South America. They include not only the one in the popular resort city, Viña del Mar, just north of Santiago, but Cachagua and Algarrobo, three hours by car from Santiago, on a scenic modern highway. Seafood lovers will find delicacies such as *congrio*, particular to Chile, and the mild and exquisitely tasteful *lenguado*. For skiers, scores of excellent resorts beckon in the Andes.

The south of Chile also has much to offer the visitor: hundreds of lakes; Easter Island (a national treasure in the southern Pacific); Valparaiso, port city and the site of the new Congress building; Neruda's homes in Bella Visita (Santiago's bohemian area) and Punta de Tralca; and Mistral's home in Valle del Elqui.

—Carl E. Meacham, Albany, New York

Official name: Republic of Chile. **Area:** 292,257 square miles (slightly larger than Texas). **Population:** 13,286,000. **Population density:** 45 inhabitants per square mile. **Capital and largest city:** Santiago (pop. 5,236,000). **Language:** Spanish. **Religion:** Roman Catholic. **Per capita income:** US$2,130. **Currency:** Peso. **Literacy rate:** 92%. **Average daily high/low:** Santiago: January, 85°F/53°F; July, 59°/37°. **Average number of days with precipitation:** Santiago: January, 0; July, 6.

TRAVEL

U.S. citizens need a passport but not a visa to enter Chile for stays of up to three months. However, those considering scientific, technical, or mountaineering activities in "frontier" areas must obtain special permission at least 90 days in advance. For further information, check with the **Embassy of Chile**, 1732 Massachusetts Avenue NW, Washington, DC 20036; (202) 785-1746. There are also Chilean consulates in Houston, Los Angeles, Miami, New York, and Philadelphia.

Getting Around

Chile's eastern border runs along the crest of the Andes. Between this and the coastal range runs a long valley, through which the **Pan-American Highway** is the main travel artery. Paved all the way from the Peruvian border, it links the main cities of Chile as far south as Puerto Montt. The region below Puerto Montt, where the ocean has flooded into the valley, is a wild coastline of rocky fjords and islands. Intermittent road access south of Puerto Montt is provided by the Carretera Austral Presidente Pinochet. Otherwise, passenger **boat** service is available to Punta Arenas on the Strait of Magellan and several points along the way. Intercity **bus** service along the Pan-American Highway is inexpensive and frequent, and several bus services link Chile and Argentina. It is also possible to rent cars in major Chilean cities. Chile's main **rail** line extends from Iquique in the desert north to Puerto Montt. However, there is no passenger service north of Santiago.

Traveling is easiest in central Chile, where most of the country's population is concentrated in and around Santiago. For tourists wishing to venture far from Santiago the most popular way of travel is by **plane**. Chile's two domestic carriers, LanChile and Ladeco, both offer separate but identical **Visit Chile Fares**. Valid for 21 days, Visit Chile Fares for northern or southern loops cost $300; for the entire continental loop the fare costs $500. Flights to Easter Island cost extra. Visit Chile Fare must be purchased in the U.S. You can call LanChile at (800) 735-5526. Ladeco can be reached at (212) 730-1002. For more information, contact Council Travel (see pages xiii–xvi).

Eating and Sleeping

There are several **youth hostels** in Chile, including three in Santiago, two in Temuco, and two in Puerto Montt. For more information, contact Hostelling International/American Youth Hostels (see page 54) or the national youth hostel organization, **Asociación Chilena de Albergues Turísticos Juveniles**, Av Providencia 2594, OF 420-421, Providencia, Santiago; (56) 2-2333220.

For Further Information

Chile and Easter Island: A Travel Survival Kit is a comprehensive guide for budget travelers interested in getting to know Chile. It's available for $11.95 from Lonely Planet Publications. An excellent book to read in preparation for your trip is *Insight Guide: Chile* ($19.95). For more information on Lonely Planet and *Insight Guide*s, see pages 56–57.

WORK

In order to work in Chile, it is necessary to obtain a temporary resident visa that is valid for one year and renewable in the country. Students interested in working must get a temporary resident visa, as the student visa does not provide you with the necessary authorization you need for employment. Applications can be made by mail or in person, but a personal appearance at the Chilean embassy is required for completion of the visa. For more information, contact the **Embassy of Chile** (see "Travel," above).

Internships/Traineeships

Two programs sponsored by members of the Council on International Educational Exchange are described below.

State University of New York at Plattsburgh. *Latin American Southern Cone Program*. Santiago, Valparaíso, and Concepción. Semester-long internships at undergraduate and graduate levels. Placements at leading newspapers, television stations, businesses, research institutes, voluntary organizations, and the National Congress. Sophomores to graduate students with intermediate Spanish. Apply by April 15 for fall and academic year; October 31 for spring. Contact: Director, Southern Cone Programs, Hawkins Hall 102, SUNY at Plattsburgh, Plattsburgh, NY 12901; (518) 564-5827/2398.

University of Illinois at Urbana—Champaign. *Political Internships in Chile*. Internships in the National Congress in Valparaíso. Courses in Chilean society, politics, and international relations. Sophomores, juniors, seniors, and graduate students with advanced Spanish language; spring semester. Contact: Study Abroad Office, 115 International Studies Building, 910 South Fifth Street, Champaign, IL 61820.

STUDY

The cultural department of the Embassy of Chile compiles the *Guide to the University System of Chile*. Updated annually, this booklet gives an overview of higher education in Chile, articulates options for foreigners, and lists all Chilean universities and their addresses for those who would like to enroll directly. To receive the guide, send a self-addressed, legal-sized envelope with $1 in postage to the cultural department of the embassy (see "Travel").

Programs sponsored by member institutions of the Council on International Educational Exchange are described below. Unless otherwise noted, consult Appendix I for the address where you can write for more information. In addition to the programs below, the University of Wisconsin at Madison offers a program open to its own students only.

Semester and Academic Year

General Studies

American University. *Santiago Semester*. Spring. Politics, economics, and society. Internships available. Homestays. Juniors and seniors with two years of college Spanish. Apply by October 15. Contact: World Capitals Programs, American University, Dunblane House—Tenley Campus, Washington, DC 20016-8083; (202) 895-4853 or 4937.

Council on International Educational Exchange. *Cooperative Latin American Studies Program at the Universidad de Chile and the Pontificia Universidad Católica de Chile*. Santiago. Fall semester, spring semester, U.S. academic year, and Chilean academic year. Sophomores to graduate students with 2.75 GPA and three years of college Spanish. Apply by April 1 for fall semester and U.S. academic year; November 1 for spring semester and Chilean academic year. Contact University Programs Department.

State University of New York at Plattsburgh. *Study Program in Chile*. Valparaiso, Santiago, or Concepción. Fall and spring semesters. General studies at a Chilean university. First-year college students to graduate students with 2.5 GPA and ability to participate in Spanish-language classroom. Apply by March 15 for fall; October 31 for spring. Contact: Director, Southern Cone Programs, Hawkins Hall 102, SUNY at Plattsburgh, Plattsburgh, NY 12901; (518) 564-5827/2398.

Political Science

University of Illinois at Urbana-Champaign. *Chilean Legislative/Public Policy Semester*. Spring semester. Juniors to graduate students with five semesters of Spanish. Apply by November 1.

University of Wisconsin at Milwaukee. *Study Abroad in Santiago*. Santiago. Semester and academic year. Offered in conjunction with the University of Michigan and the University of Wisconsin at Madison. Sophomores to seniors with 3.0 GPA and four semesters of college Spanish. Apply by March 15 for fall and academic year; October 15 for spring.

World Learning/School for International Training. *College Semester Abroad*. Santiago. Fall and spring semesters. Intensive language study, interdisciplinary seminars on Chilean life and culture, field-study methods seminar, and independent-study project. Excursions and homestays. Sophomores to seniors with 2.5 GPA and one year of college Spanish. Apply by May 7 for fall; October 7 for spring. Contact: College Semester Abroad Admissions at (800) 336-1616.

Spanish Language and Chilean Culture

Brigham Young University. *Chile Study Abroad*. Concepción. Spring semester. Homestays and excursions. First-year college students to seniors with one year of college Spanish. Apply by October 1.

Summer and Short-Term

General Studies

University of Illinois at Urbana-Champaign. *Summer Program in Chile*. Valparaiso. Summer. Study at Universidad Católica de Valparaiso. Language study and social science. Engineers welcome. Juniors to graduate students with 3.0 GPA and three semesters of college Spanish. Apply by March 15.

Villanova University. *Villanova Concepción Summer Program in Chile*. Concepción. Early July to late August. Intensive Spanish language study and general studies at the Universidad de Concepción. Sophomores to graduate students (not for graduate credit) with 2.5 GPA. Apply by March 15.

Spanish Language and Chilean Culture

State University of New York at Plattsburgh. *Latin American Southern Cone Programs—Summer Institute*. Santiago. Late July to mid-August. Two-week seminar on language and culture. School visits and excursions. Graduate students and Spanish teachers with intermediate Spanish. Apply by May 1. Contact: Director, Southern Cone Programs, Hawkins Hall 102, SUNY at Plattsburgh, Plattsburgh, NY 12901; (518) 564-5827/2398.

EXPLORING CHILEAN CULTURE

Readings

Much of modern Chilean literature deals with the 1973 coup and the subsequent military dictatorship. Isabel Allende, niece of the late President Salvador Allende, has become one of the most popular contemporary Chilean writers. Although she has lived in exile since the coup, most of her novels are set in Chile. Magical realism provides the style to Allende's novels, but the fantastic aspects of each story are securely fastened to real events in Chile. Her works include *The House of the Spirits* (1982), *Of Love and Shadows* (1984), and *Stories of Eva Luna* (1987). Another Chilean writer that presents recent Chilean history in his works is Ariel Dorfman. In *Widows*, he focuses on the women who continue looking year after year for loved ones who have "disappeared" (and are probably dead) under the military regime. Antonio Skarmeta's *Burning Patience* (1987) is set during Allende's presidency and deals with Pablo Neruda's death and the overthrow of Allende.

Mercedes Valdivieso's *Breakthrough* (1961) is regarded as the first feminist novel of Latin America. It is a novel of a rebellious woman who struggles to assert her individuality and freedom among the patriarchal Chilean bourgeoisie.

The poetry of Gabriela Mistral and Pablo Neruda, both winners of the Nobel Prize, is considered some of the best to come out of Latin America. Mistral's works are identified by a number of themes that disclose the troubled human being, the consummate teacher, the passionate crusader, and the innovative artist in her. Her books include *Desolation* (1922), *Tenderness* (1924), *Telling* (1938), and *Wine* (1954). Neruda's poetry changed over the years to reflect personal changes, from his vision of a troubled world, to a world of loneliness and solitude, to a down to earth and simple outlook on life. His books include *Residence on Earth and Other Poems* (1925), *Five Decades: Poems 1925–1970, New Poems: 1968–1970*, and *The Heights of Macchu Picchu*.

Films

Cinema in Chile moved to the cultural and political forefront during Salvador Allende's Unidad Popular government of the early 1970s. *The Promised Land* and *The Jackal of Nahueltoro*, by Miguel Littin, both explore the trials and tribulations of landless peasants, workers, and rural communities, as they contend with the country's governing bodies, industry, and the military. Perhaps the most symbolic film of this period is Patricio Guzman's epic documentary, *Battle of Chile*, which attempts to investigate the political, cultural, and economic forces that eventually resulted in the military overthrow of Salvador Allende's government and the assassination of Allende himself. Constantin Costa-Gavras's *Missing* provides an non-Chilean view of the overthrow of Allende's government, focusing on a North American father seeking his son who has disappeared in Chile during the military clampdown after the coup.

Since the fall of Allende, a number of Chilean exiles have been working actively in Europe and elsewhere in Latin America. Most prolific of these filmmakers is Raoul Ruiz, who has produced over 70 films in 15 years. Ruiz's films are informed by an intricate mix of subjective fantasy and historical episodes, cultural references, and political critique. Best known are *Tres Tigres Tristes, Three Crowns of a Sailor, Hypothesis of a Stolen Painting*, and *Of Great Events and Ordinary People*.

COLOMBIA

One of the striking themes of Gabriel García Márquez's novel *One Hundred Years of Solitude*, a mystical chronicle of one hundred years in the life of a Colombian family, is the role that nature plays in the fabric of family life. Certainly, the unusually diverse geography of Colombia has contributed to the shaping of the nation. Bordered by both the Atlantic and the Pacific and intersected on a north-south axis by three ranges of the Andes Mountains, Colombia encompasses everything from tropical swamps to snow-dusted volcanoes. Regionalism, the result of mountain barriers, has discouraged unity throughout Colombia's history and even today the country revolves around numerous regional centers such as Medellín, Cali, and Barranquilla, in addition to the national capital of Bogotá. Close proximity to the equator means that the climate in each city is roughly the same year-round, although cities at different altitudes experience radically different climates. Always a land of contradictions, this climactic predictability is unsettled all too often by earthquakes and volcanic eruptions.

Colombia's 16th-century settlers came in search of gold. A visit to the Gold

Museum (Museo de Oro) in Bogotá—an awesome vault of pre-Colombian artifacts—is proof that those pioneers found what they were looking for. Today, the country still owes its relative prosperity to its abundant natural resources. Exports of agricultural products, textiles, coal, oil, and precious stones, as well as illicit drugs, are responsible for providing the hard currency that has made Colombia one of the few countries of Latin America to keep pace with the payments on its foreign debt.

Despite the image that Colombia is out of control, an impression strengthened several years ago by a wave of political assassinations and bombings and more recently by the war between the government and the drug lords, Colombia is in fact one of South America's oldest democracies. Colombians have learned to deal creatively with recurring and violent power struggles. Some 30 years ago, for example, several years of bloodshed between members of the Liberal and Conservative parties ended with a power-sharing agreement that provided for alternating Liberal and Conservative governments from 1958 to 1974. Recently the government and opposition groups have negotiated agreements whereby insurgent groups have laid down their weapons and entered the political arena as legitimate parties. Likewise, violence between the government and drug cartels is waning. The intense national pride shared by all disparate factions in Colombia seems to be saving the nation from the total breakdown of law and order that seemed possible a couple of years ago.

In fact, Colombians have much to be proud of, and the visitor who is willing to avoid involvement in the country's political conflicts will find much to enjoy. The nation's spectacular mountains, forests, and coastline are obvious attractions. So, too, are its people and culture. And everywhere the visitor travels, exuberant Latin American hospitality and Colombian pride will welcome them.

—Sarah Wood, Brooklyn, New York

Official name: Republic of Colombia. **Area:** 439,735 square miles (almost three times the size of California). **Population:** 33,777,000. **Population density:** 76 inhabitants per square mile. **Capital and largest city:** Bogotá (pop. 4,819,000). **Language:** Spanish. **Religion:** Roman Catholic. **Per capita income:** US$1,300. **Currency:** Peso. **Literacy rate:** 80%. **Average daily high/low:** Bogota: January, 67°F/48°F; July, 64°F/50°F. **Average number of days with precipitation:** Bogotá: January, 6; July, 18.

TRAVEL

U.S. citizens need a passport and proof of an onward or return ticket to enter Colombia for stays of up to 90 days. Tourist cards are issued upon arrival. For specific regulations, check with the **Embassy of Colombia**, 2118 Leroy Place NW, Washington, DC 20008; (202) 387-8338. There are also Colombian consulates in Chicago, Houston, Los Angeles, Miami, New Orleans, New York, and San Juan.

At press time, the U.S. State Department's **Consular Information Sheet** on Colombia warned of escalating violence from narcotic traffickers and guerilla organizations. The country is also experiencing daily and nightly power outages, it states, during which violent crime greatly increases. For up-to-date information on trouble spots, obtain the latest Consular Information Sheet from the U.S. Department of State (see pages 8–9).

Getting Around

Four mountain ranges running north to south create formidable natural barriers to travel in Colombia. As a result, the country has developed one of the best domestic **air** systems in South America. The international carrier Avianca also operates the most domestic flights. Its **Discover Colombia ticket** allows 10 stops within a 30-day period for $224 or 5 stops in 14 days for $142. If you wish to visit Leticia and the island of San Andrés, the price increases. The pass must be purchased before your arrival in Colombia. For more information, contact Council Travel (see pages xiii–xvi) or Avianca, (800) 284-2622.

Good highways link the cities of the interior with each other as well as with coastal ports. The Trans-Caribbean Highway connects the cities along Colombia's northern coast. Highways also connect the country to Venezuela and Ecuador, but no roads cross Colombia's borders with Panama or Brazil. Within Colombia, **buses** are the principle means of transportation. Bus service between the major cities is good, while in more remote areas local buses provide interesting but usually slow and uncomfortable transportation. Alternatives to the buses include *busetas* (minibuses) and *colectivos* (shared taxis). **Car** rental agencies can be found in the major cities, though renting is expensive. U.S. driver's licenses are valid, but you must have an official Spanish translation.

Colombia has only a few **rail** lines, and passenger service is dwindling. Mountain passage makes journeys by rail almost painfully slow. Few Colombians take the train, preferring faster buses. Trains, however, are extremely inexpensive and afford a fascinating view of Colombia's mountainous interior.

While the Magdalena River continues to be a main transportation artery, scheduled ferry service on the river has been discontinued. However, it is possible to travel by riverboat from Colombia's Amazon port of Leticia to either Peru or Brazil.

Eating and Sleeping

There are a number of youth hostels in Colombia. For more information, contact Hostelling International/American Youth Hostels (see page 54), or the national youth hostel organization, **IDEL/ALCOM**, PO Box 3220, Carrera 7a, No 6-10, Bogotá, D.E.; (57) 1-2803318; fax (57) 1-2803460.

For Further Information

Colombia: A Travel Survival Kit is the best guidebook for the independent traveler on a budget. It's available for $11.95 from Lonely Planet Publications (see page 56). Anyone planning on spending time in the country might be interested in *Living in Colombia*, by William Hutchison and Cynthia Poznanski. The book is available for $16.95 from Intercultural Press (see page 3).

WORK

A work visa is required for U.S. citizens wishing to work in Colombia. Work visas are only granted for jobs for which no citizen of Colombia has the required training or skills. Employment is required before a work visa will be issued. Other documentation such as a birth certificate is also required. For more information, contact the **Embassy of Colombia** (see "Travel," above).

Internships/Traineeships

A program sponsored by a member of the Council on International Educational Exchange is described below.

Association for International Practical Training. *IAESTE Trainee Program.* On-the-job training for undergraduate and graduate students in technical fields such as engineering, computer science, agriculture, architecture, mathematics, and the natural and physical sciences. See page 19 for more information.

Voluntary Service

For persons interested in voluntary-service work, the Year Abroad Program sponsored by the **International Christian Youth Exchange** offers persons ages 18 to 30 voluntary-service opportunities in the fields of health care, education, the environment, construction, and more. See page 25 for more information.

STUDY

Following is an educational program offered by a member institution of the Council on International Educational Exchange. Consult Appendix I for the addresses where you can write for further information.

Semester and Academic Year

General Studies

International Student Exchange Program (ISEP). Semester and academic year. Direct reciprocal exchange between U.S. universities and institutions in Bogotá, Cali, and Baranquilla. Full curriculum options. Rolling admissions. Open only to students at ISEP-member institutions. Contact ISEP for list of members.

EXPLORING COLOMBIAN CULTURE

Readings

In *One Hundred Years of Solitude*, Gabriel García Márquez presents his image of a Latin American world of myth, sensuality, violence, and conspiracy. This book traces several generations of the Buendia family in the mythical town of Macundo. Less famous but perhaps equally fascinating are his more recent works, including *The Autumn of the Patriarch* (1975), in which he reveals the thoughts of a dying Latin American dictator who has ruled for two centuries; *Chronicle of a Death Foretold* (1983), the story of a man whose imminent murder is known to everyone in town except himself; and *Love in the Time of Cholera* (1988), a love story set at the turn of the century in Cartagena, on Colombia's Caribbean coast.

Another well-known Colombian writer is is José Eustasio Rivera. *The Vortex* (1924), the story of a couple that flees to the jungle only to be transformed and eventually destroyed there, is a powerful denunciation of exploitation in the upper Amazon during the rubber boom of the early 1900s.

ECUADOR

Ecuador derives its name from the equator, which bisects the nation; but in spite of its tropical location, the nation encompasses a wide variety of climates.

Hot, humid rain forest characterizes the northwest coast and the Amazon basin that makes up the eastern half of the country. However, equally characteristic of Ecuador are snowcapped mountains and cool plateaus. The Andes Mountains, whose peaks rise to more than 20,000 feet, run on a north-south axis through the country. In Ecuador, climate depends on altitude.

The country's geographic diversity is mirrored by its cultural diversity: the country's population includes a large number of Indian tribes, each of which retains its own clothing, way of life, and, in some cases, language. Another interesting cultural influence comes from the many mestizos, descendants of both Indians and the Spaniards who conquered the region in the 16th century. Less than 10 percent of the population is of European descent and about an equal number are blacks, whose ancestors were brought as slaves by the Spanish.

Spain, during nearly 300 years of colonial domination, left a strong imprint on Ecuador. Spanish is the official language of the country and the one most commonly spoken. Similarly, Catholicism is the religion of nearly all Ecuadorians. Churches from the colonial period are centerpieces of large cities and small villages alike. But perhaps the most interesting evidence of the Spanish conquest can be found in Ecuadorian art—a mixture of Spanish and Indian motifs, techniques, and styles. Such art continues to flourish in the handicrafts sold in busy markets in cities, towns, and villages.

The Spanish domination generated a sharp division between the upper and lower classes that continues to exist today. Richly blessed by nature, Ecuador has been at different times one of the world's leading exporters of cacao, bananas, rice, and, currently, shrimp. However, the country's wealth and power have traditionally been concentrated in the hands of a few leading families. In recent years, the development of petroleum resources in the Amazon basin has enabled the government to carry out programs beneficial to the population at large—one reason Ecuador has not suffered the bloody social upheavals and political violence that have affected many other countries of the region.

For centuries Ecuador has also been divided by the conflict between its two major cities, Guayaquil and Quito, each of which represents different economic interests, social groups, and regional ties. Guayaquil dominates the coastal region and is the country's leading port, largest city, and economic center. Quito—more isolated and more traditional—is the hub of the Andean region and the nation's capital.

No introduction to Ecuador can be complete without mentioning the Galapagos Islands. Like Darwin, current visitors to the Galapagos are amazed by the plants and animals found in these remote and sparsely populated islands.

—Hector Correa, Pittsburgh, Pennsylvania

Official name: Republic of Ecuador. **Area:** 109,483 square miles (the size of Colorado). **Population:** 10,751,000. **Population density:** 98 inhabitants per square mile. **Capital:** Quito (pop. 1,500,000). **Largest city:** Guayaquil (pop. 2,000,000). **Language:** Spanish, Quechuan, Jivaroan. **Religion:** Roman Catholic. **Per capita income:** US$1,040. **Currency:** Sucre. **Literacy rate:** 88%. **Average daily temperature:** Guayaquil: June, 76°; December, 78°. Quito: June, 55°; December, 55°. **Average number of days with precipitation:** Guayaquil: June, 4; December, 10. Quito: June, 12; December, 16.

TRAVEL

For stays of less than three months, U.S. citizens need a passport and a return or onward ticket. Visas are necessary for stays of three to six months. An AIDS test is required for stays of over three months; the U.S. test is acceptable. For specific regulations, check with the **Embassy of Ecuador**, 2535 15th Street NW, Washington, DC 20009; (202) 234-7200.

Getting Around

Frequent **air** service links the Pacific port of Guayaquil with Quito, which is located high in the Andes nearly 10,000 feet above sea level; the flight takes about 40 minutes (compared to a day-long bus journey). Very inexpensive flights are also available from Quito and Guayaquil to other major cities in Educador, as well as to several outposts in the Oriente, the eastern half of the country located in the Amazon basin.

Train service between Guayaquil and Quito is gradually being restored, after a long period of suspension following severe floods in 1983. At press time, these segments were operational: Quito to Riobamba, Guayaquil to Alausí, and Sibambe to Cuenca. This means if you want to ride from Quito to either Guayaquil or Cuenca, you'll have to take to the road between Riobamba and Alausí. Although the trains are not very comfortable, the Andean route is one of the world's most spectacular.

Most transportation is provided by **buses**, which provide frequent service throughout the country except in the Oriente, where transportation by small boat is the rule. Ecuador's road system provides easy access to the cities and points of interest in the Andean and coastal regions of the country. The road network also extends from the Andes eastward to river towns, where people and goods are transferred to boats going to points farther east. **Car** rentals can be readily arranged in Quito and Guayaquil.

Eating and Sleeping

There are several **youth hostels** in Ecuador. For more information, contact Hostelling International/American Youth Hostels (see page 54) or the **Asociación Ecuadoriana de Albergues**, 10 de Agosto y Mercadillo Of. 103, Venezuela 1459 y Oriente, Quito; (593) 2-510558; fax (593) 2-502399.

For Further Information

General tourist information is also available from the privately funded, nonprofit tourism office, **FEPROTUR**, 1390 Brickell Avenue, Third Floor, Miami, FL 33131-3324.

One of the best guidebooks for the independent traveler on a budget is *Ecuador and the Galapagos Islands: A Travel Survival Kit*, available for $16.95 from Lonely Planet Publications. An excellent book to read in preparation for your trip is *Insight Guide: Ecuador* ($19.95). For more information on Lonely Planet and *Insight Guide*s, see pages 56–57. A good source of firsthand information in Quito is the **South American Explorers Club** (see pages 547–548).

WORK

Regular salaried employment in Ecuador is possible only if you are being brought in by an Ecuadorean company for professional reasons; a work permit and a visa are required. A contract must be in place before going to Ecuador. For more information, contact the Embassy of Ecuador (see "Travel," above).

Internships/Traineeships

Two programs sponsored by members of the Council on International Educational Exchange are described below.

Ohio University. *The Consortium for Overseas Student-Teaching.* Student-teaching in local and independent schools. Quarter. Sophomores to seniors attending Ohio University only. Contact: Wes Snyder, Center for Higher Education and International Programs, 129 McCracken Hall, Athens, OH 45701; (614) 593-4445; fax (614) 593-0569.

In addition, **AIESEC-US** sponsors a reciprocal internship program for students in economics, business, finance, marketing, accounting, and computer science. See page 19 for more information.

Voluntary Service

The **Partnership for Service-Learning** and **Amigos de las Americas** sponsor voluntary-service opportunities in Ecuador; see page 26 and 22 for more information.

STUDY

The following are the educational programs offered by member institutions of the Council on International Educational Exchange. Unless otherwise noted, consult Appendix I for the addresses of the colleges and universities listed in this section.

Semester and Academic Year

Environmental Studies

Kalamazoo College. *Kalamazoo Environmental Studies.* Quito. Spring semester. University-integrated program with extensive field-research component. Juniors and seniors with four semesters of Spanish. Apply by March 15.

World Learning/School for International Training. *College Semester Abroad.* Quito, Ibarra, Ecuadorian Amazon. Fall and spring semesters. Intensive language, comparative ecology, and field-study methods seminars, homestays, and independent project. Sophomores to graduate students with 2.5 GPA and one year of college-level Spanish. Apply by May 7 for fall; October 7 for spring. Contact: College Semester Abroad Admissions at (800) 336-1616.

General Studies

Beloit College. *Ecuador Seminar.* Catholic University of Ecuador, Quito. Fall semester. Integrated study with university courses in social sciences and humanities. Homestays and excursions to Amazon and Galapagos Islands. Sophomores to graduate students with 2.75 GPA. Apply by April 1.

Brethren Colleges Abroad. Catholic University, Quito; or University of San Francisco. Full range of academic curriculum including social work. English

teaching work arranged upon request. Excursions and study tours. Sophomores to seniors with 2.8 GPA and intermediate Spanish. Apply by April 15 for fall and academic year; November 1 for spring.
Scripps College. *Scripps Program in Quito.* University of San Francisco. Semester and academic year. Sophomores to seniors with 3.0 GPA and four semesters of college Spanish. Apply by February 5 for fall and academic year; September 25 for spring.
University of Illinois at Urbana-Champaign. *Trimester in Ecuador.* Trimester and academic year. Study at the University of San Francisco. Sophomores to seniors with 3.0 GPA and four semesters of college Spanish. Apply by April 1 for fall and academic year; October 1 for winter; February 1 for spring.
University of Wisconsin at Madison. *Academic Year in Quito, Ecuador.* Fall semester and academic year. Humanities, social sciences, and Spanish language at Universidad Católica del Ecuador. Intensive language and culture orientation. Homestays and excursions. Juniors and seniors with 3.0 recommended GPA and five semesters of Spanish. Wisconsin residents or individuals attending any college or university in Wisconsin. Apply by February 11.
World Learning/School for International Training. *College Semester Abroad.* Quito and Ibarra. Fall and spring semesters. Intensive language, seminar in Ecuadorian life and culture, field-study methods seminar, homestays, and independent project. Sophomores to graduate students with 2.5 GPA and one year of college-level Spanish. Apply by May 7 for fall; October 7 for spring. Contact: College Semester Abroad Admissions at (800) 336-1616.

International Relations

University of Minnesota. *Minnesota Studies in International Development (MSID).* Academic year. Predeparture coursework at the U of M in the fall quarter; internship with development-related research or action project in Ecuador during the winter and spring quarters required. Juniors to graduates and adults with an interest in development; 2.5 GPA and two years of Spanish required. Apply by May 1. Contact: The Global Campus, University of Minnesota, 106C Nicholson Hall, 216 Pillsbury Drive SE, Minneapolis, MN 55455-0138; (612) 625-3379.

Summer and Short-Term

General Studies

University of Louisville. *Ecology, Language, and Culture in Quito.* Quito. Four weeks in summer. Spanish language study, ecology, and culture. High-school graduates to graduate students and adults. Apply by April 1.

PERU

For a thousand years before Columbus came to America, advanced empires were rising and falling in Peru. It is here that the Spanish conquerors found cities of fabulous wealth, temples whose walls were splashed with gold and studded with precious stones, and splendid palaces that even today smell of plaster and varnish. Quintessentially, Peru represents the history of the South

American continent. This can be seen best in the way different elements like man, culture, region, and language interact with each other.

Peru has three distinctive physical regions, generating contrasting social and economic features. The coast, a dry but relatively well-off region, is home of most industry and urban centers including Lima, the nation's rapidly growing capital that already contains about a fourth of Peru's people. The sierra is composed of the Andean mountain range, a world of snowcapped peaks and chilly valleys that contain such ancient provincial cities as Cuzco and Ayacucho. The Quechua-speaking Indian inhabitants of this region have been largely excluded from the political and economic life of modern Peru; here is the base for the rebel guerrilla movement, the Sendero Luminosa ("Shining Path"). The jungle region, with its tropical forests, comprises the eastern half of the country. Until recently, this region extending over the upper regions of the Amazon River had experienced little settlement because of its inaccessibility. Today, however, colonization is making it a dynamic and more populated region.

Cuzco, at 11,480 feet above sea level, was once the capital of the empire of the Incas, stretching over 12 million square miles. The Incas, who rose to power in the sierra seven or eight centuries ago, have been called the first and most successful urban planners in history. Cuzco is one of their masterpieces. It lies on a small river, which the Incas tamed, running its clear water in stone culverts throught the paved streets of the city for household use. The essential lines were preserved in the Spanish-colonial town, because Inca stone masonry proved too difficult to change. The central square remains with Inca foundations intact, but the palaces have been replaced by churches and public buildings.

About 70 miles north of Cuzco are the ruins of Machu Picchu, one of the most awesome and mysterious sights in the world. Getting to Machu Picchu is in itself an unforgettable journey. In order to get there, one must travel by train, bus, and foot. A deep valley, a sacred river, and precipitous mountains characterize this trail. However, the trip is only a prelude to what lies ahead in the "lost city of the Incas," which was discovered only in 1911.

Another highlight of any trip to Peru is Iquitos, Peru's river port with access to the Atlantic Ocean via the Amazon River. Baring little resemblance to Lima, Iquitos exists in a world of its own. Iquitos was built by Europeans during the rubber boom at the turn of the 20th century, and a traveler can still see a few architectural remainders of its former glory.

Today, Peru is slowly trying to recuperate from a decade of economic depression and internal civil strife. Austerity measures adopted by a newly elected administration have caused hardship but have yet to control inflation. Nonetheless, contemporary problems can do little to dim the beauty of Peru's dramatic landscape or the glory of its history.

—Gerardo D. Berthin, Washington, DC

Official name: Republic of Peru. **Area:** 496,222 square miles (about four times the size of Arizona). **Population:** 22,361,000. **Population density:** 45 inhabitants per square mile. **Capital and largest city:** Lima (pop. 5,826,000). **Language:** Spanish, Quechua (both official), Aymara. **Religion:** Roman Catholic. **Per capita income:** US$898. **Currency:** Sole. **Literacy rate:** 85%. **Average daily temperature:** Lima: June, 61°; December, 67°. **Average number of days with precipitation:** Lima: June, 1; December, 0.1.

TRAVEL

U.S. citizens will need a passport, but visas are not required for stays of up to 30 days. For specific regulations, check with the **Embassy of Peru**, 1700 Massachusetts Avenue NW, Washington, DC 20036; (202) 833-9860.

At press time, the U.S. State Department's latest **Consular Information Sheet** was warning against travel to Peru because of increased attacks by the Shining Path and Tupac Amaru Revolutionary Movement. A number of departments, including Lima, have been declared "emergency zones." For more up-to-date information, obtain the latest Consular Information Sheet on Peru from the U.S. Department of State (see pages 8–9).

Getting Around

AeroPeru provides service to most of Peru's cities from Lima. AeroPeru's **Visit Peru Pass** gives you up to 45 days of unlimited flight for $250. The pass must be purchased in the U.S., and all routes must be specified in advance, although you may leave the dates open. For more information, contact AeroPeru, (800) 777-7717. Faucett Peruvian Airlines offers an identical Visit Peru pass at the same price; (800) 334-3356. Two new domestic airlines, Americana and Expresso Aereo, currently service more destinations than AeroPeru or Faucett.

In general, intercity highways are paved in the coastal region of Peru, are gravel in the Andes, and are virtually nonexistent in the Amazon region (which comprises about half the country). The best roads are the coastal Pan-American Highway and the Central Highway, which goes northeast from Lima. Roads also connect Peru with Bolivia, Chile, and Ecuador, but none cross the border to Brazil or Colombia. **Buses** of various types provide the most common means of transportation for Peruvians. **Shared taxis**, called *colectivos*, serve the same routes at a slightly higher price. It is also possible to rent a car in Lima and a few other cities, though not recommended due to the cost and danger involved. Avoid driving or traveling by bus after nightfall.

Peru has a handful of **rail** lines that connect a few cities of the interior to Pacific ports. Travel on these lines is often faster and cheaper than taking the bus. A railroad from Cuzco provides access to Machu Picchu, the spectacular mountaintop city of the Incas and one of the leading tourist attractions in South America. Another of the world's most interesting railway journeys is the trip from Lima to Huancayo, which takes the traveler over 16,000 feet above sea level. Note that rail service may be scaled back due to martial law.

In the eastern half of Peru, transport is mainly by small **boat**. In fact, Iquitos, the biggest city in Peru's Amazon region, can be reached only by plane or by boat. From Iquitos, boats provide frequent passenger service down the Amazon into Brazil, stopping at towns along the way.

Eating and Sleeping

There are around 20 **youth hostels** throughout Peru. For more information, contact Hostelling International/American Youth Hostels (see page 54) or Peru's national youth hostel association, **Asociación Peruana de Albergues Turísticos Juveniles**, Casimiro Ulloa 328, San Antonio, Miraflores, Lima 18; (51) 14-465488; fax (51) 14-465488.

Especially for Students and Young People

Peru's student and youth travel bureau and issuer of the International Student Identity Card is **INTEJ**, Av. San Martin 240, Barranco, Lima 4;

(51) 14-774105; fax (51) 14-367416. INTEJ can arrange travel and accommodations, as well as provide information on student discounts available in Peru.

For Further Information

Peru: A Travel Survival Kit, designed for the independent traveler interested in truly getting to know the country, is one of the best guidebooks on the market. Last revised in 1991, it's available for $14.95 from Lonely Planet Publications. An excellent book to read in preparation for your trip is *Insight Guide: Peru* ($19.95). For more information on Lonely Planet and *Insight Guides*, see pages 56–57. Those spending a lot of time around Cusco will find a detailed guide in James and Oliver Tickell's *Cusco, Peru*. It's one of the *Travel to Landmarks* series distributed by St. Martin's Press. A good source of firsthand information in Lima is the *South American Explorers Club* (see pages 547–548).

WORK

It is difficult for foreigners to obtain regular employment in Peru. You must secure a job and obtain a work permit before leaving the U.S. When applying for a permit at the Consulate of Peru, it is necessary to present proof of employment. For more information, contact the **Consulate of Peru**, 215 Lexington Avenue, 21st Floor, New York, NY 10016.

STUDY

The Cultural Department of the Embassy of Peru (see ''Travel,'' above) has a packet of information sheets entitled ''Universities in Peru.'' The packet includes general information and lists Peruvian institutions that teach English, English schools in Lima, and Peruvian institutions of higher learning and their fields.

EXPLORING PERUVIAN CULTURE

Readings

The leading contemporary Peruvian writer is Mario Vargas Llosa, who became even better known as a presidential candidate in Peru's 1990 elections. *Aunt Julia and the Scriptwriter* (1982) is a comic novel about a Bolivian scriptwriter who arrives to work in Peru and falls in love with his older aunt (by marriage). In *Conversation in the Cathedral* (1969), two men from different social classes discuss Peruvian life, violence, and social decay in a bar called the Cathedral. *The Real Life of Alejandro Mayta* (1984) is based on the assassination of a revolutionary figure and deals with violence in Peru. Peruvian society's outdated social system is explored through life in a military academy in Llosa's *The Time of the Hero* (1962).

Ciro Alegria provides a view of Indian civilization and life in Peru in *Broad and Alien Is the World* (1941), and in *The Golden Serpent* (1935), while Jose Maria Arguedas explores a white boy's relationship with the Indians in *Deep*

Rivers (1958). Peru's contemporary poet Cesar Vallejo writes a denunciation of the brutal treatment of Andean mine workers in *Tungsten*. A novel dealing with the miners' struggle in the sierra is *Drums for Runcas* (1977), by Manuel Scorza.

A foreigner's perspective on Peru is provided by Ronald Wright in *Cut Stones and Crossroads: A Journey in Peru* (1986). He travels from the Ecuadorian border across Peru to Bolivia, providing a fascinating account of the Peruvians he meets.

URUGUAY

Uruguay, one of South America's smallest nations, is often overshadowed by its two neighboring giants, Brazil and Argentina. In fact, Uruguay owes its existence to the stalemate between its two neighbors over which one should control the area. For centuries before Uruguay's independence in 1828, Spain and Portugal had vied for control of the region as well.

Today, more than half the population of Uruguay lives in a single city, Montevideo, which dominates the political, economic, and cultural life of the country. But 90 percent of the country is still devoted to livestock raising, chiefly cattle. This has led to the description of Uruguay as "a big city with a large ranch." Of course, this oversimplification doesn't justly describe the country. Other interesting spots include the world-famous beach resort of Punta del Este and the city of Colonia, which is known for its well-preserved Portuguese colonial architecture.

The European immigrants who settled in Uruguay created an agricultural economy that generated one of the world's highest standards of living early in this century. However, with the country unable to make the transition to a successful industrial economy, the standard of living steadily eroded. Gradually, one of the world's most egalitarian and progressive countries increasingly resembled the other countries of Latin America as class divisions mounted and the role of the military heightened. In the 1970s and early '80s, hundreds of thousands of Uruguayans emigrated to Argentina, Brazil, and Spain in order to escape economic hardship and political repression. However, since 1985, when the military government turned over power to a popularly elected civilian government, attempts to revitalize the country's economy and political system have met with limited success.

—Charles Sattler, Washington, DC

Official name: Republic of Uruguay. **Area:** 68,037 square miles (about the size of Minnesota). **Population:** 3,121,000. **Population density:** 45 inhabitants per square mile. **Capital and largest city:** Montevideo (pop. 1,310,000). **Language:** Spanish. **Religion:** Roman Catholic. **Per capita income:** US$2,970. **Currency:** New Peso. **Literacy rate:** 96%. **Average daily temperature:** Montevideo: June, 52°; December, 70°. **Average number of days with precipitation:** Montevideo: June, 5; December, 7.

TRAVEL

U.S. citizens will need a passport to enter Uruguay; a visa is not required for stays of up to three months. For specific regulations, check with the **Embassy of Uruguay**, 1918 F Street NW, Washington, DC 20006; (202) 331-1313. There are also Uruguayan consulates in Chicago, Los Angeles, Miami, New Orleans, and New York.

Getting Around

There has been no passenger rail service since 1988. Several **bus** companies provide comfortable service throughout the country. Cars can be rented in Montevideo or Punta del Este, with or without a driver. Domestic flights are offered by PLUNA and Aerolíneas Uruguayas, which provide service from Montevideo to a limited number of other Uruguayan cities. In addition, a variety of boats (including hydrofoils) link Colonia, about three hours west of Montevideo, with Buenos Aires across the Rio de la Plata.

Eating and Sleeping

There are several youth hostels in Uruguay. For more information, contact Hostelling International/American Youth Hostels (see page 54) or **Asociación de Alberguistas del Uruguay (AAU)**, Pablo de María 1583/008, 11200 Montevideo; (598) 2-404245; fax (598) 2-401326.

Especially for Students and Young People

AAU (see "Eating and Sleeping," above) is also Uruguay's student travel bureau and issuer of the International Student Identity Card. Their office provides tourist information, international air tickets, and books accommodations. AAU distributes a list of discounts available to International Student Identity Card holders.

For Further Information

The best guide for the budget traveler is *Argentina, Uruguay, and Paraguay: A Travel Survival Kit*. It's available for $16.95 from Lonely Planet Publications (see page 56).

WORK

It is difficult for foreigners to obtain regular employment in Uruguay. For more information, contact the **Embassy of Uruguay** (see "Travel," above).

Internships/Traineeships

A program sponsored by a member of the Council on International Educational Exchange is described below.

Association for International Practical Training. *IAESTE Trainee Program.* On-the-job training for undergraduate and graduate students in technical fields such as engineering, computer science, agriculture, architecture, mathematics, and the natural and physical sciences. See page 19 for more information.

STUDY

A program sponsored by a member institution of the Council on International Educational Exchange is described below. Consult Appendix I for the address where you can write for more information.

Semester and Academic Year

General Studies

International Student Exchange Program (ISEP). Montevideo. Semester and academic year. Direct reciprocal exchange between U.S. universities and Universidad Católica del Uruguay. Full curriculum options. Rolling admissions. Open only to students at ISEP-member institutions. Contact ISEP for list of members.

VENEZUELA

The discovery of oil early in this century transformed Venezuela from a poor, agrarian nation into the country with the highest standard of living in South America. Oil revenues, which once made up almost eighty percent of the GNP, made possible grandiose industrial, development, transportation, mining, and agricultural projects. Oil prosperity produced an affluent middle class and helped make possible what is today South America's longest-standing and most stable democratic system. During the last decade, Venezuela has tried to reduce its dependence on petroleum production; however, about 50 percent of the gross national product still comes from oil. Falling petroleum prices in the 1980s dealt a serious blow to the nation's economy, causing massive cutbacks in government spending, inflation, and debt repayment problems, as well as political demonstrations and riots.

Venezuela, along with Colombia and Ecuador, achieved independence from Spain under the leadership of South American hero Simón Bolívar in the 1820s. Bolívar envisioned a single state stretching from Venezuela to Ecuador to be called "Gran Colombia." Local loyalties quickly fragmented Gran Colombia, even before Bolívar's death in 1830; still, he is venerated all over the continent. Nowhere is this more prevalent than in Venezuela, where the "bolivar" is the main currency unit and everywhere there are statues, squares, shopping centers, museums—and even a city—named after him.

Travelers to Venezuela will find a modern nation with glass-and-concrete office blocks, shopping malls, traffic jams, and urban air pollution. More than any other South American country, Venezuela is urbanized and industrialized. Some 80 to 85 percent of its people now live in cities. Caracas, the nation's capital and home of one out of every six Venezuelans, lies 3,000 feet above sea level, enjoying a surprisingly temperate climate. Due to an influx of immigrants in the last 30 years, one out of four *Caraqueños* are foreign-born. Immigrants from countries like Colombia and Haiti have come for economic opportunity, while others have come to escape oppression under military regimes in countries such as Argentina, Chile, and Spain.

But tourists come mainly to enjoy Venezuela's natural splendors. Margarita

Island, Venezuela's leading Caribbean beach resort, is especially popular. A sharp contrast is provided by the Andes mountains, which run eastward from Colombia across northern Venezuela. The center of the Venezuelan Andes is Mérida, a colonial city surrounded by snowcapped peaks reaching above the 16,000-foot level. Here the world's longest and highest cable car makes scaling the Andes a popular tourist attraction.

In the extreme south of the country is the Amazonas Federal Territory, a region of unexplored "cloud" forests, stone-age tribes, unmapped mesas, and remote waterfalls. The headwaters of the Orinoco are here as well as a northern section of the Amazon basin. Here also are Angel Falls, the world's highest waterfall. Venezuela has taken steps to preserve its southern wilderness; a national park the size of Belgium stretches to the borders of Brazil and Guyana.

Tropical beaches, snowcapped peaks, modern cities, unmapped wilderness—whatever your preference, Venezuela has something special to offer.

—João Castaneda, San Francisco, California

Official name: Republic of Venezuela. **Area:** 352,143 square miles (about three times the size of Arizona). **Population:** 20,189,000. **Population density:** 57 inhabitants per square mile. **Capital and largest city:** Caracas (pop. 1,290,000). **Language:** Spanish. **Religion:** Roman Catholic. **Per capita income:** US$2,150. **Currency:** Bolivar. **Literacy rate:** 88%. **Average daily temperature:** Caracas: June, 72°; December, 69°. **Average number of days with precipitation:** June, 14; December, 10.

TRAVEL

U.S. citizens will need a passport and a tourist card to enter Venezuela. Tourist cards, valid for 60 days (and nonextendable), are issued at the border or by the airlines serving Venezuela, provided the traveler has purchased a return or onward ticket. For a multiple-entry visa good for one year, proof of sufficient funds and certification of employment are also necessary. For specific requirements, check with the **Embassy of Venezuela**, 1099 30th Street NW, Washington, DC 20007; (202) 342-2214.

Getting Around

Avensa, the country's main domestic air carrier, offers the **Avensa Airpass**, which provides unlimited travel in Venezuela in a 14-day period for $333. The Avensa Airpass must be purchased outside of Venezuela. For more information, contact Council Travel (see pages xiii–xvi) or call Avensa at (800) 428-3672.

There is an excellent road system extending to all areas of the country except the south. Roads also connect Venezuela with Colombia, but there are no roads across the border to either Brazil or Guyana. **Buses** form the backbone of the nation's transportation system. Other alternatives are ***por puesto cars*** (shared taxis that leave when full) or car rentals. Passenger train service is virtually nonexistent.

For Further Information

General tourist information is available from the **Venezuela Government Tourist Center**, 7 East 51st Street, New York, NY 10022. At press time, there were no good guides to Venezuela on the market; your best bet is annually updated *South American Handbook* ($40), published in England and distributed in the U.S. by Prentice Hall. Also good is Lonely Planet's *South America on a Shoestring*. An excellent book to read in preparation for your trip is *Insight Guide: Venezuela* ($19.95). For more information on Lonely Planet and *Insight Guides*, see pages 56–57.

WORK

A work visa is required for regular salaried employment in Venezuela; application is made by the Venezuelan company seeking permission to hire a foreigner, to the **Ministry of Interior Relations**, Avenida Urdaneta, Esquina de Carmelitas, Caracas, Venezuela. Work visas can be issued for 60 days, 120 days, or a year. For more information, contact the Ministry of Interior Relations above.

STUDY

The following program is offered by a CIEE-member institution. Unless otherwise noted, consult Appendix I for the address where you can write for more information.

Semester and Academic Year

General Studies

Longwood College. *Spring Semester Spanish Studies in Mérida.* Spanish language and Latin American literature. Juniors and seniors with four semesters of college Spanish and 2.8 GPA. Apply by November 15. Contact: Dr. John F. Reynolds, International Studies Program, Longwood College, Farmville, VA 23901; (804) 395-2172.

Spanish Language and Venezuelan Culture

University of Minnesota. *Spanish in Venezuela.* Mérida. Winter quarter. Intermediate and advanced Spanish language study and Venezuelan culture. High-school students to adults with two years of college Spanish. Apply by November 1. Contact: The Global Campus, 106C Nicholson Hall, 216 Pillsbury Drive SE, University of Minnesota, Minneapolis, MN 55455-0138; (612) 625-3379.

APPENDIX

MEMBERS OF THE COUNCIL ON INTERNATIONAL EDUCATIONAL EXCHANGE

Adelphi University
International Student Services
Earle Hall, Lower Level
Garden City, NY 11530
(516) 877-4990

Adventist Colleges Abroad
12501 Old Columbia Pike
Silver Spring, MD 20904-1608
(301) 680-6444

AFS International/Intercultural Programs, Inc.
Director, International Programs
220 East 42nd Street, 3rd Floor
New York, NY 10017
(800) 237-4636

Albertson College of Idaho
Vice President of Academic Affairs
2112 Cleveland Boulevard
Caldwell, ID 83686
(208) 459-5313

Alma College
International Education
614 East Superior Street
Alma, MI 48801
(517) 463-7247

American Council on the Teaching of Foreign Languages (ACTFL)
6 Executive Plaza
Yonkers, NY 10701-6801
(914) 963-8830

American Graduate School of International Management
Vice President for Academic Affairs
Thunderbird Campus
Glendale, AZ 85306
(602) 978-7250

American Heritage Association
PO Box 147
Flavia Hall
Marylhurst, OR 97036
(503) 635-3702

American University
Vice Provost, University Programs
4400 Massachusetts Avenue NW
Washington, DC 20016
(202) 885-2398

American University in Cairo
Director of Admissions
866 United Nations Plaza
Suite 517-3W
New York, NY 10017-1889
(212) 421-6320

Antioch University
Antioch Education Abroad
Yellow Springs, OH 45387
(513) 767-6366

Arkansas College
Nichols International Studies Program
PO Box 2317
2300 Highland Road
Batesville, AR 72503
(501) 698-4397

Associated Colleges of the Midwest
18 South Michigan Avenue
Suite 1010
Chicago, IL 60603
(312) 263-5000

Association for International Practical Training (AIPT)
10 Corporate Center, Suite 250
10400 Little Patuxent Parkway
Columbia, MD 21044-3510
(410) 997-2200

Attila Jozsef University (JATE)
Associate Dean for Academic Affairs, Faculty of Arts
Egyetem u.2
Szeged H-6722 HUNGARY
(36-62) 10 108/10 894

Auburn University
International Programs
146 College of Business Building, Box P
Auburn University, AL 36849-5159
(205) 844-4504

Augsburg College
International Programs
731 21st Avenue South
Minneapolis, MN 55454
(612) 330-1159

Austin Community College
Director of Off-Campus Operations
7748 Highway 290 West
Austin, TX 78736
(512) 288-8000

Babson College
International Programs
Babson Park, MA 02157-0310
(617) 239-4566

Ball State University
Center for International Programs
Burkhardt Building
Room 321
Muncie, IN 47306
(317) 285-5422

Bates College
Associate Dean of Students
Lane Hall
Lewiston, ME 04240
(207) 786-6223

Beaver College
Center for Education Abroad
450 S. Easton Road
Glenside, PA 19038
(215) 572-2901

Beloit College
World Affairs Center
700 College Street
Beloit, WI 53511-5595
(608) 363-2269

Bentley College
International Programs
175 Forest Street
Waltham, MA 02154-4705
(617) 891-3141

Boston College
Junior Year Abroad
Gasson Hall
Chestnut Hill, MA 02167
(617) 552-3830

Boston University
International Programs
232 Bay State Road
Boston, MA 02215
(617) 353-5403

Bradford College
Director, Applied Liberal Arts Office
320 South Main Street
Bradford, MA 01835-7393
(508) 372-7161, ext. 264

Bradley University
Director of Study Abroad and Campus Internationalization
1501 W. Bradley Avenue
Bradley Hall 127
Peoria, IL 61625
(309) 677-2400

Brandeis University
Office of International Programs
Kutz Hall/215
Waltham, MA 02254-9110
(617) 736-3480

Brethren Colleges Abroad
International Studies
Box 184
Manchester College
North Manchester, IN 46962
(219) 982-5026

Brigham Young University
International Programs/Study Abroad
204 Herald Clark Building
Provo, UT 84602
(801) 378-3308

Brown University
Office of International Programs
PO Box 1973
Providence, RI 02912
(401) 863-3555

Bucknell University
Office of International Education
Lewisburg, PA 17837
(717) 524-3796

Butler University
Provost & Senior Vice President for Academic Affairs
4600 Sunset Avenue
Indianapolis, IN 46208
(317) 283-9800

California State University
International Education
400 Golden Shore
Long Beach, CA 90802-4275
(310) 985-2859

California State University—Long Beach
Center for International Education
1250 Bellflower Boulevard
Long Beach, CA 90840
(310) 985-4106

California State University—Sacramento
Office of International Programs
6000 J Street
Sacramento, CA 95819-6012
(916) 278-6686

Canadian Universities Travel Service Ltd.
171 College Street
Second Floor
Toronto, Ontario M5T 1P7
CANADA
(416) 977-5228

Carleton College
Director of Off-Campus Studies
One North College Street
Northfield, MN 55057
(507) 663-4332

Carroll College
New Cultural Experiences Program
100 North East Avenue
Waukesha, WI 53186
(414) 524-7164

Central Michigan University
Office of International Programs
Mt. Pleasant, MI 48859
(517) 774-4308

Central University of Iowa
International Education
812 University
Pella, IA 50219
(515) 628-5287

Central Washington University
International Programs
Barge Hall 308
Ellensburg, WA 98926
(509) 963-3612

Chapman University
International Student Services
333 North Glassell Street
Orange, CA 92666
(714) 997-6829

College of Charleston
International and Exchange Programs
66 George Street
Charleston, SC 29424
(803) 792-5660

Colorado College
International Programs
14 East Cache le Poudre
Colorado Springs, CO 80903
(719) 389-6802

Colorado State University
Office of International Programs
315 Aylesworth Hall
Fort Collins, CO 80523
(303) 491-5917

Cornell University
Cornell Abroad
474 Uris Hall
Ithaca, NY 14853-7601
(607) 255-6224

Curtin University of Technology
North American Office
Two Appletree Square, Suite 144
8011 34th Avenue South
Minneapolis, MN 55425
(612) 854-5800

Dartmouth College
Off-Campus Programs
6102 Wentworth Hall
Hanover, NH 03755-3526
(603) 646-3753

Davidson College
Coordinator for Study Abroad
PO Box 1719
Davidson, NC 28036
(704) 892-2250

DePaul University
Director of International Programs and Government Relations
224 South Michigan Avenue, Suite 1300
Chicago, IL 60604-2507
(312) 362-5652

DePauw University
International Education
307 East Seminary
International Center
Greencastle, IN 46135-0037
(317) 658-4373

DIS Denmark's International Study Program (University of Copenhagen)
Vestergade 7
DK 1456 Copenhagen K DENMARK
(45) 33 11 01 44

Drake University
Coordinator for Study Abroad
Des Moines, IA 50311
(515) 271-2084

Earlham College
International Programs
National Road West
Box 202
Richmond, IN 47374
(317) 983-1424

Eastern Michigan University
Director of Academic Programs Abroad
333 Goodison Hall
Ypsilanti, MI 48197
(313) 487-2424

Eberhard-Karls-Universität Tübingen
Director, International Relations
Nauklerstrasse 14
D-W 7400 Tubingen 1
GERMANY
(49) 7071-292479

Eckerd College
International Education & Off-Campus Programs
4200 54th Avenue South
St. Petersburg, FL 33711
(813) 864-8381

École Centrale de Paris (École Centrale des Arts et Manufactures)
Grande Voie des Vignes
92295 Chatenay-Malabry Cedex
FRANCE
(33) 41.13.12.46

Elmira College
Director of JYA Program
Elmira, NY 14901
(607) 735-1800

Empire State College—SUNY
International Programs
28 Union Avenue
Saratoga Springs, NY 12866
(518) 587-2100, ext. 231

Flagler College
Dean of Academic Affairs
PO Box 1027
St. Augustine, FL 32085-1027
(904) 829-6481

Florida A & M University
International Programs
Box 338
FAMU
Tallahassee, FL 32307
(904) 599-3562

Florida Atlantic University
Office of International Programs
PO Box 3091
500 NW 20th Street
Social Sciences Building, Room 310
Boca Raton, FL 33431
(407) 367-3227

Georgetown University
Office of International Programs
37th & O Streets, NW
Washington, DC 20057
(202) 687-5867

Gonzaga University
Studies Abroad Director
502 East Boone Avenue
Spokane, WA 99258-0001
(509) 328-4220, ext. 3549

Goshen College
International Education
1700 South Main Street
Goshen, IN 46526
(219) 535-7346

Great Lakes Colleges Association
Program Officer
2929 Plymouth Road
Suite 207
Ann Arbor, MI 48105-3206
(313) 761-4833

Grinnell College
Associate Dean of the College
PO Box 805
Grinnell, IA 50112-0810
(515) 269-3460

Guilford College
Study Abroad Programs
5800 West Friendly Avenue
Greensboro, NC 27410
(919) 316-2225

Gustavus Adolphus College
Office of International Education
800 W. College Avenue
St. Peter, MN 56082
(507) 933-7545

Hampshire College
International Studies
West Street
Amherst, MA 01002
(413) 549-4600, ext. 542

Hartwick College
Off-Campus Study
Oneonta, NY 13820
(607) 431-4423

Harvard College
International Experience Program
Office of Career Services
54 Dunster Street
Cambridge, MA 02138
(617) 495-2595

Hebrew University of Jerusalem
Office of Academic Affairs
11 East 69th Street
New York, NY 10021
(212) 472-2288

Heidelberg College
Academic Affairs
310 East Market Street
Tiffin, OH 44883
(419) 448-2216

Hiram College
The Center for International Studies
Mahan House
Hiram, OH 44234
(216) 569-5160

Hollins College
International Programs
PO Box 9683
Roanoke, VA 24020
(703) 362-6664

Hope College
International Education
112 East 12th Street
PO Box 9000
Holland, MI 49422-9000
(616) 394-7605

Hostelling International/ American Youth Hostels, Inc.
1426 H Street NW
Suite 800
Washington, DC 20005
(202) 783-6161

Illinois State University
Office of International Studies
Fell Hall 308
Normal, IL 61761-6901
(309) 438-5365

Indiana University
Office of Overseas Study
Franklin Hall 303
Bloomington, IN 47405-2801
(812) 855-9306

Institute of International Education (IIE)
809 United Nations Plaza
New York, NY 10017
(212) 984-5425

International Christian University
Dean of International Affairs
3-10-2, Osawa
Mitaka
Tokyo 181 JAPAN
(81) 422-33-3043

International Christian Youth Exchange
134 West 26th Street
New York, NY 10001
(212) 206-7307

International Student Exchange Program (ISEP)
3222 N Street NW
Suite 400
Washington, DC 20007-2849
(202) 965-0550

Iowa State University
Study Abroad Center
E.O. Building
Ames, IA 50011
(515) 294-6792

James Madison University
International Education
Paul Street House
Harrisonburg, VA 22807
(703) 568-6419

Kalamazoo College
Director of Foreign Study
1200 Academy Street
Kalamazoo, MI 49006-3295
(616) 337-7133

Kent State University
Center for International and Comparative Programs
124 Bowman Hall
PO Box 5190
Kent, OH 44242-0001
(216) 672-7980

Lancaster University
North American Office
Lancaster LA1 4YW ENGLAND
(44) 524-65201, ext. 2035

LaSalle University
LaSalle-in-Europe
20th & Olney Streets
Philadelphia, PA 19141
(215) 951-1200

Lehigh University
Center for International Studies
Maginnes Hall #9
9 West Packer Avenue
Bethlehem, PA 18015
(215) 758-3351

Lewis & Clark College
Overseas and Off-Campus Programs
0615 SW Palatine Hill Road
Campus Box 11
Portland, OR 97219
(503) 768-7295

Lisle Fellowship, Inc.
433 West Sterns Road
Temperance, MI 48182
(313) 847-7126

Longwood College
Office of the President
Farmville, VA 23909-1899
(804) 395-2001

Louisiana State University
Academic Programs Abroad
Baton Rouge, LA 70803
(504) 388-6801

Loyola Marymount University
Loyola Boulevard at West 80th Street
Los Angeles, CA 90045
(310) 338-2757

Macalester College
International Center
1600 Grand Avenue
St. Paul, MN 55105
(612) 696-6310

Marquette University
1217 West Wisconsin Avenue
Milwaukee, WI 53233
(414) 288-7059

Mary Baldwin College
International Studies Program
Staunton, VA 24401
(703) 887-7050

Marymount College, Tarrytown
Study Abroad Program Director
100 Marymount Avenue
Tarrytown, NY 10591-3796
(914) 332-8222

Memphis State University
Office of International Studies
300 Dunn Building
Memphis, TN 38152
(901) 678-2814

Miami University
Office of International Programs
Langstroth Cottage
Oxford, OH 45056
(513) 529-2512

Michigan State University
207 Center for International Programs
East Lansing, MI 48824-1035
(517) 355-2350

Middlebury College
Vice President for Foreign Languages
Middlebury, VT 05753
(802) 388-3711, ext. 5508

Middlesex University
Access International and Marketing
Bramley Road, London N14 4XS ENGLAND
(44) 81-362-5616

Millersville University
International Affairs
Millersville, PA 17551
(717) 872-3884

Monterey Institute of International Studies
Dean of Language Studies
425 Van Buren
Monterey, CA 93940
(408) 647-4185

Moorhead State University
Vice President for Public Affairs
Box 336
Moorhead, MN 56563
(218) 236-3287

Murdoch University
International Office
South Street
Murdoch WA 6150 AUSTRALIA
(61) 9-3602750

National Association of Secondary School Principals
1904 Association Drive
Reston, VA 22091
(703) 860-0200

National Chengchi University
Executive Secretary, Academic Cooperation Committee
64 Chih-nan Road
Sec. 2
Wenshan, Taipei 11623 TAIWAN
(886) 2-9387010

New York University
Vice President for Institutional Advancement
Elmer Holmes Bobst Library, Room 1229
70 Washington Square South
New York, NY 10012
(212) 998-2300

North Carolina State University
Study Abroad
Suite 2118 Pullen Hall
Box 7344
Raleigh, NC 27695-7344
(919) 515-2087

Northeastern University
400 Meserve Hall
360 Huntington Avenue
Boston, MA 02115
(617) 437-5172

Northern Arizona University
Office of International Studies
PO Box 5598
Flagstaff, AZ 86011
(602) 523-2409

Northern Illinois University
International and Special Programs
Lowden Hall 203
DeKalb, IL 60115-2854
(815) 753-1988

Northern Kentucky University
International Programs
Landrum Hall 217E
Highland Heights, KY 41076
(606) 572-6512

Northern Michigan University
International Education
362 Magers Hall
Marquette, MI 49855
(906) 227-1220

Northfield Mount Hermon School
International Programs
Northfield, MA 01360
(413) 498-3251

Oberlin College
Oberlin, OH 44074
(216) 775-8654

Obirin University
Center for International Studies
3758 Tokiwa-machi
Machida-shi
Tokyo 194-02 JAPAN
(81) 427-972661, ext. 421

Ohio University
Center for International Studies
56 East Union Street
Athens, OH 45701-2987
(614) 593-1840

Ohio State University
Office of International Education
Oxley Hall
1712 Neil Avenue
Columbus, OH 43210
(614) 292-6101

Old Dominion University
Office of International Programs
BAL 300
Norfolk, VA 23529-0093
(804) 683-4419

Open Door Student Exchange
250 Fulton Avenue
PO Box 71
Hempstead, NY 11551
(516) 486-7330

Pace University
International Education
Pace Plaza
New York, NY 10038
(212) 346-1368

Pennsylvania State University
International Programs
222 Boucke Building
University Park, PA 16802
(814) 865-7681

Pepperdine University
International Programs
Malibu, CA 90263
(310) 456-4532

Pitzer College
International Programs
1040 North Mills Avenue
Claremont, CA 91711
(714) 621-8104

Polytechnicum de Lille
CLARIFE
27 rue d'Armentieres
59800 Lille FRANCE
(33) 20-579219

Pomona College
Study Abroad
Sumner Hall
333 North College Way
Claremont, CA 91711
(909) 621-8154

Portland State University
International Programs
PO Box 751
Portland, OR 97207-0751
(503) 725-4011

Purdue University
International Programs
Young Graduate House, Room 111
West Lafayette, IN 47906-6207
(317) 494-2383

Ramapo College of New Jersey
Study Abroad and Continuing Education
505 Ramapo Valley Road
Mahwah, NJ 07430-1680
(201) 529-7533

Reed College
International Programs
3203 SE Woodstock Boulevard
Portland, OR 97202
(503) 777-7290

Rochester Institute of Technology
Center for International Business and Economic Growth
College of Business
One Lomb Memorial Drive
Rochester, NY 14623
(716) 475-4995

Rollins College
International and Off-Campus Programs
Box 2759
1000 Holt Avenue
Winter Park, FL 32789-4499
(407) 646-2466

Rosary College
7900 West Division Street
River Forest, IL 60305
(708) 524-6816

Rutgers, The State University of New Jersey
International Programs
172 College Avenue
New Brunswick, NJ 08903-5062
(908) 932-7263

St. John Fisher College
Foreign Study
3690 East Avenue
Rochester, NY 14618
(716) 385-8000

St. Lawrence University
International Education
Carnegie 108
Canton, NY 13617
(315) 379-5991

St. Olaf College
International and Off-Campus Studies
Northfield, MN 55057
(507) 646-3069

St. Peter's College
2641 Kennedy Boulevard
Jersey City, NJ 07306
(201) 915-9213

Scandinavian Seminar, Inc.
24 Dickinson Street
Amherst, MA 01002
(413) 253-9736

School Year Abroad
Phillips Academy
Andover, MA 01810
(508) 749-4420

Scripps College
Off-Campus Studies
1030 Columbia Avenue
Claremont, CA 91711-3948
(714) 621-8306

Shoreline Community College
Academic Affairs
16101 Greenwood Avenue North
Seattle, WA 98133
(206) 546-4651

Skidmore College
Coordinator, Foreign Study
North Broadway
Saratoga Springs, NY 12866
(518) 584-5000, ext. 2654

Southern Illinois University at Carbondale
Study Abroad Programs
International Programs and Services
Carbondale, IL 62901
(618) 453-7670

Southern Methodist University
Office of International Programs
Suite 100, McFarlin Auditorium
Dallas, TX 75275
(214) 692-2295

Southwest Texas State University
Center for International Education
San Marcos, TX 78666
(512) 245-2339

Southwestern University
Study Abroad
University at Maple
Georgetown, TX 78626
(512) 863-1857

Spelman College
Coordinator of Study Abroad
Box 1447
350 Spelman Lane, SW
Atlanta, GA 30314
(404) 223-7550

Springfield College
International Center
263 Alden Street
Springfield, MA 01109
(413) 748-3216

Stanford University
Overseas Studies
Sweet Hall, 1st Floor
Stanford, CA 94305-3089
(415) 725-0235

State University of New York
Assistant Provost for International Programs
State University Plaza, Room T801
Albany, NY 12246
(518) 443-5124

Stephens College
Study Abroad
PO Box 2053
Columbia, MO 65215
(314) 876-7154

Stetson University
Office of International Exchange
PO Box 8412
DeLand, FL 32720
(904) 822-8165/8166

Syracuse University
Division of International Programs Abroad
119 Euclid Avenue
Syracuse, NY 13244
(315) 443-3471

Texas A & M University
Study Abroad Programs
161 Bizzell West
College Station, TX 77843
(409) 845-0544

Texas Christian University
Academic Affairs
PO Box 30782
Fort Worth, TX 76129
(817) 921-7104

Texas Tech University
Overseas Opportunities Counselor
PO Box 45004
242 West Hall
Lubbock, TX 79409-5004
(806) 742-3667

Trinity College
Educational Services
300 Summit Street
Hartford, CT 06106
(203) 297-2437

Trinity University
Study Abroad and Off-Campus Study
715 Stadium Drive
San Antonio, TX 78212
(210) 736-7313

Tufts University
Tufts Programs Abroad
Ballou Hall
Medford, MA 02155
(617) 627-3152

Tulane University
200 Gibson Hall
New Orleans, LA 70118-5683
(504) 865-5261

Universidad Autonoma de Guadalajara
International Programs
Av. Patria No. 1201
Lomas del Valle
Apdo. Postal 1-440
44100 Guadalajara Jalisco MEXICO
(52) 36-417051, ext. 32807

Universidad de Belgrano
Director de la Secretaria de Relaciones Internacionales
Federico Lacroze 1959 piso 1
1426 Buenos Aires ARGENTINA
(54) 1-772-4014/17

Universidad del Salvador
Rector
Viamonte 1856
1056 Buenos Aires ARGENTINA
(54) 1-421408

Universidade Estacio de Sa
Director—CCBE
Rua dona Cecilia
25 Rio Comprido
CEP: 20251-010
Rio de Janeiro BRAZIL
(21) 273-6490

Université de Bordeaux III
Maitre de Conferences
Domaine Universitaire
33405 Talence Cedex FRANCE
(33) 56-845050

University College London
Assistant Registrar
Gower Street
London WCIE 6BT ENGLAND
(44) 1-3807007

University of Alabama
Capstone International Program Center
Box 870254
Tuscaloosa, AL 35487
(205) 348-5312

University of Alabama at Birmingham
Center for International Programs
306 University Center
Birmingham, AL 35294
(205) 934-8622

University of Amsterdam
Office of Foreign Relations
Spui 21
1012 WX Amsterdam THE NETHERLANDS
(31 20) 525 2373

University of Arkansas at Little Rock
Associate Vice Chancellor
33rd and University
Little Rock, AR 72207
(501) 569-3374

University of British Columbia
Language Institute Center for Continuing Education
5997 Iona Drive
Vancouver V6T 2A4 CANADA
(604) 228-2181

University of California
Education Abroad Program (UOEAP)
Santa Barbara, CA 93106
(805) 893-2918

University of Colorado at Boulder
Office of International Education
CB 123
Boulder, CO 80309-0123
(303) 492-7741

University of Connecticut
Study Abroad Programs
U-207
843 Bolten Road
Storrs, CT 06269-1207
(203) 486-5022

University of Denver
Study Abroad Coordinator
The College
University Park
Denver, CO 80208
(303) 871-3555

University of Essex
International Programs
Wivenhoe Park
Colchester
Essex CO4 3SQ ENGLAND
(44) 206-873777

University of Evansville
Harlaxton Coordinator
1800 Lincoln Avenue
Evansville, IN 47722
(812) 479-2146

University of Findlay
International Center for Language and Resource Development
1000 North Main Street
Findlay, OH 45840
(419) 424-4678

University of Hartford
Office of International Studies and Programs
200 Bloomfield Avenue
GSU 327
West Hartford, CT 06117
(203) 768-5101

University of Idaho
International Programs Office
Room 216, Morrill Hall
Moscow, ID 83843
(208) 885-8984

University of Illinois
Study Abroad
115 International Studies Building
910 South Fifth Street
Champaign, IL 61820
(217) 333-6322

University of Iowa
Office of International Education & Services
Iowa City, IA 52242-1802
(319) 335-0353

University of Kansas
Office of Study Abroad
203 Lippincott Hall
Lawrence, KS 66045-1731
(913) 864-3742

University of Kentucky
Office of International Affairs
215 Bradley Hall
Lexington, KY 40506-0058
(606) 257-4068

University of La Verne
Academic Affairs
1950 Third Street
La Verne, CA 91750
(714) 593-3511, ext. 4240

University of Louisville
International Center
2301 South Third Street
Louisville, KY 40292-0001
(502) 588-6602

University of Maine
International Programs
100 Winslow Hall
Orono, ME 04496
(207) 581-2905

University of Maryland
Study Abroad Office
3125 Mitchell
College Park, MD 20742
(301) 314-7746

University of Massachusetts
International Programs
William S. Clark International Center
Box 33280
Amherst, MA 01003-3280
(413) 545-2710

University of Michigan
International Center
603 East Madison Street
Ann Arbor, MI 48109-1370
(313) 747-2256

University of Minnesota
International Study & Travel Center
102 Nicholson Hall
216 Pillsbury Drive SE
Minneapolis, MN 55455
(612) 626-9000

University of Nebraska—Lincoln
1237 R Street
Lincoln, NE 68588-0221
(402) 472-5358

University of Nevada, Reno
International Programs & Services
130 Mackay Science Building
Mailstop 148
Reno, NV 89557
(702) 784-1467

University of New Hampshire
Center for International Perspectives
Department of French and Italian
Durham, NH 03824
(603) 862-3856

University of New Orleans
International Study Programs
P.O. Box 1340
New Orleans, LA 70148
(504) 286-7318

University of New South Wales
Study Abroad
PO Box 1
Kensington NSW 2033
AUSTRALIA
(61) 2-6973175

University of North Carolina at Chapel Hill
Office of International Programs for Study Abroad
207 Caldwell Hall
Chapel Hill, NC 27514-3130
(919) 962-7001

University of North Texas
Study Abroad Center
PO Box 13795
Denton, TX 76203-3795
(817) 565-2207

University of Notre Dame
International Study Programs
420 Main Building
Notre Dame, IN 46556
(219) 239-5882

University of Oklahoma
Office of International Programs
640 Parrington Oval
Room 211
Norman, OK 73019-0380
(405) 325-1607

University of Oregon
Office of International Education and Exchange
330 Oregon Hall
Eugene, OR 97403-5209
(503) 346-3206

University of the Pacific
Office of International Programs
Bechtel International Center
Stockton, CA 95211
(209) 946-2591

University of Pennsylvania
International Programs
133 Bennett Hall
Philadelphia, PA 19104-6275
(215) 898-4665

University of Pittsburgh
Study Abroad Office
4G-32 Forbes Quadrangle/UCIS
6200 Fifth Avenue
Pittsburgh, PA 15260
(412) 648-7419

University of Rhode Island
Dean of University College & Special Academic Programs
Roosevelt Hall
Kingston, RI 02882
(401) 792-5505

University of St. Thomas
International Education
Mail #44C-1
2115 Summit Avenue
St. Paul, MN 55105
(612) 962-6450

University of St. Thomas
Study Abroad
3812 Montrose Boulevard
Houston, TX 77006
(713) 525-3535

University of South Carolina
International Programs for Students
Byrnes Building, #100
Columbia, SC 29208
(803) 777-7461

University of Southern California
ADM-304
Los Angeles, CA 90089
(213) 740-5294

University of Sussex
North American Programmes
Falmer, Brighton
East Sussex BN1 9QN ENGLAND
(44) 273-678373

University of Tennessee, Knoxville
Center for International Education
201 Aconda Court
Knoxville, TN 37996-0620
(615) 974-3177

University of Texas at Austin
Study Abroad Advisor
100 West 26th Street
University Station
Austin, TX 78713-7206
(512) 471-6490

University of Toledo
Center for International Studies & Programs
2801 West Bancroft Street
Toledo, OH 43606-3390
(419) 537-3527

University of Tulsa
Dean of Students
600 South College Avenue
Holmes Student Center
Tulsa, OK 74104-3189
(918) 631-2327

University of Utah
International Center
159 Union Building
Salt Lake City, UT 84112
(801) 581-8876

University of Vermont
Office of International Educational Services
Living/Learning Center
Box #8
Burlington, VT 05405
(802) 656-4296

University of Virginia
Department of Slavic Languages & Literature
109 Cabell Hall
Charlottesville, VA 22903-3196
(804) 924-3548

University of Washington
Foreign Study Office
516 Schmitz Hall
PA-10
Seattle, WA 98195
(206) 543-9272

University of Wisconsin—Green Bay
2420 Nicolet Drive
Green Bay, WI 54311-7001
(414) 465-2491

University of Wisconsin—Madison
Division of International Education
1411 Van Hise Hall
Madison, WI 53706
(608) 262-2851

University of Wisconsin—Milwaukee
International Studies & Programs
PO Box 340
Milwaukee, WI 53201
(414) 229-5724

University of Wisconsin—Platteville
Institute for Study Abroad Programs
One University Plaza
Platteville, WI 53818
(608) 342-1726

University of Wisconsin—River Falls
International Programs
River Falls, WI 54022
(715) 425-3843

University of Wollongong
Vice-Principal (International)
Locked Bag 8844
Wollongong NSW 2521
AUSTRALIA
(61) 42-268800

University of Wyoming
International Student Services
Box 3228
University Station
Laramie, WY 82071
(307) 766-5193

University System of Georgia
International Intercultural Studies Program
One Park Placé South
Regents Global Center
Suite 817
Atlanta, GA 30303
(404) 651-2450

Utah State University
Study Abroad Office
Main 314
Logan, UT 84322-0700
(801) 750-1253

Valparaiso University
International Studies
Valparaiso, IN 46383
(219) 464-5333

Villanova University
International Studies
Tollentine Hall, Room 208
Villanova, PA 19085-1699
(215) 645-7393

Volunteers in Asia, Inc.
Box 4543
Stanford, CA 94309
(415) 723-3228

Wake Forest University
International Studies
PO Box 7385
Winston-Salem, NC 27109
(919) 759-5938

Washington College
Chestertown, MD 21620
(410) 778-2800, ext. 213

Washington State University
International Programs
Bryan Hall, Room 108
Pullman, WA 99164-5110
(509) 335-4508

Wayne State University
Junior Year in Germany
401 Manoogian Hall
Detroit, MI 48202
(313) 577-4605

Webster University
Coordinator of European Campuses
470 East Lockwood Avenue
St. Louis, MO 63119-3194
(314) 968-7469

Wesleyan University
Dean of the College
Middletown, CT 06457
(203) 344-8544, ext. 2243/4

Western Michigan University
Office of International Affairs
2090 Friedmann Hall
Kalamazoo, MI 49008-5011
(616) 387-3951

Western Washington University
International Programs & Exchanges
Old Main 530B—MS 9046
Bellingham, WA 98225-9046
(206) 650-3298

Westminster College
Old Main 102
New Wilmington, PA 16172-0001
(412) 946-7123

Whitman College
345 Boyer
Walla Walla, WA 99362
(509) 527-5132

Whitworth College
Center for International and Multicultural Education
Spokane, WA 99251
(509) 466-3733

Wichita State University
Office of International Programs
Wichita, KS 67208
(316) 689-3730

Wilmington College
International Education
Pyle Box 1282
Wilmington, OH 45177
(513) 382-6661, ext. 212

Wittenberg University
International Education
PO Box 720
Springfield, OH 45501
(513) 327-6185

Wofford College
Foreign Study Advisor
429 North Church Street
Spartanburg, SC 29303-3663
(803) 597-4510

Worcester Polytechnic Institute
Global Program Officer
100 Institute Road
Worcester, MA 01609
(508) 831-5772

World Learning
Kipling Road
PO Box 676
Brattleboro, VT 05302
(802) 258-3284

YMCA of the USA
International Program Services
71 West 23rd Street
New York, NY 10010
(212) 727-8800

Youth for Understanding International Exchange
3501 Newark Street NW
Washington, DC 20016
(202) 895-1111

INDEX